Communications
in Computer and Information Science   586

Commenced Publication in 2007
Founding and Former Series Editors:
Alfredo Cuzzocrea, Dominik Ślęzak, and Xiaokang Yang

More information about this series at http://www.springer.com/series/7899

Pascal Lorenz · Jorge Cardoso
Leszek A. Maciaszek · Marten van Sinderen (Eds.)

Software Technologies

10th International Joint Conference, ICSOFT 2015
Colmar, France, July 20–22, 2015
Revised Selected Papers

 Springer

Editors

Pascal Lorenz
University of Haute Alsace
Mulhouse
France

Jorge Cardoso
Universidade da Coimbra
Coimbra
Portugal

Leszek A. Maciaszek
Macquarie University
Sydney
Australia

Marten van Sinderen
Information Systems Group
Enschede
The Netherlands

ISSN 1865-0929   ISSN 1865-0937 (electronic)
Communications in Computer and Information Science
ISBN 978-3-319-30141-9   ISBN 978-3-319-30142-6 (eBook)
DOI 10.1007/978-3-319-30142-6

Library of Congress Control Number: 2015952534

Printed on acid-free paper

This Springer imprint is published by SpringerNature
The registered company is Springer International Publishing AG Switzerland

Preface

The present book includes extended and revised versions of a set of selected papers from the 10th International Conference on Software Technologies (ICSOFT 2015), which was sponsored by the Institute for Systems and Technologies of Information, Control and Communication (INSTICC), co-organized by the University of Haute Alsace, held in cooperation with the IEICE Special Interest Group on Software Interprise Modelling (SWIM) and technically co-sponsored by IEEE Computer Society/Technical Council on Software Engineering (IEEE CS TCSE).

The purpose of ICSOFT is to bring together researchers, engineers, and practitioners working in areas that are related to software engineering and applications. ICSOFT is composed of two co-located conferences ICSOFT-PT, which specializes in new software paradigm trends, and ICSOFT-EA, which specializes in mainstream software engineering and applications. Together, these conferences aim at becoming a major meeting point for software engineers worldwide.

ICSOFT-PT (10th International Conference on Software Paradigm Trends) focuses on four main paradigms that have been intensively studied during the last decade for software and system design, namely, "Models," "Aspects," "Services," and "Context."

ICSOFT-EA (10th International Conference on Software Engineering and Applications) has a practical focus on software engineering and applications. The conference tracks are "Enterprise Software Technologies," "Software Project Management," "Software Engineering Methods and Techniques," and "Distributed and Mobile Software Systems."

ICSOFT 2015 received 117 paper submissions from 41 countries in all continents, of which 38 % were orally presented (14 % as full papers). To evaluate each submission, a double-blind paper evaluation method was used: Each paper was reviewed by at least two internationally known experts from the ICSOFT Program Committee.

The quality of the papers herewith presented stems directly from the dedicated effort of the Steering and Scientific Committees and the INSTICC team responsible for handling all secretariat and logistics' details. We are further indebted to the conference keynote speakers, who presented their valuable insights and visions regarding areas of interest to the conference. Finally, we would like to thank all authors and attendees for their contribution to the conference and the scientific community. We hope that you will find these papers interesting and consider them a helpful reference in the future when addressing any of the research aforementioned areas.

July 2015

Pascal Lorenz
Jorge Cardoso
Leszek Maciaszek
Marten van Sinderen

Organization

Conference Chair

Pascal Lorenz University of Haute Alsace, France

Program Co-chairs

ICSOFT-PT

Jorge Cardoso University of Coimbra, Portugal and Huawei European Research Center, Germany

Marten van Sinderen University of Twente, The Netherlands

ICSOFT-EA

Leszek Maciaszek Wroclaw University of Economics, Poland and Macquarie University, Sydney, Australia

ICSOFT-PT Program Committee

Farhad Arbab CWI, The Netherlands
Colin Atkinson University of Mannheim, Germany
Maurice H. ter Beek ISTI-CNR, Pisa, Italy
Gábor Bergmann Budapest University of Technology and Economics, Hungary
Marcello M. Bersani Politecnico di Milano, Italy
Thomas Buchmann University of Bayreuth, Germany
Dumitru Burdescu University of Craiova, Romania
Jose Antonio
   Calvo-Manzano Universidad Politécnica de Madrid, Spain

Cinzia Cappiello Politecnico di Milano, Italy
Ana R. Cavalli Institute TELECOM SudParis, France
Kung Chen National Chengchi University, Taiwan
Marta Cimitile UNITELMA Sapienza, Italy
Marco Danelutto University of Pisa, Italy
Sergiu Dascalu University of Nevada, Reno, USA
Steven Demurjian University of Connecticut, USA
María J. Domínguez-Alda Universidad de Alcalá, Spain
Fikret Ercal Missouri University of Science and Technology, USA
Maria Jose Escalona University of Seville, Spain
Santiago Escobar Universidad Politécnica de Valencia, Spain
Anne Etien Université Lille 1, France

Matteo Rossi	Politecnico di Milano, Italy
Krzysztof Sacha	Warsaw University of Technology, Poland
Maria-Isabel Sanchez-Segura	Carlos III University of Madrid, Spain
Ulrik Pagh Schultz	University of Southern Denmark, Denmark
Harvey Siy	University of Nebraska at Omaha, USA
Yeong-tae Song	Towson University, USA
Cosmin Stoica Spahiu	University of Craiova, Romania
Peter Stanchev	Kettering University, USA
Clemens Szyperski	Microsoft, USA
Chouki Tibermacine	LIRMM, CNRS and Montpellier University, France
Claudine Toffolon	Université du Maine, France
Gianluigi Viscusi	EPFL-CDM, Switzerland
Christiane Gresse von Wangenheim	UFSC - Federal University of Santa Catarina, Brazil
Dietmar Wikarski	FH Brandenburg University of Applied Sciences, Germany
Andreas Winter	Carl von Ossietzky University Oldenburg, Germany
Jinhui Yao	Xerox Research, USA
Jingyu Zhang	Macquarie University, Australia
Elena Zucca	University of Genoa, Italy

ICSOFT-PT Additional Reviewers

Vincent Blondeau	Worldline, France
Sharmistha Chatterjee	Broward College, USA
Diego Rivera	Institut Telecom SudParis, France
Gustavo Santos	Université de Lille-1, France
Nikolaos Tantouris	University of Vienna, Austria
Reza Teimourzadegan	Islamic Azad University of Azarshahr Branch, Iran, Islamic Republic of
Tarck Zernadji	Biskra University, Algeria

ICSOFT-EA Program Committee

Waleed Alsabhan	KACST, UK
Nicolas Anquetil	Inria and USTL, France
Jorge Bernardino	Polytechnic Institute of Coimbra - ISEC, Portugal
Mario Berón	Universidad Nacional de San Luis, Argentina
Lisa Brownsword	Software Engineering Institute, USA
Andrea Burattin	University of Innsbruck, Austria
Dumitru Burdescu	University of Craiova, Romania
Fergal Mc Caffery	Dundalk Institute of Technology, Ireland
Antoni Lluís Mesquida Calafat	Universitat de les Illes Balears (UIB), Spain

Yeong-tae Song   Towson University, USA
Anongnart Srivihok   Kasetsart University, Thailand
Miroslaw Staron   University of Gothenburg, Sweden
Antony Tang   Swinburne University of Technology, Australia
Joseph Trienekens   TU Eindhoven, The Netherlands
László Vidács   University of Szeged, Hungary
Sergiy Vilkomir   East Carolina University, USA
Gianluigi Viscusi   EPFL-CDM, Switzerland
Christiane Gresse   UFSC - Federal University of Santa Catarina, Brazil
  von Wangenheim
Rainer Weinreich   Johannes Kepler University Linz, Austria
Murat Yilmaz   Çankaya University, Turkey
Zheying Zhang   University of Tampere, Finland
Elena Zucca   University of Genoa, Italy

ICSOFT-EA Additional Reviewers

Dominik Bork   University of Vienna, Austria
Matteo Camilli   Università degli Studi di Milano, Italy
Theodore Chaikalis   University of Macedonia, Greece
Sharmistha Chatterjee   Broward College, USA
George Digkas   University of Macedonia, Greece
Vladimir Dimitrieski   Faculty of Technical Sciences, Serbia
Hans-Georg Fill   University of Vienna, Austria
Vladimir Ivancevic   University of Novi Sad, Faculty of Technical
                            Sciences, Serbia

Invited Speakers

Eleni Karatza   Aristotle University of Thessaloniki, Greece
John Domingue   The Open University, UK
David Budgen   Durham University Mountjoy, UK

Contents

Invited Paper

What Do We Know and How Well Do We Know It? Current Knowledge About Software Engineering Practices

David Budgen[(✉)]

School of Engineering and Computing Sciences, Durham University, Durham, UK
david.budgen@durham.ac.uk

Abstract. *Context:* The 'prescriptions' used in software engineering for developing and maintaining systems make use of a set of 'practice models', which have largely been derived by codifying successful experiences of expert practitioners. *Aim:* To review the ways in which empirical practices, and evidence-based studies in particular, have begun to provide more systematic sources of evidence about what practices work, when, and why. *Method:* This review examines the current situation regarding empirical studies in software engineering and examine some of the ways in which evidence-based studies can inform and influence practice. *Results:* A mix of secondary and tertiary studies have been used to illustrate the issues. *Conclusion:* The corpus of evidence-based knowledge for software engineering is still developing. However, outcomes so far are encouraging, and indicate that in the future we can expect evidence-based research to play a larger role in informing practice, standards and teaching.

Keywords: Evidence-based · Empirical · Systematic review

1 Introduction

When teaching about software engineering (and many other topics in computing), one of the challenges we face is that much of our material requires us to provide students with knowledge which is in a 'catalogue' form. We might dress it up with models and formalism wherever possible, but basically we teach about a set of (relatively disjoint) topics that are loosely linked by such things as process models. This is contrast to most science subjects, where knowledge is imparted in a much more hierarchical fashion, with advanced topics building upon more basic knowledge.

So, one question that we might start with is where this knowledge (about design, testing, coding structures, ...) comes from? In many cases the answer is that it is largely derived from the experiences of expert practitioners, who have drawn upon observations of their own experiences (and maybe those of their colleagues too) and codified these in some way. Some examples of this are

© Springer International Publishing Switzerland 2016
P. Lorenz et al. (Eds.): ICSOFT 2015, CCIS 586, pp. 3–16, 2016.
DOI: 10.1007/978-3-319-30142-6_1

techniques such as structured programming, plan-driven design forms, design patterns, agile methods and test-first development.

This is not to imply that this is necessarily a bad thing, and indeed in computing where 'theory' is apt to be far divorced from application, it is likely to remain as the dominant way for new ideas to emerge. However, while it does mean that while we can benefit from good experiences, it is also essentially the way that a 'craft' develops rather than providing the basis needed for good engineering practice. And equally important, we are unlikely to have any reliable criteria for identifying the limitations of such knowledge. This is particularly true for software engineering where there are many confounding factors, most especially in the way that:

- software is used for a very wide range of roles in a very extensive set of application domains, so 'methods' that work in one context may be unsuitable for another.
- every practitioner has a different set of abilities and experiences, which may not always match those implicitly required for using particular techniques or methods.

So, given that this is the case, the ability to be able to *evaluate* and assess our practices is an important one, helping to move our knowledge about computing practices to an *evidence-informed* basis, rather than simply being dependent upon expert experiences. It also provides an important and valuable input to the way that we teach about our subject.

This review is therefore structured around a consideration of how we are currently able to answer the following four questions about software engineering knowledge.

1. How have our ideas about software engineering 'knowledge' been evolving?
2. How has the adoption of evidence-based studies changed the nature and quality of that knowledge?
3. How well can EBSE (evidence-based software engineering) inform practice, teaching and research?
4. What might we do to improve the quality of our knowledge?

The following sections address each of these in turn.

2   Empirical Knowledge in Computing

Q1. How have our ideas about software engineering 'knowledge' been evolving?
Software engineering knowledge covers a broad span: from process issues (project management, cost modelling, planning, lifecycles etc.) to technical issues (testing, design, programming, tools ...). And influencing most of these are human skills and experience, which may determine how the processes are performed and the technologies employed. This section briefly reviews the way that the use of empirical evaluation has evolved in computing, and in software engineering in particular.

2.1   Research Practice

We have some knowledge of how research and evaluation was conducted around the millennium from a set of studies reported in [7] that examined 1485 journal publications in computing over a five year period. For each of these the researchers identified the research methods the authors used and the *reference disciplines* that these drew upon. In particular, their study compared the practices in the three main branches of computing: computer science (CS), software engineering (SE) and information systems (IS).

The dominant research methods used were very different for each branch.

- For CS, most papers used either mathematically based *conceptual analysis* (73.4 %) or more analytically based forms of conceptual analysis (15.1 %).
- For IS, the dominant form was *field study* in various forms (24.5 %) along with some use of conceptual analysis.
- For SE, dominant forms were *conceptual analysis* (42.5 %) and *concept implementation*— "we built it and it worked" (17.1 %).

This indicates that the basis for software engineering knowledge:

- was based upon a culture of building things and using analysis rather than empirical evaluation;
- was codified in many ways, but rarely in any formal way.

In the period since this study was performed (1995–1999), empirical software engineering has been making substantial advances, both in terms of establishing accepted practice and of undertaking systematic evaluations. Indeed, this period has seen the establishment of a journal (*Empirical Software Engineering*) and two annual conferences (EASE and ESEM). Considerable effort has gone into developing and promulgating guidelines for use by researchers, and overall, there are indications that the quality of published empirical research has improved [13], although we have no recent studies to indicate how far the overall profile of research studies has changed.

2.2   Empirical Practice

For anyone with a grounding in the traditional sciences, the terms 'empirical' and 'experimental' are apt to be considered synonymous. This was probably largely the position for software engineering in the 1990s too. However, if we look more carefully, we can see that this is no longer the case. For this paper, we consider them to be defined as:

Empirical: Relying upon observation and experimental investigation rather than upon theory.
Experiment: "A study in which an intervention (i.e. a *treatment*) is deliberately controlled to observe its effects" [18].

So we can consider 'empirical' as being more of an umbrella concept that spans a wide range of forms and that it subsumes 'experimental', with experiments being simply one of these forms. Indeed, the transition from thinking about 'experiments' to thinking about'empiricism' probably reflects a growing confidence that software engineering is a distinct domain that draws upon many (often human-centric) reference disciplines.

One sign of this is the wider use of *qualitative* studies. While a quantitative study can help establish whether some form of *cause-effect* relationship exists (e.g. "does using pair programming for complex tasks require less time than when using solo programming?"), it can rarely identify *why* it might be so (or not). So to answer questions that are often stimulated by quantitative studies, such as "why different inspection groups may be more/less able to find errors, and possibly different types of error", really needs the deeper probing that can be provided by qualitative forms. For another, rather different, example, see [16].

Another sign is the use of a larger range of empirical forms, drawn from a wider set of reference disciplines. The earliest studies, starting in the 1980 s tended to be either observational (formal or informal) or involve the use of experiments or quasi-experiments. By the 1990 s researchers were also conducting some surveys, which became a more practical option with the emergence of the internet.

Post-2000 two significant developments have been increasing use of *case studies* modelled around the positivist approach developed by Robert K Yin [17,21] and of *systematic reviews*, or secondary studies [10]. Case studies provide an excellent vehicle for research 'in the field' and for investigating questions about such issues as the transition of technology into organisations. And secondary studies, discussed in the next section, provide the key underpinning of the ideas in this paper.

Overall, in terms of answering our first question, we should observe that new sources and forms of knowledge have become available, based on more systematic approaches to investigating how well our tools and techniques work, and in what circumstances they are most (or least) effective.

3   Secondary Studies

Q2. How has the adoption of evidence-based studies changed the nature and quality of that knowledge? Software engineering makes extensive use of human-centric studies in which human participants perform technical tasks, often requiring specialist training. (These are referred to as being *primary* studies.) One problem with this form of study is that the natural variability in performance by human participants, together with the many *confounding factors* that can influence the outcomes of a study, may well result in quite different results from separate studies, even when these use the same materials. Indeed, *replication* of such studies poses quite a challenging issue for empiricists, and this is currently an active research topic for empirical software engineers [20].

It is worth exploring this issue of variability a little more here, since it is an important factor when distinguishing between the use of experimentation in

Table 1. Sources of variability in experimental studies.

Form of study	Causes of variation
Natural sciences (humans as observers)	Any variation in the results of experiments tends to come from errors in measurement, and are usually relatively small
Human-centric (humans as recipients: e.g. Clinical RCTs)	We expect there to be some 'spread' of values in the outcomes because physical and physiological variability will mean that different people react differently
Human-centric (humans as participants: e.g. SE)	We expect quite a large spread in the outcome values because each participant involved will have a different combination of ability, skill and experience

traditional 'natural sciences' and its use in fields where humans are likely to be involved (medicine, social sciences, education, software engineering). Indeed, it is this very distinction that provides a strong motivating factor in favour of the use of secondary studies.

Table 1 summarises the causes for variation in experimental outcomes for three different contexts: natural sciences, where humans are primarily *observers*; fields where humans are *recipients* of some experimental treatment; and those where they actively *participate* in some way.

What this highlights is that for human-centric studies, such variation is to be expected (rather as an exam will usually produce a range of marks for a class), and it is not some artifact of measurement. So, when plotting the outcome values for a natural science study we might expect to show error bars and to see a normal distribution of values around a mean. In contrast, for human-centric studies we are more likely to use forms such as box plots (based on percentiles and the median) and expect these to show that data values might well be skewed.

3.1 Systematic Reviews

This natural variation of outcome values may well mean that an individual study has inconclusive results. One way to address this is to use a *secondary* study to aggregate the outcomes of a set of relevant primary studies in order to reduce the effects of this variability The *evidence-based* approach seeks to do this in a systematic, objective and repeatable way, and the main tool for doing so is the *systematic review*[1].

The evidence-based approach originated in clinical medicine, where one benefit of using randomised controlled trials (RCTs) is that the process of aggregation can use statistical meta-analysis. However it has spread widely to other branches of health and social care, to education, to management, and over the last decade,

---

[1] In software engineering this has often been referred to as a *systematic literature review* to distinguish it from code reviews. However, the proliferation of systematic reviews means that it is really no longer necessary to do so.

to software engineering. Software engineers have also made considerable use of *mapping studies*, which are a form of secondary study that seeks to identify what empirical knowledge exists about a topic, and in particular where there are clusters of studies, and also 'gaps' (identifying these of course requires some form of model of what aspects of the topic should be studied).

Of course the idea of the review article is not a new one, and expert reviews have long been an important element in many disciplines (perhaps rather less so in computing). However, one of the problems of the expert review is that two different experts conducting a review on the same topic may well select different studies and hence come to rather different conclusions. So an important element in the process of a systematic review is to minimise the element of individual choice. In particular, where decisions have to be made, it is customary to use two analysts, who are expected to resolve any differences and to report the degree of consistency (usually by using Cohen's *kappa* measure).

3.2   Performing a Systematic Review

So, how is a secondary study organised in software engineering? Essentially this is a five-step process, with the first three forming the *systematic review*, and the last two being the process of *knowledge translation* (KT). The steps are then as follows.

1. Convert information need into an answerable question.
2. Track down the best evidence relating to the question in a systematic and unbiased manner.
3. Critically appraise the evidence for validity, impact and applicability (usefulness).
4. Integrate the outcomes from critical appraisal with domain expertise and stakeholder requirements.
5. Evaluate the outcomes and improve the above steps.

One consequence of this is that the *research protocol* that forms the plan for any empirical study particularly needs to specify exactly how the evidence will be found and selected. With any empirical study it is important to avoid 'fishing' for results, and particularly so for a secondary study. This is usually related to the following two elements of the study:

Searching. The forms and bounds of this need to be clearly specified since the effectiveness of the search has an important effect upon the outcomes. There are arguments in favour of both manual searching and also of electronic searching using tools such as SCOPUS, IEEExplore, Web of Science etc. In addition, the use of *snowballing*, which involves following up the references of the studies initially selected can typically add a further 10 % of studies to the final set.

Inclusion/Exclusion. The candidate studies identified by the search process need to be filtered in order to determine which ones will be included in the study.

Doing so requires clear criteria that can be applied (preferably by two people). Bearing in mind that initial searches may well find several thousand candidate studies, and that the final number of studies used may well be below 50, this process needs to be clearly specified and performed systematically.

Performing both of these tasks will also be influenced by the ways in which primary studies are reported. There is an unfortunate tendency of computing researchers to re-invent the wheel (and terminology) that can complicate searching—as well as some limitations of our search engines. Ideally both searching and inclusion/exclusion can also be aided by good abstracts, and vice versa. Adoption of structured abstracts (as used at the head of this article) can help ensure that key information is provided in an abstract [3].

3.3 Influence upon Primary Studies

The relationship between primary and secondary studies is not a purely one-way flow. Secondary studies can also have an influence upon primary studies, both in terms of conduct and reporting. We can identify three important elements in this relationship.

– Since secondary studies involve expending substantial effort for data extraction, systematic reviewers are keen to encourage the use of better and more systematic *reporting standards* for primary studies. This has already occurred in domains such as clinical medicine and is an issue raised in many papers reporting systematic reviews in software engineering. The adoption of structured abstracts by a number of conferences and one journal can be considered as a useful step in this direction.
– A systematic review, and a mapping study in particular, may identify where further primary studies are needed to help provide better answers to specific research questions. At present, while this does occur in software engineering review, we lack any means of gathering this information together and making it widely available to researchers.
– A systematic review may well identify new research questions, but again, this information is not catalogued in any consistent form.

An example of identifying new research questions is the way that our systematic review examining "Empirical evidence about the UML" [2] helped to motivate the study reported in Marian Petre's award-winning paper presented at ICSE 2013, where this reported on a series of interviews with 50 experienced developers to find out how far, and in what ways, they actually *used* the UML [16].

So, returning to our second question, there are a number of ways in which EBSE has begun to change our knowledge about software engineering practices. These come primarily from the 'pooling' of the outcomes of individual studies, whether through a mapping of that knowledge, or through aggregation, as well as helping to identify how we might refine and extend our knowledge through new studies.

4   The Outcomes

Our third question (*How well can EBSE (evidence-based software engineering) inform practice, teaching and research?*) changes our focus from methodological aspects to what we can learn from the outcomes of systematic reviews in software engineering.

4.1   Tertiary Studies

In the decade since the publication of the seminal paper on EBSE [10] the number of secondary studies has proliferated, and keeping track of these has become quite a challenge. One way of checking on the number of secondary studies is to perform a systematic mapping study that identifies these—we term this a *tertiary* study. There have been three 'broad' tertiary studies reported, looking to see what existed [11,12,19], and subsequently most such studies have been more focused on specific themes rather than trying to map out the whole field.

An example of focused tertiary study is one we undertook that looked at how useful the available published systematic reviews were for use as teaching material. As a start we used the papers found by the three broad studies, and then performed a manual search of the five software engineering journals up to mid-2011 [4]. This identified 143 secondary studies (after removing duplicates where a study was reported in more than one venue), with 43 being considered as having direct value for teaching. (Obviously some of the others may also have value for teaching specialised topics, but our target was papers that could provide input to an introductory software engineering course.) We recently extended this study to the end of 2014, increasing the field to 216 studies, although only 59 of these were considered as providing useful material for teaching.

As a further backup, we conducted an electronic search for the period covered by our restricted manual search. This found over 250 further studies (the exact number is yet to be determined as we still have to remove duplicates). While many of these are very specialist in nature, and a very large proportion are mapping studies, it still leaves a likely total of over 400 secondary studies that have been published in the first decade of performing evidence-based studies in software engineering.

A fuller analysis of our dataset is still being conducted at time of writing, but it is possible to make some informal observations at this point.

- Few authors provide explicit *recommendations* based on the outcomes of their reviews, in part because the practices of knowledge translation are still immature for software engineering, but also because the effect sizes observed are often small. However, from a teaching perspective (and also that of practice), there are useful *conclusions* in many reviews that can help guide and inform learning and practice.
- Relatively few studies address the major technical issues of software engineering, such as requirements and design, although testing is covered well (most testing studies are not human-centric of course). This may be largely because

study topics are currently driven by researcher interest, rather than being commissioned by policy-making agencies (as happens in medicine, education and social sciences), although it may also reflect the nature of the available primary studies.
– Even where the outcomes of a study are limited or have only weak statistical significance, they can still offer useful insight. Indeed, part of their value may lie in helping students to be aware that software engineering is highly diverse and skill-dependent, and hence tends to lack clear 'right/wrong' answers to its questions.

Some of these points are illustrated more fully in the examples below.

4.2   Some Examples

Here we provide three brief examples of secondary studies, chosen to illustrate the range of topics addressed by such studies, their scale, and the type of outcomes that occur.

Agile Methods. The original study of the use of agile methods, published as [6], is often quoted as an excellent example of how to report such studies. The figures from searching are interesting:

– The initial search, after removal of duplicates, found 1996 studies.
– Exclusion on the basis of title reduced this to 821.
– Exclusion after reading (821) abstracts reduced the set to 270.
– After reading the full papers, the final set of studies was 36.

(We might note that secondary studies require an element of persistence!)
    Their main finding was a lack of trustworthy studies. They also found most papers were about XP (25), with only one addressing Scrum.

Pair Programming. This study is one of the rare examples where most of the primary studies were experiments and it was possible to perform a meta-analysis [9]. They again found quality issues, after reading the full papers they had 23 studies, but only 18 provided reports that were adequate for inclusion in the meta-analysis. They found limited evidence that the use of pair programming could:

– lead to higher quality code (small significance)
– be faster than conventional programming practices (small significance)
– could be less productive (moderate significance)

However, they suggest that the degree of heterogeneity in the findings does suggest that other factors could be involved.

Software Development in Startup Companies. The previous examples are rather 'technology'-focused, so this example is chosen to illustrate the wider scope of many studies [15]. As may occur with mapping studies, not all of the primary studies were actually empirical (some described frameworks or models) and none were controlled experiments. However, the paper did still suggest that there was some evidence to support the following practices:

- use of light-weight methodologies to obtain flexibility in choosing tailored practices, and to provide reactiveness so that the product could be changed to fit business strategies;
- using fast releases to build a prototype in an evolutionary way and use this to obtain users' feedback in order to help address uncertainty in the chosen market.

Overall, the outcomes from the tertiary study, as illustrated above, show that the aggregation of the outcomes from primary studies can provide a better and fuller understanding of a phenomenon or practice. As such therefore, by providing such insight, they can potentially begin to inform teaching, support practice, and help identify where new research could most usefully make a contribution.

5   Improving Knowledge

The fourth question posed at the start of this review was *Q4. What might we do to improve the quality of our knowledge?*. Inevitably this element is essentially 'informed speculation', and this section examines three factors that currently appear to be important for the development of EBSE.

5.1   Improving Empirical Quality

Over the past two decades there has been considerable effort dedicated to improving the quality of empirical studies, through books, guidelines and other activities (including the journal and conferences mentioned earlier).

A group of seven researchers recently conducted a study to see whether there was any measurable effect from these interventions [13]. The study itself formed a quasi-experiment (meaning that it was not possible to randomise the allocation of the material [18]). Its form was an 'interrupted-time-series' study, in which the team assessed the quality of a set of 70 papers describing experiments and quasi-experiments published in four major software engineering journals over the two periods:

- 1992–2002
- 2006–2010

Each paper was assessed by three members of the team (each person assessed thirty papers) using both a questionnaire with 9 quality questions, each scored on a scale of 0–3, and also providing an overall subjective quality score using the same range of values.

When analysed, the data showed a steady increase in quality over the period 1992–2010, as well as a significant linear relationship between the total quality score using the questionnaire, and the subjective assessments. However, because there were so many confounding factors, it was not possible to demonstrate that this improvement arose from the influence of the various articles and texts written by software engineering researchers, although obviously we may informally infer that these were likely to have been significant influences.

In terms of our fourth question, this is encouraging, improving the quality of primary studies can help to improve the quality of secondary studies.

5.2   Replication of Primary Studies

A concern for any experimentally-derived outcome is whether or not this has been biased by other factors. For natural sciences, results are usually not accepted until other researchers have been able to replicate them, usually in another laboratory, and much the same approach has been adopted for human-centric studies too.

Replication in software engineering has been studied quite extensively, for example as reported in [20]. There are many categorisations of replication types used in different disciplines [8], but for many purposes the two categories identified in [14] are sufficient to identify key roles:

Close replications repeat a study with a different set of participants, keeping the conditions of the study as close as possible to the original one. They are confirmatory in nature, aiming to see if the outcomes are the same when the study is repeated.

Differentiated replications seek to vary different aspects of a study in order to explore the boundaries of any observed effects.

Hence, close replications should be undertaken first, and if these are successful in confirming an effect, should then be followed by a range of differentiated studies.

Replication for software engineering has proved to be problematical, including getting the outcomes of replications published, since the importance of these has not always been understood by editors or reviewers. The systematic review reported in [20] particularly observed that:

– researchers are unlikely to publish non-confirmatory results for their own work;
– negative results are probably less likely to be accepted for publication;
– negative results might be easier to publish when these are related to the work of others.

This is an important topic, since effective replication can help improve systematic reviews. While close replications are of little use for synthesis, differentiated ones can make a valuable contribution.

5.3 Size of Studies

Many software engineering primary studies have a relatively small number of participants, making it more difficult to obtain clear outcomes where effect sizes are small. (In software engineering, the effect sizes of our interventions are usually small, and very few techniques really lead to large differences when compared with others). In part, this is because finding and recruiting participants who have relevant skills and experience can be problematical, not least because taking part in empirical studies is not an established part of our culture.

One way to improve this is to spread an experimental study across a number of different sites to obtain larger numbers of participants (for clinical studies, these are known as *multi-site trials*). For studies using human participants, the use of distributed experiments is as yet a relatively unexplored area (some initial experiences from a pilot study is reported in [5]). However, it does offer scope to help with improving the quality of primary studies, and hence secondary studies.

So, overall, there are various ways in which we might potentially improve the quality of software engineering knowledge yet further, but more work is needed to bring these into practice.

6 Conclusions

At the end of the first decade of evidence-based studies there are encouraging signs that these are achieving a greater maturity, although as yet few are really able to provide strong practice guidelines. A particular factor is the *quality* of primary studies, and in many cases, the relatively small effect sizes. Without improvements to these, the next generation of secondary studies may still be limited in their ability to inform practice and teaching as effectively as we would like. However, it is also relevant to observe that these issues are themselves stimulating further research, such as that in [16].

It is also interesting to note that evidence-based medicine (which has formed a relative avalanche in terms of its impact on the medical profession) actually started out with the mission of improving the teaching of clinical medicine [1]. The outcomes from evidence-based studies in any discipline clearly provide useful potential to inform teaching (and we ourselves are beginning to employ them in this role), and there may well be a useful lesson to learn there.

So, in terms of the question in the title—we do have more knowledge than we did ten years ago, but this is still rather 'patchy', and uneven in terms of quality. However, there are many encouraging signs that suggest that our knowledge will continue to evolve and improve over the next ten years.

Acknowledgements. This report draws upon the collective effort of many fellow researchers, and in particular the collaborative studies that I have undertaken with Barbara Kitchenham and Pearl Brereton, as well as the tertiary studies looking at teaching material with Pearl, Sarah Drummond and Nikki Williams. I would like to acknowledge all of their contributions.

More details about the practices of EBSE and empirical software engineering can also be found in *Evidence-Based Software Engineering and Systematic Reviews*, by Barbara Kitchenham, David Budgen and Pearl Brereton, Chapman & Hall, 2015.

References

1. Barends, E.G.R., Briner, R.B.: Teaching evidence-based practice: Lessons from the pioneers—An interview with Amanda Burls and Gordon Guyatt. Acad. Manag. Learn. Educ. **13**(3), 476–483 (2014)
2. Budgen, D., Burn, A., Brereton, P., Kitchenham, B., Pretorius, R.: Empirical evidence about the UML: a systematic literature review. Softw. Pract. Experience **41**(4), 363–392 (2011)
3. Budgen, D., Burn, A., Kitchenham, B.: Reporting student projects through structured abstracts: a quasi-experiment. Empirical Softw. Eng. **16**(2), 244–277 (2011)
4. Budgen, D., Drummond, S., Brereton, P., Holland, N.: What scope is there for adopting evidence-informed teaching in software engineering? In: Proceedings of 34th International Conference on Software Engineering (ICSE 2012), pp. 1205–1214. IEEE Computer Society Press (2012)
5. Budgen, D., Kitchenham, B., Charters, S., Gibbs, S., Pohthong, A., Keung, J., Brereton, P.: Lessons from conducting a distributed quasi-experiment. In: Proceedings of 2013 International Symposium on Empirical Software Engineering & Measurement, pp. 143–152. IEEE Computer Society Press (2013)
6. Dybå, T., Dingsøyr, T.: Empirical studies of agile software development: a systematic review. Inf. Softw. Technol. **50**, 833–859 (2008)
7. Glass, R., Ramesh, V., Vessey, I.: An analysis of research in computing disciplines. Commun. ACM **47**, 89–94 (2004)
8. Gómez, O.S., Juristo, N., Vegas, S.: Replications types in experimental disciplines. In: Proceedings of Empirical Software Engineering & Measurement (ESEM), pp. 1–10 (2010)
9. Hannay, J., Dybå, T., Arisholm, E., Sjøberg, D.: The effectiveness of pair programming: a meta analysis. Inf. Softw. Technol. **51**(7), 1110–1122 (2009)
10. Kitchenham, B., Dybå, T., Jørgensen, M.: Evidence-based software engineering. In: Proceedings of ICSE 2004, pp. 273–281. IEEE Computer Society Press (2004)
11. Kitchenham, B., Brereton, P., Budgen, D., Turner, M., Bailey, J., Linkman, S.: Systematic literature reviews in software engineering — a systematic literature review. Inf. Softw. Technol. **51**(1), 7–15 (2009)
12. Kitchenham, B., Pretorius, R., Budgen, D., Brereton, P., Turner, M., Niazi, M., Linkman, S.: Systematic literature reviews in software engineering — a tertiary study. Inf. Softw. Technol. **52**, 792–805 (2010)
13. Kitchenham, B., Sjøberg, D.I., Dybå, T., Brereton, P., Budgen, D., Höst, M., Runeson, P.: Trends in the quality of human-intensive software engineering experiments-a quasi-experiment. IEEE Trans. Softw. Eng. **39**(7), 1002–1017 (2013)
14. Lindsay, R.M., Ehrenberg, A.S.C.: The design of replicated studies. Am. Stat. **47**(3), 217–228 (1993)
15. Paternoster, N., Giardino, C., Unterkalmsteiner, M., Gorschek, T.: Software development in startup companies: a systematic mapping study. Inf. Softw. Technol. **56**, 1200–1218 (2014)
16. Petre, M.: UML in practice. In: Proceedings of the 2013 International Conference on Software Engineering (ICSE), pp. 722–731. IEEE Computer Society Press (2013)

17. Runeson, P., Höst, M., Rainer, A., Regnell, B.: Case Study Research in Software Engineering: Guidelines and Examples. Wiley, Hoboken (2012)
18. Shadish, W., Cook, T., Campbell, D.: Experimental and Quasi-Experimental Design for Generalized Causal Inference. Houghton Mifflin Co., Boston (2002)
19. da Silva, F.Q., Santos, A.L., Soares, S., França, A.C.C., Monteiro, C.V., Maciel, F.F.: Six years of systematic literature reviews in software engineering: an updated tertiary study. Inf. Softw. Technol. **53**(9), 899–913 (2011)
20. da Silva, F.Q., Suassuna, M., França, A.C.C., Grubb, A.M., Gouveia, T.B., Monteiro, C.V., dos Santos, I.E.: Replication of empirical studies in software engineering research: a systematic mapping study. Empirical Softw. Eng. **19**, 501–557 (2014)
21. Yin, R.K.: Case Study Research: Design & Methods, 5th edn. Sage Publications Ltd., London (2014)

Software Paradigm Trends

Filtered Model-Driven Product Line Engineering with SuperMod: The Home Automation Case

Felix Schwägerl[(✉)], Thomas Buchmann, and Bernhard Westfechtel

Applied Computer Science I, University of Bayreuth, 95440 Bayreuth, Germany
{felix.schwaegerl,thomas.buchmann,
bernhard.westfechtel}@uni-bayreuth.de

Abstract. Software Product Line Engineering promises to increase the productivity of software development. In the literature, a plan-driven process has been established that is divided up into domain and application engineering. We argue that the strictly sequential order of its process activities implies several disadvantages such as increased complexity, late customer feedback, and duplicate maintenance. SuperMod is a novel model-driven tool based upon a filtered editing model oriented towards version control. The tool provides integrated support for domain and application engineering, offering an iterative and incremental style of development. In this paper, we apply SuperMod to a well-known case study, the Home Automation System product line. We learn that the tool supports a broad variety of iterative and incremental development processes, ranging from phase-structured to feature-driven. Furthermore, it can mitigate the disadvantages of the traditional software product line development process.

Keywords: Software product line engineering · Software development process · Filtered editing · Model-driven engineering · Home automation example

1 Introduction

Software Product Line Engineering (SPLE) aims at systematic development of a family of software products by exploiting the variability among members thereof [1]. Core assets of different products are provided as the *platform*. Commonalities and differences among products are captured in *feature models* [2]. In the literature [3], a two-stage SPLE process is proposed (cf. Fig. 1): (1) During *domain engineering (DE)*, platform and variability model are defined. A *mapping*, e.g., *presence conditions* [4], specifies which part of the platform realizes which feature(s). (2) In *application engineering (AE)*, variability is resolved by specification of a *feature configuration*, and a product with the desired features is derived in a preferably automated way. For the definition of the platform, two distinct approaches exist: Using *positive variability*, a common *core* is defined to which specific features may be added. *Negative variability* proposes to specify

© Springer International Publishing Switzerland 2016
P. Lorenz et al. (Eds.): ICSOFT 2015, CCIS 586, pp. 19–41, 2016.
DOI: 10.1007/978-3-319-30142-6_2

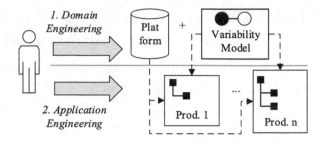

Fig. 1. The two-stage SPLE process as defined in the literature [3].

the platform as *superimposition* of product variants, from which elements must be removed to obtain a specific product.

Version Control (VC) has become indispensable for software engineers to control software evolution and to coordinate changes among a team. Version control systems *(VCS)* such as *Git* [5] or *Subversion* [6] provide an iterative three-stage editing model, which is shown in Fig. 2: (1) A developer *checks out* a specific revision of a software project from a *repository*. A copy of the project is created in the local *workspace*. (2) In the workspace, the developer *modifies* the project by implementing new functionality or by fixing bugs. (3) To make these modifications persistent and available to others, the developer *commits* his/her changes to the repository as a new revision.

Model-Driven Software Engineering (MDSE) [7] considers *models* as first-class artifacts, using well-defined languages such as the *Unified Modeling Language (UML)* [8]. Many model-driven applications are built upon the *Eclipse Modeling Framework* (EMF) [9]. The combination of MDSE with VC or SPLE is subject to many research activities, resulting in the integrating disciplines *Model Version Control* [10] and *Model-Driven Product Line Engineering (MDPLE)* [11], which improve tool support by raising the abstraction level of the artifacts subject to version control or variability.

Previous Work. In [12], we have elaborated a *conceptual framework* for the integration of SPLE and VC based on MDSE. The framework addresses the

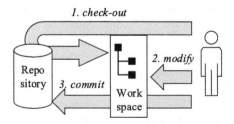

Fig. 2. The iterative three-stage editing model proposed by version control systems [5,6].

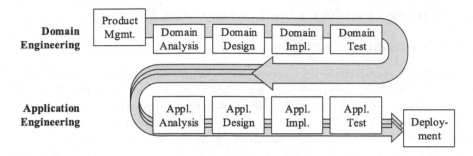

Fig. 3. Detailed phases of the traditional SPLE process as defined in the literature [3].

incremental development of a SPL in a single-version workspace using a filtered editing model that fully automates variability management. In addition to a revision graph, which describes evolution, a feature model and feature configurations are used to express logical variability. In [13], we have presented SuperMod, a model-driven tool that realizes the conceptual framework, allowing to develop a software product line in a single-version workspace step by step using the familiar version control metaphors *update*, *modify*, and *commit*.

Contribution. The current paper explores the development processes underlying existing SPLE tools relying on unfiltered editing on the one hand, and the impact of SuperMod's filtered editing model on development processes on the other hand. We apply SuperMod to a well-known SPLE example, the *Home Automation System (HAS)* product line [3], illustrating the following key observations:

- Using a filtered editing model, product lines may be developed in an iterative and incremental way, relaxing the strictly sequential order of DE and AE.
- By applying all changes representatively within one product variant, complexity is reduced when compared to multi-variant editing.
- Tool support for DE and AE is integrated, allowing to postpone the decision whether a change is product-specific or in the scope of multiple products until *commit*.
- The adaptation of the VCS-oriented editing model allows to propagate product-specific changes back to the product line.
- SuperMod is flexible with respect to the used SPLE process, ranging between phase-structured and feature-driven domain engineering.

Roadmap. Section 2 is dedicated to SPLE processes. Section 3 sketches the tool SuperMod used to carry out the HAS case study in Sect. 4. Related work is outlined in Sect. 5. Finally, in Sect. 6, open questions are discussed, before the paper is concluded.

2 Software Product Line Development Processes

2.1 The Traditional SPLE Process

The de-facto standard SPLE process has been sketched in the introduction. Figure 3 shows both sub-processes, domain and application engineering, being equally structured by the typical software development activities *analysis, design, implementation,* and *testing*. Prior to DE stands an additional activity, *product management*, where the scope of the product line is planned, including economical considerations. AE is applied repeatedly for each product; in the traditional SPLE process, it strictly follows DE and re-uses artifacts developed there, i.e., the outcomes of domain analysis, design, implementation, and testing. The sub-process terminates with the deployment of particular products.

The benefits of SPLE are obvious: Rather than developing products from scratch, they may be configured and refined based upon an existing platform. The more products are contained in the product line, the higher the return of investment will be. However, we argue that the traditional SPLE process suffers from a couple of disadvantages:

1. **Necessity of Additional Tools.** To manifest the captured variability in the platform, the toolchain must be extended by mapping tools in the case of negative variability, or composers or transformation languages in the case of positive variability. Obviously, additional tools require additional training effort and imply new sources of error. In the case of MDSE, tools need to be generic with respect to the used modeling language, which immediately leads to undesirable compromises concerning, e.g., the representation of model elements in concrete syntax.
2. **Complexity of the Multi-variant Platform.** Domain engineering requires the developers to keep track of all artifacts of the SPL. This raises complexity particularly concerning the implementation of variation points. Assuming that designing a good architecture is already a challenge for single system development, domain design and implementation become even more complex and error-prone. In many MDSE approaches, multi-variant models are constrained with single-version rules.
3. **Duplicate Maintenance.** Many tools, particularly in the context of MDPLE, aim at fully automated AE by reducing it to a simple configuration step. Frequently, product maintenance causes duplicate maintenance effort. For instance, a bug report may be at first glance specific to a single product, but then become relevant to different members of the product line. Technically, the problem is caused by the automated configuration of products being a one-way road. *Round-trip* support between DE and AE is urgently required.

2.2 Iterative and Incremental Software Product Line Engineering

Iterative SPLE. In analogy to the waterfall model for single-system development, the traditionally applied sequential SPLE process has soon been extended

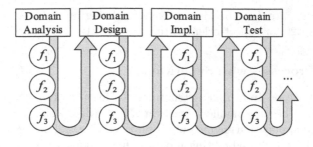

Fig. 4. Phase-structured domain engineering. The identifiers f_i refer to different features and their connected realization artifacts in the platform.

by feedback loops and *iterations*, making SPLE more flexible. Gomaa's *double spiral* development model [11] allows for alternations between the activities of DE and AE, which are executed in intertwined spirals. Similarly, Clements and Northrop [1] define an iterative SPLE process consisting of three main activities, namely *Core Asset Development*, *Product Development*, and *Management*, which coarsely correspond to DE, AE, and product management, respectively. It is assumed that all three activities are performed in parallel, evolving both the platform and individual products continuously.

Iterative SPLE still assumes that DE is performed in a strictly sequential way as shown in Fig. 4. In the beginning of each iteration, during *domain analysis*, several features are introduced. These features are further designed, implemented, and tested during the subsequent activities. This implies a *phase-structured* domain engineering process, which typically consists of long-running iterations that have to be planned extensively in advance.

Phase-structured SPLE processes allow to maintain an overview of the overall product line, easing architectural decisions necessary to anticipate variation points. For this purpose, *multi-version editing tools* are employed, e.g., preprocessor languages [14] in source-code centric approaches and mapping tools [15,16] in MDPLE.

Incremental SPLE. *Feature-Oriented Software Development (FOSD)* summarizes a plethora of different techniques and paradigms for the development of variational software in general, and SPL in particular [17]. In the sub-discipline *Stepwise and Incremental Software Development (SISD)* [18], features are described as *refinements* or *layers* of an existing software system and consecutively added to the platform as separate *increments*. The implied *feature-driven* and incremental realization of domain engineering is sketched in Fig. 5 as a counterpart to the phase-structured way. By introducing one feature at a time, this results in comparatively short-running iterations.

In the FOSD context, feature-driven development is preferred over phase-structured approaches. Rather than focusing on multi-variant architectural decisions and explicitly modeling variation points, product changes associated with a specific features are described in a preferably fine-granular way, e.g., by using composition [19, 20] or aspect-oriented techniques [21].

2.3   SPLE Processes with SuperMod

During the transition from phase-structured to feature-driven SPLE, the performed iterations become smaller. Accordingly, the distinction between domain engineering and application engineering is blurred. The tool SuperMod presented in Sect. 3 provides a filtered editing model, which makes multi-variant artifacts transparent to the SPL engineer by uniformly supporting DE and AE. An increment is performed *representatively* in a particular product variant and then propagated to the platform. Increments correspond to change sets, each referring to a partial feature configuration, which may be developed over multiple iterations. SuperMod is compatible with SPLE processes ranging between phase-structured and feature-driven. The disadvantages of the traditional process listed in Sect. 2.1 are addressed as follows:

1. **Familiar VCS and SPL Metaphors.** SuperMod is added to the toolchain as a new tool, implying the aforementioned difficulties. However, SuperMod's user interface relies on familiar concepts such as version control metaphors (*check-out* and *commit*) and established SPL abstractions (*feature models* and *configurations*).
2. **Filtered Editing.** Changes are generally performed on single-variant products, which eases architectural decisions. Variation points are created automatically and transparently. In the case of MDPLE, the variability of the invisible multi-variant model is unconstrained.
3. **Automatic Propagation of Changes.** After having finished an iteration, the performed changes are propagated to the platform automatically, removing the necessity of duplicate maintenance. In SuperMod, there is technically no distinction between DE and AE. Only at *commit* time, the user must decide whether a change is product-specific or global.

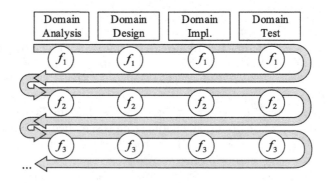

Fig. 5. Feature-driven domain engineering.

3   The Tool SuperMod

This section briefly describes SuperMod [13], a model-driven tool that allows to develop software product lines in an iterative and incremental way as proposed in the previous section. First, we explain theoretical foundations of the tool. Thereafter, SuperMod's architecture and editing model are sketched and the operations *check-out*, *modify*, and *commit* are redefined. The tool is available for evaluation as Eclipse plug-in (see installation instructions at the end of this paper). Currently, SuperMod is restricted to single-user operation; support for team collaboration is scheduled for future releases.

3.1   Underlying Principles

SuperMod realizes the conceptual framework presented in [12], which integrates MDSE, SPLE, and VC. The framework in turn specializes the *uniform version model* [22], adding higher-level representations for both the version space (i.e., feature models and revision graphs) and the product space (i.e., EMF models). Below, the core concepts of UVM and its extensions are described informally.

- **Options:** An *option* is a temporal or logical property of a software system, which may or may not be included in a specific product version. In SuperMod, two kinds of options exist: *revision options* and *feature options*.
- **Choices:** A *choice* denotes a single valid version by assigning a selection (*selected* or *deselected*) to each of the existing options. Choices are used as *read filters*, i.e., they describe product versions available in the workspace.
- **Ambitions:** An *ambition* denotes a set of versions as a subset of all valid versions. Ambitions are used as *write filters* in order to delineate the scope of a product change performed in the workspace. In contrast to a choice, an ambition may contain *unbound* options, to which the change is immaterial.
- **Version Rules:** The set of available choices and ambitions is constrained by a set of *version rules*, logical expressions over the option set. Version rules are used, e.g., in order to implement constraints such as mutual exclusion imposed by feature models, or to designate subsequent revisions.
- **Visibilities:** A visibility is a logical expression over the option set, which is attached to an element of the feature or domain model. In order to test an element's presence in a specific version, the bindings specified by the respective choice are applied. Visibilities are modified automatically during the operation *commit*.

3.2   Tool Architecture and Editing Model

Both the architecture and the editing model of SuperMod are inspired by *distributed VCS* [5]. The traditional VCS architecture is extended as follows: Firstly, the feature model is an additional artifact varying along the temporal dimension. Secondly, the domain model varies along two dimensions, the revision graph and the feature model. Figure 6 illustrates the remarks below.

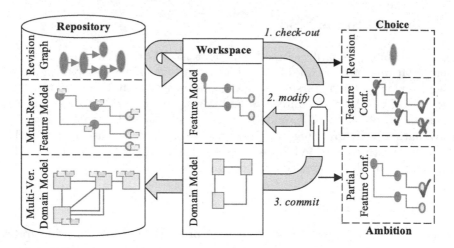

Fig. 6. SuperMod tool architecture and editing model.

Repository. A *repository* is a persistent storage transparently linked to a software project under VC. Developers communicate with it by means of the metaphors *check-out* and *commit*. A SuperMod repository consists of three layers.

– The *revision graph* is a directed acyclic graph that describes the temporal history of a SuperMod project. The graph is extended automatically each time a new revision has been committed. For each revision, a *revision option* is introduced transparently together with a *version rule* that realizes the relationship to the predecessor revision.
– The *multi-version feature model* plays a dual role: Firstly, its evolution is controlled by the revision graph. Secondly, each feature is mapped to a *feature option*, such that the feature model provides an additional version model. Feature model constraints are mapped to *version rules* transparently [12].
– The *multi-version domain model* describes the superimposition of the versioned project. Although the term "domain model" is used here, the project may comprise a file hierarchy containing model or non-model resources. Within the *visibilities* of domain model elements, both revision and feature options may occur.

Workspace. A SuperMod workspace contains the currently selected version of the domain model in its single-version representation. EMF models are represented as instances of their custom Ecore-based metamodel(s). Plain text and XML files are made available in their ordinary format, allowing SuperMod users to utilize their preferred single-version editing tools. During the sub-process *modify*, they may also edit the feature model, e.g., by introducing new features or relationships.

Version Specification. A version in the temporal dimension corresponds to a single revision. As mentioned above, *feature configurations* specify choices and ambitions in the logical dimension. When referring to an iterative and incremental development process (cf. Sect. 2.2), version specification happens in the beginning and at the end of each iteration. A feature configuration is specified on the current revision of the feature model. When provided as an ambition, the feature configuration may be *partial*[1] and typically binds only few features, in many cases only one feature. The *effective choice/ambition* is formed during check-out/commit as conjunction of the temporal and logical component.

3.3   Check-Out, Modify, and Commit

In the following, the operations *update*, *modify*, and *commit* known from VCS are redefined on top of SuperMod's architecture and editing model (cf. Fig. 6).

Check-Out. Like in ordinary VCS, the operation *check-out* is provided to select a specific version (the *choice*) from the repository, which is then copied to the workspace:

- The user selects a *revision* as the temporal component of the choice. The *feature model* is filtered by the revision, and made available for modification in the workspace.
- The user specifies a completely bound feature configuration, which forms the logical component of the choice. The *effective choice* is recorded persistently.
- The domain model is filtered by the effective choice and *exported* into the local workspace. The *export* transformation translates multi-version resources into their specific single-version representation, e.g., plain text or XMI files.
- The filtered and exported contents are made available in the workspace.

Modify. The user may *modify* both the filtered feature model and the filtered domain model within the workspace. For domain model resources, arbitrary editors may be used. For the feature model, the command *Edit Version Space* is offered, which delegates to a specific model editor for the current feature model revision.

Commit. The operation *commit*, the counterpart to *check-out*, propagates changes performed in the workspace to the repository under a user-specified scope (the *ambition*):

---

[1] Our notion of partial feature configuration only implies that there exist unbound features. This differs from the concept of *staged configurations* (as introduced, e.g., in [4]), which need to be specified in a top-down way, introducing parent-child selection constraints.

- A new *revision* is created as the successor of the revision specified for the choice and selected in the temporal component of the ambition. Within the given revision of the feature model, the logical component of the ambition is user-specified as a *partial feature configuration*. For consistency, it is required that the set of versions described by the effective ambition include the recorded choice.
- The original state of the workspace version is temporarily restored by applying the recorded choice to the repository. The new state is generated by *importing* (the inverse of *export*) the current workspace into its multi-version representation.
- *Differences* are computed between the original and the new workspace state.
- Inserted elements are copied into the repository.
- The *visibilities* of inserted/deleted feature model elements are updated automatically by adding/subtracting the temporal component of the ambition to/from the existing visibility.
- In analogy, the *visibilities* of inserted/deleted domain model elements are updated by adding/subtracting the *effective ambition*.

4   The Home Automation Case Study

We apply the tool SuperMod presented in Sect. 3 to the standard example of a product line for Home Automation Systems from [3]. The example is divided up into a phase-structured and a feature-driven part. First, the activities *analysis* (Sect. 4.1), *design* (Sect. 4.2), and *implementation* (Sect. 4.3) are executed, realizing an initial DE iteration. During implementation, a command-line application is developed based on the generated source code. Due to space restrictions, the activity *testing* has been omitted. In the second part, we transition into feature-driven DE, extending the product line by a new feature ensuing from a customer request (Sect. 4.4). Last, we present our observations and refer back to the SPLE processes from Sect. 2.

For analysis and design, we rely on UML *use case, activity, package,* and *class diagrams* [8], using the GMF[2]-based UML modeling tool *Valkyrie* [23] and its Java code generator. The remarks below are illustrated by screencasts available on our web pages; please follow the link provided at the end of this paper.

4.1   Requirements Analysis

Requirements analysis is split into two phases. To begin with, residents' interactions with the HAS are documented in a use case diagram. Subsequently, one use case is representatively refined by means of an activity diagram.

After having initialized a Valkyrie project and having connected it to Super-Mod version control, the first phase is started with an empty use case diagram. In consecutive iterations, we add actors, components, use cases, and relationships as summarized in Table 1. The table also shows that the feature model

---

[2] *Graphical Modeling Framework*, http://www.eclipse.org/modeling/gmp/.

Table 1. Commit history of the use case diagram.

Rev.	Ambition	Changes to feature model	Changes to use case diagram
1	H.A.S.	added feature H.A.S.	added actor Resident and component H.A.S.
2	Id.Mech.	added feature Id.Mech.	added component Id.Mech., contained use cases, includes, and connected use links
3	DoorLock	added feature DoorLock	added comp. DoorL., use cases Lock and Unlock
4	DoorLock	—	added missing use links for Lock and Unlock
5	AlarmAct.	added feature AlarmActivision	added component AlarmActivision, contained use cases, and connected use links
6	SMSTo-Owner	added features Ac.Sig., Vid.S., PoliceInf., and SMSToOwner	added use case Change Phone Number
7	Heat.Cont.	added feature Heat.Cont.	added component Heat.Cont. and contents

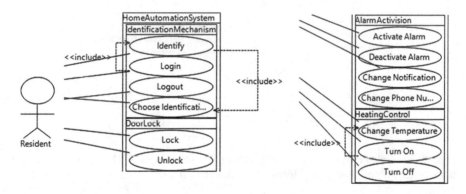

Fig. 7. The use case diagram of the HAS example after revision 7, shown in a variant that includes all mandatory and optional features available.

is developed simultaneously, introducing new features on demand in order to delineate the scope of the respective changes. Figure 7 shows a variant of the final use case diagram.

During the second analysis phase, the feature IdentificationMechanism is further refined by adding three concrete mechanisms, namely Keypad, Magnetic-Card, and FingerprintScanner. These are collected in an OR-group, meaning that at least one mechanism must be chosen in a valid configuration. In case several mechanisms are available, one of them must be chosen during identification. The

Table 2. Commit history of the activity diagram for Identify.

Rev.	Ambition	Changes to feature model	Changes to activity diagram
8	H.A.S.	added XOR groups below DoorL. and HeatingCont.	—
9	Id.Mech.	—	initialized diagram, added initial and final nodes, Choose Mech., decision/merge nodes, and flows
10	Keypad	added OR group with Keypad, Mag.Card, Fp.Scanner	added action KeypadIdentification and incoming/outgoing flow
11	Mag.Card	—	added action M.C.Id. and incoming/outgoing flow
12	Fp.Scan.	—	added action Fp.Id. and incoming/outgoing flow

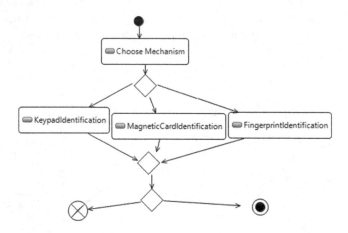

Fig. 8. The activity diagram of the use case Identify after revision 12, shown in a variant that includes all sub-features of IdentificationMechanism.

available selection should be restricted by the active features; this is realized in revisions 10 until 12 shown in Table 2. The resulting activity diagram is shown in Fig. 8; Fig. 9 shows the refined feature model.

4.2   Design

The static structure of the HAS product line is also developed in two phases. After modeling an initial package diagram, specific packages are refined by class diagrams.

Table 3 indicates that the package diagram (see Fig. 10) is developed in an iterative and incremental way by realizing one feature after another. Variation

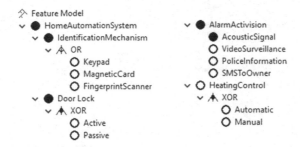

Fig. 9. The feature model after revision 12, shown in SuperMod's feature model editor. Filled circled denote mandatory features, empty circles optional child features. OR groups require the selection of at least one, XOR groups of exactly one child feature.

Table 3. Commit history of the package diagram.

Rev.	Ambition	Changes to package diagram
13	HomeAutomationS.	added package has and contained class HomeAutomationSystem
14	Ident.Mechanism	added package identification, class Id.Mech., and interface IMechanism
15	Keypad	added class Keypad
16	MagneticCard	added class MagneticCard
17	FingerprintScanner	added class FingerprintScanner
18	DoorLock	added package doorLock and interface IDoorLock
19	Active	added class ActiveLock
20	Passive	added class PassiveLock
21	AlarmActivision	added package alarm, class AlarmAct., and interface IAlarmService
22	AcousticSignal	added class AcousticSignal
23	VideoSurveillance	added class VideoSurveillance
24	PoliceInformation	added class PoliceInformation
25	SMSToOwner	added class SMSNotifier
26	HeatingControl	added package heating and contained interface IHeatingControl
27	Automatic	added class heating::Automatic
28	Manual	added class heating::Manual

points are anticipated by sketching the use of appropriate *design patterns* such as *strategy* and *command* [24], which are subsequently refined by class diagrams. Here, we refrain from introducing new features during the design phase, although permitted in general.

As shown in Table 4, the package identification is refined by a class diagram,

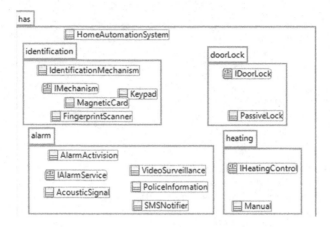

Fig. 10. The package diagram after revision 28. The shown product variant does not include features Active and Automatic, thus not classes doorLock::ActiveLock and heating::Automatic, either.

exemplifying the realization of variation points during design. In revision 29, general details are added to the class IdentificationMechanism as well as to the interface IMechanism that realizes the *command* pattern. Its specific realizations are added subsequently and scoped with the respective feature. In this example, the only necessary changes are to make the respective command classes realize IMechanism (see Fig. 11). In fact, more details could have been added to the classes here. Furthermore, similar refinements might have been applied to the packages doorLock, alarm, and heating.

4.3   Implementation

In our model-driven product line, the static part of the source code can be derived from the artifacts developed in the *design* phase using *Valkyrie*'s code generator. The main class HomeAutomationSystem shall contain the main executable as command-line application. Below, we confine the presentation to the

Table 4. Commit history of the class diagram refining package identification.

Rev.	Ambition	Changes to class diagram for package identification
29	Ident.Mechanism	initialized diagram, detailed class Ident.Mech. and interface IMech.
30	Keypad	added interface realization originating from class Keypad
31	MagneticCard	added interface realization originating from class MagneticCard
32	FingerprintScanner	added interface realization originating from class FingerprintScanner

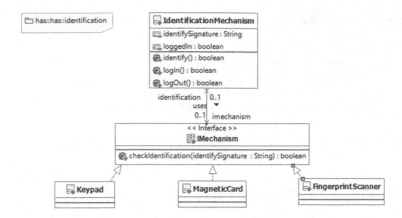

Fig. 11. The class diagram that refines package identification in its state after revision 32, with features Keypad, MagneticCard, and FingerprintScanner selected.

implementation of the method identify() of class IdentificationMechanism, which implements the activity diagram from Fig. 8.

Table 5. Overall commit history of the *implementation* phase.

Rev.	Ambition	Changes to IdentificationMechanism.java or other source files
33	HomeAutomationS.	generated Java source code
34	Ident.Mechanism	added multi-variant implementation to method identify() (l. 96 − 101)
35	**not** Fp.Scanner	removed FingerprintScanner.java and line 99
36	**not** MagneticCard	removed MagneticCard.java and line 98
37	**not** Keypad	removed MagneticCard.java and line 97

Variability is achieved by making the declarations and usages of specific mechanism classes dependent on their respective features. As shown in Table 5 and Listing 1.1, after the initial code generation run in revision 33, *negative variability* is simulated: In revision 34, a multi-variant implementation is provided. We then connect the variable constructor calls and the concrete implementation classes to their respective features by applying the *negative implementation*, i.e., by removing the corresponding source code file and the statement containing the constructor call, and by committing against the negation of the respective ambition[3]. In order to perform these deletions, it is necessary to switch to a suitable choice where the respective features are deselected, e.g., the choices presented in the screencast.

---

[3] Equivalently, we could have applied the positive realization and committed it against positively bound features; however, this would have required three additional code generation increments.

```
95   private void identify() {
96       List<IMechanism> mechs = new LinkedList<>();
97       mechs.add(new Keypad());
98       mechs.add(new MagneticCard());
99       mechs.add(new FingerprintScanner());
100      IMechanism mech = (...) // choose interactively
101      return mech.checkIdentification(getIdentifySignature());
102  }
```

Listing 1.1. Implementation of the method IdentificationMechanism.identify() in revision 34.

4.4 Handling a New Customer Request

So far, our SPL has been developed in a phase-structured way, following the classical development activities *analysis*, *design*, and *implementation*. Now, we demonstrate how SuperMod allows to quickly react to a new customer request that cross-cuts all three development activities; we realize the increment in one single iteration.

The customer requests to extend the list of identification mechanisms available in the HAS product line by a new, *biometric* mechanism that uses existing iris scanner hardware and drivers. We check-out the latest revision of the HAS project, choosing the customer's product variant, which currently includes all sub-features of IdentificationMechanism. Then, we handle the request as follows (due to space restrictions, we cannot present the modified artifacts here; please refer to the screencasts):

- **Analysis:** It is obvious that a new feature Biometric must be introduced into the OR-group below IdentificationMechanism (cf. Fig. 9). The request does not affect the use cases, but the activity diagram that details the use case Identify (cf. Fig. 8): We add a new action BiometricIdentification and connect it to the decision/merge node in analogy to the existing identification actions.
- **Design:** We add a new class Biometric as well as a realization of the interface IMechanism to the class diagram shown in Fig. 11. This transparently extends the package diagram (cf. Fig. 10).
- **Implementation:** The (incremental) code generation is re-invoked, creating a new source file Biometric.java. To the implementation of method IdentificationMechanism.identify() (cf. Listing 1.1), we add the following statement after line 99:

    ```
    mechs.add(new Biometric());
    ```
- **Deployment:** The current iteration is finalized by committing all pending changes to the repository under revision 38. As logical ambition, we specify a partial configuration that selects only the new feature Biometric. Hence, the performed modifications hold for future variants that include this feature. At last, the current product variant is deployed to the customer, without the need for an additional AE run.

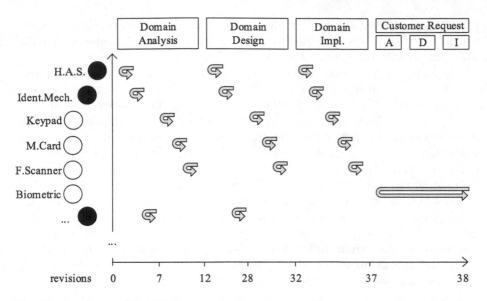

Fig. 12. Summary of the HAS example: Iterations and increments performed during specific development activities, aligned with the temporal (x-axis) and logical dimension (y-axis).

4.5 Results and Observations

Key Figures. Our example SPL has evolved over a total of 38 iterations, distributing as follows: 12 iterations for analysis, 20 for design, 5 for the implementation of a cut-out of the functionality, and one additional iteration for the new customer request. In total, the product line contains approximately 100 model elements, from which 17 source code files have been derived, the largest of which contains 137 lines of code. The final feature model contains 17 features, 10 of which are optional. The entire version management has been performed by specifying 6 choices (cf. screencasts) and 38 ambitions, respectively, during *check-out* and *commit*.

According to the mechanisms described in [12,13], 410 *visibilities* have been added to elements, attributes, and links contained in the transparent multi-variant UML model (not including its graphical representation). Necessarily, the same number of *feature expressions* or *presence conditions* would have to be manually be specified when using an explicit mapping model in a tool relying on positive variability, e.g., [15] or [16].

Remarks on SPLE Process and Tools. Figure 12 summarizes the relevant cut-out of the example. When considering DE as a whole, one could sum up revisions 1 until 37 as one process iteration, including the DE activities *analysis*, *design*, and *implementation*. Technically, a multitude of iterations have been performed using fine-grained *check-out/commit* cycles in order benefit from

SuperMod's automated variability management and filtered editing model. Note-worthily, the iterations belonging to each phase are arranged roughly diagonally when referring to the temporal and logical dimension.

Revision 37 may be considered as an initial major revision of the product line, after which we transition from phase-structured to feature-driven development in order to integrate *customer feedback* more flexibly. The change performed in revision 38 is realized in the customer's product variant and then added to the product line transparently by committing the change against the new feature Biometric. This way, *duplicate maintenance* is *avoided* by the tool-level integration of DE and AE.

In sum, the example has shown that SuperMod is compatible with both a phase-structured and a feature-driven style of iterative and incremental SPLE development. In addition to a *reduced version management overhead*, the example has demonstrated a *minimal planning effort* when referring to particular iterations; features are introduced on demand. The advantages of *tool independence* and *unconstrained variability* discussed in [12] can also be reproduced in the HAS example.

5   Related Work

This paper continues a series of previous publications on the SuperMod project and its foundations. In [12], the underlying conceptual framework for the integration of VC, SPLE and MDSE has been defined. The paper also contains a general overview of literature concerning the integrating disciplines *Model-Driven Product Line Engineering* [11], *Model Version Control* [10], and *Software Product Line Evolution* [25]. In [13], the tool SuperMod has been presented using the standard example of a product line for *graphs* [26]. Additionally, the paper contains a comparative domain analysis of VC and SPLE and aligns SuperMod with different tools that share VC and SPLE concepts. In this section, we compare our work to different iterative and/or incremental approaches to SPLE and to other occurrences of the HAS case study.

The Home Automation System example has been introduced by Pohl et al. [3] to illustrate different activities of the traditional SPLE process (cf. Fig. 3). The authors stress the importance of the activity *domain analysis*, where an initial feature model is produced. During *domain design* and *domain implementation*, a reference architecture and core implementation assets are constructed. In *domain testing*, component tests are written. These artifacts are then filtered and composed during corresponding *application engineering* activities, concluding with testing the product using respective component tests. As opposed to our version of the HAS example, the original version has been developed in a strictly phase-structured way.

Among others, the authors of [27] have observed that agile principles potentially increase the applicability of SPLE while reducing time to market. They present a bottom-up, test-driven approach inspired by *Extreme Programming* [28]. After defining a test case specific to a new feature, its realization is incorporated to the product line using systematic refactoring techniques. However, the presented solution is not as highly automated as the SuperMod approach. Furthermore, when compared to our example, the iterations are still relatively long-running. Presumably, SuperMod can also meet the requirements of agile SPLE.

In [29], an approach to filtered (*projectional*) editing of multi-variant programs is described. Like in our work, the motivation is a reduction of complexity gained by hiding variants not important for a specific change to a multi-variant model. Visibilities are managed automatically, but in contrast to our approach, the *choice* always equals the *ambition*. Furthermore, the restriction of a *completely bound choice* does not exist since the user operates on a *partially filtered* product which still contains variability. The wider the ambition, the more variability information is kept in the workspace, increasing maintenance overhead especially for wide ambitions.

Völter et al. [21] apply *aspect-oriented* techniques such as modularization and composition in order to realize the HAS example using positive variability. The platform is described at a high level of abstraction using a custom domain-specific language. During product derivation, artifacts belonging to the selected features are composed. This leads to a reduction of complexity with respect to architectural decisions of the modular artifacts, but raises new problems when it comes to conflicting composition rules.

In [15,30], the HAS example has been used to demonstrate consistency mechanisms of the MDPLE tool FAMILE, which relies on negative variability and unfiltered editing. The tool allows to connect a manually developed multi-variant domain model to a feature model in a dedicated *mapping model* using *feature expressions*, and to automatically configure products. Contradictions among feature expressions may lead to inconsistencies within the mapping model. The presented solutions, which include a domain specific language for repair actions, are interactively controlled by the SPL engineer. In contrast, SuperMod makes both the multi-variant model and feature expressions transparent, and product conflicts are resolved by the user in batch mode.

The HAS example is frequently referred to in the context of dynamically reconfiguring systems, which can be considered as product lines that use run-time variability. An example is provided in [31], where the platform itself is described using MDSE techniques. When compared to our compile-time based solution, time to market is even shorter. However, consistent component interaction must be manually ensured.

6   Discussion

Having conducted two standard examples with the tool SuperMod and having defined an appropriate development process, we are now able to discuss the potential research impact as well as the limitations of our proposed approach. The following open questions will also stimulate future research directions.

How Steep is SuperMod's Learning Curve? In the beginning, SuperMod's editing model seems quite unfamiliar, in particular to SPL engineers who are used to unfiltered editing approaches, where they fully control the multi-variant architecture. According to our own experience, planning the iterations and learning to specify a correct ambition are the most challenging parts. We have observed that small iterations and frequent commits require a fair amount of discipline. The effective training effort of SuperMod remains to be experimentally quantified and compared to unfiltered SPLE approaches.

Do We Still Require Unfiltered Editing? Intentionally, SuperMod users never get in touch with multi-version artifacts, since they always operate in a single-version view. This reduces complexity, but also awareness of the variability present in the overall product line. In some situations, one wants to inspect or modify the multi-version artifacts in an unfiltered way, e.g., in order to revise erroneously specified ambitions. A compromise between filtered and unfiltered editing is *partially filtered editing* [29]. However, preprocessor-like variability annotations are technically hard to realize for graphically represented models.

Where are Organized Reuse and Variation Points? SPL are based on the principle of *organized reuse*. When developing the multi-variant architecture, variation points are planned in advance and explicitly realized using the features of the respective programming or modeling language, e.g., inheritance. SuperMod does not require to explicitly model and document variation points; on the contrary, they are completely transparent to the user. This fact is in turn linked to the advantage of reduced complexity and the disadvantage of limited awareness of variability [12]. Furthermore, in SPLE, features are typically introduced in the beginning during *product management*. In contrast, our approach dedicates the decision, when to introduce new features, to the user.

How to Control the Multi-variant Architecture? This question is linked to the preceding two answers. Due to the single-version view and the fact that variation points are transparent, the challenge of designing a multi-variant architecture never arises. However, this also removes the chance to control the architecture, e.g., by refactoring. Does this result in a "worse" multi-variant architecture? Provided that it is transparent to the user anyway, is a "good" multi-variant architecture important at all? The properties of automatically constructed multi-variant architectures need to be further investigated.

7   Summary and Outlook

In this paper, we have revisited a well-established SPLE case study, the Home Automation System SPL. We have employed the tool SuperMod, which is focused on but not restricted to model-driven SPL. Its user interface is oriented towards version control by offering the metaphors *update*, *modify*, and *commit.* Developers may evolve the SPL in a single-version workspace, while changes are propagated to the multi-version platform transparently, obviating the need for up-front, multi-variant design. The evolution of multi-variant product artifacts is mostly automated. SuperMod's integrated tool support enables a round-trip between DE and AE, whose distinction is blurred by fine-granular *update/commit* cycles and by keeping products in the product line until deployment.

With respect to the underlying SPLE process, our example has demonstrated that SuperMod is compatible with different styles of iterative and incremental development, ranging from phase-driven domain engineering, which has been applied to create an initial major revision of the product line, to feature-driven development, which has been enforced to integrate customer feedback and to integrate the respective change to the product line transparently, without the need of duplicate maintenance.

When compared to state-of-the-art approaches, our presented solution minimizes both planning and maintenance effort. Furthermore, the amount of manually specified variability information is significantly lower. Using the presented procedure and tool, the SPLE developer may focus on product-specific design decisions, reducing the cognitive complexity in the domain engineering phase. SuperMod integrates well with existing tools, particularly in the EMF world.

Future work addresses extensions to SuperMod, including multi-user support, product conflict resolution, and difference representation. Furthermore, we aim to continue the experimental evaluation of our approach using a case study of industrial scale.

8 Accompanying Resources

The research prototype *SuperMod* is available as a set of Eclipse plug-ins under the Eclipse Public License. The plug-ins may be installed into a clean Eclipse Luna Modeling distribution using the following update site:[4]. The items *Super-Mod Core* and *SuperMod Revision+Feature Layered Version Model* should be selected for installation. Furthermore, we provide several screencasts where SuperMod's usage with both the *graph* example from [13] and the *HAS* example from this paper is demonstrated:[5].

Acknowledgements. The authors give thanks to Marco Dmitrow for adapting the HAS case study in a master project and for valuable input for the improvement of SuperMod.

References

1. Clements, P., Northrop, L.: Software Product Lines: Practices and Patterns. Addison-Wesley, Boston (2001)

---

[4] http://btn1x4.inf.uni-bayreuth.de/supermod/update.
[5] http://btn1x4.inf.uni-bayreuth.de/supermod/screencasts.

2. Kang, K.C., Cohen, S.G., Hess, J.A., Novak, W.E., Peterson, A.S.: Feature-oriented domain analysis (FODA) feasibility study. Technical Report CMU/SEI-90-TR-21, Carnegie-Mellon University, Software Engineering Institute (1990)
3. Pohl, K., Böckle, G., van der Linden, F.: Software Product Line Engineering: Foundations. Principles and Techniques, Berlin (2005)
4. Czarnecki, K., Kim, C.H.P.: Cardinality-based feature modeling and constraints: a progress report. In: International Workshop on Software Factories at OOPSLA 2005, San Diego, California, USA. ACM (2005)
5. Chacon, S.: Pro Git, 1st edn. Apress, Berkely (2009)
6. Collins-Sussman, B., Fitzpatrick, B.W., Pilato, C.M.: Version Control with Subversion. O'Reilly, Sebastopol (2004)
7. Völter, M., Stahl, T., Bettin, J., Haase, A., Helsen, S.: Model-Driven Software Development: Technology, Engineering Management. Wiley, New York (2006)
8. OMG: UML Superstructure. Object Management Group, Needham, MA. formal/2011-08-06th edn. (2011)
9. Steinberg, D., Budinsky, F., Paternostro, M., Merks, E.: EMF Eclipse Modeling Framework. The Eclipse Series, 2nd edn. Addison-Wesley, Upper Saddle River (2009)
10. Altmanninger, K., Seidl, M., Wimmer, M.: A survey on model versioning approaches. Int. J. Web Inf. Syst. (IJWIS) 5, 271–304 (2009)
11. Gomaa, H.: Designing Software Product Lines with UML: From Use Cases to Pattern-Based Software Architectures. Addison-Wesley, Boston (2004)
12. Schwägerl, F., Buchmann, T., Uhrig, S., Westfechtel, B.: Towards the integration of model-driven engineering, software product line engineering, and software configuration management. In: Hammoudi, S., Pires, L.F., Desfray, P., Filipe, J. (eds.) Proceedings of the 3rd International Conference on Model-Driven Engineering and Software Development (MODELSWARD 2015), Angers, France, pp. 5–18. SCITEPRESS (2015)
13. Schwägerl, F., Buchmann, T., Westfechtel, B.: SuperMod - A model-driven tool that combines version control and software product line engineering. In: ICSOFT-PT 2015 - Proceedings of the 10th International Conference on Software Paradigm Trends, Colmar, Alsace, France, pp.5–18. SCITEPRESS (2015)
14. Kästner, C., Trujillo, S., Apel, S.: Visualizing software product line variabilities in source code. In: Proceedings of the 2nd International SPLC Workshop on Visualisation in Software Product Line Engineering (ViSPLE), pp. 303–313 (2008)
15. Buchmann, T., Schwägerl, F.: FAMILE: tool support for evolving model-driven product lines. In: Störrle, H., Botterweck, G., Bourdells, M., Kolovos, D., Paige, R., Roubtsova, E., Rubin, J., Tolvanen, J.P. (eds.) Joint Proceedings of Co-Located Events at the 8th European Conference on Modelling Foundations and Applications. CEUR WS, Building 321, DK-2800 Kongens Lyngby, pp.59–62. Technical University of Denmark (DTU) (2012)
16. Heidenreich, F., Kopcsek, J., Wende, C.: FeatureMapper: mapping features to Models. In: Companion Proceedings of the 30th International Conference on Software Engineering (ICSE 2008), pp. 943–944. ACM, New York (2008)
17. Apel, S., Kästner, C.: An overview of feature-oriented software development. J. Object Technol. 8, 49–84 (2009)
18. Batory, D., Sarvela, J.N., Rauschmayer, A.: Scaling step-wise refinement. In: Proceedings of the 25th International Conference on Software Engineering, ICSE 2003, pp. 187–197. IEEE Computer Society, Washington, DC (2003)

19. Jayaraman, P., Whittle, J., Elkhodary, A.M., Gomaa, H.: Model composition in product lines and feature interaction detection using critical pair analysis. In: Engels, G., Opdyke, B., Schmidt, D.C., Weil, F. (eds.) MODELS 2007. LNCS, vol. 4735, pp. 151–165. Springer, Heidelberg (2007)
20. Zschaler, S., Sánchez, P., Santos, J., Alférez, M., Rashid, A., Fuentes, L., Moreira, A., Araújo, J., Kulesza, U.: VML* – A family of languages for variability management in software product lines. In: van den Brand, M., Gašević, D., Gray, J. (eds.) SLE 2009. LNCS, vol. 5969, pp. 82–102. Springer, Heidelberg (2010)
21. Völter, M., Groher, I.: Product line implementation using aspect-oriented and model-driven software development. In: Proceedings of the 11th International Software Product Line Conference, SPLC 2007, pp. 233–242. IEEE Computer Society, Washington, DC (2007)
22. Westfechtel, B., Munch, B.P., Conradi, R.: A layered architecture for uniform version management. IEEE Trans. Softw. Eng. **27**, 1111–1133 (2001)
23. Buchmann, T.: Valkyrie: A UML-based model-driven environment for model-driven software engineering. In: Hammoudi, S., van Sinderen, M., Cordeiro, J. (eds.) Proceedings of the 7th International Conference on Software Paradigm Trends (ICSOFT 2012), pp.147–157. SCITEPRESS (2012)
24. Gamma, E., Helm, R., Johnson, R., Vlissides, J.M.: Design Patterns: Elements of Reusable Object-Oriented Software, 1st edn. Addison-Wesley Longman, Amsterdam (1995)
25. Laguna, M.A., Crespo, Y.: A systematic mapping study on software product line evolution: From legacy system reengineering to product line refactoring. Sci. Comput. Program. **78**, 1010–1034 (2013)
26. Lopez-Herrejon, R.E., Batory, D.: A standard problem for evaluating product-line methodologies. In: Dannenberg, R.B. (ed.) GCSE 2001. LNCS, vol. 2186, pp. 10–24. Springer, Heidelberg (2001)
27. Ghanam, Y., Maurer, F.: Extreme product line engineering – refactoring for variability: a test-driven approach. In: Sillitti, A., Martin, A., Wang, X., Whitworth, E. (eds.) XP 2010. LNBIP, vol. 48, pp. 43–57. Springer, Heidelberg (2010)
28. Beck, K., Andres, C.: Extreme Programming Explained: Embrace Change, 2nd edn. Addison-Wesley Professional, Reading (2004)
29. Walkingshaw, E., Ostermann, K.: Projectional editing of variational software. In: Generative Programming: Concepts and Experiences, GPCE 2014, Vasteras, Sweden, 15 16 September 2014, pp. 29–38 (2014)
30. Buchmann, T., Schwägerl, F.: Ensuring well-formedness of configured domain models in model-driven product lines based on negative variability. In: Proceedings of the 4th International Workshop on Feature-Oriented Software Development, FOSD 2012, pp. 37–44. ACM, New York (2012)
31. Cetina, C., Giner, P., Fons, J., Pelechano, V.: Autonomic computing through reuse of variability models at runtime: The case of smart homes. Computer **42**, 37–43 (2009)

A Semantic Versioning Service Based on Formal Certification

Jean-Yves Vion-Dury$^{(\boxtimes)}$ and Nikolaos Lagos

Xerox Research Centre Europe, 6 Chemin de Maupertuis, 38330 Meylan, France
{jean-yves.vion-dury,nikolaos.lagos}@xrce.xerox.com

Abstract. This work describes a Version Broker Service that enables consistent management of dynamic digital resources throughout their life cycle. The service handles the association of resources with logical specifications formally expressed using an extensible logical language understood and agreed by tiers. A new version of a digital resource is considered *certified* only if the resource owner is able to formally prove that the new version satisfies the logical specifications, with the help of the service. A method is also described to both use formal proofs for qualifying changes (occurring either on the resource content or on the corresponding specifications), and for characterizing them through the evolution of version labels. While the resource owners may handle a fully detailed specification (called *internal*), the users may have a simplified view of the same resource, i.e. a particular *external* specification. The service we propose can manage changes consistently, in a sound manner, for both perspectives, all potential users, and change cases.

Keywords: Versioning model · Semantic versioning · Formal specification · Formal proofs · Change management

1 Introduction

Versioning is particularly challenging in dynamic, non-centralized architectures, as propagating changes in a consistent manner requires strict coordination of tiers. Such a case is for example service-oriented architectures, where the separation of the service interface from its implementation, often referred to as opacity, is an additional complexity (changes in the interface or the implementation may impact the contract that the service provider has with a consumer from a functional or quality-of-service (QoS) point) [1].

In our context, versioning support has two dimensions [1]: Interface versioning, which is support for the description of the behaviour expected by clients of a system, e.g. artifacts that describe the interaction of the service with its environment (for instance definitions of data in WSDL and Abstract BPEL documents in the case of service-environment); implementation versioning which is support for the code, resources, configuration files and documentation of a system.

© Springer International Publishing Switzerland 2016
P. Lorenz et al. (Eds.): ICSOFT 2015, CCIS 586, pp. 42–62, 2016.
DOI: 10.1007/978-3-319-30142-6_3

While traditional Software Configuration Management (SCM) systems, such as Subversion and GIT (among others), are being widely used for implementation versioning, interface versioning is still a not very-well studied subject.

This work presents a method towards Version Management that enables consistent management of digital resources throughout their life cycle for the benefit of both resource owners/providers (the entities offering the resource) and resource users (the entities using the resources), and exemplifies it in a service-oriented setting. As part of the method we define how resources can be associated with logical specifications written in an extensible logical formalism understood and agreed by tiers. We also describe how a Version Broker Service (VBS) can verify the well-formedness of proofs and properties when required, so that the version labels stay consistent.

2 Related Work

Version management includes defining strategies for: version naming (which should aid in recording the evolution of a resource); and for identifying/responding to different updates (which should be related to controlling the consistency of different versions). In this work we deal with both of the above issues and integrate them into a single framework.

Version naming is most typically designed to reflect consumer compatible and non-compatible (or breaking and non-breaking) changes. The former constitute major releases and the latter minor ones. The corresponding naming usually follows the "Major#.Minor#" scheme where the sequential major release version number precedes the minor one [2]. Alternatively naming schemes may incorporate a time-stamp instead of the above identifier. However, the above naming schemes provide very limited semantic information about the relationships between versions [3].

Recent work, especially in the area of web services, recognises the importance of having semantic information relevant to versioning and try to inject such information. For instance, [4] extends WSDL and UDDI with corresponding meta-data. In [5,6] a three-label version scheme is proposed, where each label is incremented in response to changes in the versioned resource (in their case each label corresponds to one of data components, message components and features). [7] goes one step further by not only assigning semantics to version labels but also using them to determine the compatibility between entities (e.g. UML processes) and source code modules. However, the naming scheme is defined by the provider and it is the job of the consumers to use this consistently. Our method allows separate identifiers for the service owner/provider and each of the users(s)/consumer(s). Based on this idea we propose the use of a dedicated versioning service implementing our method, which would ensure the consistency of the mapping between the different identifiers.

Similar work can be found, in terms of formalising the evolution of artifacts in dynamic environments, in [8], where a theoretical type-safe framework is proposed to ensure correct versioning transitions in service-oriented environments.

Although their method sketches the relation between the notion of compatibility and specifications, they do not provide any formal grounding on how the modelling of consistent change is reflected by the naming scheme of different variants. In addition, they do not refer at all to the notion of a dedicated versioning service functioning as broker, a direct versioning approach being implied to the best of our understanding. In direct approaches the consumer and provider are directly connected and each one has to manage changes to their requirements and offer respectively. In our case, we propose an intermediary-based approach, where the consumer does not have to communicate with the provider directly but only through a third service (i.e. a broker). The broker is responsible for managing the changes happening to any of the connected services (a preferred approach in the context of service-oriented environments is [9]).

Another close work is done by [10]. The author formalises the notion of component versioning to support consistent substitutability of components and falls under the umbrella of software configuration management for component-based systems. Although very interesting, the work is mainly focused on a specific architecture (widely used for software components) called CORBA [11].

3   Key Ideas

The first key idea of our method is to provide certified version evolution. Certification represents a strong guarantee that pre-defined usage properties of digital resources are preserved. In addition, the impact of changes is faithfully reflected by the version labels managed by the VBS. This desirable property is the consequence of a rigorous versioning model, operated with the help of logical tools able to verify properties and build proofs. Hence, when the data owner wants to register the evolution of a resource, or of its logical specifications, he is asked to provide proofs that the system is able to check for correctness. Thanks to the internal logic of the VBS, these proofs are minimized.

The second key idea is to clearly separate the "contract" of the resource owner (i.e. the logical specification that formally characterizes the resource) from the "contract" of the resource users (i.e. the logical specification that formally characterises the expected use of the resource). To the best of our knowledge, versioning is today associated with one unique central specification (API, contract, document) used by both the provider and the consumer of the resource. In this proposal, we consider that a resource has one provider (or *owner*) responsible for its maintenance and evolution and possibly many consumers (or *users*) able to retrieve and download the resources based on our version label based designation mechanism. Depending on their needs, users may have a more or less simplified view of the resource properties. This is a big step in our opinion, as simplified views will require less effort regarding the certification of versions, and will tune the resource to the exact needs of the user, who consequently will be less exposed to incompatible changes. Based on this distinction, the VBS will help the resource owner to propagate rigorously the changes toward a coherent labeling scheme adapted to the various needs of its consumers.

We believe that the above two innovations can enable the exploitation of the VBS with radically new business models related to the management of the evolution of resources, for the benefit of all parties.

4 The Versioning Model

4.1 Invariants, Specifications, Theories

We represent the logical characterisation of a resource via two logical formulae: the first one is the *invariant*, i.e. the logical properties that the resource must always satisfy during its life cycle; the second one, *specification*, is a logical formula that may change over time, but that the resource must satisfy in order to be *certified*. The *certification* of a resource is therefore a formally established proof that the new version is consistent with the resource logical specification. Consequently, a version increment can be generated (the choice of the increment type is left to the owner, but must satisfy specific logical properties, as explained later in the paper).

Associating an invariant with a versioned resource means that if a resource owner intends to derive versions, then something common to all versions should be preserved. Otherwise, versions are not needed, one just need to derive a new resource with a different name and different logical characteristics, and start a novel life cycle.

What is the role of the specification? We assume that versioning systems should have an abstract description that explains what is the resource and how it can be used. For instance, this can be a document describing an API (Software Engineering and Service Oriented Architectures), it can be an SQL schema for a data set, an XSD schema for an XML document, and so on. A specification can also be used to describe tests that a resource should pass in order to be considered valid.

We also distinguish between: external specification, describing the behaviour that is expected by users of the resource, e.g. an API exposing methods to a service's clients; internal specification, describing the behaviour that is expected by the owner of the resource, e.g. support for changes in the code and documentation.

Such a specification is formally expressed in this work using an underlying core logic $\mathcal{L}$ (see Sect. 5.2 and a specific, owner designed, *theory* $\mathcal{T}$, which extends the core logic with axioms and theorems suitable to handle the owner's applicative domain.

The key idea is that the versioning method, presented in this paper, is based on formal proofs to certify a versioning step. Such a proof will take the form of a proof term, i.e. a particular data structure that reflects exactly how the proof was constructed from the axioms and the theorems. Although it can be hard to build such a proof, it is easy to verify that it is well-formed and that it is indeed a proof of the claimed property.

4.2 Structure of Version Labels

A resource r represents a digital content (its digital extension as a bitstream) and is related to a unique identifier and a version label defined as $[M.m.\mu : \nu]/s$, where M, m, μ, ν, s are natural numbers greater or equal to 0. The number M stands for *major* revision, m for *minor*, μ for *micro*, ν for *variant* and s for *stamp*. Minor versions preserve the backward compatibility (while possibly offering new functionalities); micro versions have no visible impacts from the external specification point of view (improvements, bug fixes, simplifications...); while major versions may require revising the processes depending on the changing resource (this scheme is coined as *Semantic Versioning* [12]). With this it is a straightforward way to communicate to the users of a resource whether its evolutions are backward compatible or incompatible.

The stamp is incremented at each modification operation, independently of versioning mechanisms. As a consequence, a resource can be updated and never versioned, meaning that the changes can be tracked and memorized, but without any assumptions regarding its semantic properties. A resource r is *certified* when a versioning operation was able to logically establish its compliance with its semantic specification(s). The version label is designed in order to reflect this, as the variant component must be null.

4.3   Version-Based Ordering

Version labels are built in such a way that they are totally ordered for a resource. This is important since this means that one can always find the antecedent of a given version based on the label structure. We define an order $\prec$ on version labels through:

$$\forall M, M', m, m', \mu, \mu', \nu, \nu', s, s' \text{non negative integers}$$

$$
\begin{aligned}
M < M' &\Rightarrow [M.m.\mu : \nu]/s \prec [M'.m'.\mu' : \nu']/s' \\
m < m' &\Rightarrow [M.m.\mu : \nu]/s \prec [M.m'.\mu' : \nu']/s' \\
\mu < \mu' &\Rightarrow [M.m.\mu : \nu]/s \prec [M.m.\mu' : \nu']/s' \\
\nu < \nu' &\Rightarrow [M.m.\mu : \nu]/s \prec [M.m.\mu : \nu']/s' \\
s < s' &\Rightarrow [M.m.\mu : \nu]/s \prec [M.m.\mu : \nu]/s'
\end{aligned}
$$

Version labels evolve in such a way that the following property always holds.

Proposition 1. *Monotonicity of stamps*

$$\forall M', m', \mu', \nu', s' \text{non negative integers}$$
$$[M.m.\mu : \nu]/s \prec [M'.m'.\mu' : \nu']/s' \Rightarrow s < s'$$

This property says that for a resource r, the stamp $\mathbf{stamp}(r) = s$ tracks all change history regardless of the evolution of the version label. In order to abstractly handle resources, we define three *destructors* to access those attributes:

$$\mathbf{identifier}(r) = \ell \qquad \mathbf{content}(r) = c \qquad \mathbf{version}(r) = [M.m.\mu : \nu]/s$$

Similarly, versioning labels can be de-constructed with the following functions:

$$
\begin{aligned}
\mathbf{major}([M.m.\mu : \nu]/s) &= M \\
\mathbf{minor}([M.m.\mu : \nu]/s) &= m \\
\mathbf{micro}([M.m.\mu : \nu]/s) &= \mu
\end{aligned}
\qquad
\begin{aligned}
\mathbf{update}([M.m.\mu : \nu]/s) &= \nu \\
\mathbf{stamp}([M.m.\mu : \nu]/s) &= s
\end{aligned}
$$

Given the above, we can build a partial order over versioned resources as follows.

Definition 1. *Partial Ordering of Resources*

$$\forall r, r' \quad r \prec r' \quad \textit{iff} \quad \textbf{identifier}(r) = \textbf{identifier}(r') \wedge \textbf{version}(r) \prec \textbf{version}(r').$$

4.4 Designation and Selection of Resources

To be able to select and retrieve resources, we define herein the designation mechanism. Resources can be designated through a term built from the following syntax:

$$
\begin{array}{lll}
D & ::= \ell & | \quad \ell[V_1] \quad | \quad \ell/s \quad | \quad \ell/\star \quad | \quad \ell/? \\
V_1 & ::= \star & | \quad ? \quad | \quad M \quad | \quad M.V_2 \\
V_2 & ::= \star & | \quad ? \quad | \quad m \quad | \quad m.V_3 \\
V_3 & ::= \star & | \quad ? \quad | \quad \mu
\end{array}
$$

All resources $\mathcal{E}$ can be retrieved with the resolution function noted ! that takes as input the designation term, and returns a set of resources accordingly, defined in Table 1.

Table 1. Resolution of references.

Reference	Result	Comment	Certified
$!(\ell)$	$!(\ell/\star)$	shorthand	
$!(\ell/?)$	$\{r \in \mathcal{E} \mid \textbf{identifier}(r) = \ell\}$	all variants	yes/no
$!(\ell/\star)$	$\sup_{\prec}[!(\ell/?)]$	last variant	yes/no
$!(\ell/s)$	$\{r \in !(\ell/?) \mid \textbf{stamp}(r) = s\}$	a particular variant	yes/no
$!(\ell[M])$	$!(\ell[M.\star])$	shorthand	
$!(\ell[\star])$	$\sup_{\prec}[!(\ell[?])]$	last version	yes
$!(\ell[?])$	$\{r \in !(\ell/?) \mid \textbf{major}(\textbf{version}(r)) > 0\}$	all variants	yes
$!(\ell[M.m])$	$!(\ell[M.m.\star])$	shorthand	
$!(\ell[M.\star])$	$\sup_{\prec}[!(\ell[M.?])]$	last M version	yes
$!(\ell[M.?])$	$\{r \in !(\ell/?) \mid \textbf{major}(\textbf{version}(r)) = M\}$	all M versions	yes
$!(\ell[M.m.\mu])$	$\{r \in !(\ell[M.m.?]) \mid \textbf{micro}(\textbf{version}(r)) = \mu\}$	this version	yes
$!(\ell[M.m.\star])$	$\sup_{\prec}[!(\ell[M.m.?])]$	last $M.m$ version	yes
$!(\ell[M.m.?])$	$\{r \in !(\ell[M.?]) \mid \textbf{minor}(\textbf{version}(r)) = m\}$	all $M.m$ versions	yes

The jocker ? denotes all available components that match some versioning constraints, whereas $\star$ denotes the highest available component, and therefore, is always a singleton (or the empty set if the condition is not satisfied). The notation $\ell[?]$ designates the set containing all versions of the resource ℓ, $\ell[\star]$ the last qualified version, $\ell[3.\star]$ designates the last minor and micro version derived from the major revision 3 of ℓ. For some value M, m, μ the designation $\ell[M.m.\mu]$ always maps to a singleton (provided this derivation belongs to the history of the resource), as well as ℓ/s, under the same condition. The notation $\ell/?$ designates the set of all variants of ℓ regardless of any versioning information, and $\ell/\star$ the most recent element of this set, if any.

5   The Certification Model

5.1   Dynamics of Resources and Specifications

In addition to the resource r, internal I_r, and external $E_{r,c}$ specifications can also change. The triple $\langle r, I_r, E_{r,c} \rangle$ can be considered certified, if the fundamental property (Sect. 5.3) is verified. Still, uncertified resources have a versioning label and can be designated and retrieved. By construction, a version label including a non zero variant is uncertified.

Figure 1 illustrates an example where three update operations are applied on a certified resource (with version label $\ell[1.1.3 : 0]/13$). The first two steps track modifications of the resource content, whereas the third one tracks the modification of the internal specification. The last step corresponds to a minor qualification, to establish that the fundamental invariant is satisfied: the resource satisfies the modified specification and this one is a logical extension of the original specification (and is thus backward compatible). From this last property, we can deduce that the modified specification is also a logical extension of the invariant.

5.2   Underlying Logic and Its Implementations

The expressiveness of an appropriate logic depends on the requirements of the application; however, higher order logic is commonly used today, implemented with powerful proof assistants, embedding interactive/automated tactic based theorem provers [13], and is generic enough to cover practical cases.

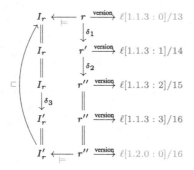

Fig. 1. Example updates for a resource r with identifier ℓ and specification I_r.

Logic $\mathcal{L}$. This logic, called $\mathcal{L}$, should be equipped with a particular relation that checks well-formedness of terms, in order to be sure that a logical specification is indeed a term that can be managed by axioms and theorems. We note this relation $\mathbf{wf}(P)$, or equivalently, using a generic typing relation, as $\mathbf{type}(P, prop)$. This logic $\mathcal{L}$ must also be equipped with a proof system able to explicitly handle proof terms. We note $\mathcal{L} \vdash \mathbf{proof}(p, P)$ the logical relation establishing that p is a proof of P in $\mathcal{L}$. Consequently, proving a property P is a process that will construct a proof term p. In general, it is much more difficult to build the proof term than to check for its correctness, the latter being usually implemented through simple and efficient algorithms (see for instance how proofs become first order entities in [14] and Dedukti [15] and how proof terms are built and computed in any logic based on the Curry-Howard correspondence [16]).

We expect also that extensions suited to domain specific applications will be expressed as additional theories $\mathcal{T}_0, \mathcal{T}_1, \cdots$ that will be designed to work on top of $\mathcal{L}$. In those cases, the $\mathcal{L}, \mathcal{T}_0, \mathcal{T}_1, \cdots \vdash \mathbf{proof}(p, P)$ will be the natural extension of the notation presented above, to express a proof in the aforementioned set of theories.

To illustrate, consider the higher order intuitionistic logic $\mathcal{L}$ (whose associated proof system is based on natural deduction [17], where elimination and introduction rules are associated with each construct). If we consider a formula like

$$\forall A.\forall B.((A \wedge B) \Rightarrow B)$$

A proof using sequents and natural deduction could be for instance

$$
\cfrac{
  \cfrac{
    \cfrac{
      \cfrac{
        \cfrac{\top}{A \wedge B \in A \wedge B, \emptyset}\in_L
        \quad
        \cfrac{
          \cfrac{
            \cfrac{\top}{B \in B, A \wedge B, \emptyset}\in_L
          }{B \in A, B, A \wedge B, \emptyset}\in_R
        }{A, B, A \wedge B, \emptyset \vdash B}I_\vdash
      }{A \wedge B, \emptyset \vdash B}E_\wedge
    }{\emptyset \vdash (A \wedge B) \Rightarrow B}I_\Rightarrow
  }{\emptyset \vdash \forall B.(A \wedge B) \Rightarrow B}I_\forall
}{\emptyset \vdash \forall A.\forall B.(A \wedge B) \Rightarrow B}I_\forall
$$

This proof can be mapped into a structurally equivalent proof term using all applied rule names

$$I_\forall(I_\forall(I_\Rightarrow(E_\wedge(\in_L, I_\vdash(\in_R (\in_L))))))$$

which can be checkedfor correctness using a dedicated predicate $\mathbf{proof}(p, P)$:

$$
\cfrac{
  \cfrac{
    \cfrac{\top}{\in_L \; \therefore \; A \wedge B \in A \wedge B, \emptyset}\in_L
    \quad
    \cfrac{
      \cfrac{\top}{\in_L \; \therefore \; B \in B, A \wedge B, \emptyset}\in_L
      \quad
      \cfrac{\in_R (\in_L) \; \therefore \; B \in A, B, A \wedge B, \emptyset}{I_\vdash (\in_R (\in_L)) \; \therefore \; A, B, A \wedge B, \emptyset \vdash B}
    }{E_\wedge(\in_L, I_\vdash(\in_R (\in_L))) \; \therefore \; A \wedge B, \emptyset \vdash B}E_\wedge
  }{I_\Rightarrow(E_\wedge(\in_L, I_\vdash(\in_R (\in_L)))) \; \therefore \; \emptyset \vdash (A \wedge B) \Rightarrow B}I_\Rightarrow
}{
  \cfrac{I_\forall(I_\Rightarrow(E_\wedge(\in_L, I_\vdash(\in_R (\in_L)))), I_\vdash(\in_L)))) \; \therefore \; \emptyset \vdash \forall B.(A \wedge B) \Rightarrow B}{I_\forall(I_\forall(I_\Rightarrow(E_\wedge(\in_L, I_\vdash(\in_R (\in_L)))))) \; \therefore \; \emptyset \vdash \forall A.\forall B.(A \wedge B) \Rightarrow B}I_\forall
}I_\forall
$$

Fundamental Logical Relations and Properties. When a resource r satisfies a logical formula F, this is noted as $r \models F$. The $\sqsubset$ relation expresses strict logical implication:

$$F_1 \sqsubset F_2 \text{ iff } F_2 \Rightarrow F_1 \wedge \neg(F_1 \Rightarrow F_2)$$

whereas $\sqsubseteq$ expresses the logical implication (therefore, is reflexive):

$$F_1 \sqsubseteq F_2 \text{ iff } F_2 \Rightarrow F_1$$

The $\sqcap_F$ relation expresses "partial disjunction", i.e., that a logical intersection F exists between two formulas:

$$F_1 \sqcap_F F_2 \text{ iff } F \sqsubset F_1 \wedge F \sqsubset F_2 \wedge \neg(F_1 \sqsubseteq F_2)$$

Defined this way, this relation produces two subcases: one where $F_2 \sqsubset F_1$ (F_2 is strictly more specific than F_1) and one where $\neg(F_2 \sqsubset F_1)$ (F_1 and F_2 are strictly conjunctive). Both situations make sense when interpreting major version evolution (which potentially can raise incompatibility issues). The first one expresses cases where a specification is restricted (producing some regression in the expectation), the second situations where a specification evolves by extending some points, but regressing on others.

The $\approx$ relation just expresses logical equivalence (but is typically used when F_1 and F_2 are syntactically distinct):

$$(F_1 \approx F_2) \text{ iff } F_2 \Leftrightarrow F_1$$

It is easy to show that the $\sqsubset, \sqsubseteq, \approx$ relations are transitive, and since the logic is expected to be sound, we also assume the following property holds:

$$(F_1 \sqsubseteq F_2 \wedge r \models F_2) \Rightarrow r \models F_1$$

We denote the change of resource r into r' by a relation δ, such that $\delta(r) = r'$.

5.3 Certification of Resources and Specifications

When a client asks that a resource r is certified (creation of a new major, minor or micro version), he/she must provide one or several proofs, depending on the past operations and the current context (some cases are detailed in Sect. 5.3). The proofs are checked for correctness, i.e., the system verifies that they indeed establish the expected properties P_i or $\mathcal{L}, \mathcal{T}_0, \mathcal{T}_1, \cdots \vdash \mathbf{proof}(p, P_i)$. Moreover, depending on the kind of change, some "structural" properties may be verified: well-formedness of changed specifications and that the resource satisfies the specifications.

Checking a proof is easy, while building the proof term (formally proving a property) can be of unbounded difficulty, depending on the application domain (and consequently on the power of theories operated by the resource owners). However, many useful scenarios can be captured by simple theories, and proofs can be established either by a proof assistant or even by specialized programs, such as type checkers. Note that run-time execution performance of such programs would not be as crucial as during development cycles, since they are used only in the certification phase. Properties such as schema membership (XML validation, database relational schema) can be processed automatically by dedicated algorithms, after those schemes are translated into $\mathcal{L}$ inside an appropriate theory. Similarly, API signatures for a software library, making use of decidable type systems, can be similarly processed through an equivalent approach.

Section 5.3 details some change cases with respect to the versioning certification. The changes involve three entities: the resource r, its internal specification I_r, and its external specification $E_{r,c}$ for a particular client c.

Version Consistency. The certification process aims at controlling the evolution of the tuple $\langle r, \mathbf{I}_r, I_r, E_{r,c} \rangle$ for all resources r, for all clients c of r and associated specifications I_r and $E_{r,c}$, and the invariant $\mathbf{I}_r$. This is achieved in a way that the resource satisfies all specifications, and the external specification visible by the client is a specialization of the internal specification (controlled by the owner). Both external and internal specifications must always specialize the initial invariant $\mathbf{I}_r$. This fundamental scheme is illustrated in the following diagram.

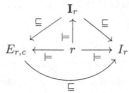

Version Co-evolution. We examine changes potentially affecting any of the three dynamic parameters (therefore, excluding the base invariant $\mathcal{I}$), focusing on the consequences both from the clients and owner perspectives, in terms of how their respective version labels will evolve. The elements with color red correspond to the logical relations that must be established, whereas the green ones express what can be deduced both from the previously established relations and from

client version	Certification scheme	owner version	required proofs	deducible properties
	(diagram)		$\mathbf{wf}(E'_{r,c})$ $E_{r,c} \sqcap_{\mathcal{I}} E'_{r,c}$ $E'_{r,c} \sqsubseteq I_r$	$r \models E_{r,c}$ $r \models E'_{r,c}$
M	(diagram)	μ	$\mathbf{wf}(E'_{r,c})$ $E_{r,c} \sqcap_{\mathcal{I}} E'_{r,c}$ $E'_{r,c} \sqsubseteq I'_r$ $\mathbf{wf}(I'_r)$ $I_r \approx I'_r$	$r \models E_{r,c}$ $r \models I'_r$ $r \models E'_{r,c}$
	(diagram)	**m**	$\mathbf{wf}(E'_{r,c})$ $E_{r,c} \sqcap_{\mathcal{I}} E'_{r,c}$ $E'_{r,c} \sqsubseteq I'_r$ $\mathbf{wf}(I'_r)$ $I_r \sqsubseteq I'_r$ $r \models I'_r$	$r \models E_{r,c}$ $r \models E'_{r,c}$
	(diagram)	**M**	$\mathbf{wf}(E'_{r,c})$ $E_{r,c} \sqcap_{\mathcal{I}} E'_{r,c}$ $\mathbf{wf}(I'_r)$ $I_r \sqcap_{\mathcal{I}} I'_r$ $r \models I'_r$ $E_{r,c} \sqsubseteq I'_r$	$r \models E_{r,c}$ $r \models E'_{r,c}$

Fig. 2. Update with changing specifications and unchanged resource: client sees a major evolution (M, m and μ stands for major, minor, micro).

the proved statements (and therefore, do not need explicit formal treatment by the service).

As many combinations exist, we present here only two cases: the first one deals with unchanged resources but evolving specifications (no change regarding the resource itself, but changes to the corresponding specifications), while in the second case the resource changes as well. See [19] for the exhaustive list of cases.

Update Describing Changing Specifications and Unchanged Resources. Figure 2 shows a certification scheme where the client considers a change as having a major effect.

Update with Changing Resources. We distinguish three cases, from the point of view of a client c, working with an external specification $E_{r,c}$ over a resource r. Figure 3 covers major changes with an evolving external specification.

6   Version Broker Service

This section presents a service-oriented application setting for the method described in the previous sections. We consider that a specialised broker can offer

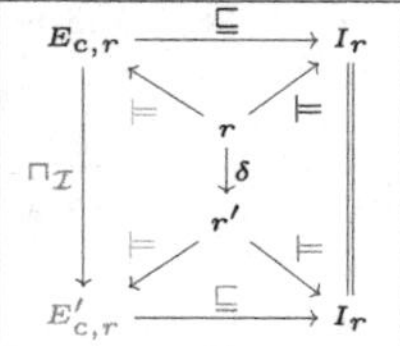

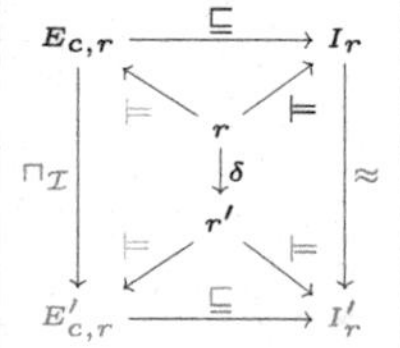

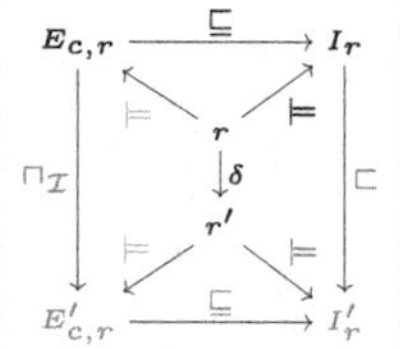

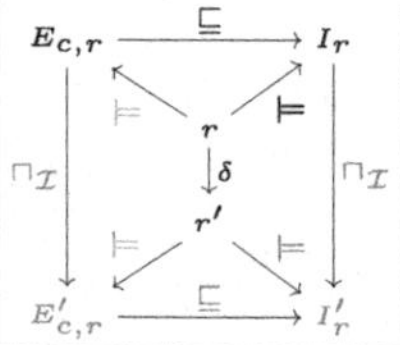

Fig. 3. Major changes with an evolving external specification (M, m and μ stands for major, minor, micro; δ denotes a modification of the resource).

services related to versioning (and generally resource lifecycle management) by implementing our method as described herein. We call that service the Version Broker Service (VBS).

We distinguish between two roles for the service's clients: the resource owner and the resource user. The resource owner publishes one or several logical descriptions, at various levels of precision, which characterize the resource and will serve as a basis for the formal agreement about its intended use. Users may subscribe to a "contract" (e.g. Quality of Service agreement) and get access to the resource through a dedicated version management scheme. Each time the owner certifies a new version, the VBS will make sure that this change is propagated to the "contracts", i.e. that each version label associated with the contracted interface is derived in a semantically consistent way. In the remaining part of the section we describe a typical example of setting up a resource certification and selection process using the VBS and what the service offers but also requires from the owners and users of the resources.

6.1   Overview of the VBS Process

In general, a broker is a common gateway/address for provider/user applications to access a wide variety of services. An example workflow of setting up a certification and selection process using the VBS is described below (Fig. 4).

– Step 1. The VBS publishes its interface to the UDDI registry that can be used by other services to locate the VBS.
– Step 2. A Resource Owner O that want to set up a certification process for a resource r contacts the UDDI registry, in order to locate the VBS.
– Step 3. Once O has located VBS, performs a binding and asks to register r. O should also send the contract definition related to the resource.
– Step 4. The VBS confirms that r is valid (i.e. well-formed, this is further explained in later sections) and responds with a confirmation to O, that r has been certified.
– Step 5. The VBS publishes r with a qualified version label (i.e. a label that represents the current state of r) by sending the information to the UDDI registry.
– Step 6. A Resource User U contacts the UDDI registry to locate a service that offers r available via the VBS. Thanks to the UDDI registry U selects the VBS.
– Step 7. Once the VBS is found, U contacts the VBS and requests a specific version or range of versions of r.
– Step 8. The VBS selects the resource r based on the information received by U related to the version label but also to the contract that U has (we assume here that the contract is also communicated to the VBS).
– Step 9. The VBS sends the response (e.g. that the specific version of the resource r is available to U).
– Step 10. In the case of a positive response U performs a binding with the VBS or O (this depends on the business model followed).

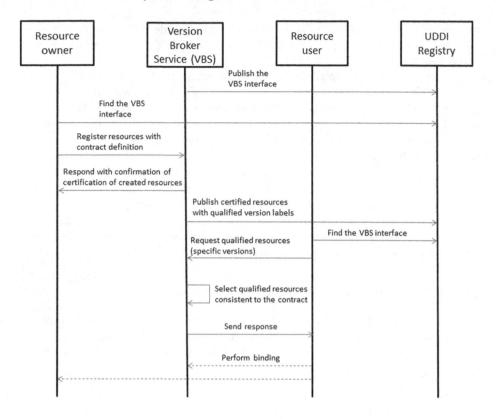

Fig. 4. VBS process (example).

Based on the above scenario, the VBS plays the role of an intermediate service between the Resource Owner and the Resource User.

6.2 The Resource Owner

The resource owner creates the resource and defines how it evolves. This includes deciding when and how to publish the resource and also what type of access and use should be allowed for different users. The owner also defines the domain specific theories needed (or use/extend those that might be proposed by the VBS), and design the properties needed to characterize the provided resource. The resource extension (its bitstream) might be directly uploaded into the VBS inner storage space, or just localized through a pointer that allows the VBS to access the content when needed. The actions that the VBS allows/expects from the resource owner are:

Theory Creation. Upload a source file compatible with the underlying logic (see Sect. 5.2) supported by the VBS, and an associated name that must be unique for this owner. This means that the VBS has a dedicated parser and computational means to verify/type the provided definitions (check for well-formedness). Once loaded and verified by the VBS the definitions can be used in other operations.

Resource Creation. Allows to specify a name uniquely associated with the target resource. This name is used to designate the revisions thanks to the version labels. For instance *cobra.socket.api*, could be subsequently referenced as *cobra.socket.api*[1.2.0].

Internal Specification Creation. VBS expects the resource name to which the specification will be attached, and a logical formula, which will be checked for well-formedness. The VBS returns a unique identifier, so that the specification can be designated without ambiguity for future operations. *External specification creation.* idem (see above).

Resource Update. Upload a novel extension for the resource, or equivalently, apply a patch; a new internal version label is computed accordingly (see *update* in Table 2).

Specification Update. Upload a novel extension for the resource (or equivalently, apply a patch); a new internal version label is computed accordingly (see *update* in Table 2).

Qualification. This corresponds to the first stage involving a logical characterization. Once certified, the resource can be derived and made visible to external users. As parameters, the VBS expects the resource label $\ell = \mathbf{identifier}(r)$, a reference to the invariant property $\mathcal{I}_\ell$ and to the internal specification S_ℓ, and the following proofs (see Sect. 5.3): (*i*) the invariant is implied by the internal specification in the defined context $\mathcal{L}, \mathcal{T}_i \vdash \mathcal{I}_\ell \sqsubseteq S_\ell$ and (*ii*) the resource satisfies the internal specification in the defined context $\mathcal{L}, \mathcal{T}_i \vdash \ell \models S_\ell$. The VBS then verifies the proofs and if correct, qualifies the resource, generating the first certified version label (Table 2).

Derivation. Compute a new version for a resource, whose name is given as a parameter, as well as the type of version: micro, minor, or major. Depending on the version type, different proofs are required by the VBS, so as to minimize the proving cost (Fig. 5).

Table 2. Operations supported by the Version Broker Service and corresponding impact on version labels.

Operation on resource	Version label (before)	Version label (after)	Certified
Creation	n.a	$[0.0.0:1]/0$	no
Qualification	$[0.0.0 : \nu]/s$	$[1.0.0 : 0]/s$	yes
Major derivation	$[M.m.\mu : \nu]/s$	$[M^+.0.0 : 0]/s$	yes
Minor derivation	$[M.m.\mu : \nu]/s$	$[M.m^+.0 : 0]/s$	yes
Micro derivation	$[M.m.\mu : \nu]/s$	$[M.m.\mu^+ : 0]/s$	yes
Update	$[M.m.\mu : \nu]/s$	$[M.m.\mu : \nu^+]/s^+$	no

certification scheme	version kind	required proofs	deducible properties
$\begin{array}{ccc} \ell & \xrightarrow{\ \models\ } & S \\ \| & & \downarrow{\scriptstyle\approx} \\ \ell & \xrightarrow{\ \models\ } & S' \end{array}$		$\mathcal{L}, \mathcal{T}_i \vdash S \approx S'$	$\mathcal{L}, \mathcal{T}_i \vdash \ell \models S'$
$\begin{array}{ccc} \ell & \xrightarrow{\ \models\ } & S \\ {\scriptstyle\delta}\downarrow & & \| \\ \ell' & \xrightarrow{\ \models\ } & S \end{array}$	**micro**	$\mathcal{L}, \mathcal{T}_i \vdash \ell' \models S$	none
$\begin{array}{ccc} \ell & \xrightarrow{\ \models\ } & S \\ {\scriptstyle\delta}\downarrow & & \downarrow{\scriptstyle\approx} \\ \ell' & \xrightarrow{\ \models\ } & S' \end{array}$		$\mathcal{L}, \mathcal{T}_i \vdash \ell' \models S'$ $\mathcal{L}, \mathcal{T}_i \vdash S \approx S'$	none
$\begin{array}{ccc} \ell & \xrightarrow{\ \models\ } & S \\ \| & & \downarrow{\scriptstyle\sqsubseteq} \\ \ell & \xrightarrow{\ \models\ } & S' \end{array}$	**minor**	$\mathcal{L}, \mathcal{T}_i \vdash S \sqsubseteq S'$	$\mathcal{L}, \mathcal{T}_i \vdash \ell \models S'$
$\begin{array}{ccc} \ell & \xrightarrow{\ \models\ } & S \\ {\scriptstyle\delta}\downarrow & & \downarrow{\scriptstyle\sqsubseteq} \\ \ell' & \xrightarrow{\ \models\ } & S' \end{array}$		$\mathcal{L}, \mathcal{T}_i \vdash \ell' \models S'$ $\mathcal{L}, \mathcal{T}_i \vdash S \sqsubseteq S'$	none
$\begin{array}{ccc} \ell & \xrightarrow{\ \models\ } & S \\ \| & & \downarrow{\scriptstyle\sqcap_{I_\ell}} \\ \ell & \xrightarrow{\ \models\ } & S' \end{array}$	**major**	$\mathcal{L}, \mathcal{T}_i \vdash \ell \models S'$ $\mathcal{L}, \mathcal{T}_i \vdash S \sqcap_{I_\ell} S'$	none
$\begin{array}{ccc} \ell & \xrightarrow{\ \models\ } & S \\ {\scriptstyle\delta}\downarrow & & \downarrow{\scriptstyle\sqcap_{I_\ell}} \\ \ell' & \xrightarrow{\ \models\ } & S' \end{array}$		$\mathcal{L}, \mathcal{T}_i \vdash \ell' \models S'$ $\mathcal{L}, \mathcal{T}_i \vdash S \sqcap_{I_\ell} S'$	none

Fig. 5. Certified evolution of a resource ℓ according to a specification S (δ denotes a modification of the resource).

Publication. Requires the resource's name as parameter and synchronizes the last certified version to generate the external version labels for all users. Proofs will be asked by the VBS according to the co-evolution schemes (see Sect. 5.3).

In the following, we use x^+ to denote $x+1$. Table 2 defines the transformations of the version label according to the operation done on a resource r, where $version(r) = [M.m.\mu : \nu]/s$.

6.3   The Resource User

The resource user accesses the bitstream extension (the resource content) corresponding to particular versions, thanks to the designation mechanism described in Sect. 4.4. The corresponding external specification may also be accessed. The operations that the VBS supports for users of the resource include:

Resource Download. The VBS expects a full version label (e.g. $dp.api[2.1.3]$), and returns a set of resource contents, associated with its exact version label. Such a label will resolve into this particular content if a subsequent access is required. As an example, a first request with $db.api[1.2.?]$ may return $\{(c_1, db.api[1.2.1]), (c_2, db.api[1.2.2])\}$ (where c_i denotes the respective bitstream contents) whereas a $db.api[1.2]$ request will be interpreted by the VBS as $db.api[1.2.\star]$ and would return the latest content available for this major and minor version in the given context, i.e. $\{\langle c_1, db.api[1.2.2]\rangle\}$.

Specification Download. Using the same communication scheme, the resource user can access external specifications associated with each version resolved by the VBS.

7   Illustrative Example

In this section we present an example that illustrates the concepts introduced in the previous sections. We assume that a provider manages a software library offering persistent storage operations. We call the library STO and assume that it is made available as a compiled module. The owner of STO chooses to expose two different views of this library: a basic one including creating/opening a persistent store, storing, deleting, and retrieving data, and a more complex one that can additionally handle transactions. We assume that the owner of STO uses an object-oriented dedicated theory to describe the resource, focusing on the naming and typing of classes and methods.

7.1   Fundamental Invariant

The fundamental invariant of STO is defined in terms of a class, three methods to deal with data, and three basic functions to create, open and delete a database.

$$
\begin{aligned}
\mathbf{I}_{STO} \equiv \quad & \mathbf{class}(\text{STOHandler}) \\
\wedge\ & \mathbf{language}(\text{Python2}) \\
\wedge\ & \mathbf{method}(\text{STOHandler}, \text{store}) \\
\wedge\ & \mathbf{method}(\text{STOHandler}, \text{retrieve}) \\
\wedge\ & \mathbf{method}(\text{STOHandler}, \text{close}) \\
\wedge\ & \mathbf{function}(\text{create}) \\
\wedge\ & \mathbf{function}(\text{open}) \\
\wedge\ & \mathbf{function}(\text{delete})
\end{aligned}
$$

Note that according to the vision of the resource owner, signatures of methods/functions are not considered as fundamental, and therefore, could change along the lifetime of the resource, however, the programming language and version must stay stable.

7.2   The External Specification

It describes a minimal view on the functionality offered by the API, namely, the signatures of methods and functions, including potential exceptions as follows.

$$
\begin{aligned}
E_{STO} \equiv\ &\mathbf{I}_{STO} \\
&\wedge\ \mathbf{signature}(\text{STOHandler.store}, [\mathbf{string}, \mathbf{string}], \mathbf{void}) \\
&\wedge\ \mathbf{signature}(\text{STOHandler.retrieve}, [\mathbf{string}], [\mathbf{string}]) \\
&\wedge\ \mathbf{signature}(\text{STOHandler.close}, [\ ], \mathbf{void}) \\[4pt]
&\wedge\ \mathbf{signature}(create, [\mathbf{string}], STOHandler) \\
&\wedge\ \mathbf{signature}(delete, [\mathbf{string}], \mathbf{void}) \\
&\wedge\ \mathbf{signature}(open, [\mathbf{string}], STOHandler) \\[4pt]
&\wedge\ \mathbf{throw}(create, \mathbf{Exception}) \\
&\wedge\ \mathbf{throw}(delete, \mathbf{Exception}) \\
&\wedge\ \mathbf{throw}(open, \mathbf{Exception})
\end{aligned}
$$

7.3   The Internal Specification

This one is typically more complex, as expected to help the designer maintaining his source code in a coherent way while hiding (potentially irrelevant) complexity to users. To illustrate this, we decided to consider three additional methods: *check* (verify the presence of a data in the store), *replace* (change a value using a known key) and *put* (store one or many values using the same key). Those methods may be used internally to build higher level operations such as the *store* method which perform storage with replacement, as in standard dictionary data structures based on a hashing algorithm.

$$
\begin{aligned}
I_{STO} \equiv\ &\mathbf{I}_{STO} \\
&\wedge\ \mathbf{signature}(\text{STOHandler.store}, [\mathbf{string}, \mathbf{string}], \mathbf{void}) \\
&\wedge\ \mathbf{signature}(\text{STOHandler.retrieve}, [\mathbf{string}], [\mathbf{string}]) \\
&\wedge\ \mathbf{signature}(\text{STOHandler.close}, [\ ], \mathbf{void}) \\[4pt]
&\wedge\ \mathbf{signature}(create, [\mathbf{string}], STOHandler) \\
&\wedge\ \mathbf{signature}(delete, [\mathbf{string}], \mathbf{void}) \\
&\wedge\ \mathbf{signature}(open, [\mathbf{string}], STOHandler) \\[4pt]
&\wedge\ \mathbf{method}(\text{STOHandler}, \text{check}) \\
&\wedge\ \mathbf{method}(\text{STOHandler}, \text{replace}) \\
&\wedge\ \mathbf{method}(\text{STOHandler}, \text{put}) \\
&\wedge\ \mathbf{signature}(\text{STOHandler.check}, [\mathbf{string}], \mathbf{integer}) \\
&\wedge\ \mathbf{signature}(\text{STOHandler.replace}, [\mathbf{string}, \mathbf{string}], \mathbf{void}) \\
&\wedge\ \mathbf{signature}(\text{STOHandler.put}, [\mathbf{string}, \mathbf{string}], \mathbf{void}) \\[4pt]
&\wedge\ \mathbf{class}(\mathbf{PathException}) \\
&\wedge\ \mathbf{subtype}(\mathbf{PathException}, \mathbf{Exception}) \\
&\wedge\ \mathbf{throw}(create, \mathbf{PathException}) \\
&\wedge\ \mathbf{throw}(delete, \mathbf{Exception}) \\
&\wedge\ \mathbf{throw}(open, \mathbf{PathException})
\end{aligned}
$$

Note that exception management is more detailed thanks to a class specialization.

$$\forall P. \qquad\qquad\qquad\qquad P:\textbf{prop} \Rightarrow \vdash P$$
$$\forall x, t. \qquad\qquad\qquad\qquad t:\textbf{type} \Rightarrow (x:t):\textbf{prop}$$

$$\textbf{void}:\textbf{type}$$
$$\textbf{any}:\textbf{type}$$
$$\textbf{type}:\textbf{type}$$
$$\textbf{prop}:\textbf{type}$$
$$\textbf{integer}:\textbf{type}$$
$$\textbf{string}:\textbf{type}$$
$$\forall t. \qquad\qquad\qquad\qquad t:\textbf{type} \Rightarrow \textbf{list}(t):\textbf{type}$$
$$\forall c. \qquad\qquad\qquad\qquad \textbf{class}(c) \Rightarrow c:\textbf{type}$$
$$\textbf{class}(\textbf{Exception})$$

$$\forall x. \qquad\qquad\qquad\qquad \texttt{integer}(x) \Rightarrow x:\textbf{integer}$$
$$\forall x. \qquad\qquad\qquad\qquad \texttt{string}(x) \Rightarrow x:\textbf{string}$$
$$\forall t. \qquad\qquad\qquad\qquad t:\textbf{type} \Rightarrow [\,]:\textbf{list}(t)$$
$$\forall e, L, t. \qquad\qquad t:\textbf{type} \Rightarrow e:t \Rightarrow L:\textbf{list}(t) \Rightarrow [e|L]:\textbf{list}(t)$$

$$\forall t_1, t_2. \qquad\qquad \textbf{subtype}(t_1, t_2) \Rightarrow \textbf{subtype}(\textbf{list}(t_1), \textbf{list}(t_2))$$
$$\forall t. \qquad\qquad\qquad\qquad t:\textbf{type} \Rightarrow \textbf{subtype}(t, \textbf{any}) \qquad \prec_{any}$$
$$\forall x, t_1, t_2. \qquad\qquad \textbf{subtype}(t_1, t_2) \Rightarrow x:t_1 \Rightarrow x:t_2$$
$$\forall c_1, c_2, m. \qquad \textbf{subtype}(c_1, c_2) \Rightarrow \textbf{method}(c_2, m) \Rightarrow \textbf{method}(c_1, m)$$
$$\forall t_1, t_2, t_3. \qquad \textbf{subtype}(t_1, t_2) \Rightarrow \textbf{subtype}(t_2, t_3) \Rightarrow \textbf{subtype}(t_1, t_3)$$
$$\forall t. \qquad\qquad\qquad\qquad \textbf{subtype}(t, t)$$

$$\forall x. \qquad\qquad\qquad\qquad \texttt{label}(x) \Rightarrow \textbf{class}(x):\textbf{prop}$$
$$\forall x, y. \qquad\qquad x:\textbf{type} \Rightarrow y:\textbf{type} \Rightarrow \textbf{subtype}(x, y):\textbf{prop}$$
$$\forall x. \qquad\qquad\qquad\qquad \texttt{label}(x) \Rightarrow \textbf{function}(x):\textbf{prop}$$
$$\forall c, m. \qquad\qquad \textbf{class}(c) \Rightarrow \texttt{label}(m) \Rightarrow \textbf{method}(c, m):\textbf{prop}$$
$$\forall c, m, i, o. \qquad \textbf{method}(c, m) \Rightarrow i:\textbf{list}(\textbf{type}) \Rightarrow o:\textbf{type}$$
$$\Rightarrow \textbf{signature}(c.m, i, o):\textbf{prop}$$
$$\forall f, i, o. \qquad \textbf{function}(f) \Rightarrow i:\textbf{list}(\textbf{type}) \Rightarrow o:\textbf{type} \Rightarrow \textbf{signature}(f, i, o):\textbf{prop}$$
$$\forall c, m, e. \qquad \textbf{method}(c, m) \Rightarrow e:\textbf{Exception} \Rightarrow \textbf{throw}(c.m, e):\textbf{prop}$$
$$\forall f, e. \qquad\qquad \textbf{function}(f) \Rightarrow e:\textbf{Exception} \Rightarrow \textbf{throw}(f, e):\textbf{prop}$$

$$\forall f, c_1, c_2. \qquad \textbf{subtype}(c_1, c_2) \Rightarrow \textbf{throw}(f, c_1) \Rightarrow \textbf{throw}(f, c_2) \qquad \prec_{throw}$$
$$\forall f, c_1, c_2. \qquad (i_1 \Rightarrow i_2) \wedge \textbf{subtype}(o_2, o_1) \Rightarrow \textbf{signature}(f, i_1, o_1)$$
$$\Rightarrow \textbf{signature}(f, i_2, o_2) \qquad \prec_{sig}$$
$$\forall t_1, t_2, T_1, T_2. \quad \textbf{subtype}(t_1, t_2) \wedge \textbf{subtype}(T_1, T_2) \Rightarrow \textbf{subtype}([t_1|T_1], [t_2|T_2]) \quad \prec_{[+]}$$
$$\textbf{subtype}([\,], [\,]) \qquad \prec_{[]}$$

Fig. 6. Example dedicated theory.

7.4 Verification of Specifications

The well-formedness of the logical specification is established by proofs using both a generic (for the basic logic operators) and a dedicated theory. In Fig. 6 we just give an idea of what the dedicated theory could be for the illustrative example presented above ($x:y$ is the infix notation of the predicate $\textbf{type}(x, y)$, and $\texttt{label}, \texttt{integer}, \cdots$ are built-in predicates to assess lexical properties of items). The formal proofs required by the VBS for the three specifications will be $\vdash \mathcal{I}_{STO}, \vdash E_{STO}$ and $\vdash I_{STO}$, which can be reduced into $\vdash \mathcal{I}_{STO}, \vdash P_1$ and $\vdash P_2$ since $I_{STO} \equiv \mathcal{I}_{STO} \wedge P_2$ and $E_{STO} \equiv \mathcal{I}_{STO} \wedge P_1$ (P_i being the additional properties illustrated by Sects. 7.2 and 7.3).

7.5 First Certification

After submitting the internal and external specifications, the owner wants to produce a first certification of STO (that is, asks the VBS to generate a certified version label $STO[1.0.0 : 0]/0)$. To that end, the owner must provide a proof that STO satisfies the specification $(STO \models I_{STO})$. The computational characterisation of the proof will depend on the characteristics of the underlying theory, on the properties of the programming language, and on the difficulty of the task (and also on the performance level of the algorithm/human operator).

In the worst case, the proof is not provided by the owner. Yet, proofs of well-formedness $(\vdash P)$, implication and partial disjunction of properties are required to control the quality of specifications and the consistency of the claimed evolution. The absence of strong compliance proofs can be compensated by offering testing infrastructure at the VBS level, and including runtime tests in the specifications, e.g. through dedicated predicates like **test**$(context, code, value)$ or **raises**$(context, code, exception)$, where $code$, $value$ and $exception$ are particular expressions of an appropriate abstract language.

In the best case, the programming language is associated with a formal specification system (e.g. based on predicate transformers) able to conduct semi-automatic proofs of correctness and to export proof terms in the VBS compliant form.

In the rest of the cases, the programming language can be associated with static analysis tools (such as type or property checkers using partial evaluation or model checking). To perform the first certification, the VBS will require $STO \models I_{STO}$, $I_{STO} \sqsubseteq E_{STO}$ (easy), $I_{STO} \sqsubseteq I_{STO}$ (easy, but longer), and $E_{STO} \sqsubseteq I_{STO}$ (a bit more difficult). The only difficulty in the last one, is about proving properties like e.g.

$$\textbf{throw}(create, \textbf{PathException}) \Rightarrow \textbf{throw}(create, \textbf{Exception})$$

which requires using appropriate subtyping oriented axioms as follows (proof scheme in abbreviated form).

$$
\begin{array}{c}
\dfrac{\top}{} \ {\in}_{\vdash L} \\
\vdots \\
\dfrac{}{} \ {\in}_{\vdash R} \\
\vdots \\
\dfrac{\textbf{subclass}(\textbf{PathException}, \textbf{Exception}) \in \gamma}{} \ {\in}_{\vdash R} \\
\dfrac{\gamma \vdash \textbf{subclass}(\textbf{PathException}, \textbf{Exception})}{\gamma \vdash \textbf{throw}(create, \textbf{PathException}) \Rightarrow \textbf{throw}(create, \textbf{Exception})} \ {}^{I_{\vdash L}} \ \prec_{throw}
\end{array}
$$

7.6   A Change and Its Co-Evolution

To illustrate the notion of co-evolution, we propose to examine a change that occurs in both the resource (modification of source code and, accordingly, of the library resource STO) and in the internal specification. Now, the $store, retrieve, put$ and $replace$ methods of the STOHandler class could accept any kind of value, and not only strings. This would constitute a major evolution from the internal side (the new specification is more specific, that is, $\delta(I_{STO}) \sqsubseteq I_{STO}$, whereas the E_{STO} need not to be upgraded. As an example, the proof for the $store$ method would be as follows.

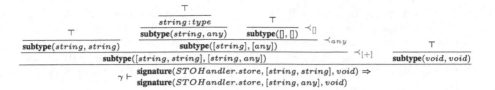

8   Conclusion

In this paper we presented a method for versioning that enables managing consistently digital resources throughout their life cycle. The method assigns explicit semantics to version labels and describes resources in terms of properties that can be checked for validity with formal logical theories. Only if these properties are valid the resource is marked as *certified*. We also sketched how this method could be implemented in a service-oriented setting. We have shown that following our versioning approach entails benefits to both resource users and owners. The resource users have a strong guarantee with respect to the versioning of certified resources. More specifically, that the versioning scheme always reflects in a consistent way the evolution of the resources they contracted for. On the other hand, resource owners receive valuable support for coherently managing changes between versions while minimizing requested proofs at each step.

We plan of extending the above work by introducing, within the same setting, the formal underpinnings for version branching and merging, and to start experimenting with the main concepts presented in this paper. The challenge of scaling such a system to a real environment should be understood more concretely, as well as the level of precision we can expect and manage regarding the various logical specifications involved in a system based on our model.

Acknowledgements. We would like to thank Jean-Pierre Chanod for his continuous support and PERICLES partners for the creative exchanges. This research is conducted in the PERICLES project [18], a four-year Integrated Project funded under EU's FP7.

References

1. Novakouski, M., Lewis, G., Anderson, W., Davenport, J.: Best Practices for Artifact Versioning in Service-Oriented Systems. Software Engineering Institute, Carnegie Mellon University, Pittsburgh, Pennsylvania, Technical Note CMU/SEI-2011-TN-009 (2012). resources.sei.cmu.edu/asset_files/TechnicalNote/2012_004_001_15356.pdf
2. Jerijrvi, K., Dubray, J.-J.:Contract Versioning, Compatibility and Composability. InfoQ Magazine, December 2008. www.infoq.com/articlescontract-versioning-comp2
3. Conradi, R., Westfechtel, B.: Version models for software configuration management. ACM Comput. Surv. **30**(2), 232–282 (1998). doi.acm.org/10.1145/280277.280280

4. Juric, M.B., Sasa, A., Brumen, B., Rozman, I.: WSDL and UDDI extensions for version support in web services. J. Sys. Soft. **82**(8), 1326–1343 (2009). dx.org/10.1016/j.jss.2009.03.001, www.sciencedirect.com/science/article/pii/S0164121209000478
5. Wetherly, C., Goring, B.R., Shenfield, M., Cacenco, M.: System and method for implementing data-compatibility-based version scheme. US Patent 8,555,272 (2013)
6. Cacenco, M., Goring, B., Shenfield, M., Wetherly, C.: Implementing data-compatibility-based version scheme. WO Patent App. PCT/CA2005/001,345 (2006)
7. Vairavan, V., Bellur, U.: Method and system for versioning a software system. US Patent App. 12/324,950 (2009)
8. Papazoglou, M.P., Benbernou, S., Andrikopoulos, V.: On the evolution of services. IEEE Trans. Soft. Eng. **38**(3), 609–628 (2012). Preprint, http://infolab.uvt.nl/~mikep/publications/IEEE-TSE%20%5Bpreprint%5D.pdf
9. Leitner, P., Michlmayr, A., Rosenberg, F., Dustdar, S.: End-to-End versioning support for web services. In: IEEE International Conference on Services Computing (SCC 2008), vol. 1, pp. 59–66 - Technical report version (2008). www.infosys.tuwien.ac.at/staff/leitner/papers/TUV-1841-2008-1.pdf
10. Brada, P.: Specification-Based Component Substitutability and Revision Identification. Ph.D. thesis, Charles University, Prague, August 2003. http://d3s.mff.cuni.cz/publications/download/brada_phd.pdf
11. CORBA 3.3, 26 June 2014. www.omg.org/spec/CORBA/3.3/
12. Semantic Versioning. Technical Whitepaper, OSGi Alliance, Revision 1.0, May 2010. www.osgi.org
13. Nipkow, T., Paulson, L.C., Wenzel, M.: Isabelle/HOL: A Proof Assistant for Higher-Order Logic. LNCS, vol. 2283. Springer, Heidelberg (2002)
14. Kirchner, F., Muñoz, C.: The Proof Monad. J. Logic Alg. Program. **79**(3), 264–277 (2010)
15. Boespflug, M., Carbonneaux, Q., Hermant, O.: The lambda-Pi-calculus modulo as a universal proof language. In: Proof Exchange for Theorem Proving, pp. 28–43 (2012)
16. De Bruijn, N.G.: On the roles of types in mathematics. In: The Curry-Howard Isomorphism, vol. 8, pp. 27–54 (1995)
17. Laboreo, D.: Introduction to Natural Deduction. Tutorial, May 2005. www.danielclemente.com/logica/dn.en.pdf
18. PERICLES: a FP7 European project (2013–2017). www.pericles-project.eu
19. Vion-Dury, J.-Y., Lagos, N.: Technical Annex (2015). www.xrce.xerox.com/content/download/34443/372476/file/SV-ANNEX.pdf

An Eclipse IDE for Teaching Java–

Lorenzo Bettini[1]($\boxtimes$) and Pierluigi Crescenzi[2]

[1] Dipartimento di Informatica, Università di Torino, Torino, Italy
bettini@di.unito.it
[2] Dipartimento di Ingegneria dell'Informazione, Università di Firenze, Firenze, Italy
pierluigi.crescenzi@unifi.it

Abstract. In this paper, we describe a new Eclipse-based IDE for teaching Java following the object-later approach. This IDE allows the programmer to write code in Java–, a smaller version of the Java language that does not include object-oriented features, and includes all the powerful features available when using an IDE like Eclipse (such as debugging, automatic building, and project wizards). With our implementation, it is also straightforward to create self-assessment exercises for students, which are integrated in Eclipse and JUnit.

1 Introduction

Java– is a smaller version of the Java language, which has been used at the University of Florence to start teaching undergraduate students to program in Java, without referring to the object-oriented features of this language [1–3]. By using Java–, students can focus, during the first few weeks, on the basic programming concepts without being distracted by complex constructs (for the educational motivation for using Java–, we refer the interested reader to [4]). In order to write, compile, and execute Java– programs, a quite simple application was also developed at the University of Florence more than ten years ago, which provides a GUI, but lacks all the advanced tooling mechanisms that are typical of an IDE like Eclipse. In this paper, we describe a new implementation of Java– that includes a full-featured Eclipse-based IDE. Our IDE provides an editor with syntax highlighting, navigation, code completion and error markers, not to mention automatic integrated building and debugging. Since the IDE is Eclipse based, the students will immediately become familiar with all the tools of Eclipse itself, which is the IDE mostly used to teach Java with all its object-oriented features. Moreover, by using our implementation of the IDE for Java–, it is straightforward for the teachers to create exercise projects that students can use for self-assessment. The teacher can, indeed, rely on existing frameworks such as JUnit, which is already integrated in Eclipse. The Java– IDE has been implemented by using Xtext [5,6], which is a modern language workbench (such as MPS [7] and Spoofax [8]) that, starting from a grammar

This work has been supported in part by MIUR (proj. CINA), Ateneo/CSP (proj. SALT), ICT COST Action IC1201 BETTY, and PRIN 2012C4E3KT national research project AMANDA (Algorithmics for MAssive and Networked Data).

P. Lorenz et al. (Eds.): ICSOFT 2015, CCIS 586, pp. 63–78, 2016.
DOI: 10.1007/978-3-319-30142-6_4

definition generates not only a parser and an abstract syntax tree, but also all the typical Eclipse-based tooling features (for more details about the technology used for implementing the Java– IDE, we refer the interested reader to [4]). Our IDE is available as an open source project starting from http://javamm.sourceforge. net, where we also provide an Eclipse update site and pre-configured Eclipse distributions with Java– installed, for several architectures. In the following we will use the term Java– for denoting both the smaller version of the Java language and the application, with or without IDE, for writing code in this language.

The rest of the paper is organised as follows. In Sect. 2 we briefly describe the original Java– application, while in Sect. 3 we describe our new Java– IDE. In Sects. 4 and 5 we focus our attention on the debugging and the self-assessment features of the Java– IDE, respectively. Finally, in Sect. 6 we refer the reader to some related work, and in Sect. 7 we conclude by suggesting some possible research open problems.

2   The Original Java– Application

In this section, we recall the main features of the original implementation of Java–. As stated in the introduction, the goal of this tool is to allow the user to focus on the basic programming concepts, without encumbering the novice student with unnecessary complex constructs. Indeed, the user can write Java code outside of any method body as shown in the left part of Fig. 1[1]. In order to appreciate the advantage of using Java–, the code shown in the figure can be compared with the code that a student should have written if Java– was not used, that is,

```java
public class Example {
  public static void main(String[] a) {
    int x = 2;
    System.out.println(x);
  }
}
```

Apart from the fact that the student is exposed since the very beginning with the object-oriented specific syntax of Java, as stated in [9] the above code can even be "harmful to development of object-thinking", since "it communicates virtually nothing about the concept of user-created objects". On the contrary, the code shown in the left part of Fig. 1 turns out to be very similar to the corresponding Python code, that is,

---

[1] As it is shown in the figure, the student is required to make a leap of faith concerning the use of the static methods to print to the standard output (such as System.out.println()). Although this could have been avoided by implementing a print() method that invokes the corresponding Java method, we preferred to ask the students to use the standard Java methods and to profess their faith in them, rather than give them a solution that is not pure Java, and which could confuse them later on.

Fig. 1. Writing a program, and defining and invoking methods in the original Java–application.

```
x = 2
print x
```

Clearly, Java– allows the programmer to define and invoke methods, as shown in the right part of Fig. 1. Once again, it is interesting to compare the code shown in the figure with the corresponding Python code defining the max method, that is,

```
def max(a,b):
  if a>b:
    return a
  else:
    return b
```

When Java– is asked to execute a code, the tool generates a temporary class where it defines the main method and copies all the methods specified by the user. Successively, the temporary class is compiled and executed: the compilation errors are shown in the Errors pane, while the output and/or the execution error are shown in the output pane. The original implementation of Java– also includes a self-assessment module, that allows the student to write methods solving simple programming problems. The behaviour of this module is very similar to other tools available on the web, such as, for example, the CodingBat tool [10]. The distribution of Java– already includes dozens of pre-defined exercises, but new exercises can be easily added by teachers.

3   The Java– IDE

We now briefly describe the new IDE, by first describing the main features of the IDE interface and by then emphasising the advantages of using these features. We would like to stress that the aim of Java– as a programming language is to target algorithmic aspects of programming, so that students can concentrate on implementing algorithms without being distracted by OO features. Thus, Java– does not target other programming contexts such as GUI programming. However, as described in more details in Sect. 7, Java– can access any existing Java type, such as container classes.

3.1   The IDE Interface

In Fig. 2 we show a screenshot of the Java– Eclipse IDE (note the complete integration of our tooling with the Eclipse mechanisms, which are basically the

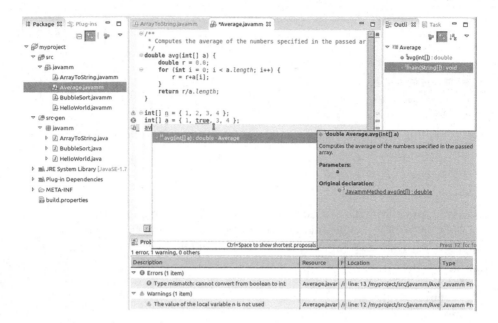

Fig. 2. Java– Eclipse IDE.

same as Eclipse JDT). First of all, in the Java– Eclipse project, the Java– compiler automatically generates Java code into the source folder `src-gen`. Such generation is integrated with the Eclipse building mechanisms: if a Java– file is modified, re-generation is automatically triggered and if a Java– file is removed, the corresponding generated Java file is automatically removed. Error markers are placed on the editor's left ruler, on the corresponding file in the "Package Explorer", and in the "Problems" view (note that warnings are generated as well, just like in Java, e.g., when a declared variable is not used). Moreover, the regions in the editor corresponding to the errors are underlined (e.g., for a type mismatch error like in the screenshot). The "Outline" view on the right reflects the one of Eclipse JDT. Code completion works as well. With that respect, note that the content assist mimics the one of Java: Javadoc comments, if present, are displayed as well. The Java– IDE also offers a project wizard to create an Eclipse project with the structure and requirements to start editing, compiling and launching Java– programs. We also provide a wizard to import a Java– project with about 40 examples (see Fig. 3).

3.2   On the Value of an IDE

Although an IDE is not a strict requirement to develop applications, it surely helps programmers to increase productivity with features like syntax colouring in the editor, compiler and debugger integration, build automation, code completion and easy navigation to definitions, just to mention a few. In an agile [11]

Fig. 3. Some examples shipped with Java–.

and test-driven context [12] the features of an IDE like Eclipse become an essential requirement. Indeed, languages such as Smalltalk have been tightly coupled with an IDE from the beginning [13]. The ability to see the program coloured and formatted with different visual styles (e.g., comments, keywords, strings, etc.) gives an immediate feedback concerning the syntactic correctness of the program. Moreover, colours and fonts help the programmer to see the structure of the program directly, making it easier to visually separate the parts of the program. The programming cycle consisting of writing a program with a text editor, saving it, switching to the command line, running the compiler, and, in case of errors, going back to the text editor is surely not productive. The programmer should not realise about errors too late: the IDE should continuously check the program in the background while the programmer is typing in the editor, even if the current file has not been saved yet. The longer it takes to realise that there is an error, the higher the cost in terms of time and mental effort to correct it. For example, the Eclipse Java plugin highlights the parts of the program with errors directly in the editor: it underlines in red only the parts that actually contain the errors; it also puts error markers (with an explicit message) on the left of the editor in correspondence to the lines with errors, and fills the Problem view with all these errors. The programmer will be able to easily spot the parts of the program that need to be fixed. With that respect, in our experience as teachers, we noted that most of the students that fail programming exams are not able to fix compilation errors since they do not use an IDE: they tend to write the whole program and then try to compile it; when they get lots of compilation errors, they are not able to understand how to fix them.

4   The Debugging Feature

When running the generated Java code in debugging mode in the Java– IDE, we can choose to debug directly the original Java– code (it is always possible to switch between the generated Java code and the original code). In Fig. 4 we show a debug session of a Java program generated by our Java– compiler (running or debugging the generated Java code can be done using context menus available directly on the original Java– source): we have set break points on the Java– file, and the debugger automatically switches to the original Java– code (note also the file names in the thread stack, the "Breakpoint" view and the "Variables" view). Indeed a well-known problem with implementations which generate Java code is that for debugging, the programmer has to debug the generated code which is usually quite different from the original program; our implementation does not have this drawback. Note that the usage of the debugging mode of the Java– Eclipse IDE has another advantage: it may indeed allow the students to get used to the debugger before using it for developing their own object-oriented more complex programs.

Fig. 4. Debugging a Java– program.

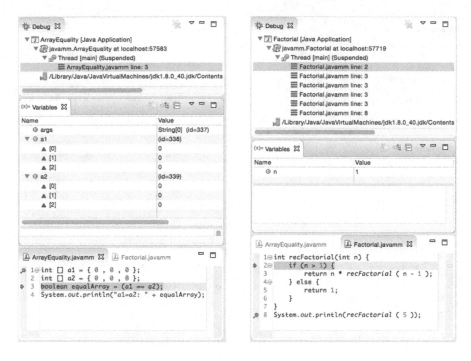

Fig. 5. Using the debug for teaching array references and the price of recursion.

The debugging feature can also be very useful, during a lecture, in order to support explanations (usually done by using the whiteboard) of a program execution. Let us now briefly describe three simple examples.

Methods and Arrays. In the left part of Fig. 5 it is shown how the debugger can be used in order to explain that an array variable is a reference variable and, hence, that the equality between two different array variables cannot be established by simply using the == operator. Indeed, in the "Variables" view it is explicitly shown that the two variables a1 and a2 are distinct, even though the elements of the two arrays they refer to are all the same.

The Price of Recursion. Another example of such a "pedagogical" utilisation of the debugger is given in the right part of Fig. 5. In this case, the "Debug" view explicitly shows the activation records corresponding to the five invocations of the recFactorial method, so that it is easier to explain to the students that recursion (and, in general, method invocation) has a "small" price to be paid, that, in certain cases, can be excessively high (just imagine the invocation of recFactorial with a large integer number as argument).

Methods and Local Variables. The last example deals with the notion of local variables inside a method, which can have the same name of another variable defined outside the method itself. As shown in Fig. 6, the variable a defined

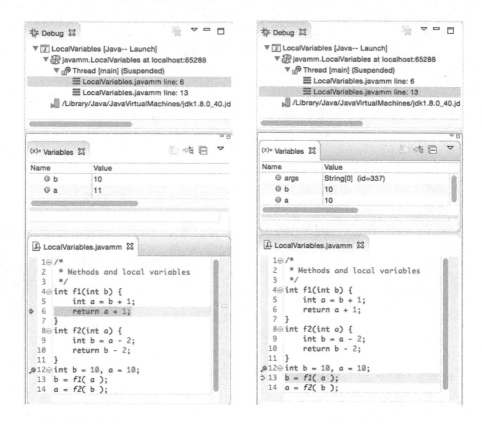

Fig. 6. Using the debug for teaching methods and local variables.

(and initialised) inside the method f1 is a local variable, which has nothing to do with the variable a defined (and initialised) before the invocation of method f1. Indeed, the value of a within the activation record corresponding to the invocation of f1 and after the execution of the first instruction of this method is 11 (see the left part of the figure) and, hence, different from the value of a within the main activation record, which is 10 (see the right part of the figure). Observe that, of course, the same reasoning applies to the variables called b and the method f2. Indeed, the value of the variable b defined outside of the methods is equal to 12 after the invocation of f1 and it is not changed by the invocation of f2.

5   The Self-Assessment Feature

By using the Java– IDE, self-assessment exercises can be straightforwardly implemented by relying on JUnit and its integration in Eclipse. The basic idea is that the teacher provides the students with Java– Eclipse projects containing a Java– file where the student implements the solution to the requested problem, the

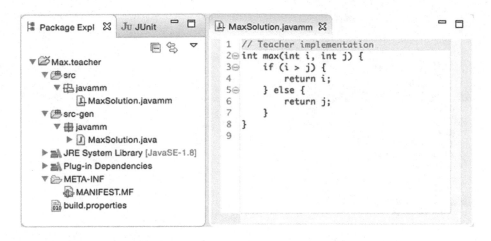

Fig. 7. An example of exercise for self-assessment: the teacher project

solution of the teacher in binary form (so that the student cannot have a look at it), and a JUnit test case that checks whether the output of the student's implementation corresponds to the teacher's implementation. Let us show this process by referring to a simple example, in which the student must implement the max function in Java–, that is, a method which, given in input two integer numbers, returns the maximum between these two integers (in the following, we will assume the reader to be sufficiently familiar with the JUnit framework).

The Teacher Side. The teacher has, first of all, to create a Java– project (called, for example, Max.teacher) and write the source code of the solution, as shown in Fig. 7. Successively, the teacher has to create another Java– project (called, for example, Max.student) and write the source code of the student solution containing only a comment explaining the exercise, and the signature of the method to be developed along with a dummy return instruction, as shown in Fig. 8. Within the Max.student project, the teacher has also to create a new folder (called, for example, solution), add this folder to the libraries of the build path of the Max.student project, and copy in this folder the javamm folder included in the bin folder of the Max.teacher project (see again Fig. 8). Finally, the teacher has to create within the Max.student project a JUnit test case: for example, in Fig. 9, the JUnit test case has been created within the folder tests and includes only one test method checking whether the method implemented by the student correctly answers with input the two values 3 and 5 (note that, by making use of the parametrized test feature of JUnit, it is easy to develop tests of the student's implementation with random inputs using the teacher's implementation as the expected output). The teacher can now distribute the Max.student project to the students.

Fig. 8. An example of exercise for self-assessment: the student project.

Fig. 9. An example of exercise for self-assessment: the JUnit test case.

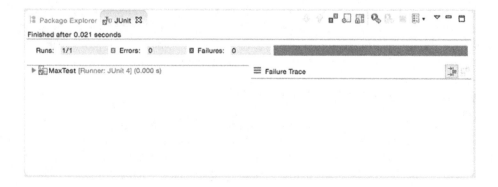

Fig. 10. An example of exercise for self-assessment: the successful case.

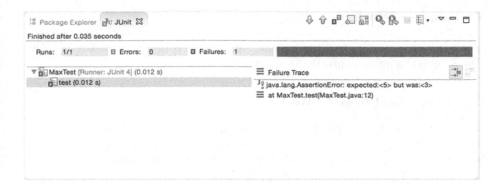

Fig. 11. An example of exercise for self-assessment: the failure case.

The Student Side. The student has to fill the body of the method, whose signature was included in the project distributed by the teacher. For example, the code written by the student could simply be the following line.

```
if (i>j) return i; else return j;
```

By running the JUnit test case included by the teacher in the `Max.student` project, the student can then verify the correctness of the proposed solution, as shown in Fig. 10. If the solution is not correct (for example, if instead of writing `i>j` the student wrote `i<j` in the previous code line), the execution of the JUnit test results in one failure, and a message is shown, specifying the expected result and the actual result returned by the student's method (see Fig. 11).

The Self-Assessment Creation Wizard. In the previous description, the setup of a self-assessment exercise has been done manually by the teacher. The manual procedure is tedious and error prone, since the teacher might forget to copy updated class files into the student's project. For these reasons, our Java– IDE supports the teacher with the following features:

- We provide a wizard that creates both projects altogether, with some initial contents, including an example of JUnit parametrized test; the student's project is also setup with the `solution` library folder, so that its contents are part of the classpath of that project.
- The teacher's project is setup with our custom Eclipse builder that automatically keeps in sync the teacher's project's `bin` folder with the student's project's `solution` folder. This way, new class files in the teacher's project are copied into the student project, updated class files in the teacher's project are updated in the student's project and if a class file is removed from the teacher's project the corresponding class file will be removed from the student's project as well.

The project wizard and the custom builder will give the teacher the usual Eclipse automatic building infrastructure experience and will avoid possible inconsistency problems.

6 Related Work

In this section we will discuss some related work, both concerning the educational context and the implementation technology.

6.1 Educational Related Work

An excellent survey of programming languages and environments for making programming accessible to beginners is contained in [14]. For what concerns Java, there is now a vast range of tools, which have been especially designed for educational purposes, in an attempt to create an environment that can help in teaching programming; we mention some of the popular ones. Alice [15] is an interactive programming environment that establishes an easy, intuitive relationship between program constructs and 3D graphics animations. BlueJ [16] is a teaching environment strictly linked to the development of object-oriented programs by means of a framework which is focused on objects (hence, applying a teaching paradigm opposite to the one followed by JOSH and Java–). JEliot 2000 [17] is a program animation system intended for teaching computer science especially to high school students but does not hide the object-oriented feature of the Java language. In [18] an approach is presented to gradually teaching programming using a programming language, e.g., Java, that grows along with the number of concepts presented to the students; however, no IDE tooling is considered in that approach. As far as we know, however, the Java– IDE is the first tool which combines the pure procedural Java syntax learning with the utilisation of all the powerful features of an IDE like Eclipse.

6.2 Implementation Framework Related Work

There are other tools for implementing DSLs and IDEs (we refer to [19–21] for a wider comparison). Tools like IMP (The IDE Meta-Tooling Platform) [22] and DLTK (Dynamic Languages Toolkit) only deal with IDE features, thus the compiler of the language has to be implemented separately, while Xtext unifies all the implementation phases. TCS (Textual Concrete Syntax) [23] is similar to Xtext, but with the latter it is easier to describe the abstract and concrete syntax at once, and it is completely open to customisation of every part of the generated IDE (besides, TCS seems to be no longer under active development). EMFText [24], instead of deriving a metamodel from the grammar, does the opposite, i.e., the language to be implemented must be defined in an abstract way using an EMF metamodel.

In general, we chose Xtext since it is basically the main standard framework for implementing DSLs in the Eclipse ecosystem, it is continuously supported, and it has a wide community. Moreover, Xtext is continuously evolving, and the main forthcoming features will be the integration in other IDEs (mainly, IntelliJ), and the support for programming on the Web (i.e., an implementation with Xtext should be easily portable on the Web, allowing programming directly in a browser).

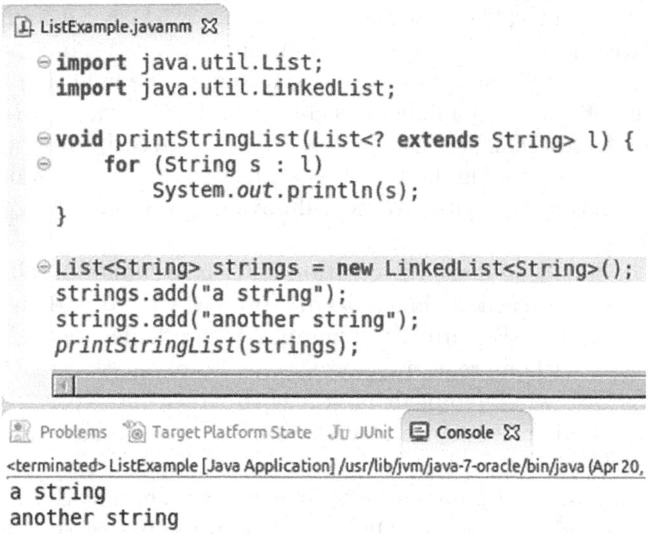

```
⌐ ListExample.javamm ⊠
  ⊖ import java.util.List;
     import java.util.LinkedList;

  ⊖ void printStringList(List<? extends String> l) {
  ⊖    for (String s : l)
            System.out.println(s);
     }

  ⊖ List<String> strings = new LinkedList<String>();
     strings.add("a string");
     strings.add("another string");
     printStringList(strings);
```

```
  Problems    Target Platform State   Ju JUnit   Console ⊠
<terminated> ListExample [Java Application] /usr/lib/jvm/java-7-oracle/bin/java (Apr 20,
a string
another string
```

Fig. 12. An example showing the use of library classes, generics and imports.

7   Conclusions

We have described a new IDE for teaching Java following the object-later approach. In particular, by using Xtext, this IDE combines the "structured programming before object oriented programming" teaching paradigm (already implemented in Java–) with all the powerful features available when using the Eclipse IDE. Observe that our IDE also allows to use all Java types, such as, e.g., the String and the Java collection classes; furthermore, the syntax for types already supports full Java generics, including wildcards. Indeed, from a Java– file one can access any Java type of any Java library available in the project's classpath. Finally, the syntax of Java– expressions corresponds to the syntax of Java expressions, except for this, super, anonymous classes and Java 8 lambdas. This means that copying Java expressions into a Java– program is allowed (of course, if the original Java expressions rely on specific OO features, like, e.g., a field reference on this, Java– will issue a validation error). An example is shown in Fig. 12: we use Java list classes, with generics (including wildcards) and imports; concerning imports, we support the automatic import statement insertion during content assist, and the typical "Organize Imports" menu. All these features turn out to be useful before migrating to the full Java syntax, in order to allow the students to familiarise with method invocation of already existing classes and with Java generics.

Adding Java 8 lambda expressions into Java– should not be a problem: Xbase supports lambda expressions with its own syntax (which we have removed from the grammar), so we would just need to introduce in the Java– Xtext grammar the syntax for Java 8 lambda expressions and then reuse Xbase's type system for lambda expressions. This is the subject of future work that would allow us to experiment with the functional programming approach as an intermediate step between object-later approach and the OO paradigm. The final step towards full Java would consist in adding anonymous classes and OO Java constructs such as interfaces and classes. This is feasible in Xtext, as proven by the programming language Xtend[2], but we think that it would not make much sense, since at that point we can directly switch to the full Java programming language and its Eclipse tooling.

As shown in Sect. 5 we make the creation and maintenance of self-assessment exercises easy for the teacher, thanks to our project wizard and the automatic building infrastructure. We are also planning to implement a dedicated DSL for defining tests, without requiring the teacher to explicitly create Junit test cases. Also this DSL will be implemented it with Xtext and Xbase. We will take inspiration from similar testing frameworks implemented in Xtext, such as, e.g., Xpect [25] and Jnario [26].

From an experimental point of view, instead, we observe that, whenever a programmer is asked whether an IDE should be used, it is very likely that the answer would be an obvious one, that is, "yes". However, as stated in [27], it might be that, for novice programmers, it can be useful "to be able to trace through the execution of the code by hand", even because, at this stage, the programs to be written will likely be pretty short. We conjecture that this is not the case. For this reason, we now plan to execute a controlled experiment in order to evaluate the efficacy of starting learning Java, by following the object-later approach, with and without an IDE (that is, by using the original Java–application and by using the IDE described in this paper).

Java– is the first project that customises Xbase grammar, type system and code generator in order to be able to deal with Java expression syntax. We believe that such customizations should be easily factored out in a more general and reusable framework: this customised Xbase expression syntax for Java expressions can be reused in other DSLs that rely on Xbase for achieving the integration with the Java platform. Indeed, our customised syntax for expressions does not depend on any specific feature of Java–: the syntax for methods is simply built on top of the syntax for expressions. It will be interesting to perform such refactoring, to extract this part from Java– and to experiment its use in other DSLs (one of such DSLs we·plan to experiment with is the one described in [28]).

References

1. Cecchi, L., Crescenzi, P., Innocenti, G.: C : C++ = JavaMM: Java. In: Proceedings of the 2nd International Conference on Principles and Practice of Programming in Java, pp. 75–78 (2003)

---

[2] Xtend, https://eclipse.org/xtend/, is a Java dialect implemented with Xtext and Xbase.

2. Bettini, L., Crescenzi, P., Innocenti, G., Loreti, M., Cecchi, L.: An environment for self-assessing Java programming skills in undergraduate first programming courses. In: Proceedings of the IEEE International Conference on Advanced Learning Technologies, pp. 161–165 (2004)
3. Crescenzi, P., Loreti, M., Pugliese, R.: Assessing CS1 Java skills: a three-year experience. SIGCSE Bull. **38**, 348 (2006)
4. Bettini, L., Crescenzi, P.: Java– meets Eclipse - an IDE for teaching Java following the object-later approach. In: Proceedings of the 10th International Conference on Software Paradigm Trends, pp. 31–42 (2015)
5. Itemis: Xtext (2015). http://www.eclipse.org/Xtext
6. Bettini, L.: Implementing Domain-Specific Languages with Xtext and Xtend. Packt Publishing, Birmingham (2013)
7. Voelter, M.: Language and IDE modularization and composition with MPS. In: Lämmel, R., Saraiva, J., Visser, J. (eds.) GTTSE 2011. LNCS, vol. 7680, pp. 383–430. Springer, Heidelberg (2013)
8. Kats, L.C.L., Visser, E.: The spoofax language workbench. Rules for declarative specification of languages and IDEs. OOPSLA **45**, 444–463 (2010)
9. Westfall, R.: Technical opinion: Hello, world considered harmful. Commun. ACM **44**, 129–130 (2001)
10. Parlante, N.: Codingbat code practice (2011). http://codingbat.com
11. Martin, R.C.: Agile Software Development: Principles, Patterns, and Practices. Prentice Hall, Upper Saddle River (2003)
12. Beck, K.: Test Driven Development: By Example. Addison-Wesley, Boston (2003)
13. Goldberg, A.: SMALLTALK-80: The Interactive Programming Environment. Addison-Wesley, Boston (1984)
14. Kelleher, C., Pausch, R.: Lowering the barriers to programming: a taxonomy of programming environments and languages for novice programmers. ACM Comput. Surv. **37**, 83–137 (2005)
15. Dann, W.P., Cooper, S., Pausch, R.: Learning to Program with Alice. Prentice Hall, Upper Saddle River (2011)
16. Barnes, D., Kölling, M.: Objects First with Java: A Practical Introduction Using BlueJ, 5th edn. Prentice Hall, Upper Saddle River (2011)
17. Levy, R.B.B., Ben-Ari, M., Uronen, P.A.: The Jeliot 2000 program animation system. Comput. Edu. **40**, 1–15 (2003)
18. Cazzola, W., Olivares, D.M.: Gradually learning programming supported by a growable programming language. IEEE Trans. Emerg. Top. Comput. **4** (2016). Special Issue on Emerging Trends in Education
19. Pfeiffer, M., Pichler, J.: A comparison of tool support for textual domain-specific languages. In: Proceedings of the DSM, pp. 1–7 (2008)
20. Voelter, M., Benz, S., Dietrich, C., Engelmann, B., Helander, M., Kats, L.C.L., Visser, E., Wachsmuth, G.: DSL Engineering - Designing, Implementing and Using Domain-Specific Languages (2013)
21. Erdweg, S., van der Storm, T., Völter, M., Tratt, L., Bosman, R., Cook, W.R., Gerritsen, A., Hulshout, A., Kelly, S., Loh, A., Konat, G., Molina, P.J., Palatnik, M., Pohjonen, R., Schindler, E., Schindler, K., Solmi, R., Vergu, V., Visser, E., van der Vlist, K., Wachsmuth, G., van der Woning, J.: Evaluating and comparing language workbenches: existing results and benchmarks for the future. Comput. Lang. Syst. Struct. **44**, 24–47 (2015)
22. Charles, P., Fuhrer, R., Sutton Jr., S., Duesterwald, E., Vinju, J.: Accelerating the creation of customized, language-Specific IDEs in Eclipse. OOPSLA **44**, 191–206 (2009)

23. Jouault, F., Bézivin, J., Kurtev, I.: TCS: a DSL for the specification of textual concrete syntaxes in model engineering. In: GPCE, pp. 249–254. ACM (2006)
24. Heidenreich, F., Johannes, J., Karol, S., Seifert, M., Wende, C.: Derivation and refinement of textual syntax for models. In: Paige, R.F., Hartman, A., Rensink, A. (eds.) ECMDA-FA 2009. LNCS, vol. 5562, pp. 114–129. Springer, Heidelberg (2009)
25. Eysholdt, M.: Xpect (2014). http://www.xpect-tests.org
26. Benz, S., Engelmann, B.: Jnario, Executable Specifications for Java (2014). http://jnario.org
27. MacDonald, B.: To IDE or not to IDE? (2014). http://radar.oreilly.com/2014/01/to-ide-or-not-to-ide.html
28. Bettini, L., Damiani, F.: Generic traits for the Java platform. In: Proceedings of the 2014 International Conference on Principles and Practices of Programming on the Java platform: Virtual machines, Languages, and Tools, pp. 5–16. ACM (2014)

Supporting Privacy Impact Assessments Using Problem-Based Privacy Analysis

Rene Meis[(✉)] and Maritta Heisel

paluno - The Ruhr Institute for Software Technology,
University of Duisburg-Essen, Duisburg, Germany
{rene.meis,maritta.heisel}@uni-due.de

Abstract. Privacy-aware software development is gaining more and more importance for nearly all information systems that are developed nowadays. As a tool to force organizations and companies to consider privacy properly during the planning and the execution of their projects, some governments advise to perform privacy impact assessments (PIAs). During a PIA, a report has to be created that summarizes the consequence on privacy the project may have and how the organization or company addresses these consequences. As basis for a PIA, it has to be documented which personal data is collected, processed, stored, and shared with others in the context of the project. Obtaining this information is a difficult task that is not yet well supported by existing methods. In this paper, we present a method based on the problem-based privacy analysis (ProPAn) that helps to elicit the needed information for a PIA systematically from a given set of functional requirements. Our tool-supported method shall reduce the effort that has to be spent to elicit the information needed to conduct a PIA in a way that the information is as complete and consistent as possible.

Keywords: Privacy impact assessment · Privacy analysis · Problem frames · Requirements engineering

1 Introduction

To provide privacy-aware software systems, it is crucial to consider privacy from the very beginning of the development. Ann Cavoukian was one of the first who promoted this idea with her concept of privacy by design [1]. Several countries prescribe or advise government departments and organizations to perform a so called privacy impact assessment (PIA). Wright et al. [2] define a PIA as follows: *"A privacy impact assessment is a methodology for assessing the impacts on privacy of a project, policy, programme, service, product or other initiative which involves the processing of personal information and, in consultation with stakeholders, for taking remedial actions as necessary in order to avoid or minimise negative impacts."* In the same document the authors review the PIA methods of seven countries, namely Australia, Canada, Hong Kong, Ireland, New Zealand, the United Kingdom, and the United States of America for the

P. Lorenz et al. (Eds.): ICSOFT 2015, CCIS 586, pp. 79–98, 2016.
DOI: 10.1007/978-3-319-30142-6_5

EU project PIAF[1]. This project had the goal to provide recommendations on how a regulation for a PIA in the EU should look like. In the draft of the EU data protection regulation [3] in article 33, the EU describes a procedure similar to a PIA called data protection impact assessment.

In this paper, we extend the problem-based privacy analysis (ProPAn) method [4] and show how this extension helps requirements engineers to elicit the information they have to provide to conduct a PIA. Wright et al. distilled from their above mentioned analysis of the PIA practice 36 points that they *"recommend for a European PIA policy and methodology"*. These points consist of 15 recommendations on how a PIA guideline document should look like, 9 points address how PIA should be integrated into policy, for the PIA report they give 6 recommendations and also 6 for the PIA process. Requirements engineers can provide valuable input for some of those points on the basis of a requirements model of the software project for which the PIA shall be conducted. Our proposed method addresses the following points which are central for the success of a PIA:

1. *"A PIA should be started early, so that it can evolve with and help shape the project, so that privacy is* built in *rather than* bolted on.*"* Our method starts at the very beginning of the software development process, namely in the analysis phase, and only needs the initial system description consisting of the functional requirements on the system.
2. *"The PIA should identify information flows, i.e., who collects information, what information do they collect, why do they collect it, how is the information processed and by whom and where, how is the information stored and secured, who has access to it, with whom is the information shared, under what conditions and safeguards, etc.,"*
3. *"The focus of a PIA report should be on the needs and rights of individuals whose personal information is collected, used or disclosed. The proponent of the proposal is responsible for privacy The proponent must "own" problems and devise appropriate responses in the design and planning phases."* With the proposed extension of ProPAn, we provide a systematic approach to identify the individuals whose personal information is collected, how it is used by the software system, and to whom it is disclosed on the basis of a given requirements model.

The rest of the paper is structured as follows. Section 2 introduces an eHealth scenario that we use to illustrate our method. The problem frames approach and ProPAn are presented in Sect. 3 as background of this paper. Our method is then described in Sect. 4. Section 5 discusses related work, and Sect. 6 concludes the paper.

2   Running Example

We use a subsystem of an electronic health system (EHS) scenario provided by the industrial partners of the EU project *Network of Excellence (NoE) on*

---

[1] http://www.piaf.eu.

Engineering Secure Future Internet Software Services and Systems (NESSoS)[2] to illustrate our method. This scenario is based on the German health care system which uses health insurance schemes for the accounting of treatments.

The EHS is the software to be built. It has to manage electronic health records (EHR) which are created and modified by doctors (functional requirement R1). Additionally, the EHS shall support doctors to perform the accounting of treatments patients received. The accounting is based on the treatments stored in the health records. Using an insurance application it is possible to perform the accounting with the respective insurance company of the patient. If the insurance company only partially covers the treatment a patient received, the EHS shall create an invoice (R2). The billing is then handled by a financial application (R3). Furthermore, mobile devices shall be supported by the EHS to send instructions and alarms to patients (R4) and to record vital signs of patients (R5). Finally, the EHS shall provide anonymized medical data to researchers for clinical research (R6).

3   Background

Problem frames are a requirements engineering approach proposed by Jackson [5]. The problem of developing the software-to-be-built (called *machine*) is decomposed until subproblems are reached which fit to problem frames. Problem frames are patterns for frequently occurring problems. An instantiated problem frame is represented as a problem diagram. A problem diagram visualizes the relation of a requirement to the environment of the machine and how the machine can influence these domains. The environment of the machine is structured into domains. Jackson distinguishes the domain types *causal domains* that comply with some physical laws, *lexical domains* that are data representations, and *biddable domains* that are usually people. A requirement can refer to and constrain phenomena of domains. Phenomena are events, commands, states, information, and the like. Both relations are expressed by dependencies from the requirement to the respective domain annotated with the referred to or constrained phenomena. Connections (associations) between domains describe the phenomena they share. Both domains can observe the shared phenomena, but only one domain has the control over a phenomenon (denoted by a "!").

We use the UML4PF-framework [6] to create problem frame models as UML class diagrams. All diagrams are stored in *one* global UML model. Hence, we can perform analyses and consistency checks over multiple diagrams and artifacts. The problem diagram (in UML notation) for the functional requirements R6 is shown in Fig. 1. The problem diagram is about the problem to build the submachine *Research* that provides medical data extracted from the *EHRs* to the *ResearchDatabaseApplication* based on the requests made by *Researchers* to perform clinical research. The functional requirement *R6* refers to the researcher that requests the medical data and to the health records from which this data

---

[2] http://www.nessos-project.eu/.

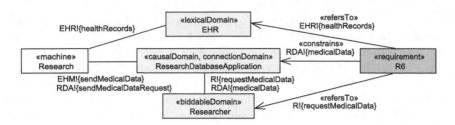

Fig. 1. Problem diagram for functional requirement R6.

is extracted. Furthermore, R6 constrains the research database application to provide the requested medical data.

ProPAn [4] extends the UML4PF-framework with a UML profile for privacy requirements and a reasoning technique. A privacy requirement in ProPAn consists of a *stakeholder* and a *counterstakeholder*, both are domains of the requirements model. A privacy requirement states that the privacy of the stakeholder shall be preserved against the counterstakeholder in the system-to-be. Note that *stakeholder* and *counterstakeholder* can be the same biddable domain because biddable domains in the problem frame model do not necessarily represent individuals, but in most cases user roles. Hence, the privacy of an individual can be threatened by another individual of the same user role. The reasoning technique identifies to which domains personal information of the *stakeholder* can potentially flow and to which domains the *counterstakeholder* may have access. For each privacy requirement, the information flows starting from the stakeholder and the access capabilities of the counterstakeholder is visualized in a privacy threat graph. This directed graph has domains as nodes and contains two kinds of edges annotated with statements (requirements, facts and assumptions) describing the origin of the edge. Information flow edges indicate a possible flow of information between the domains and access edges indicate that a domain is able to access information of the other domain. In this paper, we refine these graphs and investigate which personal information really flows between the domains due to the given requirements model.

4   Method

Our proposed method is visualized in Fig. 2 as UML2 activity diagram. The starting point of our method is a set of functional requirements in form of a UML-based problem frame model. Using this model, we first elicit further context information in the step *Context Elicitation*. The result of this step is *Domain Knowledge* that is integrated into the UML model. Then we can automatically generate *Detailed Stakeholder Information Flow Graphs* from the model and use these in the following step to identify the personal data that is put into the system by stakeholders. The result of this step is the *Personal Data of Stakeholders* and the relations between this data. In the following step, we iteratively

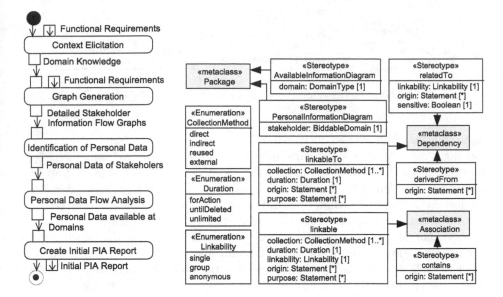

Fig. 2. Overview of the proposed method.

Fig. 3. UML profile extension of UML4PF.

analyze the flow of the previously identified personal data through the system using the previously generated graphs. During this step, we obtain information about the availability and linkability of personal data at the domains of the system. In the last step, we create artifacts for an initial PIA report based on the previously elicited information. Our method shall be carried out by requirements engineers in collaboration with privacy experts and experts in the application domain of the system to be built. We will refer to all of them using the term *user* in the rest of the paper. Our method is supported by the ProPAn-tool[3] that extends the UML4PF-framework [6]. We extended the UML4PF profile to provide the basis for our tool support as shown in Fig. 3. We will explain the stereotypes introduced by the profile where we use them the first time in our method.

4.1   Context Elicitation

Information systems often store and process data of persons who not directly interact with these systems and that hence may not be represented in the requirements model. Furthermore, there are often information flows between domains in a system that are out of the scope of the functional requirements of the system to be built. E.g., doctors and patients may exchange information without using the system to be built. To elicit these *indirect* stakeholders and *implicit* information flows between domains and stakeholders that are not covered by the

---

[3] https://www.uni-due.de/swe/propan.shtml.

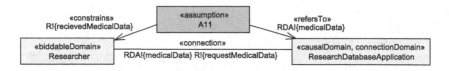

Fig. 4. Researchers receive medical data from the research database application.

requirements, we developed elicitation questionnaires [7]. The implicit information flows are captured as domain knowledge diagrams that are generated by the ProPAn-tool[4] based on the user's answers. A domain knowledge diagram is similar to a problem diagram, but it does not contain a machine and instead of a requirement it contains a *fact* (an indicative statement that is always true) or an *assumption* (an indicative statement that is may not true under some circumstances). For our proposed method, it is especially important that during the context elicitation the user elicits the domain knowledge from which domains people (biddable domains) probably gain information. Domains that are part of the same problem diagram as a biddable domain are candidates for domains from which that biddable domain may gain information. The functional requirements usually only refer to the biddable domain involved in it and hence, do not constrain that the biddable domain gains knowledge due to the functional requirement, but this is often the case. Thus, we have to add the missing domain knowledge to the model to document these implicit information flows.

Application to EHS Scenario. For the sake of simplicity, we only introduce one example for an implicit information flow. For other domain knowledge that we identified for the EHS scenario see [7]. The implicit information flow that we consider in this paper is that researchers get knowledge about the medical data they receive from the research database application based on the requests they make. This information flow is only implicit in the problem diagram for requirement R6 (cf. Fig. 1), because R6 only constrains the research database application to presents the medical data to researchers, but it does not constrain that researchers really receive this information. Figure 4 shows the domain knowledge diagram for assumption A11. It makes explicit that researchers receive the medical data (constrained phenomenon) presented to them by the research database application (referred to phenomenon).

4.2 Graph Generation

A large set of functional requirements and domain knowledge often implies complex flows of information through the system that are only visible if all requirements are considered simultaneously. Hence, it is a difficult task to analyze these information flows. To assist users to analyze the information flows implied by the given set of requirements, we generate graphs from the problem frame model. In this paper, we introduce so-called detailed stakeholder information flow

---

[4] https://www.uni-due.de/swe/propan.shtml.

graphs (DSIFGs) to identify the personal data of the stakeholder and at which domains that information is available due to the functional requirements and the elicited domain knowledge. In a problem frame model, *statements* (requirements, assumptions, and facts) refer to and constrain domains of the machine's environment. If a domain is referred to by a statement, then this implies that it is potentially an information source, and if a domain is constrained, then this implies that based on the information from the referred to domains there is a change at the domain. Hence, there is a potential information flow from the referred to domains to the constrained domains. Our tool uses this information available in the problem frame model to automatically generate the DSIFG for each biddable domain without any user interaction. In contrast to the graphs that are already used in the ProPAn-method (cf. Sect. 3), a DSIFG has a petri-net like structure with domains as places and statements as transitions. The DSIFG starts with the stakeholder under consideration. Iteratively, all statements that refer to a domain in the DSIFG are added to the DSIFG together with input edges annotated with the referred-to phenomena starting from the domain to the added statement. And for each statement in the graph, the constrained domains are added to the DSIFG together with corresponding output edges annotated with the constrained phenomena starting from the statement to the added domain.

Application to EHS Scenario. In this paper, we perform the information flow analysis for the stakeholder doctor. For the analysis of the stakeholder patient, we refer to [8]. An excerpt of the doctor's DSIFG is shown in Fig. 5. The doctor's DSIFG shows how information of the doctor possibly flows through the system based on the functional requirements R1, R2, R3, R4, R5, R6, and the assumption A11. E.g., assumption A11 (cf. Fig. 4) implies an information flow from the research database application (referred to/input domain) to the doctor (constrained/output domain) and requirement R6 (cf. Fig. 1) implies information flows from the health records (EHR) and researchers (referred to/input domains) to the research database application (constrained/output domain).

4.3   Identification of Personal Data

For the analysis of the information flow graph, the user has to identify the *personal data* of the stakeholder that is processed in the system under consideration. In the literature, often the term *personally identifiable information (PII)* is used. The International Organization for Standardization [9] defines PII as *"any information that (a) can be used to identify the PII principal to whom such information relates, or (b) is or might be directly or indirectly linked to a PII principal"*. The European Commission [3] uses the term *personal data* in the draft of the EU data protection regulation and defines *"personal data" means any information relating to a data subject*. In this paper, we use the terms *personal data* and *personal information* synonymously as more general terms than PII. Personal data is not only data that can be used to identify an individual or that is linkable to an individual, but also data related to an individual without

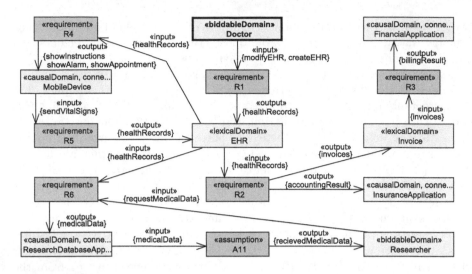

Fig. 5. Excerpt of the doctor's detailed stakeholder information flow graph.

providing any link to the related individual. E.g., knowing that there is an end-user with a specific sexual orientation will in most cases not allow one to identify or narrow down the set of end-users with that specific sexual orientation. But nevertheless, the sexual orientation of an end-user represents a sensitive personal information that needs special protection if it is processed by the system under consideration. Note that the user of the method can decide to use a more specific definition of personal data, but we decided to use the general term to capture all possibly critical processing of personal data in the system under consideration.

As starting point for the identification of personal data from the requirements model, the user has to look at the data that the stakeholder directly or indirectly provides to the system. This personal data is contained in the phenomena of the stakeholder that at least one statement refers to. Hence, the user has to consider the phenomena annotated at the edges starting from the stakeholder in his/her DSIFG. We distinguish two cases for the identification of personal data in our requirements model. A phenomenon can either be a causal or a symbolic phenomenon. Causal phenomena represent events or commands a domain issues and symbolic phenomenon represent a state, value, or information. If the phenomenon is symbolic, then the user has to check whether this phenomenon represents personal data. If the phenomenon is causal, then the user has to check whether it contains/transmits personal data.

To document the contains/transmits relationship between phenomena, we use aggregations with stereotype ≪contains≫ connecting the phenomena in the UML model (cf. Figs. 3 and 6). Besides the property that information is contained in other information, it is often the case that information is not directly contained but derived from other information. This relation is documented as dependency with stereotype ≪derivedFrom≫ (cf. Figs. 3 and 6) starting from the derived phenomenon and pointing to the phenomena which are necessary to derive it. It is possible that a personal information can be derived from different sources, e.g., the actual position of a person can be derived from the GPS coordinates of the person's smart phone or using the currently available wireless networks also provided by the person's smart phone. In such cases, we add multiple dependencies to the model.

Note that a contains relationship is naturally transitive and that if a phenomenon is derived from a set of phenomena, then each phenomenon of the set can be replaced by a phenomenon that contains it and the phenomenon can also be derived by each superset of the documented set. At the points where we need these properties, our tool computes the transitive closure of these properties. Furthermore, our tool automatically documents for traceability of decisions made, the *origin* of our decision for introducing a contains or derivedFrom relationship. The tool sets the property origin of contains and derivedFrom relations (cf. Fig. 3) automatically to the statements from which we identified the relations.

Our tool assists users to identify personal data. The tool presents for a selected stakeholder the phenomena (derived from the DSIFG) that are candidates for personal data of the stakeholder. For each symbolic phenomenon that the user identifies to be personal data, the tool documents the relation to the stakeholder by creating a dependency with stereotype «relatedTo» starting from the phenomenon and pointing to the stakeholder. To document the relation's quality, the user has to answer two questions:

1. Does the phenomenon represent sensitive personal data for the stakeholder?
2. Does the personal data identify the single individual it belongs to, does it narrow down the set of possible individuals it is related to a subgroup, or does the information not provide any link to the corresponding individual and is hence anonymous?

The answers to the above questions are stored as properties of «relatedTo» (cf. Fig. 3) and based on the values the user selects. The property origin is again automatically set by the tool by setting it to the set of statements that refer to the respective phenomenon.

Application to EHS Scenario. From the DSIFG shown in Fig. 5, we derive that *modifyEHR*, and *createEHR* are the phenomena that have to be considered to identify the personal data of doctors that is processed by the EHS. These phenomena are causal and hence, we have to decide which personal information is contained in them or transmitted by them. We identified that both *modifyEHR* and *createEHR* contain contact information (including name, address, and phone number) of the doctor represented by the symbolic phenomenon *doctorContactInformation*, details about the doctor (e.g. specialization and identification number) represented by *doctorDetails*, the *treatments* performed by doctors, the *diagnosis* doctors make, and the *notes* doctors make about the progress of the treatment. All these symbolic phenomena represent sensitive personal information related to a doctor. The contact information and the details of the doctor identify a single doctor, whereas the performed treatments, diagnosis, and notes

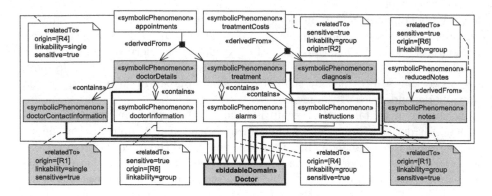

Fig. 6. Identified personal information for the doctor.

a group of possible doctors. The initially identified relations for the doctor are highlighted using bold connections and gray shapes in Fig. 6. The other relations visible in Fig. 6 are identified during the later iterative analysis.

4.4   Personal Data Flow Analysis

In this step, we analyze how the identified personal data of each stakeholder is propagated through the system based on the given requirements and domain knowledge. As a result of this process, we obtain for each domain and stakeholder of the system a projection of the identified personal data of the stakeholder that is available at the domain enhanced with some additional information.

To document that some personal data about a stakeholder is available at a domain, our tool creates for this domain a package in the UML model with stereotype «availableInformationDiagram» and adds into this package a dependency with stereotype «linkableTo» starting from the personal data to the stakeholder when the user identifies this relation during the process. We document as quality attributes of the relation linkableTo from which statements of the requirements this relation was derived (origin), for which purpose the information is available at the domain, how the collection of information took place, and how long the information will be available at the domain (duration) using the stereotype properties (cf. Fig. 3). Note that in the first place, we document for which purpose some personal information is available at a domain due to the requirements model. Whether the stakeholder gave consent to process the data for this purpose and whether the purpose is legitimate as required by some data protection regulations [3] has to be analyzed later. We distinguish four kinds of collection methods. First, direct collection from the stakeholder, e.g., the stakeholder enters the information on its own. Second, indirect collection, e.g., the information is collected by observing the stakeholder's behavior. Third, reused data that was previously collected (for another purpose). Fourth, data collected by external third parties. Note that we allow to assign multiple collection methods to a linkableTo relation. We distinguish three kinds of duration. If the duration is forAction, then the information will only be available at the domain as long as the information is needed for the action to be performed. If the duration is untilDeleted, then the information will be deleted at some point in time when it is no longer needed, but not directly after it is no longer needed. The duration unlimited expresses that once the information is available at that domain, it will stay available there.

Initialization of Personal Data Flow Analysis. At each domain, the initially available information is the information that the user identified in the previous step for this domain. I.e., the personal data related to the domain itself. The initial available information diagrams are created automatically by our tool. The tool sets the collection method for the initial available information to direct and the duration of availability to unlimited. The attribute origin is set to the value of the corresponding relatedTo relation from which the linkableTo relation is created and the attribute purpose is initially an empty collection.

During a step of the later iterative personal data flow analysis, the user selects a statement of the DSIFG for which he/she wants to investigate which personal data available at the input domains of the statement flows to which output domain of the statement and in which quality. The tool guides through the process and presents the statements that still have to be considered to the user. Initially, these are the statements for which the stakeholder under consideration is an input domain.

Application to EHS Scenario. For the stakeholder patient, we have initially to consider the statement R1 (cf. Fig. 5). The information initially available at the patient is the gray part with bold connections in Fig. 6.

Iterative Analysis of the Flow of Personal Data. Now, the user iteratively chooses a statement to be considered for the stakeholder under consideration. Our tool then collects the personal information of the stakeholder that is available at the input domains and computes the transitive closure using the contains and derivedFrom relations. The computation of the transitive closure can reveal, e.g., that a personal information a that is not available at one of the input domains, but can be derived from two pieces of personal information b available at one input domain and c available at another input domain, possibly flows to the output domain(s) due to the statement under consideration.

As mentioned before, the user may identify that only a part of or information derived from the available information is transmitted to output domains. Because of that, the tool allows the user to select available information from which only parts or derived information is transmitted. The user has only to select the available information and to enter the name of the new information. The tool then creates the newly identified phenomenon and the corresponding contains, derivedFrom, and relatedTo relations with the current statement as origin.

Then the user has to decide for each output domain which of the available information is transmitted to it and how long it will be available at the output domain (attribute duration). Based on the user's selection, our tool automatically generates the corresponding model elements. The stereotype property origin is automatically set by the tool to the statement under consideration. For the attribute collectionMethod two cases are distinguished. First, if one of the input domains is the stakeholder, then the user can choose how the information is collected due to the statement. Second, if the stakeholder is not one of the input domains, then the collection method is set automatically to the union of the collection methods specified at the input domains. For each transmitted phenomenon, the tool adds the current statement to the property purpose of the ≪linkableTo≫ dependency between the phenomenon and the stakeholder under consideration in an input domain's available information diagram if such a dependency exists. I.e., we document that the information is available at the input domain for the purpose to be made available at an output domain according to the currently considered statement.

Depending on how the information transfer is described by the current statement, it is possible that an output domain is able to link two pieces of data related to a stakeholder to each other. I.e., there is information available at the domain that allows everyone who has access to this information to know that different personal data is related to the same individual, but not necessarily to which individual. E.g., the doctor is able to link the health status of a patient to his/her demographics and hence, knows to which patient a health status is related. To document at which domain which information about the stakeholder is linkable, we use an association with stereotype ≪linkable≫ (cf. Fig. 3) that is part of the available information diagram of the domain at which this link is known and connects the phenomena which can be linked. After the user specified the information transmitted to the output domains, the tool allows to specify for each output domain which personal data available at the output domain is linkable to each other, to which degree the data is linkable to each other, how this link was collected, and how long this link will be available at the domain. The tool then creates on the basis of the user's selection the linkable relations (cf. Fig. 3) and sets the origin of the linkable relation to the statement under consideration. If such a link already existed at a input domain then the current statement is added to the attribute purpose of this linkable relation, similar to the way we set the purpose of personal data that is available at an input domain.

After the above steps, the tool removes the considered statement from the set of statements that still have to be considered and adds all statements that have one of the current output domains for which the user identified a new information flow as input domain. In this way, the user iteratively traverses the DSIFG supported by the tool until all information flows are documented.

Application to EHS Scenario. We consider the first step of the analysis for the stakeholder doctor and select statement R1. As input domain, we have the doctor and the only output domain is the EHR (cf. Fig. 5). The available phenomena are the identified personal data of the doctor, namely his/her doctor contact information, doctor details, treatment, diagnosis, and notes (cf. gray and bold part of Fig. 6). We do not identify further contained or derived personal data in

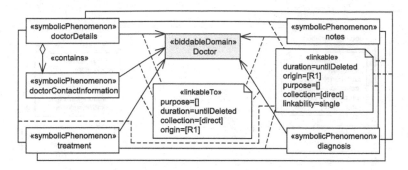

Fig. 7. Available information diagram for the EHR after the first analysis step.

the first step, but we identify that the doctor's contact information is contained in the doctor's details. R1 requires that doctors are able to create and modify health records. Doing this they enter and update contact information and details about them, and information about the treatments, diagnoses, and notes they make. All this information is entered directly by the respective doctor. Health records do not have to be deleted after the treatment is done, but there can be situations where they have to be deleted after some period. This is because some regulations prescribe to ensure that the health records are kept up to date. If this cannot be assured, e.g., because a patient does not show up for a longer time period, the respective personal data has to be deleted. Hence, we set the duration of availability to untilDeleted. Furthermore, the tool adds R1 to the property purpose of the stereotype instances ≪linkableTo≫ in the available information diagram of the doctor (input domain) for all the personal data that flows to the EHR (output domain). The personal data that doctors enter due to R1 are (and have to be) linkable to each other at the EHR for further processing. E.g., it has to be known to which doctor (determined by doctorDetails) the notes, treatments and diagnoses belong, and also it has to be known which treatments, diagnosis, and notes are related to each other. These links are recorded based on the direct input of doctors, the links allow a 1-to-1 mapping between the personal data (linkability set to single), and these links are kept until they are deleted, analogously to the personal data itself. The generated available information diagram for the EHR after the first analysis step is shown in Fig. 7.

During the further analysis, we identify additional personal information of the doctor that is processed by the EHS. This information is shown in addition to the initially identified personal data of the doctor in Fig. 6. Due to requirement R4, we identified that the alarms and instructions that are shown to patients using their mobile devices can be considered as a part of the treatment the doctor specifies for a patient and hence this information has also to be considered as personal information. Additionally, we identify from R4 that the appointments of patients are derived from the doctor's details and the specified treatment by the doctors themselves. For the accounting of patients (R2) the costs of the treatments are derived based on the treatments performed and the diagnosis of

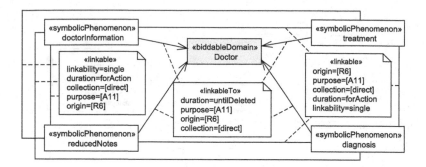

Fig. 8. Available information diagram for the research database application.

the doctor. To allow researchers to perform clinical research based on the kept health records (R6), an anonymization of the personal data to be sent to the research database application has to be performed. Only information about the doctor (phenomenon doctorInformation) which is contained in the doctor's details and which does not allow to uniquely identify a single doctor is provided to the research data base application. Additionally, the notes of doctors are reduced to ensure that these notes do not contain any information that reveals the identity of doctors. Due to limitations of space, we do not show all available information diagrams. Figure 8 shows the personal data of the doctor available at the research database application. For clinical research, the diagnoses, treatments, and anonymized information about the doctor and the reduced notes are available at the research database application. All this information is linkable to each other to be of value for clinical research. Furthermore, it was automatically documented by the tool that the purpose for which the personal data and the links between the personal data is available at the research database application is assumption A11 that we identified in the context elicitation step.

4.5   Using the Elicited Knowledge for a PIA Report

The user can now use the collected data to fill parts of a PIA report. At this point of the method, the UML model contains:

1. The personal data of stakeholders that is used in the system.
2. The information at which domain of the system which personal data is available and in which quality.
3. Traceability links to identify the requirements, facts, and assumptions that lead to the information flows.
4. For each domain, we can derive the set of counterstakeholders that possibly have access to personal data available at the domain that they should not be able to access (cf. [4]).

Wright et al. [2] propose eleven criteria that indicate the effectiveness of a PIA report. The artifacts on which our method is based and which it produces

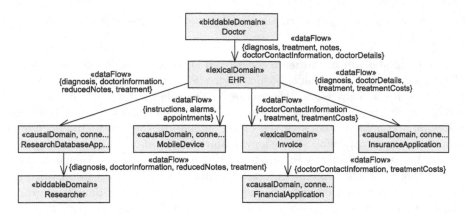

Fig. 9. Stakeholder data flow graph for the doctor.

can be used to address two of them. First, Wright et al. stress to *"include a description of the project to be assessed, its purpose and any relevant contextual information"*. By relying on the problem frames approach, we already have a description of the project to be assessed in the form of a context diagram [5] and the functional requirements. Furthermore, we extend this description in the step *context elicitation* with additional information about the environment of the software-to-be in the form of facts and assumptions. Second, Wright et al. advise to *"map the information flows (i.e., how information is to be collected, used, stored, secured and distributed and to whom and how long the data is to be retained)"*. The information about how the information is collected, used, to whom it is disclosed, and how long the data is retained is elicited during the information flow analysis and documented in the personal and available information diagrams. This information can be used for PIA reports in different ways. Several PIA guidelines suggest to visualize the information flows in the form of an information flow graph (cf. Fig. 9). Our tool is able to automatically generate such graphs (that we call *stakeholder data flow graphs*) automatically on the basis of the available information diagrams. A symbolic phenomenon p flows from a domain i to an other domain o iff p is available at both i and o, and the intersection of the purposes why p is available at i with the statements from which it was identified that p is available at o (origin) is not empty.

Furthermore, we can develop templates to automatically fill the PIA report that has to be created with the information elicited with our method. E.g., we can use the following four templates to document 1. how the information is to be collected, 2. used, 3. to whom it is disclosed and 4. how long the data is to be retained.

1. $<personalInformation>$ is $<collection>$ly collected from $<stakeholder>$ according to $<origin>$.
2. $<personalInformation>$ is used for $<origin>$ by/for the $<Domain>$.
3. $<personalInformation>$ is disclosed to $<Domain>$s according to $<origin>$.

4. *<personalInformation>* is retained *<duration>* at the *<Domain>* due to *<origin>*.

The templates are instantiated for a fixed stakeholder and a fixed personal information of that stakeholder, which represent the values of the parameters *<stakeholder>* and *<personalInformation>*. The other parameters are instantiated for specific edges of the stakeholder data flow graph (SDFG). The parameter *<Domain>* is instantiated with the target domain of the considered edge and the parameters *<collection>*, *<origin>*, and *<duration>* are the corresponding attributes of the linkableTo relation between the personal information and the stakeholder in the available information diagram of the target domain. The first template is instantiated for each edge in the stakeholder data flow graph (SDFG) that starts from the stakeholder and at which the personal information is annotated (collection), the second for each edge that does not start at the stakeholder and does not end at a biddable domain (use of collected data), the third for each edge that does not start at the stakeholder and ends at a biddable domain (flow of data to persons), and the fourth for each edge that does not end at a biddable domain (storage of data).

According to Wright et al., a PIA report shall also contain information about a privacy risk assessment and the proposed measures to reduce the identified privacy risks. Our method does not yet support a privacy risk assessment, but we think that the information our method elicits is a good starting point for the performance of a privacy risk assessment.

Application to EHS Scenario. The stakeholder data flow graph for the doctor is shown in Fig. 9. It visualizes which personal data (annotated at the edges) flows from which domains to which domains (nodes of the graph). The properties of the personal data are not visualized in the data flow graph, but this information is contained in the corresponding personal and available information diagrams.

If we apply the above mentioned templates and instantiation rules for the stakeholder *Doctor* and the personal information *treatment*, we can generate the following text automatically from the model (cf. Figs. 7, 8, and 9) in order to be used for a PIA report. The terms in *italics* represent instantiated parameters of the templates.

1. Collection
   Treatment is *direct*ly collected from *Doctor*s according to *R1*.
2. Use
   Treatment is used for *R2* by/for the *Invoice*.
   Treatment is used for *R2* by/for the *InsuranceApplication*.
   Treatment is used for *R6* by/for the *ResearchDatabaseApplication*.
3. To whom
   Treatment is disclosed to *Researcher*s according to *A11*.
4. Retention
   Treatment is retained *untilDeleted* at the *EHR* due to *R1*.
   Treatment is retained *untilDeleted* at the *ResearchDatabaseApplication* due to *R6*.

Treatment is retained *forAction* at the *Invoice* due to *R2*.
Treatment is retained *forAction* at the *InsuranceApplication* due to *R2*.

5   Related Work

Privacy-Aware Requirements Engineering. The LINDDUN-framework proposed by Deng et al. [10] is an extension of Microsoft's security analysis framework STRIDE [11]. The basis for the privacy analysis is a data flow diagram (DFD) which is then analyzed on the basis of the high-level threats Linkability, Identifiabilitiy, Non-repudiation, Detectability, information Disclosure, content Unawareness, and policy/consent Noncompliance.

The PriS method introduced by Kalloniatis et al. [12] considers privacy requirements as organizational goals. The impact of the privacy requirements on the other organizational goals and their related business processes is analyzed. The authors use privacy process patterns to suggest a set of privacy enhancing technologies (PETs) to implement the privacy requirements.

Liu et al. [13] propose a security and privacy requirements analysis based on the goal and agent-based requirements engineering approach i^* [14]. The authors integrate the security and privacy analysis into the elicitation process of i^*. Already elicited actors from i^* are considered as attackers. Additional skills and malicious intent of the attackers are combined with the capabilities and interests of the actors. Then the vulnerabilities implied by the identified attackers and their malicious intentions are investigated in the i^* model.

The above mentioned methods all support the identification of high-level privacy threats or vulnerabilities and the selection of privacy enhancing technologies (PETs) to address the privacy threats or vulnerabilities. These steps are not yet supported by the ProPAn-method. But in contrast to a problem frame model, DFDs, goal models, and business processes, as they are used by the above methods, are too high-level and lack of detailed information that is necessary to identify personal data that is processed by the system and how the personal data flows through the system. Hence, the methods proposed by Deng et al., Kalloniatis et al., and Liu et al. lack of support for the elicitation of the information that is essential for a valuable privacy analysis. Additionally, we provide a tool-supported method to systematically identify the personal data and collect the information at which domains of the system this personal data is available in a way that allows us to use the data to assist PIAs.

Omoronyia et al. [15] present an adaptive privacy framework. Formal models are used to describe the behavioral and context models, and user's privacy requirements of the system. The behavioral and context model are then checked against the privacy requirements using model checking techniques. This approach is complementary to ours, because the knowledge collected by our method can be used to set up adequate models, which is crucial to obtain valuable results.

Methodologies Supporting PIA. Oetzel and Spiekermann [16] describe a methodology to support the complete PIA process. Their methodology describes which steps have to be performed in which order to perform a PIA. Hence, their methodology covers all necessary steps that have to be performed for a PIA. In contrast to our method, Oetzel and Spiekermann's methodology does not give concrete guidance on how to elicit the relevant information needed for a PIA which is the focus of this work.

Tancock et al. [17] propose a PIA tool for cloud computing that provides guidance for carrying out a PIA for this domain. The information about the system has to be entered manually into the tool. The PIA tool by Tancock et al. covers more parts of a PIA then our method. In contrast, our method can use the information provided by an existing requirements model and provides in this way more guidance for the elicitation of the information essential for a PIA.

6   Conclusions

To assist the creation of a PIA report for software projects, we developed a tool-supported method that derives necessary inputs for a PIA from a requirements model in a systematic manner. This method is based on a requirements model in problem frame notation and hence, can be started at the very beginning of the software development process, when it is still possible to influence the software project. Our method assists requirements engineers and domain experts to systematically identify the personal data processed by the system to be built and how this personal data flows through the system. We sketched how this information can be used to create parts of a PIA report. Additionally, it can also serve as starting point for a privacy risk assessment. Our proposed UML profile can be extended with further stereotype properties and values to capture additional information that has to be documented for a specific PIA report.

Our method has some limitations. As starting point of the analysis, we rely on a complete model of functional requirements. Hence, changes in the functional requirements generally imply a re-run of our method and all collected information has to be elicited again. To overcome this limitation, we could enhance our method as follows. If a requirement is removed from the mode, then all information flows that originate from this requirement could be automatically removed from the model by the tool. This is possible due to the attributes origin (cf. Fig. 3). And if a requirement is added then we would have to check whether this requirement introduces new relevant domain knowledge, and whether the requirement together with the new domain knowledge introduce new information flows to the already elicited information flows. In this way, the already collected information from the unchanged requirements could be kept. Another limitation is that our proposed tool is only a prototype implementation that needs to be further analyzed for usability and user acceptance.

As future work, we want to further support the generation of PIA reports based on the elicited information. For this, we will extend our tool support with the possibility to define templates that can be filled with the information contained in the UML model and then be used as part of a PIA report. We also want to extend our proposed method with a privacy risk assessment and to integrate a privacy threshold assessment that indicates which level of detail the PIA shall have. Furthermore, we plan to empirically validate our method, the tool support, and the outputs produced by our method.

References

1. Cavoukian, A.: Privacy by design - the 7 foundational principles (2011). https:// www.ipc.on.ca/images/resources/7foundationalprinciples.pdf
2. Wright, D., Wadhwa, K., Hert, P.D., Kloza, D.: A privacy impact assessment framework for data protection and privacy rights - Deliverable D1. Technical report, PIAF Consortium (2011)
3. European Commission: Proposal for a regulation of the european parliament and of the council on the protection of individuals with regard to the processing of personal data and on the free movement of such data (general data protection regulation) (2012). http://eur-lex.europa.eu/legal-content/EN/TXT/?uri=CELEX: 52012PC0011
4. Beckers, K., Faßbender, S., Heisel, M., Meis, R.: A problem-based approach for computer-aided privacy threat identification. In: Preneel, B., Ikonomou, D. (eds.) APF 2012. LNCS, vol. 8319, pp. 1–16. Springer, Heidelberg (2014)
5. Jackson, M.: Problem Frames: Analyzing and Structuring Software Development Problems. Addison-Wesley, Boston (2001)
6. Côté, I., Hatebur, D., Heisel, M., Schmidt, H.: UML4PF - a tool for problem-oriented requirements analysis. In: Proceedings of RE, pp. 349–350. IEEE Computer Society (2011)
7. Meis, R.: Problem-based consideration of privacy-relevant domain knowledge. In: Hansen, M., Hoepman, J.-H., Leenes, R., Whitehouse, D. (eds.) Privacy and Identity 2013. IFIP AICT, vol. 421, pp. 150–164. Springer, Heidelberg (2014)
8. Meis, R., Heisel, M.: Systematic identification of information flows from requirements to support privacy impact assessments. In: ICSOFT-PT 2015 - Proceedings of the 10th International Conference on Software Paradigm Trends. SciTePress (2015)
9. ISO/IEC: ISO 29100 Information technology - Security techniques - PrivacyFramework (2011)
10. Deng, M., Wuyts, K., Scandariato, R., Preneel, B., Joosen, W.: A privacy threat analysis framework: supporting the elicitation and fulfillment of privacy requirements. RE **16**, 3–32 (2011)
11. Howard, M., Lipner, S.: The Security Development Lifecycle. Microsoft Press, Redmond (2006)
12. Kalloniatis, C., Kavakli, E., Gritzalis, S.: Addressing privacy requirements in system design: the PriS method. RE **13**, 241–255 (2008)
13. Liu, L., Yu, E., Mylopoulos, J.: Security and privacy requirements analysis within a social setting. In: Proceedings of 11th IEEE International Requirements Engineering Conference, pp. 151–161 (2003)
14. Yu, E.: Towards modeling and reasoning support for early-phase requirements engineering. In: Proceedings of the 3rd IEEE International Symposium on RE, pp. 226–235. IEEE Computer Society, Washington, DC (1997)
15. Omoronyia, I., Cavallaro, L., Salehie, M., Pasquale, L., Nuseibeh, B.: Engineering adaptive privacy: on the role of privacy awareness requirements. In: Proceedings of the 2013 International Conference on SE, ICSE 2013, pp. 632–641. IEEE Press, Piscataway (2013)

16. Oetzel, M., Spiekermann, S.: A systematic methodology for privacy impact assessments: a design science approach. Eur. J. Inf. Syst. **23**, 126–150 (2014)
17. Tancock, D., Pearson, S., Charlesworth, A.: A privacy impact assessment tool for cloud computing. In: IEEE 2nd International Conference on Cloud Computing Technology and Science (CloudCom), pp. 667–676 (2010)

Integrating Model Driven and Model Checking to Mine Design Patterns

Mario L. Bernardi[1], Marta Cimitile[2], Giuseppe De Ruvo[1],
Giuseppe A. Di Lucca[1(✉)], and Antonella Santone[1]

[1] Department of Engineering, University of Sannio, Benevento, Italy
{mlbernar,gderuvo,dilucca,santone}@unisannio.it
[2] Unitelma Sapienza University, Rome, Italy
marta.cimitile@unitelma.it

Abstract. The use of Design Patterns has constantly grown in the development of Object Oriented systems, due to the well-known advantage they offer to improve the quality of software design. However, lack of documentation about which Design Patterns are actually adopted and implemented in the code and about the code components involved in the implementation of each Design Pattern instance can make harder any operation of maintenance, reuse, or evolution impacting those components. Thus, several Design Pattern Mining approaches and tools have been proposed to identify the instances of Design Pattern implemented in an Object oriented system. Nevertheless, the results produced by these approaches can be not fully complete and precise because of the presence of false positive/negative. In this paper we propose to integrate a Model Driven based Design Pattern mining approach with a Formal Method technique to automatically refine and improve the precision of results of traditional mining tool. In particular Model checking is used to refine the results of the Design Pattern Finder (DPF) tool implementing a Model Driven based approach to detect Design Pattern instances Object Oriented systems. To verify and validate the feasibility and effectiveness of the proposed approach we carried out a case study regarding four open source OO systems. The results from the case study showed that actually the technique allowed to raise significantly the precision of the instances that the DPF tool was able to identify.

Keywords: Software engineering · Design patterns · Model checking · Formal methods · Models · Mining

1 Introduction

In the last two decades we have seen a growth on the usage of Design Patterns (DPs) [1] in the development of Object Oriented (OO) software systems, because their adoption contributes to greatly improve the software quality [2,3]. Unfortunately, the lack of adequate documentation may make difficult to understand which are the adopted Design Patterns and where they are implemented

© Springer International Publishing Switzerland 2016
P. Lorenz et al. (Eds.): ICSOFT 2015, CCIS 586, pp. 99–117, 2016.
DOI: 10.1007/978-3-319-30142-6_6

(i.e., which code components implement each instance of a DP) in a system. Thus, several approaches have been proposed to support the automatic identification of DPs instances in an existing OO software system, linking each detected instance to the OO components implementing it [4–6]. The automatic detection of DPs provides software engineers the needed knowledge to better comprehend the system reducing the effort to modify and evolve it [3,7,8].

However, the results obtained by the existing DP detection approaches can suffer a lack of completeness or precision due to the presence of false positive/negative. The precision of the DP's instances detected by a tool can be improved by Model Checking (MC) techniques that can automatically refine the results the tool produces. Model checking has been applied to several fields. For instance, it has been used in bioinfomatics to infer gene regulatory networks from time series data [9] or to analyse wiki quality [10]. In this paper we proposed to integrate Model Driven based DP mining approaches with Formal Method techniques to improve the precision and quality of the DP detection task. Formal methods are exploited to automatically refine the results produced by an existing DP mining tool implementing a Model based mining approach. In particular we employ Model Checking using the Language of Temporal Ordering Specification (LOTOS) and selective-μ-calculus (we interchangeably refer to either μ or MU). The MC methodology [11] aims to analyze the DPs' instances, detected by the Model based mining tool, evaluating their correctness with respect to formally encoded properties checked against the entire system model represented with (basic) LOTOS. This allows to reduce the number of wrongly detected patterns (false positives) with respect to the original approach.

We apply the proposed MC technique to the Design Pattern Finder (DPF) approach presented in [12,13]. The DPF approach is based on a meta-model and a Domain Specific Language (DSL) to represent both the software system and the searched DPs. The DPs models are organized as a hierarchy of declarative specifications and expressed as a wide set of high level properties that can be added, removed or relaxed obtaining new pattern variants. Moreover, the DPF approach with respect to the existing ones: (i) allows to easily specify variant forms of the classic DPs; (ii) takes into account a wider set of high level properties (including also the behavioural properties to better characterize DPs) to specify a pattern. The DPF effectiveness, was evaluated by applying it to several systems and the obtained results are reported in [13]. Even if the obtained results are good, we observed that the precision of the DPF can be further improved. Indeed, DPF, as any other existing DPs detecting approach, can suffer in lacking of precision and completeness. We decided to apply the MC refinement to the DPF, because: (i) the authors of DPF made available both the tool and the results of previous analysis they made; (ii) DPF seems to perform better than other similar tools as shown in [13]; (iii) DPF is based on a meta-model that can be exploited by the MC refinement to create (basic) LOTOS processes.

Therefore, we embodied a new refinement step along the DPF detection process, where the DPF outcomes are the inputs. From the DPF model we create (basic) LOTOS processes and from DPF detected patterns we generate selective-μ-calculus properties in order to verify the actual existence of design patterns instances through model checking.

The approach has been assessed by applying it to some systems of open benchmarks proposed in [14, 15].

Of course, the proposed refining approach can be extended to any other DP mining approach. The remainder of this paper is organized as follows. Section 2 discusses related work. Section 3 gives definitions of basic LOTOS and selective-μ-calculus. Section 4 presents and discusses the proposed detection approach, the implemented tools and their integration aspects. Section 5 introduces and describes the case study. Finally, in Sect. 6, conclusive remarks and future work are presented.

2   Related Work

In the last years, many design pattern recovery techniques and tools have been proposed. In [5, 6] reviews regarding some of the main existing approaches can be found.

Several approaches, as the ones in [16–18], use UML structures, represented as matrices, to model structural and behavioral information of software systems. These techniques are applied to match a DP template matrix with the matrix generated for the system. In particular, a DP detection methodology based on similarity scoring between graph vertexes is proposed in [16]. The approach is able to also recognize patterns that are slightly modified from their standard representation. It exploits the fact that patterns reside in one or more inheritance hierarchies (in order to reduce the size of the graphs to which the algorithm is applied). These approaches are computationally efficient and have good precision and recall rates. Their limit is that they miss to detect patterns variants of similar design patterns. Furthermore, they are only limited to the patterns coded as matrices and hence it is not suitable to be easily extended.

Some DP mining approaches are based on metric techniques: program related metrics (i.e. generalizations, aggregations, associations, interface hierarchies) are computed from different source code representations and their values compared with source code DP metrics [18–20]. These techniques are computationally efficient because metric computation is less expensive than structural pattern recognition and do not require heuristic approach to reduce search space through filtration [21]. Their precision and recall are usually low; moreover they were experimented on few design patterns in literature.

Other DP detection approaches exploit other techniques (such as, fuzzy reasoning, bit vector compression, minimum key structure method, dynamic analysis using run-time execution traces, machine learning based approaches and concept analysis) that are good as a complement to improve the DP detection based on structural methods. For example, in [22], De Lucia et al. use a recovery technique based on the parsing of visual languages, and supported by a visual environment automatically produced by a grammar based visual environment generator. A tool, using a mixed structural and metric approach, for design pattern detection and software architecture reconstruction is proposed in [23].

Other studies [17,24] have been focused on the formalization of empirical evaluation criteria [17,24].

There is few work, at best of our knowledge, that exploits formal methods (model checking) based approaches to detect DP instances in existing OO systems. In [25] formal framework to specify the DPs at different levels of abstraction is proposed. The framework uses stepwise refinement to incrementally add details to a specification after starting from the most abstract one. Moreover, a validation through model checking will verify that a specification in a given level of abstraction is indeed a refinement of a specification of a higher level. The limit of this approach is that a domain specific language to describe DPs is missing and applications in real systems has been never performed. In [26], authors propose an approach aiming to validate DPs using formal method. Similarly, in [27] formal methods are used to demonstrate that a particular design conforms to a given DPs. Both these approaches, are not validated on real software systems. Finally, in [28], a fully automated DPs mining approach performing both static and dynamic analysis to verify the behavior of pattern instances, is proposed. The static analysis exploits model checking to analyze the interactions among objects, while the dynamic analysis of the pattern behavior is performed through a code instrumentation and monitoring phase, applied on the candidate pattern instances. This approach, differently from ours, requires the analysis of the collaboration among objects at runtime by identifying and executing test cases on the software system.

3   Background

Historically, process algebras have been developed as formal descriptions of complex computer systems, and in particular of those involving communicating, concurrently executing components. The crucial idea in the definition of Process Algebras is the algebraic structure of the concurrent processes. This uses a state-based approach with labeled transitions, where states and transitions correspond to processes and actions, respectively. There are many examples of process algebras, like for example Milner's Calculus of Communicating Systems (CCS) [29] and Language of Temporal Order Specification (LOTOS) [30], which we will use in this paper.

3.1   Basic LOTOS

Let us now recall the main concepts of Basic LOTOS. A Basic LOTOS program is defined as:

```
process ProcName := B
    where E
endproc
```

where B is a *behaviour expression*, `process ProcName := B` is a *process declaration* and E is a *process environment*, i.e., a set of process declarations. A behaviour expression is the composition, by means of a set of operators, of a finite set $\mathcal{A} = \{$i,a,b, ...$\}$ of atomic *actions*. Each occurrence of an action in $\mathcal{A}$ represents an event of the system. An occurrence of an action a $\in \mathcal{A}-\{$i$\}$ represents a communication on the gate a. The action i does not correspond to a communication and it is called the *unobservable action*.

The syntax of behaviour expressions (also called *processes*) is the following:

```
B ::= stop | a;B | B[]B| P | B|[S]|B | B[f] | hide S in B | exit
            | B>>B | B[>B
```

where P ranges over a set of process names and a ranges over $\mathcal{A}$. The operational semantics of a behaviour expression B is a labelled transition system, i.e., an automaton whose states correspond to behaviour expressions (the initial state corresponds to B) and whose transitions (arcs) are labeled by actions in $\mathcal{A}$. The meaning of the operators composing behavior expressions is the following:

– The *action prefix* a;B means that the corresponding process executes the action a and then behaves as B.
– The *choice* B1 [] B2 composes the two alternative behavior descriptions B1 and B2.
– The expression **stop** cannot perform any move.
– The *parallel composition* B1|[S]|B2, where S is a subset of $\mathcal{A}-\{$i$\}$, composes in parallel the two behaviors B1 and B2. B1 and B2 interleave the actions not belonging to S, while they must synchronize at each gate in S. A synchronization at gate a is the simultaneous execution of an action a by both partners and produces the single event a. If S = $\emptyset$ or S = $\mathcal{A}$, the parallel composition means pure interleaving or complete synchronization.
– Cyclic behaviors are expressed by recursive process declarations.
– The *relabeling* B[f], where f: $\mathcal{A} \rightarrow \mathcal{A}$ is an action relabeling function, renames the actions occurring in the transition system of B as specified by the function f. This function is syntactically defined as: a0 -> b0,...,an->bn, meaning that:
  f(a0) = b0,...,f(an) = bn, and f(a) = a for each a not belonging to $\{$a0,...,an$\}$. Note that each relabelling function has the property that f(i) = i.
– The *hiding* hide S in B renames the actions in S, occurring in the transition system of B, with the unobservable action i.
– The expression **exit** represents successful termination; it can be used by the enabling (B >> B) and disabling (B[> B) operators: B >> B represents sequentialization between B1 and B2 and B[> B models interruptions. For the sake of simplicity, we do not discuss these operators in the paper.

Assume the precedence of the operators as specified by the following list, ordered in decreasing order:

```
;  [f]  hide  |[S]|   []
```

Table 1. Standard operational semantics of Basic LOTOS.

$a \in \mathcal{A},\, l \in \mathcal{A} - \{\texttt{i}\}$

$$\textbf{pre}\ \frac{}{a; B \xrightarrow{a}_S B} \qquad\qquad \textbf{choice}\ \frac{B_1 \xrightarrow{a}_S B_1'}{B_1\,[]\,B_2 \xrightarrow{a}_S B_1'}$$

$$\textbf{inst}\ \frac{B \xrightarrow{a}_S B'}{P \xrightarrow{a}_S B'}\, P := B \in E \qquad \textbf{rel}\ \frac{B \xrightarrow{a}_S B'}{B[f] \xrightarrow{f(a)}_S B'[f]}$$

$$\textbf{par}\ \frac{B_1 \xrightarrow{a}_S B_1'}{B_1\,|[S]|\,B_2 \xrightarrow{a}_S B_1'\,|[S]|\,B_2}\, a \notin S$$

$$\textbf{com}\ \frac{B_1 \xrightarrow{a}_S B_1',\ B_2 \xrightarrow{a}_S B_2'}{B_1\,|[S]|\,B_2 \xrightarrow{a}_S B_1'\,|[S]|\,B_2'}\, a \in S$$

$$\textbf{hide}_1\ \frac{B \xrightarrow{a}_S B'}{\text{hide S in B} \xrightarrow{a}_S \text{hide S in B}'}\, a \notin S$$

$$\textbf{hide}_2\ \frac{B \xrightarrow{l}_S B'}{\text{hide S in B} \xrightarrow{i}_S \text{hide S in B}'}\, l \in S$$

The semantics of a process B is precisely defined by means of the structural operational semantics (in Table 1). The semantic definition is given by a set of conditional rules describing the transition relation of the automaton corresponding to the behavior expression defining B. This automaton is called *standard transition system* for B and is denoted by $\mathcal{S}(B)$. In Table 1 the symmetrical rules for choice and parallel composition are not shown.

We consider only finite Basic LOTOS programs, i.e., programs with finite standard transition systems. A sufficient condition for finiteness is that the parallel operator does not occur inside recursive process declarations. From now on, we write LOTOS instead of Basic LOTOS.

3.2 Selective-μ-Calculus

The selective-μ-calculus, introduced in [31], is a branching temporal logic to express behavioral properties of systems. It is equi-expressive to μ-calculus [32], but it differs from it in the definition of the modal operators.

Given a set $\mathcal{A}$ of actions and a set *Var* of variables, the syntax of the selective mu-calculus logic is the following, where K and R range over sets of actions:

$$\varphi ::= \texttt{tt} \mid \texttt{ff} \mid \varphi \wedge \varphi \mid \varphi \vee \varphi \mid [K]_R\,\varphi \mid \langle K \rangle_R\,\varphi \mid \mu Z.\varphi \mid \nu Z.\varphi$$

The satisfaction of a formula φ by a state s of a transition system, written $s \models \varphi$, is defined as follows:

- each state satisfies tt and no state satisfies ff;
- a state satisfies $\varphi_1 \vee \varphi_2$ ($\varphi_1 \wedge \varphi_2$) if it satisfies φ_1 or (and) φ_2;
- $[K]_R \, \varphi$ is satisfied by a state which, for every performance of a sequence of actions not belonging to $R \cup K$, followed by an action in K, evolves to a state obeying φ.
- $\langle K \rangle_R \, \varphi$ is satisfied by a state which can evolve to a state obeying φ by performing a sequence of actions not belonging to $R \cup K$, followed by an action in K.

The selective modal operators $\langle K \rangle_R \, \varphi$ and $[K]_R \, \varphi$ substitute the standard modal operators $\langle K \rangle \, \varphi$ and $[K] \, \varphi$. The basic characteristic of the selective-μ-calculus is that each formula allows us to immediately point out the parts of the transition system that do not alter the truth value of the formula itself. More precisely, *the only actions relevant for checking a formula are the ones explicitly mentioned by the selective modal operators used in the formula itself.* Thus, the result of checking the formula is independent from all other actions. This information can be exploited to obtain reduced transition systems on which the formula can be equivalently checked (see, for example, [33]). The precise definition of the satisfaction of a closed formula φ by a state of a transition system can be found in [31].

4   The Integrated Approach

In this section we introduce the integrated Design Pattern mining approach.

The process is structured in two main sub-processes. The first one performs the Model Driven design pattern detection applying the Graph-Matching approach implemented by DPF, discussed in [13]. The second sub-process performs the refinement of the results by DPF using the Model Checking approach defined in this paper.

In the following there is a short description of the main process activities, according to the sequence they are performed:

- **Source Code Analysis** — The source and bytecodes of the system under study are parsed and the complete ASTs of the system are produced.
- **Model Instantiation** — A traversal of the system AST is performed to generate an instance of the system model (i.e. the system graph S), conforming to the meta-model defined for DPF. Rapid type analysis (RTA), class flattening and inlining of not public methods are exploited in order to build a system's representation suitable for the matching algorithm.
- **Graph-Matching DPs Detection** — The DPF graph matching algorithm, described in [13], is performed to match the system model, built in the previous step, with the pattern specifications graphs of the DPs to be detected.
- **Pattern Property Generation** — Each pattern specification to be detected is written as a set of templated μ-properties. These properties involve the patterns roles and their relationships. The template parameters are bound to the concrete system elements using information extracted from the pattern instances found in the detection step (i.e. roles and the system elements related to them).

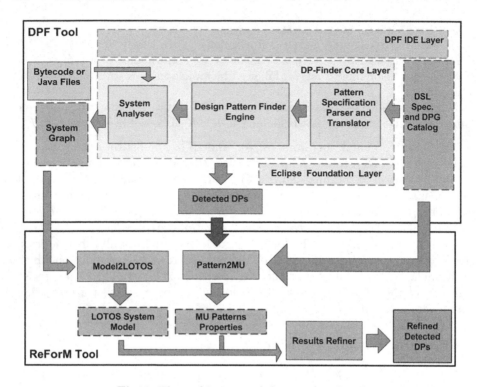

Fig. 1. The architecture of the integrated tool.

- **LOTOS System Model Creation** — In order to check if a given set of parametrized μ-properties holds, the system model graph has to be expressed in a suitable model (in our approach LOTOS was exploited). Hence this step takes the system model graph as input and translates it to a LOTOS model instance. This translation has to be performed only one time for each system to be mined.
- **Pattern Matching Through Model Checking** — This step checks the parametrized sets of μ-properties obtained from the pattern specifications catalogue against the LOTOS model of the system in order to reduce the number of false positives in the results by DPF.

The Fig. 1 shows the overall architecture of the tool implementing the proposed approach. The tool integrates the DPF tool with the ReForM (Refining by Formal Methods) tool exploiting Model Checking to improve the precision of the DPF's results.

The DPF tool implements the three steps of the first sub-process described before. It was developed as a set of Eclipse plug-ins based upon Java Development Tools (JDT) and upon the Eclipse Modeling Framework. It has a layered architecture.

The bottom layer includes the Eclipse Foundation Components: the tool uses the JDT and the Eclipse Modeling Platform (Xpand, Xtext, and MoDisco) to extract.

The DP-Finder Core layer includes three main sub-systems. The Pattern Specification Parser and Translator module supports the activities related to the specification of DPs by the Domain Specification Language defined at this aim. It registers the DSL specifications of each DP and parses them to produce the corresponding DPGs. Each DSL specification is translated, by means of the Xtext-based DSL translator in a set of constraints. The specifications (both DSLs and corresponding DPGs) of the DPs to be mined are stored in a Catalog.

The System Analyzer produces an instance of the meta-model (i.e., the System Graph) of the analyzed system by static analysis.

The Design Pattern Finder Engine module executes the detection algorithm to identify the DP instances by searching the System Graph for sub-graphs matching a defined DPG. The detection algorithm produces a model of the system elements annotated with information on the detected patterns (e.g., their internal members and roles played in the pattern). Each identified pattern instance is traced to the source code elements implementing it.The results of the identification process are stored in the central repository.

The DPF IDE layer allows interactions with users, that can select which DPs are to be searched and analyzed in a system by means of a tree viewer or using the Eclipse Visualizer. The Visualizer also shows a summary of patterns found in the analyzed system at different levels (package or class).

The ReForM tool is composed by three main modules. The Pattern2MU is devoted to activities for writing the set of templated μ-properties for each DP to detect.

The module Model2LOTOS supports the translation of the System Model Graph into a LOTOS model instance.

The Results Refiner component executes the check of the μ-properties against the LOTOS model of the subject system.

At the time of writing this paper, just a first prototype of ReForM has been developed: some activities/operations (mainly for the Pattern2MU and Model2LOTOS) are not fully automated and require human intervention to be performed.

4.1   Graph-Matching DPs Detection

The detection of the DPs instances is performed according to the DPF approach [13]. The DPF approach is based on a meta-model and a Domain Specific Language (DSL) to model the structure of both OO systems and DPs. The meta-model uniformly describes the DPs and systems in terms of relationships among code elements, and allows to trace down to the DPs Properties and Types components both the structural and behavioral relationships among the types. The meta-model defined in [13] is exploited to define the DSL to represent structural and behavioral relevant properties of OO software systems, as well as to express the specifications of the DPs to be detected. Each pattern, in order to be detected, has been modeled writing a DSL pattern specification stored into a repository. The current repository stores a catalog composed of 18 patterns with 56 variants. Each DSL specification can be translated into a graph, called

DP Graph (DPG), in which elements are nodes and properties are labeled edges. The DPG is part of the input for the graph-matching detection algorithm.

Along the execution of the DPF Graph Matching algorithm, the system graph (i.e., the instance of the system model) is traversed and each pattern instance sub-graph is mapped to the corresponding matching DPG (to identify the actually implemented patterns). More insights and details about the DPF approach can be found in [13].

4.2   DPF Refinement

The proposed approach is based on the use of formal methods. From the DPF outcomes we derive LOTOS processes, which are successively used to perform model checking to increase the precision of DPs mining results produced by DPF. The following activities are to be performed:

1. LOTOS System model creation.
2. Pattern Property generation.
3. Pattern Matching through Model Checking.

LOTOS Model Creation. We use, as internal representation, the LOTOS language. Thus, LOTOS specifications are generated starting from the internal representation of DPF. This is obtained by defining a DPF-to-LOTOS transform operator T. The function T directly applies to Java system outcomes of DPF and translates them into LOTOS process specifications. The function T is defined for each part of a Java system such as classes, interfaces, methods, fields. Each one has been translated into LOTOS processes. First of all, a System is composed of a set of Types. A Type may be a ClassType or an InterfaceType. A ClassType is made up of Methods. Types may be tied by inheritance relations and a ClassType may implement an InterfaceType, as usually occurs in OO software systems.

System. The generic Java *System* containing k types is translated into the following LOTOS process:

$$T(C) = \begin{array}{l} process\ SYSTEM := \\ Type_1\ []\cdots[]\ Type_k \\ endproc \end{array}$$

where $Type_i$ is written using the fully qualified Java name. The LOTOS process $SYSTEM$ represents the parent process of all the types. Each translated LOTOS model has a *System* process.

Type. As stated, a Type may be a ClassType or an InterfaceType. If FQN is the fully qualified name of a Type, a ClassType is translated into the following LOTOS process:

$\mathcal{T}(T) = process\ FQN\_ClassType :=$
$name\_ClassType;$
$(FQN\_\ Method_i; FQN\_\ Method_{i\_}\ Method\ []\cdots[]$
$FQN\_\ Method_k; FQN\_\ Method_{k\_}\ Method\ []$
$implements; (FQN\_\ InterfaceType_j\ []\cdots[]$
$FQN\_\ InterfaceType_w)\ []$
$inherits; (FQN\_\ ClassType_l\ []\cdots[]$
$FQN\_\ ClassType_y)\ []$
$field; (FQN\_\ InterfaceType_h\ []\cdots[]\ FQN\_\ ClassType_z))$
$endproc$

Instead, an InterfaceType is translated into the following LOTOS process:

$\mathcal{T}(I) = processFQN\_InterfaceType :=$
$name\_InterfaceType; (FQN\_\ Method_i;$
$FQN\_\ Method_{i\_}\ Method\ []\cdots[]$
$FQN\_\ Method_k; FQN\_\ Method_{k\_}\ Method\ []$
$inherits; (FQN\_\ InterfaceType_l\ []\cdots[]\ FQN\_\ InterfaceType_y))$
$endproc$

where *implements* and *inherits* are actions which respectively indicate implementation of interfaces and inheritance relation between types.

Method. A method is represented with its own arguments and with a modifier, thus it is translated into the following LOTOS process:

$\mathcal{T}(M) = process\ FQN\_\ Method := name\_Method;$
$(arg_i; stop\ []\cdots[]\ arg_k; stop\ []\ modifier\_mod; stop)$
$endproc$

where arg_i is the name of the argument and mod is the type of modifier such as public, private, protected.

Pattern Property Generation. After the LOTOS processes of the Java software system are generated, we can use selective-μ-calculus logic to specify desired properties. A pattern is translated into a selective-μ-calculus property. Each design pattern leads to a different property, although a set of common properties are used as building blocks:

1. Existence of Interface Implementation:
   $\langle implements \rangle_\emptyset\ \langle name\_\ InterfaceType \rangle_\emptyset\ \mathsf{tt}$
2. Existence of Inheritance:
   $\langle inherits \rangle_\emptyset\ \langle name\_\ ClassType \rangle_\emptyset\ \mathsf{tt}\ \wedge \langle inherits \rangle_\emptyset\ \langle name\_\ InterfaceType \rangle_\emptyset\ \mathsf{tt}$
3. Existence of a Method:
   $\langle name\_\ Method \rangle_\emptyset\ \mathsf{tt}$
4. Existence of a Field:
   $\langle field \rangle_\emptyset\ \langle name\_InterfaceType \rangle_\emptyset\ \mathsf{tt}\ \wedge\ \langle field \rangle_\emptyset\ \langle name\_ClassType \rangle_\emptyset\ \mathsf{tt}$
5. Existence of an Argument:
   $\langle arg \rangle_\emptyset\ \langle name\_\ InterfaceType \rangle_\emptyset\ \mathsf{tt}\ \wedge\ \langle arg \rangle_\emptyset\ \langle name\_\ ClassType \rangle_\emptyset\ \mathsf{tt}$

Pattern Matching Through Model Checking. Once we have created the LOTOS model of a Java software system and we also have built all the properties which represent the design patterns, we can proceed with model checking. As aforementioned, in this paper both model and properties (patterns) come out translating the ones of DPF. Such translations have been completely automated.

One of the most popular toolbox for the design of asynchronous concurrent systems is CADP [34]. It supports high-level descriptions written in various languages, mainly LOTOS. In the CADP the verification of temporal logic formulae is based on model checking [35], a formal technique for proving the correctness of a system with respect to a desired behavior. This is accomplished by checking whether a structure representing the system (typically a labelled transition system) satisfies a temporal logic formula describing the expected behaviour.

The CADP model checker is applied verifying each pattern against the System model. When the result is TRUE, it means that the pattern has been found, FALSE otherwise. Thanks to a very detailed LOTOS model we are able to identify false positives among the DPs detected by DPF. Eventually, we have all the necessary information to improve the precision of the overall results, as explained in the following section.

5   Case Study

The effectiveness and efficiency of the proposed approach has been validated applying it to some middle-sized OO systems. These systems were available from the publicly available benchmarks proposed in [14,15].

We present the results for the four systems reported in Table 2 and the 4 GoF patterns (Command, Composite, Factory methods and Strategy) for which the DPF method provides the lowest precision.

According to [36], in order to assess effectiveness and correctness of the proposed approach, we evaluated precision and recall. To compute recall and precision we assume that a pattern instance can be classified into one of four categories (T_P: true positive, F_P: false positive, T_N: true-negative, and F_N false-negative).

Precision is defined as the ratio of correctly found occurrences to occurrences provided by the tool whereas recall is defined as the ratio of correctly found occurrences to all correct occurrences:

$$Precision = T_P/(T_P + F_P) \tag{1}$$

$$Recall = T_P/(T_P + F_N) \tag{2}$$

Table 2. Analyzed systems characteristics.

System name	Version	Size (KLOC)	#Types	#Methods
JHotDraw	5.1	8,9 K	174	1316
QuickUML	2.1	9,2 K	230	1082
Nutch	0.4	23,6 K	335	1854
PMD	1.8	41,5 K	519	3665

Table 3. Results obtained on JHotDraw and QuickUML.

Step →		Detection						Refinement					
↓Design Pattern	GS	D	T_P	F_P	F_N	P	R	D	T_P	F_P	F_N	P	R
System→		JHotDraw											
Composite/spec{GoF}	16	19	14	5	2	0,74	0,88	17	14	3	2	0,82	0,88
Factory Method/spec{Parametrized}	15	14	12	2	3	0,86	0,8	14	12	2	3	0,86	0,8
System→		QuickUML											
Command/spec{GoF}	10	8	7	1	3	0,88	0,7	7	7	0	3	1	0,89
Strategy/spec{GoF}	15	18	12	6	3	0,67	0,8	12	12	0	3	1	0,8

Table 4. Results obtained on Nutch before and after refinement.

System→	Nutch (using DPF)							System→	Nutch (after refinement)					
↓Design Pattern	GS	D	T_P	F_P	F_N	P	R	↓Design Pattern	GS	D	T_P	F_P	F_N	P	R
Command/spec{GoF}	50	47	46	1	4	0,98	0,92	Command/spec{GoF}	50	46	46	0	4	1	0,92
Factory Method/spec{Parametrized}	26	30	26	4	0	0,87	1	Factory Method/spec{Parametrized}	26	27	26	1	0	0,96	1
Strategy/spec{GoF}	39	36	36	0	3	1	0,92	Strategy/spec{GoF}	39	36	36	0	3	1	0,92

Table 5. Results obtained on PMD before and after refinement.

System→	PMD (using DPF)							System→	PMD (after refinement))					
↓Design Pattern	GS	D	T_P	F_P	F_N	P	R	↓Design Pattern	GS	D	T_P	F_P	F_N	P	R
Command/spec{GoF}	10	6	6	0	4	1	0,6	Command/spec{GoF}	10	6	6	0	4	1	0,6
Composite/spec{GoF}	8	8	7	1	1	0,88	0,88	Composite/spec{GoF}	8	7	7	0	1	1	0,88
Factory Method/spec{Parametrized}	7	6	5	1	2	0,83	0,71	Factory Method/spec{Parametrized}	7	5	5	0	2	1	0,71
Strategy/spec{GoF}	29	28	28	0	1	1	0,97	Strategy/spec{GoF}	29	28	28	0	1	1	0,97

To verify the correctness of the results we considered as Gold Standard (GS) the union of both the benchmarks cited in [14,15] (assumed to be correct) with the correct results produced by DPF approach (i.e., also the instances not present in the benchmarks, mainly due to DP variants, but correctly detected by DPF as verified by manual code inspection).[1]

Since in this context we are interested to assess the improvement in precision obtained after the model-checking driven refinement, we evaluate and compare precision and recall at the end of both DPs Matching and DPF Refinement steps.

Tables 3, 4, 5 report, for each of the analyzed systems: the name of the DPs searched in the code (first column), the number of true positive instances as provided by the benchmark (GS), and two groups of columns for the DPs detection performed by DPF and the DPF Refinement steps performed using the model checker. Each group contains the number of detected patterns (column D), the number of true positive (column Tp), the number of false positive and negative ones (columns F_p and F_n). The last two columns report respectively precision (P) and recall (R).

---

[1] Of course, the different formats of the benchmarks were translated into a unique common format to store the considered GS.

In the Composite-GoF pattern, for the JHotDraw system, the model-checking step reduced the number of false positive from five to three raising the precision from 0.74 to 0.82. Looking at the three remaining false positive we can see that these are cases in which the assignment of the element to a role in the pattern can be only done looking at the semantics of the element. This is confirmed by the presence in the results of two methods of 3 concrete composite classes (*read()* and *readObject()* in subclasses of CompositeFigure) that were mistakenly bound to Operation role by both the steps but are not part of the interface. This is also the case for the parametrized Factory Method for which the two false positives have the same structure and behaviour of the defined property but cannot be considered as factory methods (*decompose(...)* and *flip(...)* method of Figure class).

In QuickUML system in both cases properties were able to consider structural or behavioral relationships that the original approach was unable to take into account. For instance, for the Strategy pattern several false positive (e.g. the ToolPalette, Clipboard Tool, PropertyChangeHandler and SelectioModel contexts) were detected since the properties were able to better identify indirect relationships and type nesting relationships.

In Nutch system, the model checking step reduced the number of false positives from 1 to 0 in the Command-GoF pattern, and from 4 to 1 in the FactoryMethod-Parametrized. Such reductions lead respectively to a precision of 1 and 0.96, without affecting the recall.

Finally, in PMD, the model checking step improved the precision leading to 1 in either Composite-GoF pattern or FactoryMethod-Parametrized. Even in this case the recall was not affected.

The overall average improvement for all the considered patterns and systems was above 20 %, thanks to the model checking step.

5.1   Motivation of the Use of the Selective-μ-Calculus Logic

We use the selective-μ-calculus logic to express design patterns to improve both the ReForm performance, i.e., the speed at which the model checker returns its results, and its scalability, i.e., the extent to which the model checker can manage increasingly large systems. In the following, we discuss the results of these tests.

The basic characteristic of the selective mu-calculus is that the actions relevant for checking a formula ϕ are those ones explicitly mentioned in the modal operators used in the formula itself. Thus, we define the set $\mathcal{O}(\phi)$ of *occurring actions* of a formula ϕ as the union of all sets K and R appearing in the modal operators ($[K]_R\psi$, $\langle K \rangle_R\psi$) occurring in ϕ.

In the work [31] ρ-equivalence is defined, formally characterizing the notion of "the same behavior with respect to a set ρ of actions":

> *two transition systems are ρ-**equivalent** if a ρ-bisimulation*
> *relating their initial states exists.*

The definition of ρ-bisimulation is based on the concept of α-*ending path*: an α-ending path is a sequence of transitions labeled by actions not in ρ followed by a transition labeled by the action α in ρ. Two states S_1 and S_2 are ρ-bisimilar if and only if for each α-ending path starting from S_1 and ending into S_1', there exists an α-ending path starting from S_2 and ending into a state ρ-bisimilar to S_1', and vice-versa. In [31] it is proved that *"two transition systems are ρ-equivalent if and only if they satisfy the same set of formulae with occurring actions in ρ"*. As a consequence, a formula of the selective mu-calculus with occurring actions in ρ can be checked on any transition system ρ-equivalent to the standard one. Thus, improvements in model checking can be obtained by minimizing the transition system with respect to the actions in ρ. Obviously, the degree of reduction depends on the size of ρ with respect to the size of the whole set A of actions. Consider the transition systems illustrated in Fig. 2. $S1$ is $\{a, b\}$-equivalent to $S3$. The two transition systems give the same value for the formulae containing only actions in $\{a, b\}$. In particular, they satisfy ψ_2, while they do not satisfy ψ_1. Note that $\mathcal{O}(\psi_1) = \{a, b\}$ and $\mathcal{O}(\psi_2) = \{a\} \subseteq \{a, b\}$. On the contrary $S2$ is not $\{a, b\}$-equivalent to $S3$, since it can perform an action b without performing an action a. In [33] a method is defined, which, given a process p and a set of interesting actions ρ occurring in a formula ϕ to be checked, transforms p into another process q, corresponding to a smaller transition system than that of p, on which ϕ can be equivalently checked. The tool is based on a set of syntactic transformations rules. A prototype tool which implements the algorithm has also been defined; it is written in SICStus Prolog [37]. The tool can be easily used both for the CCS [29] and for LOTOS. We discuss our experience with the above methodology to verify the effectiveness in improving the precision of design pattern instances identification. The aim is to evaluate the performances of the approach and compare it against the CADP. First, we apply our tool to transform the specification into a smaller one, where the reduction is driven by the actions occurring in the formulae. Then, we check the properties on the reduced specification. All properties have been checked on reduced LOTOS processes; below we will show only the application on a single property, just to give the reader the flavor of the approach followed.

Consider the following property:

$$
\begin{aligned}
P_1 &= LEAF \wedge COMPOSITE \\
COMPOSITE &= MC \wedge (IC \vee HC) \wedge FC \\
IC &= \langle implements\_CH\_ifa\_draw\_framework\_Figure \rangle_\emptyset\, \mathbf{tt} \\
HC &= \langle inherits\_CH\_ifa\_draw\_framework\_AbtractFigure \rangle_\emptyset\, \mathbf{tt} \\
FC &= \langle field\_fFigures \rangle_\emptyset\, \mathbf{tt} \\
LEAF &= MO \\
MC &= MO \wedge MA \wedge MR \wedge MGC \\
MO &= \langle CH\_ifa\_draw\_standard\_BouncingDrawing\_animationStep \rangle_\emptyset\, \mathbf{tt} \\
MA &= \langle CH\_ifa\_draw\_standard\_BouncingDrawing\_add \rangle_\emptyset\, AC \\
MR &= \langle CH\_ifa\_draw\_standard\_BouncingDrawing\_remove \rangle_\emptyset\, \mathbf{tt} \\
AC &= \langle arg\_CH\_ifa\_draw\_framework\_Figure \rangle_\emptyset\, \mathbf{tt} \\
MGC &= \langle CH\_ifa\_draw\_standard\_CompositeFigure\_findFigure \rangle_\emptyset\, \mathbf{tt}
\end{aligned}
$$

P_1 is the selective-μ-calculus logic formulation of the Composite-GoF pattern. It holds that the set of interesting actions of the above property is:

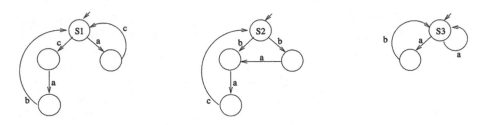

Fig. 2. Three transition systems.

$\rho_1 = \mathcal{O}(P_1) = \{implements\_CH\_ifa\_draw\_framework\_Figure,$
$inherits\_CH\_ifa\_draw\_framework\_AbtractFigure, field\_fFigures,$
$CH\_ifa\_draw\_standard\_BouncingDrawing\_animationStep,$
$CH\_ifa\_draw\_standard\_BouncingDrawing\_add,$
$CH\_ifa\_draw\_standard\_BouncingDrawing\_remove,$
$arg\_CH\_ifa\_draw\_framework\_Figure,$
$CH\_ifa\_draw\_standard\_CompositeFigure\_findFigure\}$

Table 6. State-Space reduction.

JHotDraw (without reduction)		P_1-reduction	
states	trans.	states	trans.
1964	9210	15	33

Table 6 shows the number of states and transitions of the P_1-reduction, i.e., is the reduced LOTOS process obtained by applying the property-based methodology with ρ_1. It is worth noting that the reduction we perform of the states and transitions is significant. Note that also for all the other properties we obtain great reductions. Obviously, a reduction of the state-space implies also a reduction of the time employed by CADP to check the formulae. In almost the cases we obtain a reduction more than 90 %. In general, the usefulness of our tool depends both on the number of actions occurring in the formula and on the structure of the formula to be checked.

6   Conclusions and Future Works

In this work we exploited formal methods to automatically refine the results produced by an existing DP mining approach. In particular, we proposed an integration of model driven and model checking techniques, namely DPF and ReForM. On the one hand, DPF approach introduces a meta-model to represent both the patterns and the system under study as graphs in order to apply a graph matching algorithm. On the other hand, the detection process is enriched using ReForM, a model-checking refinement step in which the system model is represented using LOTOS and patterns as selective-μ-calculus properties checked against it. The defined LOTOS model allows to check a wider set of properties that lead to a reduction of the number of false positives. The performed experiments confirmed the feasibility, correctness, and effectiveness of the approach showing, on the analyzed systems, an improvement of the precision (20 % on average) with a very reduced impact on the original recall. As future work, a more complete translation of pattern specifications to selective-μ-calculus properties will be defined. Moreover, we will perform the translation of the entire DP catalogue defined in [13] as selective-μ-calculus properties allowing the experimentation on the complete benchmark comprised of 12 OO systems. Finally, we want to assist software engineers providing "What You See Is What You Get" (WYSIWYG) tools that support our approach as done in [38].

References

1. Gamma, E., Helm, R., Johnson, R., Vlissides, J.: Design Patterns: Elements of Reusable Object-Oriented Software. Addison-Wesley Longman Publishing Co., Inc., Boston (1995)
2. Ampatzoglou, A., Frantzeskou, G., Stamelos, I.: A methodology to assess the impact of design patterns on software quality. Inf. Softw. Technol. **54**, 331–346 (2012)
3. Bergenti, F., Poggi, A.: Improving uml designs using automatic design pattern detection. In: Proceedings of the 12th International Conference on Software Engineering and Knowledge Engineering (SEKE 2000), pp. 336–343 (2000)
4. Peng, T., Dong, J., Zhao, Y.: Verifying behavioral correctness of design pattern implementation. In: Proceedings of the Twentieth International Conference on Software Engineering & Knowledge Engineering (SEKE 2008), pp. 454–459 (2008)
5. Dong, J., Zhao, Y., Peng, T.: Architecture and design pattern discovery techniques - a review. In: Arabnia, H.R., Reza, H. (eds.) Software Engineering Research and Practice, pp. 621–627. CSREA Press, Las Vegas (2007)
6. Rasool, G., Streitfdert, D.: A survey on design pattern recovery techniques. IJCSI Int. J. Comput. Sci. Issues **8**, 251–260 (2011)
7. Beyer, D.: Relational programming with crocopat. In: Proceedings of the 28th International Conference on Software Engineering, ICSE 2006, pp. 807–810. ACM, New York (2006)
8. Prechelt, L., Unger-Lamprecht, B., Philippsen, M., Tichy, W.: Two controlled experiments assessing the usefulness of design pattern documentation in program maintenance. IEEE Trans. Softw. Eng. **28**, 595–606 (2002)
9. Ceccarelli, M., Cerulo, L., De Ruvo, G., Nardone, V., Santone, A.: Infer gene regulatory networks from time series data with probabilistic model checking. In: FormaliSE 2015 (2015)
10. De Ruvo, G., Santone, A.: Analysing wiki quality using probabilistic model checking. In: 2015 IEEE 24th International WETICE Conference, WETICE 2015, Larnaca, Cyprus, 15–17 June 2015
11. Bernardi, M.L., Cimitile, M., De Ruvo, G., Di Lucca, G.A., Santone, A.: Model checking to improve precision of design pattern instances identification in OO systems. In: ICSOFT-PT 2015 - Proceedings of the 10th International Conference on Software Paradigm Trends, Colmar, Alsace, France, 20–22 July 2015, pp. 53–63 (2015)

12. Bernardi, M., Cimitile, M., Di Lucca, G.: A model-driven graph-matching approach for design pattern detection. In: 20th Working Conference on Reverse Engineering (WCRE), pp. 172–181 (2013)
13. Bernardi, M., Cimitile, M., Di Lucca, G.: Design patterns detection using a dsl-driven graph matching approach. J. Softw. Evol. Process. Published online in Wiley Online Library (wileyonlinelibrary.com). doi:10.1002/smr.1674 (2014)
14. Guéhéneuc, Y.G.: P-mart: pattern-like micro architecture repository. In: Michael, W., Birukou, A., Giorgini, P. (eds.) Proceedings of the 1st EuroPLoP Focus Group on Pattern Repositories (2007). http://www.ptidej.net/tool/designpatterns/
15. Rasool, G., Philippow, I., Mäder, P.: Design pattern recovery based on annotations. Adv. Eng. Softw. **41**, 519–526 (2010)
16. Tsantalis, N., Chatzigeorgiou, A., Stephanides, G., Halkidis, S.T.: Design pattern detection using similarity scoring. IEEE Trans. Softw. Eng. **32**, 896–909 (2006)
17. Dong, J., Zhao, Y., Sun, Y.: A matrix-based approach to recovering design patterns. Trans. Sys. Man Cyber. Part A **39**, 1271–1282 (2009)
18. Paakki, J., Karhinen, A., Gustafsson, J., Nenonen, L., Verkamo, A.I.: Software metrics by architectural pattern mining. In: Proceedings of the International Conference on Software: Theory and Practice (16th IFIP World Computer Congress), pp. 325–332 (2000)
19. von Detten, M., Becker, S.: Combining clustering and pattern detection for the reengineering of component-based software systems. In: Proceedings of the Joint ACM SIGSOFT Conference QoSA-ISARCS, QoSA-ISARCS 2011, pp. 23–32. ACM, New York (2011)
20. Antoniol, G., Fiutem, R., Cristoforetti, L.: Design pattern recovery in object-oriented software. In: Proceedings of the 6th International Workshop on Program Comprehension, IWPC 1998, p. 153. IEEE Computer Society, Washington, DC (1998)
21. Guéhéneuc, Y.G., Guyomarc'H, J.Y., Sahraoui, H.: Improving design-pattern identification: a new approach and an exploratory study. Softw. Qual. Control **18**, 145–174 (2010)
22. De Lucia, A., Deufemia, V., Gravino, C., Risi, M.: Design pattern recovery through visual language parsing and source code analysis. J. Syst. Softw. **82**, 1177–1193 (2009)
23. Arcelli, F., Zanoni, M.: A tool for design pattern detection and software architecture reconstruction. Inf. Sci. **181**, 1306–1324 (2011)
24. Tonella, P., Torchiano, M., Du Bois, B., Systä, T.: Empirical studies in reverse engineering: state of the art and future trends. Empirical Softw. Engg. **12**, 551–571 (2007)
25. Taibi, T., Herranz-Nieva, Á., Moreno-Navarro, J.J.: Stepwise refinement validation of design patterns formalized in TLA+ using the TLC model checker. J. Object Technol. **8**, 137–161 (2009)
26. Aranda, G., Moore, R.: A formal model for verifying compound design patterns. In: Proceedings of the 14th International Conference on Software Engineering and Knowledge Engineering, SEKE 2002, pp. 213–214. ACM, New York (2002)
27. Flores, A., Moore, R., Reynoso, L.: A formal model of object-oriented design and gof design patterns. In: Oliveira, J.N., Zave, P. (eds.) FME 2001. LNCS, vol. 2021, pp. 223–241. Springer, Heidelberg (2001)
28. De Lucia, A., Deufemia, V., Gravino, C., Risi, M.: Improving behavioral design pattern detection through model checking. In: 2010 14th European Conference on Software Maintenance and Reengineering (CSMR), pp. 176–185 (2010)

29. Milner, R.: Communication and Concurrency. PHI Series in Computer Science. Prentice Hall, Upper Saddle River (1989)
30. Bolognesi, T., Brinksma, E.: Introduction to the iso specification language lotos. Comput. Netw. **14**, 25–59 (1987)
31. Barbuti, R., De Francesco, N., Santone, A., Vaglini, G.: Selective mu-calculus and formula-based equivalence of transition systems. J. Comput. Syst. Sci. **59**, 537–556 (1999)
32. Stirling, C.: An introduction to modal and temporal logics for CCS. In: Yonezawa, A., Ito, T. (eds.) Concurrency: Theory, Language, and Architecture. LNCS, pp. 1–20. Springer, Heidelberg (1989)
33. Barbuti, R., De Francesco, N., Santone, A., Vaglini, G.: Reduced models for efficient CCS verification. Formal Methods Syst. Des. **26**, 319–350 (2005)
34. Garavel, H., Lang, F., Mateescu, R., Serwe, W.: CADP: a toolbox for the construction and analysis of distributed processes. STTT **15**(2013), 89–107 (2011)
35. Clarke, E.M., Grumberg, O., Peled, D.: Model Checking. MIT Press, Cambridge (2001)
36. Pettersson, N., Lowe, W., Nivre, J.: Evaluation of accuracy in design pattern occurrence detection. IEEE Trans. Softw. Eng. **36**, 575–590 (2010)
37. SICStus Prolog User's Manual. Swedish Institute of Computer Science. Release 3.7.1, October 1998. Swedish Institute of Computer Science. http://www.sics.se/isl/sicstus.html
38. De Ruvo, G., Santone, A.: An eclipse-based editor to support lotos newcomers. In: 2014 IEEE 23rd International Conference on Enabling Technologies: Infrastructure for Collaborative Enterprises (WETICE) (2014)

R-UML: An UML Profile for Verification of Flexible Control Systems

Mohamed Oussama Ben Salem[1,2($\boxtimes$)], Olfa Mosbahi[2], Mohamed Khalgui[2],
and Georg Frey[3]

[1] Polytechnic School of Tunisia, University of Carthage, Tunis, Tunisia
`bensalem.oussama@hotmail.com`
[2] LISI Laboratory, INSAT, University of Carthage, Tunis, Tunisia
`olfamosbahi@gmail.com, khalgui.mohamed@gmail.com`
[3] Chair of Automation and Energy Systems, Saarland University,
Saarbrücken, Germany
`georg.frey@aut.uni-saarland.de`

Abstract. Unified Modeling Language (UML) is currently accepted as
the standard for modeling software and control systems since it allows to
highlight different aspects of the system under design. Nevertheless, UML
lacks formal semantics and, hence, it is not possible to apply, directly,
mathematical techniques on UML models in order to verify them. Furthermore, UML does not feature explicit semantics to model flexible control systems sharing adaptive shared resources either. Thus, this work
proposes a new UML profile, baptized R-UML (Reconfigurable UML),
to model such reconfigurable systems. R-UML is enriched with a PCP-
based solution for the management of resource sharing. The paper also
presents an automatic translation of R-UML into R-TNCES, a Petri
Net-based formalism, in order to support model checking.

Keywords: UML · R-TNCES · Model transformation · Modeling ·
Model-based verification · PCP · Shared resource

1 Introduction

The Unified Modeling Language (UML) is a semi formal language developed
by the Object Management Group to specify, visualize and document models of both software and non-software systems. Driven by software engineering
industries, it became well developed and supported with dozens of tools [1].
UML provides two types of diagrams to create a specific profile for a given system: structural and behavioral. The first is designed to visualize and document
the static aspects of systems, while the second aims at visualizing the dynamic
aspects [2]. UML has unquestionable advantages as a technique for visual modeling, nevertheless, it does not guarantee that the generated models are correct.
Actually, no step of system development, including the modeling one, is spared
from human errors. Consequently, the cost to detect and remove such defects
considerably increases through the system development [3].

© Springer International Publishing Switzerland 2016
P. Lorenz et al. (Eds.): ICSOFT 2015, CCIS 586, pp. 118–136, 2016.
DOI: 10.1007/978-3-319-30142-6_7

The idea of being able to, more or less automatically and systematically, verify and validate UML-based models has been around for a while, so there is a rather large body of literature on the topic. For example, the authors in [4] use statecharts and sequence diagrams in a combined manner to check temporal logic formulas over a statechart-based description of the system, and the model checker produces, then, counterexamples through sequence diagrams. Another approach is described in [5] where sequence diagrams are formally translated into Petri nets, based on the UML collaborations package metamodel. The authors check the correctness of the sequence diagrams through the resulting Petri nets. A work described in [6] uses the sequence diagram in conjunction with use cases and deployment diagrams to obtain queuing network models for performance evaluation. An execution graph from the sequence diagram is later obtained thanks to a given algorithm. Another work reported in [7] translated Statecharts into PROMELA, the input language of SPIN verification system, whereas [8] formally analyzed activity diagrams using NuSMV model checker to determine the correctness of activity diagrams. The authors in [9] produce Petri net models starting from UML diagrams, however, they only describe the methodology at an intuitive level, through an example and no translation procedure is described. The work described in [10] proposed new UML stereotypes to enrich UML diagrams with dependability aspects. The purpose is to exploit the latter to build generally distributed stochastic Petri net models. The authors didn't focus on an automatic translation, but rather on detecting the dependability aspects from the UML diagrams.

We see in the previous related works that no one of our community was interested in modeling the reconfiguration aspect which is featured by many control systems and their shared resources. Nevertheless, reconfiguration has become, nowadays, a crucial feature to consider when designing new embedded systems. It is actually the ability to dynamically improve the latter's performance and quality of service at run-time, according to well defined conditions [11]. Increasing safety constraints and growing expected flexibility pushed developers to focus on designing systems that are able to fit their environment and shifting user requirements under functional and temporal constraints [12]. In this work, a reconfiguration scenario is assumed to be any run-time automatic operation that modifies the system's structure by adding or removing tasks or resources according to user requirements in order to adapt the whole architecture to its environment [13]. Whence, we propose, in this work, a new UML profile, baptized R-UML (Reconfigurable UML), endowed with a formal semantics enabling UML to model flexible control systems sharing adaptive shared resources. R-UML relies on UML's extensibility mechanisms to enhance class and statechars diagrams, respectively called R-CD and R-StD henceforth. The latter are extended to support Priority Ceiling Protocol (PCP), a well-known synchronization protocol for shared resources. It was proved in [13] the relevance of this protocol to solve the issue of concurrent access to adaptive shared resources in reconfigurable control systems. We propose then a new solution to translate R-UML into Reconfigurable Timed Net Condition/Event Systems

(R-TNCES) [14], a Petri net-based formalism to model flexible control systems. An application of formal verification is, then, performed and aims to (dis)prove certain properties of the system using a formal model. This contribution is original since R-TNCES is a new and original formalism for reconfigurable systems, and no one in our community worked on the translation of UML into R-TNCES to combine their respective assets, i.e. the easiness and relevance of UML for visual modeling and the formal semantics of R-TNCES to verify and validate models.

This paper is organized as follows: the next section describes useful preliminaries for the reader. Section 3 introduces a running example which will be used throughout the paper to prove the relevance of our contribution. We expose, in Sect. 4, the new profile R-UML and a solution to translate the latter into R-TNCES. We finish the paper in Sect. 5 by a conclusion and an exposition of our future works.

2   Background

We start, in this section, by presenting the formalisms TNCES [15] and R-TNCES [14] which extend Petri nets for the modeling of adaptive control systems. We provide, then, an overview of the well-known PCP.

2.1   Timed Net Condition/Event System

The formalism was introduced by [15]. A TNCES is a tuple:

$$TNCES = \{P, T, F, m_0, \Psi, CN, EN, DC\} \tag{1}$$

where (i) $P = \{p_1, p_2, ..., p_n\}$ is a finite set of places; (ii) $T = \{t_1, t_2, ..., t_m\}$ is a finite set of transitions; (iii) $F \subseteq (P \times T) \cup (T \times P)$ is a finite set of flow arcs between places and transitions; (iv) m_0 is initial marking; (v) $CN \subseteq (P \times T)$ is a finite set of condition arcs; (vi) $EN \subseteq (T \times T)$ is a finite set of event arcs.

Ψ is input/output structure of TNCES module which is represented by the following tuple:

$$\Psi = \{C^{in}, E^{in}, C^{out}, E^{out}, Bc, Be, Cs, Dt\} \tag{2}$$

where (i) C^{in} defines a finite set of TNCES module condition input signals; (ii) E^{in} defines a finite set of TCNES module event input signals; (iii) C^{out} defines a finite set of TNCES module condition output signals; (iv) E^{out} defines a finite set of TCNES module event output signals; (v) $Bc \subseteq C^{in} \times T$ is a set of TNCES module input condition arcs; (vi) $Be \subseteq En \times T$ is a set of TNCES module input event arcs; (vii) $Cs \subseteq P \times C^{out}$ is TNCES module output condition arcs; (viii) $Dt \subseteq T \times E^{out}$ is a set of TNCES module output event arcs.

Time intervals are assigned to the pre-transition flow arcs $F \subseteq P \times T$, which impose time constrains to the firing of the transition:

$$DC = \{DR, DL, D_0\} \tag{3}$$

where (i) DR represents the set of minimum times that the token should spend at particular place before the transition can fire; (ii) DL is the final set of limitation time that defines maximum time that the place may hold a token (if all the other conditions for transition firing are met); (iii) D_0 is the initial set of the clocks associated with the places.

2.2 Reconfigurable Timed Net Condition/Event System

An R-TNCES, as defined in [14], is a structure $RTN = (B, R)$, where R is the control module consisting of a set of reconfiguration functions $R = r_1,...,r_n$ and B is the behavior module that is a union of multi TNCESs, represented as

$$B = (P, T, F, W, CN, EN, DC, V, Z) \tag{4}$$

where: (i) P (respectively, T) is a superset of places (respectively, transitions), (ii) $F \subseteq (P \times T) \cup (T \times P)$ is a superset of flow arcs, (iii) W: $(P \times T) \cup (T \times P) \to \{0,1\}$ maps a weight to a flow arc, $W(x,y) < 0$ if $(x,y) \in F$, and $W(x, y)=0$ otherwise, where $x, y \in P \cup T$, (iv) $CN \subseteq (P \times T)$ (respectively, $EN \subseteq (T \times T)$) is a superset of condition signals (respectively, event signals), (v) $DC : F \cap (P \times T) \to \{[l_1, h_1], ..., [l_{|F \cap (P \times T)|}, h_{|F \cap (P \times T)|}]\}$ is a superset of time constraints on output arcs, where $i \in [1, |F \cap (P \times T)|], l_i, h_i \in N$, and $l_i < h_i$, (vi) $V : T \to \{\vee, \wedge\}$ maps an event-processing mode (AND or OR) for every transition, (vii) $Z = (M_0, D_0)$, where $M_0 : P \to \{0,1\}$ is the initial marking and $D_0 : P \to \{0\}$ is the initial clock position.

2.3 Priority Ceiling Protocol

The Priority Ceiling Protocol (PCP) [16] in real-time computing is a synchronization protocol for shared resources to avoid unbounded priority inversion and mutual deadlock due to wrong nesting of critical sections. In this protocol, each resource R is assigned a priority ceiling $Cl(R)$, which is equal to the highest priority of the tasks that may lock it. A task can acquire a resource only if the resource is free and has a higher priority than the priority ceiling of the rest resources in lock by other tasks.

Let us assume a system to be composed of the tasks T_1, T_2, T_3 and T_4 (having respectively the increasing priorities 1, 2, 3 and 4) and two resources R and Q: R can be used by T_1 and T_2 and Q by T_1 and T_4. Then, Cl(R) = 2 and Cl(Q) = 4. Thus, T_2 is blocked if it tries to block R which is free when Q is locked.

3 Running Example

Let us assume a reconfigurable discrete event system to be composed of two tasks A and B. We suppose that these two tasks share initially the resources Q and R (as shown in Fig. 1) before applying a reconfiguration scenario which will add a new resource S (to be used by both A and B). This case was not treated in any related work and forms a new problem dealing with reconfigurable resources. We suppose that B has the highest priority ($B > A$). We suppose that the system is safe before the reconfiguration scenarios. But, once the reconfiguration is applied, a deadlock certainly occurs according to Fig. 2. In fact, A starts by using R and then S before being interrupted by B due to the latter's higher priority. B is then blocked because it tries to lock R ($P(R)$) which is dill hold by A. A continues progressing until it frees R ($V(R)$) and B interrupts it. When B asks for S ($P(S)$), it is interrupted because S is hold by A. A is in its turn blocked because it is asking for Q which is hold by B. A deadlock occurs thus, because A is waiting for Q while B for S. Regarding to this situation, we apply the PCP on this running example which solves the deadlock issue as illustrated in Fig. 3.

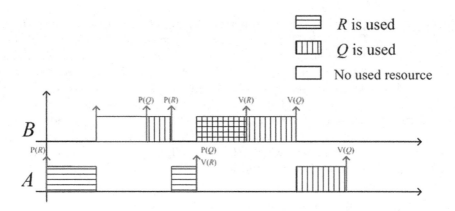

Fig. 1. Behavior of A and B before a reconfiguration scenario.

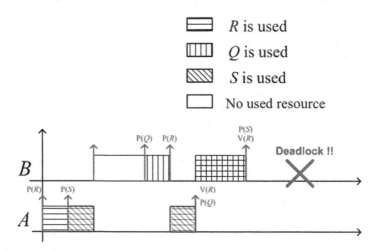

Fig. 2. Behavior of A and B after a reconfiguration scenario.

This running example features two tasks sharing three adaptive resources like in [13], however, the tasks' behavior and the reconfiguration scenario are different. Besides, in [13], a deadlock occurs because A is waiting for S while B for Q, whereas, in this work, it occurs because A is waiting for Q while B for S.

4 Conception and Validation of Flexible Control Systems

We expose, in this section, the new profile R-UML to model and validate flexible control systems sharing adaptive resources. A new solution is proposed, then, to transform an R-UML into an R-TNCES.

4.1 R-UML

In this section, we define how to model the structure and the behavior of a flexible control system using R-UML. The contribution is applied on the running example of Sect. 3.

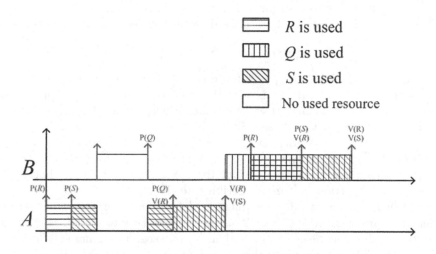

Fig. 3. A and B behaviors after using PCP.

Structure Modeling. UML provides the class diagram to show the logical structure of a system. This diagram highlights conceptual connections showing the relations between the system's modules or components, each of which having its distinctive properties defined by a class. It is possible to extend the core semantics of UML and express new properties by using stereotypes. The latter is a mechanism to categorize an element. Thus, we extend the contribution proposed in [17] and define the following eight stereotypes of the class's attribute:

- $<<$ *input* $>>$: the given attribute is a system input;
- $<<$ *output* $>>$: the given attribute is a system output;

- $<< in >>$: the given attribute is a system module input;
- $<< out >>$: the given attribute is a system module output;
- $<< eventInput >>$: the given attribute is a system module event input;
- $<< eventOutput >>$: the given attribute is a system module event output;
- $<< integer >>$: the given attribute is an integer;
- $<< boolean >>$: the given attribute is a boolean attributed which can be evaluated to TRUE or FALSE.

The description above distinguishes between *system* and *module*. *System* denotes the whole system under control, whereas *module* a part of the system. A system may actually have internal connections between the modules specified by means of the stereotypes $<< in >>$ and $<< out >>$, and a module may provide to the controller the connections that are specified by means of the stereotypes $<< input >>$ and $<< output >>$. Two system modules may also be interconnected by an event which is an action which occurrence may be detected by another module in the system. An event is different from an input/output, since the first is just a signal informing that a certain action took place. The $<< eventInput >>$ and $<< eventOutput >>$ stereotypes respectively represent the event inputs and outputs that a module may have.

The information provided by a class diagram can be formally written as a tuple:

$$ClD = \{C, A, M, S, \alpha, \beta\} \tag{5}$$

where (i) $C = \{cl_1, cl_2, ..., cl_n\}$ is a finite set of classes in class diagram ClD; (ii) $A = \{attr_1, attr_2, ..., attr_n\}$ is a final set of attributes that belong to the classes; (iii) $M = \{setInput, resetInput, setOutput, resetOutput, setCeiling\}$ is a set of methods of the classes; (iv) S is a set of stereotypes / $S = \{<< in >>, << out >>, << input >>, << output >>, << eventInput >>, << eventOutput >>, << integer >>, << boolean >>\}$; (v) $\alpha : st_i \rightarrow attr_j$ is a function that maps the stereotype st_i from S to the $attr_j$ from A; (vi) $\beta : attr_i \rightarrow cl_j$ is a function that maps attribute to the class.

According to the previous class diagram definition, we create two classes to model the running example of Sect. 3: a class named *Task* to model, as its name suggests, the different tasks of the system, and a second one, named *Resource*, to model the different reconfigurable shared resources. We instantiate for each task or resource an object from the corresponding class.

The class *Task*, as showed in Fig. 4, has an integer-stereotyped attribute, named *priority*, translating the task's priority. It also has a boolean-stereotyped one, *added*, indicating whether the task in added to the system (*added=TRUE*) or not (*added=FALSE*), depending on the applied reconfiguration scenario. The Fig. 5 shows that the class *Resource* features an integer-stereotyped attribute, named *ceiling*, translating the ceiling that each resource has according to PCP definition in Sect. 2.3. The class also features a method named *setCeiling* that recompute a resource's ceiling after applying a reconfiguration scenario. This method's code will be detailed later. Just as tasks, resources have a boolean-stereotyped attribute, *added*, because a reconfiguration scenario may add or remove a task or a resource [13].

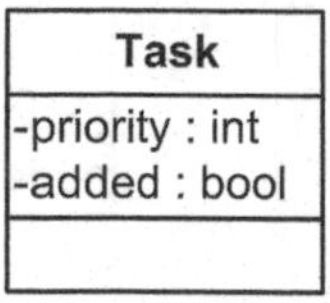

Task
-priority : int
-added : bool

Fig. 4. The Task class.

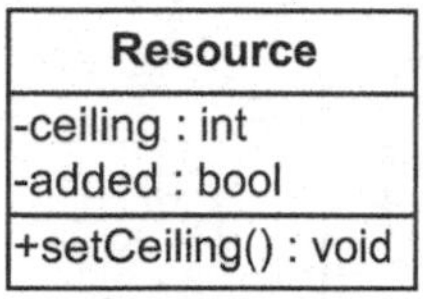

Resource
-ceiling : int
-added : bool
+setCeiling() : void

Fig. 5. The Resource class.

Running Example 1. The static description of a system is often made through the class diagram. This simplifies the modeling by synthesizing the common characteristics and covering a large number of objects. However, it is sometimes useful or even necessary to add an object diagram. The latter allows, depending on the situation, to illustrate the class diagram (showing an example that explains the model), clarify certain aspects of the system (by highlighting imperceptible details in the class diagram), express an exception (by modeling specific cases of non-generalizable knowledge) or take an image (snapshot) of a system at a given time. The class diagram models the rules, whereas the object diagram models facts. Often the class diagram is a model to instantiate the binders in order to obtain the object diagram [18]. Thus, we propose here to realize the object diagram of the running example described in Sect. 3. The said diagram illustrated in Fig. 6 features two objects of the Task class (modeling the tasks A and B) and three of the Resource class (modeling the resources R, Q and S) while highlighting the links between them.

Behavior Modeling. UML features the State diagram as powerful tool to represent the behavior of an object which is the implementation of a particular class. We define for the system or its components a set of states which they may take. Each state is distinguished by its name. The change of the states is represented via transitions. The latter specify the laws that cause the change of the state and the consequences of the change. The rules which fire transitions may be expressed by event and guard which is a boolean expression that has to be evaluated to TRUE to fire the transition. A given transition may be fired through three manners: an event (if a certain action took place somewhere in the system), a guard (if the certain properties are assigned with the particular values) or combination of both. The different states are interconnected by transitions which determine the rules that cause transition to fire and the consequences of a transition's firing. Events, guards and the combination of both

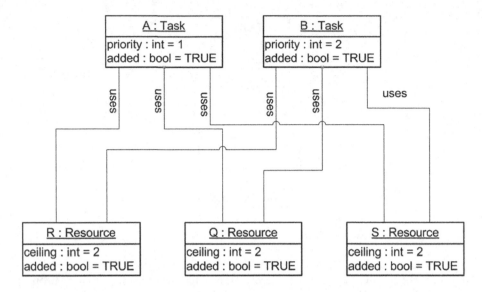

Fig. 6. The running example's object diagram.

specify these rules. A time event, after (n) where n is a positive integer, is also used to specify that n time units should elapse before the transition may fire. Events may also be specified by $<< eventInput >>$ or $<< eventOutput >>$ stereotyped attributes. A transition firing may be accompanied by the activation of an action which can modify some properties of the system. This activation may call attribute-modifying methods defined in the classes, such as setInput, resetInput, setOutput, resetOutput and setCeiling.

We extend the contribution proposed in [17] and formally represent a state diagram by the tuple:

$$StD = \{St, Tr, Ev, G, Ac, \gamma, \delta, \epsilon, \zeta\} \tag{6}$$

where (i) $St = \{st_1, st_2, ..., st_n\}$ is a finite set of states in a state diagram StD; (ii) $Tr = \{tr_1, tr_2, ..., tr_m\}$ is a finite state of transitions in a state diagram StD; (iii) Ev is a finite set of events in transitions of StD; (iv) G is a finite set of the guards in StD; (v) Ac is a final set of actions; (vi) $\gamma : ev_i \rightarrow tr_j$ is a function that maps the event ev_i of Ev to the transition tr_j of Tr; (vii) $\delta : gr_k \rightarrow tr_j$ is a function that maps the guard gr_k of Gr to the transition tr_j of Tr; (viii) $\epsilon : act_l \rightarrow tr_j$ is a function that maps the action act_l of Ac to the transition tr_j of Tr; (ix) $\zeta : trj \rightarrow \{st_b, ste\}$ is a function that maps transition tr_j of Tr to the pair of states st_b and st_e, where st_b is the state from which the transition is taken and st_e is the next state if tr_j fires.

According to the reconfiguration feature expected from the system, we define a reconfigurable state diagram as a structure:

$$R - StD = (B, R) \tag{7}$$

where (i) B is the behavior module that is a union of multi StD; (ii) R is the control module consisting of a set of reconfiguration functions $R = \{r_1,...,r_n\}$.

A reconfiguration function r_i makes the necessary changes to the system after a reconfiguration scenario in accordance with the definition given in Sect. 1. Hence, we define r as the structure:

$$r = (\eta, \theta, \iota) \tag{8}$$

where (i) $\eta : t_i \rightarrow \{0,1\}$ is a function controlling tasks, $\eta(t_i) = 1$ if the task t_i is added to the system, $\eta(t_i) = 0$ otherwise; (ii) $\theta : res_j \rightarrow \{0,1\}$ is a function controlling resources, $\theta(res_j) = 1$ if the resource res_i is added to the system and $\theta(res_j) = 0$ otherwise; (iii) $\iota : (res_j, t_i) \rightarrow \{0,1\}$, $\iota(res_j, t_i) = 1$ if res_j is used by t_i in this triggered reconfiguration scenario, $\iota(res_j, t_i) = 0$ otherwise.

According to the previous definitions, we define in this section the Resource class's method, *setCeiling*, as follows:

```
if  θ(res) == 1
   for i:=1 to |Tasks|
      if  η(tᵢ) == 1 AND ι(res, tᵢ) == 1
      AND tᵢ.priority > res.ceiling
         res.ceiling := tᵢ.priority
```

We propose, then, R-StD diagrams to model a task and a resource on the basis of PCP definition and the reconfiguration feature expected from the system. Thus, we propose the R-StD illustrated in Fig. 7 to model a reconfigurable shared resource:

A resource may actually be free or hold by a task T_i. Thus, we propose the states "Free", "Hold by T_i" and "Hold by T_n" where R may be exclusively hold by a task from a set of n different tasks (n is an integer $\in (1, +\infty)$). The guards associated to the transitions leaving the state *Free* guarantee the respect of PCP rules before locking a resource, i.e. a task T may hold a given resource if, first, the latter is free and, secondly, the resources hold by other tasks have a ceiling

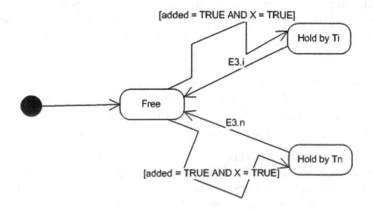

Fig. 7. The shared resource's R-StD.

lower than T's dynamic priority, a condition verified by the guard named X. $E3.i$ is an event coming from T_i and asking to unlock R.

We propose, then, a second R-StD, illustrated in Fig. 8 to model a reconfigurable task:

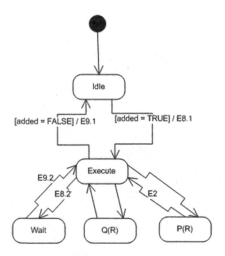

Fig. 8. The task's R-StD.

The task's R-StD is composed of the following states: (i) *Idle*: as its names suggests, the task is idle, (ii) *Execute*: the task is running, (iii) *Wait*: the task was interrupted by another one, so it is waiting, (iv) *P(R)*: the task T is asking to lock a resource R, (v) *Q(R)*: the task T is unlocking the resource R. The R-StD of a task T should include as many *P(R)* and *Q(R)* as the resources it may lock, but, in this running example, we decide that T will use just one resource (R). The different events indicated on the figure above stand for: (i) *E2*: an event confirming the lock of R by T, (ii) *E8.1* and *E8.2*: when T switches from *Idle* to *Execute*, the event *E8.1* forces the running tasks with lower priorities to switch from *Execute* to *Wait*. T's *E8.1* is actually the *E8.2* of tasks with lower priorities. Whence, the *E8.2* on Fig. 8 is an event announcing that a task with a higher priority than T's switched from *Idle* to *Execute*, (iii) *E9.1*: when T switches from *Execute* to *Idle*, the event *E9.1* will force the waiting tasks with lower priorities to switch from *Wait* to *Execute*. T's *E9.1* is actually the *E9.2* of tasks with lower priorities. Whence, the *E9.2* is translating that a task with a higher priority that T's has switched from *Execute* to *Idle*.

Running Example 2. Now that we formalized R-StD and proposed patterns to model control tasks and shared resources, we can model our running example. We propose, as examples and respectively in Figs. 9 and 10, the modeling of the control task A, which uses the resources Q, R and S, and the resource R which is shared by the tasks A and B.

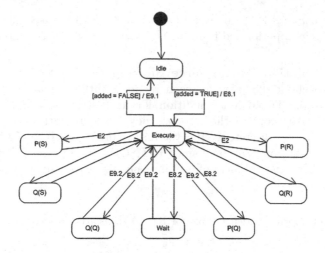

Fig. 9. The task A's R-StD.

In our case study, the different resources have the same modeling since they have the same ceiling and are used by the same tasks. We choose to model the resource R as shown in Fig. 10. The guards named X are used to guarantee that, when a task T tries to lock the resource, all the other resources, whose ceilings are not lower than the task's priority, are free or hold by T. Thus, we avoid any eventual deadlock and see the relevance of the PCP.

4.2   Tranformation

We present, in this section, R-TNCES-based models using PCP to solve the issue of concurrent access to adaptive shared resources. We propose, then, a new

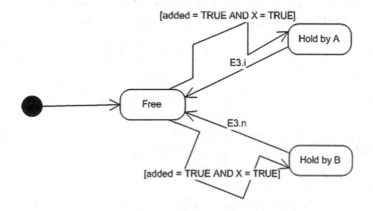

Fig. 10. The resource R's R-StD.

solution to translate R-StD models into the said R-TNCES-based ones. A formal verification is, then, performed to prove the relevance of our contribution.

PCP-based Solution for Resource Sharing in R-TNCES. We aim in this section to check the safety of each reconfiguration scenario by enriching the Reconfigurable Timed Net Condition/Event System (R-TNCES) with the PCP protocol. We propose, then, to use new patterns introduced in [13] to model reconfigurable discrete event systems according to R-TNCES by using PCP. This contribution is original since R-TNCES is an original formalism for reconfigurable systems, but lacks of useful mechanisms to manage reconfigurable shared resources.

Table 1. Correspondence table for R-StD translation into R-TNCES.

Rules	R-StD	R-TNCES
Rule 1	St (6)	P (4)
Rule 2	Tr (6)	T (4)
Rule 3	$\{st_b, st_e\} := \zeta(tr)$ (6)	$\{p_{out}, p_{to}\} \subseteq P$; $\{fa_1, fa_2\} \subseteq F$ (4)
Rule 4	$gr := \delta^{-1}(tr)$ (6)	$ci \in C^{in}$ (2); $co \in C^{out}$ (2); $ca \in CN$ (1)
Rule 5	$ac := \epsilon^{-1}(tr)$ (6)	$ei \in E^{in}$ (2); $eo \in E^{out}$ (2); $ea \in EN$ (1)
Rule 6	$ev := \zeta^{-1}(tr)$ (6) AND << $eventInput >>:= \alpha^{-1}(ev)$ (5)	$ei \in E^{in}$ (2); $eo \in E^{out}$ (2); $ea \in EN$ (1)
Rule 7	$ev := \zeta^{-1}(tr)$ (6) AND ev is an after(n) event	$n \in DR$; $\infty \in DL$ (1) (2) (3)

Formalization. We present in this section the formalization of Distributed Reconfigurable Control Systems (DRCS) sharing resources.

<u>DRCS.</u> The authors in [13] assume a DRCS D to be composed of n_1 networked reconfigurable sub-systems sharing n_2 resources. They extend the formalization of DRCS in [14] by adding the new set of resources as follows:

$$D = (\sum R - TNCES, \varpi, \sum M, \sum R) \qquad (9)$$

where: (i) $\sum R - TNCES$ is a set of n_1 R-TNCES, (ii) ϖ a virtual coordinator handling $\sum M$, a set of Judgment Matrices, (iii) $\sum R$, a set of n_2 shared resources.

<u>Shared Resources.</u> On the basis of PCP's definition and the flexibility expected from the DRCS, a resource R is defined as follows :

$$R = (Rec, S, Cl) \qquad (10)$$

where: (i) *Rec* (Reconfiguration) indicates whether R is added to the system /$Rec \in \{added, !added\}$, (ii) S indicates the state of R /$S \in \{free, hold\_by\_a\_task\_i\}$, (iii) Cl is used for the ceiling of R.

Tasks. Based on the expected reconfiguration of the system, the authors in [13] defines a task T by:

$$T = (Rec, S) \tag{11}$$

where: (i) *Rec* (Reconfiguration) indicates whether T is added to the system $/R \in \{added, !added\}$, (ii) S indicates the state of T $/S \in \{idle, execute, wait, P(R_i), V(R_i)\}$ and $P(R_i)$ means locking R and $V(R_i)$ unlocking it.

Modeling. The authors in [13] proposes new solutions to introduce PCP in R-TNCES to avoid any blocking problem after reconfiguration scenarios. An R-TNCES model is proposed for each resource of $\sum R$ and task of $\sum R - TNCES$.

Shared Resources. Each shared resource is modeled by an R-TNCES as shown in Fig. 11. The latter is composed of three TNCES modeling the resource's reconfiguration (*Rec*), state (*S*) and ceiling (*Cl*). Here is the modeling of a resource R:

Control Tasks. The authors in [13] model each task T by an R-TNCES to be composed of two TNCESs as shown in Fig. 12: the first one is illustrating its reconfiguration (*Rec*), the second its state (*S*).

R-Std Translation into R-TNCES. The paper proposes Table 1 which is given above to show the correspondence between R-StD and R-TNCES. The numbers given in parentheses show the reference to the formulas that give details on the syntax used in the table.

The seven translation rules are explained hereafter:

- Rule 1: A state *St* in an R-StD corresponds to a place P in an R-TNCES;
- Rule 2: A transition *Tr* in an R-StD corresponds to a transition too (T) in an R-TNCES;

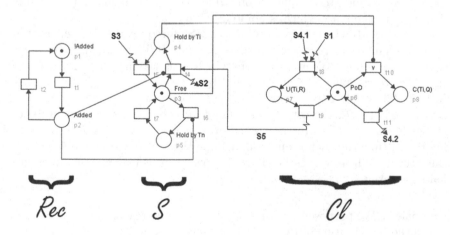

Fig. 11. A shared resource's modeling.

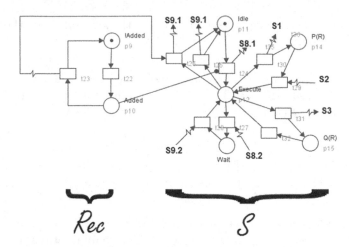

Fig. 12. A task's modeling.

- Rule 3: Each transition tr in an R-StD is mapped to a pair of states, st_b and st_e, where the first is the state from which tr is taken and the second is the next state if tr fires. The corresponding transition (t) and two places (p_{out} and p_{to}) will be created using, respectively, Rule 2 and Rule 1. Rule 3 creates actually in the R-TNCES a flow arc, fa_1, linking p_{out} to t, and another one, fa_2, linking t to p_{to};
- Rule 4: In an R-StD, some guards can be mapped to some transitions. A guard gr corresponds to a condition arc, ca, in an R-TNCES. A condition output signal, co, is added to the place from which ca is leaving and a condition input signal, ci, to the place which is pointed by ca;
- Rule 5: In an R-StD, some actions can be mapped to some transitions. An action ac corresponds to an event arc, ea, in an R-TNCES. An event output signal, eo, is added to the place from which ea is leaving and an event input signal, ei, to the place which is pointed by ea;
- Rule 6: In an R-StD, each <<eventInput>>-stereotyped event, ev, is translated into an event arc, ea, in the corresponding R-TNCES. An event output signal, eo, is added to the place from which ea is leaving and an event input signal, ei, to the place which is pointed by ea;
- Rule 7: An R-StD may feature after(n)-typed events, where $n \in \mathbf{N}^*$. If so, n is added to DR, the set of minimum times that the token should spend at particular place before the transition can fire, and ∞ to DL, the set of limitation time that defines maximum time that the place may hold a token, since the place from which the after(n)-typed event is leaving may indefinitely hold the token.

Verification. We propose in this section to check the relevance of the our solution and the contribution of PCP in solving several issues threatening a DRCS's safety and deadlock-freedom. Thus, we start by modeling the running example of

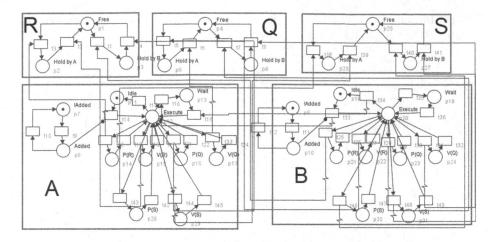

Fig. 13. The illustrative example's R-TNCES.

Fig. 14. Screenshot from SESA.

Sect. 3 in UML and then transforming the latter in R-TNCES according to [14]. Thus, we don't call out the PCP. We obtain the model illustrated in Fig. 13. To verify it, we use model-checking which is a technique for automatically verifying the correctness properties of finite-state systems. Model checking for R-TNCES is based on its reachability graphs. ZiZo [11] is a new and effective software environment for the analysis of R-TNCES, which computes the set of reachable states exactly. It exports, then, files exploitable by the model-checker SESA [19]. Typical properties which can be verified are boundedness of places, liveness of transitions, and reachability of states. In addition, temporal/functional properties based on Computation Tree Logic (CTL) specified by users can be checked manually. We apply, then, the CTL formula AG EX TRUE which checks the deadlock-freedom of the system. The said formula turned out to be false as shown in Fig. 14, meaning that the system features a deadlock issue.

Whence, we call out the solution we proposed in the previous sections. We start by modeling the two tasks and the three resources in R-StD and transform, then, the models to R-TNCES based on the transformation rules specified in Sect. 4.2. We obtain, thus, the R-TNCES model of the tasks A and B illustrated in Fig. 15.

Once the R-TNCES model of the DRCS is enriched with PCP, the next step is to verify whether the models meet users requirements. So, any reconfiguration scenario dealing with adding/removal of resources does not lead to a blocking situation. The following e-CTL formula is applied:

$$AG\ EX\ true \tag{12}$$

This formula is proven to be true by SESA as shown in the screenshot in Fig. 16, so there is no deadlock in our R-TNCES.

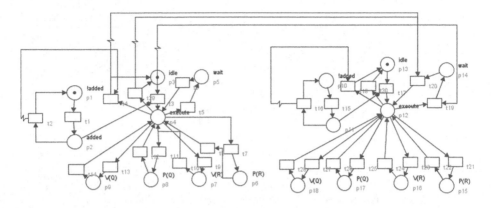

Fig. 15. The taks A and B's modeling using PCP.

Fig. 16. Screenshot from SESA.

We also check the safety property by checking if a given resource may be simultaneously locked by two different tasks. The following CTL formula is checked:

$$EF\ p22\ AND\ p23 \tag{13}$$

where $p22$ is the place translating that the resource R is locked by the task A; $p22$ means that B locks R. This formula is proven to be false as illustrated in Fig. 17.

The formula 13 is applied six times of the R-TNCES modeling, changing at each time $p22$ and $p23$ by the places which correspond to the ones translating that the resource R (and then Q and S) is locked by the task A (and then B). We check thus whether a given resource can be locked by the two tasks at the same time. The six formulas turned out to be false. We are sure, then, that our system doesn't feature a deadlock issue caused by a concurrent access to shared resources after a reconfiguration scenario.

5   Conclusions

Our work consisted, through this paper, in proposing a new UML profile, the R-UML, to model and verify flexible control systems sharing adaptive resources.

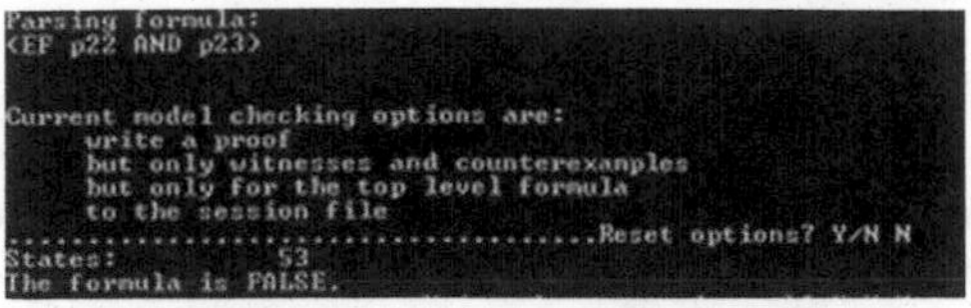

Fig. 17. Screenshot from SESA.

Whence, we chose to enhance class and statecharts diagrams to support PCP. We proposed, then, a new and original solution to translate the generated R-UML models into R-TNCES-based patterns which were proposed in [13]. This aims at proving the correctness of the R-UML models by performing model-checking on the generated R-TNCES models. The relevance of our contribution was proved thanks to model-checking using ZiZo, a new R-TNCES editor, simulator and model-checker [11]. This approach is original since R-TNCES is a new formalism dedicated to flexible control systems modeling and ZiZo is a new tool supporting the said formalism.

The next step is to apply this contribution on BROS, a new surgical robotic platform [12]. BROS is a flexible system since it can run under different operating modes: it is reconfigurable. The concurrent access to adaptive shared resources is present in the said system, which can be rather hazardous in such medical systems. Whence, applying our contribution on BROS can be very relevant to certify that the robotic platform is safe and does not run any risk after any reconfiguration scenario.

Acknowledgements. This research work is carried out within a MOBIDOC PhD thesis of the PASRI program, EU-funded and administered by ANPR (Tunisia). The BROS national project is a collaboration between the Children Hospital of Bchir Hamza (Tunis), eHTC and INSAT (LISI Laboratory) in Tunisia.

References

1. Bahill, T., Daniels, J.: Using objected-oriented and UML tools for hardware design: a case study. Syst. Eng. **6**(1), 28–48 (2003)
2. Warmer, J.B., Kleppe, A.G.: The Object Constraint Language: Precise Modeling With UML. Addison-Wesley, Boston (1998). (Addison-Wesley Object Technology Series)
3. Fenton, N.E., Neil, M.: A critique of software defect prediction models. IEEE Trans. Softw. Eng. **25**(5), 675–689 (1999)
4. Lilius, J., Paltor, I.P.: The production cell: an exercise in the formal verification of a UML model (1999)
5. Cardoso, J., Sibertin-Blanc, C.: Ordering actions in sequence diagrams of UML. In: Proceedings of the 23rd International Conference on Information Technology Interfaces, ITI 2001, pp. 3–14. IEEE, June 2001
6. Cortellessa, V., Mirandola, R.: Deriving a queueing network based performance model from UML diagrams. In: Proceedings of the 2nd International Workshop on Software and Performance, pp. 58–70. ACM, September 2000

7. Mikk, E., Lakhnech, Y., Siegel, M., Holzmann, G.J.: Implementing statecharts in PROMELA/SPIN. In: Proceedings of the 2nd IEEE Workshop on Industrial Strength Formal Specification Techniques, pp. 90–101. IEEE (1998)
8. Lam, V.S.: A formalism for reasoning about UML activity diagrams. Nord. J. Comput. **14**(1), 43–64 (2007)
9. King, P., Pooley, R.: Using UML to derive stochastic Petri net models. In: Proceedings of the 15th UK Performance Engineering Workshop, pp. 45–56, July 1999
10. Bondavalli, A., Majzik, I., Mura, I.: Automated dependability analysis of UML designs. In: Proceedings of the 2nd IEEE International Symposium on Object-Oriented Real-Time Distributed Computing, 1999 (ISORC 1999), pp. 139–144. IEEE (1999)
11. Ben Salem, M., Mosbahi, O., Khalgui, M., Frey, G.: Modeling, simulation and verification of reconfigurable real-time control tasks sharing adaptive resources - application to the medical project BROS. In: Proceedings of the International Conference on Health Informatics, pp. 20–31 (2015). ISBN: 978-989-758-068-0
12. Ben Salem, M., Mosbahi, O., Khalgui, M., Frey, G.: BROS - a new robotic platform for the treatment of supracondylar humerus fracture. In: Proceedings of the International Conference on Health Informatics, pp. 151-163 (2015). ISBN 978-989-758-068-0
13. Salem, M.O.B., Mosbahi, O., Khalgui, M.: PCP-based solution for resource sharing in reconfigurable timed net condition/event systems
14. Zhang, J., Khalgui, M., Li, Z., Mosbahi, O., Al-Ahmari, A.M.: R-TNCES: a novel formalism for reconfigurable discrete event control systems. IEEE Trans. Syst. Man Cybern. Syst. **43**(4), 757–772 (2013)
15. Hanisch, H.M., Thieme, J., Luder, A., Wienhold, O.: Modeling of PLC behavior by means of timed net condition/event systems. In: Proceedings of the 1997 6th International Conference on Emerging Technologies and Factory Automation, ETFA 1997, pp. 391–396. IEEE, September 1997
16. Goodenough, J.B., Sha, L.: The priority ceiling protocol: a method for minimizing the blocking of high priority Ada tasks. ACM **8**(7), 20–31 (1988)
17. Lobov, A., Lastra, J.L.M., Tuokko, R.: Application of UML in plant modeling for model-based verification: UML translation to TNCES. In: 3rd IEEE International Conference on Industrial Informatics, INDIN 2005, pp. 495–501. IEEE, August 2005
18. Rumbaugh, J., Blaha, M., Premerlani, W., Eddy, F., Lorensen, W.E.: Object-oriented Modeling and Design. Prentice-hall, Englewood Cliffs (1991). vol. 199(1)
19. Starke, P.H., Roch, S.: Analysing signal-net systems. Professoren des Inst. fr Informatik (2002)

Invariant Implementation for Domain Models Applying Incremental OCL Techniques

Alberto-Manuel Fernández-Álvarez, Daniel Fernández-Lanvin[(⊠)],
and Manuel Quintela-Pumares

Computing Science Department, University of Oviedo,
Oviedo, Asturias, Spain
{alb, dflanvin, quintelamanuel}@uniovi.es

Abstract. Constraints for rich domain models are easily specified with the Object Constraint Language (OCL) at model level, but hard to translate into executable code. We propose a solution which automatically translates the OCL invariants into aspect code able to check them incrementally after the execution of a Unit of Work getting good performance, a clean integration with programmers' code being respectful with the original design and easily combined with atomic all-or-nothing contexts (data base transactions, STM, ORM, etc.). The generated code solves some difficult issues: how to implement, when to check, over what objects and what to do in case of a violation.

Keywords: Constraint · Invariant · Incremental checking · Domain model · Object orientation · Ocl · Aspect oriented programming

1 Introduction

Domain modeling is a well-known practice to capture the essential sematic of a rich domain. The advantages of this approach have been widely discussed in the software engineering literature [1–3]. The most popular tool to model both static and dynamic aspects of the domain model during the development is UML. Even though UML is proven as an effective and powerful resource, it is lacking in mechanisms to represent efficiently some aspects of the system under design. For instance, some complex domain constraints cannot be easily graphically expressed in UML.

Those constraints can be expressed in natural language or by means of OCL expressions that complement the UML models. Afterwards, the developer will transform these OCL expressions into source code.

Although the use of OCL fills the gap of UML limitations, the subsequent implementation of these constraints usually involves some difficulties that can complicate the work of the programmers: (1) *how* to write the invariant check, (2) *when* to execute the constraint verification, (3) over *what objects* should be executed and (4) *what to do* in case of a constraint violation.

Constraints that affect only to one attribute or set of attributes on the same object can be easily checked. However, those that affect to more than one object of the domain (domain constraints) are determined by the state and relationships of every concerned object. As changes in any of the involved objects state can be produced by different

© Springer International Publishing Switzerland 2016
P. Lorenz et al. (Eds.): ICSOFT 2015, CCIS 586, pp. 137–154, 2016.
DOI: 10.1007/978-3-319-30142-6_8

method calls it is difficult to know where to place the constraint checking code. There may be several methods that need to check the constraint, or part of it, as a postcondition. That could lead to code scattering, code tangling and thigh coupling [4].

Regarding the *when* problem, in case of domain constraints, immediate checking after every single method call could simply not be possible as low-level method calls may produce transient illegal states that, eventually, will evolve to a final legal state. That means the checking must be delayed until the higher-level method finishes. Again, it may be difficult to foresee at programming time whether a high-level method is being called by another higher-level call or not.

The third issue (over *what objects*) that developers must solve is to delimit the scope of the checking. A complete checking of every constraint after any modification would involve unfeasible performance rates. Ideally the programmer must keep track of those constraints that might be compromised and over what objects they should be checked and then, at the end of the high-level method call check as few constraints, over as few objects, as possible.

Finally, developers must guarantee the consistency of the model in case a domain constraint violation happens. There are many works on this topic. Some applies backward error recovery techniques (BER) that provide *Atomicity*, that is the case of *Reconstructors* [5]. With that property in place, programmers can assume that modifications are done in an all-or-nothing way.

Although all these issues could be solved by manual implementation, their high complexity makes its development and maintenance an error prone task that can suppose a source of implementation problems in the project.

This paper describes the implementation of a tool that (1) translates invariants code (OCL) into executable code (aspect code), (2) optimizes the constraints by generating simpler (incremental) versions regarding the events that affect the constraint, (3) delays the execution of those constraints until the close of the atomic context or a high-level operation, (4) is easy to integrate with atomic contexts such as *Reconstructors* or an STM and (5) generates non-invasive code (aspect code), and thus easy to add to programmer's code.

The remaining of this paper is organized as follows: the second chapter summarizes the proposal, the third presents the difficulties a programmer must solve, the fourth introduces a running example the tool is deep detailed in chapter five and chapter six shows the results of applying the proposed processing to the running example, the seventh chapter comments related work and the eighth closes with the conclusions.

2 Proposal

We think that all the aforementioned difficulties could be avoided and automatized by means of appropriate consistency checking mechanisms that complement atomicity contexts. Checking all pending constraints when the atomic context is about to close solves the *when* difficulty (2). *What-to-do* (4) in case of failure is then solved due to the atomicity property of the context. The other two, *how* (1) and over *what object* (3), can be solved applying OCL analysis techniques and code generation. Those techniques are able to convert the original constraints into new incremental versions (*how*) optimized for the events and objects affected (*what object*). Consequently, programmers' effort would be reduced.

Developers must implement the domain model classes as Plain Old Java Objects (POJO), and provide all constraints expressed in OCL in a separate unit.

The tool (Fig. 1) analyzes the model implementation and the OCL constraints. The constraint engine generates the code implementing an incremental checking of the given constraints. The output is the AspectJ code to be weaved with the programmer's code.

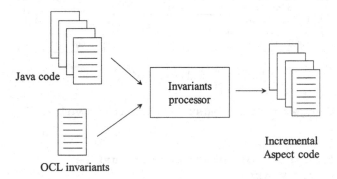

Java code

OCL invariants

Invariants processor

Incremental Aspect code

Fig. 1. A tool to generate invariants checking code.

The programmer must also delimit the context of the business operations, in the same way he/she delimits transactions. At the end of the context every check will be done. If any constraint is violated, an exception will be raised indicating a constraint violation in the business operation.

```
Context ctx = Context.createContext();
try {
    <business operations here>
    ctx.close();
} catch (...) {
    ctx.dispose();
}
```

Fig. 2. Execution of business code inside a context.

Ideally this consistence integrity checking will be done in combination with some kind of atomicity handling context able to restore the model to its previous state. The tool currently integrates with *Reconstructors* [5], and with the Hibernate ORM [6]. The design would easily integrate also software transactional memory solutions [7, 8].

3   Constraint Implementation Issues

Depending on the model elements involved we could classify constraints on four different categories: (1) attribute, (2) object, (3) class and (4) domain constraints.

Let us use the example in Fig. 3 for illustrating purposes in which we add three constraints as OCL invariants to a small UML model.

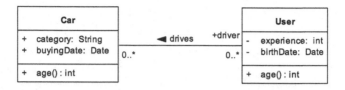

Fig. 3. Car and driver UML diagram.

- **I1: The age of a user must be a positive value**
context User inv I1:
      self.age() > = 0
- **I2: If a car is gold class then it must be**
- **less than 4 years old**
context Car inv I2:
      self.category = 'gold' implies self.age() < 4
- **I3: There can only be 10 cars of gold class at maximum**
context Car inv I3:
      Car.allInstances- > select(category = 'gold')- > size
() < 10
- **I4: Gold class cars can only be driven by**
- **drivers with more than 10 years of experience.**
context Car inv I4:
      self.category = 'gold' implies self.drivers- > forAll(d |
            d.experience > 10
)

Attribute constraints are those that only depend on the value of an object attribute, for example the I1 constraint. *Object constraints* involve several attributes of the same object, as example the I2. Here the constraint depends on the category and age attributes. *Class constraints* (I3) depend on all instances of a class (extent). *Domain constraints* are those affected by the state of a subgraph of objects (I4).

Attribute and object constraints can be safely checked after any attribute modification. Those changes are typically done by object methods and, thus, the enumerated difficulties have a straight solution. These constraints can be checked after (*when*) the execution of the object method that changes the attribute (as a postcondition). The implementation of the constraint checking will be a plain translation into the implementation language (*how*). The concerned object is clearly located (*what object*). The last issue (*what to do*) may also be easily solved provided we have an atomic execution context.

Class constraints are more difficult to check properly. As more than the currently-being-modified object is involved, the constraint is not only sensitive to the modification of object's attributes it depends on, but also to insertions and deletions of other objects. When to check the constraint has more affecting events (updates, inserts and deletes) and the *what-object* difficulty is also more complex as more objects are involved. The complexity of the implementation (*how*) of this kind of constraints is related to the architecture; in the case of plain model to code translation, it is usually hard to maintain the extent of the class. Not many languages maintain such a collection of objects, and in those with garbage collection, it is hard to control if an object has been functionally deleted (unreferenced) or not.

Domain constraints management involves even more problems. Several linked objects may be involved, so any change in any of them might violate the constraint. Let's see a trivial example of two entities, A and B, which have a bidirectional association. There is an implicit constraint: if an object of A has a reference to an object of B, then this object of B must have a reference to the A object. If we check the constraint after setting the reference to B in A (a.setB(b)), the object A will be in a valid state, but B is not linked to A yet, thus the constraint is not meet. If we do the reverse we end in a similar situation. The obvious solution here is to delay the checking until the high-level operation has finished (*when*). As the constraint might be affected by different objects, through different method calls, there could be various objects on which we have to check the constraint (more difficult over *what-object*). The implementation of the constraint (*how*) have to consider more than one class. Combining this with every possible method that may affect it would lead to a combinational explosion. That kind of situations are error-prone since a programmer can easily forget some of those methods. This quickly leads to code scattering, code tangling, and strong coupling of code [4]. Besides, as an attribute may be involved in several constraints (in the previous examples the car class attribute), the implementations of the modifier methods will end up even more tangled.

All those difficulties acquire a new dimension if performance is another concern. The programmer should analyze the constraint looking for affecting modifications (relevant events). Consider again the example constraint I4 "gold class cars can only be driven by drivers with more than 10 years of experience". We will conclude that we only need to check that constraint if there is an updating of the car class attribute, or a change in the driver experience field, or when a car and a driver are linked. The rest of all possible modifications in the model will never affect it, so it is unnecessary to check the constraint. Note that checking the constraint after an effective attribute modification is more precise than checking it after a method execution that might have changed the attribute or not.

Another efficiency gap comes from the checking of more objects than those really affected by the changes. For instance, to check the constraint over all cars after modifying the category attribute in one of them clearly has no point. Note that the processing of the relevant instances for a constraint must consider not only the entities of the context type directly modified by the structural events, but also those entities related directly or indirectly to certain modified entities of other types.

Furthermore, depending on the type of event, the body of the constraint could be different, better focused. For instance, if the case of a linking event between a car and a driver, then an equivalent and more efficient constraint body would be:

– I4: better focused for class-driver linking
```
context Drives inv:
    self.car.category <>'gold' or self.driver.experience > 10
```

That redefinition only requires the two linked objects. Neither needs to check all the drivers related with the car nor all the cars related with the driver.

As another example for the case of User::experience modification, we could check this other redefined constraint:

– I4: better focused for driver.experience changes
```
context User inv: self.cars- > forAll(c |
        c.category <> 'gold' or self.experience > 10
    )
```

This performs better given that it only involves the cars related with the driver. Note the context change from Car to User.

As a conclusion, we can state that implementing constraints avoiding code tangling, scattering or high coupling, with an efficient (incremental) checking and ensuring the stability of the system in case of constraint violation is not a trivial task for the developer.

4 Running Example

In order to illustrate different stages of the constraints processing we will use a running example based on the well-known *Royal&Loyal* model proposed by Jos Warmer and Anneke Kleppe [9]. We show a reduced version of the *Royal&Loyal* system in Fig. 4.

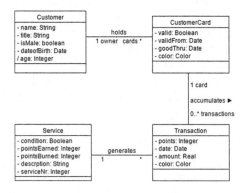

Fig. 4. Reduced version of the Royal&Loyal model.

Consider the following example restrictions expressed as OCL invariants over this domain model:

– I1 Owner's card must be an adult
```
context CustomerCard inv I1:
    validFrom.diffYears(owner.dateOfBirth) > = 18
```
– I2 Every senior citizen's card must have a positive
```
credit in all his transactions
context Customer inv I2:
    self.age() > = 65 implies self.cards- > forAll(c |
        c.transactions- > collect(t | t.points)- > sum() > = 0
)
```

5 The Tool

The tool makes use of Dresden OCL ToolKit (DOT) [10]. DOT provides a set of tools to parse and evaluate OCL constraints on various models like UML, EMF and Java. The tool is also able to generate Java equivalent code. We take advantage of the model loading feature to build a representation of the domain model from Java classes. The OCL parsing capabilities are also used to build an AST representation of every OCL constraint.

Over that AST representation we apply the processing proposed by [11]. They propose an incremental checking of constraints. I.e., if the system is currently in a valid state and we apply some modification over it, we do not need to check all constraints over all instances (that would be extremely inefficient), but just over the instances affected and only those constraints that could possibly be violated by the modification. The algorithm transforms the original constraints into an equivalent set of simpler and optimized constraints according to the type of modification (event type).

5.1 Processing Every Constraint

The processing of constraint AST consists of several stages, as depicted in Fig. 5.

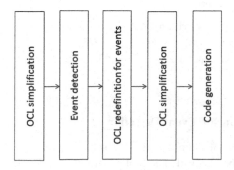

Fig. 5. Processing of constraints.

During the first stage OCL expressions are simplified by translating them into a canonical form. During this step some logical equivalences are applied. An extensive relationship of this equivalences can be found in [12]. The process uses here a rule engine that recursively applies every matching rule over the AST until no more rules can be applied.

The second stage computes all possible structural events that can affect a constraint. For this we follow the process explained in [11]. Our implementation can detect five different types of events:

- *Insert*: the creation of a new entity (call to new operator)
- *Delete*: the deletion of an entity. There are some extra difficulties here as in Java we cannot delete an object. More on this later.
- *Link*: indicates the linking of two objects over an association.
- *Unlink*: signals the unlinking of two objects.
- *UpdAtt*: indicates a change in the value of an attribute (update attribute).

The third stage computes for each constraint-event pair a new alternative equivalent to the first but probably simpler and with fewer entities involved. This new constraint is specialized for that specific type of event.

After this transformation the simplification rule engine is executed again with the addition of some new rules [11].

As a result of this process we end up with some simpler constraints regarding every event for each constraint. These new constraints will be simpler and consequently, more efficient in execution.

Consider again the invariant example I1, it is affected by the events *UpdAtt(CustomerCard.validFrom)*, *Link(Holds)*, *Insert(CustomerCard)* and *UpdAtt(Customer.dateOfBirth)*. Being the two last events better checked by the redefinition I1-2 of the original invariant.

```
context Customer inv I1-2:
  self.cards- > forAll(v |
    v.validFrom.diffYears( v.owner.dateOfBirth ) > = 18
  )
```

The invariant I2 is affected by the events *Link(Accumulates)*, *Unlink(Accumulates)*, *Link(Holds)* and *UpdAtt(Transaction.points)*. For all those events the I2-2 redefinition is better focused then the original.

```
context CustomerCard inv I2-2:
  not (self.customer.age() > = 65
  or self.transactions- > collect(t | t.points)- > sum
() > = 0
```

5.2   Code Generation for Event Detection

The output of the previous processing is a set of classes, with the events and the invariants that should be checked. The tool generates aspect code to detect those events over the objects that form the domain graph.

Attribute Modification To detect this type of modification we create pointcuts following this pattern:

```
protected pointcut < att > Set(< cl > obj):
    set(* < cl > .<att >) && this(obj);
```

Where < *cl* > and < *att* > are placeholders for the class name and the attribute name. We advise that pointcut with a block of code as shown in Fig. 6.

```
after(<cl> obj): <att>Set(obj) {
    if (! Context.hasActiveContext())  return;
    Method method = getInvariantMethod(<cl>.class,
        "<invariant_name>");
    Context.getCurrentContext().add(
        new Invariant(obj, method));

}
```

Fig. 6. Insertion into the context of an invariant checker method after event detection.

That code creates and registers an object in charge of checking and invariant when invoked (*new Invariant(...)*). This object will receive as argument the affected object and the reflective representation of the checking method to be executed. It is then stacked on the context waiting for context *close()* operation to be executed.

Linkage of Objects. We need to distinguish between linking to unique association ends and many association ends. The former are represented in Java by a reference to an object, while the latter are usually supported by a collection. One-side linking is detected with the same pattern as for attribute modification detection.

In case of a many side, we need to detect additions and removals to the underlying collection. The tool introduces a proxy for the collection to generate callbacks when a modification to the underlying collection is done. That proxy must be configured with the event types it has to notify (additions or deletions). It is injected after the assignment of the collection to the object's field during construction time. The pointcut we use here follows a pattern like this:

```
pointcut < att > ColSetter(< cl > obj):
    set(Set < att >) && within(< cl >) && target(obj);
```

With and *after* advise for that pointcut the proxy is inserted:

The last line of code configures the proxy with the events it must notify and an invariant builder object whose mission is to create and insert into the context an invariant checker (*new Invariant(...)*) whenever one of the specified events occurs.

```
after(<cl> obj) : <att>ColSetter(obj){
   Field field = getField(<cl>.class, "<att>");
   IncContainer ic = newProxy(obj, field);
   applyValueToField(obj, field, ic);

   ContainerEvent[] events;
   Method method;
   method = reflectivelyGetMethod(
      <cl>.class, "<invariant>");
   events = new ContainerEvent[]{<evnts>};
   InvariantBuilder builder =
      new InvariantBuilder(obj, method);
   ic.registerInvariantBuilderForEvents(builder, events);

}
```

Fig. 7. *After* advise pattern for many side linking and unlinking.

5.3 Creation and Deletion of Objects: Extent of a Class

Those OCL constraints that involve an *allInstances* expression are especially difficult to compute due to the fact that not all created objects are valid objects. Just by detecting the construction of an object (with a pointcut on the constructor execution) will not be enough. Some objects could be created just as temporal values (variables in methods) and others could be unreferenced objects waiting for the garbage collector to be removed. Several questions come to the fore here: Which objects are valid objects? When does an object become invalid (i.e. it is no longer used)? Where is the collection of valid objects?

In our understanding, the objects that must be considered valid are those in the domain object graph. More precisely, those objects reachable from the graph. In that way we can detect the addition of a new object when it is linked to another object already in the graph. Conversely an object deletion will be produced after the removal of all links that maintain the object linked to the graph.

We consider an object to be *in-the-graph* when it is reachable though "any" link of "any" association type its class can have. Using another aspect we crosscut the domain entity classes with two collections, one for forward references, and another for the backward ones.

```
privileged aspect GraphNodeAspect {
   boolean GraphNode.isInRepository;
   List < GraphNode > GraphNode.forward;
   List < GraphNode > GraphNode.backward;
   ...
}
```

When an insertion or deletion (Insert or Delete events) is detected the affected object is then added or removed to/from the corresponding *allInstances* collection.

```
void GraphNode.removeFromAllInstances(){
  Extents.get(this.getClass()).remove(this);
  for(GraphNode entity: forward) {
    if (! entity.isInGraph()) {
      entity.removeFromAllInstances();
    }
  }
}
```

We already know how to detect when two objects are linked or unlinked. Now we need to augment the body of the previous after advise pattern (Fig. 7) to check the reachability of both objects after the link/unlink operation.

```
after(< cl > obj) : < cl > ColSetter(obj){
  //same code as Fig. 7
  //extra code to detect Insert
  events = new ContainerEvent[]{Insert};
  method = getInvariantMethod(< cl > .class, "< inv_name > ");
}
```

The system maintains a collection for every domain class. The contents of these collections are updated after the additions and removals.

There is one remaining question. A graph is a set of interrelated objects, but there could be many independent graphs. What is the real graph? In our conception the graph must have some root nodes (objects) to which other objects are connected after. Those root nodes are usually well localized in the design and stored in some type of collection (Repository pattern in [1]). With that in place we can state the condition an object must meet to be considered *in-the-graph*: *An object will be in the graph if it is directly stored in a repository or is reachable from another object that is already in the graph.*

```
public boolean GraphNode.isInGraph() {
  return isInRepository || anyRelatedIsInGraph();
}
boolean GraphNode.anyRelatedIsInGraph() {
  for(GraphNode n: backward) {
    if (n.isInGraph() && n.forward.contains( this )) {
      return true;
    }
  }
  return false;
}
```

In this tool we use an annotation (*@Repository*) to mark those collections that act as repositories. Finally, by proxying those collections with and aspect advise we are able to detect additions or removals of root objects. Whenever a new object is added, its *inRepository* attribute is set to true and the opposite when it is removed. Consequently, all objects reachable from this object will acquire or lose their *in-the-graph* condition by reachability (and will fire the respective Insert/Delete event).

5.4   Code Generation of Invariants

Once the invariants have been transformed in their incremental versions they can be translated into Java. For this step we use again the Dresden OCL Toolkit. The output DOT code generator is a list of strings, being the last one the final Boolean expression used to raise and exception in case it evaluates to false. The invariant checker method will follow this pattern:

```
public void < inv_name > (<class > obj) {
  <DOT generated lines>
  if (! < DOT generated last line >) {
   throw new ConstraintException(...);}}
```

5.5   Execution Context

All business operations must be executed within a context (similar idea as a transaction). This functionality is represented by the *Context* interface.

```
public interface Context {
  public void add(Invariant i);
  public void close() throws ...
  public void dispose() throws ...
}
```

The developer must invoke the business operations within an opened context as shown in Fig. 2. Explicitly context handling can be avoided by annotating the business methods with @Context. The tool put the context handling code behind the scenes.

```
@Context public void doBusiness(...){...}
```

Context objects are obtained from a factory class that maintains the *Context* object linked to the current running thread. The *add()* method is invoked from the event detectors to insert the corresponding invariant checker method that, along with other pending invariants, must be checked at the end of the context (when the close() method is called).

Event Simplification. During the execution of the business operation some events may arise, and consequently the event handler inserts an invariant checker method to verify the corresponding constraint. The context stores every checker object classified by its origin object, event type and invariant method to call. With this information in place there are some optimizations that can be done to improve efficiency.

* In the case of *UpdAtt* events repeated over the same object attribute, the context just store one. If there is a previous *Insert* event then the *UpdAtt* is irrelevant, as all invariant checkings related to *UpdAtt* events are always verified by an *Insert* event.

- With *Delete* events we must delete all previous invariants for the same instance. Besides, if there already an Insert event for the same entity we do not even need to store the *Delete* event.
- The case of *Unlink* event is similar to the previous one, if there already is a *Link* event for the same association and object in the context the *Link* event must be deleted. And if *Link* and *Unlink* are in the same context, none of them deserve to be checked.
- Finally, as different events could raise the same invariant checking, the context object should avoid registering the same object-invariant more than once.

Final Execution. When the business operation is finished, the context is closed and every pending check is executed. The context catches and stacks every possible violation. After that, all the accumulated exceptions are gathered together in one final exception raised with all that information in place. That way the programmer can obtain information about every broken constraint in one single shot.

6 Results

We have tested our tool with the full version of the *Royal&Loyal* model already presented [9]. For that purpose we take the invariant definitions available as example in the Dresden Toolkit [13]. The full domain model consists of 11 entity classes and 2 extra types. It also has 20 OCL invariants of which 6 are of attribute or object type, 12 are of domain type and 2 of class type.

Consider a use case in which a *Customer* consumes a *Service* offered by a *Program Partner* of a *Loyalty Program* to which both are associated and is paid with the points accumulated on the *Loyalty Account* by the previous customer's *Transaction*s. During the operation the system has to register a new *Burning* transaction for a number of points specified by the service. Figure 8 shows the involved invariants.

```
(1)  context Burning inv burningAsTransaction:
         points = oclAsType(Transaction).points
(2)  context ProgramPartner inv totalPointsEarning:
     self.services.transactions
       ->select(t| t.oclIsTypeOf(Earning))
       ->collect( tt | tt.points)->sum() < 10000
(3)  context ProgramPartner inv totalPoints:
     self.services.transactions
       ->collect(t | t.points)->sum() < 10000
(4)  context LoyaltyAccount inv oneOwner:
         self.transactions.card.owner->size()=1
(5)  context LoyaltyAccount inv transactionsWithPoints:
         self.points <= 0
         or self.transactions->select(t | t.points > 0)
            ->size() > 0
```

Fig. 8. New generated versions of invariants.

As discussed before, in case of using a DbC approach the object's invariants would only be checked due to object's methods executions, and thus the invariant's affected object could be unaware of possible invariants violations due to changes in other linked objects. As shown in Table 3, just one invariant is of attribute or object type, therefore the other invariants will not be checked (unless some other methods of the related *ProgramPartner* and *LoyaltyAccount* objects are executed).

Alternatively we can use an OCL interpreter, widely used in some scenarios such as model to model transformations. An interpreter checks all the constraints against all objects in the model instance. We can use the amount of objects visited as an indicator for comparing the three approaches mentioned.

After executing the tool we get 36 new invariants related to 25 affecting events and 11 new AspectJ files ready to be weaved with the entities[1].

Table 1. Events raised by the use case execution.

Ev id	Ev type	Over entity type
1	Insert	Transaction (base class of Burning)
2	Insert	Burning
3	Link	Transaction and Service
4	Link	Transaction and CustomerCard
5	Link	Transaction and LoyaltyAccount
6	UpdAtt	LoyaltyAccount.points

During the execution of the use case, several affecting events will be produced indicating a potential violation of their related constraints.

Table 2. Invariants stacked onto the context due to the previous events (Id column relates with the id column of Table 1).

Ev id	Context	Invariant
1	Burning	burningAsTransaction
2	ProgramPartner	totalPointsEarning
3	ProgramPartner	totalPoints
4	LoyaltyAccount	**oneOwner**
5	LoyaltyAccount	**oneOwner**
6	LoyaltyAccount	transactionsWithPoints-19

In During the execution of the use case, several affecting events will be produced indicating a potential violation of their related constraints.

---

[1] The tool and all related code for this testing can be downloaded from http://www.di.uniovi.es/~alberto_mfa/constraints.proto.zip.

Table 2 we can observe that event 1 has no invariant associated, while event 3 has two of them. Besides, the oneOwner invariant is raised by two different events. Thanks to context optimization those repetitions are avoided and eventually only 5 invariants require to be checked.

Table 3. Type of each invariant and number of objects accessed by each one (id refers to Table 1). The symbol (.) indicates the formula in the "Proposed Tool" column.

Inv id	Inv type	Proposed tool	OCL intrpr.
1	Attribute	1	N_B * (.)
2	Domain	$1 + S_{PP} * (1 + T_S)$	N_{PP} * (.)
3	Domain	$1 + S_{PP} * (1 + T_S)$	N_{PP} * (.)
4	Domain	$1 + (3 * T_{LA})$	N_{LA} * (.)
5	Domain	$1 \parallel 1 + T_{LA}$	N_{LA} * (.)

Table 3 relates the invariant, the type and number of objects accessed for its verification. The third column indicates the number of objects using the proposed tool while the fourth do the same for an OCL interpreter. Here SPP stands for the average number of Service objects linked to a ProgramPartner object, TS represents the average number of Transactions linked to a Service, and TLA means the average number of Transactions linked to a LoyaltyAccount.

The OCL interpreter must execute each invariant for every context class object in the system. That is represented in the right column where N_B stands for the total number of *Burning* transactions in the system; N_{PP} represents the total number of *ProgramPartners* and N_{LA} the total of *LoyaltyAccounts*.

7 Related Work

This idea of objects having to satisfy a set of invariants traces back to the work of Hoare [14]. Later Meyer continued the idea with his Design by Contract (DbC) methodology [15]. Nowadays this idea was also applied to many other languages such as JML for Java [16], Spec# for C# [17], etc.

Design by Contract is based on the principle of an object being responsible for its own consistency. This rule is practical for single objects not associated with others (attribute and object constraints in our classification), or just having references to its owned objects (composition), but does not match with class and domain constraints. Therefore, DbC is enough for attribute and object constraints, but is not practical for class and domain constraints.

There are also many works using OCL based contracts. Some tools translate them into Java, AspectJ [18–21] or other contract languages such as JML [22, 23] or CleanJava [24]. All this works differ from our approach in their adherence to DbC (attribute and object constraints only). However, those that generate AspectJ suggest techniques and templates. In [25] the authors offers a complete report and comparison of those techniques. We take the idea of using proxies for them.

Henrique Rebêlo et al. [26], propose a JML to AspectJ compiler able to solve one the problems addressed with our proposal, the scattering of the contract specification among different methods that may violate it. Their work avoids contract scattering by centralizing the contract specification in a common advice complemented with JML. Our approach also avoids scattering and promotes the invariants specification as documentation by centralizing all invariants in one single file.

Dzidel et al. [20] present another OCL-contract to AspectJ tool, but leave as future work some problems we try to solve with our proposal: (1) the challenge of translating the OCL *allInstances* expression into target code, and (2) the runtime overhead of checking OCL collection expressions as *forAll*, *collect*, etc. We have proposed a possible solution to the *allInstances* problem using the idea on being in-the-graph.

Another type of OCL tools are the interpreters [27]. They are aimed to check a model instance against its model and constraints. That may seem a solution but they work in a one shot fashion: they check every constraint against the whole model instance. This solution is practical for those situations in which the whole model instance is created at once, for example in model transformations (MDA). But this strategy will lead to unfeasible performance rates for a domain model being incrementally updated by business logic method executions.

A common point in all these DbC and OCL tools is that they do not perform any analysis of constraints, thus the generated code is not incremental. Although some of them can generate code able to detect plain attribute modifications, they insert the checking right after the modification [13] or allow the programmer to call the checking method later, leading to the programmer the responsibility to explicitly decide *when* and *what* method to call. They help with the *how* difficulty, partially with the over *what object*, but neither with the *when* nor with the *what to do* difficulties.

8   Conclusions

The proposed tool aids developers with the four discussed difficulties. The generated code is able to detect those potentially affecting events (*what object*) which combined with the delayed checking (*when*) and the transformed invariants translated to executable code (*how*) is a key difference with all DbC-like implementations for the specific case of programs built around the domain model pattern. The integration with atomicity contexts such as *Reconstructors* [5] or Hibernate [6] solves the problem of restoring the model to a previous state (*what to do*), although that integration is not mandatory; the generated code could work without that capability.

As we can conclude from results section the efficiency is quite good. Due to the incremental approach followed, every constraint is executed over as few objects as necessary and the context simplification process may reduce the number of constraint verifications.

The tool also gives a possible implementation for the *allInstances* problem, a classical problem when translating OCL to Java code.

Finally, by maintaining all invariants in a single source file it also helps with the problem of invariant scattering while it preserves the invariants as documentation for programmers.

Acknowledgements. This work has been funded by the European Union, through the European Regional Development Funds (ERDF); and the Principality of Asturias, through its Science, Technology and Innovation Plan (grant GRUPIN14-100).

References

1. Evans, E.: Domain-Driven Design-Tackling Complexity in the Heart of Software. Addison-Wesley Professional, Boston (2003)
2. Fowler, M.: Patterns of Enterprise Application Architecture. Addison-Wesley Longman Publishing Co., Inc., Boston (2003)
3. Olivé, À.: Conceptual schema-centric development: a grand challenge for information systems Research. In: Pastor, Ó., Falcão e Cunha, J. (eds.) CAiSE 2005. LNCS, vol. 3520, pp. 1–15. Springer, Heidelberg (2005)
4. Cachopo, J.M.P.: Development of Rich Domain Models with Atomic Actions, UNIVERSIDADE TÉCNICA DE LISBOA (2007)
5. Fernández Lanvin, D., Izquierdo Castanedo, R., Juan Fuente, A.A., Fernández Álvarez, A. M.: Extending object-oriented languages with backward error recovery integrated support. Comput. Lang. Syst. Struct. **36**, 123–141 (2010)
6. Bauer, C., King, G., Gregory, G.: Java Persistence with Hibernate. Manning Publications Co., Greenwhich (2014)
7. Harris, T., Marlow, S., Peyton-Jones, S., Herlihy, M.: Composable memory transactions. In: Proceedings of the Tenth ACM SIGPLAN Symposium on Principles and Practice of Parallel Programming - PPoPP 2005, p. 48. ACM Press, New York (2005)
8. Dice, D., Shalev, O., Shavit, N.: Transactional locking II. Distrib. Comput. **4167**, 194–208 (2006)
9. Warmer, J., Kleppe, A.: The Object Constraint Language: Getting Your Models Ready for MDA. Addison-Wesley Professional, Reading (2003)
10. Wilke, C., Thiele, M.: Dresden OCL2 for Eclipse Manual for Installation, Use and Development (2010)
11. Cabot, J., Teniente, E.: Incremental integrity checking of UML/OCL conceptual schemas. J. Syst. Softw. **82**(9), 1459–1478 (2009)
12. Cabot, J., Teniente, E.: Transformation techniques for OCL constraints. Sci. Comput. Program. **68**, 179–195 (2007)
13. Wilke, C., Demuth, B., Aÿmann, U.: Java Code Generation for Dresden OCL2 for Eclipse (2009). http://dresden-ocl.sourceforge.net/downloads/pdfs/gb_claas_wilke.pdf
14. Hoare, C.A.R.: Proof of correctness of data representations. Acta Inform. **1**, 271–281 (1972)
15. Meyer, B.: Applying "design by contract". Computer **25**, 40–51 (1992). (Long. Beach. Calif)
16. Leavens, G.T., Cheon, Y.: Design by Contract with JML. Draft. 1, 4 (2005). www.jmlspecs. org
17. Barnett, M., Leino, K.R.M., Schulte, W.: The Spec# programming system: an overview. In: Barthe, G., Burdy, L., Huisman, M., Lanet, J.L., Muntean, Traian (eds.) CASSIS 2004. LNCS, vol. 3362, pp. 49–69. Springer, Heidelberg (2005)

18. Cheon, Y., Avila, C., Roach, S., Munoz, C., Estrada, N., Fierro, V., Romo, J.: An aspect-based approach to checking design constraints at run-time. Presented at the November (2008)
19. Gopinathan, M., Rajamani, S.K.: Runtime monitoring of object invariants with guarantee. In: Leucker, M. (ed.) RV 2008. LNCS, vol. 5289, pp. 158–172. Springer, Heidelberg (2008)
20. Dzidek, W.J., Briand, L.C., Labiche, Y.: Lessons learned from developing a dynamic OCL constraint enforcement tool for java. In: Bruel, J.M. (ed.) MoDELS 2005. LNCS, vol. 3844, pp. 10–19. Springer, Heidelberg (2006)
21. Rebêlo, H., Soares, S., Lima, R., Ferreira, L., Cornélio, M.: Implementing java modeling language contracts with AspectJ. In: Proceedings of 2008 ACM Symposium Applied Computing, SAC 2008, pp. 228–233 (2008)
22. Avila, C., Flores, G., Cheon, Y.: A library-based approach to translating OCL constraints to JML assertions for runtime checking. In: International Conference on Software Engineering Research and Practice, Las Vegas, Nevada, 14-17 July 2008, pp. 403–408 (2008)
23. Hamie, A.: Translating the object constraint language into the java modelling language. In: Proceedings of 2004 ACM Symposium Applied Computing - SAC 2004, pp. 1531–1535 (2004)
24. Cheon, Y., Avila, C.: Automating Java program testing using OCL and AspectJ. In: ITNG2010 - 7th International Conference on Information Technology: New Generations, pp. 1020–1025 (2010)
25. Froihofer, L., Glos, G., Osrael, J., Goeschka, K.M.: Overview and evaluation of constraint validation approaches in Java. In: Proceedings - International Conference on Software Engineering, pp. 313–322. IEEE Computer Society, Los Alamitos (2007)
26. Rebêlo, H., Leavens, G.T., Bagherzadeh, M., Rajan, H., Lima, R., Zimmerman, D.M., Cornélio, M., Thüm, T.: AspectJML: modular specification and runtime checking for crosscutting contracts. In: Proceedings of the 13th International Conference on Modularity, pp. 157–168. ACM, Lugano (2014)
27. Chimiak-Opoka, J., Demuth, B., Awenius, A., Chiorean, D., Gabel, S., Hamann, L., Willink, E.D.: OCL Tools Report based on the IDE4OCL Feature Model. Eceasst. **44**, (2011)

An Ontological Analysis of a Proposed Theory for Software Development

Diana Kirk[1](✉) and Stephen MacDonell[2]

[1] Independent Research Consultancy, Auckland, New Zealand
dianakirk@acm.org
[2] Software Engineering Laboratory (SERL),
Auckland University of Technology (AUT), Auckland, New Zealand
stephen.macdonell@aut.ac.nz

Abstract. There is growing acknowledgement within the software engineering community that a theory of software development is needed to integrate the myriad methodologies that are currently popular, some of which are based on opposing perspectives. We have been developing such a theory for a number of years. In this paper, we overview our theory and report on a recent ontological analysis of the theory constructs. We suggest that, once fully developed, this theory, or one similar to it, may be applied to support situated software development, by providing an overarching model within which software initiatives might be categorised and understood. Such understanding would inevitably lead to greater predictability with respect to outcomes.

Keywords: Software development · Software engineering · Theoretical model · Ontology · Software context

1 Introduction

The term *Software Engineering* was coined in 1968 at a conference whose aim was to discuss the need for the software development discipline to be more strongly based on theoretical and engineering principles [46]. The *Waterfall* model, a then-popular model used in manufacturing, was adopted as the standard approach for developing computer software. As time progressed, it became apparent that a strict implementation of this model was not appropriate for all software. A number of modifications, for example *Spiral* [8], and alternative models, for example *XP* [7], have emerged. The authors of the various models have different viewpoints on what kind of activity software development actually *is*. Earlier models view software development as an engineering activity and focus on control. More recent models adopt the viewpoint of 'software-as-a-service' and focus on effective communications. However, regardless of the huge variation in approach, until recently, the accepted wisdom by all methodology architects was that, in order to be fully effective, their approach must be followed exactly, with nothing added and nothing missed [12].

© Springer International Publishing Switzerland 2016
P. Lorenz et al. (Eds.): ICSOFT 2015, CCIS 586, pp. 155–171, 2016.
DOI: 10.1007/978-3-319-30142-6_9

We have long understood from experiences in industry that this 'wisdom' is not based on what actually happens in the field, and have advocated with others the need to more deeply understand the process of developing computer software in order to support industry in its need to select practices in a flexible way, according to objectives and context [4,15,25,30,35,36]. This viewpoint has now become the accepted one [2,3,44,49,55]. The traditional viewpoint — that methodologies and practices should be adopted and used as prescribed — has thus been superseded by one of acceptance that tailoring is both necessary and unavoidable.

If tailoring is of the essence, we clearly must strive to fully understand the nature of the relationships between objectives, process and context. Only then will we be in a position to advise industry on which practices might be most suitable or to predict project outcomes based on context and practices implemented. The sole route to this kind of general understanding is through theory-building [16]. Without an understanding of the relationships between objectives, practices, context and outcomes, we can at best expose patterns based on data or observations. Such patterns represent *correlations* and correlations can not be used to predict in a general way. For consistent prediction, we must create frameworks based on causal relationships i.e. theoretical models. Indeed, Basili et al. remind us that, when carrying out controlled experiments, "... it is hard to know how to abstract important knowledge without a framework for relating the studies" [6].

The role of theory in software engineering (SE) has been investigated from a number of perspectives. Sjøberg et al. observed that there is very little focus on theories in software engineering and remind us of the key role played by theory-building if we wish to accumulate knowledge that may be used in a wide range of settings [51]. Hannay et al. conducted a review of the literature on experiments in SE and found that fewer than a third of studies applied theory to explain the cause-and-effect relationship(s) under investigation, and that a third of the theories applied were themselves proposed by the article authors [24]. Gregor examined the nature of theory in Information Systems (IS) and found multiple views on what constitutes a theory [17]. Stol and Fitzgerald argue that SE research does, in fact, exhibit traces of theory and suggest that the current focus on evidence based software engineering (EBSE) must be combined with a theory-focussed research approach to support explanation and prediction [52].

While there is general agreement within the research community that an increased focus on theory building would produce benefits, there remains uncertainty about how to proceed. Wand et al. remind us that "To employ conceptual modeling constructs effectively, their meanings have to be defined rigorously" and that achievement of this requires an articulation within the context of *ontology* [56]. The authors apply an ontological framework developed by Bunge [9] to analyse the relationship construct in entity-relationship modelling. A number of authors have used their approach to investigate various aspects of IS, for example, UML [47] and reference models [14]. A key aspect of the approach is the ability to confirm that a model is complete and without redundancy.

Our aim is to establish a conceptual model to describe a *software initiative*. By *software initiative*, we mean the software-related processes implemented to achieve specified outcomes. We suggest that the existence of such a model would support the software industry in the selection of appropriate practices, according to an organisation's specific objectives and contexts.

In this paper, we report on an ontological analysis of our proposed theory. We analysed the theoretical constructs with respect to the Unified Foundational Ontology (UFO) [21] with a view to identifying issues relating to meaning. The aim of our analysis was to gain a better understanding of the constructs that form the basis of our model. In Sect. 2 we discuss other efforts towards providing a theoretical foundation for software development. In Sect. 3, we overview our proposed model prior to ontological analysis. In Sect. 4, we present the results of our analysis based on the UFO and in Sect. 5, we summarise the paper and discuss limitations and future work.

2   Related Work

As far as we are aware, the only initiative to create a theory specifically for software is the SEMAT initiative, launched in 2009 by Ivar Jacobson, Bertrand Meyer and Richard Soley [27]. The approach proposes a *SEMAT kernel* comprising three parts. The first is a means of measuring project progress and health, the second categorises the activities required to effect progress, and the third defines the competencies required to effect the activities [26]. There are seven top-level 'alphas' - *Requirements, Software System, Work, Team, Way of Working, Opportunity* and *Stakeholders*. It is claimed that these concepts support determination of a project's health and facilitate selection of a suitable set of practices.

Although the authors of the SEMAT approach state that the initiative promotes a "non-prescriptive, value-based" philosophy that encourages selection of practices according to context, we suggest that the approach is, in fact, prescriptive in intent. Each of the SEMAT elements has a number of states "which may be used to measure progress and health" [28], and this implies that the health of every software project can be measured in a common way. We do not believe this to be the case, because of the vast number of possible objectives and contexts. In addition, the SEMAT model appears to offer no guidance on *how* to choose activities. Other than mentioning competencies required for activities, there is no link between activities and objectives or context. How do we know if an activity is suitable when the developers are in different countries or when the team comprises multiple cultures? The authors state that gaps and overlaps in activities can be easily identified, but it is not clear how this can be achieved in an objective way. We also note that the theory relates to a software *project*, a scope we have identified as being too narrow. For the above reasons, we have issue with the claim that a general theory is being developed. We cannot see how the approach will help researchers better understand practice limitations.

Weiringa, discussing the field of requirements engineering, reminds us of the dangers of confusing solution design with research [57]. We suggest that SEMAT, at this point, represents a design initiative rather than a theory building exercise.

3   Theory Overview

Our first observation is that we must scope our model to include *any* software initiative i.e. the scope is larger than a software *project*. Our rationale is the need to consider in a holistic way the entire *software-in-a-system (SIAS)* i.e. the software product or service as part of a larger whole. This 'whole' will vary in time as the software is first created and then used. The larger system during creation will include the development organisation, test environments (possibly stand-alone) and the client. After deployment, the software will become part of a system comprising any of hardware, software, humans and processes. The job is to create, deliver and sustain healthy software systems over a lifetime of operation. The reason behind our viewpoint of a need for greater holism has its roots in the uncertainty that results from the growing complexity of software systems. This complexity makes it impossible to categorise in a simple way the environment during development and makes it difficult to anticipate all future conditions under which the software will run i.e. we can no longer assume a stable and bounded operating environment. Conditions such as technology change and inappropriate use will probably affect the in-situ efficacy of the software. Uncertainty also characterises delivery mechanisms — in the past, a *project* developed a software product and then delivered this to a known client base. More recently, the web-based mechanism of 'deliver a little, solicit immediate client feedback, and deliver the next increment' has become popular [53], leaving the concept of a 'project-to-develop-then-deliver' no longer tenable.

As early as 1987, Basili and Rombach believed that "Sound tailoring requires the ability to characterise ... goals ..., the environment ..., and the effect of methods and tools on achieving these goals in a particular environment" [5]. Our efforts thus far have focused on clarifying what this might mean when considering flexibility in software initiatives. We thus begin with a consideration of *objectives*, *process* and *context*. In the following sections, we overview our efforts and comment on understandings achieved.

3.1   Objectives

We first observe the need to consider more than one objective for an initiative [33,36]. The reason is that a focus on a single outcome may lead to the identification of a local maximum and a possible sub-optimisation of the whole system [40,42,43]. We next observe that there are many possible objectives, including the common product-related ones of minimisation of cost and maximisation of quality, but also including the people-related ones such as 'increase developer subject-area knowledge', 'retain developers' or 'keep a specific customer happy'. For some of these, an associated numerical value will change throughout the initiative, for example, when spending increases throughout a project. For others, the goal is less definitive and a more fuzzy measure may be appropriate, for example, developer satisfaction levels may be described as 'Low', 'Medium' and 'High' [31]. A third observation is that most software initiatives are characterised by uncertainty [1,48] and this means that values cannot be represented in a deterministic way. A probabilistic distribution is a more suitable measure for some kinds of objective [11,39,50]. Our proposal is that a set of objectives may be modelled by a set of *values*, the type of value for each depending upon the nature of the objective. An implementation would involve representing an objective by a name, a description and a desired value.

Monitoring of progress, i.e. 'current state', will involve a consideration of the current value for each objective in the set. This takes into account the fact that state values are generally not 'empty' at commencement. For example, developers will have a certain 'satisfaction' level at commencement; in a product line situation, there is an existing code base that is characterised by a level of quality. While we believe this to be a sound approach, we have as yet taken this investigation no further i.e. the structure of *objectives* is an open research question.

3.2 Process

We view a *process* as a set of *practices*. Each *Practice* has the effect of moving the initiative closer to (or further away from) its *Objectives*. We observe that, in addition to the accepted practices such as 'design inspection', our definition includes anything that has an effect. For example, in a small startup organisation, an informal, unplanned practice such as 'chat over lunch' may be crucial for supporting the developer's understanding of what is to be built and is thus an acceptable 'practice' in our model. According to our model, a desired practice is one that successfully moves the initiative in the right direction. A 'lean' process is one in which every practice is effective.

The space of all possible practices is huge, and includes practices for identifying the target audience for a proposed product and understanding what the product should do, practices for designing, implementing and delivering the product, and practices for supporting product use in the target environment(s). We clearly need to introduce some structure, but found that the standard reference models did not suit when attempting to elicit information from individuals in smaller, less formal organisations [37]. It was clear that, if we wanted to capture practices-as-implemented-in-the-real-world, some new perspective was required.

Our approach considers what organisations *need to achieve* at a high level when involved in a software initiative. Our top-level functional categories are

- Define what is to be made.
- Make it.
- Deliver it.

We extended these categories to be what we believe are the main subcategories for software. These are shown in Table 1.

Table 1. Categories for practices.

Define	Roadmap
	Scope
Make	Design
	Implement
	Integrate
Deliver	Release
	Support

Because we have structured based on *function*, the categorisation will support any practice deemed to be relevant for meeting objectives. Informal meetings in the lunch room that help developers understand scope clearly fit into the 'scope' category. We hypothesise that the proposed categorisation addresses *all* software practices. A precondition that an objective be met is that each category must contain one or more effective practices. To illustrate, for a 'Quality' objective, including quality considerations during product design, implementation and integration will fail to achieve the objective if quality expectations are not included during scoping. The identification of gaps is straightforward.

The categorisation above does *not* imply any ordering of practices. Such ordering would exist at a higher level and might be used to describe strategies of iteration and incremental delivery. We also submit that the categorisation is 'paradigm-agnostic' — whether an initiative is run in a traditional or agile way, the basic functions of defining, making and delivering the product must be carried out. Of note is the fact that the sub-categories 'Roadmap' and 'Support' lie outside of a traditional development project and sub-categories 'Scope' and 'Release' relate to practices that span development organisation and client.

Our work on the *practices* aspect of the proposed theory is embryonic. Testing thus far is limited to a single, exploratory study in which we captured practices in three New Zealand software organisations [37,38]. We did expose some interesting areas for further study. For example, all participating organisations reported a dependence on practices that involved having to actively search for information, possibly implying some inefficiency as individuals must spend time. However, the study was exploratory in nature and this is an open research area.

3.3 Context

This represents the most challenging aspect of any theory for software development. There have been many attempts to relate project outcomes to specific contextual factors, for example, [2,10,41,53]. Our main critique of existing approaches is that they remain factors based [32]. We suggest that such an approach is misguided because

- there are simply too many possible factors to take into consideration, and this number will increase as new paradigms for software are introduced.

– it is unlikely that any two projects will be exactly the same and so understanding key factors for some is unlikely to be of use in a general way.

We believe that it is crucial that we develop an operationalisation of *context* that will be relevant for all software initiatives i.e. takes into account the situated nature of a software product throughtout its lifetime. It seems clear that the required model must comprise a number of orthogonal dimensions in order that an initiative can be plotted as a point in the dimensional space. In order to remove the 'factors-based' aspect, it is necessary to also find suitable abstractions for each dimension, abstractions that support a straight-forward identification of value for a given initiative. For example, rather than define a number of factors such as 'developer experience', 'developer subject area knowledge', we must abstract in such a way as to render it irrelevant if we have missed a factor out (for example, 'developer commitment').

Our first efforts at modelling this space involved a consideration of the dimensions *Who*, *Where*, *What*, *When*, *How* and *Why* [32]. These dimensions have been applied by others to ensure orthogonality [13,58]. Of course, the usefulness of the abstraction depends upon the choices about what these dimensions *mean*. Our assigned meanings are [34]:

Who: associates with peoples' *ability to perform*. Personal characteristics, culture and group structure are relevant, as these affect levels of understanding and conceptual sharing.

Where: associates with peoples' *availability*. The degrees of temporal and physical separation are relevant.

What: associates with *product* characteristics. Standards expectations, product interfaces and achieved quality are relevant.

When: associates with *product life cycle*. Examples are in-development, recently deployed, near retirement [45].

How: associates with *engagement expectations*. Client and developer expectations for the mechanisms for product specification and delivery will affect which practices are most appropriate.

Why: associates with *establishing objectives*.

We carried out some 'proof-of-concept' studies on this model, each involving categorising contextual factors from a small number of studies from the software engineering literature [29,34]. These studies caused us to refine our understanding of context in the following ways. In the first instance, it became clear that the dimension *why* addresses *objectives* and is thus not part of a model for *context*. We also found that many contextual factors mentioned in the literature are vague or ambiguous, and so must be clarified prior to categorising. For example, when considering the commonly-mentioned factor 'Company size', we suggest that it is not size itself that affects practice selection and/or outcomes, but rather what this means in terms of culture and physical and temporal separation. We labelled such factors as 'Secondary'. Some factors, such as 'requirements uncertainty', may be the result of one of a number of possible scenarios. For example, perhaps the client is not clear about what the product exactly is; perhaps (s)he is simply weak on decision-making; perhaps (s)he is unable to state what is wanted because of client-internal processes i.e. (s)he is waiting for a decision from someone else. We cannot know which practices will be effective until we understand which meaning is relevant. A practice of 'regular client meetings with prototypes' will not help if the client is waiting for someone else. We labelled this kind of factor as 'ambiguous'. Finally, we noticed that some factors were more 'high level' in that they could be more usefully viewed as affecting strategy. For example, 'lack of funds' would likely force some consideration about strategy, and the resulting decision may, in turn, affect objectives and/or context. It might be decided that the project should be abandoned, that some developers should be removed, or that a minimal product only should be delivered. We recognise these factors as *Strategic factors* and remove from our discussion of *context*.

Our current status is that, with our refined definition of *context*, we are well into a study to categorise contextual factors from the literature into our dimensional model. Thus far, we have met no obstacles. However, we have as yet included only literature from the *software engineering* domain and have constrained the study to the *development project*. Although we are optimistic, there clearly is much scope for research in this area, research that must be carried out before we can be confident in our proposed structure for *context*.

4   Ontological Considerations

As a preliminary to investigating the efficacy of our model in the field, we sought to more deeply understand its constructs from a *meaning* perspective. In order to achieve this, we turned to the field of *ontology*.

Ontology is primarily a long-established branch of philosophy that deals with the nature and structure of reality [19]. With the more recent growing interest in the semantic web, the term has been more generally used to represent a single domain in some knowledge representation language, for example, RDF and OWL [20]. However, the data modelling community has continued to apply the term in its more philosophical sense i.e. as a "philosophically well-founded domain-independent system of formal categories that can be used to articulate domain-specific models of reality" [20]. The claim is that, unless a domain model is based on the *meaning* of the domain concepts, the model will be flawed and open to mis-interpretation. One implication is that the use of logics for capturing systems is insufficient because logics do not address *meaning*. When discussing classifications of modelling primitives in knowledge representation, Guarino suggests that an ontological level for modelling is required to ensure meaning is adequately represented [18].

Guizzardi and Wagner suggest that an ontologically sound model is characterised by *truthfulness to reality (domain appropriateness)* and *conceptual clarity (comprehensibility appropriateness)* [23]. Without these constraints, a model may have several interpretations and cause misunderstandings in communication. These properties can be guaranteed if an isomorphism (one-to-one mapping) exists between abstraction and domain models. Specifically, an abstraction must exhibit:

Soundness — each modelling construct maps to a domain construct.
Completeness — each domain construct is represented by a modelling construct.
Lucidity — each modelling concept represents at most one domain concept.
Laconicity — each domain construct is represented by at most one modelling construct.

Foundational ontologies are "theoretically well-founded domain-independent systems of categories that have been successfully used to improve the quality of conceptual ... models" [23]. They thus enable the description of general concepts to be used in conceptual modelling. To our knowledge, there are two main foundational ontologies that have been adopted by the Information Systems community. Each of these has been applied to expose issues in current modelling methods. The *Bunge-Wand-Weber* model is an ontology based on the work of the philosopher Bunge [9] and adapted by Wand and Weber for use in information systems [56]. The approach has been applied to expose issues with the relationship construct in entity-relationship modelling [56], and to analyse shortcomings in UML [47] and reference models [14]. The *Unified Foundational Ontology (UFO)* represents a "synthesis of a selection of foundational ontologies" with the goal of creating a foundational ontology that is "tailored towards applications in conceptual modelling" [21]. As the UFO appears to have been more fully developed, with greater consideration for process-related entities, we have chosen to use this as a basis for our analysis.

In the next section, we overview the UFO, including only those aspects that we believe are relevant to this research. In the following section, we categorise the components of our proposed theory in terms of the UFO.

4.1   Unified Foundational Ontology (UFO)

The Unified Foundational Ontology (UFO) aims to define a range of domain-independent ontological categories to be used as a basis and elaborated for specific domains. There are three layered sets [22]:

UFO-A: defines the core set and addresses *endurants* i.e. entities that do not depend upon time for identification, for example, a person or a document.
UFO-B: extends UFO-A to include *perdurants* i.e. entities that are critically time-dependent, for example, events and processes.
UFO-C: extends UFO-B to include terms relating to intentional and social things.

Endurants are changed by perdurants. For example, a document may be altered by the enactment of an editing procedure.

Some relevant terms are introduced below [23]. A fundamental distinction is made between the categories of *Particular (Individual)* and *Universal (Type)*.

Particulars (Individuals) are entities that possess a unique identity. Examples are 'person', 'apple'.

Universals (Types) are patterns of features which can be realised in a number of different particulars. Examples are 'Person', 'Apple'.

Substantials are existentially independent particulars, for example 'apple'.

Moments are particulars that can exist only in other particulars and are thus existentially dependent upon them. These relate to the *properties* or *qualities* of a substantial. Examples, are a colour, a symptom.

Intrinsic Moments are dependent upon a single individual, for example, the *colour* of a rose.

Relators (Relational Moment) are dependent upon multiple individuals, for example, *an employment*. A relator can be viewed as the sum of the moments (properties) acquired by the participating individuals.

Substance Universals include, for example, 'Apple', 'Person'.

Moment Universals include, for example, 'Colour', 'Headache'.

Relations are universals that glue together other entities, for example, 'Employment'.

Material Relations have a material structure, for example, 'being employed by'.

Formal Relations hold between two or more entities directly, for example, 'part-of'.

Quality Structure provides the means for representing intrinsic moments, for example, a one-dimensional structure for representing 'height'.

Quale is a point in a quality structure.

Conceptual Space is a collection of quality structures, for example, a 'Colour' conceptual space may comprise structures for 'red', 'green' and 'blue'.

Mode is an intrinsic moment that can be conceptualised in terms of multiple separable quality dimensions, for example 'beliefs', 'symptoms', skills'.

At first glance, it would appear that the UFO-C would also be relevant, as we are aiming to model a software development initiative and this inherently includes teams, goals, etc. However, our aim is not to fully describe a software initiative, but is rather to find an abstraction that will support selection of suitable practices. As we consider *all* contextual aspects as simply affecting practice efficacy, we have no need of the social aspects covered in UFO-C. In the next section, we report the results of considerng our proposed abstraction in the light of the UFO-A and UFO-B.

4.2   Application of UFO to Proposed Theory

The concepts identified above as being relevant for our abstraction are *Software Initiative*, *Objectives*, *Context* and set of *Practice*.

In keeping with the convention of naming particulars and universals above, we use first letter uppercase for naming universal concepts and first letter lowercase for naming particulars.

We categorise Software Initiative as a substance universal i.e. a type, and software initiative as a substantial particular i.e. an instantiation.

When considering 'Objectives', we notice that objectives are closely bound to a software initiative i.e. are existentially dependent upon the initiative. We also observe that a software initiative has a current status, which changes as the initiative progresses and which has the same structure as objectives. It would seem reasonable to categorise both *Objectives* and *Current Status* as properties of Software Initiative i.e. as moment universals. As these constructs comprise multiple separable quality dimensions, for example, 'Time to market', 'Developer satisfaction', we represent as a *mode*.

We now consider Practice. We view as a substantial i.e. uniquely identifiable entity, with properties such as 'name', 'description' and 'category' (see Table 1). Torres reminds us that "sometimes we become so enamored with our favorite tools and techniques that we lose sight that they ... have a nominal operating range" [54]. We recognise that a practice is inherently associated with an operating specification, for example, 'client must be available' or 'effective change management for a fast-changing product but not for a stable one'. These constraints would be modelled as intrinsic moments of Practice. We observe that the operating specification relates directly to context, and revisit below.

On considering Context, our first analysis results in viewing as a substantial, with moments (properties) such as 'name' and 'description'. We have suggested in Sect. 3.3 that context is 'made up of' a number of parts i.e. a who-part, a where-part, etc. Each of these parts would be represented as a substantial. A material relation 'implement practice within a context and software initiative', exemplified by a relator entity, let's say 'practice implementation', would then bind a specific software initiative, practice and context.

However, we noticed in the previous paragraph that a practice's operating specification is closely related to the concept of *context* in that an operating specification will comprise the same kinds of values as are found in context. If we view Operating Specification as an intrinsic moment (property) of Practice, we cannot easily relate this to Context-as-a-Substantial. We are applying different kinds of modelling construct to model domain constructs that have the same basis. This would compromise the conceptual clarity of our model.

Another viewpoint is to consider that Context might be better viewed as an intrinsic moment of Software Initiative i.e. is existentially dependent upon Software Initiative. However, the moment comes into being only when a practice is carried out within a software initiative i.e. it is externally dependent upon the Relation 'implement practice within a software initiative' and the associated relator (relational moment) 'practice implementation'. To illustrate, the developer characteristics and lifecycle stage associated with a software initiative become relevant only in relation to a practice implementation. For example, a developer may be extremely skilled in playing chess and in designing software systems, but neither of these is relevant for a task of contract negotiation with a potential client.

We now have both context and operating specification viewed as intrinsic properties of substantials. As Context comprises several separable dimensions (who, when, what, where and how), we model as a mode, each dimension of which is a quality structure. This supports analysis of whether a practice is being implemented within its operating constraints.

From UFO-B, which extends UFO-A, we can consider the perdurant 'practice implementation' as an event that causes a change of state in its participating substantials. In our abstraction, change is effected to both current status and context (both intrinsic moments of software initiative). For example, current status may have become closer to some objectives and developer experience may have increased.

In summary, our abstraction is:

Software Initiative is a substantial universal with moment universals Objectives and Current Status. The moments are described as a *Software Status* mode. For a specific software initiative, software status comprises the quality dimensions appropriate for the initiative (for example, cost) and the elements of each as quales.

Practice is a substantial universal with moment universals Category and Operating Constraints. The latter has a structure similar to that of *Context*.

Practice Implementation is a relational moment (relator), relating Software Initiative and Practice and described as 'a practice is implemented within a software initiative'. As a relator, Practice Implementation is characterised by the properties of the participating substantials that become relevant as a result of participation in the relationship. The relevant property is Context, a moment of software initiative. Context is a mode, with dimensions modelled as quality structures.

4.3   Discussion

We submit that the above abstraction complies with the requirements that a model be characterised by *domain appropriateness* and *comprehensibility appropriateness* [23]. We believe the exercise has been beneficial in that the need for separation of 'practice' and 'practice implementation' has been exposed. We have had to think more clearly about the roles of objectives and current status. We have exposed a need for the concept 'operating specification' and have considered its link with context.

Although the UFO extension, UFO-C, would appear to be relevant, in that it includes ideas such as 'objective' and 'intentions', we submit that, because we are not trying to describe a software development process, the concepts are not necessary for our purpose. We wish to more deeply understand how to support practice selection and at this point believe that the influence of human attributes can be viewed in the same way as, for example, lifecycle stage for this purpose. Each of these affects which practices are (contra-)indicated for the software initiative.

An observation from the above analysis, is that the relational moment *context* is dependent upon the participation of a software intiative in a practice implementation relationship. As noted above, a developer's experience and location have meaning only in relation to the task being carried out. The implication is that discussing a software initiative's context in general has no meaning. This is potentially problematic from a practical perspective in that we cannot ascertain practice implementation efficacy without understanding which contextual elements are relevant and we cannot know which contextual elements are relevant without considering a practice implementation. We believe the key lies in how the dimensions of context are abstracted, and this is clearly an area for further research.

Although our approach has shown benefits, we are clear that this does not mean our proposed theory is correct, or useful i.e. if our abstraction does not model a software initiative in a way that supports practice selection, its adherence to ontological requirements is irrelevant. Our goal is rather to expose potential issues with theory structure before embarking on a more extensive and situated evaluation.

5   Summary

We have proposed an embryonic theory for software development with the aim of more deeply understanding which practices might be indicated and contraindicated within specific contexts. One characteristic of a successful theory is that opposing viewpoints can be seen as facets of a larger whole. Our conceptualisation must address the traditional versus agile dichotomy. It is not difficult to see that, as a situated practice is defined simply as a transformation of current state, many different practices will exist that implement the same kind of transformation. For example, in relation to Table 1, the practices 'Formally document requirements' and XP's 'Planning Game' both result in an increased understanding of what is to be built. However, if we consider the objectives 'Reliability' and 'Increase developer subject area knowledge', it is likely that the formal documentation approach will address the former (as non-functional requirements are an inherent part of formal requirements documents) while 'Planning Game' will not. The XP approach may require additional practices to address quality expectations.

Before embarking on a more exhaustive consideration of the efficacy of our theory, we deemed it necessary to gain confidence in the proposed constructs from a 'meaning' perspective and have completed a preliminary ontological analysis. When mapping the theoretical constructs to constructs in the UFO (Unified Foundational Ontology), we identified Software Initiative and Practice as basic entities, understood that a relator entity 'Practice Implementation' is required and established that Objectives and Context can be represented as multi-dimensional modes. We believe our analysis has been of benefit in that we now have a mechanism for associating a software initiative's objectives and current state and a practice's operating constraints and implementation context.

In summary, we have presented an overview of the theoretical approach we have been pursuing for several years and a report of our recent ontological analysis. Our work is in-embryo. Our contribution is that we are making an honest attempt to tackle an extremely difficult problem, and have set a new direction for exploration. We believe we have made pockets of progress in some areas. Our hope is that the efforts we have made thus far will be used as a starting point for other researchers. We submit that, if the community does not take the theory-building initiative seriously, we are doomed to endless cycles of 'new' process paradigms and architectures, each of which has some merit and many shortfalls.

References

1. Atkinson, R., Crawford, L., Ward, S.: Fundamental uncertainties in projects and the scope of project management. Int. J. Proj. Manage. **24**, 687–698 (2006)
2. Avison, D., Pries-Heje, J.: Flexible information systems development: designing an appropriate methodology for different situations. In: Filipe, J., Cordeiro, J., Cardoso, J. (eds.) Enterprise Information Systems: 9th International Conference, ICEIS 2007. LNBIP, pp. 212–224. Springer, Heidelberg (2008)
3. de Azevedo Santos, M., de Souza Bermejo, P.H., de Oliveira, M.S., Tonelli, A.O.: Agile practices: an assessment of perception of value of professionals on the quality criteria in performance of projects. J. Softw. Eng. Appl. **4**, 700–709 (2011)
4. Bajec, M., Vavpotic, D., Krisper, M.: Practice-driven approach for creating project-specific software development methods. Inf. Softw. Technol. **49**, 345–365 (2007)
5. Basili, V.R., Rombach, H.D.: Tailoring the software process to project goals and environments. In: Proceedings of the Ninth International Conference on Software Engineering, pp. 345–357. IEEE, IEEE Computer Society Press (1987)
6. Basili, V.R., Shull, F., Lanubile, F.: Building knowledge through families of experiments. IEEE Trans. Softw. Eng. **25**(4), 456–473 (1999)
7. Beck, K.: eXtreme Programming eXplained - Embrace Change. Addison-Wesley, USA (2000)
8. Boehm, B.W.: A spiral model of software development and enhancement. IEEE Comput. **21**(5), 61–71 (1988)
9. Bunge, M.A.: Treatise on Basic Philosophy 3. Ontology 1: The Furniture of the World. D. Reidel Publishing Company, Dordrecht (1977)
10. Clarke, P., O'Connor, R.V.: The situational factors that affect the software development process: towards a comprehensive reference framework. Inf. Softw. Technol. **54**, 433–447 (2012)
11. Connor, A.: Probabilistic estimation of software project duration. N. Z. J. Appl. Comput. Inf. Technol. **11**(1), 11–22 (2007)
12. Cusumano, M., MacCormack, A., Kemerer, C., Crandall, B.: Software development worldwide: the state of the practice. IEEE Softw. **20**(6), 28–34 (2003)
13. Dybå, T., Sjøberg, D.I., Cruzes, D.S.: What works for whom, where, when and why? on the role of context in empirical software engineering. In: Proceedings of the 6th International Symposium on Empirical Software Engineering and Measurement (ESEM 2012), Lund, Sweden, pp. 19–28, September 2012
14. Fettcke, P., Loos, P.: Ontological evaluation of reference models using the Bunge-Wand-Weber model. In: Proceedings of the Ninth Americas Conference on Information Systems (AMCIS 2003), pp. 2944–2955. Association for Information Systems (2003)
15. Fitzgerald, B.: The use of systems development methodologies in practice: a field study. Inf. Syst. J. **7**, 201–212 (1997)
16. Gilmore, D.J.: Methodological issues in the study of programming. In: Hoc, J.M., Green, T., Samurcay, R., Gilmore, D. (eds.) Psychology Of Programming, pp. 83–98. Academic Press Ltd., London (1990)

17. Gregor, S.: The nature of theory in information Systems. MIS Q. Manage. Inf. Syst. **30**(3), 611–642 (2006)
18. Guarino, N.: The ontological level: revisiting 30 years of knowledge representation. In: Borgida, A.T., Chaudhri, V.K., Giorgini, P., Yu, E.S. (eds.) Conceptual Modeling: Foundations and Applications. LNCS, vol. 5600, pp. 52–67. Springer, Heidelberg (2009)
19. Guarino, N., Oberle, D., Staab, S.: What is an Ontology? In: Staab, S., Studer, R. (eds.) Handbook on Ontologies. International Handbooks on Information Systems, vol. 4171, pp. 1–17. Springer, Heidelberg (2009)
20. Guizzardi, G., Falbo, R., Guizzardi, R.S.: Grounding Software Domain Ontologies in the Unified Foundational Ontology (UFO): The case of the ODE Software Process Ontology. http://www.inf.pucrio.br/~cibse/CIBSEPapers/artigos/artigos_IDEAS08/13_paper_58_GiancarlGuizzardi-fmra.pdf (2008)
21. Guizzardi, G., Wagner, G.: A Unified Foundational Ontology and some Applications of it in Business Modeling. http://ceur-ws.org/Vol-125/paper2.pdf
22. Guizzardi, G., Wagner, G.: Towards ontological foundations for agent modelling concepts using the unified fundational ontology (UFO). In: Bresciani, P., Giorgini, P., Henderson-Sellers, B., Low, G., Winikoff, M. (eds.) AOIS 2004. LNCS (LNAI), vol. 3508, pp. 110–124. Springer, Heidelberg (2005)
23. Guizzardi, G., Wagner, G.: Using the unified foundational ontology (UFO) as a foundation for general conceptual modeling languages. In: Poli, R., Healy, M., Kameas, A. (eds.) Theory and Applications of Ontology: Computer Applications, Chap. 8, pp. 175–196. Springer, Heidelberg (2010)
24. Hannay, J.E., Sjøberg, D.I.K., Dybå, T.: A systematic review of theory use in software engineering experiments. IEEE Trans. Softw. Eng. **33**(2), 87–107 (2007)
25. Hansson, C., Dittrich, Y., Gustafsson, B., Zarnak, S.: How agile are software development practices? J. Syst. Softw. **79**, 1295–1311 (2009)
26. Jacobson, I., Seidewitz, E.: A new software engineering. Commun. ACM **57**(12), 49–54 (2014)
27. Jacobson, I., Meyer, B., Soley, R.: Software Engineering Method and Theory (2013). http://www.semat.org
28. Jacobson, I., Spence, I., Ng, P.W.: Agile and SEMAT - perfect partners. Commun. ACM **56**(11), 53–59 (2013)
29. Kirk, D., MacDonell, S.G.: Categorising software contexts. In: Proceedings of 20th Americas Conference on Information Systems, AMCIS 2014 (2014). http://aisel.aisnet.org/amcis2014/Posters/ITProjectManagement/8/
30. Kirk, D.: A Flexible Software Process Model. Ph.D. thesis, University of Auckland, Auckland, New Zealand (2007)
31. Kirk, D., MacDonell, S.: A simulation framework to support software project (re)planning. In: Proceedings of the 35th Euromicro Conference on Software Engineering Advanced Applications (SEAA), pp. 285–292. IEEE Computer Society Press (2009)
32. Kirk, D., MacDonell, S.: A model for software contexts. In: Proceedings of the Eighth International Conference on Evaluation of Novel Approaches in Software Engineering (ENASE 2013), pp. 197–204, July 2013
33. Kirk, D., MacDonell, S., Tempero, E.: Modelling software processes - a focus on objectives. In: Proceedings of the 24th ACM SIGPLAN Conference Companion on Object Oriented Programming Systems Languages and Applications (OOPSLA), Session: Onward Short Papers Session 2, pp. 941–948. ACM Press, Orlando (2009)

34. Kirk, D., MacDonell, S.G.: Investigating a conceptual construct for software context. In: Proceedings of the Conference on Empirical Assessment in Software Engineering (EASE), no. 27 (2014)
35. Kirk, D., Tempero, E.: Proposal for a flexible software process model. In: Proceedings of the 5th International Workshop on Software Process Simulation and Modeling (ProSim 2004), Edinburgh, Scotland (2004)
36. Kirk, D., Tempero, E.: A conceptual model of the software development process. In: Proceedings of the 6th International Workshop on Software Process Simulation and Modeling (ProSim 2005), Fraunhofer IRB, St. Louis, Missouri (2005)
37. Kirk, D., Tempero, E.: A lightweight framework for describing software practices. J. Syst. Softw. 85(3), 581–594 (2012)
38. Kirk, D., Tempero, E.: Software development practices in New Zealand. In: Proceedings of the Nineteenth Asia-Pacific Software Engineering Conference (APSEC 2012), pp. 386–395, Hong Kong, December 2012
39. Kitchenham, B., Linkman, S.: Estimates, uncertainty and risk. IEEE Softw. 14(3), 69–74 (1997)
40. Kitchenham, B.A., Pfleeger, S.L., Hoaglin, D.C., El Emam, K., Rosenberg, J.: Preliminary guidelines for empirical research in software engineering. IEEE Trans. Softw. Eng. 28(8), 721–734 (2002)
41. Kruchten, P.: Contextualizing agile software development. J. Softw. Evol. Process 25(4), 351–361 (2013)
42. Lakey, P.B.: A hybrid software process simulation model for project management. In: Proceedings of the 2003 International Workshop on Software Process Simulation and Modeling (ProSim 2003), Portland, Oregan, U.S.A. (2003)
43. Lehman, M.: Process modelling - where next. In: Proceedings of the 1997 Conference on Software Engineering. IEEE Computer Society Press (1997)
44. MacCormack, A., Crandall, W., Henderson, P., Toft, P.: Do you need a new product-development strategy? Res. Technol. Manage. 55(1), 34–43 (2012)
45. MacDonell, S., Kirk, D., McLeod, L.: Raising healthy software systems. In: The 4th International ERCIM Workshop on Software Evolution and Evolvability (Evol 2008). The European Research Consortium for Informatics and Mathematics (ERCIM), L'Aquila, Italy, pp. 21–24. IEEE Computer Society Press (2008)
46. Naur, P., Randell, B.: NATO Software Engineering Conference 1968. Conference report, NATO Science Committee (1969), Report on a conference sponsored by the NATO SCIENCE COMMITTEE held in Garmisch, Germany, October 1968
47. Opdahl, A.L., Henderson-Sellers, B.: Ontological evaluation of the UML using the Bunge-Wand-Weber model. Softw. Syst. Model. 1(1), 43–67 (2002)
48. Perminova, O., Gustaffson, M., Wikstrom, K.: Defining uncertainty in projects a new perspective. Int. J. Proj. Manage. 26, 73–79 (2007)
49. Petersen, K., Wohlin, C.: A comparison of issues and advantages in agile and incremental development between state of the art and an industrial case. J. Syst. Softw. 82, 1479–1490 (2009)
50. Rao, U.S., Kestur, S., Pradhan, C.: Stochastic optimization and modeling and quantitative project management. IEEE Softw. 25, 29–36 (2008)
51. Sjøberg, D.I., Dybå, T., Anda, B.C., Hannay, J.E.: Building theories in software engineering. In: Shull, F., et al. (eds.) Guide to Advanced Empirical Software Engineering, pp. 312–336. Springer, London (2008)
52. Stol, K., Fitzgerald, B.: Uncovering theories in software engineering. In: Proceedings of the 2nd Workshop on Grand Theory in Software Engineering (GTSE 2013), Colocated with ICSE 2013, San Francisco, USA, pp. 5–14 (2013)

53. Stuckenberg, S., Heinzl, A.: The impact of the software-as-a-service concept on the underlying software and service development processes. In: Proceedings of the 2010 Pacific Asia Conference on Information Systems (PACIS 2010), pp. 1297–1308 (2010). http://aisel.aisnet.org/pacis2010/125

54. Torres, F.: Context is King; what's your software's operating range. IEEE Softw. **32**, 9–12 (2015)

55. Turner, R., Ledwith, A., Kelly, J.: Project management in small to medium-sized enterprises: matching processes to the nature of the firm. Int. J. Proj. Manage. **28**, 744–755 (2010)

56. Wand, Y., Storey, V.C., Weber, R.: An ontological analysis of the relationship construct in conceptual modeling. ACM Trans. Database Syst. **24**(4), 494–528 (1999)

57. Wieringa, R.: Requirements researchers: are we really doing research? Requirements Eng. **10**, 304–306 (2005)

58. Zachman, J.A.: Engineering the Enterprise: The Zachman Framework for Enterprise Architecture (2009). http://www.zachmaninternational.com/index.php/the-zachman-framework

Software Engineering and Applications

Specifying Business Process Outsourcing Requirements

Mouna Rekik[1,3](✉), Khouloud Boukadi[1,3], and Hanene Ben-Abdallah[2,3]

[1] Sfax University, Sfax, Tunisia
mouna.isims@gmail.com
[2] King Abdulaziz University, Jeddah, Kingdom of Saudi Arabia
[3] Mir@cl Laboratory, Sfax, Tunisia

Abstract. Outsourcing enterprises' data, business processes and applications to the Cloud is emerging as a major trend thanks to the Cloud offerings and features. Basically, enterprises expect when outsourcing to save cost, improve software and hardware performance and gain more flexibility by responding to the dynamic customers' requirements. However, adopting the Cloud as an alternative environment for the management of the business processes leads to a radical change in the enterprise IT infrastructure. Furthermore, additional challenges may appear such as data security, vendor-lock-in and labor union rendering the outsourcing decision require a deep analysis and knowledge about the business processes context. Assisting enterprises' experts in the business process outsourcing to the Cloud decision is the focus of this paper: it extends the BPMN 2.0 language to explicitly support the specification of outsourcing concepts, and it presents an automated approach to help decision makers identify those parts of their business process that benefit most from outsourcing to the Cloud. Using this extension helps also in identifying Cloud services considered as the most suitable to support the outsourced business process requirements.

Keywords: Business process outsourcing · Cloud computing · BPMN extension · Genetic algorithm

1 Introduction

Face to the increasingly stringent business competition, small and medium size enterprises strive to excel in the marketplace by adopting different strategies and solutions. Outsourcing their business processes has been among the most widely adopted strategies [20]. Business Process Outsourcing (BPO) is seen as a means to save costs, improve the business process performance and make it more flexible, etc. These advantages along with others explain the exponentially growing number of manufacturers which are outsourcing substantial parts of their supply chain processes to outside contractors [1].

In the recent years, the Cloud became the most chosen outsourcing environment. Indeed, according to the National Institute of standards and technology

© Springer International Publishing Switzerland 2016
P. Lorenz et al. (Eds.): ICSOFT 2015, CCIS 586, pp. 175–190, 2016.
DOI: 10.1007/978-3-319-30142-6_10

(NIST) [12], Cloud computing is a model for enabling convenient, on-demand network access to a shared pool of configurable computing resources that can be rapidly provisioned and released with minimal management effort or service provider interaction. It is a pay-as-you-go model providing customers with the possibility of using its various offerings and pay only for the used resources. When thinking about the suitability of BPO, business experts must address several issues to properly choose those parts of the business process to outsource. This explains the fact that enterprises decision makers spend almost 80 % of their time to decide about the suitability to outsource theur business processes [20]. Indeed, BPO affects and depends on several aspects of an enterprise: social, economic, legal, and IT (information technology) aspects. To make a judicious outsourcing decision, business experts must have a clear specification of each of these aspects; we believe that such specification should be through a set of valued criteria integrated as much as possible with the business process model. For example, it is easier to delimit the social/economic/IT effects of an outsourcing decision when the business expert has an explicit description of the personnel in charge, costs and IT requirements of each business activity. Currently available business process modeling languages, and in particular the standard BPMN [13], do not provide for most of these criteria; this is justified by the fact that these languages' primary concern is the business modeling and not the outsourcing.

To overcome this expressive power shortage, this paper proposes OutyBPMN, a lightweight BPMN extension for the specification of outsource-ability characteristics of business processes. Because our research work deals with the Cloud as an outsourcing environment, OutyBPMN extends BPMN with outsourcing concepts pertinent to the Cloud, e.g., cost as cloud may be a pertinent solution to save overhead cost, security to prevent outsourcing sensitive data, etc. In a second contribution, this paper presents an automated approach that uses OutyBPMN to identify the business process parts that benefit most from outsourcing to the Cloud. The identification is in fact a multi-objective optimization problem that can be resolved through evolutionary algorithms such as genetic algorithms, neuroevolution, genetic programming, etc. [3]. The herein presented approach applies the penalty based genetic algorithm [8] to select the activities candidate to outsourcing according to the criteria specified in OutyBPMN. Initially randomly selected activities are generated as potential solutions. According to their quality, only best ones are kept from generation to another allowing thus to keep solutions that best meet specified criteria. Using the proposed extension helps also in identifying Cloud services considered as the most suitable to support the outsourced business process requirements.

The remainder of this paper is structured as follows. Section 2 enumerates the criteria pertinent to business process outsourcing to the Cloud. Section 3 presents how OutyBPMN extends BPMN to provide for the explicit specification of these criteria. Section 4 presents the proposed solution design whose evaluation is discussed in Sect. 5. Section 6 summarizes the work status and highlights its extensions.

2   Business Process Outsourcing Criteria

BPO is the process of delegating one or more ITintensive business processes to third parties that may perform the business process more effectively and efficiently. Deciding whether to outsource ones business process is not a trivial task. To assist with the outsourcing decision making, [20] suppose that a set of potential determinants have been gathered from experts. Indeed, enterprises expect from the outsourcing to save costs, focus on core competence and gain flexibility in management. Other dimensions may urge enterprises to outsource their business processes such as speeding the time to market and improving service quality [11]. Despite these advantages, some drawbacks may prevent enterprises from outsourcing their business processes. BPO inconveniences are related to security issues, loss of management control, and vendor's service quality. In fact, cost saving is not always guaranteed owing to an inadequate business case or the inability to predict all business requirements. Moreover, security concerns, loss of control and vendor lock-in are among risks that may prohibit enterprises from outsourcing their business processes. More detailed risks are exposed in the research elaborated by [6]. A judicious outsourcing decision needs to fix a set of criteria that can help decision maker in weighing the pros and cons of each outsourcing solution. In the next sections, we provide a detailed definition for the most important set of criteria that are widely considered when outsourcing business processes to the Cloud.

2.1   Cost Saving

Almost all researchers and practitioners, agree on the fact that cost saving is the most determinant factor that attracts enterprises to outsource their related business processes. In their analysis of data collected from trade reports, [16] showed that outsourcing may yield a cost saving of 20 %. [20] argue that outsourcing is guided essentially by overhead costs; that is, parts of a business process to be outsourced are selected by ascertaining firstly how much money they may save. To calculate the cost of a business process, one should have a knowledge about expenditure of setting up, executing and monitoring each of its a tasks/activities. An activity's cost is calculated essentially by investigating on expenditure related to its enactment cost (EC) and realization cost (RC). The former corresponds to the cost necessary for achieving essential steps in the business process management life-cycle starting from its design to the monitoring of its behavior. The latter corresponds however, to the data transfer rate, transaction, or pre-payment for a period of time [17].

2.2   Focus on Core Competence

Focusing on core competencies means that enterprises are spending financial expenditure and business efforts on activities expected to bring competitive advantage. As stated by Tom Peters, an expert in the outsourcing area, an enterprise should follow the rule of "Do what you do best and outsource the rest" [18]. The activities which are typical for outsourcing are those considered as noncore. More specifically, the less strategic the activity is, the more likely it can be outsourced. In this sense, business activities can be categorized into three types according to their strategic importance, listed from most to least critical:Core competence, critical noncore and noncritical noncore. Although the general attempts when outsourcing is to delegate noncore activities/processes to external provider, some enterprises are trying to outsource also some of their related core business processes [19].

2.3 Security Concerns

When outsourcing its business processes, an enterprise should be aware about risks that may lead to undesirable outcome. Security concerns are the most prominent factor that may prohibit enterprises from outsourcing to external provider [20]. This concern is due to the fact that service providers have control over the outsourced activities including those dealing with the confidential data of costumers. This risk increases when the service provider lacks the means to encrypt data of outsourcing enterprises [6]. Moreover, the Internet-based connectivity between the outsourcing enterprise and its service provider can present vulnerabilities of unauthorized access to personal data, intrusion and hackers. To overcome this situation, an outsourcing enterprise should think to keep confidential business data or activities dealing with high level security data in premise. This way, it will be sure that vital information and data are secured and protected [14]. It is worth noting that, in spite of the existence of multitude solutions, security issues still remain a serious problem when outsourcing due to lack of trust in service providers.

2.4 Quality Improvement

Besides cost reduction, outsourcing relies on the hypothesis that the service providers are capable of performing the outsourced activities more efficiently and effectively. The satisfaction of this hypothesis presumably leads to an increased customer satisfaction [5]. Indeed, the majority of outsourcing cases are elaborated after making sure that the quality of the services provided by the external party is better compared to internal outcomes [20]. In addition, outsourcing enterprises may benefit from external expertise as the service supplier may have skills, platforms specialists and technical staff for enacting business processes; the outsourcing enterprise is often unable to provide such human resources.

3   BPMN 2.0 Extension with Outsourcing Concerns

Business processes are devoted to present the workflow of activities within enterprises. In a service oriented architecture, the business process is considered as a set of logically interrelated services. In this context each service is supposed to perform an activity [17]. Modeling a business process is considered as a means to improve the way of the business process operation. In general, the prominence of modeling processes is due to the possibility it offers for sharing knowledge between enterprise stakeholder which allows to work harmoniously towards goals [4]. Several number of process modeling languages and notations have been emerged in the aim to assist enterprises in the documentation and presentation of their processes. However, BPMN (Business Process Modeling Notation) [13] is considered as the de facto standard [15] approved by ISO/OSI [9]. BPMN is defined by OMG in order to make the understanding of business processes easier from business analysts to technical developers. Its elements can be classified into five categories: Data, Flow Objects, Connection Objects, Swimlanes and Artifacts; we refer readers to [13] for more details. BPMN2.0 introduces an extensibility mechanism for extending standard BPMN elements with additional attributes and elements to specify a specific need. The BPMN2.0 extension consists essentially on four different elements which are: Extension, ExtensionDefinition, ExtensionAttributeDefinition, and ExtensionAttributeValue. The ExtensionDefinition class defines additional attributes, however ExtensionAttributeDefinition presents the list of attributes that can be attached to any BPMN element. ExtensionAttributeValue contains attribute value. Finally the extension element imports the ExtensionDefinition and its related attributes to a BPMN model definition. Several works focus on the BPMN extension for different purposes. In fact, the extension allows to give additional comprehension for business process models. Moreover, adding new concepts to business process modeling allows to switch the way to use the BPMN from the contemplative manner to the productive one by automating the analysis of the business process or even its implementation [2]. In this context, [15] presents a new extension of BPMN to incorporate security requirements to business process diagrams. Additionally, the adding of the quality of service into the business process modeling is considered in [17]. Despite the multitude researches dealing with business process extension, there is no work which deals with the extension of BPMN for outsourcing concerns. In our elaborated extension, we propose a generic concepts that helps experts to decide the suitability of BPMN elements to be outsourced such as cost, business criticality, security and specific concepts such as the location side concept (in premise, in the cloud) and defaulting service concept as we aim to enhance the web service quality by enacting it in the Cloud environment. Furthermore, the extension specifies the business processes features requirements which enable to identify which Cloud service is most suitable for supporting the outsourced part. For instance, when enterprise decide to outsource its related databases to Cloud services, the programming language, the schema, and the database model should be compliant so the business process enactment will be held in the best circumstances. This paper adopts BPMN2.0 to support the aforementioned outsourcing concerns. Figure 1 presents the proposed class diagram corresponding to the meta model used for illustrating the outsourcing concerns. The outsourcing concerns class presents the ExtensionDefinition class containing extension attributes classes which are: Cost, BusinessCriticality, SecurityLevel and DefaultingService. Another class presenting the feature requirements is proposed specifying the hardware and software features for the business process enactment. It is straightforward to mention that the enterprise aim when outsourcing is to keep as much as possible the same programming language and the databases model so to avoid any compliancy problems.

These latter classes present the ExtensionAttributeDefinition illustrated in details in Fig. 2.

The extension proposed is intended for adding new concepts to the activity element as our aim is to identify then which activities are the most suitable for outsourcing. The activity is the generic term for work that enterprise performs. Table 1 presents the graphical representation of the extensions over activity element and their corresponding description. Only information about location side (in premise/in cloud) are designed to be on the pool element. In fact, we aim to group activities selected to be outsourced into one BPMN element which is the pool. The implementation of the proposal is done using Eclipse Modeler as a tool.

4   Outsourced Activity Identification

Our work aims to find a good solution corresponding to the appropriate set of activities suitable for outsourcing respecting the enterprise experts preferences. These latter are specified in OutyBPMN. Our solution search adopts penalty based genetic algorithm. In this section, we first present the problem model. Secondly, we present our algorithm for the identification of activities to be outsourced. A report on the algorithm performance is presented in Sect. 5.

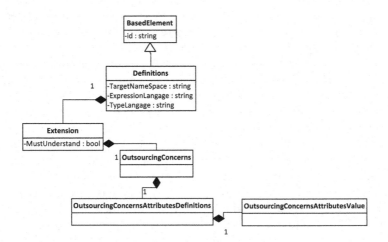

Fig. 1. Outsourcing concerns extension metamodel [13].

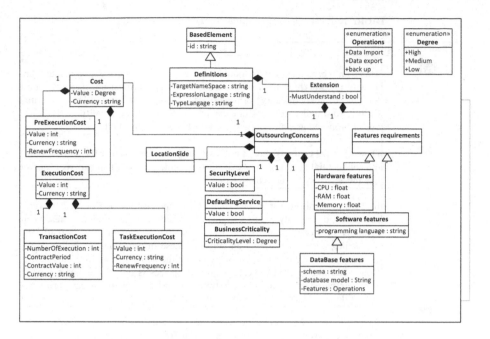

Fig. 2. OutyBPMN metamodel: BPMN2.0 extensions with outsourcing concerns.

4.1   Problem Formulation

The input to our search algorithm is an OutyBPMN model identifying in particular, the following activities:

- Expensive when executed in premise compared to when executed in the cloud;
- Noncore;
- Handling and processing non sensitive data;
- Presenting a defaulting behavior when executed as a service within the enterprise.

To look for an optimal set of activities best outsourced, we will use the following problem formulation:

1. $A = \{A_1, A_2, A_3, ..., A_n\}$ is a set of activities composing the business process.
2. The weights for outsourcing concerns, W_1, W_2, W_3 and W_4 for Cost (C), Business Criticality (BC), Defaulting Service (DS), and the number of activities composing the solution (L) respectively.

$$\sum_{k=1}^{4} W_k = 1 \tag{1}$$

3. $S = \{S_1, S_2, S_3, ..., S_n\}$ is a set of security constraints imposed on data handled by corresponding activities.

Table 1. Extensions graphics for BPMN elements.

Graphical extension	Description
	This icon means that experts should precise the business criticality, namely the activity is core {high level of business criticality}, critical noncore {medium level of business criticality} or noncritical noncore {low level of business criticality}. To simplify for users, one can precise the level of criticality by choosing one of proposed graphics presented in the last row of this table.
	IT and business experts should collaborate to identify whether the activity handle confidential data or not. The security graphic is used when experts observe that the activity proceed sensitive data .
$	In the context of this paper, IT experts should precise the cost of the hardware supporting the activity. More specifically, experts should be able to present in detail required expenditure of hardware maintenance, monthly bills, and all corresponding costs for realizing an activity. These information will help next to compare between financial cost of executing the activity in premise and in the cloud. Techniques used for calculating two prices is out of this paper scope. However, based on the difference between two prices, experts can categorize the cost of doing the activity internal {high,medium,low}.
	As previously said, among potential determinants urging enterprises to outsource their business processes, is the need to improve service quality. As we focus on business processes running within Small and Medium Enterprises (SME) that lack sufficient IT expertise, cost and required determinants for well realizing their business processes, we decide to choose defaulting services most suitable for outsourcing. Defaulting services are those have leading to the degradation of the business process performance, more specifically, those preventing business processes from attaining their goals. Discovering defaulting services is done in our previous work. We use "defaulting service" term and "activities presenting a default behavior when executed as service" interchangeably to refer the same thing.
	Whenever the algorithm of selecting appropriate activities to be outsourced is done, experts should analyze results and precise on each activity its location side {in premise, in the cloud}.
	IT developers are supposed to indicate to indicate the programming language of business processes fractions whenever they notice the importance of this information.
	These graphics help experts to specify level of importance of the extended elements (business criticality, security, and cost). They refer respectively to, high , medium and low level.

Our aim is to give a set A' of activities that are most suitable for outsourcing where A'⊂ A. We should notice all the process may merit to be outsourced which make A' = P where P is the entire business process although it is not a preferable case. A' is selected according to the fitness function (4).

We convert the optimization problem from a multi-objective to single objective one by assigning weights to each objective function composing the function (2).

$$\text{Max } F' = W_1 * F_1'(A') + W_2 * F_2'(A') + W_3 * F_3'(A') + W_4 * F_4'(A') \quad (2)$$

where

- $F_1'(A') = \frac{\sum_{i=1}^{N} C(a_i)}{N}$
- $F_2'(A') = \frac{\sum_{i=1}^{N} BC(a_i)}{N}$
- $F_3'(A') = \frac{\sum_{i=1}^{N} DS(a_i)}{N}$

$$F_4'(A') = \begin{cases} 1 + (\frac{(N-N')}{(N'-1)}) & if\ 1 < N < N' \\ 1 - (\frac{(N-N')}{(L(P)-N')}) & if\ N' < N < L(P) \end{cases} \quad (3)$$

- a_i is an activity that belongs to A'.
- N is the number of activities composing the solution A'.
- N' is the preferred length of the solution A'. This metric is added to F_4' to prevent foster solutions having greater number of activities. The value of this metric is automatically calculated by counting the number of activities having a defaulting behavior when executed as services and not dealing with sensitive data.
- L(P) is the number of activities composing the process.

4.2   Implementation of Genetic Algorithm to Select Suitable Activities for Outsourcing

Genetic algorithms (GAs) [6] are evolutionary algorithms. Their main idea is to simulate the evolution of population composed of diversified individuals. These individuals are subject to operations such as recombination and mutation allowing thus, by selecting best individuals, to enhance the population quality. Choosing to work with GA is due to the fact that it allows to find solutions which best meet different criteria. The genetic algorithm presents solutions as individuals in a population that varies each time its quality is enhanced. The individuals composing a population vary when undergoing a set of operations such as crossover and mutation. Their quality is evaluated using a fitness function.

Individuals Encoding. To find out suitable solutions for the optimization problem, appropriate encoding of individuals is necessary. First of all, we should note that individuals composing a population have variable lengths. Each gene, composing an individual, corresponds to an integer referring an activity that belongs to the business process. Figure 3 presents examples of individuals encoding.

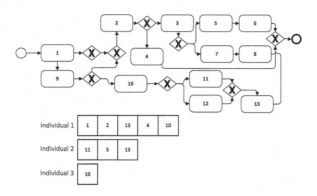

Fig. 3. Individuals encoding.

Infeasible Solutions. In our research case, some solutions are infeasible as they violate security constraint. An individual may be composed of one or more activities handling sensitive data, we consider each activity dealing with sensitive data as a constraint violation.

Crossover and Mutation. We apply in our proposal the crossover and the mutation operations. We adopt the classical one-point crossover to generate each time two offsprings. Concerning the mutation operator, we have use it in three different ways:it can select randomly a position in the individual and replace it by another activity, add an activity, or delete existing one. An additional control should be done in this level to prevent repeating the same activity within an individual.

Fitness Function. An individual composed of activities requiring securing their data is considered as infeasible. To guaranty that GA reaches an optimal or near-optimal solution, these infeasible individuals should be kept as their presence is essential in the building of solutions. Thus, the idea is to give a penalty to fitness values relative to infeasible solutions. This leads to lower fitness values compared to those corresponding to feasible solutions. Moreover, infeasible solutions having more activities requiring security are more harshly penalized. This process helps to reenforce the presence of feasible solutions and the disappearance of the infeasible ones from generation to another. The Eq. (4) presents the definition of the fitness function.

$$\text{Fitness(X)} = \begin{cases} F' * 0,5 + 0,5 & \text{if} \quad v(X) = 0 \\ F' * 0,5 - (0,1 * v(X)/v_{max}) & \text{otherwise} \end{cases} \quad (4)$$

F' is the objective function presented in Sect. 4, $v(X)$ presents the total number of activities composing an individual requiring security, and v_{max} stands for the total number of activities requiring security in the entire business process. The presented fitness guaranties that infeasible solutions have always less fitness values compared to feasible ones.

5   Experiment and Result

We applied the penalty based genetic algorithm using Java as a development language. Simulations were conducted on a laptop computer with 2.5 GHz Intel Core i7 CPU and 4 GB RAM.

The business process illustrated in Fig. 4 presents an example of a case study that we analyzed. As shown, the business process is composed of 13 activities. The suitable activities appropriate for outsourcing is unknown rendering the research space huge despite that experts define the preferred number of activities to be outsourced. Preferred number of activities to be outsourced in this example is 4 (the number of activities presenting defaulting behavior when executed as services and not requiring security constraints). As shown, three activities require high level of security which are: 2, 4, and 7. Individuals encompassing one or more of these three activities are penalized but they still present solutions of our problem. The evaluation of our penalty based GA is twofold: we evaluated firstly the performance of our genetic algorithm and then we verified the pertinence of the results. A comparison between our algorithm and a greedy algorithm was also elaborated in terms of performance and the pertinence of results.

5.1   Experiment A

Table 2 presents parameters values we used to experiment our algorithm. We evaluate the validity of our penalty based genetic algorithm by comparing its time cost in different computing scale. We begin by observing the execution time consumed by our algorithm when increasing the number of constraints. Figure 5 shows that the number of constraints influences the execution time of the algorithm which can be explained by the additional number of treatment to be

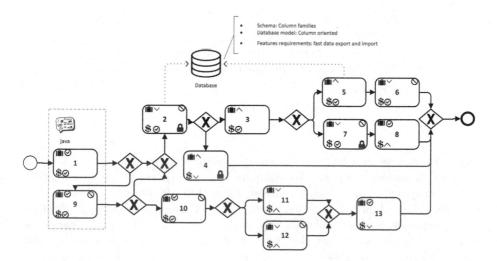

Fig. 4. The business process used for the evaluation of the proposed GA.

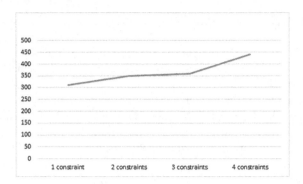

Fig. 5. The execution time consumed when increasing the number of constraints.

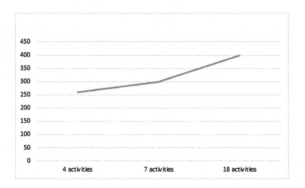

Fig. 6. The execution time consumed when increasing the number of activities.

Table 2. Parameters used for our penalty based genetic algorithm.

Parameters	Description
Population size	50
Selection technique	Tournament selection
Termination condition	Number of generation = 100
Crossover probability	0.5
Mutation probability	0.015

done. The number of activities composing a business process increases the time of execution as shown in Fig. 6. We compared our genetic algorithm with another optimization algorithm namely the greedy algorithm [10]. Greedy algorithms are known by their ability to find quickly solutions. Generally, generated solutions are approximate, and optimal ones are founded in few cases. The comparison was done by testing the execution time of both algorithms when applied to different number of business processes. As shown in Fig. 7, the GA consumed a bit more time to generate results compared to greedy algorithms.

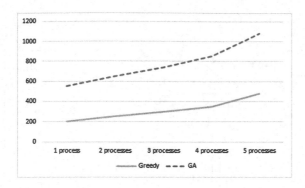

Fig. 7. Comparison between the execution time consumed corresponding to both algorithms.

5.2   Experiment B

To evaluate the pertinence of our algorithm, we interviewed 5 business experts having knowledge on business processes. We first asked experts to rank the outsourcing concerns according to their preferences, the results of this interview are shown in Table 3. According to the experts preferences, we attributes to the weights explained in Sect. 4.1, the following values: $W1 = 0.4$ for (BC), $W2 = 0.25$ for (DS), $W3 = 0.25$ for (C) and $W4 = 0.1$ for (L).

Table 3. Ranks of outsourcing concerns according to experts.

Rank	Outsourcing Concern (OC)	% experts how select the corresponding OC
1	BC	100 %
2	DS & C	60 %
3	L	100 %

Table 4. Evaluation of our GA.

Precision of GA	Recall of GA	Precision of greedy	Recall of greedy
100 %	66 %	33 %	33 %

The extended BPMN illustrated in Fig. 4 is presented to the same experts to depict, according to them, the most appropriate activities to be outsourced. Among the thirteen activities, four experts chose the activities 12 and 6 and one expert select in addition to these activities, the activity 11. When we applied the GA, the individual having the best quality according to its fitness is composed of

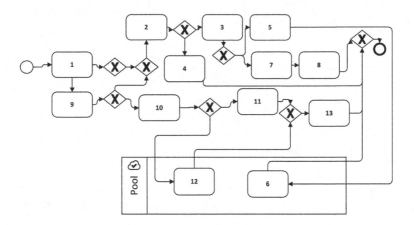

Fig. 8. BPMN with deployment location data.

two activities: {6,12} where fitness = 0.8437. The greedy algorithm generated an individual composed of 3 activities {12,9,1}. Table 4 presents the precision and recall of our penalty-based genetic algorithm and the same values corresponding to greedy algorithm. As shown in above table, the GA has a high value of recall and precision which make it a relevant and pertinent way to assist experts in the decision of business process outsourcing. Moreover, despite that the greedy algorithm take less time to generate results, our GA generate better results if we refer to the comparison of the recall and precision of the two algorithms. According to experiments, we can affirm that the proposed genetic algorithm is a pertinent way to decide about the business process activities to be outsourced. However, in term of performance and more specifically the response time, the genetic algorithm may not be the most suitable one.

In the context of our research, when applying the GA on the business process, the BPMN should be redesigned so that, activities selected to be outsourced are putted within a pool element designed to be entirely in the cloud as presented in Fig. 8. The next step consists on the selection of the most suitable cloud offering that well support the business process execution. Regarding the huge number of cloud services and models, the proposed extension and more specifically the features requirements, contributes to the filtration of the Cloud offerings that are not suitable for the outsourced business process part. In the example illustrated in Fig. 4, referring to the features requirements of the presented database, the Amazon's simpleDB [7] cannot be a suitable Cloud offering. This is due to the fact that the Amazon's simpleDB offers different schema and database model from the business process' database requirements.

6   Conclusions

This paper presents a method to assist experts in the fastidious task of BPO to the cloud decision. The method offers a modeling language, OutyBPMN, an extension of the BPMN to take into consideration the outsourcing criteria. In addition it uses a penalty based genetic algorithm to identify most appropriate activities of a business process to be outsourced. In the herein presented work, activity appropriateness is determined based on its business criticality, cost, its quality when executed and constrained by security level of handled data. Based on our preliminary experimental results, the proposed penalty based genetic algorithm generates satisfactory results. Indeed, the evaluation of the method presents its accuracy and the similarity with experts preferences. We are elaborating a deployment model for the execution of the business process when part of it is located in the cloud. Moreover, we are working on defining a decision model to weight the importance of outsourcing the selected pool against keeping it in premise. Additional experimental evaluations are needed to adjust the fitness function and its related parameters to thoroughly examine the performance of the proposed algorithm.

References

1. Adesta, E., Agusman, D.: The evolution of supply-chain management into extended enterprise. In: Proceedings of the 2004 IEEE International Conference on Engineering Management, vol. 3, pp. 1298–1302 (2004)
2. Bocciarelli, P., D'Ambrogio, A.: A BPMN extension for modeling non functional properties of business processes. In: Proceedings of the 2011 Symposium on Theory of Modeling & Simulation: DEVS Integrative M & S Symposium, TMS-DEVS 2011, pp. 160–168. Society for Computer Simulation International, San Diego (2011)
3. Deb, K., Kalyanmoy, D.: Multi-Objective Optimization Using Evolutionary Algorithms. Wiley, New York (2001)
4. Eriksson, H.-E., Penker, M.: Business Patterns at Work, 1st edn. Wiley, New York (1998)
5. Gewald, H., Dibbern, J.: Risks and benefits of business process outsourcing: a study of transaction services in the German banking industry. Inf. Manag. **46**(4), 249–257 (2009)
6. Gewald, H., Rouse, A.: Comparing business process and IT outsourcing risks–an exploratory study in Germany and Australasia. In: 2012 45th Hawaii International Conference on System Science (HICSS), pp. 275–284 (2012)
7. Ramanathan, S., Goel, S., Alagumalai, S.: Comparison of cloud database: Amazon's SimpleDB and Google's bigtable. In: 2011 International Conference on Recent Trends in Information Systems (ReTIS), pp. 165–168 (2011)
8. Hu, Y.-B., Wang, Y.-P., Guo, F.-Y.: A new penalty based genetic algorithm for constrained optimization problems. In: Proceedings of the 2005 International Conference on Machine Learning and Cybernetics, 2005, vol. 5, pp. 3025–3029 (2005)
9. ISO 10303-203:1994: Information technology – object management group business process model and notation (1994)
10. Kodaganallur, V., Sen, A.: Greedy by chance - stochastic greedy algorithms. In: 2010 Sixth International Conference on Autonomic and Autonomous Systems (ICAS), pp. 182–187 (2010)
11. Li, H., Meissner, J.: Improving quality in business process outsourcing through technology. Working Papers MRG/0009, Department of Management Science, Lancaster University (2009)

12. Mell, P.M., Grance, T.: Sp 800-145. the nist definition of cloud computing. Technical report, Gaithersburg, MD, United States (2011)
13. (OMG), O. M. G.: Business process model and notation (bpmn) version 2.0. Technical report (2011)
14. Pathak, R., Joshi, S.: Secured communication for business process outsourcing using optimized arithmetic cryptography protocol based on virtual parties. In: Ranka, S., Aluru, S., Buyya, R., Chung, Y.-C., Dua, S., Grama, A., Gupta, S.K.S., Kumar, R., Phoha, V.V. (eds.) IC3 2009. CCIS, vol. 40, pp. 205–215. Springer, Heidelberg (2009)
15. Rodríguez, A., Fernández-Medina, E., Piattini, M.: A BPMN extension for the modeling of security requirements in business processes. IEICE - Trans. Inf. Syst. **E90–D**(4), 745–752 (2007)
16. Rouse, A.C., Corbitt, B.J.: It-supported business process outsourcing (BPO): the good, the bad and the ugly. In: PACIS, p. 126. AISeL (2004)
17. Saeedi, K., Zhao, L., Sampaio, P.: Extending BPMN for supporting customer-facing service quality requirements. In: 2010 IEEE International Conference on Web Services (ICWS), pp. 616–623 (2010)
18. Soiva, J.: Business process outsourcing case study: how to develp Deloitte S2G's shared service activities in the Bercelona costumer response centre. PhD thesis, Lahti university of applied sciences (2007)
19. Lynn, T., Carroll, N.O., Mooney, J., Helfert, M., Corcoran, D., Hunt, G., Van Der Werff, L., Morrison, J., Healy, P.: Towards a framework for defining and categorising business Process-As-A-Service (BPaaS). In: 21st International Product Development Management Conference. Citations: Not Avail. (2014)
20. Yang, D.-H., Kim, S., Nam, C., Min, J.-W.: Developing a decision model for business process outsourcing. Comput. Oper. Res. **34**(12), 3769–3778 (2007). Operations Research and Outsourcing

Supporting Deviations on Software Processes: A Literature Overview

Manel Smatti[1]([✉]), Mourad Oussalah[2], and Mohamed Ahmed Nacer[1]

[1] LSI-USTHB, BP 32-Bab Ezzouar, Algiers, Algeria
manel.smatti@univ-nantes.fr, anacer@mail.cerist.dz
[2] LINA-Universite de Nantes, CNRS UMR 6241, 2 Rue de la Houssiniere BP 92208, 44322 Nantes, France
mourad.smatti@univ-nantes.fr

Abstract. Software Process (SP) models are the results of the efforts deployed by the software Engineering community to guarantee an advanced level of the SP quality. However, experience has shown that SP agents often deviate from these models to cope with new environments' challenges. Unfortunately, the appearance of such situations, if not controlled, often lead to the process failure. Since the 90s, several research works have been conducted to handle this problem. Through this paper, we aim at gathering these approaches around a single classification that puts in advance their strengths and their weaknesses. To achieve this goal, we propose two classification frameworks that highlight how existing approaches deal with deviations from two different axes: detection and correction. As a result of this classification, a covering graph is drawn for each framework, which gives an insight about what has been left by the existing approaches and worth to be considered, further. Finally, we introduce briefly the general outlines of a new contribution that we are currently working on to face the shortcomings of the existing approaches.

1 Introduction

PSEEs (Process-centered Software Engineering Environment) [1] are special environments dedicated to support (large) software development projects that are conducted through a set of steps that define their *processes*. The goal of proposing such environments is to assess software agents through the development steps in order to achieve the desired quality within the final products. Moreover, as they are often endowed of the process model description using a Process Modeling Language (PML) [2], and in ideal situation a clear view of what is carried out in real world, PSEEs play an important role in process understanding, training, when hiring new engineers, and even organization strategies improvement, they are the core of any software development process [3].

Because of their significant importance, PSEEs have gotten a great interest within the software engineering field. Many prototypes have been proposed to cater for all the needs of software development projects by offering means to

© Springer International Publishing Switzerland 2016
P. Lorenz et al. (Eds.): ICSOFT 2015, CCIS 586, pp. 191–209, 2016.
DOI: 10.1007/978-3-319-30142-6_11

model processes and enacting them, but the lack of flexibility, to cope with unforeseen situations, within these environments has led to their failure in being widely adopted within industry.

Deviations on Software Processes (SP) are known as unexpected situations that could arise during software development projects. They are either actions that violate the SP model constraints or those performed out of the control of the PSEE. In both cases, the PSEE becomes unable to support the software development and useless, though.

Many solutions have been proposed to address this issue that is related to the evolution aspect of software processes [4,5]. Most approaches deal with deviations at two different levels: (1) how to detect them, at a first time and (2) how to cope with them. Several methods have been used to address the first point like logic formulas evaluation [6–8] and algebraic-based analysis [9]. On the other hand, correcting the occurred deviations has not been much considered except of some proposals that aim at changing the process model so it could further support the software development as done in [4] or the reconciliation approach adopted in [8].

Through this paper, we aim at offering an original analysis of most approaches that have addressed the problem of deviations on software processes. Our main goal is to have a suitable classification that highlights a set of important features we believe they should be considered when choosing an existing approach or proposing a new one. Such classification would be very useful to have a clear insight on what has been achieved so far and what has been left and worth to be considered by future works. Although we have looked over several studies that have considered the problem of deviations within different kinds of processes, we will focus through this paper on studying the most *representative* approaches that have *explicitly* considered this issue in the context of software processes.

The paper is structured as follows. Section 2 gives a general overview of deviations on software processes, the deviation concept is introduced as well as the motivations that have raised the interest devoted to this research area. In Sect. 3, we focus on how deviations are detected within the existing approaches. The comparison framework we have elaborated at this aim is introduced after defining each item belonging to the set of criteria we have selected for this purpose. Another comparison framework is given in Sect. 4. Unlike the first one, this second framework is concerned with solutions proposed to correct deviations. This framework is also built around a set of criteria we define. Section 5 discusses the results achieved within both frameworks. A covering graph is elaborated for each classification framework in order to get a clear insight about what criteria have been covered/ignored by each approach. Through Sect. 6, we introduce the general outlines of a new contribution that we are currently working on to overcome some shortcomings of the existing approaches. Section 7 concludes the paper.

2   Deviations on Software Processes

2.1   Deviation Concept

A deviation is an action that violates the process model constraints. It is the difference between what is expected and what is carried out in real world.

In [7], a consistency relationship, which describes an ideal SP enactment, has been defined based on the interactions between SP agents and the PSEE. Thus, deviations have been defined as actions that break this consistency relationship.

When a deviation occurs, the PSEE becomes unable to support SP agents through the development steps. The state resulting from such situation is called *inconsistency* [7]. Such situations are very likely to arise within any software development project. Moreover, experience has shown that the appearance of such situations is not an exception [10] because SP agents have often to deviate from the software process model. Thus, deviations are unescapable situations that need to be considered from the beginning of the software development process.

2.2 Motivation

The huge software applications that companies claim nowadays have increased the interest devoted to the software process area. This interest results in many contributions especially in SP modeling and SP enactment fields [11]. The SP modeling field has reached an advanced level thanks to the wide panoply of PMLs that have been proposed [2]. Furthermore, the proposition of the standard SPEM [12] by the OMG has facilitated the integration of such formalisms within industry. Whereas, most PSEEs have failed to gain such success because of multiple reasons, among them:

- PSEEs are built around SP models that are very rigid while SP agents are requiring more and more flexibility to be able to act using their skills and their previous experiences;
- New ways of development, like agile methods, are based on customers' implication within all of the software development steps. Thus, final requirements are often changed or modified during the software development life cycle, which often leads to deviate from the SP model in order to cope with these changes;
- Organizations often change their structures and their strategies within (large-scale) software development. New people are engaged while others left, new tools are integrated and much certifications are required. All these are important factors that need to be considered within software processes and their dedicated supports;
- Competition within software development companies to gain international markets is based on two important factors: time and cost of software development. Thus, having special environments that are able to support SP agents in a controlled fashion has become very challengeable.

3 Detecting Deviations

The most important research works that have been led during the last twenty years to deal with deviations on software processes are considered through this paper. These approaches are classified and discussed through a set of criteria we have selected.

At a first time, we start by classifying the addressed approaches based on how they proceed to detect the encountered deviations. To achieve this goal, we project each solution on the set of criteria designed for this purpose. We define within the next subsection each criterion, its role and the values it could have.

3.1 Criteria

1. **Deviation Object:** We believe that it is very important to have information about the responsible element for the deviation occurrence. Based on the SPEM conceptual meta-model [13], the deviation object could be the *activity*, SP agent through his *role* or the *artefacts* consumed and/or generated within a software process activity. Getting a clear insight about the identity of this element would make the correction much easier.

2. **Deviation Type:** Based on their causes/consequences, several kinds of deviations could be distinguished. Even if there is no standard classification, most approaches have been built around a precise set of deviations they define. Through the classification framework we have elaborated (Sect. 3.2), we will highlight the most relevant deviation classes by enumerating the different types that have been proposed by the existing approaches.

3. **Deviation Cause:** Enumerating the possible causes makes the analysis much easier and the solution much effective. Based on the existing approaches, deviations may occur because of different reasons. Depending on the nature/size of the process, the chosen process model and the SP agents skills, a deviation may occur because of:
   - A bad choice of the process model;
   - Misunderstanding of customers needs or misallocation of resources;
   - Wrong execution of activities or a bad sequencing;
   - etc.

4. **Deviation Moment:** Most approaches define deviations as a problem related to SP enactment and/or SP evolution. In fact, most deviations are detected while the process is enacting but they are not all the reason of an execution problem. Deviations could be *static*, which means that they are related to the SP specification and that the problem has been encountered within the software process model before any deployment. Deviations may also occur during deployment due to a misunderstanding of the SP model constraints or even because of a bad assignment of roles.

5. **Detection Process:** Detecting the occurred deviations within software processes falls into finding mechanisms to analyze and evaluate the software process along all its steps. Based on the chosen process model, the PML used to describe it and the tools integrated within the PSEE, several methods have been implemented for this purpose. For instance, visualization-based method and evaluation of first order logic formulas are two options that have been widely adopted by the existing approaches.

6. **Automation Level:** PSEEs are supposed to support SP agents to achieve the desired quality within the final products. The automation level offered

by these environments play a key role in the success of any software development project. Thus, the ability of the PSEE to detect incorrect actions or transitions without human intervention is very important. In spite of the great number of prototypes that have been designed to support deviations on software processes, we have noticed that detecting such situations still require human intervention in most cases. As a result, the detection operation is often *semi-automatic* or *manual*.

7. **Execution Environment:** A software process could be enacted either within a *mono machine* environment or a *distributed* one. Moreover, some recent research works are focusing on finding out solutions to easily integrate nomadic users within software development projects. Thus, proposing a support for deviations, or for any other problem encountered within the software engineering field, requires a good estimate of the runtime environment. It is obvious that the larger is the environment, the more difficult is the solution to implement.

3.2   Classification Framework

Deviations have been considered by researchers from the beginning of the 90s. Since that, several approaches have been proposed to address this problem within the different kinds of processes. The most relevant approaches are listed in Table 1. To select the appropriate papers, our work was partially inspired from the methodology followed in [11] when performing a systematic review. The papers related to our study have been selected based on a rigorous search using one of the three words: deviation, inconsistency, evolution conjointly with the software process expression. Searchers were performed on the most known digital libraries such: IEEE Digital Library, Springer and ACM Digital Library. As

Table 1. Approaches dealing with deviations.

	Year		
	1990–2000	2000–2010	2010–Today
Proposed Approach	Bandinelli et al. [4]	Thompson et al. [14]	Yong & Zhou [15]
	Cugola et al. [6]	Yang et al. [9]	Almeida da Silva et al. [8]
	Bolcer & Taylor [16]	Egyed et al. [17]	Cugola et al. [18]
	Dami et al. [19]	Kabbaj et al. [7]	Ge et al. [20]
			Bendraou et al. [21]
			Zhang et al. [22]
			Hull et al. [23]
			Rangiha & Karakostas [24]

a second step, papers that have not treated the studied issue as a main subject, but have just given an insight about it, have been discarded.

Moreover, As we are interested to the Software Process area, and to not have a cluttered tables and graphs, we consider through this study only the most representative approaches that have been proposed within this field.

We start within this section by classifying the selected approaches based on how they proceed to detect deviations on software processes. Each solution is projected on the aforementioned set of criteria. The results obtained from this classification are presented in Table 2. Some of the values listed in this table have been *explicitly* extracted from their sources while others constitute the outcome of the analysis we have performed on each of the selected works.

Table 2. Classification framework for detecting deviations on SP.

	Deviation object	Deviation type	Deviation causes	Deviation moment	Detection process	Automation level	Execution environment
[4]	-Activity	-Static	-Changing in requirements	-Execution	Ad-hoc analysis	Manual	Mono machine
		-Dynamic	-Changing in the environ-ment/organization				
[6]	-Role	-Environment level	Violation of activities' constraints	Deployment	Evaluation of logic formulas	Semi-automatic	Mono machine
		-Domain level					
[14]	-Activity	**None**	A predefined set of seven causes	-Deployment	Evaluation of SQL queries	Semi-automatic	Mono machine
	-Role		-Execution				
[7]	-Activity	-Environment level	-Violation of activities' constraints	Execution	Evaluation of logic formulas	Automatic	Mono machine
	-Role	-Domain level	-Misallocation of roles				
[8]	-Activity	**None**	-Sequencing	Execution	Evaluation of logic formulas	Automatic	Mono machine
[21]	-Activity	-Organizational	-Activities' sequencing	-Deployment	Comparing the execution trace to a prede-fined set of rules	Automatic	Distributed
	-Artefact	-Behavioral	-Violation of methodologi-cal guidelines	-Execution			
		-Structural					

Discussion. As we have mentioned before, the problem of deviations on SP enactment is not recent. SPADE [4] and SENTINEL [6] are the most known approaches that have dealt with this issue. Based on the SLANG and LATIN languages respectively, these two prototypes have been the basis of all the approaches that have been proposed later. Although they have reached an advanced level, especially after the proposition of their successors SPADE-1 [25] and PROSYT [26] respectively, these prototypes have failed in being adopted within industry because of multiple reasons such as the complexity of the languages used to conceive them and the lack of flexibility within SPADE that does not support deviations until the process model is changed. Moreover, the wide panoply of PMLs that have been proposed in addition of the proposition of SPEM has led to consider new features to model software processes and enacting them.

On the other hand, recent approaches take advantage from what has been achieved within the software engineering field and its dedicated tools and languages. For instance, [7] propose to support deviations within software processes described as a UML profile. Authors use XMI (XML Metadata Interchange) to automatically generate first order logic formulas from the UML description of the SP model. The analysis performed upon the obtained formulas enable authors to easily detect the occurred deviations.

4 Correcting Deviations

Detecting the unexpected situations that could arise during a given software development project is very important but the most important is to be able to handle them. Among all the approaches considered within this study, few have proposed a *correction* plan to fix the occurred deviations. Through this section, correction mechanisms that have been adopted by the covered approaches are highlighted. First, we start by enumerating some motivations that have incited to propose these correction plans. Then, we provide a brief definition of the possible solutions that have been widely adopted to deal with deviations on software processes. Finally, as done for the detection aspect, a classification framework is elaborated after defining each item belonging to the selected set of criteria.

4.1 Motivation

Offering a suitable development environment that meets all the SP agents requirements, including flexibility, still remains a big challenge within the Software Engineering field.

Deviations are very likely to occur within any software development project. At each moment, SP agents may decide not to follow the software process model because they think they are able to accomplish things better than as described within the SP model. Thus, they decide to act based on their skills or on their previous experiences. Such deviations, even if they are performed with a good faith, could be the main reason of any software project failure. Offering a good support for software processes results in:

– Considering the SP model as a plan that is supposed to guide SP agents to achieve the final goals without imposing a specific manner;
– Offering a suitable tool that brings together all the SP modeling benefits and the required flexibility within a single environment;

– Obtaining a *complete* environment that could be easily integrated into industry.

4.2   Correction Plans

After detecting the occurred deviations, three possible solutions have been distinguished in [27], these solutions have been adopted by all the approaches that have been proposed later:

1. **Nothing to Do:** In this case, deviations are detected but ignored. The software project is pursued without correcting deviations consequences. The PSEE has an erroneous view of what is carried out in real world and becomes useless, though.
2. **Changing the Model:** The process model is changed to meet the new requirements that have led to the triggered deviation. This solution is very costly and may generate other problems especially if there are several running instances of that model. In addition, a deviation may occur temporarily and does not require changing the entire SP model.
3. **Tolerating the Deviation:** In this case, the SP model is not changed but mechanisms are integrated within the PSEE to *tolerate* deviations under its control. Moreover, the PSEE supports SP agents to reconcile the *observed* process (the observed process is the partial view, of what is carried out in real world, owned by the PSEE [7,27], the expression *Process definition enactment* has been used in [9,27] to indicate the same view) with the process model (the planned process in [28]).

Unlike Sect. 3 where we have focused on the problem itself. Through this section, we will be dealing with deviations from a solution perspective. To be on the same wavelength, we start within the next subsection by defining each item belonging to the chosen set of criteria. Approaches that have proposed a correction plan are then discussed according to these criteria.

4.3   Criteria

1. **Correction Object:** A deviation is always caused within one (or more) of the SP elements: *activity*, *role* or *product*. As well, the correction step is applied within one, or more, of these items. It could be the same that has caused the deviation or another one. For instance, the deviation may be detected within an output product while the correction is applied within the activity that has produced it.
2. **Correction Type:** Based upon the correction plans we have explained above. SP managers may decide even to change the model to cope with the triggered deviations or to change just the running instance within which the deviation has occurred. Thus, we are talking about *static* and *dynamic* changes, respectively. We consider the first kind of corrections as *preventive correction* while the second as *curative correction*.

3. **Correction Reason:** While interested to deviations on software processes, most researchers have focused their studies on how to detect these deviations and how to correct their consequences. We believe that holding this problem may have more benefits than just correction. For instance, the implementation of a given correction could have a *perfective* effect by improving the process functionalities. Moreover, such correction may improve the reusability of SP models by offering reusable configurations.

4. **Correction Process:** When deviations occur, SP agents/managers may choose multiple options while performing their correction plans. For instance, changing the component (activity, role or product) parameters could be very useful to reconcile the enacting process with the process model. The problem may also be solved by applying a set of transformations or even by changing the component by another one to add new concepts while keeping the old ones (inheritance concept).

5. **Correction Moment:** To correct a given deviation, changes could be applied to the process specification, while deployment or even during the process enactment. Thus, the deviation is not necessarily corrected at the *same* moment where it has been detected. For instance, the deviation may be detected at enactment time while changes are applied to the process specification (process model) to correct it or to avoid it in future time.

6. **Automation Level:** As for the detection process, correcting the occurred deviations may be done *manually* by SP agents. In best cases, the correction is *automatic* if it is entirely done by the PSEE without any human intervention. However, based on what has been achieved by former research works, this is almost impossible. Thus, a suitable correction always involves both the PSEE and SP agents (semi-automatic).

7. **Execution Environment:** Through the different approaches that have been proposed in the literature, we have noticed that the solution, when proposed, is not always applicable at the same level within which the process is conducted. Therefore, the process may be led trough a distributed environment while the deviation support is implemented in a *mono machine* environment.

4.4 Classification Framework

The approaches that have proposed a correction policy are considered in this section. As mentioned before, we are interested at those approaches that have *explicitly* proposed a correction plan within the context of software processes. These approaches are classified according to the set of criteria listed above. The results obtained from this classification are summarized in Table 3.

Discussion. As we can notice from this classification, in spite of the great number of contributions that have addressed the problem of deviations on software processes, just few of them have been interested at proposing correction mechanisms. The others have been much concerned with studying the problem itself than finding out solutions for it. The results are several classifications and prototypes that aim at detecting those deviations.

Table 3. Classification framework for correcting deviations on SP.

	Correction object	Correction type	Correction reason	Correction moment	Correction process	Automation level	Execution environment
SPADE [4,5]	All SP elements	Static	Perfective	Specification	Transformation	Manual	Mono machine
SENTINEL [6]	All SP elements	-Static	-Perfective	-Specification	Transformation	Semi-automatic	Mono machine
		-Dynamic	-Corrective	-Execution			
Almeida Da Silva et al. [8]	All SP elements	Dynamic	Corrective	Execution	Restructuring	Semi-automatic	Mono machine

Through this section, we have highlighted those approaches that aim at proposing some policies to correct deviations. Approaches like [28] have been discarded from this classification because they do not propose an *explicit* solution except pieces of advice authors give to help SP managers finding out some resolutions that are supposed to fix the occurred deviations once applied.

Almost all approaches that have proposed correction mechanisms have been validated on simple prototypes within *mono machine* environments. Some authors have focused on studying the problem of deviations within distributed environments as done in [21] but, as we have already mentioned, they have been much concerned with the problem than the solution.

5   Results and Discussion

Within the previous sections, we have highlighted the most relevant approaches that have dealt with the problem of deviations on software processes. These approaches have been classified according to two different axes: (1) how they detect deviations and; (2) how they correct them.

As we may decide to choose one method or one tool among the existing ones, and since this choice is strongly based on the constraints (criteria) that are most relevant to us, offering an explicit covering graph for both detection and correction aspects is very important to make the choice much effective.

Through this section, and based on the results obtained within Sects. 3 and 4, we draw a *covering graph* for each classification framework. For a sake of simplicity, each criterion, in both graphs, will have three possible values: *low*, *medium* and *high*[1]. For instance, for the Deviation Object criterion, if a given approach is able to detect the occurred deviations within just one SP element, the value *low* is assigned to this criterion. If two SP elements are considered within the detection mechanisms, this criterion would have *medium* as value. Otherwise, if all SP elements are covered, the value *high* is assigned to this criterion. On the other hand, when correcting a deviation, we are interested at involving as less components as possible into the correction procedure. This is because the more components are involved, the more expensive the correction is to apply,

---

[1] This is a choice of our own, authors may prefer to assign other values for both sets of criteria.

Table 4. Signification of Covering Graphs values.

Qualification	Detection		Correction	
	Criterion	Description	Criterion	Description
Low	Deviation object	Detecting deviations within just one SP element	Correction object	All the SP elements
Medium		Two SP elements are considered		Two SP elements are considered
High		All the basic SP elements are considered		One SP element is corrected
Low	Deviation type	Behavioral	Correction type	Static
Medium		Functional		Dynamic
High		Behavioral & Functional		Static & Dynamic
Low	Deviation causes	One kind of deviations	Correction reasons	Corrective or Perfective
Medium		A predefined set of possible causes		Corrective & Perfective
High		Causes related to each SP elements are distinguished		Promote reusing
Low	Deviation moment	Execution or deployment	Correction moment	Specification
Medium		Execution and deployment		Deployment
High		Execution, deployment and specification		Execution
Low	Detection process	Ad-hoc	Correction process	Transformation or restructuring
Medium		Using external tools		Inheritance or parametrizing
High		Integrated within the process specification		Design pattern
Low	Automation level	Manual	Automation level	Manual
Medium		Semi-automatic		Semi-automatic
High		Automatic		Automatic
Low	Execution environment	Mono machine	Execution environment	Mono machine
Medium		Distributed		Distributed
High		Mobile		Mobile

especially if there are several instances of that SP model. Thus, if a given approach proposes to change/modify just one SP element to correct the occurred deviation, the criterion Correction Object gets *High* as value, if two elements are involved, *Medium* is assigned to this criterion. Otherwise, *Low* is assigned.

The signification of all the adopted values for each criterion is summarized in Table 4.

To not have cluttered graphs, we will project three approaches on each covering graph: *detection* and *correction*. The results are shown on Fig. 1. We have intentionally projected the same three approaches on both graphs. Thus, the reader may have a clear insight on how the same approach proceeds to treat both detection and correction aspects.

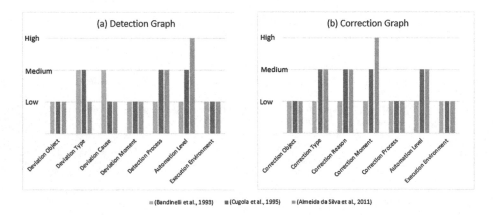

Fig. 1. Coverings Graphs for detecting and correcting deviations on SP.

As we may decide to choose one method or one tool among the existing ones, and since this choice is strongly based on the constraints (criteria) that are most relevant to us, offering an explicit covering graph for both detection and correction aspects is very important to make the choice much effective.

6   New Trends to Support Deviations on Software Processes

From the study conducted though this paper, we have noticed that all of the existing approaches consider the problem of deviations from two different perspectives: detection and correction. However, most of them have focused on finding out mechanisms to detect deviations than to correct them.

Unfortunately, despite the great number of approaches dealing with the detection issue, some interesting observations could be pointed out:

– Most of researchers have not considered the process model concept while dealing with this problem. Moreover, within the former approaches, some authors do not give any insight about how they define their processes [6,29] (which are the different conceptual parts that build up the process). Through recent approaches, more interest has been devoted to process modelling and most of authors have explicitly defined their processes as the interaction between activities responsible for delivering the products and the agents that perform them. These concepts (activity, agent, and artefact) are considered as the core of SPEM [12], the OMG standard. However, despite the interest that process modelling has acquired, holding the problem of deviations has not been much concerned with this aspect and much research works still consider them as problem related to SP execution and have no relationship with the process model. Thus, no approach has focused on integrating the solution into the process model, consequently;

– As the approaches are very dependent to the tools they invoke, the reusing aspect has not been considered at all. In each approach, authors treat deviations within just one context: the process they consider. No insights have been given about how to extend a solution to another process kind and no approach has offered a concrete flexibility about the choice of tools to implement, differently, the solution introduced. In other words, authors have not been concerned with proposing conceptual solutions or giving an abstraction of the prototypes they introduced, so they could be reused.

Through this section, we aim at introducing, through an informal description, a new approach to deal with deviations on software processes. Our main objective is not just to propose a support for this problem but also to be able to integrate it into the process model. Thus, as deviations are very likely to happen within any software process, project managers would be given a solution that is already integrated within the process model they choose. Moreover, such solution would be very useful because of the abstraction level it offers. As the solution is endowed within the process model, and have no relationship with the tools used to define it, it promotes to be reusable.

To achieve our goal, we proceed differently from the existing works. First, we consider deviations as a problem related to the *evolution aspect* of software processes. Thus, we assume that even if most deviations are detected during execution time, they are not all the results of an execution problem. The need to deviate from the SP model could be noticed during different phases of the development project. Therefore, as much as the process evolves in time, the need to deviate from the process model becomes much required.

In addition, within the approach we conceive, we do not define the SP model as the starting point of the development project, it is considered as the target result. Thus, to prevent the occurrence of deviations, the goal is to ensure that the SP agents are performing the right transitions while enacting the different activities of the process.

6.1 Deviation Identity

We start by giving a complete definition of the deviation as we consider it. The most relevant information required to treat deviations are covered within this identification. We define the following features as the most important to consider (Fig. 2):

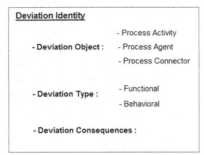

Fig. 2. Deviation Identity.

- *The Deviation Object:* That depicts the SP element within which the deviation has been detected; based on the SPEM meta model, the deviation object could be either the *activity*, the *process agent* or the *artefact*;
- *The Deviation Type:* In spite of the great number of classifications proposed in the literature, we have gathered these classes, because of their similarities, into *behavioral* and *functional*. Thus, a behavioral deviation concerns the actions performed by the SP agents whereas a functional deviation is related to the SP activities and transitions between them;
- *The Deviation Consequence:* Instead of focusing on the deviations causes, as done by most of the existing approaches, we focus within the approach we conceive on the deviations consequences. Thus, the most important for us is not what has caused the deviation but what its results are. Therefore, our goal is to answer the question: what constraints have been violated by the deviation occurrence?

6.2   Detecting deviations

Through our proposal, we consider the software process as a set of steps or *sub-processes*. Each sub-process is either an activity or a set of activities. The process manager does the definition of each sub-process, and the activities that make it up. Theses sub-processes are linked though a set of *transitions*; we define a transition as the ending of a sub-process and the starting of the one(s) that succeeds it.

In order to detect the occurred deviations, a set of analysis should be performed at different phases of the process. Most of the existing approaches propose to perform the required analysis upon each elementary activity of the process [7,14,21]. Moreover, in [8] authors propose to perform three kinds of analysis for each activity: when it is launched, during its execution and when it finishes. We believe that performing too much analysis could be very costly, especially within large-scale processes.

To face this problem, we propose to minimize the number of analysis phases. Thus, instead of performing them upon each elementary activity, an analysis step is executed at the end of each sub process (it is up to the process manager to define the boundaries of each sub process and the number of activities involved within it). We assume that if we are able to control the right ending of each step of the process (outputs and costs), we would be able to control the whole process. The ending of a sub process is notified whenever its outputs are delivered.

As the deviation occurs due to a constraints violation, appropriate mechanisms should be provided to enable a suitable verification in order to detect such violation. Within our approach, constraints are defined for each sub process; they are integrated at the same time of the process modeling.

6.3 Correcting Deviations

When a deviation is triggered, the process has to be adapted. We define an adaptation pattern as a set of steps/actions that are supposed to restore the consistency state of the process once applied. We admit that one or several adaptation patterns could exist for a single deviation. Thus, based on the deviation identification, the most appropriate adaptation pattern is selected.

Within some of the existing approaches [7,21], the proposed correction mechanisms are strongly based on the languages/tools used to enact the process. However, as the occurrence of deviations is unavoidable within most of the processes, we believe that for a solution to be feasible; it has to be integrated to the process model at the same time as its design.

Through the adaptation patterns we introduce, we aim at proposing a reusable approach to solve the problem of deviations on software processes. An adaptation pattern should be endowed with the required information that enable its use. We consider the following features as the most important to identify an adaptation pattern (Fig. 3):

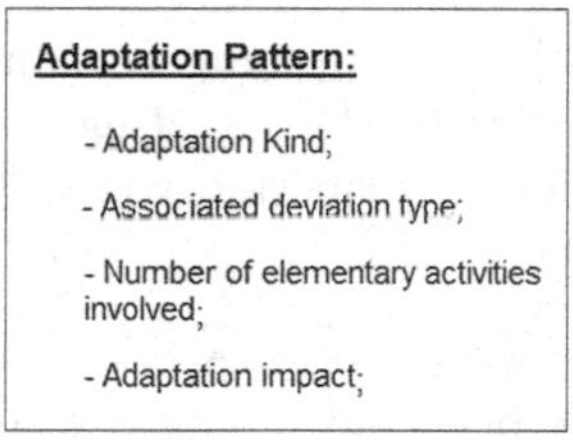

Adaptation Pattern:

- Adaptation Kind;

- Associated deviation type;

- Number of elementary activities involved;

- Adaptation impact;

Fig. 3. Adaptation pattern.

- *The Adaptation Kind:* many alternatives could exist to adapt the process. For instance, operating changes upon the existing SP elements, changing the SP activities sequencing or adding new elements (activities or agents) are some examples of the possible solutions;
- *The Associated Deviation Type:* each adaptation pattern is designed to treat either behavioral or functional deviations;
- The number of activities involved within the adaptation process;

– The adaptation impact: all the possible consequences of the adaptation patterns application on the remaining SP elements.

In addition of these main features, an adaptation pattern must ensure the following basic functionalities:

– Restore the SP model consistency that has been violated by the deviation occurrence;
– Applying the required actions/changes upon the SP elements within which the deviation has occurred without affecting the remaining elements;
– Avoid the appearance of new deviations while adapting the existing ones.

7   Conclusion

Through this paper, we have highlighted the problem of deviations on Software Processes. The most relevant approaches that have dealt with this issue have been considered within this study.

The paper starts by introducing the deviation concept. A deviation is an unexpected situation that could arise within a software development process. The appearance of such situation, if not corrected, often leads to the violation of SP model constraints and to the software development failure, consequently. The paper gives also an insight about the relevant reasons that have incited to devote such interest to this research area.

As it is almost impossible to cover, in one study, all what has been achieved within a given research field. We have covered, through this paper, the most important approaches that have *explicitly* considered the deviation issue as a separate problem. Moreover, approaches that have been concerned with this issue within business processes have been discarded.

We have classified the selected approaches using two comparative frameworks. These frameworks deal with: (1) detecting deviations and (2) correcting them. Our choice to make such a distinction while developing this study is justified by the following reasons:

– Holding the problem on software processes falls into two important directions: finding ways to detect the occurred deviations and offering mechanisms to correct them;
– Separating the classification from these two perspectives makes the analysis much effective. The reader would be easily awards of what has been achieved and what has been left within both directions.

For both classification frameworks, we have conceived a set of criteria. Then, we have detailed every set by defining each item belonging to it. After that, we have projected the selected approaches on each set. To facilitate the comprehension of each classification, we have listed the obtained results within tables.

As a result, we can notice that besides the great number of approaches proposed to deal with deviations within software processes, just few works have explicitly offered mechanisms to correct them. Moreover, we have realized that most of approaches are *tool-dependent*. For instance, in [21], authors say *"Having different modeling languages would not change anything to the proposed solution because of the use of Praxis"*. On the other side, within the Software Engineering field, we are not interested at having the same execution tool. The goal has always been to offer *generic* solutions and let the developers free about the choice of the execution features.

To consider this last issue, we have introduced at the end of this paper a general description of a new contribution of our own. To make this contribution effective, we are currently working on proposing a *platform-independent* solution to detect deviations and correcting them at a second time. Our main objective is to offer a *conceptual-level* approach that facilitate the detection of deviations within a large spectrum of software processes. Moreover, the challenge for us is to offer a *reusable* approach since it is one of the main objectives within the Software Engineering field. This new approach is strongly based on the Software Architecture field that has reached an advanced level regarding the reusing aspect.

References

1. Matinnejad, R., Ramsin, R.: An analytical review of process-centered software engineering environments. In: 2012 IEEE 19th International Conference and Workshops on Engineering of Computer Based Systems (ECBS), pp. 64–73 (2012)
2. García-Borgoñon, L., Barcelona, M., García-García, J., Alba, M., Escalona, M.: Software process modeling languages: a systematic literature review. Inf. Softw. Technol. **56**, 103–116 (2014)
3. Fuggetta, A.: Software process: a roadmap. In: Proceedings of the Conference on the Future of Software Engineering, pp. 25–34. ACM (2000)
4. Bandinelli, S., Fuggetta, A., Ghezzi, C.: Software process model evolution in the spade environment. IEEE Trans. Softw. Eng. **19**, 1128–1144 (1993)
5. Bandinelli, S., Di Nitto, E., Fuggetta, A.: Policies and mechanisms to support process evolution in PSEEs. In: Proceedings of the Third International Conference on the Software Process, 'Applying the Software Process', 1994, pp. 9–20 (1994)
6. Cugola, G., Nitto, E., Ghezzi, C., Mantione, M.: How to deal with deviations during process model enactment. In: 17th International Conference on Software Engineering, 1995, ICSE 1995, p. 265 (1995)
7. Kabbaj, M., Lbath, R., Coulette, B.: A deviation management system for handling software process enactment evolution. In: Wang, Q., Pfahl, D., Raffo, D.M. (eds.) ICSP 2008. LNCS, vol. 5007, pp. 186–197. Springer, Heidelberg (2008)
8. Almeida da Silva, M., Bendraou, R., Robin, J., Blanc, X.: Flexible deviation handling during software process enactment. In: 2011 15th IEEE International Enterprise Distributed Object Computing Conference Workshops (EDOCW), pp. 34–41 (2011)
9. Yang, Q., Li, M., Wang, Q., Yang, G., Zhai, J., Li, J., Hou, L., Yang, Y.: An algebraic approach for managing inconsistencies in software processes. In: Wang, Q., Pfahl, D., Raffo, D.M. (eds.) ICSP 2007. LNCS, vol. 4470, pp. 121–133. Springer, Heidelberg (2007)

10. Almeida Da Silva, M.A., Blanc, X., Bendraou, R., Gervais, M.P.: Experiments on the impact of deviations to process execution. Ingénierie des systèmes d'information **18**, 95–119 (2013)
11. Ruiz-Rube, I., Dodero, J.M., Palomo-Duarte, M., Ruiz, M., Gawn, D.: Uses and applications of spem process models. a systematic mapping study. J. Softw. Maintenance Evol. Res. Pract. **1**, 999–1025 (2012)
12. Object Management Group: Software Process Engineering Metamodel (SPEM) 2.0 (2008)
13. Object Management Group: Software Process Engineering Metamodel (SPEM) 1.1 (2005)
14. Thompson, S., Torabi, T., Joshi, P.: A framework to detect deviations during process enactment. In: 6th IEEE/ACIS International Conference on Computer and Information Science, 2007, ICIS 2007, pp. 1066–1073 (2007)
15. Yong, Y., Zhou, B.: Software process deviation threshold analysis by system dynamics. In: 2010 The 2nd IEEE International Conference on Information Management and Engineering (ICIME), pp. 121–125 (2010)
16. Bolcer, G.A., Taylor, R.N.: Endeavors: a process system integration infrastructure. In: Proceedings of the Fourth International Conference on the Software Process, 1996, pp. 76–89. IEEE (1996)
17. Egyed, A., Letier, E., Finkelstein, A.: Generating and evaluating choices for fixing inconsistencies in UML design models. In: 23rd IEEE/ACM International Conference on Automated Software Engineering, 2008, ASE 2008, pp. 99–108 (2008)
18. Cugola, G., Ghezzi, C., Pinto, L.: Process programming in the service age: old problems and new challenges. In: Tarr, P.L., Wolf, A.L. (eds.) Engineering of Software, pp. 163–177. Springer, Heidelberg (2011)
19. Dami, S., Estubler, J., Amiour, M.: Apel: a graphical yet executable formalism for process modeling. In: Di Nitto, E., Fuggetta, A. (eds.) Process Technology, pp. 61–96. Springer, US (1998)
20. Ge, X., Paige, R.F., McDermid, J.A.: Failures of a business process in enterprise systems. In: Cruz-Cunha, M.M., Varajão, J., Powell, P., Martinho, R. (eds.) CENTERIS 2011, Part I. CCIS, vol. 219, pp. 139–146. Springer, Heidelberg (2011)
21. Bendraou, R., Almeida da Silva, M.A., Gervais, M.P., Blanc, X.: Support for deviation detections in the context of multi-viewpoint-based development processes. In: CAiSE Forum, pp. 23–31 (2012)
22. Zhang, H., Kitchenham, B., Jeffery, R.: Toward trustworthy software process models: an exploratory study on transformable process modeling. J. Softw. Evol. Process **24**, 741–763 (2012)
23. Hull, R., Su, J., Vaculin, R.: Data management perspectives on business process management: tutorial overview. In: Proceedings of the 2013 International Conference on Management of data, pp. 943–948. ACM (2013)
24. Rangiha, M., Karakostas, B.: Process recommendation and role assignment in social business process management. In: Science and Information Conference (SAI), pp. 810–818 (2014)
25. Bandinelli, S., Di Nitto, E., Fuggetta, A.: Supporting cooperation in the SPADE-1 environment. IEEE Trans. Softw. Eng. **22**, 841–865 (1996)
26. Cugola, G., Ghezzi, C.: Design and implementation of PROSYT: a distributed process support system. In: Proceedings of the IEEE 8th International Workshops on Enabling Technologies: Infrastructure for Collaborative Enterprises, 1999 (WET ICE 1999), pp. 32–39 (1999)
27. Cugola, G.: Tolerating deviations in process support systems via flexible enactment of process models. IEEE Trans. Softw. Eng. **24**, 982–1001 (1998)

28. Zazworka, N., Basili, V., Shull, F.: Tool supported detection and judgment of non-conformance in process execution. In: 3rd International Symposium on Empirical Software Engineering and Measurement, 2009, ESEM 2009, pp. 312–323 (2009)
29. Bandinelli, S., Ghezzi, C., Fuggetta, A., Lavazza, L.: SPADE: an environment for software process analysis, design, and enactment. In: Software Process Modeling and Technology, pp. 223–248. Wiley (1994)

Protection of Customers' and Suppliers' Knowledge in Software Development Projects with Fixed-Price Contract: Using Property Rights Theory

Cornelia Gaebert[✉]

Research Group on Strategic Information Management,
European Research Center for Information Systems,
University of Muenster, Leonardo Campus 11, 48149 Muenster, Germany
cg@indal.de

Abstract. In software development projects (SDP), both the supplier and the customer must share their business knowledge for reaching the project success. However, this business knowledge is an essential intellectual property, and thus needs protection from misuse. In this paper, we present an analysis of knowledge difficult to protect. We enact a strategy to achieve SDPs success despite these barriers. Our theoretical and empirical analysis also found that SDP success is largely an uncertainty problem between the contractual parties on the management level, and thus technical-organizational approaches alone are inadequate for achieving success. Based on property rights theory, we introduce two models for protecting knowledge depending on uncertainties. Our findings offer managers important insights how they can design and enact especially fixed-price contracts. Moreover, we show how the economic theories can enhance understanding of SDP dynamics and advance the development of a theory of effective control of SDP success.

Keywords: Software development project · Information · Knowledge · Intellectual property rights · Property rights theory

1 Introduction

The number of failing software development projects (SDP) has remained high for decades [1–3] notwithstanding of the professionalization of the software development process and project management improvements. Due to researchers and practitioners, changing requirements are the main reason for failure (cf. [4, 5]). Organizations expect to mitigate this risk by outsourcing [6]. The supplier shall take the risk for the project failing when working independently. Researchers recommend that in this situation a fixed-price contract (FPC) with a predetermined price for the software system is not suitable for completion of the SDP in line with the expectations of the contractual parties [7, 8]. Indeed, the contract influences the success or failure of SDPs [9]. This is not a question of trust, but an economic issue of uncertainty due to incomplete information on both sides [10].

© Springer International Publishing Switzerland 2016
P. Lorenz et al. (Eds.): ICSOFT 2015, CCIS 586, pp. 210–227, 2016.
DOI: 10.1007/978-3-319-30142-6_12

Against this background, we argue that ineffective contract provisions regarding the protection of property rights (PR) on information and knowledge (I&K) are at the root of causes for ineffective FPCs. This is because both contractual parties must share business I&K to be successful in software development outsourcing (SDO), at least if the project regards a novelty [11]. Nevertheless, this I&K belongs to the organizations' intellectual properties [12]. Consequently, both sides have an interest in protecting their I&K for securing their intellectual PR (cf. [13]). Problems arise, because the contract does not contain effective instruments securing these PR. We conclude that among others the inadequate protection of I&K causes changing requirements. However, there is a paucity of research on how contractual parties can improve SDP performance or outcome by protecting PR on I&K under FPC.

In this paper, we bring different research fields together: Information Management, Requirement Engineering, and New Institutional Economics. First, we analyze I&K in general by means of insights from Information Management Research. Second, for I&K in SDPs in particular, we draw from Requirement Engineering special insights. Finally, we can use PR Theory from New Institutional Economics to develop theoretical models describing the situation. From these models, we will derive suggestions for an adequate use of FPCs for SDPs.

The PR theory is directed to the available rights on the exchange object, a central approach of New Institutional Economics [14, 15]. The research focuses on the incentives triggered by regulatory, ownership and the institutional framework; the use of economic theories proved to be appropriate (cf. [16–19]). In this paper, we will investigate how the PR theory can improve our understanding of the options of protection of PR to attenuate reasons for requirement change and therefore, reasons for failure of SDPs.

We have conducted an empirical investigation regarding the role of sharing I&K in SDPs, the fears and worries of customers and suppliers. The collected empirical data will guide our theoretical considerations. Therefore, we start with a brief description of our empirical study in Sect. 2. Afterwards, we will discuss the kind of knowledge and information customers and suppliers must share and protect within the project in Sect. 3. We will distinguish this from other kinds of information needed to share between the parties without the problem of protecting it from misuse. In addition, we will tell it apart from intellectual PR. We will develop a schema of knowledge kinds of both contractual parties that are worth to protect. However, the parties have to share this knowledge to facilitate the project success.

The conflict description between the need of sharing the knowledge and the necessity of protecting it by means of the PR theory is in the focus of Sect. 4. We will develop two new theoretical models, a rent and a wage model concerning the PR on I&K in SDPs under FPC, depending on the net gain of the cooperation.

In Sect. 5 we will finally discuss possible decision criteria regarding the derived options. Above all, we will suggest instruments for securing PR on I&K while sharing it during the project phases.

2   The Empirical Support

Throughout this paper, we use an abductive research approach [20, 21]. We are "in the discovery stage of scientific hypothesis formation and testing" [22]. For the collection of empirical data on the I&K role in SDPs under FPC, we conducted a two-step evaluation. First, we developed a questionnaire in the form of a standardized online survey as a special kind of standardized survey [23]. Next, we conducted personal interviews to deepen our understanding of the questionnaire results. The evaluation period lasted one year.

For the questionnaire, we chose the standardized online survey to give the respondents an opportunity to reflect and to question their own companies [24]. The format of the online survey itself was legitimate because the interviewees were an IT-savvy group. Open answers supplemented closed questions so the questionnaire would not be too restrictive. In addition, they helped gather the covered information [25].

We interviewed experienced project participants on both sides (customer and supplier side). The questionnaire had to take into account the management perspective as well as the project management's view. Since it is not possible to address the population of all SDP customers and suppliers, and given that questioning the population about any associated and unacceptably high cost is not realistic, we chose a smaller population. Therefore, we could not achieve complete representativeness [24]. For practical reasons, we addressed the 45 members of an IT company's network in Germany. Fifty additional addressees were available from other contacts. To expand the circle of respondents and to amplify the customer side, we used contacts in social networks such as Facebook (approximately 30), Xing (approximately 20), and Twitter (approximately 50). This ensured that the respondents had experience in different possible project contexts. Of the 200 addressees requested to participate in the survey, 29 actually completed the questionnaire (14 suppliers, 5 customers, 9 suppliers and customers, and 1 other).

An independent survey evaluating the willingness to participate in the survey suggested a conscientious answering of the questions. 48.3 % of the respondents indicated that they belong to management and have contract responsibility; 27.6 % are project managers; 6.9 % are employees at the working level, and 17.2 % perform other activities, such as consulting. 89.7 % of the respondents had 10 or more years of SDP experience. The participants represented a broad range of project sizes with regard to duration and number of employees.

For the exemplary and in-depth interviews, we conducted semi-structured expert interviews. On the one side, we questioned a consultant with an SDP experience of approximately 15 years. He supports big companies in defining and organizing the contractual issues of SDPs. On the other side, we spoke with a supplier having an SDP experience of approximately 20 years. He is the owner of a software development company employing 10 programmers. Considering the sensitivity of failure research and the resulting difficulty in gaining access to project details, this methodology was most appropriate. The incomplete script of the semi-structured interview format left room for improvised questions [26]. The first interview lasted approximately 3 h, the second 1.5 h. We made extensive notes during the interviews, which we evaluated afterwards through a qualitative content analysis. Since we demanded appointed circumstances and facts, we were able to avoid free interpretation problems [27].

We designed the investigation in preparation of the following analyses. We draw our legitimation for the subsequent sections. Therefore, we will use some study results in connection with the corresponding theoretical considerations in the next sections.

3 Knowledge and Information in Software Development Projects

Before we can develop models for the protection of knowledge from misuse in Sect. 4, we need to analyze I&K in SDPs. Therefore, in this section we link insights from Information Management literature with Requirement Engineering. The requirement specification is a fundamental document for the FPC and the SDP itself, and it consists in particular of the customer's I&K. However, the supplier must also provide I&K. In this section, we show that not all provided I&K are worthy of protection. For this, we will discuss at first the difference between knowledge and information using the literature. Second, we will detect which kinds of I&K are worthy of protection in the context of SDPs. Finally, we will summarize the chain of reasoning derived from that. Concerning both parties' interests, we enhance the research. We will identify a symmetrical distribution of protection worthy knowledge.

3.1 Knowledge and Information

According to Information Management literature, it is difficult to distinguish between knowledge and information in a way that for every single situation it is clear, if some set of statements, documents, or data contains knowledge or information [28]. For systematic reasons, we will clearly differentiate between information and knowledge as follows.

According to Ackoff [29], an information contains useful data and provides answers to questions like who, where, when, and what, whereas knowledge is an application of information, which answers how questions. In addition, Zeleny [30] describes information as knowing what, whereas knowledge as knowing how. One can describe a business process by saying who is the process actor, what the actor does within this process, and in which situation (where and when) he does it. These descriptions are information about the business process. On the other hand, one can describe how the actor meets a business goal by carrying out a business process. This provides knowledge, the know how to reach the goal. In order to have knowledge it is therefore not enough to be able to describe process details, but you must also know the goal, for which the process is a tool on the way to reach it.

Both Ackoff and Zeleny point out further kinds of knowing something. If one not only knows what (where, when, who) and how, but also has the answer to the why question, then, according to Ackoff, the person has understanding. Zeleny calls the ability to provide answers to why questions wisdom. As knowledge is inherited from information, understanding and wisdom are inherited from knowledge. Thus, data is the quasi common denominator of information, knowledge, understanding, and wisdom.

There is a broad discussion going on regarding the differences between information, knowledge, understanding, and wisdom [28, 31]. It is not the supplier's task to understand the customer's business model in the broadest sense. However, there is no clear divide between knowledge and understanding. The purpose of a software system is in some sense connected to the customer's business goal. For our purposes, it is therefore sufficient to mark the difference between information and knowledge. For that reason, we will use the notion of information for data regarding processes, events, objects, and methods without answering how these described data are used to reach a goal, and why these data are necessary as a means for someone's purpose. On the other hand, knowledge offers us such answers. He who has knowledge knows the purposes the data are used for. He knows how these data should be used to reach these purposes, and why these data are suitable for the purposes.

In the next section, we will use these findings for an analysis of I&K in an SDP context.

3.2   Knowledge and Information in Software Development Projects

Our empirical study shows that during the proposal phase and during contract-negotiations, both sides must provide detailed information on the customer's requirements and the supplier's abilities. We aim to clarify which kind of I&K is a property the contractual parties wish to protect against misuse by the other side. During SDP preparation and execution, the customer and the supplier must share different kinds of I&K.

For analyzing purposes, we will first take the customer's perspective. There is broad research in the field of software engineering regarding I&K provided by the customer in SDPs. After that, we will be able to develop a consistent view of the supplier's perspective. From this contribution of research, we will summarize which are the kinds of I&K worthy of protection in the context of an SDP.

The Customer's Perspective: Requirements. The research about customer-delivered information focuses on requirements representation and specification [32]. Researchers have been distinguishing for long three kinds of requirements: project requirements (a), process requirements (b), and system requirements (c) [33, 34].

(a) We have to consider information on the project's timeline, the budget, and milestones to be met (what, when, where, and who). These are the project requirements. Obviously, the customer must share this information, because the supplier will set up the project plan based on it. In our expert interview, the business side consultant stated that the customer shares this information in the early phases, and mostly long before signing the contract. Often the customer delivers such information to more than one potential supplier. Obviously, there is no problem as long as it is only information as defined in the previous section. However, problems arise during the project if it gets impossible to achieve the needed milestones. Due to external reasons, meeting a milestone is sometimes prioritized, but in other cases, it may be possible to shift the timeline if changes in requirements or other problems arise. To find the right decisions, the customer must share more than information with the supplier. It is necessary to deliver the answer to the question why a milestone was set to a special due date. According to our definition in the previous section, this is part of the customer's knowledge. This knowledge may be connected with other knowledge from the customer's side, for instance a marketing strategy for a new product launch. There is good reason to hide this knowledge from external suppliers.

(b) There is information needed directly for work processing and for the coordination of the involved staff's activities. From the customer's perspective, such information is part of process requirements. Due dates, contact persons' names and data as well as the meeting schedule are examples of such information, which controls the process. This kind of information is not in the focus of our study. There is no reason to hide such information, because it is only valuable during the project and in case the contractors share it.

(c) When we use the notion of requirements during SDPs, we mostly refer to system requirements. Requirement specification is mostly the first part of each project. Since changing and ambiguous requirements are one of the main reasons for project failure (cf. Introduction and our empirical investigation), researchers have been focusing on methods of software requirements engineering during the last decades.

System requirements are divided into functional and non-functional requirements, and constraints. Functional requirements define what the system is bound to do. In the sense of Ackoff and Zeleny, these requirements belong to *information* to be shared by the customer. Obviously, this information is crucial for producing the right software system. On the other hand, the customer is often not able to define in a clear and detailed way how the system should look like, how it should react to user input, or how it should process data. As the manager from the supplier's side stated in our interview, in order to design an appropriate system it is useful to share *knowledge* about how the users do their work, about what the business processes are, and why they need support from the required software system. This knowledge is the know-how of the customer's organization.

Consequently, we must consider not only information, but also knowledge of the customer. There are good reasons for sharing this knowledge with the supplier, but on the other hand, there are also reasons to hide this know-how: it is the internal knowledge of an organization and it is its competitive advantage.

The customer may also define non-functional requirements as information. Requirement specifications must contain statements about needed response times or data volumes. Sometimes it is necessary to prioritize non-functional requirements. For this, it is useful to know why the customer needs the defined system parameters, and why it is important to meet these requirements. Then, it is not enough to deliver information, but it is also useful to deliver knowledge about the business know-how.

Last, we have to consider constraints. Constraints are legal or cultural restrictions that the supplier must take into consideration during the software system development.

Such information is mostly publicly available, and is not the customer's private property. Therefore, we must not examine it in detail in this study.

Table 1 shows an overview of the I&K to be provided and shared by the customer during an SDP. As our analysis shows, the customer may share nearly each input either as information or as knowledge. At the knowledge level, the customer may have an interest in protecting it from usage by external parties [13]. Therefore, we can depict this knowledge as customer property. Properties are worthy of protection. We will further develop this idea and its consequences in Sect. 4 of this paper. Before, we will take the supplier's perspective.

Table 1. Kinds of information and knowledge provided by the customer.

	Information	Knowledge	Protection-relevant
Project requirements	Project's due dates	Project business goals	Relevant, maybe interesting for competitors
Process requirements	Project internal due dates availability of resources	Current business processes and activities outside the project	Not relevant, because only valid during a short time period
System requirements	Functional and non-functional requirements, constraints	business goals, business knowledge	Relevant, interesting for competitors, usable by the supplier in other projects, define the customer's competitive advantage

The Supplier's Perspective: Abilities. In order to achieve a suitable and systematic description of I&K provided and shared by the supplier, we will develop in the following this description in analogy to the kinds of I&K found for the customer. In the previous section, we have identified three kinds of I&K for the customer to deliver during the SDP. These are (a) project requirements: organizational project embedding within the organization's processes, its connections with customer strategies and business goals, (b) process requirements: project management and organization, (c) system requirements: the organization's business know-how as far as it is relevant for the development of the needed software system.

On the suppliers' side, we can identify three corresponding kinds of I&K.

(a) Project requirements: The supplier has to embed the single project within his production processes. He must answer the following questions: When is the needed staff available? Which experts are necessary? When will they be able to work on the project? Which other resources, like development and test systems, are needed for the project?
This information influences the overall project plan. The supplier must deliver these data to the customer by at least partly committing to timelines and milestones. Sometimes, the sequence of the project's working steps will depend on

such external basic conditions. If the supplier does not just deliver the plain information, but also the reasons underlying the decisions for a certain setting, the supplier shares organizational knowledge with the customer. This knowledge concerns the supplier's organization ability to handle and process projects as needed in order to produce the desired software system.

(b) Process requirements: As in the customers' case, sharing project management information is not worthy of protection because it has no value outside the project. This information is in no way connected with the organization's knowledge. Therefore, we will not consider this information in our study.

Table 2. Supplier's knowledge and information.

	Information	Knowledge	Protection-relevant
Project abilities	Commitment of project's due dates	Supplier's overall strategy	Relevant, maybe interesting for competitors
Process abilities	Project internal due dates availability of resources	Current business processes and activities outside the project	Not relevant, because only valid during a short time period
System abilities	Development methods, used tools and frameworks	Know-how in development, experiences, problem- solving strategies	Relevant, interesting for competitors, make the customer independent, define the supplier's competitive advantage

(c) System requirements: We must consider information regarding the core of the supplier's business expertise. During the proposal and negotiation phase, the supplier must deliver information to show that the organization is able to produce the needed software system. Therefore, the supplier shares relevant parts of the business expertise. Furthermore, during system development of the system, it may be useful to share information on the used employed tools and methods. In addition, the supplier has to share technical implementation details to justify prioritizing the implementation of non-functional requirements. Often, the customer and the supplier must make such decisions in common. In order to make possible such decisions, the supplier must share the information in a way that the customer can generate knowledge regarding the underlying technical facts, methods, and constraints. This knowledge is worthy of protection for the supplier, because the generation of such knowledge makes the customer more independent from the supplier's services [35]. Furthermore, the customer may use this knowledge in other projects and may share it with the supplier's competitors [36]. We have summarized the supplier's perspective on I&K he has to share in Table 2.

3.3 Summary: The Character of Information and Knowledge as Properties

Summarizing the theoretical analysis of I&K needed in SDPs, we have to accept the fact that both parties have reason to protect knowledge from misuse by the other side. We substantiate our empirical investigation. There is knowledge regarding the internal business processes, regulations, experiences, and goals making the organization powerful and successful in the market and in the context of competition with other firms. These are intellectual properties of the firm [12].

Consequently, this knowledge is an important asset for both firms as long as each organization protects it against competitors. The customer possibly maintains a relationship with the supplier's competitors and vice versa. Therefore, both contractual parties have reason to protect their own knowledge. Both parties may withhold the needed I&K as long as possible.

On the other hand, sharing this knowledge is crucial for a successful project. Knowledge is needed to make the right decisions in designing the right system. In addition, at the beginning of an SDP both parties do not know the exact I&K is needed. Therefore, both parties deliver I&K as late as possible, a reason for changing requirements. With the next section, we develop a possibility for a balance of the protection of I&K in spite of the FPC.

4 The Protection of Knowledge: The Property Rights Model for the SDP

In this section, we will provide the announced theoretical ex-ante investigation of the contract impact on reaching customer and supplier-specific economic outcome goals in an SDO project. We will investigate how PR theory can improve our understanding of how the protection of PR can attenuate reasons for changing requirements and therefore, reasons for failure.

First, we will give a summary of our literature review on efforts made to date. We argue that the protection of knowledge needs further research; this paper will contribute to that. Second, we are adopting Barzel's [37] classical landowner model on our situation under investigation. We will develop two new models describing the property rights situation in SDPs. With this, we can get a balance of knowledge protection.

4.1 Excursus: Protection of Knowledge by Credible Commitments

Copyright or patent laws are formal protection measures, yet they are not suitable for protecting knowledge in an SDP context [38, 39]. As shown by Liebeskind [38], the firm itself has the power to protect the knowledge, making it invisible from the outside. Friesike [39] calls these options "informal protection measures". However, contractors have to share knowledge in an SDP. Consequently, preventing visibility is not useful.

In long-term collaborations, contractual parties can reach trustworthy behavior by credible commitments [40–42]. For that, reciprocal specific investments are most effective.

Reciprocal specific investments create a mutual hostage situation that serves as a safe-guard against the misuse of knowledge. However, these investments are not suitable for a single SDP. This also applies to non-disclosure agreements; they are effectively reachable only in long-term collaborations [43, 44]. Thus far, the contractual parties are aware that the SPD's end is within the range of vision. Therefore, trustworthy behavior is hardly to ensure, especially after the project's end.

Consequently, we must search for alternative incentives to secure knowledge protection during an SDP. In the next section, we will find such options by starting from models of the economic PR theory.

4.2   Protection of Knowledge by Property Rights: The Landowner Model

A classic model introduced by Barzel [37] analyzes the contractual situation between a landowner having PR on land and a worker having PR on labor. In order to produce goods, at least one of them must assign the PR to the other. They have three options: first, the landowner may assign the land-using right to the worker through a fixed-rent contract. Second, the worker may assign the labor-using right to the landowner via a wage contract. Finally, they can sign a shared tenancy contract to share the profit from the crop sale. In each case, both parties will overuse the contractual partner's resources, which they control themselves. On the contrary, each party will reduce its support for resources, which are now under control of the other side. Therefore, the decision for a contract type depends on the net gain of the cooperation. No contract type will always be the best under all circumstances. With a fixed-rent contract, the landowner will maintain his land less improved; with a wage contract, the tenant will shirk more. Half way between both of them, there is a bit of everything. In this case, output specification and monitoring will be additionally necessary.

I&K does not need maintenance in the sense of physical wear and tear. At first sight, I&K cannot be overused, because it cannot be damaged by using and sharing. Nevertheless, we can interpret it as an overuse when a party, having received I&K from the other side, shares this with a third party or uses it in another project. In such cases, I&K as a property of the owner may lose its value.

The fixed-price contract, as under our investigation, is the most commonly chosen contract design [45] in SDPs; our empirical investigation supports this. However, we must be careful: using the fixed-rent model for managing the usage of I&K in an SDP does not imply a FPC for the SDP, such as a wage model does not imply a time and material contract. We will see as follows that the crucial question does not relate to the price model of the underlying contract. It is the question who controls the usage of I&K and labor.

However, with respect to SDPs, the landowner model has some weaknesses. First, the I&K needed by the other party plays the role of the land. This raises the question whether someone is willing to pay for the use of a requirement specification. Second, in our case landowner and crop buyer are the same party. Consequently, no independent third party (the market) will validate the value of the I&K. Incidentally, this explains why shared contracts are unusual in SDPs.

Therefore, we will analyze the consequences of these problems in the following, and discuss the fixed-rent model as well as the wage model.

4.3   The Fixed-Rent Model

In the most obvious application of Barzel's model to the situation of an SDP, the customer plays the role of the landowner, whereas the supplier is the worker. Requirement specification and the business knowledge behind it are customer properties. In case of a rent model, the supplier rents this knowledge. After finalizing software development, the supplier sells the software solution to the customer.

However, according to Sect. 3, we must consider the opposite situation, too. We will look for situations in the SDP, when the customer uses supplier's knowledge to contribute to the project success.

In the next section, we discuss the following questions: is it possible to rent the knowledge needed by the other party inside the SDP? How can we interpret the model in this situation, and what are the consequences of that? In the following two sections, we will analyze both cases where supplier or customer rent knowledge.

Knowledge Regarding Requirements. At first glance, it seems to be an unusual idea for a supplier in an SDP to rent knowledge from the customer. Two questions arise: (a) Should the supplier pay a rent for the knowledge, which is necessary for the SDP? (b) How it is possible to give the knowledge back to the owner after finalizing the project?

Concerning the first question (a), we can take the view that the parties offset the knowledge rent against the price for the software solution delivered at the end of the project. Customer information on business goals and the business knowledge lying behind this information is valuable for the supplier. This knowledge helps the supplier in understanding and thus developing the required software. Consequently, customer knowledge is valuable for the supplier, and the supplier can rent this knowledge. The contractors can offset this rent with the calculated overall SDP fixed-price.

Nonetheless, we must discuss the possibility of project failure. The supplier does not deliver any software and the customer will not pay the agreed price. Should the contractors stipulate a penalty regarding the delivered knowledge? We are facing the same question as in the landlord-worker model: should the worker pay a rent after crop failure, if he cannot harvest grain? The answer the rent model gives us is yes, because the landowner does not know the reasons for the failure. Therefore, it is the worker's risk. Dispensing the rent would be only possible in the case of a sharing model. Thus, also in an SDP, the parties should agree on a penalty in case the customer shares business knowledge, but the supplier delivers no software system.

We are now coming to the more interesting second question (b). Here, the parties must avoid that the supplier integrates the knowledge rented from the customer into the knowledge of his own organization. As our empirical study shows, 77 % of the suppliers admit using received information outside the project. If the knowledge given from customer to supplier becomes a part of the suppliers' business knowledge, the supplier cannot give back this knowledge when the rent ends. We can interpret this as an overuse of information as defined by Barzel [37]. If the supplier uses the customer's business knowledge in other projects, namely to support competitors of the customer, the value of this knowledge decreases as does the value of overused land.

One can argue that the supplier must integrate knowledge into his own knowledge in order to develop the required software. Nevertheless, we must distinguish three cases: integration of knowledge into the knowledge of the supplier as a knowing organization (i) [46], integration of knowledge into the knowledge of a project team (ii), and integration of knowledge into the knowledge of a single person (iii), for instance the requirements engineer or solution designer. (i) For software system development, it is not necessary for the supplier to integrate knowledge about requirements into the knowledge of his own organization. The contract should contain rules to avoid this. (ii) In our empirical online survey, 77 % of the interview partners say that such knowledge will be discussed in joint project teams. The project team knowledge disappears when the project ends. (iii) Last, a person's knowledge about complex facts often requires this person to have access to detailed documentation. We can interpret this documentation as the expert's extended mind [47]. For proper use of the knowledge, the expert needs access to the documentation. If this access is denied after the end of the project, the value of such knowledge decreases within short periods.

Furthermore, we must take into account the different kinds of information as discussed in the previous section of this paper. As we have seen there, two kinds are likely to raise problems: the knowledge behind the information regarding project requirements, and the knowledge behind the information concerning functional and non-functional requirements.

First, the knowledge regarding project requirements, such as reasons for timelines or customer business goals, which the customer will only deliver to project leaders. This knowledge should remain inside the project management team. These people should sign a non-disclosure agreement regarding this knowledge. Since the value of such knowledge decreases very fast after the project is finished, it is possible to supervise this agreement and to demand a penalty in the case of knowledge misuse.

Second, functional, and non-functional requirements and the associated knowledge are mostly very complex and recorded in voluminous documents. Making impossible to copy these documents is a technical issue. Consequently, the experts from the supplier's side can only use this knowledge without integrating it into the knowledge of their organization. At the end of the project, the customer must prevent the supplier's experts from having access to the documents.

Therefore, it is possible to rent relevant knowledge to the supplier. A prerequisite for this lies in agreeing on some special contract regulations and in securing that the documents delivered be difficult to copy. This is just a technical issue [48].

Renting Knowledge Regarding Abilities. Following the same arguments, we can apply the rent model to knowledge about the abilities of the supplier as analyzed in the previous section. First, the parties may also offset the rent with the delivered software price. We suggest calculating the rent within the project price. If possible, the parties should agree that the customer pays a certain amount of the overall price for this knowledge. It is particularly worth noting that this amount is even due if the customer cancels the SDP.

Nonetheless, we have to consider knowledge regarding the supplier's technical abilities, especially regarding the core of business expertise. The customer may be interested in this information for two reasons. First, it may help in negotiations and cooperation with other suppliers, namely with direct competitors of the supplier who delivers the knowledge. Second, the customer may use it to be more independent from the supplier after finishing the project, especially in the field of maintenance and when it comes to developing future software releases. In our empirical survey, 50 % of the interview partners, acting at least partly as customers, admit using received knowledge outside the project.

Especially in the case that the customer cancels the contract, the supplier will fear that the customer uses the knowledge he has got during the project for future developments. Therefore, the parties should agree on a price for the delivered knowledge, which must be paid by the customer also in case of cancellation.

However, the supplier can protect his knowledge, too. This knowledge about the supplier's abilities is also very complex and mostly documented in repositories and libraries. In order to use this information outside the single project, the customer must get permanent access to these documents. The supplier should present this knowledge without really sharing it. It is possible to show the needed knowledge proving that the needed knowledge is available, and without delivering all the documents specifying details of the supplier's business know-how.

Consequences of Renting Knowledge. As shown by Barzel [36], the rent of a property is connected with the problem of overusing this property. In the case of knowledge, this means that using it outside the project may reduce its value dramatically. Therefore, both parties, customer and supplier, should assess the situation and the potential for such misuse before signing the contract. If they know the value of their business knowledge, they can agree on a rent model on knowledge as described before.

To sum up the Sect. 4.3, both parties signing a fixed-price SDP contract must be aware of the fear of delivering part of one's own business knowledge to the other side. As we have shown, it is possible to offset a rent of this knowledge with the agreed fixed-price. For some kinds of knowledge, a penalty can be agreed upon in case of misuse or if the project fails and the customer do not pay the agreed price.

To implement a rent model regarding this knowledge it is necessary to secure that the other party has no permanent access to the documents containing the knowledge. This is just a technical issue. "Show and present, but do not deliver your documents" may be seen as the golden rule of implementing the rent model for PR on business knowledge.

We will now discuss the opportunity for a wage model agreement under FPC.

4.4 The Wage Model

Let us recall that the parties sign a fixed-price contract in most SDP cases. Therefore, at first glance, there is no place for a wage model regarding knowledge. However, we claim that this view is wrong in connection with knowledge in SDPs.

First, we must face the problem that also in the case of a time and material contract the factual PR on knowledge may go over to the other side. If the customer completely delivers all the documents to the supplier, the sender cannot be sure that the receiver might use it in other projects. Therefore, also in this case the customer may lose PR on own knowledge. This is the same problem as in the case of the fixed-price contract.

Second, we can also apply Barzel's wage model to the FPC in SDPs. It is not about an overall fixed-price connected with the project result, it is about knowing if the PR on I&R are rented to the other side, or if the owner uses the other side's labor just to produce some goods.

The goods produced by using the customer's business knowledge are the technical specifications and the software designs needed by the programmers for software realization. In an SDP, it is possible to integrate the business analysts, the requirement engineers, and the system designers needed for this work into the customer's organization for the time required to produce these specifications. It is not important whether the work of these experts is paid by time and material or if the wage is part of the overall fixed-price. The crucial fact is that they lose the PR on used knowledge when they leave the location where they had access.

One might object that they will mentally take this knowledge with them. Nonetheless, as discussed before, in cases of complex business information the value of the individual knowledge decreases fast if this person has no longer access to the documents containing knowledge details and describing information connections and relations.

Consequently, if the supplier's business analysts are working under the control of the customer, with no option of taking away business information from the customer's offices, we can see this part of the project as work done with a wage model, and with or without payment of an overall fixed-price.

Following Barzel [37], the customer must be aware of possible shirking from the supplier's side in this case. Given that the supplier's experts produce technical specifications for the software and even software architecture under the customer's control, the customer is responsible for the quality of these documents. It is difficult to identify the origin problems with the result of the software development: they might be due to low information quality delivered by the customer, or to poor work of the experts producing the specifications, or to that of developers.

On the other hand, the supplier must face potential misuse of the intellectual property under the customer's control. In the case of an SDP, this means that the customer might try to use the abilities. There can especially be a transfer of the experts' knowledge to the customer. Consequently, the customer will be more independent as foreseen by the supplier.

According to Barzel's conclusion, the customer should only use the wage model if the quality of his own property is unclear. In the SDP case, this means that the customer is not sure about the quality of the specified requirements and the availability of the needed information and business know-how. However, the customer must in this case be capable of effectively controlling the work of the supplier's experts and of evaluating the quality of the produced results. However, the last mentioned issue will be difficult because specifications and designs are not testable in the same way as developed software [49].

Finally, we will discuss the case of a wage model regarding the supplier's business knowledge. This is possible when experts from the customer's side are working under the supplier's control, using the supplier's information and knowledge. In an SDP, there are a few cases where such a setting can happen, for instance during the design of user interfaces or during software system integration tests. We can interpret this part of the project as a wage model, in which the supplier must pay the customer a wage. We can expect the parties to offset this wage with the overall fixed-price. We suggest that the parties evaluate the value of this work during the contract negotiation.

4.5   Summary: Rent and Wage Model

We have described two models, considering two options: a rent model and a wage model. From our theoretical consideration, in both cases, we face two issues for the application of these models in practice: how to pay the rent respectively the wage, and how to protect PR, especially after the project is finished.

We suggest offsetting the price for the delivered knowledge with the overall fixed-price in the case of knowledge renting. Consequently, the parties should consider the value of the needed knowledge during contract negotiation. The price should take into account the risk of knowledge misuse outside the project. If both parties are aware of these problems, they are able to arrive at a satisfactory solution.

On the other side, the parties should prefer technical solutions for the protection of PR, granting knowledge access just for the time needed. Such technical restrictions are possible by the implementation of knowledge management software and the use of document management systems. Considering the fact that knowledge about complex business processes rapidly decreases if the access to documentations is denied, an effective rent system is possible if such a system is used.

A rent model option is a possible model for using both customer and supplier knowledge, however, the wage model is just an option for the use of customer knowledge during technical specification and system design. The customer might pay the wage as part of the overall fixed-price. Designers and analysts may work under the customer's control and use the customer's facilities. Then, it is easy to protect knowledge from misuse, because controlling the access to customer documentations and knowledge management systems is easy to organize.

5   Conclusions

In SDPs with FPCs, the protection of contractual parties' knowledge is at risk. Our paper shows possibilities to get protection in spite of the FPC using Information Management and Requirement Engineering Research, and New Institutional Economics. We have analyzed the different kinds of I&K needed in SDPs that customers and suppliers have to share. The supplier must deliver I&K regarding his own abilities. The customer must deliver I&K derived from business goals. Sometimes, delivering only the pure *information* is sufficient. Confirmed through our empirical investigation we have shown, that the parties must often share their business *knowledge*, which can lead to misuse outside the project by the party receiving the knowledge. Our empirical study shows that the contractual parties fear of this misuse. Hence, both sides need protection.

The knowledge of an organization is an intellectual property of its owner. However, the owner cannot protect most of the knowledge needed in an SDP by copyright, patent, or trademark. Consequently, we have developed theoretical models (rent or wage) for the protection of PR on knowledge straight from a classic model of the PR theory.

Which option the parties should prefer? The answer to this question will depend on the quality of the needed knowledge and on the possibilities of securing it by technical means. If the knowledge is contained in documents and if it is possible to protect these delivered documents by technical means from misuse, the parties should prefer the rent model. Such protection systems are possible especially by granting limited online access by using digital documents in document management systems.

Otherwise, the wage model is a better way to share knowledge. In this case, both parties give only access to the knowledge inside their own properties. The knowledge delivering party will provide equipment and working places for the experts of the other party. The experts can do their job, using and transforming the knowledge for contributing to the project's success without taking the knowledge away from the owner.

In both cases, the parties should be aware of the following principles.

(a) Both sides have protection-worthy knowledge.
(b) Both sides have to set a price for this knowledge. They should agree upon the value of the shared knowledge during contract negotiation and offset it with the overall price.
(c) The parties should agree upon payment for received and used knowledge in case the project fails and the customer does not pay the negotiated price for the software system.

The customer as well as the supplier can minimize the risks resulting from sharing knowledge in SDPs by using these suggestions. Further research can just tie here.

References

1. Manifesto, C.: The Laws of Chaos and the CHAOS 100 Best PM Practices. The Standish Group International, Boston (2010)
2. El Emam, K., Koru, A.G.: A replicated survey of IT software project failures. IEEE Softw. **25**(5), 84–90 (2008)
3. Dijkstra, E.W.: The humble programmer. Assoc. Comput. Mach. **15**(10), 859–866 (1972)
4. Al-Ahmad, W., Al-Fagih, K., Khanfar, K., Alsamara, K., Abuleil, S., Abu-Salem, H.: A taxonomy of an IT project failure: root causes. Int. Manage. Rev. **5**(1), 93–104 (2009)
5. Dwivedi, Y.K., Ravichandran, K., Williams, M.D., Miller, S., Lal, B., Antony, V., Muktha, K.: IS/IT project failures: a review of the extant literature for deriving a taxonomy of failure factors. IFIP Adv. Inf. Commun. Technol. **402**, 73–88 (2013)
6. Chua, C.E.H., Lim, W.K., Soh, C., Sia, S.K.: Client strategies in vendor transition: a threat balancing perspective. J. Strateg. Inf. Syst. **21**(1), 72–83 (2012)

7. Dey, D., Fan, M., Zhang, C.: Design and analysis of contracts for software outsourcing. Inf. Syst. Res. **21**(1), 93–114 (2010)
8. Fink, L., Lichtenstein, Y.: Why project size matters for contract choice in software development outsourcing. Data Base Adv. Inf. Syst. **45**(3), 54–71 (2014)
9. Chen, Y., Bharadwaj, A.: An empirical analysis of contract structures in IT outsourcing. Inf. Syst. Res. **20**(4), 484–506 (2009)
10. Williamson, O.E.: The Economic Institutions of Capitalism. Firms, Markets, Relational Contracting, New York (1985)
11. Tiwana, A.: Beyond the black box: knowledge overlaps in software outsourcing. IEEE Softw. **21**(5), 51–58 (2004)
12. Teece, D.J.: Strategies for managing knowledge assets: the role of firm structure and industrial context. Long Range Plan. **33**(1), 35–54 (2000)
13. Norman, P.M.: Are your secrets safe? knowledge protection in strategic alliances. Bus. Horiz. **44**(6), 51–60 (2001)
14. Hart, O., Moore, J.: Property rights and the nature of the firm. J. Polit. Econ. **98**(6), 1119–1158 (1990)
15. Cole, D.H., Grossman, P.Z.: The meaning of property rights: law versus economics? Land Econ. **78**(3), 317–330 (2002)
16. Benaroch, M., Lichtenstein, Y., Wyss, S.: Contract Design Choices in IT Outsourcing: New Lessons from Software Development Outsourcing Contracts, 20 April 2012. http://ssrn.com/abstract=2137174 or http://dx.doi.org/10.2139/ssrn.2137174
17. Aubert, B.A., Patry, M., Rivard, S.: A tale of two outsourcing contracts. An agency-theoretical perspective. Wirtschaftsinformatik **45**, 181–190 (2003)
18. Lichtenstein, Y.: Puzzles in software development contracting. Commun. ACM **47**(2), 61–65 (2004)
19. Beulen, E., Ribbers, P.: IT Outsourcing contracts: practical implications of the incomplete contract theory. Proceedings of the 36th HICSS (2003)
20. Osei-Bryson, K.M., Ngwenyama, O.: Using decision tree modelling to support Peircian abduction in IS research: a systematic approach for generating and evaluating hypotheses for systematic theory development. Inf. Syst. J. **21**(5), 407–440 (2011)
21. Schurz, G.: Patterns of abduction. Synthese **164**(2), 201–234 (2008)
22. Walton, D.: Abductive reasoning. University of Alabama Press, Tuscaloosa (2014)
23. Klammer, B.: Empirische Sozialforschung. Eine Einführung für Kommunikationswissenschaftler und Journalisten. Utb, Konstanz (2005)
24. Schnell, R., Hill, P., Esser, E.: Methoden der Sozialforschung, 9th edn. Oldenbourg Wissenschaftsverlag, München (2011)
25. Mayer, H.: Interview und Schriftliche Befragung. Entwicklung, Durchführung und Auswertung. Oldenbourg Wissenschaftsverlag, München (2012)
26. Myers, M.D., Newman, M.: The qualitative interview in IS research: Examining the craft. Inf. Organ. **17**(1), 2–26 (2007)
27. Gläser, J., Laudel, G.: Experteninterviews und Qualitative Inhaltsanalyse, 4th edn. VS Verlag, Wiesbaden (2010)
28. Rowley, J.: The wisdom hierarchy: representations of the DIKW hierarchy. J. Inf. Sci. **33**(2), 163–180 (2007)
29. Ackoff, R.L.: From data to wisdom. J. Appl. Syst. Anal. **16**, 3–9 (1989)
30. Zeleny, M.: Management support systems: towards integrated knowledge management. Hum. Syst. Manage. **7**(1), 59–70 (1987)
31. Swigon, M.: Personal knowledge and information management – conception and exemplification. J. Inf. Sci. **39**(6), 832–845 (2013)

32. Pohl, K.: The three dimensions of requirements engineering. In: Bubenko, J., Krogstie, J., Pastor, O., Pernici, B., Rolland, C., Sølvberg, A. (eds.) Seminal Contributions to Information Systems Engineering, pp. 63–80. Springer, Heidelberg (2013)

33. IEEE Recommended Practice for Software Requirements Specifications. Institute of Electrical and Electronics Engineers (1998)

34. Glinz, M.: On non-functional requirements. In: Requirements Engineering Conference, pp. 21–26 (2007)

35. Gassmann, O., Kausch, C., Ellen, E.: Negative side effects of customer integration. Int. J. Technol. Manage. **50**(1), 43–63 (2010)

36. Paasi, J., Luoma, T., Valkokari, K., Lee, N.: Knowledge and intellectual property management in customer–supplier relationships. Int. J. Innov. Manage. **14**(04), 629–654 (2010)

37. Barzel, Y.: Economic Analysis of Property Rights. Cambridge University Press, Cambridge (1997)

38. Liebeskind, J.P.: Knowledge, strategy, and the theory of the firm. Strateg. Manage. J. **17**(S2), 93–107 (1996)

39. Friesike, S.: Profiting from Innovation by Managing Intellectual Property. Doctoral Dissertation, University of St. Gallen (2011)

40. Williamson, O.E.: Credible commitments: using hostages to support exchange. Am. Econ. Rev. **73**, 519–540 (1983)

41. North, D.C.: Institutions and credible commitment. J. Inst. Theor. Econ. (JITE)/Zeitschrift für die gesamte Staatswissenschaft **149**, 11–23 (1993)

42. Ebers, M., Semrau, T.: What drives the allocation of specific investments between buyer and supplier? J. Bus. Res. **68**(2), 415–424 (2015)

43. Crasswell, R.: Taking information seriously: misrepresentation and nondisclosure in contract law and elsewhere. Va Law Rev. **92**, 565–632 (2006)

44. Bogers, M.: The open innovation paradox. knowledge sharing and protection in R&D collaborations. Eur. J. Innov. Manage. **14**(1), 93–117 (2011)

45. Badenfelt, U.: Fixing the contract after the contract is fixed: A study of incomplete contracts in IT and construction projects. Int. J. Project Manage. **29**, 568–576 (2011)

46. Choo, C.W.: The knowing organization: how organizations use information to construct meaning, create knowledge and make decisions. Int. J. Inf. Manage. **16**(5), 329–340 (1996)

47. Clark, A., Chalmers, D.: The extended mind. Analysis **58**, 7–19 (1998)

48. Krogh, G.V.: How does social software change knowledge management? toward a strategic agenda. J. Strateg. Inf. Syst. **21**, 154–164 (2012)

49. Wiegers, K., Beatty, J.: Software Requirements. Pearson Education, Boston (2013)

GQM-Based Definition and Evaluation of Software Project Success Indicators

Luigi Lavazza[1,2(✉)], Enrico Frumento[2], and Riccardo Mazza[3]

[1] Dipartimento di Scienze Teoriche e Applicate,
Università degli Studi dell'Insubria, Varese, Italy
luigi.lavazza@uninsubria.it
[2] CEFRIEL, Milano, Italy
enrico.frumento@cefriel.com
[3] WIND, Ivrea, Italy
riccardo.mazza@wind.it

Abstract. KPI (Key Process Indicators) are usually defined very early in the project's life, when little details about the project are known. Moreover, the definition of KPI does not always follow a systematic and effective methodology. As a result, KPI and project success indicators are often defined in a rather generic and imprecise manner. We need to precisely define KPI and project success indicators, guarantee that the data upon which they are based can be effectively and efficiently measured, and assure that the computed indicators are adequate with respect to project objectives, and represent the viewpoints of all the involved stakeholders. In this paper a complete and coherent process for managing KPI and success indicators lifecycle is proposed. The process is instrumented by well integrated techniques and tools, including the Goal/Question/Metrics (GQM) method for the definition of measures and the R statistic language and environment for analyzing data and computing indicators. The proposed process was applied in the evaluation of the research project MUSES. The MUSES case study shows that the proposed process provides an easy and well supported path to the definition and implementation of effective KPI and project success indicators.

Keywords: Software measurement process · Goal/Question/Metrics · GQM · Key performance indicators · KPI · Success indicators

1 Introduction

KPI and success indicators are usually defined very early in the project's life, often even before starting the project. As a consequence, they tend to be defined in a rather generic way and with no precise context. Important details –such as the data upon which they have to be computed, or how such data are measured– are very often omitted, just because the knowledge that is necessary to clarify these details is not yet available. Therefore, it is generally convenient (sometimes

© Springer International Publishing Switzerland 2016
P. Lorenz et al. (Eds.): ICSOFT 2015, CCIS 586, pp. 228–249, 2016.
DOI: 10.1007/978-3-319-30142-6_13

even necessary) to revise the definitions of the KPI and success indicators in the light of such increased knowledge.

In this paper, we describe a process of refining KPI and success indicators' definitions and the consequent data collection, analysis and evaluation activities. The methods that can be used in process activities are also described. The considered process is expected to provide convincing answers to the following questions, which usually are left unanswered (sometimes they are not even explicitly formulated):

– What is the purpose of each specific KPI or indicator, i.e., what does it mean, actually?
– Do the KPI or indicators represent the actual needs of the project?
– Is there agreement on the definition of the KPI or indicators? In particular, is there agreement between the people in charge of developing the software product, end users and those who pay for the product?
– KPI or indicators' definitions typically involve the measurement of products or processes. Are the required measures well defined and viable?
– How are KPI and indicators computed and visualized?

In many cases, even though the project owners have a fairly good knowledge of the project, they do not use such knowledge effectively in the definition of KPI and success indicators, just because they do not follow a proper methodology that guides the definition and computation of KPI and success indicators.

In this paper we illustrate and evaluate –via a case study– a process that can be used to define KPI and success indicators in software development projects. Namely, the process is applied to the evaluation of the MUSES (Multiplatform Usable Endpoint Security) project. MUSES is a research project partly funded by the EU [1]. The purpose of MUSES is to foster corporate security by reducing the risks introduced by user behavior. To this end, MUSES provides a device-independent, user-centric and self-adaptive corporate security system, able to cope with the concept of seamless working experience on different devices, in which a user may start a session on a device and location and follow up the process on different ones, without loss of corporate digital assets.

The remainder of the paper is organized as follows. Section 2 presents a complete process for the definition of KPI and the enactment of the activities through which measures are collected and indicators are computed. Section 3 describes the definition of KPI and success indicators via GQM. Section 4 shows how the schema of the measure database can be defined on the basis of the knowledge gained during the definition of GQM plans. Section 5 deals with the interpretation of the collected data, and the precise definition of how KPI and success indicators have to be computed. Section 6 illustrates the obtained indicator values and their visualization and discusses the final evaluation of the delivered KPI and success indicators. Section 7 accounts for related work, while Sect. 8 draws the conclusions and outlines future work.

2   The Evaluation Process

To achieve the objectives mentioned in the introduction, a coherent and comprehensive process is needed: the UML activity diagram in Fig. 1 describes such process.

Activity `GQM_goal_definition` aims at specifying the purpose of KPI or success indicators, i.e., what they actually mean. This activity is performed according to the GQM method. Usage of tools supporting the GQM is advisable, but not mandatory.

Activity `Product&Process_modelling` assures that the KPI and success indicators are coherent with the properties of the product or process they refer to. Product or process analysis is performed according to typical analysis methodologies; models are written in UML.

Activity `GQM_plan_definition` assures that the measurements required by KPI and success indicators are well defined and can be performed at reasonable cost. This activity is performed according to GQM. Usage of tools supporting the GQM is advisable, but not mandatory.

Activity `Measure_DB_schema_design` is carried out with the purpose that evaluators and developers agree on the data to be provided by measurement activities; it guarantees that the right data are provided, and the data are provided right, i.e., as required for evaluation. UML class diagrams can be used for conceptual modelling.

In activity `Project_Trials`, the process to be evaluated is carried out, and measures are collected. Actually, "Project trials" is MUSES terminology to indicate beta testing. The process is instrumented to provide the required measures.

Review and validation of measures are also performed before using the collected data, to further increases the confidence on the validity of the representativeness of measures, hence of the derived indicators. Depending on the specific process/product, measurement tools, questionnaires, monitoring activities, etc. can be used.

Activity `Indicator_definition` provides a well defined (actually, a formal and executable) (re)definition of KPI and success indicators, also highlighting what data are used and how. The R language is used to code the data analysis and processing that yields KPI and success indicators.

Activity `Indicator_computation` presents indicators in a form that can be easily understood by users and stakeholders, and whose representativeness of the actual product and process can be easily assessed. The R environment is used to compute KPI and success indicators and graphically represent them.

3   Using GQM to Define KPI and Success Indicators

KPI and success indicators are (re)defined as GQM goals. We start from the indications given in the MUSES Description of Work (DoW): *The achievement of the project objectives will be measured based on the success and progress indicators given in* Table 1. *The indicators will be revised and updated in the course of the project in order to reflect the detailed user needs and related technical objectives of the project.*

In Table 1, the success and progress indicators are given without specifying why they have been introduced and what quality they are intended to represent. In an evaluation activity, one should always start from the definition of the evaluation goal, so that the data to be collected and the indicators to be used can be consequently defined. The GQM technique [2–4] formalized these ideas.

3.1   The GQM

In general, every project calls for specific measures and evaluation criteria, depending on the specific goals of the projects. The GQM method is a general purpose, goal-driven method, which has been successfully used in several

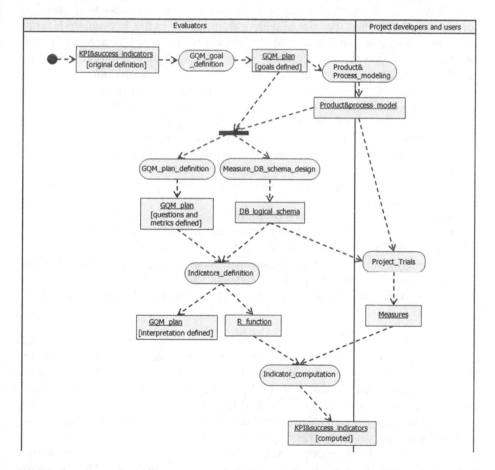

Fig. 1. A process for the systematic definition and computation of KPI and project success indicators.

Table 1. A few success indicators from MUSES DoW.

	Success & Progress Indicators	Measuring and verification form	Target value
Effectiveness	Applicability of the MUSES model	Successful application of MUSES in multiple non overlapping and independent settings • Functional user cases • Domain	At least 4 Functional Use Cases within the selected domain successfully conducted
Usability	User perception	Perceived improvement in user experience (e.g., ease of use, usability, ...)	Over 70% of user satisfaction
	User response	MUSES cancelled by user requests	<10%

evaluation activities [5,6,8]. The GQM provides a systematic approach to formalize the goals of a project and to refine them into a measurement plan.

A GQM plan is organized into a few levels: at the topmost level, one or more goals are specified. Each goal includes: an object (what is evaluated: typically a process, an activity or a product); a quality (i.e., the characteristic(s) of the object that have to be evaluated); a purpose (such as evaluation, analysis, understanding, etc.); a point of view (since the same objective may be evaluated differently by different stakeholders); an environment (where is the object evaluated: the environment can affect the evaluation).

As shown in Fig. 2, a GQM goal is always the formalization of needs: it must be clear where each goal comes from and why it was conceived.

An example of a goal is: "Evaluate the throughput of a given process, from the point of view of the process manager, in environment X".

For every goal, an "abstraction sheet" is built. It identifies 4 groups of items:

1. Quality foci (QF): the qualities of interest.
2. Variation factors (VF): variables that are not of interest themselves, but can affect the values of the measures associated to the quality foci.
3. Baseline hypotheses (BH): the expected values for quality foci and variation factors. These will be used in the analysis of the data.
4. Impact of variation factors on baseline hypothesis: how VF are expected to affect BH.

The abstraction sheets are a preparation step to address the operational level of the plan: for every element of the abstraction sheet, one or more questions are defined. These are used to describe the object of the study and the attributes, properties, characteristics and aspects that should be taken into considerations. Accordingly, questions have to be defined having in mind –as shown in Fig. 2– a model of the objects of measurement and of the environment where the measurement will take place and the results will be used.

The final level is the metric level, which is quantitative. According to the model defined at the questions level, a set of metrics is identified. Measurement activities will provide data (i.e., a quantitative knowledge of the elements of the model) that will allow answering the questions. The process of defining a GQM

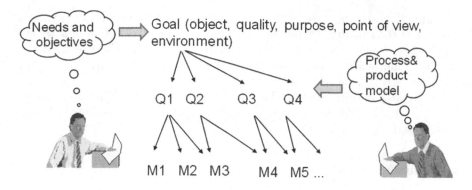

Fig. 2. GQM goal, questions and metrics.

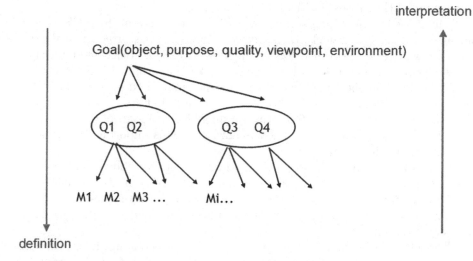

Fig. 3. GQM goal top-down refinement and bottom-up interpretation.

plan is thus a top-down refinement, from goals to metrics. Once the measurement has been performed, the GQM plan guides the interpretation of data in a bottom-up way (Fig. 3). Measures provide the data associated with the metrics definitions. The analysis of such data provides answers to questions. The answers contribute to achieving the goal.

The GQM method is general-purpose; however, it has been proposed in the software engineering arena, as a reaction to the idea of predefined measures and criteria for interpreting them. The spirit of the GQM is that individual processes and products call for specific sets of measures and criteria for interpreting them. A possible strategy is to identify the measures that characterize the process or product being examined, and set target values for the measures that characterize it. The measurements are performed only a-posteriori, to check if the target has been reached. In any case, the GQM is an extremely flexible conceptual tool, which can be easily adapted to a great variety of situations.

Finally, it has to be noted that GQM plans are conceptual plans, without indication of the resources to be employed, the timing and duration of activities, etc. All these issues have to be tackled in the creation of the execution and evaluation plan, which will provide traditional planning instruments like Work Breakdown Structure, Gantt charts, etc.

The GQM has been used in the evaluation of several EU funded projects (including CEMP, SACHER, CASCADOSS projects and others) as well as in industrial settings [5,6,8–10]

3.2   Definition of KPI as GQM Goals

In this section we show how KPI and success indicators can be redefined at a high level as GQM goals. This section describes in detail activity `GQM_goal_definition` of the process in Fig. 1.

To limit the length of the paper, we considered only a few of the MUSES KPI and success indicators (namely, those given in Table 1). We started by analyzing the first row of Table 1 critically, considering how MUSES is structured internally and in which contexts it is intended to be used. We found that MUSES is shaped around several different general working scenarios (named "use cases", or "UC" in the project). Not all UC are exercised in all domains, but are generic enough to adapt to different situations; UC are the building blocks of most of the situations where MUSES adds layers of security. Accordingly, it is important to evaluate all the relevant (UC, domain) pairs.

The analysis revealed also that the evaluation activity had to address two complementary aspects: (1) the applicability of MUSES in all the scenarios in which it is intended to be used, (2) the success of the application of every MUSES UC. By the way, in the original definition, it was not clear what "successfully conducted" should mean.

Although MUSES will be usable in many application domains, in the context of the research project only a couple of domains were considered. Accordingly, the KPI and success indicators evaluated within the project have to apply only to the domains in which the tests are carried out.

So, the first row of Table 1 can be stated as a GQM goal as follows:

Goal 1. Evaluate the applicability of MUSES UCs in selected domain-specific scenarios from the point of view of the companies operating in such domains.

To define KPI and success indicators we use the GQM, therefore we start from GQM goals. Part of the knowledge about the product acquired during the definition of the GQM goals is not embedded in the goal definition, rather it is used in the definition of the GQM plan, which is discussed in Sect. 3.3.

In the MUSES project, we reformulated all the indications given in Table 1, even when the resulting GQM goal definition is very close to the original definition. For instance, the second row in Table 1 led to formulating the following GQM goal:

Goal 11. Evaluate the MUSES framework with respect to perceived user experience, in the selected industry domains from the point of view of domain users.

In this goal, the "perceived user experience" has to be further specified, since there are so many factors that can affect the user experience. The detailed definition of "user experience" within MUSES is specified in Sect. 3.3.

3.3 Detailing KPI and Success Indicators in a GQM Plan

Having defined the GQM goals, the next step consists of refining the goals into questions and metrics. Here is where the GQM is most useful: via a step-by-step refinement, we make sure that the metrics definitions obtained at the end of the process are coherent with the goals, and take into consideration (a) all the issues connected with the product or process to be evaluated, and (b) the points of view of the involved stakeholders.

Product and Process Modelling – MUSES Goal 1 Activities. The definition of an effective measurement plan must include the definition of a model of the empirical, real-world context in which the measurement is to take place [7].

The GQM does not prescribe how one should represent or document such model, which includes the knowledge of the relevant product and process. It was suggested that such knowledge can be represented via UML models [11]: here we follow such proposal.

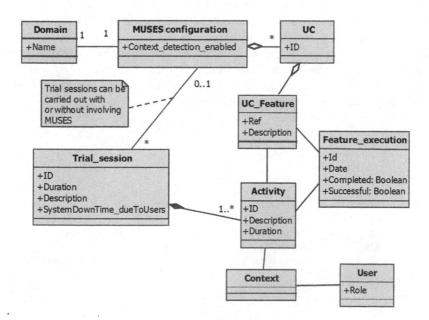

Fig. 4. Conceptual model of MUSES Goal 1 testing and evaluation activities.

The class diagram given in Fig. 4 illustrates the elements of the MUSES testing and evaluation activities, upon which the evaluation of the project is based. The diagram specifies that in each domain, a specific configuration of MUSES is used. Every configuration includes a possibly different set of UC. These are the UC that are useful in the domain where the particular MUSES configuration will be used.

Every MUSES configuration is used in one or more trial session. There are trial sessions where no MUSES configuration is used. These sessions are useful to get data on the behaviour of a domain not equipped with MUSES, to enable comparisons between the without-MUSES and with-MUSES situations.

MUSES UC are characterized in terms of UC features. Trial activities exercise UC features. The execution of UC features within an activity is observable, hence it can be classified with respect to completeness and correctness. Trial activities are carried out in specific contexts, whose main characterization is given by the participating users' roles.

GQM Plan Definition – Goal 1. By taking into account the situation described in Fig. 4, we can identify QF Application of MUSES UC and VF Application domain. Then, still making reference to Fig. 4, we can derive the following questions:

Q1.1. How many UC were executed per domain?
Q1.2. How many UC were successfully applied in each domain?

Figure 4 indicates that although the MUSES evaluation is carried out at the granularity level of UC, we need to consider that every trial activity involves a set of UC features. Accordingly, question Q1.1 was associated with metrics that account for both UC and UC features (see Fig. 5).

Question Q1.2 was associated with the metrics shown in Fig. 5, which account for the fact that the absolute number of successful executions of UC features is not relevant per se, rather it is the ratio of successful execution to total executions that provides a clear idea of MUSES success rate.

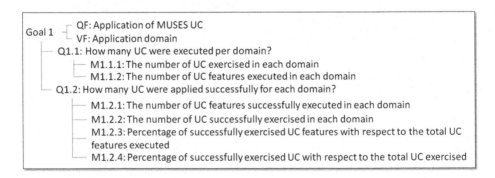

Fig. 5. GQM plan of Goal 1.

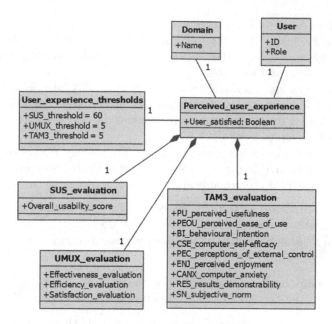

Fig. 6. Conceptual model of MUSES Goal 11 testing and evaluation activities.

Product and Process Modelling – MUSES Goal 11 Activities. When considering the second row in Table 1 –which was formalized by the definition of Goal 11 in Sect. 3.2– we found different problems than with the indicators considered previously:

- The characterization of user experience is incomplete, as only a few properties –namely, ease of use, usability and flow– are mentioned. Besides, the mentioned properties are not precisely defined: for instance, the meaning of "usability" (and how it differs from "ease of use") is not defined.
- Having multiple experience aspects, a single satisfaction measure can be obtained via multiple composition criteria. It should also be decided if it is the user who has to express a single satisfaction measure, or the user evaluates separately his/her satisfaction with respect to ease of use, usability, etc. and the global user satisfaction is computed later by the project evaluators.
- The measure of user satisfaction is not defined. In particular, user satisfaction is hardly expressible as a Boolean value. Usually values of this type are measured via Likert scales [12], in which case the satisfaction threshold has to be identified. If scale rates are "Very dissatisfied", "Moderately dissatisfied", "Moderately satisfied", "Very satisfied", one could place the threshold either at the "Moderately satisfied" or at the "Very satisfied" level.

To clarify all these issues, we proceeded as for the previously described goals, i.e., we built a conceptual model of perceived user experience. Such model – derived with the help of experts– is given in Fig. 6 (where the connections of the Perceived_user_experience to the trial activities have been omitted to simplify the picture).

Perceived usability of the MUSES applications is assessed with the 10-item System Usability Scale (SUS) [13], including usability and learnability [14]. The goal for MUSES is to achieve the score of 60 for the overall usability (combining the factors usability and learnability).

Complementary aspects are assessed via the Usability Metric of User Experience (UMUX) [13] to address effectiveness, satisfaction and efficiency. A 7 level Likert scale is used for the measurement: evaluations are considered successful when the grade is above level 4.

Technology acceptance is measured via the Technology Acceptance Model 3 (TAM3) [15]. Also in this case a 7 level Likert scale is used: evaluations are considered successful if the grade is above level 4.

GQM Plan Definition – Goal 11. Based on Fig. 6, for Goal 11 we can identify QF MUSES user experience and VF Application domain.

Then, still making reference to the situation described in Fig. 6, we can derive the following questions:

Q11.1. How many users used MUSES in each domain?
Q11.2. What is the percentage of satisfied users, for each domain?

The definition of user experience given in Fig. 6 suggests that overall users' satisfaction is evaluated based on SUS, TAM-3 and UMUX evaluations. Accordingly, the metrics shown in Fig. 7 were defined.

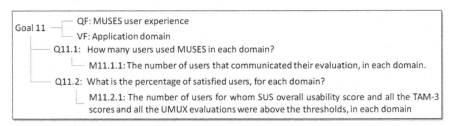

Fig. 7. GQM plan of Goal 11.

3.4   Validating the Plans: Involving Stakeholders

The conceptual definition of the product and process –as given in Figs. 4 and 6– is the basis for the definition of the GQM plan and project evaluation. Of course, someone has to supply the data and/or carry out the activities described in the model, otherwise the required measures will not be available and the evaluation will not be possible.

In general, people in charge of project evaluation (i.e., those aiming at computing KPI and showing to what extent the project outcomes satisfy the original objectives) and those participating in carrying out research and development activities (i.e., those who make the "real work") belong to disjoint subsets. Accordingly, the conceptual definition of the product and process can be seen as a "contract" between evaluators on one side and researchers, developers, users, stakeholders, etc. on the other side. Hence, it is necessary that everybody agrees that the conceptual model is a faithful representation of the project product and processes, and that the corresponding data and measures will be provided.

In some cases the agreement on the model is achieved *a priori*: for instance the model of the data that are relevant for Goal 11 (Fig. 6) was defined with the help of the people working in the project, who had a clear idea of both the type of usability that MUSES had to provide, and how to characterize it. In other cases, the conceptual model was derived by the evaluators, who had in mind the need of getting data that could support the KPI and success indicator defined in the DoW. In fact, we should remember that the DoW is the technical annex of the contract, thus the project *must* deliver all what is described in the DoW, including the measures of the KPI and success indicators.

Discussions and adjustments of the model were caused by Goal 12:

Goal 12. Evaluate the MUSES framework with respect to acceptance by users involved in trials, in the selected industry domains from the point of view of domain users.

In this case, the issue raised by the people in charge of the project trials concerned the type of activity in which the users had to be involved in order to provide the required data concerning the acceptance of the MUSES framework. This is a particularly interesting case, because the metric is defined in a straightforward way: it is a Boolean, representing the fact that the user continued using MUSES for his/her work throughout the trials period, or he/she preferred to drop MUSES and go on working without its support. The concerns of project people were that the trials could not be carried out in a real production environment, and trials could not last so long as to allow users appreciate all MUSES features in all possible conditions.

The solution was that the trials were organized in a way that relevant situations occurred in a realistic environment, rather than in real production environments. So, the benefits of modelling, documenting and discussing the KPI and success indicators did not result in a better definition of the indicators themselves, but in clarifying the activities that had to provide the raw measures. In any case, the important point is that an agreement on what had to be done for evaluating MUSES was achieved.

4   The Measure DB Schema

Data are usually measured from the field and collected into a database. This is a good practice for several reasons, including the fact that data measurement activities are isolated from the evaluation activities. Actually, the definition of the database acts as a "contract" between the parties: people in charge of data collection do not need to worry about the technicalities concerning the usage of the collected data and measures. Similarly, people in charge of the project evaluation do not need to worry about how data and measures are collected, provided that the measured data have the meaning that has been agreed upon.

The GQM plan usually provides precise indications about the needed data: it is thus easy to derive the measure database schema from the GQM plan. More precisely, the conceptual descriptions of the product and process provided by UML diagrams like the one in Fig. 4 can be used as conceptual data models for the design of the measure database. For instance, class Feature_execution in Fig. 4 suggests the definition of the table shown in Table 2.

Table 2. Feature_execution table.

Attribute	Type
Feature_execution_ID	Int
UC_feature_ID	Int
Feature_execution_date	Date
Feature_completely_executed	Boolean
Feature_successfully_executed	Boolean

The definition of the GQM metrics tells us also how the relevant data should be derived from the database tables. For instance, by properly joining the tables designed on the basis of UML class diagrams it is possible to get the view described in Table 3.

Table 3. Goal 1-oriented data view.

Attribute	Type
Domain_name	Text
UC_ID	Int
UC_feature_ID	Int
Feature_completely_executed	Boolean
Feature_successfully_executed	Boolean

Given such view, the data associated to the metrics of Goal 1 are obtained very easily. E.g., the number of UC features successfully executed in domain "Domain_A" is obtained via the following query:

```
SELECT Count(UC_feature_ID) AS M1
FROM SELECT DISTINCT View1.UC_feature_ID
FROM View1
WHERE (((View1.Domain_name)="Domain_A")
  AND ((View1.Feature_completely_executed)=Yes)
  AND ((View1.Feature_successfully_executed)=Yes));
```

Other metrics are obtained via similar queries.

5 Implementing Indicators

5.1 Determining the Interpretation of Measures

Most importantly, the GQM plan can be used as a basis for specifying the interpretation of the questions, goals, and –ultimately– the indicators that represent the KPI and success indicators. We face two needs: (1) computing the numbers needed to answer the questions, and (2) specifying how such numbers have to be interpreted to provide suitable indicators at the goal level.

Considering the metrics associated to question Q1.2 of Goal 1 (How many UC were applied successfully in each domain?), it is quite evident that we have to solve the problem of determining if a given UC was successful or not, given the results of its features' executions. Do we need that all UC feature executions are successful? If not, what is the criterion for deciding if a given mix of UC features executions should be considered an overall success of the UC they belong to? Consider the following case: a given UC includes two UC features: fA and fB; fA has been executed 10 times: it was successful 8 times and it failed 2 times; fB has been executed 4 times: it was successful 3 times and it failed once. Should the UC be considered successful? To decide, we need to establish success thresholds for UC features. There are several ways to do it; here it is not important how you define the success thresholds, instead, it is important stressing that considering the definitions of questions and metrics leads to realizing the need for aggregating results obtained at the UC feature level into results at the UC level.

When moving to the goal level, we can observe that the role of Goal 1 questions is different: Q1.2 quantifies the achievements of the project in terms of successful UC, while Q1.1 quantifies the extent of the work done and –by difference– it indicates how many tested UC were not successful. The MUSES DoW indicates that at least 4 UC must be successfully applied in each domain, therefore we stick to such interpretation: the indicator is simply the result of checking if the number of successfully applied UC is not smaller than 4.

From a strictly contractual point of view, we could stop here, as far as Goal 1 is concerned, since showing that at least 4 UC per domain have been successfully tested is enough to comply with the contract. However, answering question Q1.1 could provide additional insight to project participants: in fact, knowing that one or more UC were tested but were not successful provides indications that could foster improvements in the concerned research area.

5.2 Implementing KPI

The definitions of KPI and success indicators have to be translated into actual code that processes measures and yields the values of the KPI and success indicators. In doing this, it is useful considering that graphical, easy to read representations of KPI and indicators are usually very welcome, especially by non technical managers.

This step can be performed in several ways. In this paper we use the statistical language and programming environment R [25, 26]. We use R because it is open-source, reliable, extremely well supported and very flexible.

A general consideration concerning the implementation of KPI and indicators is that there is always some processing that can be effectively performed by the database management system. Therefore, a decision to be taken concerns the amount of processing that is demanded to the DBMS: at one extreme we get from the DB raw data, and all the processing is carried out in the data analysis and elaboration environment (in our case, R); at the other extreme the DBMS makes most of the required computation, and the data analysis and elaboration environment has just to carry out some –possibly trivial– data elaboration and visualization task.

Also in this case the GQM plan helps: a very simple and effective choice is that the DBMS provides exactly the metrics data as defined in the GQM plan, while the rest of the elaboration is carried out by R programs. For instance, metric M1.1.1 can be easily extracted from the DB by the following R code:

```
library(RODBC)
channel <- odbcConnect("MUSES",uid="root",pwd="**",believeNRows=FALSE)
Domains <- as.matrix(sqlQuery(channel
                    "SELECT Dom_name FROM MUSES.Domains"))
Num_tested_UC = c()
for(i in 1:length(Domains)) {
  query_text = sprintf("SELECT DISTINCT View1.UC_ID FROM MUSES.View1
    WHERE(((View1.Domain_name)=\"%s\") AND
          (View1.Feature_completely_exec=1))", Domains[i])
  S1 <- as.matrix(sqlQuery(channel, query_text))
  Num_tested_UC = append(Num_tested_UC, length(S1))
}
print(Num_tested_UC)
```

The R code shown above works in a rather straightforward way:

1. Package rodbc [16] is loaded.
2. A connection to the DB is created.
3. A first query retrieves the list of domain names from the Domain table.
4. For each domain, the set of UC identifiers for which at least one feature was completely executed is also retrieved. The cardinality of the set is added to vector Num_tested_UC.
5. Vector Num_tested_UC is printed.

The shown R code does very little more than retrieving data via a query. The R code shown below performs slightly more complex processing: on the one hand the queries are more complex (they do not just retrieve data, but group UC_features per UC), on the other hand, the percentages of successful UC feature per UC and per domain are computed.

```
library(RODBC)
channel <- odbcConnect("MUSES",uid="root",pwd="**", believeNRows=FALSE)
Domains <- as.matrix(sqlQuery(channel,
                    "SELECT Domain_name FROM MUSES.Domains"))
for(i in 1:length(Domains)) {
```

```
cat("domain:", Domains[i], "\n")
query_text = sprintf("SELECT View1.UC_ID, Count(View1.UC_feature_ID)
  AS Num_UC_feature_ID FROM View1 WHERE (((View1.Domain_name)=\"%s\"))
  GROUP BY View1.UC_ID;", Domains[i])
All <- sqlQuery(channel, query_text)
cat("============================\n");
query_text = sprintf("SELECT View1.UC_ID, Count(View1.UC_feature_ID)
  AS Num_UC_feature_ID FROM View1 WHERE (((View1.Domain_name)=\"%s\")
  AND ((View1.Feature_completely_executed)=1) AND
  ((View1.Feature_successfully_executed)=1)) GROUP BY View1.UC_ID;",
  Domains[i])
Good <- sqlQuery(channel, query_text)
query_text = sprintf("SELECT View1.UC_ID, Count(View1.UC_feature_ID)
  AS Num_UC_feature_ID FROM View1 WHERE (((View1.Domain_name)=\"%s\")
  AND (((View1.Feature_completely_executed)=0) OR
  ((View1.Feature_successfully_executed)=0))) GROUP BY View1.UC_ID;",
  Domains[i])
Bad <- sqlQuery(channel, query_text)
for (j in 1:length(All[,1])) {
  x = subset(Good, Good$UC_ID==j);
  num_good=ifelse(length(x[,1])==0, 0, x$Num_UC_feature_ID);
  x = subset(Bad, Bad$UC_ID==j);
  num_bad=ifelse(length(x[,1])==0, 0, x$Num_UC_feature_ID);
  cat("UC_ID =", j, ": UC feature success =",
      100*num_good/(num_good+num_bad), "%\n")
}
cat(" \n")
}
odbcCloseAll()
```

The output of this code is shown in Fig. 8. Of course, it is possible to represent the output in a more sophisticated and easy to read way, e.g., graphically, as illustrated Sect. 6.1.

```
domain: Domain A
================================
UC_ID = 1 : UC feature success = 66.66667 %
UC_ID = 2 : UC feature success = 50 %

domain: Domain B
================================
UC_ID = 1 : UC feature success = 50 %
UC_ID = 2 : UC feature success = 50 %
UC_ID = 3 : UC feature success = 100 %
```

Fig. 8. Indicators concerning UC feature success in each domain, generated by the code shown above.

6   Indicator Computation

6.1   Computing Results

When the measure database has been populated (in the case of MUSES by project trials) R programs can read data from the DB and produce both textual and graphical results, possibly in comprehensive reports. For instance, the results yielded by the R programs associated to Goal 11 are given in Fig. 9. In the examples reported here, R is used for its basic data manipulation and graphic display capabilities. When necessary, R –being provided with numerous libraries, which implement almost any desirable statistical function– can perform more complex statistical computations. An example is given in Fig. 10, where Goal 10 indicators are given: communication delays are plotted, with respect to security violations occurrence times (the red line is the maximum delay threshold, while

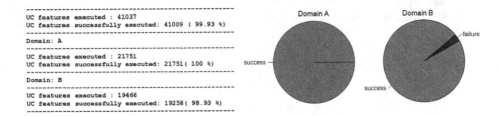

Fig. 9. Results of Goal 11.

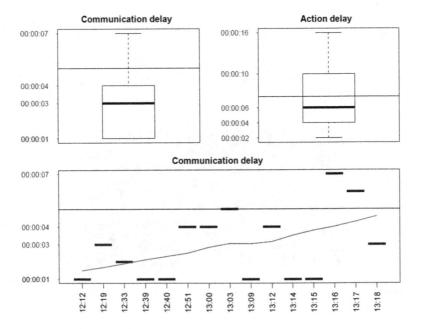

Fig. 10. Results of Goal 10 (Color figure online).

the blue line indicates the "lowess" –locally weighted scatterplot smoothing– line, which can be interpreted as the trend of the delays.

Quite noticeably, the R code that computes the required KPI and success indicators can get the needed data directly from the measurement DB and then process them to produce the required indicators. This approach is very effective, because when new measures are inserted in the database, it is sufficient to re-run the R program to get updated indicators.

6.2   Final Evaluations

The KPI and success indicators computed as shown in the previous sections make the effectiveness of the project apparent. However, to be sure that these indications are reliable, some validation is advisable To this end, we found that two-fold validation is usually quite effective.

First, during the trial activities that generate measures, project people examine the computed indicators and verify that the computed KPI and success indicators actually reflect reality (i.e., what happened in the trials). To this end, it is essential that the KPI and success indicators are provided as soon as the measurement data are available; in fact, if the delay between the events in the field and their effects on the indicators is too long, it is possible that project people do not remember precisely the situation against which the correctness of indicators must be verified. With the considered process, indicators are computed and visualized as soon as measurement data are loaded in the database, hence real-time feedback is available to people running the product to be evaluated, so that they can evaluate the current indicators against the current situation.

Second, the proposed process instrumentation allows for presenting users and stakeholders with KPI that are very easy to understand. In the case of MUSES, the EU officer and reviewers could easily realize that the KPI actually represented what they needed to know about the product/process.

The two-fold validation assures not only that KPI and success indicators are correct, but also that they represent well the situation they are meant to disclose, i.e., that we have built the right KPI, and that we have built them right.

7   Related Work

The definition and implementation of indicators concerning the performance of processes has received a great deal of attention in the past. Initially, the literature concentrated on the definition of KPI and the associated measurement plans, but gave little or no attention to measurement, data collection and actual computation of KPI [17].

Researchers also addressed the role of techniques like the GQM in process evaluations [7]. In general, these proposals focused on the generation and execution of measurement plan at a quite high level of abstraction, without mentioning the tools to be used, or the techniques that could help reasoning about the product and process to be measured, or how to ensure that the measurement plans actually matched the objects of measurement and the users' goals. Even a rather extensive guidebook like [20] does not deal with the aforementioned details.

A more comprehensive and detailed view of software project measurement illustrated software project control centers (SPCC) [18]. SPCC are sets of activities and tools aiming at collecting, interpreting, and visualizing measures to provide purpose- and role-oriented information to all parties involved in project development and quality assurance. Although our approach has some similarities with the SPCC described by Muench and Heidrich (for instance, some of the activities of our process comply with their classification) a fundamental difference is that SPCC are meant primarily to provide indications to project people during the execution of a project, while we address a broader objective, including providing useful indications to end users and payors of the project. Thus, making KPI understandable and evidently coherent with the project scope and aims is a primary objective. Issues such as supporting multiple types of visualizations for different stakeholders, and making indicators easy to understand are typical of the situation we target, while they are not relevant in SPCC.

A more recent proposal [19] addresses IT governance by proposing the integration of CoBIT [21] and GQM.

The point of view of stakeholders is introduced in project monitoring as a central issue in [22]. Although Tsunoda et al. have the merit of introducing stakeholder-oriented concepts like the stakeholder's goal and the key goal indicator, they describe the project measurement and monitoring process at a quite abstract level.

Several researchers are addressing KPI for software-supported business processes: see for instance [24]. When dealing with business processes, the problem of defining and computing KPI is the same as discussed in this paper, but the object of the evaluation –i.e., business processes instead of software development processes– makes a big difference. In the former case, the KPI are more homogenous and easy to describe than in the case of software development; moreover software is given, and KPI tend to consider its qualities only with reference to supporting a specific process rather than development project goals, as in the case of MUSES. Consequently, the literature on KPI for software-supported business processes is hardly interesting for software projects.

When dealing with business processes, it is often the case that software is involved as an instrument to achieve business goals. The GQM+strategies technique [23] was introduced as a way for linking indicators to business goals in a systematic and structured way. In any case, the need for addressing hierarchies of business goals and related strategies (possibly supported by software) is out of the scope of this paper. Adapting the approach proposed here to hierarchies of business goals and related strategies is a subject for future work.

Overall, none of the mentioned articles addresses in an organic and systematic manner all of the issues we dealt with in the paper, namely: Defining stakeholders' goals; Connecting measures to goals that are relevant for stakeholders; Assuring that measures are coherent with the product and/or process of interest; Making the relationships between measurement data, measure definitions and process and product properties explicit; Making the definition of indicators explicit, formal and supported by tools that can be used to retrieve data, compute and visualize indicators.

In summary, we can state that our proposal provides practitioners with guidelines –encompassing well defined activities, which are effectively supported by tools– more extensively and at a much more concrete level than previous work.

8   Conclusions

Defining adequate KPI and project success indicators for software development projects is made difficult by several concurrent issues:

- We need that indicators are really representative of the project's achievements, and account for the viewpoints of all the involved stakeholders.
- Indicators have to be precisely defined, otherwise they can be misinterpreted, both in the data collection and indicator computation phase and in the usage phase (i.e., when the project's success has to appear).
- Indicators must be feasible, i.e., the measures upon which they are based have to be obtainable effectively and efficiently.
- Activities ranging from defining indicators to delivering results (i.e., indicators' values based on measures) call for specific techniques and tools, otherwise they can be quite time and effort consuming and error-prone.

As a consequence, we need to provide people in charge of software project evaluation with guidelines, techniques and tools to effectively manage the KPI and success indicator lifecycle.

In this paper, we have described the phases of the lifecycle of KPI and project success indicators, highlighting problems and suggesting techniques and tools that can be used to support the various activities. We have also proposed a model of the KPI and success indicator definition and computation process.

Our process model and guidelines are derived from a careful analysis of the problems connected with the KPI and success factor lifecycle; such analysis – which in principle can be applied in any software development process– led to identifying techniques, tools and practices that can make the process efficient and relatively easy. In fact, the identified activities and the supporting methods and techniques are highly integrated and work in a quite cooperative manner: UML models describe the elements of the GQM plan; the GQM plan indicates the measures to be collected, while UML diagrams indicate their logical structure; the measurement database schema is coherent with both UML models ad GQM plans; R procedures implement the interpretation criteria that are implicit in the GQM plan; R procedures are fed by the measure database (actually they can directly query the database). Thanks to this tight integration, the process of defining and computing KPI and success indicators is fairly smooth and easy to enact.

The described process, techniques, tools and practices have been used in the research project MUSES. Despite its research nature, MUSES is like any other software development project, with respect to KPI and success indicators: developers had difficulties in defining proper indicators, and had no systematic approach to measurement and indicator computation and visualization.

The results achieved within the MUSES project were very satisfactory, especially in that project people were challenged to thoroughly discuss –and eventually approve– the definitions of indicators and the measures to be collected and their interpretations. Finally, the measurement plan provided several hints for the organization of the project trials, and even suggested a few data collection and logging features to be included in the MUSES platform and tools.

In conclusion, we believe that whoever has to evaluate the success of a software development process can get several useful suggestions from this paper, both at the methodological level –e.g., concerning the activities to be carried out and the overall process– and practically –e.g., concerning the usage of the methods and tools described in the paper to make activities easier and cheaper.

Future work includes the construction of a toolset that integrates the GQM plan management, the measure database and the R environment.

Acknowledgements. The work presented here was partly supported by the EU Collaborative project MUSES – Multiplatform USable Endpoint Security, under grant agreement n. 318508 and by project "Metodi, tecniche e strumenti per l'analisi, l'implementazione e la valutazione di sistemi software," funded by Università degli Studi dell'Insubria.

References

1. MUSES project. https://www.musesproject.eu/
2. Basili, V., Weiss, D.: A methodology for collecting valid software engineering data. IEEE Trans. Softw. Eng. **10**(6), 728–738 (1984)
3. Basili, V., Rombach, H.D.: The TAME project: towards improvement-oriented software environments. IEEE Trans. Softw. Eng. **14**(6), 758–773 (1988)
4. Basili, V., Caldiera, G., Rombach, H.D.: Goal/Question/Metric paradigm. In: Marciniak, J.J. (ed.) Encyclopedia of Software Engineering, vol. 1. Wiley, New York (1994)
5. Fuggetta, A., Lavazza, L., Morasca, S., Cinti, S., Oldano, G., Orazi, E.: Applying G/Q/M in an industrial software factory. ACM Trans. Softw. Eng. Methodol. **7**(4), 411–448 (1998)
6. Birk, A., van Solingen, R., Jarvinen, J.: Business impact, benefit, and cost of applying gqm in industry: an in-depth, long-term investigation at Schlumberger RPS. In: 5th International Symposium on Software Metrics (1998)
7. Birk, A., Hamann, D., Pfahl, D., Jrvinen, J., Oivo, M., Vierimaa, M., van Solingen, R.: The Role of GQM in the PROFES Improvement Methodology (1999)
8. van Solingen, R., Berghout, E.: Integrating goal-oriented measurement in industrial software engineering: industrial experiences with and additions to the Goal/Question/Metric method (GQM). In: 7th International Software Metrics Symposium (2001)
9. Lavazza, L.: Multi-scope evaluation of public administration initiatives in process automation. In: 5th European Conference on Information Management and Evaluation (2011)

10. Lavazza, L., Mauri, M.: Software process measurement in the real world: dealing with operating constraints. In: Wang, Q., Pfahl, D., Raffo, D.M., Wernick, P. (eds.) SPW/ProSim 2006. LNCS, vol. 3966, pp. 80–87. Springer, Heidelberg (2006)
11. Lavazza, L., Barresi, G.: Automated support for process-aware definition and execution of measurement plans. In: International Conference on Software Engineering (2005)
12. Likert, R.: Technique for the measure of attitudes. Arch. Psychol. **22**(140), 1–55 (1932)
13. Brooke, J.: SUS: a "quick and dirty" usability scale. In: Jordan, P., Thomas, B., Weerdemeester, B. (eds.) Usability Evaluation in Industry. Taylor and Francis, London (1996)
14. Lewis, J.R., Sauro, J.: The factor structure of the system usability scale. In: Kurosu, M. (ed.) HCD 2009. LNCS, vol. 5619, pp. 94–103. Springer, Heidelberg (2009)
15. Venkatesh, V., Bala, H.: Technology acceptance model 3 and a research agenda on interventions. Decis. Sci. **39**(2), 273–312 (2008)
16. Ripley, B., Lapsley, M.: Package RODBC - ODBC Database Access (2014)
17. Basili, V.: Applying the Goal/Question/Metric paradigm in the experience factory. In: 10th Annual CSR Workshop, Application of Software Metrics and Quality Assurance in Industry (1993)
18. Muench, J., Heidrich, J.: Software project control centers: concepts and approaches. J. Syst. Softw. **70**(1), 3–19 (2004)
19. Nicho, M., Cusack, B.: A metrics generation model for measuring the control objectives of information systems audit. In: 40th Annual Hawaii International Conference on System Sciences (2007)
20. Park, R.E., Goethert, W.B., Florac, W.A.: Goal-Driven Software Measurement. A Guidebook. Software Engineering Inst., Carnegie-Mellon Univ. (1996)
21. ISACA: COBIT 5: A Business Framework for the Governance and Management of Enterprise IT (2012)
22. Tsunoda, M., Matsumura, T., Matsumoto, K.I.: Modeling software project monitoring with stakeholders. In: 9th International Conference on Computer & Information Science (2010)
23. Basili, V., Lindvall, M., Regardie, M., Seaman, C., Heidrich, J., Munch, J., Rombach, D., Trendowicz, A.: Linking software development and business strategy through measurement. Computer **43**(4), 57–65 (2010)
24. Souza Cardoso, E.C.: Towards a methodology for goal-oriented enterprise management. In: Enterprise Distributed Object Computing Conference Workshops (2013)
25. Ihaka, R., Gentleman, R.: R: a language for data analysis and graphics. J. Comput. Graphical Stat. **5**(3), 299–314 (1996)
26. The R Project for Statistical Computing. http://www.r-project.org

Dynamic Analysis Techniques to Reverse Engineer Mobile Applications

Philippe Dugerdil[(✉)] and Roland Sako

Geneva School of Business Adminsitration,
University of Applied Sciences Western Switzerland,
7 route de Drize, 1227 Geneva, Switzerland
philippe.dugerdil@hesge.ch, roland.sako@gmail.com

Abstract. Nowadays mobile applications have moved to mainstream. Service companies such as IBM advise us to develop on the "Mobile First". Although earlier mobile apps were simple data access front ends, today's apps are quite complex. Therefore the same problem of code maintenance and comprehension of poorly documented apps, as in the desktop world, happen to the mobile today. Hence we need techniques to reverse engineer mobile applications starting from the mere source code. In this paper we present the methodology and suite of tools we developed that helps with the reverse engineering and understanding of mobile apps. The performance of these tools is demonstrated on two case studies of iPhone applications. The contribution of the paper is to show how dynamic analysis techniques can be applied to mobile applications and the techniques we develop to make educated guesses about the role and structure of the classes that make up the app.

Keywords: Mobile application · Dynamic analysis · Reverse engineering · Program understanding

1 Introduction

According to several surveys, mobile business applications are the trend of the day, although not all surveys agree on the strength of the trend [2, 17, 30]. With the growing interest in B2B and B2E mobile apps [17], mobile development becomes mainstream [14, 16]. Then the very same problems of application maintenance and understanding arise as in desktop applications. There are no reasons to believe that mobile apps will be any easier to maintain than desktop ones. In particular the lack of documentation could even be higher, on average, than on traditional desktop platform since these applications are notoriously developed using agile approaches such as Scrum which leaves a lot of freedom to the developer as to what documentation to produce. Then we decided to develop a mobile version of our methodology for the reverse engineering of applications. This is a complete set of techniques and tools to analyze the functional structure of an application [8] to improve its understanding hence its maintenance. Indeed it is known for a long time that to "understand" a large software system, the structural aspects of the system are more important than any single algorithmic component [29]. Since there are several views of software architecture [5], each targeting

© Springer International Publishing Switzerland 2016
P. Lorenz et al. (Eds.): ICSOFT 2015, CCIS 586, pp. 250–268, 2016.
DOI: 10.1007/978-3-319-30142-6_14

a particular purpose, we propose new ones specifically targeted at software under-standing. First we developed the functional structure view of the system [8] i.e. the classes, their relationships and the methods that implement some business relevant scenario. Second we developed the classes' time series that let us observe when a given class or set of classes are involved in the execution of some business relevant scenario. These views rests on dynamic analysis techniques i.e. the analysis of the execution trace of the program corresponding to some scenarios (use-cases) relevant to the business. One key problem in dynamic analysis is to cope with the amount of data to process. In fact, the execution trace file can contain several hundreds of thousands of events. To cope with this data volume, we developed a trace segmentation technique [6] that has showed to be very efficient at analyzing the interactions between the components of the system. In [26] we investigated the way to apply our tools and techniques to the analysis of iPhone apps. This led us to extend the interpretation of our tools' and methodology's results in the mobile environment. In this paper we first present our reverse engineering framework for software system (Sect. 2). Section 3 presents the technique we use to recover the use-cases from users of the apps. Next we show the tools we developed specifically to adapt our framework to the reverse engineering of Objective-C applications on the iPhone (Sect. 4). In Sect. 5, we present two case studies and the way the results can be interpreted to make educated guesses about the structure and roles of the classes of the app. Section 6 presents the related work and Sect. 7 concludes the paper.

2 Reverse Engineering Technique

The goal of our reverse engineering process is to recover the functional structure of the program [8] i.e. to analyze what classes or components support the business relevant function of the application. The process starts with the recovery of the use-cases of the system, if they are not readily available from the documentation of the app (which is generally the case), by watching the users interacting with the system. We simply ask a user to go through all the business-relevant scenario and we take note of all the actions he does with the app. In the case of legacy desktop applications we even video-record the actions of the user. But this is not required here because the use-cases for mobile apps are usually much simpler. Next we instrument the source code of the app to be able to generate the execution traces (i.e. the sequence of method calls in a given run of the system). Code instrumentation consists of inserting extra statements in the source code to record events when the methods are executed. An event is generated when the method is entered and exited. Next, the system is run according to the use-cases and the corresponding execution trace is recorded. Finally, an off-line analysis of the execution trace is performed to recover the functional structure of the system using many views. Figure 1 illustrates a simplified version of the reverse engineering process with only the key tasks. This process has been implemented using a set of tools that are presented in Fig. 2. To instrument the source code, many variants exist among which:

- Developing an instrumentor for the programing language of the system;
- Leveraging an AOP environment to inject the "instrumentation aspects" into the code.

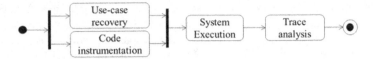

Fig. 1. Reverse engineering process.

Depending on the programming language considered, the second option may not be available. For Objective-C (iPhone) it is indeed the case and we developed our own code instrumentor that will be detailed in the next section. Once the code has been instrumented it is compiled and shipped onto the mobile phone. Then the app is run according to the use-cases and the execution trace is recorded in a file on the device. Next, the file is downloaded from the device and uploaded into a trace database using a trace loader which performs a few integrity checks. Finally, the trace is analyzed using our trace analysis tools. The latter is able to present the information from the trace using several views. There are two formats for the events to be recorded in the execution trace. The first is for method entry and the second for method exit. By recording these two kinds of events, we can reconstruct the call graph with the call hierarchy.

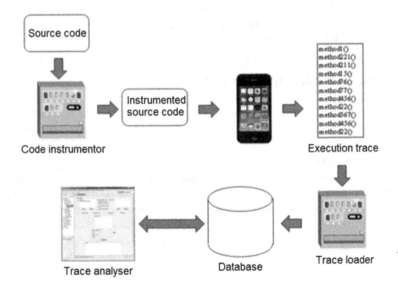

Fig. 2. Tools workflow.

The syntax of the events is the following:
[SCI] [DCI] '['[TN] ']' [Sign] 'AS' [Type] '['[TS] ']' [Param]
or
'END' [SCI] [DCI] '['[TN] ']' [Sign] 'AS' [Type] '['[TS] ']'
With:
[SCI]:   Static class identifier: the package name and class name in which the executed method is implemented.

[DCI]:   Dynamic class identifier: the package name and class name corresponding
            to the class of the instance that executed the method.
[TN]:   Thread number.
[Sign]:   Method signature.
[Type]:   Type of the element returned by the method.
[TS]:   Time stamp of the event.
[Param]:   List of the comma-separated values for the primitive-typed parameters of
            the method. Non primitive-typed values are replaced by '_'.

The first event represents the entry into a method and the second, headed by the keyword 'END', indicates the exit from the method. The thread number allows us to gather all the events that belong to the same thread for further analysis. Since Objective-C does not have any package construct, the class identifiers of the events uses only the class name (in our tool we append the "default" keyword to replace the package name in the long name of the class).

3 Use Case Recovery

The first step of our approach is to recover the use-cases of the app. This is compulsory since the dynamic analysis rests on the execution of a relevant business scenario. If no user documentation is available, which is the common situation, the technique is first to identify all the user categories (the actors in the UML parlance). Then, we ask each representative of each user categories what he would use the app for, what is for him the expected result of using the app. This represents the "business goal" of each use-case to recover. Next, starting from each of these goals, we ask each representative to show the manipulations of the app they would perform get the expected result, with the main variants. This allows us to re-document the use-cases with the main flow and the alternative flows. In complex situations (like in the reverse engineering of large desktop application) we even video-recorded the interaction of the users with the application to make sure we remembered all the interactions. Then by slowly watching the video we can write down the sequence of action the user made to get the expected result from the app. Then we abstract the manipulations and write down the use-cases. The last step it to present the use cases to the users for validation. In particular we ask each user to manipulate the device according to the recovered use-case in order to get the expected result. Then we can immediately observe if the user feels comfortable with the scenario or if something is missing.

4 App Instrumentation

4.1 Introduction

Dynamic analysis as opposed to static analysis aims at observing the application's behavior while it is running. Although many techniques can be used [15] we decided to use code instrumentation because, on the mobile device, there are not many alternatives. Indeed one cannot install any profiling or debugging environment without deeply impacting the behavior of the code. The least intrusive technique is simply to add lightweight tracing statements in the application source code to write the events in a flat file. Each of the recorded events must contain the signature of the method called. As for the class identifier we record the name of the class and, in case of the languages using module or package declarations, the package or module in which the class is defined. Once the trace file is generated (that could hundreds of thousands of events), it is loaded into a database for further processing. Many of the existing dynamic techniques focus on the monitoring of the low level instructions of the program, in particular when the purpose is to analyze an app for which only the compiled code is available. Since we wish to reverse engineer and understand the source code of the app, access to the source code is a must. The first step to build our own instrumentor is to be able to parse the source code. To build such a parser, several possibilities exist. Tools like JavaCC [21] YaCC [31] or ANTLR [1] are capable of generating a parser given the syntax definition of the programming language in the EBNF format. Such parser is completed by adding some extra parsing instructions in the target language. The main difference between these tools is the language in which the parser is generated. Our choice was JavaCC which generates a parser in Java. This is because JavaCC-encoded grammars are available for several programming languages, including Objective-C, and also because we had some previous successful experience with it. However we do not only need to parse the code, we also need to build an abstract syntax tree (AST) of the code in memory so that we could add the extra trace event generation code to some of the nodes in the AST. We used the Java Tree Builder [22] to produce the AST. Some Visitor [10] classes are generated by the same tool to visit each node of the AST. We use these "Visitor" classes to add the instrumentation instructions at the proper locations in the code. For the method start event we add the instrumentation instruction as the first statement of the method. For the method end event we enclose all the statements of the method in a try-finally construct and write the instrumentation instruction in the finally block. With this technique we can catch the method end whatever the way the method is ended. The output of the parser generation process is represented by two packages named "syntaxtree" and "visitor" which respectively contain the AST elements and their associated "visitors". Because every single abstract syntax tree element comes with its own "visitor" class, we focused on the ones responsible for the handling of methods. The added instructions in the source code must satisfy two conditions:

1. Do not produce any changes to the application semantics;
2. Limit as much as possible the impact on the application processing time.

The first constraint is self-evident. The second constraint aims at avoiding any impact on the scheduling of multi-threaded applications. To be able to record the events during the execution of the app, we need to build a little runtime program to write the events to a flat file. This is specific to each programming language. The instrumentation instructions we insert in the source code of the methods are simple calls to the functions of the run time. Because of the above constraint on the processing time, using a database to record the events is not an option. We must record them as fast as possible hence the choice of a flat file.

4.2   The Case of Objective-C

In the case of Objective C, the runtime program contains:

- A class with two methods to write an event at the entry and at the exit of the instrumented method.
- A class responsible for converting the primitive-typed values of the parameters into NSString, to write these values in the trace event (see the [Param] element of the trace event grammar).

Every iOS application has its own set of directories in which it can read and write files. An application's private file system is called a Sandbox [3] and it is specific to the application. Inside a sandbox, there are three predefined directories: Documents, Library and tmp. To store a trace file, the runtime program can write in either the Library or Documents directory. But we should avoid tmp, since its content may be cleared away by the system when the application stops running. Because these folders generally contain user-generated content and other resources used by the application's logic, we need to make sure the trace files we write will not interfere with the existing files. To do so, we create the trace files in a custom folder inside the Library folder:

< Application_Home> /Library/HEG_TRACE/trace_[timestamp].

This will not only ensure that our tool does not hamper the application's behavior but also allows the running of our use-cases in sequence to get several trace files all at once. Next, to upload the trace file into the desktop machine for further analysis we pull it out of the iPhone using iExplorer [18] which gives access to the part of the device's file system where the applications reside. A technique to shortcut the creation of the trace file could have been to embed a socket communication module in our runtime program to "pipe" all the data in real time to a listening socket. However this would require a permanent connection to server and this would not respect our second constraint to have as little an impact on the processing time as possible. Another alternative technique to trace file writing could have been to monitor the application execution using an embarked version of a debugger such as GDB [11]. Unlike C++ or Java, the runtime of Objective-C [24] uses a specific syntax to do message sending. A message sending is a statement like "[object1 foo:@ arg]" meaning that object1 is sent a message whose "selector" is foo: and whose argument is "arg". This syntax is converted to: "objc_msgSend(object1,foo(arg))" by the Objective-C runtime. Then, using the debugger, we would set a breakpoint on every "objc_msgSend" to monitor the execution. As the iOS devices use the ARM processor, fetching the right registers could give access to all the methods' execution context. But this technique would delay the program execution at each message sending and then would exaggeratedly slow down the whole application, therefore not respecting the second constraint. The chosen instrumentation technique using our own instrumentor has the extra advantage to be applicable to any programming language provided that a LALR-analyzable grammar is available. Hence the technique presented in this paper can be extended to the Android platform [25] since it uses Java as the programming language.

5   Case Studies

5.1   Data Access Application

We will first present the technique and tool we developed on a simple app that allows the user to search and display the acts and articles of the Swiss Law recorded in a database on the phone. With our reverse engineering technique we can quickly identify what classes are involved in the delivery of a given functionality and what are the dynamic caller-callee relationships for the use-case. As an example, here is the analysis of the classes involved in the use-case "Read a judgment of the Swiss Federal Court". The execution trace is rather short ($\sim$ 2000 calls) and the number of classes involved is small (6 classes). But this app is well suited to show the power of the analysis we may perform with our tools. Once we loaded the execution trace in our analysis tool, we can display the main features of the execution.

Fig. 3. Trace analyzer.

For example, in Fig. 3 the trace analyzer tool displays the classes involved in the use-case and specifically what class calls what other classes.

As we can see in the display, the class RootViewController is called by 3 other classes:

- CPCAppDelegate   12 times
- homeViewController   only once
- RootViewController   170 times.

Figure 4 displays the call graph with all the involved classes. In this figure we can see that four classes are coupled bi-directionally which, on the point of view of code quality, could be something to investigate further. But this is neither the case of the ArticleViewController nor the Preferences classes. The call graph is generated by our tool using the Graphviz open source library [13].

Now we are interested to know when, in the course of the execution, the classes are involved. Then our trace analysis tool could display a "time series" graph of the classes' execution in the trace. But the problem is that the trace could be quite huge. Then the display of each and every method in the trace would lead to a very dense graph. To overcome the problem we introduced a little bit of statistical processing: we segment the trace in contiguous segments of a predefined size and, for each segment, we count the number of times a given class is called. Figure 5 presents such a time series graph for the Preference class.

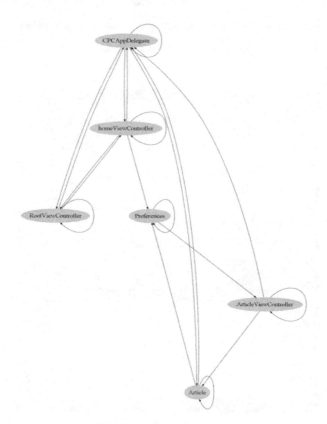

Fig. 4. Caller-callee graph.

On the top of the window we see the segment size (35 calls in this example). The horizontal axis shows the location of each of the segment. To make the time series comparable between use-cases, we normalize the horizontal axis to 100. The position of a class execution is therefore relative to the trace size.

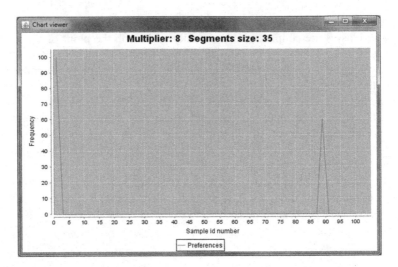

Fig. 5. Preference class time series.

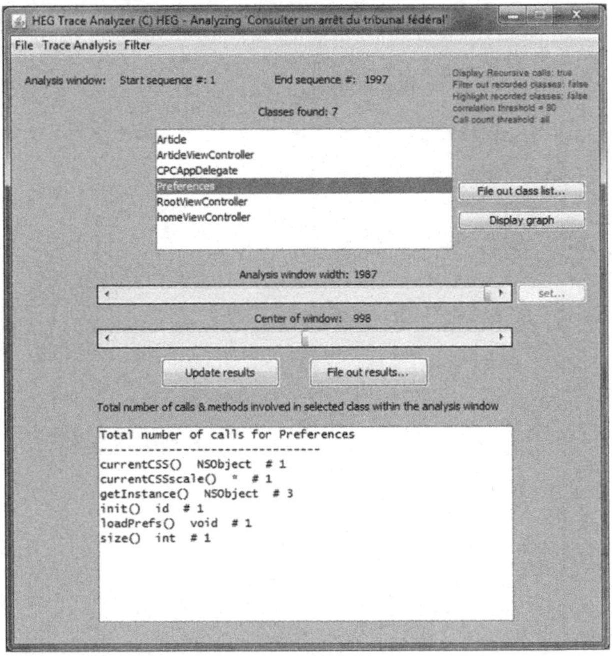

Fig. 6. Methods called in preference class.

As we can see, the Preference class is executed at the beginning of the processing and close to the end. Figure 6 displays the methods that are called in the Preferences class. We observe that very few calls are made in this class. Indeed this class holds the

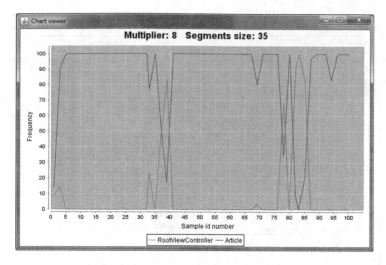

Fig. 7. Joint time series for 2 classes.

application's preferences parameters. All the behavior, showed by Figs. 5 and 6, rightfully represents what we could expect from a class which holds preferences information. Next, we could compare the time series of two classes. Figure 7 shows the joint time series for the classes RootViewController and Article.

Interestingly, the involvement of these two classes seems opposite. In the few segment where the Article class is much less involved then the RootViewController class is heavily involved. A further source code investigation revealed that the hundreds of Article instances (i.e. articles of the law) to be loaded in memory from a file are loaded all at once. Because this process is not in a dedicated thread, it blocks everything else until it is finished. The RootViewController contains a UITableView and implements its delegate and datasource protocols [4]. Because the structure of the law acts and articles is hierarchical, a RootViewController is reclusively created every time the user browses a subcategory of the law acts and articles. Then the relevant Article objects are accessed in memory, inserted into the UITableView cells and the RootViewController is quit. This explains the sudden "bursts" of activity of the RootViewController following the activity on Article objects. With this information we can now reconstruct the UML class diagram corresponding to the executed use case (Fig. 8). This diagram represents the implementation classes of the functional structure of the system in relation to the use-case. It contains the classes, methods and dynamic associations involved in the execution of the use-case. In some sense this represents a "projection" of the use-case to the whole system (in the relational database sense). Today, this UML class diagram is built by hand from the output of the tool. We intend however to integrate our tool with the software modeling environment we use (IBM's Rational Software Architect) so that this class diagram could be created automatically.

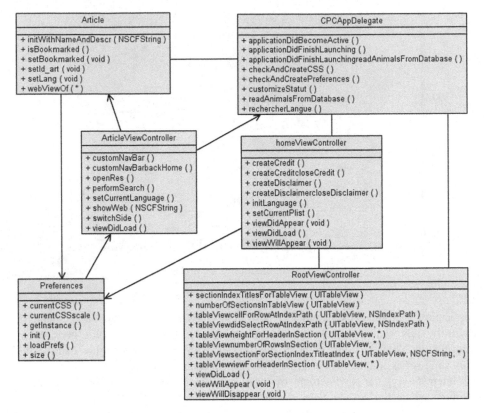

Fig. 8. Class diagram of the functional structure.

5.2 Word Press

As a second example, we ran the WordPress framework to create a blog from the iPhone. This open source framework was instrumented, compiled and then shipped to the iPhone. Then we used the app to create a blog ("create blog" use case). The execution trace is about 1 Mb long and has 4252 calls which involve 53 classes. First we can analyze the diversity of methods called per class (the number of different method called in the classes). While more than half of the classes (30) have 5 of less distinct methods called, a single class, ReaderPostsViewController, has 55 distinct methods called and CreateAccountAndBlogViewController has 29. Table 1 shows the 15 classes that get 10 or more distinct method executed.

Next we can analyze the coupling between the classes: what are the classes called by each of the classes. A class that calls many classes may play the role of a "controller" class i.e. a class that organizes the work of other classes (following the MVC

Table 1. Number of distinct method executed per class, for classes with 10 methods or more.

Class	#methods
ReaderPostsViewController	55
CreateAccountAndBlogViewController	29
WordPressAppDelegate	24
ReaderPostView	21
ReaderPostService	19
LoginViewController	18
NotificationsViewController	16
ReaderPostServiceRemote	15
WPStyleGuide	13
WPAvatarSource	12
WPAnalyticsTrackerMixpanel	11
WPNUXUtility	11
ReaderPostTableViewCell	10
WPTableImageSource	10
WPWalkthroughTextField	10

Table 2. Classes calling other classes.

Class name	# class called
ReaderPostsViewController	17
WordPressAppDelegate	17
LoginViewController	16
WPImageSource	15
CreateAccountAndBlogViewController	12
ReaderPostView	10

style). A close look at the classes that call the most of other classes show that their name include the term "controller" in 50 % of the cases (Table 2).

If one displays the location where these classes are involved one finds that ReaderPostsViewController is involved in almost every part of the execution trace while WordPressAppDelegate is much more localized (Fig. 9) although the number of classes they call is similar. ReaderPostsViewController seems to be a key class in the implementation of the use-case.

On Fig. 10 we compare ReaderPostsViewController and LoginViewController whose number of class it calls is close (16). The execution of LoginViewController is somewhat more localized than ReaderPostsViewController and seems to play less of a central role.

The sequence of screens that we get when the use-case is executed is presented in

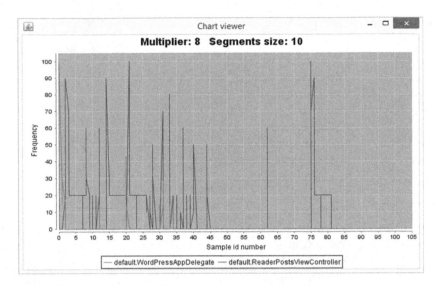

Fig. 9. Time series comparison of WordPressAppDelegate and ReaderPostViewController.

Fig. 11 (as recorded on September 20st, 2015). The screen on the left is displayed for a short period of time (1 s) after wich the second screen is displayed. Once the information have been entered into this screen and the account created the third screen opens to sign in.

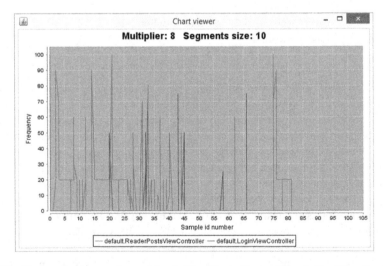

Fig. 10. Time series comparison of LoginViewController and ReaderPostViewController.

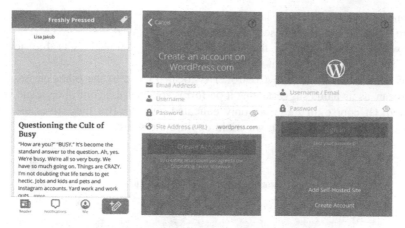

Fig. 11. Sequence of screen in the create blog use-case.

Since we suspect the classes whose name start with "UI" to be involved in the implementation of the displays we draw their time series in the same graph. These may represent screens or parts of screens. This is presented on Fig. 12.

We see that UIDevice, which represents the current device and which is used to retrieve the device parameters, is called at the beginning of the use-case as we could have guessed. On the other hand UIColor is used to manage the colors and could be involved in every screen. There is not much information to infer from the location of the execution of this class in the time series except that each time it is executed there must be some screen involved. UITableView is a class used to display a list of items as a single column that is vertically scrollable. But the first screen in Fig. 11 has exactly this kind of behavior. Therefore we can identify where in the execution trace this screen is located. It is at coordinates 13 in the time series. Finally, UILabel represents a

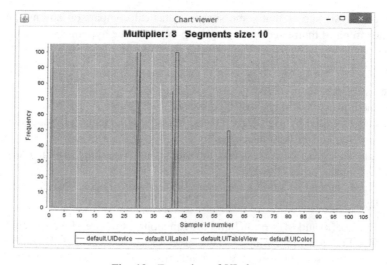

Fig. 12. Execution of UI classes.

read-only text view. Since the last two screen are full of these, the time series let us observe where in the trace these screens might be displayed.

Now we could observe the execution of the UILabel, UITableView and LoginViewController classes in the trace (Fig. 13).

We remark that LoginViewController is located close to the other classes which could mean, as its name suggests, that it performs some access control once the view is displayed. Of course all these are only educated guesses. But they gives us a good starting hypotheses from which we could explore the source code.

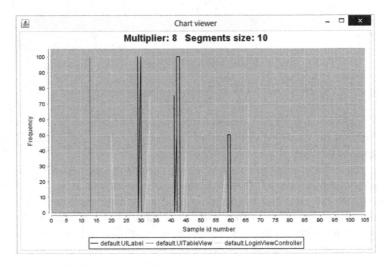

Fig. 13. UI classes and login view controller.

5.3   Interpretation Process

The above analysis shows that some simple statistical comparison among classes as well as the timing of their executions may help us formulate hypotheses when trying to understand some unknown code. Here are the steps of our interpretation process. From each execution trace we identify:

(a)   The list of classes involved
(b)   The methods called in each of the classes
(c)   The classes called by each class (i.e. the classes implementing the methods called by some method in the other classes)
(d)   The classes calling each class (i.e. the classes implementing the methods calling methods in the other classes)
(e)   The places in the execution trace where the methods of each classes are executed, displayed as a time series.

From (a), (b), (c) and (d) we can build the functional structure of the system for each use-case (see Fig. 8 as an example). This gives us an overview of the classes, their methods and their associations required to implement each use case. But such a structure may not be complete since we usually do not recover all the alternative flows of a use-case. From (c) and (d) we can see if some class interacts with a lot of other classes. This would suggest the role of a controller in the MVC paradigm. The time series of the executions let us find classes that work closely together. Indeed if the execution of some classes is repeatedly adjacent in the time series, forming a pattern of executions, we can make the hypothesis that these classes together implement some function or subfunction. Of course, this is not directly observable in the source code since it is difficult to infer when a given class will call a method in another class. In contrast, the time series let us observe when the classes are called in the context of a business relevant use-case. For example, we leveraged this dynamic technique to retrieve the functional components of a system using a clustering algorithm [7]. From (c) and (e) we could infer the scope of a controller class. If the number of class called in high but the activity of the class is spread all over the time series, then it is probably a global controller class, whereas if the activity of this class is localized it is more like a subfunction controller.

6   Related Work

Dynamic analysis of apps has been a subject of interest for a few years. For example, it has been used to check the security of the app when its source code is unavailable and specifically to do black-box penetration testing. However, when the source code of the app is available, the tester generally turns to static code review and white box testing. Gianchandani [12] uses snoop-it [27] to hook into a chosen application's process and to monitor network and file system activities. He also uses Introspy [19] which is composed of a tracer module and an analyzer module. After having selected the API to trace, the tracer will log the corresponding calls to a database.

Next, the analyzer will produce a human readable report in HTML. However the tool does not target all the custom application classes but focuses on the specific ones related, but not limited to cryptography, data storage and networking. Szydlowski et al. [28] proposed a technique to perform automatic dynamic analysis of iOS applications by hooking to the application's delegate and triggering all of the UI controls on every view. The result is a state model of the application. However, most of the dynamic analysis methods operate on the low level instructions. Hence, hooking to the running process is needed. But Apple does not include any default debugger on the device and installing one requires to jailbreak the iPhone. An alternative consists of running the application on the iOS Simulator [20] that comes with XCode then monitoring its process using GDB [11] or LLDB [23]. But the dynamic analysis of a simulated application using a debugger does not provide as much information as is available when writing the trace events to a file and analyzing the file off-line. Indeed the latter method let us perform statistical analysis which is difficult when using a debugger. Moreover, working on a simulated device, the technique does not allow analyzing apps that involve sensors such as accelerometer, compass or camera as they cannot be reproduced in the iOS Simulator.

7 Conclusion

The contribution of this paper is to present a reverse-engineering process and the associated tools to reverse-engineer and mobile applications. Indeed the technique is not limited to iPhone apps since the only specific part is the generation of the trace file. Hence the technique is applicable to whatever environment, provided that we can build a source code instrumentor for the associated programming language to generate an application trace in a standard format. In particular, since we already developed an instrumentor for Java, we are ready to analyze any Android application. The trace analyzer we developed provides a rich set of views through which the maintenance engineer can study the running of the code. In our case studies, we observed that the "time series" technique can visually present the mutual behavior of the classes in a convenient format. It provides some useful clues as to how classes interact when running the use-cases. The UML class diagram of the functional structure of the use-case summarizes all the programming elements involved in the execution of some use-case. It is important to highlight that our technique is based first and foremost on business relevant use-cases, i.e. whole scenarios that make sense for the user of the app, and not on the execution of some arbitrary function. This allows us to make hypothesis about the business semantics of the observed patterns of classes' execution. But the difficulty of the technique comes from the very same reason. Since we are not sure to recover all the relevant alternative paths in each of the scenarios, because the use-cases are drawn from the observation of the user, the analysis will be incomplete. To overcome the problem, in the case of legacy desktop applications, we investigated a semi-automated technique to recover the use cases directly from the legacy code [9] with moderate success however, due to the complexity of the task. Indeed, use-case recovery from source code is still an open problem. As future work we will integrate our tool with IBM's RSA to be able to generate the UML class diagram of the functional structure automatically. We also intend to develop new views to directly represent the dynamic business-level application semantics. Indeed we are building domain concept ontologies whose concepts will be dynamically identified in the executed code. This technique will help us to close the semantic gap between the high level business domain concepts and the code level.

References

1. ANTLR: ANother Tool for Language Recognition (2014). http://www.antlr.org/. Accessed 12 October 2014
2. Appcelerator/IDC: Mobile Developer report (2013). www.appcelerator.com.s3.amazonaws. com/pdf/developer-survey-Q2-2013.pdf. Accessed 5 March 2015
3. Apple iOS: File System Programming Guide (2014). https://developer.apple.com/library/ mac/documentation/FileManagement/Conceptual/FileSystemProgrammingGuide/ FileSystemOverview/FileSystemOverview.html. Accessed 12 October 2014
4. Apple UITableView: UITableView Class Reference (2014). https://developer.apple.com/ library/ios/documentation/UIKit/Reference/UITableView_Class/. Accessed 12 October 2014

5. Bachmann, F.: Documenting Software Architectures: Views and Beyond, 2nd edn. Addison-Wesley, Reading (2010)
6. Dugerdil, P.: Using trace sampling techniques to identify dynamic clusters of classes. IBM CAS Software and Systems Engineering Symposium (CASCON) October 2007
7. Dugerdil, P., Jossi, S.: Computing dynamic clusters. In: 2nd Indian Conference on Software Engineering (ISEC) 2009. ACM Digital Lib (2009)
8. Dugerdil, P., Niculescu, M.: Visualizing software structure understandability. In: 23rd Australasian Software Engineering Conference (ASWEC) 2014. IEEE Digital Library, Sydney (2014)
9. Dugerdil, P., Sennhauser, D.: Dynamic decision tree for legacy use-case recovery. In: 28th ACM Symposium On Applied Computing (SAC 2013), Coimbra, Portugal, 18–22 March 2013
10. Gamma, E., Helm, R., Johnson, R., Vlissides, J.: Design Patterns Elements of Reusable Object Oriented Software. Addison-Wesley, Reading (1995)
11. GDB: GNU Debugger (2014). http://www.gnu.org/software/gdb/ Accessed 12 October 2014
12. Gianchandani, P.: Damn Vulnerable iOS Application (DVIA) (2014). http://damnvulner ableiosapp.com/#learn. Accessed 12 October 2014
13. Graphviz (2015). http://www.graphviz.org/Home.php. Accessed 17 April 2015
14. Hammond, J.S.: Development Landscape: 2013, Forrester Research (2013)
15. Hamou-Lhadj, A., Lethbridge, T.C.: A Survey of Trace Exploration Tools and Techniques. In: Proceedings of the IBM Conference of the Centre for Advanced Studies on Collaborative Research (2004)
16. IBM: IBM Mobile First initiative (2014). www.03.ibm.com/press/us/en/presskit/39172.wss. Accessed 12 October 2014
17. IDC: IDC Predictions 2013 Competing on the 3rd Platform (2013). www.idc.com/getdoc. jsp?containerId=WC20121129. Accessed 5 March 2015
18. iExplorer (2014). http://www.macroplant.com/iexplorer/. Accessed 12 October 2014
19. Introspy-iOS (2014). https://github.com/iSECPartners/Introspy-iOS. Accessed 12 October 2014
20. iOS Simulator (2014). https://developer.apple.com/library/ios/documentation/IDEs/Conceptal/iOS_Simulator_Guide/GettingStartedwithiOSStimulator/GettingStartedwithiOSStimulator.html. Accessed 12 October 2014
21. JavaCC: Java Compiler Compiler – The Java Parser Generator (2014). https://www.javacc.java.net/. Accessed 12 October 2014
22. JTB: Java TreeBuilder (2014). http://compilers.cs.ucla.edu/jtb/. Accessed 12 October 2014
23. LLDB: LLDB Debugger (2014). http://lldb.llvm.org/. Accessed 12 October 2014
24. Objective, C: Runtime Reference (2014). https://developer.apple.com/library/mac/documentation/Cocoa/Reference/ObjCRuntimeRef/Reference/reference.html. Accessed 12 October 2014
25. Parada, A.G., de Brisolara, L.B.: A model driven approach for android applications development. In: Proceedings of the Brazilian Symposium on Computing System Engineering (SBESC) (2012)
26. Sako, R.: Reverse engineering d'une application mobile Apple. Bachelor Thesis (2011)
27. Snoop-it (2014). https://code.google.com/p/snoop-it/. Accessed 12 October 2014
28. Szydlowski, M., Egele, M., Kruegel, C., Vigna, G.: Challenges for dynamic analysis of iOS applications. In: Camenisch, J., Kesdogan, D. (eds.) iNetSec 2011. LNCS, vol. 7039, pp. 65–77. Springer, Heidelberg (2012)
29. Tilley, S.R., Santanu, P., Smith, D.B.: Toward a framework for program understanding. In: Proceedings of the IEEE International Workshop on Program Comprehension (1996)

30. Wasserman, A.I.: Software engineering issues for mobile application development. In: Proceedings of the 2nd Workshop on Software Engineering for Mobile Application Development MobiCase 2011 (2011)
31. YaCC: Yet Another Compiler-Compiler (2014). http://dinosaur.compilertools.net/yacc/. Accessed 12 October 2014

Annotating Goals with Concerns in Goal-Oriented Requirements Engineering

Shinpei Hayashi[1]([✉]), Wataru Inoue[1], Haruhiko Kaiya[2], and Motoshi Saeki[1]

[1] Department of Computer Science, Tokyo Institute of Technology,
Ookayama 2-12-1-W8-83, Meguro-ku, Tokyo 152-8552, Japan
{hayashi,inouew,saeki}@se.cs.titech.ac.jp
[2] Department of Information Sciences, Kanagawa University,
Tsuchiya 2946, Hiratsuka, Kanagawa 259-1293, Japan
kaiya@kanagawa-u.ac.jp

Abstract. In goal-oriented requirements analysis, goals specify multiple concerns such as functions, strategies, and non-functions, and they are refined into sub goals from mixed views of these concerns. This intermixture of concerns in goals makes it difficult for a requirements analyst to understand and maintain goal refinements. Separating concerns and specifying them explicitly is one of the useful approaches to improve the understandability of goal refinements, i.e., the relations between goals and their sub goals. In this paper, we propose a technique to annotate goals with the concerns they have in order to support the understanding of goal refinement. In our approach, goals are refined into sub goals referring to the annotated concerns, and these concerns annotated to a goal and its sub goals provide the meaning of its goal refinement. By tracing and focusing on the annotated concerns, requirements analysts can understand goal refinements and modify unsuitable ones. We have developed a supporting tool and made an exploratory experiment to evaluate the usefulness of our approach.

Keywords: Goal-oriented requirements engineering · Concern · Goal refinement

1 Introduction

In information system development, it is necessary to elicit requirements from customers and users as early in the development process as possible, in order to reduce the development cost and to develop the information system of higher quality. To support requirements elicitation, various techniques and/or methods have been studied and made some of them into practice.

Goal-oriented requirements engineering (GORE) is one of the promising approaches to elicit requirements, and in this approach, elicited requirements and their relationships are represented with a graph, called a goal graph [6]. We can reason about how a goal is derived by means of tracing the edges incoming to and outgoing from it. However, as elicited requirements are increasing more and more

© Springer International Publishing Switzerland 2016
P. Lorenz et al. (Eds.): ICSOFT 2015, CCIS 586, pp. 269–286, 2016.
DOI: 10.1007/978-3-319-30142-6_15

in a goal graph, it is more difficult to analyze them using the graph because the numbers of the goals and their relationships are larger. As a result, the structure of the goal graph is more complicated. A case study of analyzing a large-scale system was reported where goals exceeded more than 500 in a goal graph [6]. The complicated graph results in the difficulties of analyzing it, especially of finding specific goals and of tracing their relationships to the other goals such as their parent and/or sub goals. As a result, maintaining the goal graph can be error-prone tasks for human analysts. In addition to the larger number of goals and edges, goal refinements cause the difficulties in maintaining the goal graph.

A (parent) goal is refined into the sub goals that contribute to its achievement. More precisely, the achievement of the parent goal is a logical entailment of its sub goals' achievement from logical view [2,5,10], i.e., if the achievement of the sub goals holds, that of the parent goal also holds. This rule on the logical entailment of goal achievement dominates the formal meaning of goal refinements. Although some techniques propose the patterns of goal refinements such as Divide-and-Conquer and Guard-Introduction [6], most of them are based on logical entailment. For requirements analysts as practitioners, they refine goals into sub goals from various views not only from the view of logical entailment. In some cases, analysts may refine a goal into actions or tasks that can realize its achievement, and in other cases they may do the goal into the conditions or constraints that should hold for achieving it. The former case is based on operational view of goal refinements, i.e., a sequence of actions or tasks is necessary to be executed for the achievement of the goal, and the latter is on a logical view of the conditions or assumptions of the goal. The wide variety of goal refinement views causes the difficulties in analysts' constructing and/or maintaining a goal graph. To use GORE practically, it is necessary for analysts to understand goal refinements well [9].

The paper proposes a technique to classify goal refinement views and show them for analysts so as to understand the goal graph easily. The basic idea of our approach is annotating goals with concerns that they have. Goals specify multiple concerns such as functions, strategies, and non-functions, and they are refined into sub goals from mixed views of these concerns. This intermixture of concerns in goals causes the wide varieties of goal refinement views and makes it difficult for a requirements analyst to understand and maintain goal refinements, i.e., relations between goals and their sub goals. Separating concerns and specifying them explicitly is one of the useful approaches to clarify goal refinements to improve their understandability. In our approach, a concern of requirements analysts corresponds to annotations and the analysts attach their concerns as annotations to the goals that specify the concerns during constructing a goal graph. Suppose that an analyst has a goal "Deliver stock to franchise stores just-in-time" in the development of an information system for convenience store chains. It has two concerns: functional aspect (stock delivery) and business strategic one (just-in-time). The analyst picks up one concern, say strategic one, and consider what sub goals can achieve this goal from a single view of the picked concern, strategic one, without considering another concern. As a result, sub goals to achieve "just-in-timeliness", e.g., "Coordinate supply chain

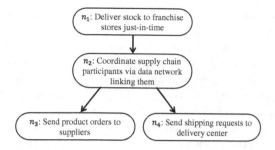

Fig. 1. Part of a goal graph in B-SCP: excerpt from [1].

participants" can be obtained. Our approach can help analysts derive sub goals, i.e., goal refinements and provide the explicit meaning of goal refinements. In the above example, the goal refinement from "Deliver stock to franchise stores just-in-time" to "Coordinate supply chain participants" represents the derivation of more concrete strategic goal. By tracing and focusing on the annotated concerns of goals, the requirements analysts can understand goal refinements and furthermore correct unsuitable ones.

The rest of the paper is organized as follows. In Sect. 2, we show a motivating example and clarify where our problem to be solved is. Section 3 presents our approach, and in Sect. 4, we show the supporting tool based on our approach. We assess our approach with an experiment and discuss its effectiveness based on the experimental results in Sect. 5. Sections 6 and 7 are for related work and concluding remarks.

2 Motivating Example

In GORE, the customers' and users' abstract needs can be considered as goals to be achieved, and the goals are decomposed or refined into more concrete sub goals. The achievement of the sub goals contributes to the achievement of their parent goals. We have two types of goal refinement; one is AND refinement, and the other is OR. In AND refinement, if all of the sub goals are achieved, their parent goal can be achieved, while in OR refinement, the achievement of at least one sub goal leads to the achievement of its parent goal. The meaning of refinement is "logical entailment" only.

Figure 1 illustrates a part of the goal graph excerpted from [1], which was the result of analyzing the business strategy of Seven Eleven Japan [7]. In the figure, rounded boxes and arrows stand for goals and goal refinements, respectively. For example, the goal n_2 is refined into sub goals n_3 and n_4 in OR refinement. Considering the meaning of these goals, their goal refinement is not easy to understand underlying ideas on how these sub goals n_2, n_3, and n_4 had been derived from the root goal n_1. The goal n_1 specifies stock delivery *just-in-time*, and it includes both a functional aspect (stock delivery) and a strategic one (just-in-time)[1]. Its direct sub goal n_2 specifying the coordination of supply chain

---

[1] Here, we regard the constraints of goals as strategic.

contributes to the achievement of the strategic aspect of n_1, just-in-timeliness of stock delivery, but less contributes to its functional aspect, i.e., stock delivery. Rather, n_3 and n_4, which are direct sub goals of n_2 not n_1, seem to directly contribute to the achievement to the stock delivery of n_1. It can be considered that the refinement of n_1 to n_2 is done based on a strategic aspect, and on the other hand, the refinement of n_2 to n_3 and n_4 is on functional aspect of n_1, not of n_2. Thus, n_3 and n_4 are not so suitable as the result of refining directly the goal n_2, rather it is better to consider that the goal n_1 is directly refined into them following a functional viewpoint. The point is that this example includes mixed views of a goal refinement, strategic view, and functional view in a goal graph. More concretely, goals derived from multiple views are intermixed in the same graph, and this intermixture leads the difficulty of understanding and furthermore maintaining the goal graph.

We call the aspects that a goal specifies and that a requirements analyst has an interest for her/his analysis *concerns*, and the analyst refines the goal into its sub goals from the view of these concerns. The goal refinements based on these concerns are more natural for human analysts rather than based on the view of logical entailment. A goal specifies more than one concern as shown in the goal n_1, and a requirements analyst tries to refine it into sub goals from the view of its concerns. Suppose that the analyst refines the goal n_1 directly into n_3 and n_4 from the view of a functional concern and into n_2 from the view of a strategic concern. The resulting goal graph includes two types of goal refinement, and as a result, it is difficult to understand the meaning of the relationships between the parent goal n_1 and its sub goals (n_2, n_3, and n_4) because of the intermixture of goal refinement having different meaning. This paper addresses this problem, and the next section presents how to tackle it.

3   Our Approach

3.1   Basic Idea

The problem that we address in this paper is the intermixture of multiple goal refinements based on the concerns related to information systems development. We adopt the idea of annotating goals with concerns and clarifying the meaning of goal refinements using the annotations in order to address this problem. In our technique, we construct a goal graph annotating goals with concerns, and we concentrate on goal refinements for a single concern by tracing them along the concern. The aim of our work is to develop the supporting technique to maintain goal graphs, especially to understand the relationships among goals through the meaning of goal refinements.

3.2   Concerns of Goals

Let C be a set of concerns: $C = \{c_1, \ldots, c_n\}$. An annotation or annotation value is a n-tuple $\langle v_1, \ldots, v_n \rangle$ where $v_i \in \{c_i, -\}$ $(1 \le i \le n)$. As shown in

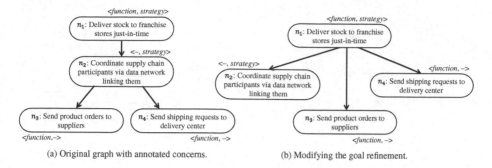

(a) Original graph with annotated concerns.　　(b) Modifying the goal refinement.

Fig. 2. Concerns of the motivating example.

Fig. 2(a), the goals of the motivating example in Fig. 1 can have two concerns: a function concern and a strategy one, so $c_1 = function$ and $c_2 = strategy$. Since n_1 specifies these two concerns, on one hand, we set its annotation value to be $\langle function, strategy \rangle$. On the other hand, n_2 specifies only one concern, i.e., strategy, and so its value is $\langle -, strategy \rangle$. The value "$-$" denotes a null value, and it means that the goal does not specify the corresponding concern. In the example, n_2 does not specify the function concern. The annotations are similar to the attributes or semantic tags attached to goals [4,11,12].

Our approach has three beneficial points to support maintaining goal graphs. The first one is that we can reason about the meaning of goal refinements and can understand how sub goals are derived. For example, the refinement from n_1 into n_2 has a meaning of the refinement of the strategy "just-in-time" because both of these goals have a strategy concern. If a requirements analyst tries to focus on a strategy concern, she/he can trace the goals having a concern "strategy" and their refinements. As a result, she/he can understand why and how the strategic goals were derived while constructing the goal graph. We can classify the meaning of goal refinements as follows, and this clarification is useful to reason about how goals specifying a certain concern are derived.

- A parent: *strategy*, a sub goal: *strategy* (both a parent goal and its sub goal specify strategy concerns)
  → The parent goal is divided or refined into a more concrete strategy denoted by the sub goal.
- A parent: *strategy*, a sub goal: *function*
  → The sub goal is a function or an operation to realize the strategy denoted by the parent goal.
- A parent: *function*, a sub goal: *strategy*
  → The sub goal is a strategy to implement the function denoted by the parent goal.
- A parent: *function*, a sub goal: *function*
  → The function denoted by the parent goal has the sub function denoted by the sub goal.

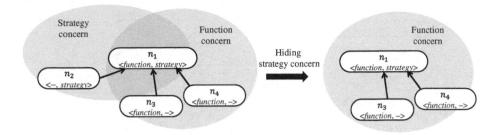

Fig. 3. Focusing on a concern.

In the first category of the above classification, if both a parent and a sub goal specify a strategy concern, the parent goal is divided or refined into the strategy denoted by the sub goal. By reading these meaning descriptions on tracing a sequence of goal refinements, a requirements analyst can reason about the derivation process of the related goals.

The second benefit is to support the detection of unsuitable goal refinements in a goal graph as shown in Fig. 1. Suppose that we have the rule of goal refinement "A goal should be refined into sub goals from the view of at least one of the concerns that it specifies". In our approach, this rule can be translated into "If the i-th element of the annotation of a parent goal is null, i.e., $\langle v_1, \ldots, v_{i-1}, -, v_{i+1}, \ldots, v_n \rangle$, then the i-th element of its sub goals should also be null". Figure 2(a) violates this rule at the refinement from n_2 into n_3 and n_4, because the annotation at the function concern in n_1 is null while its value is neither null at n_3 nor at n_4. Thus, we can obtain the modified version as shown in Fig. 2(b) by letting n_3 and n_4 be direct sub goals of n_1. This approach allows us to automate detecting the occurrences of semantically unsuitable goal refinements. Note that this rule is an extreme but comprehensive example. We used it only for the explanation of the second benefit.

The third beneficial point is the mechanism to filter out the goals specifying irrelevant concerns, i.e., the goals that a requirements analyst has less interest in can be hidden. For a human analyst, it is difficult to analyze a goal graph recognizing many types of concerns at the same time, especially in the case when the graph is larger and more complicated. The analyst can select a small number of the concerns that she/he wants to focus on at first. Figure 3 illustrates hiding a strategy concern from the motivating example. As a result, the analyst can devote herself/himself to focusing on goals and their refinements from the viewpoint of a function concern.

We can summarize the beneficial points to improve the existing GORE approach by using our approach as follows:

1. understandability on why and how sub goals are derived by clarifying the meaning of goal refinements,
2. detectability of unsuitable goal refinements by considering the concerns annotated at goals, and

3. easiness to analyze goal graphs by reducing their size by means of hiding the goals having less interesting concerns.

Goal refinements are subjective tasks of requirements analysts in the sense that the results greatly depend on the analysts. The aim of our research is not automating goal refinements but assisting in the analysts' tasks. Although our approach can improve the quality of goal refinements, it does not provide a mean to automate them. Our approach allows an analyst to focus on a single and simple concern, not on multiple and intermixture concerns, when she/he refines goals, and to be assisted in getting goal refinements of higher quality because she/he can avoid considering varieties of aspects of a goal at its refinement. Although she/he can refine a goal along a single concern, the task of its refinement is still subjective. The efforts of subjective tasks can be reduced in our approach.

3.3 Applying Our Approach

In this subsection, we mention how to apply our approach to GORE. There are two alternatives to apply it. The first alternative is its application to the construction of a goal graph specifying no unsuitable goal refinements. A requirements analyst decides what concerns she/he has an interest and then starts constructing a goal graph. While constructing the graph, the analyst can find and add new concerns that she/he must consider. She/he considers what concerns that a goal represents and annotates it with the suitable concerns. The annotations play a role of the guideline on goal refinements. Suppose that a requirements analyst has a goal n_1 shown in Fig. 2 and that she/he focuses on a function concern and a strategy one. The analyst recognizes that n_1 has both of function and strategy concerns, and for each concern, the analyst tries to decompose n_1 into sub goals. As a result, as shown in Fig. 2(b), the analyst refines n_1 into n_3 and n_4 from the viewpoint of a function concern, while into n_2 from a strategy view.

The second alternative is the application of our approach to already constructed goal graphs. A requirement analyst has constructed a goal graph by using an existing technique such as KAOS, the strategic rationale model in i^*, or AGORA, and then she/he identifies what concerns each goal in the graph has. After finishing annotating the goals with the concerns, the analyst checks the suitability of goal refinements and improves them by changing sub goals or adding new sub goals if any unsuitability exists. To understand the goal graph for maintaining it, the analyst can trace the goal graph along a goal refinement of a certain concern. In addition, the analyst can remove goals having the other concerns from her/his view. These supports result from the three beneficial points mentioned in the previous subsection.

4   Supporting Tool

We have implemented a tool for supporting our approach by using an AGORA tool that had been developed before by the authors' group [11]. Figure 4 illustrates the screenshot for editing a goal graph. The example goal graph shown in

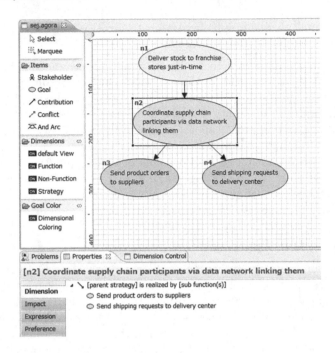

Fig. 4. Screenshot of the supporting tool (Color figure online).

this screenshot is the same as the one shown in Fig. 2(a). The following is a list of the functions of this tool.

1. **Getting a Concern Definition File:** Before starting and/or while constructing a goal graph, a requirements analyst can define new coordinates. The tool can obtain a file having information on the concerns that the analyst (also the tool user) newly defines in XML form. The definition of a concern includes the name of the concern, new goal refinement rules in which the concern participate, and semantic information on the goal refinements related to the concern. The refinement rules are represented in a matrix form whose entries are suitable goal refinements, and are used to detect the occurrences of unsuitable goal refinements. The semantic information is written in text and presents the explanations of the goal refinements as shown in the previous section. It is shown to an analyst and useful for her/him to understand how the corresponding sub goals have been derived.

2. **Attaching Annotations to a Goal and Displaying Them:** An analyst selects a goal that she/he tries to attach annotations, i.e., concerns, by clicking it with a pointing device and chooses suitable concerns from a pop-up menu. In the screen of the tool, concerns are differentiated by coloring a goal. For example, a function, a strategy, and a non-function concern are assigned to red, green, and blue respectively, and goals specifying these concerns are colored following this color assignment. Like the goal n_1 specifying function

and strategy concerns, it is colored with yellow, which is the mixture of red and green.

3. **Hiding Goals:** When an analyst selects the concerns that she/he likes or does not like to focus on, the tool displays the goals specifying the selected concerns or not specifying them.

4. **Showing Semantic Information of a Goal Refinement:** See the Properties tab in the bottom screen of Fig. 4. This tab is for the area where the meaning of the selected goal refinements is displayed in a textual form. More precisely, when an analyst points a goal, the tool displays the meaning of its refinement to sub goals and their contents in a tree form. In the figure, the analyst points the goal n_2, and the tool shows the meaning of the refinements to n_3 and n_4 "[parent strategy] is realized by [sub function(s)]". This means that strategy n_2 is realized by sub function(s) n_3, etc. The analyst considers if the strategy "Coordinate supply chain participants via data network linking them" (n_2) can be realized by "Send product orders to suppliers" (n_3) or not. Perhaps, she/he may be doubtful for this refinement and consider that it is not sufficient from the view of realizing a strategy by functions. In this way, considering the meaning of goal refinements, the analyst may also find an unsuitable goal refinement.

5   Exploratory Experiment

As mentioned in Sect. 3, our approach and tool have three beneficial points:

- understandability on why and how sub goals are derived by clarifying the meaning of goal refinements,
- detectability of unsuitable goal refinements by checking annotations of goals, and
- easiness to analyze goal graphs by reducing their size by means of hiding the goals having less interesting concerns.

In this section, we made an experiment to assess if these beneficial points are obtained or not.

5.1   Procedure

The aim of our experiment is to confirm that our approach including the supporting tool can have the above three beneficial points. To do, we made a comparative experiment with two settings; one is the situation that our subjects analyze goal graphs using the existing technique, and the other is that they analyze the goal graphs using the supporting tool. Their processes and outcomes are compared. Figure 5 illustrates this experimental procedure. Our subjects were provided with goal graphs and questions about them, and they answered the questions by analyzing the goal graphs. The subjects were grouped into two sets; one is for the subjects who use the existing goal graph editor such as [11], and the other is for the subjects who use our tool mentioned in Sect. 4. Subjects made answers to

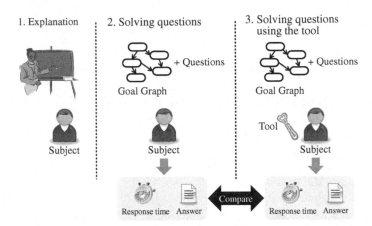

Fig. 5. Experiment.

the several questions related to sample goal graphs that might include unsuitable goal refinements. We observed their answering processes and their resulting answers and extracted the following information.

1. The numbers of wrong answers and missing answers: We checked if the answers of a subject using our approach included wrong answers and missing ones less than those of a subject not using our approach.
2. The time spent in making answers (response time): We measured the time when a subject spent in making answers. This is for checking if our subjects could reduce their efforts or not.

We made questions to observe and evaluate the following items;

Item (a): our subjects can understand goal refinements,
Item (b): our subjects can detect unsuitable goal refinements, and
Item (c): our subjects can focus on goals specifying a certain concern.

We designed three types of questions to obtain the information on the above items from our subjects as follows.

– **Question Type 1 (QT 1): Selecting Goals Playing the Specific Roles on Deriving the Given Goals.** Given two goals that are connected in a goal graph, a subject is required to identify the goals having specific roles on deriving these given two goals. Since the given two goals, letting a descendant goal and its ancestor be n_1 and n_2 respectively, are connected, one goal n_1 is transitively derived from the other goal n_2. There are goals on the path between n_1 and n_2 that more contribute to the derivation of n_1 from n_2 based on a certain concern. The subjects were asked to look for such goals as these. To find them correctly, the subjects should understand the derivation process from n_2 to n_1, i.e., how and why n_1 is derived from n_2 from a view of a certain concern. The example of the question of this type is "Goal n_1

Fig. 6. Modifying edges in a goal.

can contribute to the achievement of Goal n_2. Which can goals on the path between n_1 and n_2 play a role of Function for their achievement?".

– **Question Type 2 (QT 2): Identify Goals Refinements to be Modified.** We gave goal graphs of lower quality that had been artificially generated and asked our subjects to find the goal refinements to be modified. To generate the goal graphs of lower quality, we picked up original goal graphs whose quality was high and deteriorate them by reconnecting some of sub goals to wrong parent goals so that we got goal graphs having unsuitable goal refinements. See Fig. 6. Given the produced unsuitable goal graphs, a subject is required to identify unsuitable goal refinements.

– **Question Type 3 (QT 3): Identifying Insufficient Derivation of Sub Goals from a Certain Concern.** Given a certain concern and a goal specifying it, a subject is required to check if there exist the goals that contribute to the given goal from the view of the other relevant concerns, or not. The example of the question of this type is "Where are the goals specifying the non-function concern whose their achievement as function are not considered, if any?" In a completed goal graph, the goals representing non-functional requirements should be finally refined into sub goals that denote the functions to implement these non-functional requirements. If these sub goals do not exist yet in a goal graph, the goals of the non-functional requirements should be analyzed and refined further. This type of questions is for the subjects to select the goals necessary to be analyzed and refined further.

These types of questions correspond to the observation Items (a), (b), and (c) mentioned above. For example, to answer QT 1 correctly, a subject should understand the meaning of goal refinements between the given two goals, e.g., the goal n_1 and n_2 in the example question. We prepared 3, 1, and 2 questions for QT 1, 2, and 3, respectively. Some of the questions correspond to multiple solutions. For example, the question of QT 2 for each graph correspond to 8 solution goals.

In our experiments, we use three concerns: function, non-function, and strategy. Note that we did not use goal refinement rules, i.e., any concern combination was allowable in this example, and we made the textual explanations of the meaning of 9 (= 3 concerns × 3) types of goal refinements. The textual explanations of the meaning of refining a strategy concern into a function concern are displayed to our subjects on the screen of the tool, as shown in Sect. 4. The reason we did not use the rules is as follows. It is obvious that our tool can detect

Table 1. Details of used goal graphs.

	# goals	# functions	# non-functions	# strategies	# edges
G_{SEJ}	50	26	11	15	61
G_{CRE}	50	22	15	16	60

Table 2. Goal graphs that subjects used.

	No support	Our approach
Subject A	G_{CRE}	G_{SEJ}
Subject B	G_{CRE}	G_{SEJ}
Subject C	G_{SEJ}	G_{CRE}
Subject D	G_{SEJ}	G_{CRE}

the violation of the rules in an instant, and the comparison of correct answers and answering time is not so meaningful. Rather, we would like to show our semantic information of goal refinements can contribute to detecting unsuitable goal refinements as well.

We used two goal graphs G_{SEJ} and G_{CRE}. G_{SEJ} is for the strategies of Seven Eleven in Japan [7], and G_{CRE} is for an information system where university students apply for class credits. Table 1 shows their size such as the numbers of goals, edges and the occurrences of concerns. For example, the graph G_{SEJ} had 50 goals and 61 edges, and a function concern was attached to 26 goals out of the 50 ones.

We had four student subjects of the computer science department who had learned requirements engineering. All of them had experiences in developing information systems, but were not expertized to requirements analysis techniques. Thus, as shown in Fig. 5, we gave the subjects a short lecture of GORE and the existing goal graph editor, which had no support of our approach and our tool in 20 min. They tried out these tools in this lecture. Table 2 shows the assignment of the goal graphs G_{SEJ} and G_{CRE} to our subjects. For example, Subject A analyzed G_{CRE} with the existing goal graph editor and G_{SEJ} with our tool, i.e., she/he proceeded the step 2 with G_{CRE} and the step 3 with G_{SEJ}. We use the term "No support" to express the group of the subjects who did not use our tool but the existing goal graph editor.

5.2 Results

Table 3 shows the results of the subjects' answers. The numerals of the table represent the average numbers of correct answers, wrong answers, and missing answers over the four subjects. In the case where a subject did not find a correct answer, we count it as a missing answer. Suppose that a goal n is one of the correct answers. If a subject answered as n, we count this answer as a correct one in the table. On the other hand, if she/he did not, we count it as a missing

Table 3. Average of correct and wrong answers.

		G_{SEJ}			G_{CRE}		
		Correct	Wrong	Missing	Correct	Wrong	Missing
QT 1	No support	2.5	2.5	0.5	1	3.5	2
	Our approach	2.5	1	0.5	3	4.5	0
QT 2	No support	3	0	5	3	0	5
	Our approach	3.5	0	4.5	3.5	0	4.5
QT 3	No support	2	1	3	1	2	2
	Our approach	5	1	0	3	3	0

Table 4. Average time spent in answering.

		G_{SEJ}	G_{CRE}
QT 1	No support	2'48"	1'44"
	Our approach	2'39"	2'16"
QT 2	No support	10'15"	10'34"
	Our approach	10'47"	10'44"
QT 3	No support	3'14"	4'44"
	Our approach	3'31"	3'59"

answer, but if she/he did the different goal n', it is a wrong answer. In the example of QT 1 and the goal G_{SEJ}, each subject answered three questions, and two subjects of four used our approach. The total number of *real* correct answers to these questions was just 3. Subject A answered the three questions correctly, i.e., she/he could find all three goals that were correct answers to the questions. However, Subject B listed four goals as her/his answers, and two of the four were correct. She/he identified two wrong goals and missed one *real* correct goal. For the two subjects using our approach, 2.5 in average were correct one, and they selected one wrong answer and missed 0.5 correct answers in average.

Table 4 shows the average time spent on subjects' answering the questions. In the example of the graph G_{SEJ} and QT 1, the average time of the subjects was 2 min 48 s.

5.3 Discussion

According to the experimental results, we can consider that our approach allows to prevent requirements analysts from missing the goals necessary to understand goal refinements from the viewpoint of a certain concern. In QT 1 to the graph G_{CRE} of Table 3, our approach was successful in reducing missing answers at two and increasing correct answers. However, for G_{SEJ} we could not observe the same result, so we need more experiments and investigations further. In addition, we could not observe considerable differences on wrong answers between no support and our approach, so we cannot conclude that our approach reduced misunderstanding of goal refinements.

As for detectability of unsuitable goal refinements, we could not obtain positive results. We can conclude that our approach might be useful to reduce the efforts of our subjects because the time spent in finding the unsuitable goal refinements was decreasing. See the column QT 2 of Table 4. Our subjects using the tool could reduce their average times of G_{SEJ} and G_{CRE} at only 32 and 10 s respectively, and we could not conclude that the difference is enough large. Also, in QT 1 and QT 3, we could not obtain the evidence of the benefits of our approach. Rather, in these cases the time spent in making answers was increasing. The manipulation time of our tool, e.g., the manipulation time for retrieving the goals specifying certain coordinates, might cause additional time. As a goal graph to be analyzed is larger and more complicated, we might obtain clearer results.

Let us turn back to Table 3 and see the column of QT 3. For the subjects using our tool, the number of missing correct answers was reduced at 3 in G_{SEJ} and 2 in G_{CRE} respectively, and the correct answers were increasing. Thus, we can conclude that our approach reduced missing the goals necessary to be analyzed.

To sum up, our approach has possibilities of preventing analysts from missing goal refinements to be recognized and goals to be analyzed. Regarding the reduction of the efforts in detecting unsuitable goal refinements in a goal graph, the new usages of the tool might be the obstacle to detecting such refinements quickly.

5.4   Threats to Validity

External Validity. External validity is related to generalization of our experimental results. We used students as subjects of the experiment, and in this sense, it may be doubtful whether the experimental results can hold in practitioners. However, our subjects had been involved in practical projects and had experiences in system development. Although they were not practitioners of requirements analysis or GORE, they took lectures related to requirements engineering. Thus, although experiments for practitioners may be necessary, we do not consider that experimental results extremely different. In addition, the two goal graphs and the concerns that we used are limited. The domain of the goal graphs was business application. We need to make experiments using goal graphs in different problem domains and different concerns. In particular, we consider concerns more than three: Function, Strategy, and Non-Function. Interrelated concerns and the larger number of them may result in more positive effects of our approach.

Internal Validity. It may be a problem that the questions that we made really reflect on the items to be evaluated. For example, we made a question like "Where are the goals specifying the concern Non-Function whose their achievement as Function are not considered?" to check if the subjects could identify insufficient goal refinements or not. Suppose that we have a goal specifying a Non-Function concern and that it should be achieved. The Non-Function concern should be implemented by functions in an information system, so the goal graph should include some goals specifying a Function concern that can contribute to the Non-Function goal. If this kind of a Function goal does not exist, the goal refinement can be insufficient, and we should add sub goals specifying Function concern to achieve the Non-Function goal. To identify these insufficient refinements, the subjects should understand the meaning of goal refinements in the goal graph well. Thus, the question can contribute to evaluating Item (c) (our subjects can understand goal refinements) mentioned in Sect. 5.1. In this way, we designed the questions carefully, but we do not consider that the used questions can cover all the aspects of the items to be evaluated. Thus, we should consider wide varieties of questions that cover more aspects of the evaluation items in further experiments.

Construct Validity. Our experiment was based on a comparative way, i.e., we had two experiments where only one factor was different from them. This factor is the usage of the supporting tool for our approach, and the other factors such as the characteristics of subjects should be the same in the two experiments. Construct validity guarantees that nothing but the difference of this factor causes the experimental results. We chose the subjects who had the same experiences and skills as prudently as possible. We used two tools having editing functions of goal graphs. One is the AGORA editor [11] as the tool having no functions of our approach. The other is the tool supporting our approach and is an extended version of AGORA editor. That is to say, two tools have the same user interface and the functions except for the functions related to annotating and manipulating concerns. Thus, we do not consider there are any effects of the experimental results caused by the differences on the tools.

6   Related Work

The idea of separating concerns is not new. Tarr et al. proposed a technique to manage software documents by separating them from the multiple viewpoints based on concerns [13]. Our approach is the extension of this basic idea to goal graphs. Moreira et al. developed a technique of handling multiple concerns to analyze cross-cutting functional requirements [8]. In their approach, concerns are separated and relationships among them are defined. These relationships are helpful to understand cross-cutting functional requirements. Their aim and concrete approach are similar to ours. However, it applied to XML documents, not goal graphs. Rather, they tried to support the selection of software architectures to implement the functional requirements. Giorgini et al. introduced the concept of *perspective* into Tropos method in order to model data warehouse systems [3]. In their method, a perspective is attached to a goal, and it looks like a check item that is necessary to confirm the achievement of the goal. They set up two perspectives for modeling: organizational perspective and decisional one, and these perspectives are conceptually closer to the idea of annotations. i^* approach adopts different notations of graph nodes, e.g., Hard Goal, Soft Goal, Task, and Resource [14]. It may be useful for requirements analysts to understand the meaning of goal refinements, e.g., they can understand that the refinement from a soft goal to tasks via Means-End links expresses the implementation of the soft goal. However, in this approach varieties of notation are limited, and the goals derived from multiple concerns cannot be handled. In addition, it is difficult for human analysts to understand at a glance the underlying various intents of goal refinement. In i^* and NFR, it is also possible to tag goals, e.g., via contribution links to soft goals. However, our approach can use varieties of semantic tags as annotations, and furthermore requirements analysts can individually define them.

Similarity to the proposed approach, our previous work [4,12] can handle semantic information to goals. Although this approach aims to support the change impact analysis of a goal graph, the proposed approach aims to obtain the goal refinement of higher quality.

7   Conclusion

This paper addresses the problem of the intermixture of goals specifying various concerns in a goal graph so as to make it difficult to understand the goal graph, especially goal refinements. Our approach is to adopt the idea of annotating goals with concerns. Goals are refined following the rules of concerns. We provide the meaning of a goal refinement based on concerns, more concretely combinations of the concerns of a parent goal and those of sub goals. Furthermore, we developed a supporting tool, where a requirements analyst can define her/his interesting concerns and annotate goals with them. The tool also has functions for displaying the meaning of goal refinements, of retrieving goals having a specific concern, of hiding the goals having irrelevant concerns, etc. These functions are embedded to the existing goal graph editor AGORA as a plug-in. Although our experimental results did not show positive observations for all beneficial points that we expected, some of them were observed.

Our future work can be listed up as follows:

More Case Studies. As future work, we have to make more experiments using various problem domains, more concerns, and practitioners.

Considering Separation of Concerns. The basis underlying our approach is that concerns are not interrelated and can be clearly separated. However, some concerns may be interrelated to each other and although we can separate them, we should consider them concurrently when we refine a goal. In our approach, some kinds of dependencies among concerns in goal refinement can be handled by means of goal refinement rules on these concerns. However, more elaborated techniques to handle interrelated concerns and interactions among concerns should be developed.

Improving the Usability of the Tool. When the number of concerns would increase, the usability of the technique might decrease because the effects of hiding and showing goals become large. A further technique to visualize and analyze a goal graph on a display screen of the tool should be considered in the future.

Using Different Types of Concerns. Using new types of concerns can be used. For example, some quality attributes of goals, such as performance or security [12], can also be regarded as the concerns. Moreover, we are also able to regard the view from a stakeholder as a specific concern.

Handling the Type of Refinements. Although we adopted the three concerns in this paper as an example, our approach can handle with various types of goal refinements such as causality relationship. Its reason is that a concern denotes an atomic meaning of goal relationship on refinement, and requirements analysts can define the concerns that they will use. Furthermore, by combining concerns, we can express complex meaning of goal relationships. It is also one of the future work to illustrate this issues and to show an additional effectiveness of our approach.

Acknowledgements. This work was partly supported by JSPS Grants-in-Aid for Scientific Research (#15K00088 and #15K00109).

References

1. Bleistein, S.J., Cox, K., Verner, J., Phalp, K.T.: B-SCP: a requirements analysis framework for validating strategic alignment of organizational it based on strategy, context, and process. Inf. Softw. Technol. **48**(9), 846–868 (2006)
2. Giorgini, P., Mylopoulos, J., Nicchiarelli, E., Sebastiani, R.: Reasoning with goal models. In: Spaccapietra, S., March, S.T., Kambayashi, Y. (eds.) ER 2002. LNCS, vol. 2503, pp. 167–181. Springer, Heidelberg (2002)
3. Giorgini, P., Rizzi, S., Garzetti, M.: Goal-oriented requirements analysis for data warehouse design. In: Proceedings of the 8th ACM International Workshop on Data Warehousing and OLAP (DOLAP 2005), pp. 47–56 (2005)
4. Hayashi, S., Tanabe, D., Kaiya, H., Saeki, M.: Impact analysis on an attributed goal graph. IEICE Trans. Inf. Syst. **E95–D**(4), 1012–1020 (2012)
5. van Lamsweerde, A.: Goal-oriented requirements engineering: a guided tour. In: Proceedings of the 5th IEEE International Symposium on Requirements Engineering (RE 2001), pp. 249–263 (2001)
6. van Lamsweerde, A.: Requirements Engineering: From System Goals to UML Models to Software Specifications. Wiley, Hoboken (2009)
7. Makino, N., Suzuki, T.: Convenience stores and the information revolution. Jpn. Echo **24**(1), 44–49 (1997)
8. Moreira, A., Rashid, A., Araujo, J.: Multi-dimensional separation of concerns in requirements engineering. In: Proceedings of the 13th IEEE International Conference on Requirements Engineering (ICSE 2005), pp. 285–296 (2005)
9. Munro, S., Liaskos, S., Aranda, J.: The mysteries of goal decomposition. In: Proceedings of the 5th International i* Workshop (iStar 2011), pp. 49–54 (2011)
10. Mylopoulos, J., Chung, L., Nixon, B.: Representing and using non-functional requirements: a process-oriented approach. IEEE Trans. Softw. Eng. **6**(4), 489–497 (1992)

11. Saeki, M., Hayashi, S., Kaiya, H.: A tool for attributed goal-oriented requirements analysis. In: Proceedings of the 24th IEEE/ACM International Conference on Automated Software Engineering (ASE 2009), pp. 670–672 (2009)
12. Tanabe, D., Uno, K., Akemine, K., Yoshikawa, T., Kaiya, H., Saeki, M.: Supporting requirements change management in goal oriented analysis. In: Proceedings of the 16th IEEE International Requirements Engineering Conference (RE 2008), pp. 3–12 (2008)
13. Tarr, P., Ossher, H., Harrison, W., Sutton Jr., S.M.: N degrees of separation: multi-dimensional separation of concerns. In: Proceedings of the 10th International Conference on Software Engineering (ICSE 1999), pp. 107–119 (1999)
14. Yu, E.: Towards modeling and reasoning support for early-phase requirements engineering. In: Proceedings of the 3rd IEEE International Symposium on Requirements Engineering (RE 1997), pp. 226–235 (1997)

A Model-Based Approach for Integrating Executable Architectural Design Patterns in Space Flight Software Product Lines

Julie Street Fant[1,2], Hassan Gomaa[1(✉)], and Robert G. Pettit[2]

[1] George Mason University, Fairfax, VA, USA
hgomaa@gmu.edu
[2] The Aerospace Corporation, Chantilly, VA, USA
{julie.s.fant,robert.g.pettit}@aero.org

Abstract. The unmanned space flight software (FSW) domain contains a significant amount of variability within its required capabilities. Because of the large degree of architectural variability in FSW, it is difficult to develop a FSW software product line (SPL) architecture that covers all possible variations. In order to address this challenge, this paper presents a model-based SPL approach for FSW SPLs that manages variability at a higher level of granularity using executable software architectural design patterns and requires less modeling during SPL engineering but more modeling at the application engineering phase. The executable design patterns are tailored to individual FSW applications during application engineering. The paper describes in detail the application and validation of this approach to FSW.

Keywords: Software product lines (SPL) · UML · Software architectural design patterns · Executable patterns · Application engineering · Unmanned space flight software

1 Introduction

The unmanned space Flight Software (FSW) domain is well-suited for applying Software Product Line (SPL) modeling approaches due to its commonalities and variability. All FSW must be able to communicate with ground stations, to execute ground commands, and to control spacecraft attitude. However, within each of the capabilities there is a significant amount of variability, such as the volume of commands that must be processed, the amount of control that is given to the ground station versus onboard autonomy, and the amount and type of hardware that requires controlling. Choices made on this variability will affect the underlying software architectures and component interactions. This degree of architectural variability makes it difficult to develop a FSW Software Product Line (SPL) architecture that covers all possible variations.

Leveraging the benefits of software design patterns is particularly important in the FSW domain. The FSW industry is experiencing a growing number of software related spacecraft anomalies. In fact, it is reported that "in the period between 1998 and 2000

© Springer International Publishing Switzerland 2016
P. Lorenz et al. (Eds.): ICSOFT 2015, CCIS 586, pp. 287–306, 2016.
DOI: 10.1007/978-3-319-30142-6_16

nearly half of all observed spacecraft anomalies were related to software" [1]. This trend has continued as FSW continues to grow in complexity. This challenge can be addressed through this research. First, this research effort uses software design patterns to produce higher quality designs. Second, this research provides validation during the design phase. Therefore, design flaws that lead to in-flight software anomalies can be identified and remedied early in the software lifecycle. Additionally, this research aligns with a recommendation from the National Aeronautics and Space Administration (NASA) to help improve FSW acquisitions by performing early analysis and architecting of FSW [2].

This paper addresses the needs of FSW SPL architectures by reducing the amount of SPL engineering modeling through the incorporation of variable architectural design patterns and giving the application developer the capability of customizing the patterns to the needs of the application. Variable design patterns contain customizable components, connectors, and interactions rather than specific components, connectors, and interactions. Therefore several different combinations of specific components, connectors, and interactions are abstracted into one design pattern and do not need to be individually modeled. Thus less modeling is required during the SPL engineering phase. The trade-off is that the application engineering phase does require additional modeling since the application specific components, connectors, and interactions must be derived from the design patterns. However, guidance is provided to help assist the application engineer and ensure the SPL architecture is maintained. A key piece of this approach lies in the ability to interconnect design patterns to form software architectures. This paper specifically addresses how to systematically interconnect design patterns to create a FSW SPL software architecture.

This paper is organized as follows. After surveying related work, it describes the overall approach, including the interconnection of variable design patterns during SPL engineering and how this approach was applied to the FSW SPL. Then the application engineering process is described and illustrated using a real world case study. Next, discuss how this FSW SPL derived applications were validated. Finally, this paper includes a discussion on conclusions and areas of future work.

2   Related Work

There are many notable SPL approaches including [3–6]. Many existing SPL approaches typically focus on capturing all possible SPL variability in the SPL engineering phase. This becomes challenging in the FSW domain because all possible variability in components, connectors, and interactions must be individually modeled. On the other hand, other approaches focus on modeling the commonality of the SPL and define variation points where variability is permitted to be introduced during application engineering [7]. However, this approach defers most development of variable components to application engineering. The approach described and applied in this paper takes an intermediate approach in between modeling all variability and limited variability by modeling SPL variability at the architectural design pattern level.

Currently, there are very few works that discuss building FSW from software architectural design patterns [8–11]. These works describe the application of a small number of design patterns to FSW, but do not provide an overall approach for building FSW from design patterns. There are several reference architectures for FSW that can be used as a starting point for building FSW [12–14]. However, none of the reference architectures are design pattern based and therefore they do not guarantee that the benefits of design patterns will be leveraged in the architectures produced using them.

Finally, Bennett et al. [15, 16] are working on related research called the Mission Data System (MDS) project. The MDS provides a system level control architecture, framework, and systems engineering methodology for developing state-based models for planning and execution. The approach described in this paper can be used to complement and support this work.

A second set of related work describes approaches to build real-time and embedded software architectures from design patterns [5, 17–20] and software architectural design patterns [21–24]. While these approaches identify several useful patterns for this domain, they only provide high-level guidance on their application to develop variable software architectures. In particular, they do not explicitly capture SPL variability in the patterns to assist with selection of SPL members.

This paper builds on the authors' previous work in [5, 25, 26]. In [25] executable design patterns were used to build FSW architectures for single systems. This paper extends this work by addressing variability in the FSW domain and describing how variable design patterns are interconnected to form SPL and SPL member architectures. In [27], we addressed the concept of a design pattern based SPL at a very high level and did not include the specific details about the approach. This paper extends the previous works to describe the details of how variable design patterns are interconnected to form SPL architectures and relates this information to the validation.

3   SPL Engineering with Architectural Design Patterns

The design pattern approach to SPL engineering involves creating domain specific patterns, which are based on well-known general-purpose patterns [20, 21] during the domain-engineering phase. The purpose of creating SPL architectural design patterns is to add SPL domain knowledge and variability to the general-purpose architectural design patterns as described next. The architectural design patterns need to be related to the feature model in order to allow the selection of the appropriate design patterns for application engineering. The main steps include: (1) Build a set of variable distributed real-time and embedded (DRE) architectural design patterns that can be leveraged as a starting point, (2) Develop a set of use cases and features that are used to define SPL, (3) Perform use case activity modeling to precisely capture the sequencing in use cases, (4) Create a feature to design pattern mapping, (5) Customize the variable DRE design patterns to become variable SPL specific design patterns, (6) Define the design pattern sequencing and interconnection. The subsections below describes each of the main steps in more detail and describe the application to the FSW SPL's command and data handling (C&DH) subsystem.

3.1   Variable Distributed Real-time and Embedded (DRE) Design Patterns

The first step in our approach is to create variable DRE architectural and executable design patterns, which serve as the foundation for the developed SPLs. Each variable DRE architectural pattern contains several UML views including collaboration diagrams, interaction diagrams, and component diagrams. Variable design patterns are modeled at the DRE level so that they can be reused and customized across multiple domains. Each variable DRE design pattern is supplemented by an executable design pattern that consists of interacting objects that execute state machines. The purpose of the executable version of the design pattern is to specify the internal behavior of a representative set of the pattern's objects and to facilitate validation of the pattern. Each executable design pattern is individually simulated and validated using Harel's approach of executable object modeling with statecharts [28] We created a total 21 DRE design patterns [25] using this approach, including the centralized control, distributed control, hierarchical control and layers design patterns. The approach enables architectures produced by interconnecting these design patterns to be fully executable and validated, as described in Sect. 5.

The process to create executable DRE design patterns is illustrated using a centralized control design pattern. The centralized control design pattern involves a single controller that provides overall control by conceptually executing a state machine [5] The first view is a collaboration diagram that captures the components that participate in the design pattern and their variability. At the DRE level, the design patterns are composed of domain components that will be later customized to first the SPL and then the SPL member. Variability is captured using SPL stereotypes from the PLUS method [5]. A collaboration diagram for the Centralized Control design pattern [19] is given in Fig. 1. This depicts the kernel Centralized Controller and optional Input, Output, and IO components, as well as the multiplicity of the components.

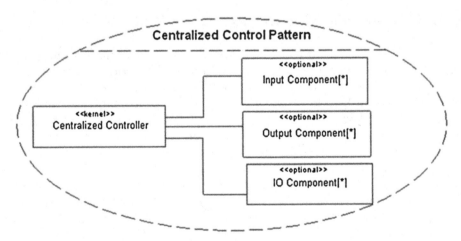

Fig. 1. Collaboration diagram for DRE level Centralized Control executable design pattern.

The second architectural view uses interaction diagrams, which capture how the objects within the design pattern interact. Because of the wide range of variability in which DRE design pattern can be applied, the interaction diagrams only capture a representative set of object interactions. For instance, the interaction diagram will show the Centralized Controller receiving an input from an Input_Component and in response it will invoke an action on an Output_Component.

The third architectural view uses a component diagram that models the interconnection between components in the DRE design pattern. The component diagram shows the components with required ports, provided ports, and connectors that interconnect the components. Component variability is modeled with SPL stereotypes.

Finally, an executable version of the design pattern is also created using communicating state machines. The purpose of the executable version of the design pattern is to specify the internal behavior of a representative set of the pattern's objects and to facilitate validation of the pattern. Each executable design pattern is individually simulated and validated using Harel's approach [28]. The state machine for the Centralized Controller component is depicted in Fig. 2.

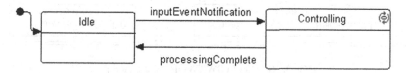

Fig. 2. Centralized Controller state machine.

3.2   Use Case and Feature Modeling

Next, SPL use cases are developed applying the PLUS method [5]. This involves identifying the use cases and variability within the use cases through variation points, optional and alternative use cases. From the use case variability, an initial feature model can be developed [5]. Features represent common and variable characteristics or requirements of the SPL. Features are analyzed and categorized as common, optional, or alternative. Related features can be grouped into feature groups, which constrain how features are used by a SPL member [5].

When use case modeling was applied to the FSW SPL C&DH subsystem, three kernel use cases with internal variability were identified. Within these use cases, numerous variation points were identified. These variation points resulted in identifying 52 features. A subset of the FSW C&DH feature model is shown in Fig. 3. This feature model contains an «exactly-one-of feature group» called Command Execution that is based on the Command Execution use case's Command Volume variation point. This feature group has three «alternative» features. The Low Volume Command Execution feature is used when a small amount of commands needs processing, the High Volume Command Execution feature is used when a large amount of commands needs processing, and Time Triggered Command Execution is used when commands must be executed with strict temporal predictability. There is also a significant amount of variability in the amount and type of hardware that must be commanded, which are captured in variation points.

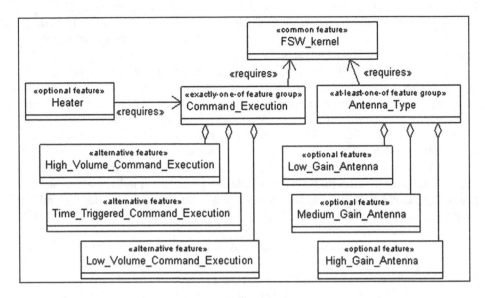

Fig. 3. Subset of FSW C&DH feature model.

3.3   Use Case Activity Modeling

The next step is to create variable use case activity models [25]. Use case activity models are activity diagrams that make the sequencing of interactions between actor(s) and system in a use case description more precise. In variable use case activity diagrams [25], SPL variability is captured in two ways. First, feature based conditions are used when the flow in activity is associated with SPL features. Feature based conditions, such as [CommandExecution = "LowVolume"], are modeled as branches from decision nodes. Second, steps with variability, which are denoted using the «adaptable» stereotype, can be successively refined in separate sub-activity diagrams. Our approach only refines adaptable steps when they are impacted by a small number of variation points. If an adaptable step has a significant amount of variation points, then modeling is deferred until the application engineering phase.

   Use case activity modeling was performed on three uses cases of the FSW SPL's C&DH subsystem. The FSW SPL's Execute Commands use case involves executing commands from the ground station to ensure the spacecraft is not put into an unsafe state and the actions taken are appropriate for the spacecraft's mode. This use case is impacted by the Command Execution feature condition as it influences which steps are performed. Thus the path taken through the Execute Commands use case activity diagram (see Fig. 4) is heavily impacted by the Command Execution feature condition.

As seen in Fig. 4, several variation points including modes and spacecraft IO devices (listed in parentheses after the step's description) influence the adaptable steps in the use case activity diagram. The Spacecraft IO device variation point specifies variations in the optional and alternative I/O devices. These devices include antennas, antenna gimbals, memory storage devices, power appendages, power devices, attitude control devices, attitude determination devices, payload devices, thrusters, heaters, louvers, and temperature sensors. Since all adaptable steps in this use case have significant amount of variability as seen by the multitude of variation points, more detailed activity modeling was deferred to application engineering.

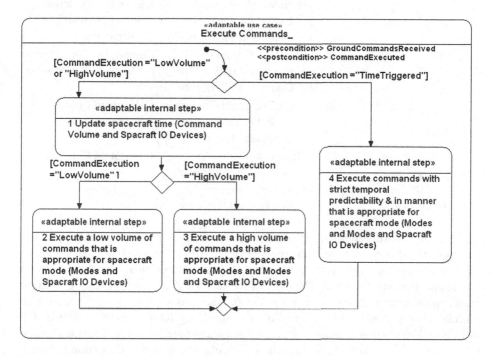

Fig. 4. Execute Commands use case activity model.

3.4   Feature to Design Pattern Mapping

The next step is to create a feature to design pattern mapping. The purpose of the feature to design pattern mapping is to determine which variable design patterns could be mapped to SPL features. To accomplish this goal, a dynamic SPL interaction model [5] is created for each feature, which captures the objects and object interactions that realize each feature. Then the dynamic interaction models are analyzed to identify where variable design patterns can be applied in the SPL and then relates these patterns back to the SPL features. Features that are mapped to variable design patterns are called pattern specific features. *Pattern specific features* are coarse grained features that relate to a

Table 1. Subset FSW SPL C&DH feature to design pattern mapping.

Feature Group	Var.	Feature	DRE Design Pattern
<<exactly-one-of feature group>> Command Execution	alt.	High Vol. Command Execution	Hierarchical Control
	alt.	Low Vol. Command Execution	Centralized Control
	alt.	Time-Triggered Command Execution	Distributed Control
	alt.	High Vol. Command Execution with Command Flexibility	Hierarchical Control with Command Dispatcher
	alt.	Low Vol. Command Execution with Command Flexibility	Centralized Control with Command Dispatcher
	alt.	Time-Triggered Command Execution with Command Flexibility	Distributed Control with Command Dispatcher
<<exactly-one-of feature group>> Telemetry Storage and Retrieval	alt.	High Vol. Telemetry Storage and Retrieval	Compound Commit
	alt.	Low Vol. Telemetry Storage and Retrieval	Client Server

design pattern and differentiate among other related features. *Pattern variability features* are fine grained features, which influence the variability within a pattern specific feature.

The feature to design pattern mapping is demonstrated using the Low Volume Command Execution feature. The interaction model for the Low Volume Command Execution alternative feature is shown in Fig. 6. Since this feature is typically associated with small spacecraft, only the kernel input, output, and IO devices are modeled. The objects and interaction sequence supporting this feature are consistent with the Centralized Control design pattern [5]. Thus the Low Volume Command Execution feature is categorized as a pattern specific feature and is mapped to the Centralized Control design pattern.

When this step was applied to the FSW SPL, a SPL interaction model was created for each of the pattern specific features, 24 in total. A subset of the FSW C&DH feature to design pattern mapping is shown in Table 1.

3.5 Executable Design Patterns

The next step is to derive the variable SPL architectural and executable design patterns from the variable DRE architectural and executable design patterns for each of the pattern specific features. The purpose of the variable SPL design patterns is to add domain specific knowledge to the design patterns so they can be systematically incorporated into SPL architectures. This process involves systematically updating the components, interactions, and component behavior to reflect the SPL specific components and variability based on the SPL features.

This process is illustrated using the DRE Centralized Control design pattern (Fig. 1) in the FSW SPL (Fig. 5). This design pattern captures the I/O devices the FSW interacts with based on the ground commands it receives. To realize this mapping, the Centralized Controller and the I/O components in Fig. 1 are updated to give the CDH Centralized Controller and FSW I/O components in Fig. 5. SPL components are categorized as kernel, optional, or variant.

For example, the SPL requires ground commands that adjust the spacecraft's attitude by invoking actions on attitude control devices. This is achieved by updating an Output_Component in the DRE level design pattern to become an Attitude_Control_Device_OC kernel component. Since there can be different versions of attitude control in different missions, different attitude control devices are modeled as variants. Additionally, since a heating device is optional, another Output_Component is updated to an optional Heater_OC. The Centralized Control design pattern is only used when there are a small amount of commands to execute and hardware to control. Therefore, when this pattern is customized to an application, only an application specific subset of the optional devices is selected.

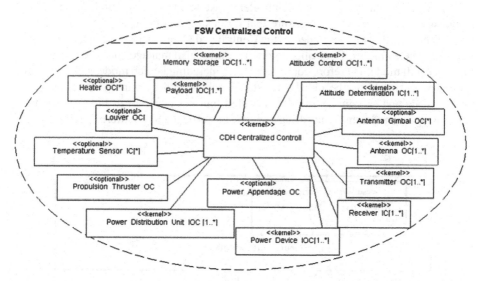

Fig. 5. FSW SPL centralized control collaboration diagram.

Second, the interaction diagrams capture the object interactions within a design pattern. If the precise sequence of object interactions is known, then it should be modelled. However, in design patterns where there is variability in the object interactions, then only a subset of object interactions is modelled, as shown in Fig. 3. Detailed interaction modelling, in which other application specific I/O objects and interactions might be added to the pattern, is deferred to the application engineering phase. For the FSW SPL's C&DH subsystem, 24 interaction diagrams were created, one for each of the pattern specific features. As an example, Fig. 3 shows an interaction diagram for the FSW Centralized Control design pattern that is mapped to the specific feature.

This feature captures the FSW processing and execution for a set of ground commands, which involves invoking actions on the input, output, and IO components. The type and amount of input, output, and IO components in the FSW Centralized Control design pattern is influenced by several pattern variability features. For example, the optional Heater pattern variability feature captures whether or not the spacecraft has heaters. This results in an optional Heater superclass component, as seen in Fig. 6. The specific Heater subclasses are not modeled until the application engineering phase.

Next, the component diagrams, which capture the interconnection between components, must be updated. This involves updating the diagram with the required components identified in the collaboration diagram. Then subsequently, updating all the required ports, provided ports, and connectors that interconnect the components.

Finally, state machines [5] capture the internal behavior of each active component in the design pattern. For the FSW SPL's C&DH subsystem, a state machine was created for each active component in the FSW SPL's 24 patterns. A subset of the state machine for the CDH Centralized Controller from the Centralized Control Design pattern is illustrated in Fig. 7, which is derived from the DRE Centralized Control Pattern in Fig. 1. In FSW the Centralized Controller must validate all ground commands or responses to onboard events to ensure that it does not put the spacecraft in an unsafe state. Therefore this logic is added to the Centralized Controller's state machine. Additionally, the Centralized Controller component must also manage and take into account the spacecraft mode. Therefore common modes, including launch mode, safe mode, and normal mode should also be added to the state machine. Other common modes including launch mode and safe mode are also modeled, but not depicted in Fig. 7. The states comprising the modes and controlling logic are based on the SPL pattern specific feature.

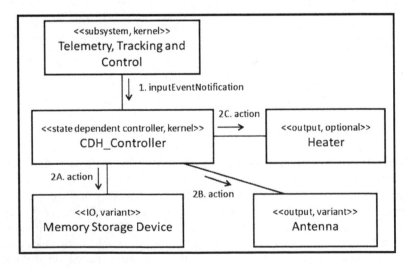

Fig. 6. Interaction diagram for the Low Volume Command Execution pattern.

The actions within the states, which are not depicted in Fig. 7, are determined from the pattern specific and pattern variability features.

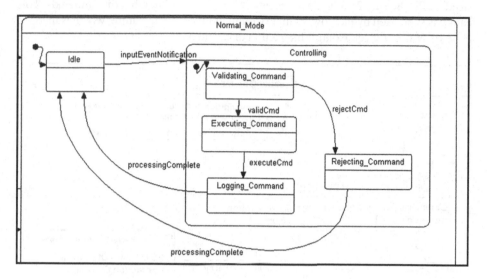

Fig. 7. State machine subset for centralized controller.

3.6   Design Pattern Interconnection

The next step is to capture how the variable design patterns are integrated together to form software architectures. A use case scenario driven approach is used to interconnect variable design patterns to achieve the SPL functionality. For each use case scenario, an interaction overview diagram is created based on the use case activity diagram. This is accomplished by using the same control flow in the use case activity diagrams but replacing each activity with a reference to the variable SPL design pattern's interaction diagram that supports that step. On feature based condition paths, the variable design pattern used to achieve one or more of the steps along the path can be determined from the feature to design pattern mapping.

After an interaction overview diagram is created, the design pattern interconnections are determined. When the interaction diagrams for two design patterns appear sequentially, they must communicate with each other and must be interconnected. Interaction modeling and the design pattern integration process is illustrated using the FSW SPL Execute Commands use case. An interaction overview diagram is created using the same control flow in the use case activity diagram. For instance, since the Execute Commands use case activity diagram (Fig. 4) begins with a feature based decision, the Execute Commands interaction overview diagram (Fig. 8) also begins with this same decision point. Each of the steps in the use case activity diagram in Fig. 4 is updated to reflect the supporting variable design pattern's interaction diagram using the feature to design pattern mapping table, as depicted in Fig. 8. For example, Step 1 on Fig. 4 involves sending a time update. This step is supported by the Spacecraft Clock pattern specific feature, which is mapped to the FSW Spacecraft Clock Multicast executable design pattern. Therefore the FSW Spacecraft Clock Multicast's interaction diagram is referenced on Fig. 8. Step 2 on Fig. 4 involves executing a small number of commands. This feature is supported by the Low Volume Command Execution feature, which is mapped to the FSW Centralized Control interaction diagram, as shown in Fig. 8.

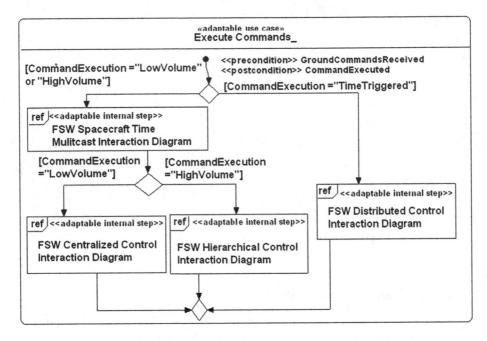

Fig. 8. Execute Commands interaction overview diagram.

After all the FSW SPL interaction overview diagrams were created, they were analyzed. If there are two sequential variable design patterns, then these design patterns must be interconnected. For instance, in Fig. 8, the FSW Spacecraft Clock Multicast executable design pattern interconnects with the FSW Centralized Control and FSW Hierarchical Control executable design patterns. Patterns are interconnected using connectors. The last interacting component (client or producer) of one pattern sends a message to the receiving component (consumer or server) of the other pattern. The appropriate provided and required interfaces are specified during architectural design.

4   Application Engineering

After the development of the FSW SPL architecture and components, applications are derived from them. This is accomplished by first selecting the appropriate FSW SPL features based on the application's requirements. From the feature to design pattern mapping, the appropriate FSW SPL executable design patterns are then determined and customized to create the application executable design patterns. This approach is illustrated with the case studies described in the next section.

5   Case Studies

This section describes case studies of the application engineering process, where FSW applications are derived from the FSW SPL assets. The process is applied to the Student Nitric Oxide Explorer (SNOE) and Solar TErrestrial RElations Observatory (STEREO) application case studies, which are real-world space programs [29, 30]. SNOE mission involves using a small spin stabilized spacecraft in a low earth orbit to measure thermospheric nitric oxide and its variability. SNOE is a low earth orbit and relies heavily on the ground station to control the spacecraft's small amount of hardware. STEREO mission involves using two nearly identical three-axis stabilized spacecraft orbiting around the sun to study the studying the nature of coronal mass ejections. Since STEREO is not in constant communication with the ground station, it relies on a significant amount of autonomy and stored ground commands to control the spacecraft. These case studies were selected because they cover a wide variety of spacecraft in the FSW domain.

5.1   Feature Selection

SPL pattern specific and pattern variability features are selected based on the application's requirements. SNOE's C&DH subsystem is derived from the FSW SPL by choosing a total of seven pattern specific features and seven pattern variability features. Because SNOE is only required to process a low volume of ground commands, the Low Volume Command Execution alternative feature is selected from the Command Execution pattern specific feature group. Since this feature depends on the Spacecraft Clock pattern specific feature, SNOE must also select this feature.

For STEREO's C&DH subsystem's derivation from the FSW SPL, a total of 10 pattern specific features and 15 pattern variability features were chosen. Because STEREO must store and process a large number of commands from the ground station, the High Volume Command Execution alternative feature was selected from the Command Execution pattern specific feature group. Some pattern variability features are also selected. Because STEREO is required to have onboard active thermal control, the optional Heater pattern variability feature is selected.

5.2   Design Pattern Customization

The next step in application engineering process is to determine the design patterns that an application utilizes. This information is derived from the SPL feature to design pattern mapping and the application's selected features.

When this step is applied to SNOE, seven variable design patterns were selected based on SNOE's seven pattern specific features. STEREO selected a total of 10 variable design patterns based on its pattern specific features selection. For example, SNOE selected the FSW Centralized Control design pattern since it is mapped to its Low

Volume Command Execution pattern specific feature, as shown in Fig. 9. In contrast, STEREO selected the FSW Hierarchical Control design pattern since it is mapped to the High Volume Command Execution pattern specific feature.

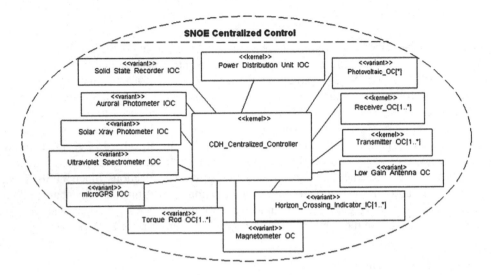

Fig. 9. SNOE specific centralized control collaboration diagram.

The interaction diagrams for SNOE are also systematically updated. Figure 10 depicts a subset of the SNOE specific interactions for Command Execution interaction diagram. This interaction diagram is based on the FSW SPL execute low volume commands interaction diagram in Fig. 6, which contains a representative set of object interactions. First, the SNOE specific variant components are selected based on SNOE's pattern variability features. There are selected SPL pattern variability features for the specific type of antenna and memory storage device, see Fig. 10. The variant components are developed during the application derivation process and customized to meet the needs of the application. After the interaction diagram is updated with the application specific variants, the object interactions are also updated. In Fig. 10, the CDH Controller receives an input EventNotification to reinitialize the spacecraft's low gain antenna. Since the specific antenna and memory storage device variants are known based on the pattern variability feature selection, the specific interactions with this output component can now be modeled in Fig. 10, which depicts different commands that can be invoked on a device.

Next, the application's executable design patterns are derived from the variable SPL executable design patterns. This involves systematically customizing the variable SPL design pattern specification and executable pattern based on the application's features. As part of this process, if an SPL design pattern's interaction diagram only contained a representative set of interactions, then the interaction diagram must be updated to reflect the precise sequence of interactions.

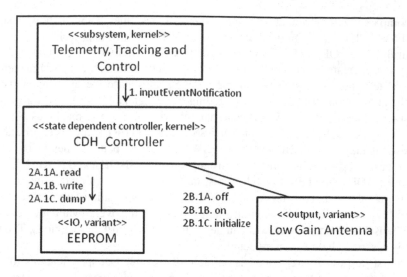

Fig. 10. SNOE command execution interaction diagram.

5.3   Design Pattern Interconnection

The application's design pattern interconnections are determined based on the application feature selection. The interaction overview diagrams from the FSW SPL's C&DH subsystem were customized for each application. As SNOE selected to use the Low Volume Command Execution feature, therefore only the feature based conditions corresponding to this feature are selected for SNOE. This includes the FSW Spacecraft Time Multicast interaction diagram and the FSW Centralized Control interaction diagram.

STEREO's interaction overview modeling follows the same customization process. However, STEREO selected the High Volume Command Execution feature, therefore only the feature-based conditions corresponding to this feature are selected. This includes the FSW Spacecraft Time Multicast interaction diagram and the FSW Hierarchical Control interaction diagram.

6   Validation

The approach to validate the DRE patterns, the FSW product line, and the SNOE and STEREO application case studies involved several validation steps throughout the development. First, the individual DRE design patterns were validated by ensuring functional correctness of the individual executable design patterns. This was accomplished by creating test cases to cover all states, transitions, and actions for the state machines of all the components in the DRE executable design pattern. Input data to the test cases included source states and event sequences that trigger a test case and output data including the expected destination states and actions.

Second, the FSW SPL individual design patterns were also validated for functional correctness. Again, test cases were created that covered all states, transitions, and actions for the state machines of all the components. Then the expected results of the test cases were compared with the actual behavior of the state machines. Table 2 shows a subset of the FSW SPL design patterns that were validated using this approach.

Thirdly, the SNOE and STEREO design patterns were individually validated. Again, test cases were created to cover all states, actions, and transitions for the design patterns. However, test cases are different from the FSW SPL test cases because they must test all of the application customizations, including data, logic, and additional states. Then the test cases were compared with the actual behavior of the state machines. A subset the design patterns that were validated for SNOE and STEREO are listed in Table 2. The design patterns are listed next to the FSW SPL design patterns they were derived from, in order to show which SPL patterns are reused in SNOE and STEREO. Finally, the entire SNOE and STERO architectures, including the design pattern interconnections, were validated. To achieve this, a feature based validation approach based on CADeT [27] was applied. This approach helps to reduce the overall validation effort by created reusable SPL test assets that can be customized for SPL applications. The validation is described below in more detail.

The first step was to create a decision table of reusable test specifications for each SPL use case activity diagram and sub-activity diagram. This step is demonstrated using the Execute Commands' activity diagram from Fig. 2. Each unique path through the use case activity diagram is given a test specification column in the decision table. The «adaptable» stereotype on the test specifications implies it contains adaptable steps. The feature condition rows indicate under what feature selections this test specification applies. The action rows indicate what steps are executed for the test specification.

The second step is to customize the FSW SPL test specifications for SNOE and STEREO. This is accomplished by updating the decision tables to include just the test specifications that are applicable the application.

The next step in the validation process is to refine the adaptable steps in the test specifications to the application. This involves refining each adaptable test specification into non-adaptable steps based on the application's feature selection and populating the steps. Steps are made into non-adaptable steps by using the application's specific variants, such as replacing the Antenna superclass with the Low Gain Antenna variant and listing the application specific actions, such as turn on Low Gain Antenna.

Next, the test specifications input data, steps, and output data are populated with the state, transitions, and actions from the design pattern component state machines. Creating this level of test specifications detail ensures that integration testing of individual design patterns is performed at application testing, as well as testing interconnected design patterns.

The final step in the functional validation is to execute the tests against the software architecture, which consists of concurrent executable state machines. This testing is different from validation of the individual design patterns because it not only tests the design patterns, but also how the design patterns are integrated together. A total of 22 feature-based test specifications were created and passed for SNOE and 32 feature-based test specifications were created and passed for STEREO.

Table 2. Subset of design patterns validation.

FSW SPL Design Patterns	SNOE Design Patterns	STEREO Design Patterns
FSW Hierarchical Control		STEREO Hierarchical Control
FSW Distributed Control		
FSW Centralized Control	SNOE Centralized Control	
FSW Hierarchical Control with Command Dispatcher		
FSW Centralized Control with Command Dispatcher		
FSW Distributed Control with Command Dispatcher		
FSW Telemetry Storage and Retrieval Compound Commit		STEREO Telemetry Storage and Retrieval Compound Commit
FSW Telemetry Storage and Retrieval Client Server	SNOE Telemetry Storage and Retrieval Client Server	
FSW Telemetry Formation Master Slave with Pipes and Filters		
FSW Telemetry Formation Master Slave with Pipes and Filters & Strategy		
FSW Telemetry Formation Pipes and Filters	SNOE Telemetry Formation Pipes and Filters	
FSW Telemetry Formation Pipes and Filters with Strategy		STEREO Telemetry Formation Pipes and Filters with Strategy
FSW Telemetry Formation Reliability Protected Single Channel		
FSW Telemetry Formation Reliability Sanity Check		STEREO Telemetry Formation Reliability Sanity Check

7   Benefits and Limitations

Our design pattern based SPL solution has several benefits. First, it offers a practical and scalable SPL approach for domains that have significant architectural variability, such as the FSW domain. This means that there is less modeling required during the SPL engineering and maintenance phases. This makes developing and maintaining a SPL that must cover a wide amount of variability less time consuming. The tradeoff is that additional work is required during the application engineering phase. This tradeoff is acceptable in FSW domain where maintaining a traditional SPL can be too cumbersome and time consuming. A second benefit of the solution is that the design patterns and architectures produced can be validated for functional correctness. This is accomplished by executing the components' state machines to validate that the actual behavior follows the expected behavior. Finally, the last major benefit of our solution is the architectures produced are composed of software architectural design patterns, which are best practice solutions. Therefore the benefits associated with the design patterns are included in the architecture. The stakeholders that can most benefit from this approach are acquisition, development, and over-sight organizations involved in the development of FSW. However, our solution is not limited to the FSW domain. Other domains that experience similar architectural variability in the products could also benefit from our solution. Our current solution does have some limitations. First, the SPL product derivation process and application customization process are manual processes. However, the SPL product derivation process could be automated using existing approaches, such as [18–20]. These approaches should be evaluated and applied to our solution. Another limitation of our approach is that is currently does not include information to perform model-driven software performance analysis. In the FSW domain, meeting the software performance requirements is just as important as meeting the functional requirements. Therefore, approaches and tool support for performing model-driven software performance analysis should also be explored.

8 Conclusions

This paper has described the application of a design pattern based SPL approach for building FSW SPL. This approach is useful in the FSW domain because architectural variability is captured at a larger degree of granularity using software architectural design patterns, thus less modeling is required during the SPL engineering phase. The trade-off with this approach is that additional modeling is required during the application engineering phases. This trade-off is acceptable in domains such as FSW, where modeling all possible variations during the SPL engineering phase can be time consuming and may not always be known in advance.

In addition, in certain domains, application variability, such as payload variability in FSW, is mission specific and hence specific to a single application. It is thus considered an advantage to develop mission specific components during application engineering rather than domain engineering.

Using the design pattern based approach for the FSW SPL required significantly less component modeling during SPL Engineering than a component/connector based SPLE approach. In the FSW SPL, during the SPL Engineering phase, the design pattern based approach required modeling only 29 components containing representative SPL behavior, while the component/connector based SPLE approach required 53 components containing parameterized or specialized behavior for all the different SPL variants. As previously discussed, the trade-off is that additional modeling is required during the application engineering phases. During the application engineering of SNOE, 10 FSW SPL components were customized to the application and in STEREO 22 FSW SPL components were customized.

The approach described in this paper has several benefits. First, the approach provides domain specific architectural design patterns that can be applied to FSW product lines. Second, executable versions of the patterns are developed to allow the patterns to be validated. Third, providing domain specific design patterns provides a systematic approach, which leverages best design practices, for incorporating these patterns into the SPL architecture and its member applications. Furthermore, executable architectures produced from these patterns using executable state machines can be validated during the design phase for functional correctness.

Several avenues of future investigation could be pursued. First, this work should be extended to address model-driven software performance validation since meeting performance requirements is as important as meeting functional requirements in DRE systems. Additionally, this approach can be applied to other distributed real-time application domains to illustrate its applicability across other domains. Finally, future work should address additional automation to increase the practicality of this work.

References

1. Hecht, M., Buettner, D.: Software Testing in Space Programs. Crosslink **6**(3), 58–64 (2005)
2. Dvorak, D. (ed.): NASA Study on Flight Software Complexity, NASA Office of Chief Engineer (2009)
3. Clements, P., Northrop, L.: Software Product Lines: Practices and Patterns. Addison-Wesley, Boston (2002)
4. Pohl, K., Böckle, G., van der Linden, F.: Software Product Line Engineering Foundations, Principles, and Techniques. Springer, Heidelberg (2005)
5. Gomaa, H.: Designing Software Product Lines with UML: From Use Cases to Pattern-Based Software Architectures. Addison-Wesley, Boston (2005)
6. Weiss, D.M., Lai, C.T.R.: Software Product-Line Engineering: A Family-Based Software Development Process. Addison Wesley, Reading (1999)
7. Webber, D., Gomaa, H.: Modeling variability in software product lines with the variation point model. J. Sci. Comput. Program. **53**(3), 305–331 (2004)
8. Herrmann, A., Schöning, T.: Standard telemetry processing – an object oriented approach using software design patterns. Aerosp. Sci. Technol. **4**(4), 289–297 (2000)
9. van Katwijk, J., Schwarz, J.-J., Zalewski, J.: Practice of real-time software architectures. In: IFAC Conference on New Technologies for Computer Control, Hong Kong (2001)
10. Wilmot, J.: A core flight software system. In: 3rd IEEE/ACM/IFIP International Conference on Hardware/software Codesign and System Synthesis, Jersey City, NJ, USA (2005)
11. Wilmot, J.: Implications of responsive space on the flight software architecture. In: 4th Responsive Space Conference, Los Angles, CA (2006)
12. Bass, L., Clements, P., Kazman, R.: Software Architecture in Practice. Addison-Wesley Professional, Boston (2003)
13. Gomaa, H.: Software Modeling and Design: UML, Use Cases, Architecture, and Patterns. Cambridge University Press, New York (2011)

14. Selic, B., Gullekson, G., Ward, P.T.: Real-Time Object-Oriented Modeling. Wiley, New York (1994)
15. Bennett, M., Dvorak, D., Hutcherson, J., Ingham, M., Rasmussen, R., Wagner, D.: An architectural pattern for goal-based control. In: IEEE Aerospace Conference. IEEE Computer Society (2008)
16. Bennett, M., Knight, R., Rasmussen, R., Ingham, M.: State-based models for planning and execution. In: 15th International Conference on Planning and Scheduling (ICAPS 2005). Jet Propulsion Laboratory, National Aeronautics and Space Administration (2005)
17. Selic, B.: Architectural patterns for real-time systems: using UML as an architectural description language. In: Lavagno, L., Martin, G., Selic, B. (eds.) UML for Real, pp. 171–188. Springer, New York (2004)
18. Douglass, B.: Real-Time Design Patterns. Addison-Wesley, Boston (2003)
19. Bellebia, D., Douin, J.-M.: Applying patterns to build a lightweight middleware for embedded systems. In: 2006 Conference on Pattern Languages of Programs, Portland, Oregon, USA (2006)
20. Fliege, I., Geraldy, A., Gotzhein, R., Kuhn, T., Webel, C.: Developing safety-critical real-time systems with SDL design patterns and components. Comput. Netw. **49**, 689–706 (2005)
21. Gamma, E., Helm, R., Johnson, R., John, V.: Design Patterns: Elements of Reusable Object-Oriented Software. Addison-Wesley, Reading (1995)
22. Buschmann, F., Henney, K., Schmidt, D.C.: Pattern Oriented Software Architecture. On Patterns and Pattern Languages, vol. 5. Wiley, Hoboken (2007)
23. Pettit IV, R., Gomaa, H.: Modeling behavioral design patterns of concurrent objects. In: Proceedings of ICSE 2006, Shanghai, China (2006)
24. Kalinsky, D.: Design patterns for high availability. Embed. Syst. Prog., Aug 2002 [18]. Dupire, B., Fernandez, E.B.: The command dispatcher pattern. In: 8th Conference on Pattern Languages of Programs, Monticello, Illinois, USA (2001)
25. Fant, J., Gomaa, H., Pettit IV, R.: Architectural design patterns for flight software. In: 2nd IEEE Workshop on Model-Based Engineering for Real-Time Embedded Systems, Newport Beach, California (2011)
26. Fant, J.: Building domain specific software architectures from software architectural design patterns. In: Presented at the 33rd International Conference on Software Engineering (ICSE) ACM Student Research Competition (SRC) 2011, Honolulu, Hawaii USA (2011)
27. Olimpiew, E.M., Gomaa, H.: Reusable model-based testing. In: Edwards, S.H., Kulczycki, G. (eds.) ICSR 2009. LNCS, vol. 5791, pp. 76–85. Springer, Heidelberg (2009)
28. Harel, D.: Executable object modeling with statecharts. In: 18th International Conference on Software Engineering (ICSE), Boston, MA (1997)
29. Laboratory For Atmospheric and Space Physics at the University of Colorado at Boulder. Student Nitric Oxide Explorer Homepage. http://lasp.colorado.edu/snoe/ 21 April 2010
30. Johns Hopkins University Applied Physics Laboratory. STEREO Web Site, 26 April 2010. http://stereo.jhuapl.edu/index.php

Model Checking Feature Interactions

Thibaut Le Guilly$^{(\boxtimes)}$, Petur Olsen, Thomas Pedersen, Anders P. Ravn,
and Arne Skou

Department of Computer Science, Aalborg University,
Selma Lagerlofs Vej 300, 9220 Aalborg, Denmark
{thibaut,petur,tpd,apr,ask}@cs.aau.dk

Abstract. This paper presents an offline approach to analyzing feature interactions in embedded systems. The approach consists of a systematic process to gather the necessary information about system components and their models. The model is first specified in terms of predicates, before being refined to timed automata. The consistency of the model is verified at different development stages, and the correct linkage between the predicates and their semantic model is checked. The approach is illustrated on a use case from home automation.

1 Introduction

Some of the first large scale embedded software was for telephone exchanges. The flexibility of software allowed a modular realization of much new functionality. One example is call forwarding from one number to another, another is putting a call on hold in a waiting queue. These and many others are seen as a matter of course today. These functionalities were programmed in a modular way, independent of each other, so they could be introduced gradually in the software. They were developed by competent professionals and of course tested very carefully, so they did not introduce errors in the system, when they were put into operation. Everything seemed well; but nevertheless there were something reminiscent of defects in the systems. A standard example for a phone is when call on hold and call forward are activated. What happens if a new call comes, when there is already one active, should it be on hold or should it be forwarded? The outcome of such conflicts can be arbitrary and timing dependent. The result is certainly a puzzled user who believes to have found a bug. This type of error was named by Pamela Zave from ATT Bell Lab in the early 1990's [1], as being a "feature interaction", an (unwanted) interaction of functionality. The problem attracted much attention, see for example the survey by Keck and Kuhn a few years later [2]. Since then the phenomenon has been detected in many other systems where functionality is built incrementally using parallel programs. A recent example is the work on software product lines, where features are added incrementally [3].

The motivation for studying feature interactions in this paper is from the domain of Smart Homes. In this application domain it is also called policy conflicts, because it appears as a consequence of network protocol conflicts, see for instance the paper [4], as well as [5]. An example of a feature interaction in a

© Springer International Publishing Switzerland 2016
P. Lorenz et al. (Eds.): ICSOFT 2015, CCIS 586, pp. 307–325, 2016.
DOI: 10.1007/978-3-319-30142-6_17

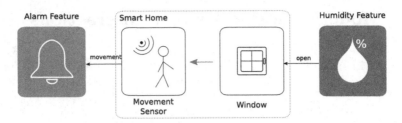

Fig. 1. Example of a feature interaction in a Smart Home.

Smart Home is shown in Fig. 1. In this example, the system is composed of two features. The first is an alarm feature, which uses a movement sensor to monitor movements and trigger an alarm when needed. The second is a humidity feature, keeping the humidity at an acceptable level using a window to let some fresh air in the home when needed. Here the interaction problem is that when the humidity feature opens the window, it creates a movement detected by the movement sensor, which then triggers the alarm.

Detecting these interactions in complex systems with independently developed modules is not an easy task, and there is thus a need for methods and tools to assist in detecting them, see for example the discussion in [6]. Ideally this should be done before the system is put into operation.

In this paper, which extends a previous contribution [7][1], we propose to use model checking to detect feature interactions. However, as with any model based approach, it is essential to obtain a sufficiently accurate model of the system for the analysis to be of interest. Deriving such a model is not trivial and requires rigorous methodology. In Sect. 2, we propose a general model for systems with features, that includes the necessary and sufficient information to detect interactions. Also sanity checks are proposed to ensure that the model is rational and consistent. This generic model must then be mapped to a concrete environment, which consists of a specific configuration of components. This mapping is thus a recurring task that needs to be done for each specific environment. To support this process, Sect. 3 introduces a list of activities that will help carefully gathering the information required to build a realistic system model. This paper uses Timed Automata [8] to model the system. Timed Automata fit well with the dynamic nature of embedded systems, and can be model checked for reachability, safety and liveness. Furthermore they admit checking for interaction of extra-functional features, see [9]. Section 4 shows a translation of the information gathered on the system into formal models, and a translation of the requirements into logic to verify the models against them, and to ensure that the models are correct with respect to their specifications. The approach

---

[1] Note to reviewers only: The entire paper was rewritten. The model in Sect. 2 was refined, and consistency checks are detailed. The identification process in Sect. 3 was extended to include considerations about requirements. In Sect. 4 we add information on how to link the predicates to the timed automata model. Finally the use case in Sect. 5 was extended and updated to take into account the changes.

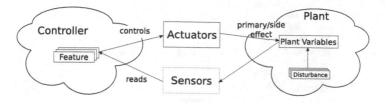

Fig. 2. A feature based control system model.

is then illustrated through a use case in a Smart Home in Sect. 5, using the
UPPAAL model checker for verifying the correctness of the system. We continue
by discussing related work, before concluding and presenting further work.

2   System Model

Modeling a system makes it possible to understand its components, their behaviors and properties. The model proposed here is inspired by the online feature
manager from [10] but aims at adapting it to home automation and other similar control systems. A system is a tuple (F, Pl) where F is a set of features
or controls and Pl a plant or environment. We prefer the control engineering
terminology and thus see the uncontrolled home as a plant. The plant represents
the system to control and is a tuple $Pl = (V, A, P)$, where:

- V is a set of controllable variables that define its state space. They are functions of time, and thus at any point of time the plant is in a specific state.
  The behavior of the plant is its possible trajectories through time.
- A is a set of actuators that enable control by affecting the plant state; their
  state is defined by a set of variables representing set points or configurations
  for example.
- P is a set of disturbances that influence the variables in an uncontrollable,
  although defined manner. Their state is also represented by a set of variables.

A feature is a concrete and well defined component that controls the evolution
of some of the variables in V through the set of actuators A, as illustrated in
Fig. 2. A feature f_i is specified by a tuple (R_i, S_i), where R_i is a predicate on V
that specifies its requirements, and S_i is its specification which is a predicate on
V and A.

An example of such a system is a Smart Home. In this case, the plant is
the house with a set of variables such as temperature, humidity or luminosity,
a set of actuators that can be used to control them (heater, AC, lights...), and
the disturbances created by its walls or windows for example. Note that in this
paper we do not include sensors in the model, and instead consider directly
plant variables. The plant state is thus directly observable. The approach can
be generalized to consider sensors in a similar way as actuators. It would then
be reasonable to assume that the sensors provided full observability of the plant
state. Figure 3 shows an example of a control system controlling a Smart Home.

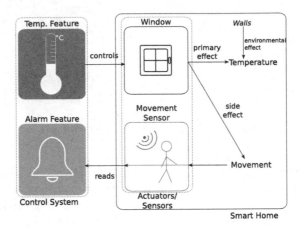

Fig. 3. Example of a control system with two features controlling a Smart Home.

2.1 Assumptions

The assumptions define the effect that actuators and disturbances have on plant variables V. They are composed of assumptions on actuators, $W_a(V)$ with $a \in A$, and on disturbances, $W_p(V)$ with $p \in P$. For a system the combined assumptions are:

$$W = \bigwedge_{a \in A} W_a(V) \wedge \bigwedge_{p \in P} W_p(V)$$

Assumptions can describe interactions on common plant variables, and actuators can have multiple effects. For actuators, we distinguish between their primary and side effects [11]. A primary effect is one that is the primary function of an actuator. A side effect is one that is induced by the actuator but is not part of its function. For example, a fridge cools down its compartment as a primary effect. But to do so, it needs to dissipate heat to its environment, thus warming up the room as a side effect. Side effects are generally acceptable, but need to be considered in the model to ensure that they don't lead to undesired interactions. This could be the case for example if we place a large fridge in a small room with little ventilation. Finally, the effect of disturbances on plant variables is called an environmental effect. In order to specify each type of effect on each plant variable, we assign to each variable a set of dynamic boolean variables that represent a certain effect being applied to it, increasing or decreasing it. These variables depend on the behavior of actuators and are thus function of time. For each plant variable $v \in V$:

v_inc_pe: represents an increase of v by an actuator as a primary effect;
v_dec_pe: represents a decrease of v by an actuator as a primary effect;
v_inc_se: represents an increase of v by an actuator as a side effect;
v_dec_se: represents a decrease of v by an actuator as a side effect;
v_inc_env: represents an increase of v by a disturbance as an environmental effect;
v_dec_env: represents a decrease of v by a disturbance as an environmental effect.

Using these booleans, we can for example represent an assumption for a heater in the form $Heater.On \implies temp\_inc\_pe$, to indicate that when the heater is on, it increases the variable $temp$ as a primary effect. Note that we do not detail here communication errors and delays that could arise from home automation middleware, but these could be introduced using stochastic transitions as shown in [12]. It is possible to specify assumptions that are inconsistent, resulting in an ill-formed plant model, without any trajectories. The plant state cannot be continued in such cases, or it may even be that it cannot be initialized. Validation of a model is considered in the next section.

2.2   Feature and System Consistency

We say that a feature f_i is consistent when its specifications S_i validate its requirements R_k with respect to the assumptions W. A consistent feature is then defined as follow:

Definition 1 (Feature Consistency). *A feature f_i is consistent, if and only if, given S_i, W and R_i as predicates, then $S_i, W \vdash R_i$.*

S_i is usually a disjunction of specifications each specifying a particular behavior for a certain value of the plant variables it considers. For our analysis, it is important that specifications be complete, that is, they consider all possible values of the plant variables they use, subject to constraints imposed by W. R_i here represents a conjunction of requirements that need to be satisfied by a specification S_i. From the definition of feature consistency follows the definition of system consistency.

Definition 2 (System Consistency). *Let C be a system with n features. Let the tuple (R, W, S) be the combination of those features such that: $S = \bigwedge_{i=1}^{n} S_i$, and $R = \bigwedge_{k=1}^{p} R_i$. C is consistent if and only if $S, W \vdash R$, and S is in itself consistent in the context of W.*

Assuming the consistency of each feature does not imply the consistency of their combinations. This is in fact the feature interaction problem. Let us assume that $S_i, W \vdash R_i$ is satisfied for any feature f_i. First the requirements can be trivially satisfied if there exists two specifications S_i and S_j that contradict each other, such that: $S_i \wedge S_j \wedge W$ cannot be satisfied. To avoid contradiction, sufficient conditions are:

– No two actuators can be used simultaneously in a contradicting manner;
– No variable can be updated by a primary effect simultaneously in a contradicting manner.

To ensure the absence of contradiction and errors in the model, we propose the following sanity checks:

S 1. $S \wedge W$ is satisfiable; this ensures that there is no contradiction in the state of actuators when controlled by the features. This check is somewhat similar to the consistency proofs in [13]. It can be checked by verifying the satisfiability of the following formula:

$$\forall v_1, \cdots, v_n \in V \cup P \; \exists z_1, \cdots, z_k \in A : \; S \wedge W$$

The universal quantifier is used for uncontrollable variables - the plant and disturbances variables - and the existential quantifier for controllable variables - actuator variables. This makes sure that there exist a consistent control for each valuation of the uncontrollable variables.

S 2. The second sanity check ensures the absence of conflicting effect on a plant variable. It is somewhat similar to the lock used in the online feature manager [10], but here used offline. It can be checked by verifying the satisfiability of the following formula:

$$\forall v_1, \cdots, v_n \in V \cup P \; \exists z_1, \cdots, z \in A :$$
$$S \wedge W \wedge \neg((v_1\_inc\_pe \wedge v_1\_dec\_pe) \wedge \cdots (v_n\_inc\_pe \wedge v_n\_dec\_pe))$$

This ensures that a plant variable cannot be increased and decreased simultaneously as a primary effect. Some feature interactions can thus already be caught at this stage. However, these two checks do not ensure the absence of feature interaction, as the system can be underspecified, but ensure the absence of contradictions in the specifications. Moreover, they do not take into consideration extra functional requirements, which is why they will be refined to timed automata as shown in Sect. 4. They can be checked using a theorem prover as we will demonstrate in Sect. 5.

3   Identifying Components

To obtain a sound and useful model, it is essential to clearly identify each component of the system as well as its behavior. This task is specific for each system and each plant, and can hardly be automated. It needs to rely on the knowledge of practitioners. However, following a systematic process to derive the information necessary to model each component can help and reduce the likelihood of errors. This section proposes such a process based on a series of questions.

Question 1: What are the Requirements? The requirements represent the expected behavior of the plant when the features control it. To be usable in the consistency proof, it is important that requirements be refined to testable requirements, precise, unambiguous, and not divisible into lower level requirements. The first level of requirements are usually informal and derived from either customer expectations or use cases. The requirements are then refined to semi-formal requirements or testable requirements, and finally to formal requirements which constrain the behavior of the plant variables. This is a common step in formal engineering methodology as in SOFL [14] for example.

Question 2: What are the Plant Variables? From the semi-formal requirements, the set V of plant variables that will have to be controlled by the features are identified.

Question 3: What are the Features? The next step is then to group the requirements that should be satisfied by a single feature. Thus for each group is defined a feature that will have to satisfy them.

Question 4: What are the Actuators? For each feature, the actuators required to satisfy its requirements must be determined. The choice of actuators depends on availability and cost or performance constraints that are not discussed here. However, at this point features may be further refined based on the choice of actuator. For example, the set of requirements { *"temperature > 19°C"*, *"temperature < 24°C"*} could be realized by a single feature using a single HVAC actuator capable of heating and cooling, or by two features, one using a heater and the other an air conditioner.

Question 5: What are the Disturbances? We need to identify the disturbances that can affect the plant variables in V. This is dependent on the specificity of the plant and its dynamics.

Question 6: What are the Assumptions? The next step is to identify the assumptions. Following the identification of the set V of plant variables, A of actuators, and P of disturbances, their behaviors are described. This step is specific to each set of actuator and each plant. Note that only assumptions involving controlled variables are of interest for the analysis.

Question 7: What are the Features Specifications? Once the set of actuators is determined, the action of the features on actuators must be specified. At this stage will be defined the different states of the feature and its behavior.

4   Timed Automata Model

To build the model, we use timed automata. The interest of this formalism is that it can capture the dynamics of the system by the use of timing constraints, and can be formally model checked against a set of properties. Recall that the objective is to verify the consistency proof of a system C with n features, combined in: $S = \bigwedge_{i=1}^{n} S_i$.

At this stage the specifications are implemented in the form of timed automata. Each predicate in S and W is thus assigned a timed automata semantics, and the requirements are assumed written in a temporal logic. The consistency proof thus becomes:

$$\mathcal{M}(S_i) \parallel \cdots \parallel \mathcal{M}(W_j) \parallel \cdots \models \bigwedge_{i=1}^{p} R_i$$

Thus the parallel composition of the specifications (modeling the behavior of the features) with the assumptions (modeling the behavior of the plant) need to satisfy the conjunction of requirements. We will now look into the details of creating the model of each constituent.

4.1 Variables

The first elements to introduce in the model are the plant variables in V. Each plant variable is declared in the model as an integer value, representing its state, as well as a guardian automaton per boolean variable representing the dynamics of the effect applied by actuators and disturbances. The guardian automata are introduced to monitor the effect applied to the boolean variables. However, we allow them to be read directly as it does not affect their behavior. An example of a guardian automaton is shown in Fig. 4. The act? in the first transition denotes receiving a synchronization on communication channel act (! is used to trigger synchronizations). A communication channel in UPPAAL allows processes to synchronize and exchange information (see [15] for more details). Here they enable the models to update the plant variables by applying an effect, but they also enable the features to change the state of actuators for example. When triggered, the caller needs to specify the duration for which the effect is being applied, and the value is updated (+1 for increase −1 for decrease). The mapping between the channels, variables and update values is done by the parameters

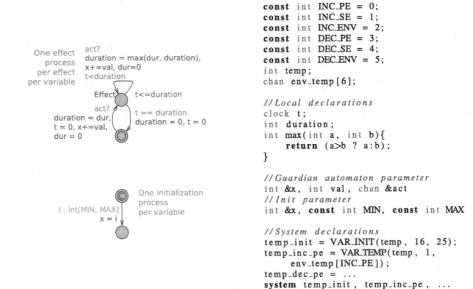

Fig. 4. A guardian automaton constraining and observing the actions on the temperature variable, and the associated variables declaration.

given to each process shown in the system declaration. A separate process also initializes the variable at random within a given interval to cover a range of initial values. Using the guardian automaton makes it possible to check if different effects can be applied simultaneously, which can be a feature interaction.

4.2   Assumptions

Once the variables are declared in the model, we add the set of assumptions W, that define the influence of actuators and disturbances on plant variables. To each actuator and disturbance is associated a timed automaton model that interacts with the variables using the guardian automata. The models define their behavior with respect to the variables they influence and their own state. Actuator models also contain transitions equipped with channel communications so features can change their states. An example of an actuator model is shown in Fig. 5. When this heater is On, it increases the temperature as its primary effect every time unit, and does nothing while it is Off. We can see here the use of communication to a guardian automaton to increase the temperature. Two communication channels are defined to enable features to turn it On or Off. Channels for controlling actuators are defined as urgent to force the feature to react immediately.

Fig. 5. Example of a timed automata representing the behavior of a heater.

4.3   Features

The set of feature F is then added to the model. A feature essentially reads the values of plant variables, which they read directly, and sends control commands to actuators using their communication channels. An example is shown in Fig. 6.

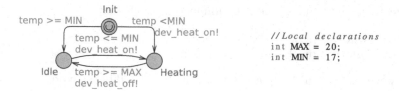

Fig. 6. An example of a feature model.

In this example, a heating feature monitors the temperature and turns the heater on when it goes below 17°C, and off when it goes above 20°C.

4.4 Requirements

The requirements are properties that should be verified by the system. As we have chosen timed automata as a modeling formalism, a temporal logic is used for representing them. In this case a subset of Timed Computational Tree Logic (TCTL), used by the UPPAAL [15] model checker that we will use to perform the model checking. TCTL formulae are composed of state formulae, expressions that can be evaluated for a state such as $temp \geq 19$, and path formulae that quantify state formulae over paths or traces. UPPAAL also makes use of the keyword `deadlock` to denote deadlocking states. Path formulae are generally separated into three categories:

Reachability. Properties are used to check whether a state formula is satisfied by any reachable state. For a state formula φ, the query is encoded as $E\Diamond\,\varphi$.

Safety. Properties are used to express that "something bad should never happen", or "something will possibly never happen". For a state formula φ, $A\Box\varphi$ expresses that φ should be true for all reachable states, while $E\Box\varphi$ expresses that there should exist a maximal path (infinite or whose last state has no outgoing transition) such that φ is always true. A common safety query is to check for the absence of deadlock: $A\Box\neg deadlock$.

Liveness. Properties are used to express that "something good will eventually happen". For state formula φ and ψ, $A\Diamond\varphi$ expresses that φ is eventually satisfied, and $\varphi \rightsquigarrow \psi$ that whenever φ is satisfied, then ψ is eventually satisfied.

Typically, formal requirements are translated into liveness properties that ensure that the desired control is correctly applied by the system. Examples of formal requirements and their translation will be shown in Sect. 5. Sanity checks will usually take the form of safety properties ensuring the absence of conflicts at any state of the system, but can also take the form of liveness properties in certain cases.

4.5 Correctness of Models

After constructing the models, it is important to validate that they verify the specifications and assumptions they implement, such that:

- for each feature $f_i \in F : \mathcal{M}(S_i) \models S_i$;
- for each assumption $W_j \in W : \mathcal{M}(W_j) \models W_j$.

However, due to the temporal dimension introduced in the models, we cannot directly verify the predicates, but have transform them into temporal logic. The translation from predicates to temporal logic is dependent on the model and the semantics of the specifications and assumptions. In general liveness queries are well suited for checking that the system will eventually satisfy its specification or requirements. Finally we define some sanity checks to ensure that the models are rational:

S 3. The models do not contain deadlock: $A\square\neg deadlock$. This is a basic requirements for a model, as deadlock can make some properties trivially satisfiable, because it indicates an inconsistent system with trajectories that are only partial and stop after a time.

S 4. The model is a model for the specifications: $S_i \in S : \mathcal{M} \models S_i$. Similarly for the assumptions: $W_i \in W : \mathcal{M} \models W_i$.

S 5. For each variable $v \in V : A\square\neg(v\_inc\_pe \wedge v\_dec\_pe)$; this is the translation of S2, ensuring that a variable is not simultaneously increased and decreased by primary effects.

5   Use Case

This section illustrates the proposed methodology through a use case in the domain of home automation. In this use case there are two main actors: a company specialized in home automation system and a home owner who desires a number of intelligent features to be implemented in his house. The company can potentially have many customers each with a different set of requirements and a different house. Before buying the equipments required to build a control system that satisfy the requirements, the company would like to ensure that its design will behave as expected once deployed. Here performing an offline analysis of the system can help at detecting unwanted behavior and in particular feature interactions. If undesired behavior is detected, the company can update it until it is fixed, avoiding having to debug already deployed components. The company starts the process by asking the first question, what are the requirements?

5.1   Requirements

The requirements are first obtained from a discussion between the company and the home owner in the form of informal requirements written in natural language. The home owner has three requirements, all related to a single room. The first is related to Heating, Ventilation and Air-Conditioning (HVAC), the second to Humidity Control (HC) and the last one to Home Security (HS).

u_{HVAC}: The temperature shall be kept between 17°C and 24°C.
u_{HC}: An automatic ventilation system, that will improve humidity.
u_{HS}: An alarm that should be triggered when an intruder is detected, but only
  when the intruder is actually present.

The requirements are then refined into formal requirements:

u_{HVAC}: $17 < temp < 24$.
u_{HC}: $hum < 50$.
u_{HS}: $burglar \Longleftrightarrow alarm.on$.

5.2   Plant Variables

In this simple example, the variables to be controlled are easily identified:

v_{temp}: The indoor temperature, initialized in $[16, 25]$ to cover cases above and under every set points.
v_{hum}: The indoor humidity, initialized in $[40, 60]$ to cover above and under 50%.
v_{move}: The detection or not of movement in the room initialized at zero.

5.3   Features

The features can be directly mapped to the three requirements. We thus have three features:

- F_{HVAC}.
- F_{HC}.
- F_{HS}.

5.4   Actuators

The company decides to use:

- a window motor to let fresh air in and control the humidity, with two states, *open* and *close*;
- an alarm which can be triggered;
- a heater and an Air Conditioner (AC) to control the temperature.

Based on this, the F_{HVAC} feature is refined into two features, one using a heater and the other the AC. Another company could choose a single actuator to control the temperature and keep this feature as one. The refined feature results in two requirements:

u_{HVAC_Heat}: $temp > 17$.
u_{HVAC_Cool}: $temp < 24$.

5.5   Disturbances

This use case considers two disturbances:

p_{wall}: the disturbance on the temperature and humidity created by the thermodynamics of the walls, dependent on the outdoor temperature;
$p_{burglar}$: which represents the action of a burglar breaking into the house.

5.6   Assumptions

With the set of actuators, disturbances and variables in place, the assumptions are defined:

$W(p_{wall}, \{temp\})$: $(temp > temp\_out \implies temp\_dec\_env) \land (temp < temp\_out \implies temp\_inc\_env) \land hum\_inc\_env$

$W(p_{burglar}, \{move\})$: $burglar \implies move\_inc\_env$

$W(heater, \{temp\})$: $on \implies temp\_inc\_pe$

$W(ac, \{temp\})$: $on \implies temp\_dec\_pe$

$W(window, \{temp, move\})$: $((open \land temp\_out < temp) \implies temp\_dec\_env) \land ((open \land temp\_out > temp) \implies temp\_inc\_env) \land (opening \implies move\_inc\_se)$.

5.7 Specifications

The specifications determine how the features will use the actuators to satisfy the requirements:

S_{HVAC_Heat}: $(temp < 17 \implies heater.on) \land (temp > 20 \implies heater.off)$

S_{HVAC_Cool}: $(temp > 24 \implies ac.on) \land (temp < 20 \implies ac.off)$

S_{HS}: $(active \land move) \iff alarm.on$

S_{HC}: $hum > 50 \implies window.open$

With all the components of the system specified, the consistency of the model can be checked. We use the Z3 theorem prover to verify that it passes the two sanity checks[2].

Note that the specifications are still under-specified, and do not validate the requirements, as the behavior of the plant variables are not specified, and the assumptions do not take into account the dynamics of the system. Therefore a network of timed automata is used to give this information.

5.8 Modeling

The plant variables v_{temp}, v_{hum} and v_{move} are first introduced, using the templates shown in Fig. 4. The assumptions for actuators are shown in Fig. 7 and the assumptions for disturbances in Fig. 8. The models are described in more details in [7]. The biggest changes are related to the use of the guardian automata and minor changes to adapt to the various checks that the model must satisfy, as well as the specification of duration for the effect by actuators and disturbances models.

The UPPAAL queries and their results are shown in Table 1[3]. Queries q_{0-18} ensure the rationality of the model and that the assumptions and specifications are correctly modeled. Queries q_{19-22} show that the corresponding requirements are satisfied while query q_{23} shows that u_{HS} is not satisfied. The window movement can in fact trigger the alarm while the burglar is still inactive. Query q_{24} shows an example of queries that can be perform to check for interaction with side effect for example. Here the window can decrease the temperature while the heater is on. One can then decide if this side effect is an acceptable or not.

---

[2] Code available at http://rise4fun.com/Z3/q9Vd.

[3] Max execution time per query 47.3 s on a regular laptop.

Table 1. UPPAAL queries and their results.

	UPPAAL Query	Result	What
q_0	`A[] not deadlock`	✓	S3
q_1	`temp<17 --> Heater.On`	✓	S4: S_{HVAC_Heat}
q_2	`temp>20 --> Heater.Off`	✓	S4: S_{HVAC_Heat}
q_3	`temp<20 --> AirCon.Off`	✓	S4: S_{HVAC_Cool}
q_4	`temp>24 --> AirCon.On`	✓	S4: S_{HVAC_Cool}
q_5	`((F_HS.Active && move) --> Alarm.On)`	✓	S4: S_{HS}
q_7	`hum > 50 --> Window.Open`	✓	S4: S_{HC}
q_8	`temp>temp_out --> (temp_dec_env.Effect || temp == temp_out)`	✓	S4: $W_{wall}(temp)$
q_9	`temp<temp_out --> (temp_inc_env.Effect || temp == temp_out)`	✓	S4: $W_{wall}(temp)$
q_{10}	`true --> (hum_inc_env.Effect)`	✓	S4: $W_{wall}(temp)$
q_{11}	`Burglar.Active --> move_inc_env.Effect`	✓	S4: $W_{burglar}(move)$
q_{12}	`Heater.On --> (temp_inc_pe.Effect || Heater.Off)`	✓	S4: $W_{heater}(temp)$
q_{13}	`AirCon.On --> (temp_dec_pe || AirCon.Off)`	✓	S4: $W_{ac}(temp)$
q_{14}	`(Window.Open && temp_out < temp) --> (temp_dec_se || temp == temp_out)`	✓	S4: $W_{window}(temp)$
q_{15}	`(Window.Open && temp_out > temp) --> (temp_inc_se || temp == temp_out)`	✓	S4: $W_{window}(temp)$
q_{16}	`Window.Open --> hum_inc_pe.Effect`	✓	S4: $W_{window}(move)$
q_{17}	`Window.Opening --> move_inc_se.Effect`	✓	S4: $W_{window}(move)$
q_{18}	`A[] !(temp_INC_PE && temp_DEC_PE)`	✓	S5
q_{19}	`temp < 17 --> temp > 17`	✓	u_{HVAC_Heat}
q_{20}	`temp > 24 --> temp < 24`	✓	u_{HVAC_Cool}
q_{21}	`hum > 50 --> hum < 50`	✓	u_{HC}
q_{22}	`Burglar.Active --> Alarm.On`	✓	u_{HS}
q_{23}	`Burglar.Inactive --> Alarm.On`	✗	u_{HS}
q_{24}	`A[] !(temp_inc_pe.Effect && temp_dec_se.Effect)`	✗	side effect

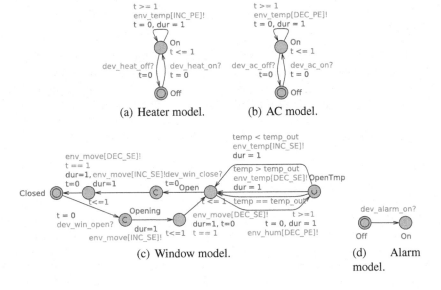

(a) Heater model.   (b) AC model.

(c) Window model.   (d) Alarm model.

Fig. 7. Actuator models.

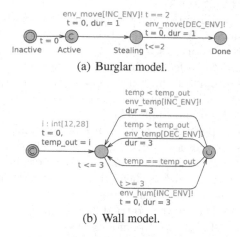

(a) Burglar model.

(b) Wall model.

Fig. 8. Disturbance models.

6 Limitations

The proposed approach has some limitations. The first is that the detection of interactions and inconsistencies in the system relies on information about the plant that may not be trivial to obtain. Moreover, one might argue that once the information about primary, side and environmental effect are obtained, detecting interactions is easy. However, this is a common drawback for any analytical approach to the feature interaction problem. For example, the feature manager in [16], even though being an online approach, also relies on that type of knowledge. We also note that the series of question proposed in this paper aims at facilitating the analysis and reducing the risk of omission. The second limitation comes from the use of model checking, that faces the state space explosion problem when system specifications become too large. Two solutions can be considered for it. Firstly a static pruning of the models, isolating the models having common variables. In fact, interactions can only occur between components sharing a common plant variable. This can lead to considerable reduction of the state space to explore. Secondly Statistical Model Checking (SMC) can be used, to obtain estimates of the satisfaction of properties. As SMC relies on runs on the system and not a systematic exploration of its states, it does not encounter issues with state space explosions. Examples of using SMC are shown in [12,17]. The drawback is of course that it gives only probabilities about the satisfiability of the queries. However with a large enough number of runs, the confidence in the result is usually sufficient.

7 Related Work

The definitions of feature, consistency and interaction were originally proposed in [13]. They also use a SAT solver to verify the consistency of the system. In this paper they are reused and refined, and we show how the predicates can be linked to timed automata models. We extended also the proofs to include consideration about primary effects of actuators.

Online approaches to the feature interaction problem are shown in [10,11]. The notions of primary and side effect are reused in this paper. The use of lock on plant variables is also similar to the check performed for contradicting primary effects on plant variables in our approach.

An object-oriented approach to feature interaction analysis is shown in [18]. The view of features, devices and variables is essentially similar to ours, except that their early work did not include branches, loops or time. These were later added to the language [19], which is checked using the SMV model checker [20]. The language, as well as the queries used are similar to ours, except that time is not part of the models. They have also tried to use the Java Modeling Language (JML) [21], but the verification of the models was uneasy, long and not always successful. An interesting point they make however, is on the need to abstract from implementation specific details and on requirements elicitation by reading safety instructions. Chains of services are also considered using Event Condition Action rules in [22]. They propose to quantify the impact of assumptions in [23].

An approach based on requirements analysis using an existing development platform is shown in [24]. They use dependency graphs, and hint at possible interactions at the requirement level. Compared to our approach, they consider larger systems at a more abstract level, and do not model the internals of the features.

Verification of intelligent environments is discussed also in [25]. The methodology is similar to the one we propose, but the steps are not in the same order. In fact their analysis is based on existing systems, while ours starts from requirements. However the details for each step of the process are of interest and could be applied to our approach as well.

Modeling home automation systems in UPPAAL has also been shown in [26], even though the focus is not on feature interactions. Using stochastic and hybrid models for modeling the dynamics of a heating system is shown in [17,27], and could be applied to our approach as well. UPPAAL is also used in [9] to detect non functional feature interactions in the automotive domain.

We also mention work on software product line and safe configuration as shown in [28]. The focus there is on feature composition and efficient algorithms for the combinatorial problem of composition in software product lines. Similar is the work on componentization of timed automata in [29].

8   Conclusion and Future Work

An offline approach to analyzing feature interactions has been presented. The approach helps ensuring consistency of the models along the development process, and the absence of undesired interactions. It is shown how to link the predicates obtained from the formalization of requirements to their timed automata models. Timed automata makes it possible to include time constraints, and to verify system properties using temporal logic. The approach is applied to a use case from home automation, showing how to use a SAT solver to ensure the correctness of the system when in the form of predicates, and the UPPAAL model checker for verifying that the timed automata model of the system satisfies its requirements.

We foresee different improvements to this work. A first one is the introduction of a quantification of the effect that actuators and disturbances have on plant variables, as done in [23]. A second one would be to provide more details on how to obtain the system requirements. Inspiration could be taken from [30] where requirements are obtained by eliciting safety properties. Another interesting question that was not discussed in this paper is how to resolve the interactions once detected. Here one could have a look at controller synthesis using timed games for example [31,32]. Another interesting direction would be to consider the proposed models for online feature interaction detection. This could be done using previous work on interpreting and abstracting timed automata [33,34]. Finally, as mentioned in Sect. 6, SMC could be introduced to improve the scalability of the approach.

References

1. Zave, P.: Feature interactions and formal specifications in telecommunications. Computer **26**, 20–28 (1993)
2. Keck, D., Kuehn, P.: The feature and service interaction problem in telecommunications systems: a survey. IEEE Trans. Softw. Eng. **24**, 779–796 (1998)
3. Lochau, M., Oster, S., Goltz, U., Schürr, A.: Model-based pairwise testing for feature interaction coverage in software product line engineering. Softw. Qual. J. **20**, 567–604 (2012)
4. Maternaghan, C., Turner, K.J.: Policy conflicts in home automation. Comput. Netw. **57**, 2429–2441 (2013)
5. Al-Baltah, I.A., Ghani, A.A.A., Ab Rahman, W.N.W., Atan, R.: Semantic conflicts detection of heterogeneous messages of web services: challenges and solution. J. Comput. Sci. **10**, 1428 (2014)
6. Calder, M., Kolberg, M., Magill, E.H., Reiff-Marganiec, S.: Feature interaction: a critical review and considered forecast. Comput. Netw. **41**, 115–141 (2003)
7. Pedersen, T., Le Guilly, T., Ravn, A., Skou, A.: A method for model checking feature interactions. In: Proceedings of the 10th International Conference on Software Engineering and Applications, pp. 219–228 (2015)
8. Alur, R., Dill, D.L.: A theory of timed automata. Theor. Comput. Sci. **126**, 183–235 (1994)
9. Répási, T., Giessl, S., Prehofer, C.: Using model-checking for the detection of non-functional feature interactions. In: 2012 IEEE 16th International Conference on Intelligent Engineering Systems (INES), pp. 167–172. IEEE (2012)
10. Kolberg, M., Magill, E.H., Wilson, M.: Compatibility issues between services supporting networked appliances. IEEE Commun. Mag. **41**, 136–147 (2003)
11. Wilson, M., Kolberg, M., Magill, E.H.: Considering side effects in service interactions in home automation-an online approach. In: Feature Interactions in Software and Communication Systems IX, p. 172 (2008)

12. Le Guilly, T., Olsen, P., Ravn, A.P., Skou, A.: Modelling and analysis of component faults and reliability. In: Petre, L., Sekerinski, E. (eds.) From Action System to Distributed Systems: The Refinement Approach (2015, accepted for publication)
13. Classen, A., Heymans, P., Schobbens, P.-Y.: What's in a *feature*: a requirements engineering perspective. In: Fiadeiro, J.L., Inverardi, P. (eds.) FASE 2008. LNCS, vol. 4961, pp. 16–30. Springer, Heidelberg (2008)
14. Liu, S.: Formal Engineering for Industrial Software Development. Springer, Heidelberg (2004)
15. Behrmann, G., David, R., Larsen, K.G.: A tutorial on Uppaal 4.0 (2006)
16. Wilson, M., Magill, E.H., Kolberg, M.: An online approach for the service interaction problem in home automation. In: Consumer Communications and Networking Conference, CCNC. 2005 Second IEEE, pp. 251–256. IEEE (2005)
17. David, A., Larsen, K.G., Legay, A., Mikučionis, M., Poulsen, D.B.: Uppaal SMC tutorial. Int. J. Softw. Tools Technol. Transf. **17**, 1–19 (2015)
18. Nakamura, M., Igaki, H., Matsumoto, K.I.: Feature interactions in integrated services of networked home appliances. In: Proceedings of International Conference on Feature Interactions in Telecommunication Networks and Distributed Systems (ICFI05), pp. 236–251 (2005)
19. Leelaprute, P., Nakamura, M., Tsuchiya, T., Matsumoto, K.I., Kikuno, T. : Describing and verifying integrated services of home network systems. In: Software Engineering Conference, APSEC 2005. 12th Asia-Pacific, p. 10 (2005)
20. Cimatti, A., Clarke, E., Giunchiglia, F., Roveri, M.: Nusmv: a new symbolic model checker. Int. J. Softw. Tools Technol. Transfer **2**, 410–425 (2000)
21. du Bousquet, L., Nakamura, M., Yan, B., Igaki, H.: Using formal methods to increase confidence in a home network system implementation: a case study. Innovations Syst. Softw. Eng. **5**, 181–196 (2009)
22. Inada, T., Igaki, H., Ikegami, K., Matsumoto, S., Nakamura, M., Kusumoto, S.: Detecting service chains and feature interactions in sensor-driven home network services. Sensors **12**, 8447–8464 (2012)
23. Nakamura, M., Ikegami, K., Matsumoto, S.: Considering impacts and requirements for better understanding of environment interactions in home network services. Comput. Netw. **57**, 2442–2453 (2013)
24. Metzger, A., Webel, C.: Feature interaction detection in building control systems by means of a formal product model. In: FIW, pp. 105–122 (2003)
25. Corno, F., Sanaullah, M.: Modeling and formal verification of smart environments. Secur. Commun. Netw. **7**, 1582–1598 (2014)
26. Augusto, J.C., McCullagh, P.: Ambient intelligence: concepts and applications. Comput. Sci. Inf. Syst. **4**, 1–27 (2007)
27. David, A., Du, D., Guldstrand Larsen, K., Legay, A., Mikučionis, M.: Optimizing control strategy using statistical model checking. In: Brat, G., Rungta, N., Venet, A. (eds.) NFM 2013. LNCS, vol. 7871, pp. 352–367. Springer, Heidelberg (2013)
28. Classen, A., Heymans, P., Schobbens, P.Y., Legay, A., Raskin, J.F.: Model checking lots of systems: efficient verification of temporal properties in software product lines. In: Proceedings of the 32nd ACM/IEEE International Conference on Software Engineering, vol. 1, pp. 335–344. ACM (2010)
29. David, A., Larsen, K.G., Legay, A., Nyman, U., Wasowski, A.: Timed I/O automata: a complete specification theory for real-time systems. In: Proceedings of the 13th ACM International Conference on Hybrid Systems: Computation and Control, pp. 91–100. ACM (2010)

30. Yan, B., Nakamura, M., du Bousquet, L., Matsumoto, K.: Characterizing safety of integrated services in home network system. In: Okadome, T., Yamazaki, T., Makhtari, M. (eds.) ICOST. LNCS, vol. 4541, pp. 130–140. Springer, Heidelberg (2007)
31. Jessen, J.J., Rasmussen, J.I., Larsen, K.G., David, A.: Guided controller synthesis for climate controller using UPPAAL TIGA. In: Raskin, J.-F., Thiagarajan, P.S. (eds.) FORMATS 2007. LNCS, vol. 4763, pp. 227–240. Springer, Heidelberg (2007)
32. Behrmann, G., Cougnard, A., David, A., Fleury, E., Larsen, K.G., Lime, D.: UPPAAL-Tiga: time for playing games!. In: Damm, W., Hermanns, H. (eds.) CAV 2007. LNCS, vol. 4590, pp. 121–125. Springer, Heidelberg (2007)
33. Dalsgaard, P.H., Le Guilly, T., Middelhede, D., Olsen, P., Pedersen, T., Ravn, A.P., Skou, A.: A toolchain for home automation controller development. In: 2013 39th EUROMICRO Conference on Software Engineering and Advanced Applications (SEAA), pp. 122–129. IEEE (2013)
34. Le Guilly, T., Smedegard, J.H., Pedersen, T., Skou, A.: To do and not to do: constrained scenarios for safe smart house. In: 2015 International Conference on Intelligent Environments (IE), pp. 17–24 (2015)

Deriving Tailored UML Interaction Models from Scenario-Based Runtime Tests

Thorsten Haendler[✉], Stefan Sobernig, and Mark Strembeck

Institute for Information Systems and New Media,
Vienna University of Economics and Business (WU), Vienna, Austria
{thorsten.haendler,stefan.sobernig,mark.strembeck}@wu.ac.at

Abstract. Documenting system behavior explicitly using graphical models (e.g. UML activity or sequence diagrams) facilitates communication about and understanding of software systems during development and maintenance tasks. Creating graphical models manually is a time-consuming and often error-prone task. Deriving models from system-execution traces, however, suffers from resulting model sizes which render the models unmanageable for humans. This paper describes an approach for deriving behavior documentation from runtime tests in terms of UML interaction models. Key to our approach is leveraging the structure of scenario-based runtime tests to render the resulting interaction models and diagrams tailorable by humans for a given task. Each derived model represents a particular view on the test-execution trace. This way, one can benefit from tailored graphical models while controlling the model size. The approach builds on conceptual mappings (transformation rules) between a test-execution trace metamodel and the UML2 metamodel. In addition, we provide means to turn selected details of test specifications and of testing environment (i.e. test parts and call scopes) into views on the test-execution trace (scenario-test viewpoint). A prototype implementation called KaleidoScope based on a software-testing framework (STORM) and model transformations (Eclipse M2M/QVTo) is available.

Keywords: Test-based documentation · Scenario-based testing · Test-execution trace · Scenario-test viewpoint · UML interactions · UML sequence diagram

1 Introduction

Scenarios describe intended or actual behavior of software systems in terms of action and event sequences. Notations for defining and describing scenarios include different types of graphical models such as UML activity and UML interaction models. Scenarios are used to model systems from a user perspective and ease the communication between different stakeholders [3,17,18]. As it is almost impossible to completely test a complex software system, one needs an effective procedure to select relevant tests, to express and to maintain them, as well as to automate tests whenever possible. In this context, scenario-based testing is a

© Springer International Publishing Switzerland 2016
P. Lorenz et al. (Eds.): ICSOFT 2015, CCIS 586, pp. 326–348, 2016.
DOI: 10.1007/978-3-319-30142-6_18

means to reduce the risk of omitting or forgetting relevant test cases, as well as the risk of insufficiently describing important tests [21,32].

Tests and a system's source code (including the comments in the source code) directly serve as a documentation for the respective software system. For example, in Agile development approaches, tests are sometimes referred to as a *living documentation* [35]. However, learning about a system only via tests and source code is complex and time consuming. In this context, graphical models are a popular device to document a system and to communicate its architecture, design, and implementation to other stakeholders, especially those who did not author the code or the tests. Moreover, graphical models also help in understanding and maintaining a system, e.g., if the original developers are no longer available or if a new member of the development team is introduced to the system. Alas, authoring and maintaining graphical models require a substantial investment of time and effort. Because tests and source code are primary development artifacts of many software systems, the automated derivation of graphical models from a system's tests and source code can contribute to limiting documentation effort. Moreover, automating model derivation provides for an up-to-date documentation of a software system, whenever requested.

A general challenge for deriving (a.k.a. reverse-engineering) graphical models is that their visualization as diagrams easily becomes too detailed and too extensive, rendering them ineffective communication vehicles. This has been referred to as the problem of *model-size explosion* [1,33]. Common strategies to cope with unmanageable model sizes are filtering techniques, such as element sampling and hiding. Another challenge is that a graphical documentation (i.e. models, diagrams) must be captured and visualized in a manner which makes the resulting models *tailorable* by the respective stakeholders. This way, stakeholders can fit the derived models to a certain analysis purpose, e.g., a specific development or maintenance activity [9].

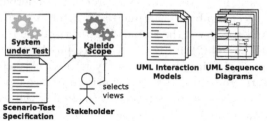

Fig. 1. Deriving tailored UML interaction models from scenario tests.

In this paper, we report on an approach for deriving behavior documentation (esp. UML2 interaction models depicted via sequence diagrams) from scenario-based runtime tests in a semi-automated manner (see Fig. 1). Our approach is independent of a particular programming language. It employs metamodel mappings between the concepts found in scenario-based testing, on the one hand, and the UML2 metamodel fragment specific to UML2 interactions [27], on the other hand. Our approach defines a *viewpoint* [4] which allows for creating different views on the test-execution traces resulting in partial interaction models and sequence diagrams. Moreover, we present a prototypical realization of the approach via a tool called KaleidoScope[1]. This paper is a revised and extended version of our paper from ICSOFT 2015 [15]. This post-conference revision incorporates important changes in response to comments by reviewers and by conference attendees. For example, we included the OCL consistency constraints for the derived UML interaction models.

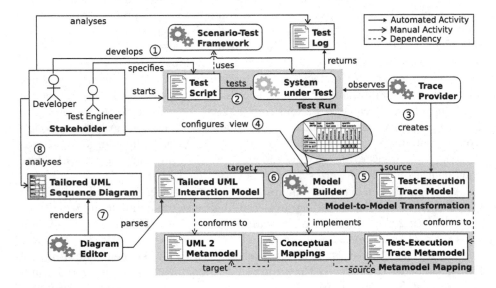

Fig. 2. Conceptual overview of deriving tailored UML interaction models from scenario-based runtime tests.

Figure 2 provides a bird's-eye view on the procedure of deriving tailored interaction models from scenario-based runtime tests. After implementing the source code of the SUT and specifying the scenario-test script, the respective tests are executed (see steps ① and ② in Fig. 2). A "trace provider" component instruments the test run (e.g. using dynamic analysis) and extracts the execution-trace data[2] for creating a corresponding scenario-test trace model (see step ③). After test completion, the test log is returned (including the test result). Based on a view configuration and on the extracted trace model (see steps ④ and ⑤), an interaction model (step ⑥) is derived. This transformation is executed by a "model builder" component, which implements the conceptual mappings between the test-execution trace metamodel and the UML2 metamodel. The concrete source and target models are instances of the corresponding metamodels. Notice that based on one trace model (reflecting one test run), multiple tailored interaction models can be derived in steps ④ through ⑥.[3] Finally,

---

[1] Available for download from our website [14].

[2] For the purposes of this paper, a *trace* is defined as a sequence of interactions between the structural elements of the system under test (SUT), see e.g. [38].

[3] The process described so far is supported by our KaleidoScope tool [14].

the models can be rendered by a diagram editor into a corresponding sequence diagram (step ⑦) to assist in analysis tasks by the stakeholders (step ⑧).

The remainder of this paper is structured as follows: In Sect. 2, we explain how elements of scenario tests can be represented as elements of UML2 interactions. In particular, we introduce in Sect. 2.1 our metamodel of scenario-based testing and in Sect. 2.2 the elements of the UML2 metamodel that are relevant for our approach. In Sect. 2.3, we present the conceptual mappings (transformation rules) between different elements of the scenario-test metamodel and the UML2 metamodel. Subsequently, Sect. 3 proposes test-based tailoring techniques for the derived interaction models. In Sect. 3.1, we explain the option space for tailoring interaction models based on a scenario-test viewpoint and illustrate a simple application example in Sect. 3.2. Section 3.3 explains how tailoring interaction models is realized by additional view-specific metamodel mappings. In Sect. 4, we introduce our prototypical implementation of the approach. Finally, Sect. 5 gives an overview of related work and Sect. 6 concludes the paper.

2 Representing Scenario Tests as UML2 Interactions

2.1 Scenario-Test Structure and Traces

We extended an existing conceptual metamodel of scenario-based testing [34]. This extension allows us to capture the structural elements internal to scenario tests, namely test blocks, expressions, assertions, and definitions of feature calls into the system under test (SUT; see Fig. 3). A trace describes the SUT's responses to specific stimuli [4]. We look at stimuli which are defined by an executable scenario-test specification and which are enacted by executing the corresponding scenario test. In the following, we refer to the combined structural elements of the scenario-test specifications and the underlying test-execution infrastructure as the scenario-test framework (STF). This way, an execution of a scenario-based `TestSuite` (i.e. one test run) is represented by a `Trace` instance. In particular, the respective trace records instances of `FeatureCall` in chronological order, describing the SUT feature calls defined by the corresponding instances of `FeatureCallDefinition` that are owned by a block. Valid kinds of `Block` are `Assertion` (owned, in turn, by `Pre-` or `Postcondition` block) or other STF features such as `Setup`, `TestBody` or `Cleanup` in a certain scenario test. In turn, each SUT `Feature` represents a kind of `Block`. A block aggregates definitions of SUT feature calls. Instances of `FeatureCall` represent one interaction between two structural elements of the SUT. These `source` and `target` elements are represented by instantiations of `Instance`. Every feature call maintains a reference to the calling feature (`caller`) and the corresponding called feature (`callee`), defined and owned by a given class of the SUT. Features are divided into structural features (e.g. `Property`) and behavioral features (e.g. `Operation`). Moreover, `Constructor` and `Destructor` owned by a class are also kinds of `Feature`. A feature call additionally records `Argument` instances that are passed into the

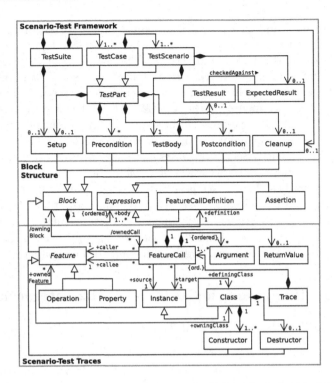

Fig. 3. Test-execution trace metamodel extends [34] to include test-block structure and scenario-test traces.

called feature, as well as the return value, if any. The sum of elements specific to a call is referred to as "call dependencies".

2.2 Interaction-Specific Elements of UML2

UML interaction models and especially sequence diagrams offer a notation for documenting scenario-test traces. A UML `Interaction` represents a unit of behavior (here the aforementioned trace) with focus on message interchanges between connectable elements (here SUT instances). In this paper, we focus on a subset of interaction-specific elements of the UML2 metamodel that specify certain elements of UML2 sequence diagrams (see Fig. 4). The participants in a UML interaction model are instances of UML classes which are related to a given scenario test. The sequence diagram then shows the interactions between these instances in terms of executing and receiving calls on behavioral features (e.g. operations) and structural features (e.g. properties) defined for these instances via their corresponding UML classes. From this perspective, the instances interacting in the scenario tests constitute the SUT. Instances which represent structural elements of the scenario-testing framework (STF; e.g. test cases, postconditions), may also be depicted in a sequence diagram; for example as

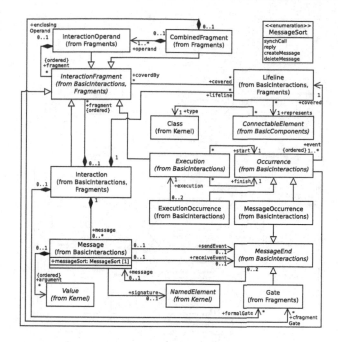

Fig. 4. Selected interaction-specific elements of the UML2 metamodel.

a test-driver lifeline [5]. The feature calls on SUT instances originating from STF instances rather than other SUT instances represent the aforementioned stimuli. This way, such feature calls designate the beginning and the end of a scenario-test trace.

2.3   Mapping Test Traces to Interactions

To formalize rules for transforming scenario-test traces into UML interactions, we define a metamodel mapping between the scenario-test trace metamodel, on the one hand, and the corresponding excerpt from the UML2 metamodel, on the other hand. For the purposes of this paper, we specified the corresponding mappings using transML diagrams [13], which represent model transformations in a tool- and technology- independent manner compatible with the UML. In total, 18 transML mapping actions are used to express the correspondences. These mapping actions (M1–M18) are visualized in Figs. 5, 6 and 12. The transML mapping diagrams are refined by OCL expressions [24] to capture important mapping and consistency constraints for the resulting UML interaction models. The mapping constraints are depicted below each related transML mapping. The mapping action represents the context for the OCL constraints and, this way, allows for navigating to elements of the source and target model. The OCL consistency constraints are fully reported in the Appendix of this paper.

In general, i.e. independent of a configured view, each Trace instance, which comprises one or several feature calls, is mapped to an instance of UML

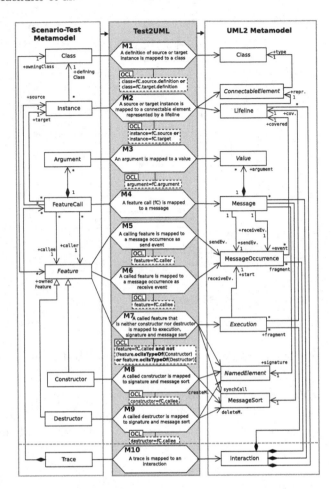

Fig. 5. Mapping elements of scenario-test traces (specific to a feature call fC) to UML2 elements.

Interaction (see M10 in Fig. 5). This way, the resulting interaction model reflects the entire test-execution trace (for viewpoint mappings, see Sect. 3.3). However, each instance of FeatureCall (fC) contained by a given trace is mapped to one UML Message instance (see M4). Each of the mappings of the other trace elements (i.e. "call dependencies") depends on mapping M4 and is specific to fC. Each instance that serves as source or target of a feature call is captured in terms of a pair of a ConnectableElement instance and a Lifeline instance. A Lifeline, therefore, represents a participant in the traced interaction, i.e., a ConnectableElement typed with the UML class of the participant. See the transML mapping actions M1 and M2 in Fig. 5. An instance of MessageOccurrence in the resulting interaction model represents the feature call at the calling feature's end as a sendEvent (see M5). Likewise, at the called feature's end, the feature call maps to a receiveEvent (see M6). Depending on the kind of the feature call, the resulting Message instance is annotated differently. For constructor and destructor calls, the related message has a create or delete signature, respectively. In addition, the corresponding message is marked using messageSort createMessage or deleteMessage, respectively (see M8 and M9). Note that in case of a constructor call, the target is represented by the class of the created instance and the created instance is the return value. This way, in this specific case, the return value is mapped to life-line and connectable element typed by the target (see M8). Other calls map to synchronous messages (i.e. messageSort synchCall). In this case, the name of the callee feature and the names of the arguments passed into the call are mapped to the signature of the corresponding Message instance (see M7). In addition, an execution is created in the interaction model. An Execution represents the enactment of a unit of behavior within the lifeline (here the execution of a called feature). The resulting Execution instance belongs to the lifeline of the target instance and its start is marked by the message occurrence created by applying M6. For the corresponding OCL consistency constraints based on mapping M4, see Listing 1.3 in the Appendix.

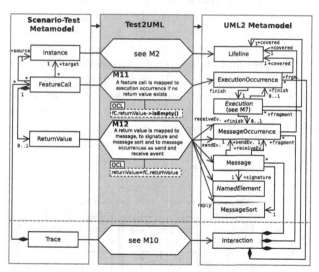

Fig. 6. Mapping return value (specific to a feature call fC) to UML2 elements.

If a given feature call fC reports a return value, a second Message instance will be created to represent this return value. This second message is marked as having messageSort reply (see M12 in Fig. 6). Moreover, two instances of MessageOccurrence are created acting as the sendEvent and the receiveEvent (covering the lifelines mapped from target and source instance related to fC, respectively). An instance of NamedElement acts as the signature of this message, reflecting the actual return value (see M12). In case of a missing return value, an ExecutionOccurrence instance is

provided to consume the call execution (`finish`) at the called feature's end
(see `M11`). Listing 1.4 in the Appendix provides the corresponding OCL consistency constraints based on mapping `M12`.

The chronological order of the `FeatureCall` instances in the recorded trace
must be preserved in the interaction model. Therefore we require that the message occurrences serving as `send` and `receiveEvents` of the derived messages (see `M5`, `M6`, `M12`) preserve this order on the respective lifelines (along
with the execution occurrences). This means, that after receiving a message
(`receiveEvent`), the send events derived from called nested features are added
in form of events covering the lifeline. In case of synchronous calls with owned
return values, for each message, the receive event related to the reply message
enters the set of ordered events (see `M12`) before adding the send event of the
next call.

3   Views on Test-Execution Traces

In this section, we discuss how the mappings from Sect. 2 can be extended to
render the derived interaction models tailorable. By tailoring, we refer to specific
means for zooming in and out on selected details of a test-execution trace; and
for pruning selected details. For this purpose, our approach defines a scenario-
test viewpoint. A viewpoint [4] stipulates the element types (e.g. scenario-test
parts, feature-call scopes) and the types of relationships between these element
types (e.g. selected, unselected) available for defining different views on test-
execution traces. On the one hand, applying the viewpoint allows for controlling model-size explosion. On the other hand, the views offered on the derived
models can help tailor the corresponding behavior documentation for given
tasks (e.g. test or code reviews) and/or stakeholder roles (e.g. test developer,
software architect).

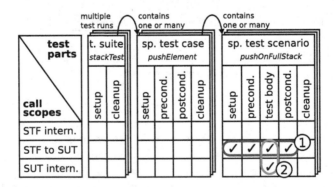

Fig. 7. Example of an option space for configuring views on test-execution traces by
combining scenario-test parts and feature-call scopes.

3.1   Scenario-Test Viewpoint

To tailor the derived interaction models, two characteristics of scenario tests and the corresponding scenario-test traces can be leveraged: the whole-part structure of scenario tests and trackable feature-call scopes.

Scenario-Test Parts. Scenario tests, in terms of concepts and their specification structure, are composed of different parts (see Sect. 2.1 and Fig. 3):

- A *test suite* encompasses one or more test cases.
- A *test case* comprises one or more test scenarios.
- A test case, and a *test scenario* can contain assertion blocks to specify *pre-* and *post-conditions*.
- A test suite, a test case, and a test scenario can contain exercise blocks, as *setup*, or *cleanup* procedures.
- A test scenario contains a *test body*.

Feature-Call Scopes. Each feature call in a scenario-test trace is scoped according to the scenario-test framework (STF) and the system under test (SUT), respectively, as the source and the target of the feature call. This way, we can differentiate between three feature-call scopes:

- feature calls running from the STF to the SUT (i.e. test stimuli),
- feature calls internal to the SUT (triggered by test stimuli directly and indirectly),
- feature calls internal to the STF.

The scenario-test parts and feature-call scopes form a large option space for tailoring an interaction model. In Fig. 7, these tailoring options are visualized as a configuration matrix. For instance, a test suite containing one test case with just one included test scenario offers 14,329 different interaction-model views available for configuration based on one test run (provided that the corresponding test blocks are specified).[4]

3.2   Example

In this section, we demonstrate *by example* the relevance of specifying different views on the test-execution traces for different tasks and/or stakeholder roles. A stack-based dispenser component (one element of an exemplary SUT) is illustrated in Fig. 8. A Stack provides the operations push, pop, size, and full as well as the attributes limit and element, which are accessible via corresponding getter/setter operations (i.e. getElements, getLimit and setLimit).

---

[4] The number of views computes as follows: There are $(2^3 - 1)$ non-empty combinations of the three feature-call scopes (SUT internal, STF internal, STF to SUT) times the $(2^{11} - 1)$ non-empty combinations of at least 11 individual test parts (e.g. setup of test case, test body of test scenario).

Stack
-limit: Integer [1]
-element: Double [*]
+push(e:Double): Boolean
+pop(): Double
+size(): Integer
+full(): Boolean
-getElements(): Double[]
+getLimit(): Integer
+setLimit(l:Integer)

Fig. 8. Excerpt from a UML class diagram of an exemplary SUT.

Listing 1.1. Natural-language notation of scenario pushOnFullStack.

```
1 Given: 'that a specific instance of Stack contains elements of the size of 2
          and has a limit of 2'
2 When:  'an element is pushed on the instance of Stack'
3 Then:  'the push operation fails and the size of elements is still 2'
```

Listing 1.2. Excerpt from an exemplary test script specifying test scenario pushOnFullStack.

```
1  set fs [::STORM::TestScenario new -name pushOnFullStack -testcase pushElement]
2  $fs expected_result set 0
3  $fs setup_script set {
4     [::Stack info instances] limit set 2
5  }
6  $fs preconditions set {
7     {expr {[[::Stack info instances] size] == 2}}
8     {expr {[[::Stack info instances] limit get] == 2}}
9  }
10 $fs test_body set {
11    [::Stack info instances] push 1.4
12 }
13 $fs postconditions set {
14    {expr {[[::Stack info instances] size] == 2}}
15 }
```

Consider the example of a test developer whose primary task is to conduct a test-code review. For this review, she is responsible for verifying a test-scenario script against a scenario-based requirements description. The scenario is named pushOnFullStack and specified in Listing 1.1. The excerpt from the test script to be reviewed is shown in Listing 1.2. To support her in this task, our approach can provide her with a partial UML sequence diagram which reflect only selected details of the test-execution trace. These details of interest could be interactions triggered by specific blocks of the test under review, for example. Such a view provides immediate benefits to the test developer. The exemplary view in Fig. 9 gives details on the interactions between the STF and the SUT, i.e. the test stimuli observed under this specific scenario. To obtain this view, the configuration pulls feature calls from a combination of setup, precondition, test body and postcondition specific to this test scenario. The view from Fig. 9 corresponds to configuration ① in Fig. 7.

As another example, consider a software architect of the same SUT. The architect might be interested in how the system behaves when executing the test body of the given scenario pushOnFullStack. The architect prefers a behavior documentation which additionally provides details on the interaction between SUT instances. A sequence diagram for such a view is presented in Fig. 10. This second view effectively zooms into a detail of the first view in Fig. 9, namely the inner workings triggered by the message push(1,4). The second view reflects configuration ② in Fig. 7.

3.3 Viewpoint Mappings

UML interaction models and corresponding sequence diagrams allow for realizing immediate benefits from a scenario-test viewpoint. For example, sequence

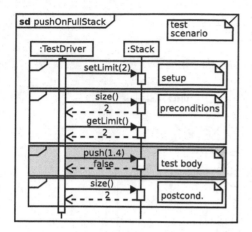

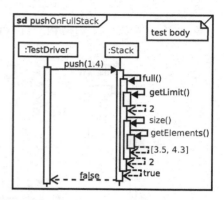

Fig. 9. Sequence diagram derived from pushOnFullStack highlighting calls running from STF to SUT.

Fig. 10. Sequence diagram derived from pushOnFullStack zooming in on test body and representing both, calls running from STF to SUT and calls internal to the SUT.

diagrams provide notational elements which can help in communicating the scenario-test structure (suite, case, scenario) to different stakeholders (architects, developers, and testers). These notational features include combined fragments and references. This way, a selected part can be visually marked in a diagram showing a combination of test parts (see, e.g., Fig. 9). Alternatively, a selected part of a scenario test can be highlighted as a separate diagram (see Fig. 10). On the other hand, interaction models can be tailored to contain only interactions between certain types of instances. Thereby, the corresponding sequence diagram can accommodate views required by different stakeholders of the SUT. In Fig. 9, the sequence diagram highlights the test stimuli triggering the test scenario pushOnFullStack, whereas the diagram in Fig. 10 additionally depicts SUT internal calls.

Conceptually, we represent different views as models conforming to the view metamodel in Fig. 11. In essence, each view selects one or more test parts and feature-call scopes, respectively, to be turned into an interaction model. Generating the actual partial interaction model is then described by six additional transML mapping actions based on a view and a trace model (see M13–18 in Fig. 12). In each mapping action, a given view model (view) is used to verify whether a given element is to be selected for the chosen scope of test parts and call scopes. Upon its selection, a feature call with its call dependencies is processed according to the previously introduced mapping actions (i.e. M1–M9, M11, and M12).

Mappings Specific to Call Scope. As explained in Sect. 3.1, a view can define any, non-empty combination of three call scopes: *STF internal*, *SUT internal*, and *STF to SUT*. In mapping action M18, each feature call is evaluated according

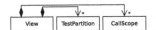

Fig. 11. View metamodel.

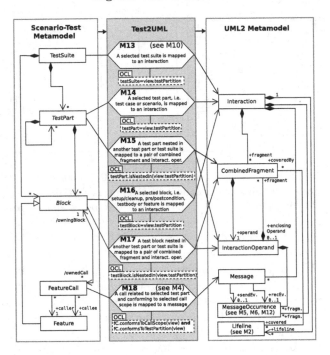

Fig. 12. Mappings specific to a given configured view with callScope and testPartition. For clarity, the case for configuring a view with one call scope and one test partition is depicted.

to the structural affiliations of the calling and the called feature, respectively. For details, see the OCL helper operation conformsToCallScope(v:View) in Listing 1.5 shown in the Appendix. Note that in case of explicitly documenting SUT behavior (i.e. *SUT internal* and *STF to SUT*), lifelines can alternatively just represent SUT instances. In this case, the sendEvent of each call running from STF to SUT (and, in turn, each receiveEvent of the corresponding reply message) is represented by a Gate instance (instead of MessageOccurrence) which signifies in the UML a connection point for relating messages outside with inside an interaction fragment.

Mappings Specific to Test Partition. The viewpoint provides for mapping structural elements of the STF to structural elements of UML interactions to highlight feature calls in their scenario-test context. Relevant contexts are the STF and scenario-test blocks (see M13–M17 in Fig. 12). Feature calls relate directly to a test block, with the call definition being contained by a block, or indirectly along a feature-call chain. This way, the STF and the respective test parts responsible for a trace can selectively enter a derived interaction as participants (e.g. as a test-driver lifeline). Besides, the scenario-test blocks and parts nested in the responsible test part (e.g. case, scenario, setup, precondition) can become structuring elements within an enclosing interaction, such as combined fragments. Consider, for example, a test suite being selected entirely. The trace obtained from executing the `TestSuite` instance is mapped to an instance of `Interaction` (M13 in Fig. 12). Scenario-test parts such as test cases and test scenarios, as well as test blocks, also become instances of `Interaction` when they are selected as active partition in a given view (M14, M16). Alternatively, they become instances of `CombinedFragment` along with corresponding interaction operands (M15, M17), when they are embedded with the actually selected scenario-test part (see `isNestedIn(p:Partition)` in Listing 1.5 in the Appendix). Hierarchical ownership of one (child) test part by another (parent) part is recorded accordingly as `enclosingOperand` relationship between child and parent parts. The use of combined fragments provides for a general structuring of the derived interaction model according to the scenario-test structure. All feature calls associated with given test parts (see M18 in Fig. 12 and the mapping constraint `conformsToTestPartition(v:View)` in Listing 1.5 in the Appendix) are effectively grouped because their corresponding message occurrences and execution occurrences (both being a kind of `InteractionFragment`) become linked to a combined fragment via an enclosing interaction operand. Combined fragments also establish a link to the `Lifeline` instances representing the SUT instances interacting in a given view. To maintain the strict chronological order of feature calls in a given trace, the resulting combined fragments must apply the `InteractionOperator` *strict* (see Sect. 2.1).[5]

4   Prototype Implementation

The KaleidoScope[6] tool can derive tailored UML2 interaction models from scenario-based runtime tests. Figure 13 depicts a high-level overview of the derivation procedure supported by KaleidoScope. The architectural components of KaleidoScope (STORM, trace provider, and model builder) as well as the diagram editor are represented via different swimlanes. Artifacts required and resulting from each derivation step are depicted as input and output pins of the respective action.

4.1   Used Technologies

The "Scenario-based Testing of Object-oriented Runtime Models" (STORM) test framework provides an infrastructure for specifying and for executing

---

[5] The default value *seq* provides weak sequencing, i.e. ordering of fragments just along lifelines, which means that occurrences on different lifelines from different operands may come in any order [27].

[6] Available for download from our website [14].

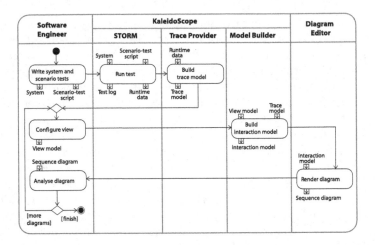

Fig. 13. Process of deriving tailored interaction models with KaleidoScope.

scenario-based component tests [34]. STORM provides all elements of our scenario-based testing metamodel (see Fig. 3). KaleidoScope builds on and instruments STORM to obtain execution-trace data from running tests defined as STORM test suites. This way, KaleidoScope keeps adoption barriers low because existing STORM test specifications can be reused without modification. STORM is implemented using the dynamic object-oriented language "Next Scripting Language" (NX), an extension of the "Tool Command Language" (Tcl). As KaleidoScope integrates with STORM, we also implemented Kaleido-Scope via NX/Tcl. In particular, we chose this development environment because NX/Tcl provides numerous advanced dynamic runtime introspection techniques for collecting execution traces from scenario tests. For example, NX/Tcl provides built-in method-call introspection in terms of message interceptors [36] and callstack introspection. KaleidoScope records and processes execution traces, as well as view configuration specifications, in terms of EMF models (Eclipse Modeling Framework; i.e. Ecore and MDT/UML2 models). More precisely, the models are stored and handled in their Ecore/XMI representation (XML Metadata Interchange specification [26]). For transforming our trace models into UML models, the required model transformations [6] are implemented via "Query/View/Transformation Operational" (QVTo) mappings [25]. QVTo allows for implementing concrete model transformations based on conceptual mappings in a straightforward manner.

4.2   Derivation Actions

Run Scenario Tests. For deriving interaction models via KaleidoScope, a newly created or an existing scenario-test suite is executed by the STORM engine. At this point, and from the perspective of the software engineer, this derivation-enabled test execution does not deviate from an ordinary one.

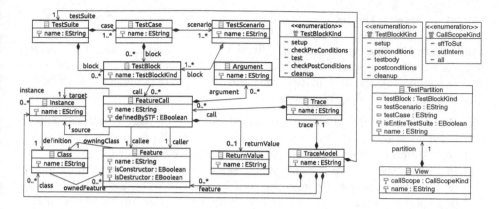

Fig. 14. Trace metamodel, EMF Ecore.   **Fig. 15.** View meta-
model, EMF Ecore.

The primary objective of this test run is to obtain the runtime data required to
build a trace model. Relevant runtime data consist of scenario-test traces (SUT
feature calls and their call dependencies) and structural elements of the scenario
test (a subset of STF feature calls and their call dependencies).

Build Trace Models. Internally, the trace-provider component of KaleidoScope
instruments the STORM engine before the actual test execution to record the
corresponding runtime data. This involves intercepting each call of relevant features and deriving the corresponding call dependencies. At the same time, the
trace provider ascertains that its instrumentation remains transparent to the
STORM engine. To achieve this, the trace provider instruments the STORM
engine and the tests under execution using NX/Tcl introspection techniques.
In NX/Tcl, method-call introspection is supported via two variants of message
interceptors [36]: mixins and filters. Mixins [37] can be used to decorate entire
components and objects. Thereby, they intercept calls to methods which are
known a priori. In KaleidoScope, the trace provider registers a mixin to intercept
relevant feature calls on the STF, i.e. the STORM engine. Filters [23] are used by
the trace provider to intercept calls to objects of the SUT which are not known
beforehand. To record relevant feature-call dependencies, the trace provider uses
the callstack introspection offered by NX/Tcl. NX/Tcl offers access to its operation callstack via special-purpose introspection commands, e.g. `nx::current`,
see [22]. To collect structural data on the intercepted STF and SUT instances, the
trace provider piggybacks onto the structural introspection facility of NX/Tcl,
e.g., `info` methods, see [22]. This way, structural data such as class names, feature names, and relationships between classes can be requested. The collected
runtime data is then processed by the trace provider. In particular, feature calls
at the application level are filtered to include only calls for the scope of the
SUT. This way, calls into other system contexts (e.g., external components or
lower-level host language calls) are discarded. In addition, the execution traces
are reordered to report "invocations interactions" first and "return interactions"

second. Moreover, the recorded SUT calls are linked to the respective owning test blocks. The processed runtime data is then stored as a trace model which conforms to the Trace metamodel defined via Ecore (see Fig. 14). This resulting trace model comprises the relevant structural elements (test suite, test case and test scenario), the SUT feature calls and their call dependencies, each being linked to a corresponding test block.

Configure Views. Based on the specifics of the test run (e.g. whether an entire test suite or selected test cases were executed) and the kind of runtime data collected, different views are available to the software engineer for selection. In KaleidoScope, the software engineer can select a particular view by defining a view model. This view model must conform to the View metamodel specified using Ecore (see Fig. 15). KaleidoScope allows for configuring views on the behavior of the SUT by combining a selected call scope (SUT internal, STF to SUT, or both) and a selected test partition (entire test suite or a specific test case, scenario, or block), as described in Sect. 3.

Build Interaction Models. The model-builder component of KaleidoScope takes the previously created pair of a trace model and a view model as input models for a collection of QVTo model transformations. The output model of these QVTo transformations is the UML interaction model. The conceptual mappings presented in Subsects. 2.3 and 3.3 are implemented in QVT Operational mappings [25], including the linking of relationships between the derived elements. In total, the transformation file contains 24 mapping actions.

Display Sequence Diagrams. Displaying the derived interaction models as sequence diagrams and presenting them to the software engineer is not handled by KaleidoScope itself. As the derived interaction models are available in the XMI representation, they can be imported by XMI-compliant diagram editors. In our daily practice, we use Eclipse Papyrus [8] for this task.

5   Related Work

Closely related research can be roughly divided into three groups: reverse-engineering sequence diagrams from system execution, techniques addressing the problem of model-size explosion in reverse-engineered behavioral models and extracting traceability links between test and system artifacts.

Reverse-Engineering UML Sequence Diagrams. Approaches applying dynamic analysis set the broader context of our work [2,7,12,28]. Of particular interest are model-driven approaches which provide conceptual mappings between runtime-data models and UML interaction models. Briand et al. [2] as well as Cornelissen et al. [5] are exemplary for such model-driven approaches. In their approaches, UML sequence diagrams are derived from executing runtime tests. Both describe metamodels to define sequence diagrams and for capturing system execution in form of a trace model. Briand et al. define mappings between these two metamodels in terms of OCL consistency constraints.

Each test execution relates to a single use-case scenario defined by a system-level test case. Their approaches differ from ours in some respects. The authors build on generic trace metamodels while we extend an existing scenario-test metamodel to cover test-execution traces. Briand et al. do not provide for scoping the derived sequence diagrams based on the executed tests unlike Cornelissen et al. (see below). They, finally, do not capture the mappings between trace and sequence model in a formalized way.

Countering Model-Size Explosion. A second group of related approaches aims at addressing the problem of size explosion in reverse-engineered behavioral models. Fernández-Sáez et al. [10] conducted a controlled experiment on the perceived effects of derived UML sequence diagrams on maintaining a software system. A key result is that derived sequence diagrams do not necessarily facilitate maintenance tasks due to an excessive level of detail. Hamou-Lhadj and Lethbridge [16] and Bennett et al. [1] surveyed available techniques which can act as counter measures against model-size explosion. The available techniques fall into three categories: *slicing* and *pruning* of components and calls as well as *architecture-level filtering*. *Slicing* (or sampling) is a way of reducing the resulting model size by choosing a sample of execution traces. Sharp and Rountev [33] propose interactive slicing for zooming in on selected messages and message chains. Grati et al. [11] contribute techniques for interactively highlighting selected execution traces and for navigating through single execution steps. *Pruning* (or hiding) provides abstraction by removing irrelevant details. For instance, Lo and Maoz [20] elaborate on filtering calls based on different execution levels. In doing so, they provide hiding of calls based on the distinction between triggers and effects of scenario executions. As an early approach of *architectural-level filtering*, Richner and Ducasse [31] provide for tailorable views on object-oriented systems, e.g., by filtering calls between selected classes. In our approach, we adopt these techniques for realizing different views conforming to a scenario-test viewpoint. In particular, slicing corresponds to including interactions of certain test parts (e.g., test cases, test scenarios) only, selectively hiding model elements to pulling from different feature-call scopes (e.g., stimuli and internal calls). Architectural-level filtering is applied by distinguishing elements by their structural affiliation (e.g., SUT or STF).

Test-to-System Traceability. Another important group of related work provides for creating traceability links between test artifacts and system artifacts by processing test-execution traces. Parizi et al. [29] give a systematic overview of such traceability techniques. For instance, test cases are associated with SUT elements based on the underlying call-trace data for calculating metrics which reflect how each method is tested [19]. Qusef et al. [30] provide traceability links between unit tests and classes under test. These links are extracted from trace slices generated by assertion statements contained by the unit tests. In general, these approaches do not necessarily derive behavioral diagrams, however Parizi et al. conclude by stating the need for visualizing traceability links. These approaches relate to ours by investigating which SUT elements are covered by a specific part of the test specification. While they use this information, e.g., for calculating coverage metrics, we aim at visualizing the interactions for documenting system behavior. However, Cornelissen et al. [5] pursue a similar goal by visualizing the execution of unit tests. By leveraging the structure of tests, they aim at improving the understandability of reverse-engineered sequence diagrams (see above), e.g., by representing the behavior of a particular test part in a separate sequence diagram. While they share our motivation for test-based partitioning, Cornelissen et al. do not present a conceptual or a concrete solution to this partitioning. Moreover, we leverage the test structure for organizing the sequence diagram (e.g., by using combined fragments) and consider different scopes of feature calls.

6   Conclusion

In this paper, we presented an approach for deriving tailored UML interaction models for documenting system behavior from scenario-based runtime tests. Our approach allows for leveraging the structure of scenario tests (i.e. test parts and call scopes) to tailor the derived interaction models, e.g., by pruning details and by zooming in and out on selected details. This way, we also provide means to control the sizes of the resulting UML sequence diagrams. Our approach is model-driven in the sense that test-execution traces are represented through a dedicated metamodel. Conceptual mappings (transformation rules) between this metamodel and the UML metamodel are captured by transML diagrams refined by inter-model constraint expressions (OCL). To demonstrate the feasibility of our approach, we developed a prototype implementation called KaleidoScope. The approach is applicable for any software system having an object-oriented design and implementation, provided that suitable test suites and a suitable test framework are available. A test suite (and the guiding test strategy) is qualified if tests offer structuring abstractions (i.e. test parts as in scenario tests) and if tests trigger inter-object interactions. The corresponding test framework must offer instrumentation to obtain test-execution traces.

In a next step, we will investigate via controlled experiments how the derived interaction models can support system stakeholders in comprehension tasks on the tested software system and on the test scripts. From a conceptual point of view, we plan to extend the approach to incorporate behavioral details such as measured execution times into the interaction models. From a practical angle, we seek to apply the approach on large-scale software projects. For this, our KaleidoScope must be extended to support runtime and program introspection for other object-oriented programming languages and for the corresponding test frameworks.

Appendix

Listing 1.3. OCL consistency constraints based on mapping M4 in Fig. 5.

```
1  context M4 inv:
2  message.name=featureCall.name and
3  (featureCall.argument->notEmpty() implies message.
       argument.name=featureCall.argument.name) and
4  message.sendEvent.oclIsTypeOf(
       MessageOccurrenceSpecification) and
5  message.sendEvent.name=featureCall.caller.name and
6  message.sendEvent.covered.name=featureCall.source.
       name and
7  message.sendEvent.covered.represents.name=
       featureCall.source.name and
8  message.sendEvent.covered.represents.type.name=
       featureCall.source.definingClass.name and
9  message.receiveEvent.oclIsTypeOf(
       MessageOccurrenceSpecification) and
10 message.receiveEvent.name=featureCall.callee.name
       and
11 if(featureCall.callee.oclIsTypeOf(Constructor)) then
       {
12 message.messageSort=MessageSort::createMessage and
13 message.signature.name='create' and
14 message.receiveEvent.covered.name=featureCall.
       returnValue.value and
15 message.receiveEvent.covered.represents.name=
       featureCall.returnValue.value and
16 message.receiveEvent.covered.represents.type.name=
       featureCall.target.name
17 } else {
18 message.receiveEvent.covered.name=featureCall.
       target.name and
19 message.receiveEvent.covered.represents.name=
       featureCall.target.name and
20 message.receiveEvent.covered.represents.type.name=
       featureCall.target.definingClass.name and
21 if (featureCall.callee.oclIsTypeOf(Destructor))
       then {
22 message.messageSort=MessageSort::deleteMessage and
23 message.signature.name='delete'
24 } else {
25 message.messageSort=MessageSort::synchCall and
26 message.signature.name=featureCall.callee.name and
27 (featureCall.returnValue->isEmpty() implies
       message.receiveEvent.execution.finish.
       oclIsTypeOf(ExecutionOccurrence))
28 } endif
29 } endif
```

Listing 1.4. OCL consistency constraints based on mapping M12 in Fig. 6.

```
1  context M12 inv:
2  message.messageSort=MessageSort::reply and
3  message.name=returnValue.value and
4  message.signature.name=returnValue.value and
5  message.argument->isEmpty() and
6  message.sendEvent.oclIsTypeOf(
       MessageOccurrenceSpecification) and
7  message.sendEvent.name=returnValue.featureCall.
       callee.name and
8  message.sendEvent.covered.name=returnValue.
       featureCall.target.name and
9  message.sendEvent.covered.represents.name=
       returnValue.featureCall.target.name and
10 message.sendEvent.covered.represents.type.name=
       returnValue.featureCall.target.definingClass.
       name and
11 message.receiveEvent.oclIsTypeOf(
       MessageOccurrenceSpecification) and
12 message.receiveEvent.name=returnValue.featureCall.
       caller.name and
13 message.receiveEvent.covered.name=returnValue.
       featureCall.source.name and
14 message.receiveEvent.covered.represents.name=
       returnValue.featureCall.source.name and
15 message.receiveEvent.covered.represents.type.name=
       returnValue.featureCall.source.definingClass.
       name
```

Listing 1.5. OCL helper operations applied in mappings M15, M17 and M18 in Fig. 12.

```
1  context FeatureCall
2  def: conformsToCallScope(v:View) : Boolean =
3  if (v.callScope='sutIntern') then {
4    self.isDefinedByStfBlock=false and
5    self.calleeOwnedByStfClass=false
6  } else {
7    if (v.callScope='stfToSut') then {
8      self.isDefinedByStfBlock and
9      self.calleeOwnedByStfClass=false
10   } else {
11     if (v.callScope='stfIntern') then {
12       self.isDefinedByStfBlock and
13       self.calleeOwnedByStfClass
14     } else { false } endif
15   } endif
16 } endif
17 def: conformsToTestPartition(v:View) : Boolean =
18   self.owningBlock.isNestedIn(v.testPartition)
19 def: isDefinedByTestBlock : Boolean =
20   block.oclIsTypeOf(Setup) or
21   block.oclIsTypeOf(TestBody) or
22   block.oclIsTypeOf(Cleanup) or
23   (block.oclIsTypeOf(Assertion)implies(block.block.
       oclIsTypeOf(Precondition) or
24   block.block.oclIsTypeOf(Postcondition))
25 def: calleeOwnedByStfClass : Boolean =
26   Set{TestSuite, TestCase, TestScenario, Setup,
       Precondition, TestBody, Postcondition,
       Cleanup}->includes(self.callee.owningClass.
       name)
27 def: block : Block = self.definition.Block
28
29 context TestPart
30 def: isNestedIn(p:TestPartition) : Boolean =
31 if (p.oclIsTypeOf(TestSuite)) then {
32   true
33 } else {
34   if (p.oclIsTypeOf(TestCase)) then {
35     (self.oclIsTypeOf(TestCase) implies p.name=self.
       name) and
36     (self.oclIsTypeOf(TestScenario) implies p.name=
       self.testCase.name) and
37     (self.oclIsTypeOf(Block) implies (
38       (self.testCase->notEmpty() and p.name=self.
       testCase.name) or
39       (self.testScenario->notEmpty() and p.name=self.
       testScenario.testCase.name)))
40   } else {
41     if (p.oclIsTypeOf(TestScenario)) then {
42       (not self.oclIsTypeOf(TestCase)) and
43       (self.oclIsTypeOf(TestScenario) implies (
44         p.name=self.name and
45         p.testCase.name = self.testCase.name
46       )) and
47       (self.oclIsTypeOf(Block) implies (
48         p.name=self.testCase.name and
49         p.testCase.name=self.testScenario.testCase.name
       ))
50     } else {
51       if (p.oclIsTypeOf(Block)) then {
52         self.oclIsTypeOf(Block) and p.name=self.name
       and
53         ((p.testCase->notEmpty() and self.testCase->
       notEmpty()) implies p.testCase.name =
       self.testCase.name) and
54         (p.testScenario->notEmpty() and self.
       testScenario->notEmpty()) implies p.
       testScenario.name = self.testScenario.
       name))
55     } else { false } endif
56   } endif
57 } endif
58 } endif
```

References

1. Bennett, C., Myers, D., Storey, M.A., German, D.M., Ouellet, D., Salois, M., Charland, P.: A survey and evaluation of tool features for understanding reverse-engineered sequence diagrams. Softw. Maint. Evol. **20**(4), 291–315 (2008). doi:10.1002/smr.v20:4

2. Briand, L.C., Labiche, Y., Miao, Y.: Toward the reverse engineering of UML sequence diagrams. In: Proceedings of WCRE 2003, pp. 57–66. IEEE (2003). doi:10.1109/TSE.2006.96

3. Carroll, J.M.: Five reasons for scenario-based design. Interact. Comput. **13**(1), 43–60 (2000). doi:10.1016/S0953-5438(00)00023-0

4. Clements, P., Bachmann, F., Bass, L., Garlan, D., Ivers, J., Little, R., Merson, P., Nord, R., Stafford, J.: Documenting Software Architecture: Views and Beyond. SEI, 2nd edn. Addison-Wesley, Boston (2011)

5. Cornelissen, B., Van Deursen, A., Moonen, L., Zaidman, A.: Visualizing testsuites to aid in software understanding. In: Proceedings of CSMR 2007, pp. 213–222. IEEE (2007). doi:10.1109/CSMR.2007.54

6. Czarnecki, K., Helsen, S.: Classification of model transformation approaches. In: WS Proceedings of OOPSLA 2003, pp. 1–17. ACM Press (2003)

7. Delamare, R., Baudry, B., Le Traon, Y., et al.: Reverse-engineering of UML 2.0 sequence diagrams from execution traces. In: WS Proceedings of ECOOP 2006. Springer (2006)

8. Eclipse Foundation: Papyrus (2015). http://eclipse.org/papyrus/. Accessed 25 September 2015

9. Falessi, D., Briand, L.C., Cantone, G., Capilla, R., Kruchten, P.: The value of design rationale information. ACM Trans. Softw. Eng. Methodol. **22**(3), 21:1–21:32 (2013). doi:10.1145/2491509.2491515

10. Fernández-Sáez, A.M., Genero, M., Chaudron, M.R., Caivano, D., Ramos, I.: Are forward designed or reverse-engineered UML diagrams more helpful for code maintenance? a family of experiments. Inform. Softw. Tech. **57**, 644–663 (2015). doi:10.1016/j.infsof.2014.05.014

11. Grati, H., Sahraoui, H., Poulin, P.: Extracting sequence diagrams from execution traces using interactive visualization. In: Proceedings of WCRE 2010, pp. 87–96. IEEE (2010). doi:10.1109/WCRE.2010.18

12. Guéhéneuc, Y.G., Ziadi, T.: Automated reverse-engineering of UML v2.0 dynamic models. In: WS Proceedings of ECOOP 2005. Springer (2005)

13. Guerra, E., Lara, J., Kolovos, D.S., Paige, R.F., Santos, O.M.: Engineering model transformations with transML. Softw. Syst. Model. **12**(3), 555–577 (2013). doi:10.1007/s10270-011-0211-2

14. Haendler, T.: KaleidoScope. Institute for Information Systems and New Media. WU Vienna (2015). http://nm.wu.ac.at/nm/haendler. Accessed 25 September 2015

15. Haendler, T., Sobernig, S., Strembeck, M.: An approach for the semi-automated derivation of UML interaction models from scenario-based runtime tests. In: Proceedings of ICSOFT-EA 2015, pp. 229–240. SciTePress (2015). doi:10.5220/0005519302290240

16. Hamou-Lhadj, A., Lethbridge, T.C.: A survey of trace exploration tools and techniques. In: Proceedings of CASCON 2004, pp. 42–55. IBM Press (2004). http://dl.acm.org/citation.cfm?id=1034914.1034918

17. Jacobson, I.: Object-Oriented Software Engineering: A Use Case Driven Approach. ACM Press Series. ACM Press, New York (1992)
18. Jarke, M., Bui, X.T., Carroll, J.M.: Scenario management: an interdisciplinary approach. Requirements Eng. **3**(3), 155–173 (1998). doi:10.1007/s007660050002
19. Kanstrén, T.: Towards a deeper understanding of test coverage. Softw. Maint. Evol. **20**(1), 59–76 (2008). doi:10.1002/smr.362
20. Lo, D., Maoz, S.: Mining scenario-based triggers and effects. In: Proceedings of ASE 2008, pp. 109–118. IEEE (2008). doi:10.1109/ASE.2008.21
21. Nebut, C., Fleurey, F., Le Traon, Y., Jezequel, J.: Automatic test generation: a use case driven approach. IEEE Trans. Softw. Eng. **32**(3), 140–155 (2006). doi:10.1109/TSE.2006.22
22. Neumann, G., Sobernig, S.: Next scripting framework. API reference (2015). https://next-scripting.org/xowiki/. Accessed 25 September 2015
23. Neumann, G., Zdun, U.: Filters as a language support for design patterns in object-oriented scripting languages. In: Proceedings of COOTS 1999, pp. 1–14. USENIX (1999). http://dl.acm.org/citation.cfm?id=1267992
24. Object Management Group: Object Constraint Language (OCL) - Version 2.4 (2014). http://www.omg.org/spec/OCL/2.4/. Accessed 25 September 2015
25. Object Management Group: Meta Object Facility (MOF) 2.0 Query/View/Transformation Specification, Version 1.2, February 2015. http://www.omg.org/spec/QVT/1.2/. Accessed 25 September 2015
26. Object Management Group: MOF 2 XMI Mapping Specification, Version 2.5.1, June 2015. http://www.omg.org/spec/XMI/2.5.1/. Accessed 25 September 2015
27. Object Management Group: Unified Modeling Language (UML), Superstructure, Version 2.5.0, June 2015. http://www.omg.org/spec/UML/2.5. Accessed 25 September 2015
28. Oechsle, R., Schmitt, T.: JAVAVIS: Automatic program visualization with object and sequence diagrams using the java debug interface (JDI). In: Diehl, S. (ed.) Dagstuhl Seminar 2001. LNCS, vol. 2269, pp. 176–190. Springer, Heidelberg (2002). doi:10.1007/3-540-45875-1_14
29. Parizi, R.M., Lee, S.P., Dabbagh, M.: Achievements and challenges in state-of-the-art software traceability between test and code artifacts. Trans. Reliab. IEEE **63**, 913–926 (2014). doi:10.1109/TR.2014.2338254
30. Qusef, A., Bavota, G., Oliveto, R., de Lucia, A., Binkley, D.: Recovering test-to-code traceability using slicing and textual analysis. J. Syst. Softw. **88**, 147–168 (2014). doi:10.1016/j.jss.2013.10.019
31. Richner, T., Ducasse, S.: Recovering high-level views of object-oriented applications from static and dynamic information. In: Proceedings of ICSM 1999, pp. 13–22. IEEE (1999). http://dl.acm.org/citation.cfm?id=519621.853375
32. Ryser, J., Glinz, M.: A scenario-based approach to validating and testing software systems using statecharts. In: Proceedings of ICSSEA 1999 (1999)
33. Sharp, R., Rountev, A.: Interactive exploration of UML sequence diagrams. In: Proceedings of VISSOFT 2005, pp. 1–6. IEEE (2005). doi:10.1109/VISSOF.2005.1684295
34. Strembeck, M.: Testing policy-based systems with scenarios. In: Proceedings of IASTED 2011, pp. 64–71. ACTA Press (2011). doi:10.2316/P.2011.720-021
35. Van Geet, J., Zaidman, A., Greevy, O., Hamou-Lhadj, A.: A lightweight approach to determining the adequacy of tests as documentation. In: Proceedings of PCODA 2006, pp. 21–26. IEEE CS (2006)
36. Zdun, U.: Patterns of tracing software structures and dependencies. In: Proceedings of EuroPLoP 2003, pp. 581–616. Universitaetsverlag Konstanz (2003)

37. Zdun, U., Strembeck, M., Neumann, G.: Object-based and class-based composition of transitive mixins. Inform. Softw. Tech. **49**(8), 871–891 (2007). doi:10.1016/j. infsof.2006.10.001

38. Ziadi, T., Da Silva, M.A.A., Hillah, L.M., Ziane, M.: A fully dynamic approach to the reverse engineering of UML sequence diagrams. In: Proceedings of ICECCS 2011, pp. 107–116. IEEE (2011). doi:10.1109/ICECCS.2011.18

Documenting and Designing QVTo Model Transformations Through Mathematics

Ulyana Tikhonova[✉] and Tim Willemse

Technische Universiteit Eindhoven,
P.O. Box 513, 5600 MB Eindhoven, The Netherlands
{u.tikhonova,t.a.c.willemse}@tue.nl

Abstract. Model transformations play an essential role in Model Driven Engineering (MDE), as they provide the means to use models as first-class artifacts in the software development process. While there exist a number of languages specifically designed to program model transformations, the practical challenges of documenting and designing model transformations are hardly addressed. In this paper we demonstrate how QVTo model transformations can be described and designed informally through the mathematical notation of set theory and functions. We align the QVTo concepts with the mathematical concepts, and, building on the latter, we formulate two design principles of developing QVTo transformations: structural decomposition and chaining model transformations.

Keywords: Model driven engineering · Model transformation · QVTo · Documentation · Software design

1 Introduction and Motivation

Model transformations are the key technology of Model Driven Engineering (MDE). Model transformations make models meaningful and exploitable and, thus, allow for (software) development using models as first-class artifacts. Employing model transformations as the key development technology poses challenges typical for software engineering, such as design, documentation, and maintenance. To address these challenges one needs to be able to describe model transformations in an unambiguous and clear way.

Nowadays, there exist a number of languages specifically devoted for implementing model transformations, such as: ATL (Atlas Transformation Language), QVT (Query/ View/Transformation) family of languages, ETL (Epsilon Transformation Language), etc. These languages can be viewed as DSLs for model transformations. Consequently, a notation for designing and documenting programs written in such languages should be specifically tailored to describing model transformations, more or less disqualifying general purpose notations such as UML. In the current practice there exist no specific notation for describing model transformations (except those provided by the model transformation languages themselves). The common approach for documenting and/or explaining

P. Lorenz et al. (Eds.): ICSOFT 2015, CCIS 586, pp. 349–364, 2016.
DOI: 10.1007/978-3-319-30142-6_19

model transformations is to use concrete examples of their inputs and the corresponding outputs. Clearly, this approach provides an incomplete picture of the transformation and it fails to provide an overview of the transformation design, which are essential for describing complex model transformations bridging big semantic gaps and/or having complex organizational structures.

In this paper we focus on QVT-Operational (QVTo), that was introduced as part of the MOF (Meta Object Facility) standard [1]. QVTo allows for imperative implementations of model transformations using various tool support, such as plug-ins of Eclipse Modeling Project. The language comprises both high-level concepts specific for model transformation development, such as constructs of the Object Constraint Language (OCL), traceability, inheritance of subroutines; and low-level concepts of the imperative languages, such as loops, conditional statements, explicit invocation of subroutines. Consequently, using QVTo requires strong language expertise. However, in practice QVTo is used by engineers who are experts in their own domains but typically have little to no computer science training and lack the required language expertise. Moreover, gaining the required expertise in QVTo is hampered by the fact that the language is poorly documented and especially lacks documentation on its pragmatics.

Following our experience of developing and maintaining a complex QVTo model transformation and of teaching QVTo to students, we propose to adopt functions and set theory as a notation-independent approach for documenting, explaining, and designing QVTo model transformations. Typically such mathematical concepts are familiar to most engineers. In this paper we demonstrate how this notation can be aligned with the QVTo concepts, and thus can be used for explaining QVTo concepts and for documenting model transformations (Sect. 3). Moreover, using this notation we formulate two common design principles of developing model transformations and show how the corresponding organization structure and information flow can be described (Sect. 4). In the rest of the paper, in Sect. 5 we discuss and assess the proposed approach based on interviews with QVTo practitioners. Related work is discussed in Sect. 2. Conclusions and directions for future work are given in Sect. 6.

2   Related Work

The broad problem of supporting the whole life-cycle of the model transformation development with a proper description notation is raised by Guerra et al. in [2]. In this study they propose a family of different visual languages for various phases of the development process: requirements, analysis (testing), architectural design, mappings overview and their detailed design. Although the authors state that the resulting diagrams should guide the construction of the software artifacts, there is no discussion in the paper on how to design model transformations. In contrast, in our paper we use a single mathematical notation for describing three of the listed phases: architectural design (transformation chains), mappings overview (function signatures) and their detailed design (formulas). The mathematical notation of function signatures applied in our paper is close to the notation of rewrite rules of the Stratego language [3].

The earlier works on a notation for describing and designing model transformations, such as [4,5], propose graphical representations that are based on UML class diagrams. The major disadvantage of such approaches is the difficulty to describe the organizational structure of a transformation and the information flow through this structure from source to target models. This challenge is managed in the visual notation of the MOLA transformation language [6], that combines 'structured flowcharts' for describing a transformation algorithm with (model) patterns for defining input and output of a transformation. Though MOLA aims for describing model transformations in a 'natural and easy readable way', it introduces a number of specific visual means, which might require certain experience from a user.

The existing studies that specify model transformations using mathematical formalisms, e.g. [7], mostly aim for formal analysis of transformations rather than for designing and maintaining them. An exception to this is [8,9] by Lano and Rahimi, who define a systematic development process for model transformations with the focus on their formal specification and further verification. They propose to describe a model transformation as a set of abstract constraints on the relation between source and target models that is realized by this transformation. For this, they identify and classify common patterns for specifying constraints on model transformations [10]. The authors also give guidelines on how the (implementation) design of a model transformation can be derived based on the pattern that has been applied for its specification - using one of the proposed implementation patterns, or implementation strategies. The structural decomposition approach—the design principle that we discuss in Sect. 4.1—is similar to the recursive pattern in [8]. In particular, our decomposition method can be used to determine the structural dependency ordering of the target model, which is required when applying this implementation pattern. Chaining of model transformations—our second design principle, discussed in Sect. 4.2—is similar to the auxiliary metamodels pattern in [8].

The principle of structuring a program (or in our case, a transformation) according to the structure of its input and/or output goes back to the method proposed by M. Jackson in 1970s and known as Jackson Structured Programming (JSP) [11,12]. This method was developed in the domain of data processing systems, where an input data stream is processed and an output data stream is produced as a result. JSP gives guidelines on how to decompose, i.e. to design, a program that performs such processing. According to JSP, program structure should be dictated by the structure of its input and output data streams. The JSP method uses diagrams to represent structures of input and output streams, to merge them and to derive a corresponding program structure. We apply ideas, similar to those of the JSP method, to structure model transformations along the structure of its input and output metamodels (Sect. 4.1).

3 Notation for Describing Model Transformations

A model transformation takes as an input one or more source models and generates as an output one or more target models. An algorithm for such generation is defined in terms of source and target metamodels. In particular, the smallest units of a model transformation (such as *mappings* in QVTo, or *rules* in ATL and ETL) are defined in terms of *classes* and *associations* specified in the source and target metamodels. In order to provide a description of a model transformation using the mathematical notation of set theory, we need to specify how we refer to the metamodel concepts in this notation.

3.1   Describing Metamodel Concepts

In the context of MDE, a metamodel is usually defined using the MOF standard. This standard can be seen as a subset of UML class diagrams. There have been a number of studies on formalizing UML class diagrams, see *e.g.* [13]. A common approach is to view a class as a set of objects that instantiate this class, and the associations between classes as relations on the corresponding sets of objects. Following this approach, we notate classes as sets and objects of classes as elements of sets. For instance, the example metamodel depicted in Fig. 1 introduces the sets *StateMachine, State, Transition, CompositeState,* etc. In model transformations, associations are used as references to access and assign the associated objects, rather than elements of relations on the sets of objects. Therefore, we do not use the notation of relations, but stick to the notation common in object-oriented languages (including QVTo), and refer to the associated classes using association names and dot notation; for instance *s.states* where $s \in StateMachine$.

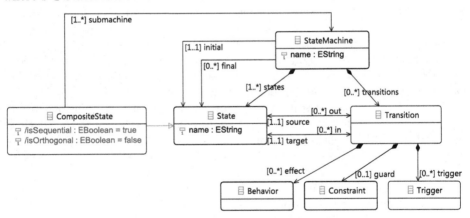

Fig. 1. Metamodel of the UML state machine.

Associations between classes are the key metamodel elements that determine the structure of the resulting models. From the point of view of a model structure, we may treat an object as a tuple of its referenced objects and its attributes. This permits a different view on classes: a class can be seen as a relation on the classes it is associated with. For example, the class *StateMachine* is determined by a relation on the classes with which it is associated through the associations *states, transitions, initial,* and *final*:

```
1   mapping Transition  ::  CloneTransition()  :  Transition  {...}
2
3   mapping Transition  ::  MultiplyTransByState(in state  :  State)
4                           :  Transition  {...}
5
6   mapping Tuple(s1:  State ,  s2:  State)  ::  MultiplyTwoStates()
7                                           :  State  {...}
8
9   mapping Set(StateMachine)  ::  MultiplySTMs()
10                             :  StateMachine  {...}
```

Listing 1.1. Mapping declarations of the example QVTo transformation.

$$StateMachine \subseteq \mathbb{P}(State) \times \mathbb{P}(Transition) \times State \times \mathbb{P}(State) \qquad (1)$$

Note that here we use the powerset $\mathbb{P}(S)$ of a set S to indicate that multiplicity of an association end has an upper bound greater than one. We will use the inclusion relationship (1) as a rewriting rule when constructing transformations in Sect. 4.1.

3.2 Describing Model Transformations

In general, a model transformation defines a relation between a set of source models and a set of target models [14]. A QVTo mapping is more restrictive, realizing a function that maps one or more source model objects into one or more target model objects. Thus, we can denote a QVTo mapping as a function from a set representing the source class to a set representing the target class. For example, the simple mapping depicted in the line 1 of Listing 1.1 can be viewed as a function with the following signature:

$$CloneTransition : Transition \rightarrow Transition \qquad (2)$$

Mappings with multiple inputs and/or outputs can be treated in the same way, using Cartesian products of sets to indicate these inputs and/or outputs; *e.g.* the QVTo mappings of lines 3 and 6 in Listing 1.1 can be represented as follows:

$$MultiplyTransByState : Transition \times State \rightarrow Transition \qquad (3)$$

$$MultiplyTwoStates : State \times State \rightarrow State \qquad (4)$$

Note, that in QVTo multiple inputs and outputs for a mapping can be realized in two different ways: using *in/out* parameters of the mapping (lines 3–4 in the Listing 1.1) or using tuples as source/target types (lines 6–7 in the Listing 1.1).[1]

QVTo also allows a collection of objects to be used as an input and/or output of a mapping (line 9 in Listing 1.1). We treat an instance of a collection defined on a class as a set of objects of this class[2], meaning that we treat the collection class as a power set of the set that represents the class of the collection elements:

---

[1] This syntactic difference influences results of the traceability and resolving mechanisms of QVTo, as only the object before the symbol '::' is traced and resolved.

[2] Note, that strictly speaking a collection can be realized as a list or a bag, and thus cannot be formally specified as a set. We use this notation rather as an approximation in order to describe a transformation conceptually.

```
1   mapping Transition :: CloneTransition() : Transition {
2       result.trigger := self.trigger -> map CloneTrigger();
3       result.guard := self.guard. map CloneConstraint();
4       result.effect := self.effect -> map CloneBehavior();
5       result.source := self.source. map CloneState();
6       result.target := self.target. map CloneState();
7   }
```

Listing 1.2. QVTo code of the *CloneTransition* mapping.

$$MultiplySTMs : \mathbb{P}(StateMachine) \rightarrow StateMachine \qquad (5)$$

Function signatures allow us to concisely capture the purpose of a mapping in terms of source and target metamodels, and in line with the QVTo code. However, they do not suffice to describe what a mapping actually does. For this, we need to describe how elements of target objects are calculated from the elements of source objects. We use formulas of the following form (which we explain below) to achieve this:

$$CloneTransition(self) : trigger = \bigcup_{t \in self.trigger} \{CloneTrigger(t)\},$$

$$guard = CloneConstraint(self.guard),$$

$$effect = \bigcup_{e \in self.effect} \{CloneBehavior(e)\}, \qquad (6)$$

$$source = CloneState(self.source),$$

$$target = CloneState(self.target)$$

Formula 6 describes the QVTo mapping depicted in Listing 1.2. It shows how each element of the target object is calculated by the invocation of other mappings on elements of the source object. We denote a calculation that is performed on a collection by a quantified union over elements of the collection (lines 1 and 3 of the formula)[3]. The invocation of a mapping is indicated by the application of the corresponding function, such as *CloneConstraint(self.guard)*.[4] This formula moreover specifies the order of invocation of the mappings, which might be essential due to the operational nature of QVTo.

---

[3] In QVTo invocation of a mapping on a collection is denoted by arrow "-> **map**", while invocation on a single object uses dot-notation: ". **map**".

[4] According to the execution semantics of QVTo implemented in the Eclipse project, the result of a mapping invocation is the corresponding target object, which is newly constructed or resolved depending on whether this mapping has been already invoked on this source object.

4   Design of Model Transformations

Designing model transformations is a challenging part of the model transformation development process. When designing a model transformation one must answer questions such as 'what are the mappings that constitute a model transformation?' and 'how are these mappings related with each other, *i.e.* invoked by each other?'. In practice, there exist a number of design principles that developers can follow when creating their model transformations [8,15]. In this section we demonstrate how the presented mathematical notation can facilitate application of some of these design principles.

4.1   Structural Decomposition of Model Transformations

Model transformations construct target models from source models. Such models typically consist of objects connected with each other by associations. Therefore, mappings that constitute a model transformation should construct both target objects and the associations between them. In QVTo each mapping constructs a new object via assigning values to its properties, *i.e.* by constructing objects it is associated with. This observation is captured by the following principle for designing model transformations:

> mappings should be related to (invoked by) each other in the same way as the objects that they construct are associated with (composed of) each other.

In other words, the structure of a model transformation follows the structure defined by the target metamodel. In [15], this was identified as one of the best practices for understandability and maintainability of transformations. To apply this principle in our design process we take the following steps:

1. We identify the inputs and outputs of the transformation and define their structures,
2. We establish the correspondence between the elements in input and output structures,
3. We capture these correspondences in signatures of the constituent mappings,
4. We decompose the transformation into constituent mappings.

In what follows, we illustrate and explain these steps through the following example: we show how these steps help design a mapping that takes two state machines and constructs a state machine representing their product. The source and target metamodel of this transformation is depicted in Fig. 1. The function signature of the mapping is as follows.

$$MultiplyTwoSTMs : StateMachine \times StateMachine \rightarrow StateMachine \qquad (7)$$

The task of writing such a transformation may not seem challenging, taking into account that we know the definition of a product of two state machines. However, it might be not so obvious how to implement this transformation in QVTo code.

Identifying the Structure of the Inputs and Outputs. That is, we establish what kind of objects we have to implement the transformation. For this we 'rewrite' each of the classes in the initial function signature with the classes that are associated with this one. The rule we use to rewrite is based on the inclusion relation captured in Formula (1). According to this formula, an object of the class *StateMachine* can be viewed as a tuple of objects referenced through the associations *states*, *transitions*, *initial*, and *final*, *i.e.* as an object that belongs to $\mathbb{P}(State) \times \mathbb{P}(Transition) \times State \times \mathbb{P}(State)$. Thus, as a result of rewriting signature (7), we obtain the following:

$$
\begin{aligned}
&(\mathbb{P}(State) \times \mathbb{P}(Transition) \times State \times \mathbb{P}(State)) \times \\
&(\mathbb{P}(State) \times \mathbb{P}(Transition) \times State \times \mathbb{P}(State)) \to \\
&\mathbb{P}(State) \times \mathbb{P}(Transition) \times State \times \mathbb{P}(State).
\end{aligned}
\tag{8}
$$

Connecting Elements in Input to Output Structures. Compared to signature (7), signature (8) is much richer, but it is still very 'monolithic'. We next strive towards breaking down the structure in the formula, allowing for a modular solution. To this end, we redistribute the inputs on the left of the arrow and the outputs on the right of the arrow according to our understanding of *which input elements are required to construct which output elements*. For example, we know that the states of the resulting state machine are constructed from the states of the input machines. We capture this by grouping the input collections of *States* and the output collection of *States* in a separate *sub-signature* in Formula (9).

$$
\begin{aligned}
&(\mathbb{P}(State) \times \mathbb{P}(State) \to \mathbb{P}(State)) \times \\
&(\mathbb{P}(Transition) \times \mathbb{P}(Transition) \times \mathbb{P}(State) \times \mathbb{P}(State)) \to \mathbb{P}(Transition)) \times \\
&(State \times State \to State) \times \\
&(\mathbb{P}(State) \times \mathbb{P}(State) \to \mathbb{P}(State))
\end{aligned}
\tag{9}
$$

We do the same for the output transitions, the initial state, and the final states. The output transitions depend both on the input transitions and on the input states, thus we duplicate the input state collections on the left of the arrow for the second sub-signature. The resulting initial state is composed of the input initial states, see the third sub-signature in Formula (9). The same holds for the collection of final states, see the fourth sub-signature in Formula (9).

Deriving Signatures of the Constituent Mappings. Each sub-signature, underlying the signature obtained in the previous step, captures a correspondence between source and target objects. We decompose the mapping *MultiplyTwoSTMs* into invocations of the constituent mappings according to these correspondences. This means that, as a first approximation, each sub-signature of signature (9) corresponds to an invocation of a constituent mapping.

To derive signatures of the constituent mappings, we consider each sub-signature separately. The first sub-signature of Formula (9) is

$$
\mathbb{P}(State) \times \mathbb{P}(State) \to \mathbb{P}(State)
\tag{10}
$$

In QVTo a $\mathbb{P}$-symbol that appears evenly on both sides of an arrow corresponds to the invocation of a mapping on an input collection and assigning the result of this mapping to an output collection. If the mapping operates on elements of the collections rather than on the collections, then we can reduce the corresponding collection symbols $\mathbb{P}$ that appear evenly on both sides of an arrow. Mathematically, such a reduction of $\mathbb{P}$-symbols corresponds to an *inverse of function lifting*. After applying this technique to signature (10), we derive the following underlying signature:

$$MultiplyTwoStates : State \times State \rightarrow State \qquad (11)$$

The resulting mapping *MultiplyTwoStates* constructs a state of the target state machine as a pair of states from the two source machines. The initial and final states are constructed in the same way. Thus, the signature of *MultiplyTwoStates* can be derived from the first, third, and fourth sub-signatures of formula (9).

Using our knowledge of what the transformation should do, we can further refine the sub-signature from the second line of Formula (9). Each output transition is a copy of an input transition duplicated as many times as its *source* and *target* states have been duplicated to construct the output states. As each state of an input machine is paired with all states of the other input machine, we conclude that each transition of an input machine is paired with all states of the other input machine. This knowledge is captured by regrouping the corresponding collections in the second line of formula (9):

$$(\mathbb{P}(Transition) \times \mathbb{P}(State)) \times (\mathbb{P}(Transition) \times \mathbb{P}(State)) \rightarrow \mathbb{P}(Transition) \quad (12)$$

The described pairing of transitions with states is applied symmetrically to both input machines. The target collection of transitions is constructed as the *union* of the two resulting collections. Therefore, we reduce signature (12) to the following underlying signature:

$$\mathbb{P}(Transition) \times \mathbb{P}(State) \rightarrow \mathbb{P}(Transition) \qquad (13)$$

Observing that we can once more use a reverse function lifting, we finally arrive at the following signature for a constituent mapping:

$$MultiplyTransByState : Transition \times State \rightarrow Transition. \qquad (14)$$

Describing the Implementation of a Mapping. Function signature (9) helps to identify signatures of the mappings that compose the *MultiplyTwoSTMs* mapping, but it does not capture how this composition is implemented. Therefore, as a final step of the design procedure, we describe the implementation of the *MultiplyTwoSTMs* mapping in a formula using the notation we introduced in Sect. 3.2. Such formula should capture our knowledge of the transformation functionality discussed above using invocations of the constituent mappings *MultiplyTwoStates* and *MultiplyTransByState*.

$$MultiplyTwoSTMs(m1, m2):$$

$$states = \bigcup_{s1 \in m1.states} \bigcup_{s2 \in m2.states} \{MultState(s1, s2)\},$$

$$transitions = \bigcup_{t \in m1.transitions} \bigcup_{s \in m2.states} \{MultTrans(t, s)\} \cup$$
$$\bigcup_{t \in m2.transitions} \bigcup_{s \in m1.states} \{MultTrans(t, s)\}, \tag{15}$$

$$initial = MultState(m1.initial, m2.initial),$$

$$final = \bigcup_{f1 \in m1.final} \bigcup_{f2 \in m2.final} \{MultState(f1, f2)\}$$

After we have come up with the design of the mapping and captured it in a formula, we *write the QVTo code according to this formula*. Listing 1.3 corresponds to formula (15).

```
1  mapping Tuple(stm1: StateMachine, stm2: StateMachine)
2            :: MultiplyTwoSTMs()  : StateMachine
3  {
4    result.states := stm1.states -> collect(s1 |
5                     stm2.states -> collect(s2 |
6               Tuple{st1=s1, st2=s2}.map MultiplyTwoStates()));
7
8    result.transitions := stm1.transitions -> collect(t |
9                     stm2.states -> collect(s |
10                      t.map MultiplyTransByState(s)) )
11              -> union (
12                     stm2.transitions -> collect(t |
13                     stm1.states -> collect(s |
14                      t.map MultiplyTransByState(s))) );
15
16   result.initial := Tuple{st1=stm1.initial, st2=stm2.initial}.
17                            map MultiplyTwoStates();
18   result.final := stm1.final -> collect( f1 |
19                   stm2.final -> collect( f2 |
20             Tuple{st1=f1, st2=f2}.map MultiplyTwoStates()));
21  }
22
23  mapping Tuple(st1: State, st2: State) :: MultiplyTwoStates()
24                            : State
25  { ... }
26
27  mapping Transition :: MultiplyTransByState(in state: State)
28                  : Transition
29  { ... }
```

Listing 1.3. QVTo code of the *MultiplyTwoSTMs* transformation.

In this section, we derived the structured design of a mapping by gradual refinement of our knowledge about the mapping implementation. The same procedure can be applied recursively for designing the constituent mappings *MultiplyTwoStates* and *MultiplyTransByState*.

4.2   Chaining Model Transformations

In the previous section we discussed how a model transformation can be decomposed into constituent mappings by following the structure of the target model(s) and matching it with the corresponding elements of the source model(s). However, this principle is difficult to apply if source and target models have very different structures; for example, if mappings that match source and target elements are scattered over the metamodels structures, or if there are mutual dependencies between constructed objects. This type of situation is described in the literature as *structure clash* [12], or *semantic gap* [16]. Such design difficulty is usually solved using a *chain of model transformations*. One or more intermediate structures (or metamodels) are introduced to split a model transformation into two or more steps (links of the chain). In this way, a structure clash is managed in a chain of separate model transformations each of which with a minimal clash.

Using our notation this design principle can be explained as follows. Consider a model transformation $f : A \to B$, where the gap between structures A and B is too wide to manage in a one-step transformation. Therefore, we split this model transformation by introducing an intermediate structure C that mediates between A and B. We develop two model transformations $f_1 : A \to C$ and $f_2 : C \to B$. Then we connect those into a chain using *function composition*: $f(m) = f_2(f_1(m))$. A function composition can be denoted in a more 'chain-like' style using the 'o' operator, allowing us to write $f(m) = (f_1 \circ f_2)(m)$. We prefer to use the latter notation, as it is more readable when we have more than two steps in a transformation chain. Function composition cannot always be applied immediately. For instance, if the result of a function application is of a form that is different from the form that is accepted by the next function, then the function composition fails. An indispensable tool in many such cases is to use *currying*. Currying basically entails the translation of a function of the form $f : A \times B \to C$ to a function of the form $g : A \to (B \to C)$, by setting $g(a)(b) = f(a,b)$.

Below, we illustrate through an example transformation how the concepts of function composition and currying can be used to design a transformation chain. The example transformation *flattens* a UML state machine (specified by the metamodel in Fig. 1) by removing its composite states and replacing them with equivalent sets of simple states and transitions. The mapping that performs such replacement can be described by the following signature:

$$SimplifyComposite : CompositeState \to \mathbb{P}(State) \times \mathbb{P}(Transition) \qquad (16)$$

According to our metamodel in Fig. 1, each composite state can be either sequential or orthogonal. A sequential composite state contains only one submachine, while an orthogonal (or parallel) composite state contains more than one submachine. Intuitively, when transforming a sequential state, we can simply substitute its submachine into the parent machine by 'erasing' borders of the submachine and redirecting and adding the necessary transitions. When transforming an orthogonal state, we need to consider its parallel nature and express it in terms of simple states. In other words, we first need to transform parallel submachines into one sequential submachine. After this we can apply the same transformation as for a sequential state. This is a simple example of a transformation chain that constitutes the mapping (16). The transformation chain will therefore consist of two mappings: *Orthogonal2Sequential* and *SubstituteMachine*. The first mapping transforms a collection of parallel state machines into one state machine and can thus be described as follows:

$$Orthogonal2Sequential : \mathbb{P}(StateMachine) \rightarrow StateMachine \qquad (17)$$

The second mapping substitutes a nested state machine into the parent state machine. When substituting a nested machine from a composite state we need to update two sets of transitions: those that have the composite state as a *target*, and those that have the composite state as a *source*. The former should be redirected to the initial substate of the composite state; the latter should be exiting from all substates of the composite state. Therefore, we consider these sets of transitions as an input of the mapping. As an output, the mapping thus creates a set of new states and a set of new and updated transitions:

$$SubstituteMachine : \mathbb{P}(Transition) \times \mathbb{P}(Transition) \times StateMachine \rightarrow$$
$$\mathbb{P}(State) \times \mathbb{P}(Transition) \qquad (18)$$

Observe that the output of the *Orthogonal2Sequential* mapping does not directly match with the input of the *SubstituteMachine* mapping. Therefore, we cannot connect these two mappings using a function composition. To overcome this problem, we apply currying: we rewrite Function (18), which takes a tuple of inputs, as a sequence of functions, each of which takes a single input. Put simply, we replace the Cartesian products on the left of the arrow with a sequence of arrows to obtain the following:

$$SubstituteMachine : \mathbb{P}(Transition) \rightarrow \mathbb{P}(Transition) \rightarrow StateMachine \rightarrow$$
$$\mathbb{P}(State) \times \mathbb{P}(Transition) \qquad (19)$$

When calculating such function, we calculate each of the functions in the sequence separately and as a result of each separate calculation we get a new function. For example, if we calculate Function (18) for a tuple (x, y, z), we start from the first function in the sequence (19) and apply it for the first argument of the tuple. As a result we get a new function:

$$SubstituteMachine(x) : \mathbb{P}(Transition) \rightarrow StateMachine \rightarrow$$
$$\mathbb{P}(State) \times \mathbb{P}(Transition) \qquad (20)$$

Then we do the same for function (20) and the rest of the tuple (y, z). As a result we get a new function:

$$SubstituteMachine(x, y) : StateMachine \rightarrow \mathbb{P}(State) \times \mathbb{P}(Transition) \qquad (21)$$

```
1  helper CompositeState :: SimplifyComposite()
2              : states: Set (State), transitions: Set(Transition)
3  {
4    return self.submachine -> map Orthogonal2Sequential().
5           map SubstituteMachine(self._in, self._out);
6  }
```

Listing 1.4. QVTo code of the *SimplifyOrthogonal* transformation.

Note that input of function (21) matches with the output of function (17). Therefore, we can apply function composition to these two functions. The resulting definition of the *SimplifyComposite* mapping connects the mapping *SubstituteMachine* (with two fixed inputs) and the mapping *Orthogonal2Sequential* into a transformation chain:

$$SimplifyComposite(state) = (Orthogonal2Sequential(state.submachine)$$
$$\circ SubstituteMachine(state.in, state.out)) \quad (22)$$

Formula (22) demonstrates how the notation of function composition can enhance the description of a model transformation chain and the flow of information through the separate steps of this chain. The corresponding QVTo code is depicted in Listing 1.4.

5 Discussion and Validation

In the previous section, we demonstrated how the mathematical notation of set theory can be used to describe QVTo mappings, their signatures and implementations, to derive organizational structure of mappings, and to describe the information flow in chains of model transformations. While the proposed approach requires further investigation and experiments, we have applied it to a large practical example, and we performed an early evaluation of its potential by consulting with QVTo practitioners through interviews.

Applications. The proposed approach for describing and designing model transformations was formulated while developing, documenting, and refactoring a model transformation that implements the semantics of a high-level metalanguage. According to the taxonomy proposed in [17], this model transformation can be classified as an exogenous vertical semantical transformation with multiple source and target models; and it can be characterized as a fully automated and complex (about 40 mappings and one thousand lines of code). This means that the transformation is objectively sophisticated, which corresponds to our subjective experience. The proposed approach helped us in streamlining the development of this transformation.

Applying the proposed approach, we found that:

– the described design principles can assist in the creative process of designing model transformations;

- designing a model transformation in the form of formulas prior to coding it in QVTo improves readability and understandability of the resulting code;
- describing a model transformation using the proposed notation facilitates explaining its meaning to peers.

Interviews. We conducted *three interviews* with developers from three different affiliations and different engineering domains. The interviews were based on 25 open questions aiming to (1) assess an interviewee's experience of developing and maintaining QVTo transformations, (2) gauge his understanding of the employed mathematical notation, and (3) get the interviewee's feedback on the usability and usefulness of the proposed approach. The interviewees used QVTo in the following situations:

1. developing large-scale software systems for further industrial usage in a team of software developers that also continues to maintain and extend the QVTo source code;
2. prototyping software architectures for further delegation of found solutions to software developers, without need for documentation and long-term maintenance of the QVTo code;
3. developing a domain specific language for conducting research in the field of electrical engineering by an engineer without computer science expertise.

In the first situation, the developers find the maintenance and documentation of their model transformations especially challenging and experience a lack of notation for this. The developers believe that the proposed notation can be used for these purposes. In the second situation, the architect does not see the need for notation for describing his transformations and, moreover, presumes that the proposed design guidelines might restrict his experiments. Thus, we conclude that our proposed approach may not be suited for situations such as this one. In the third situation, the (non-software) engineer finds it especially important to discover the pragmatics of QVTo and to have guidelines on how to design a model transformation. He believes that the proposed decomposition principle and the corresponding design process can be very useful. Furthermore, all interviewees find the description of QVTo mappings in the form of formulas clear and understandable. This includes the engineer with no computer science expertise.

Discussion. In addition to these results, we conclude that for the successful application of the proposed notation the following questions require further investigation:

- does the proposed notation restrict the resulting design of a model transformation;
- what are the limits of the proposed notation, whether all essential situations and QVTo constructs can be naturally described using mathematical concepts;[5]

---

[5] For instance, there is no mathematical operator that naturally matches the QVTo concept of inheritance of mappings.

– how scalable is the proposed approach, how much effort it might require in general to apply the proposed notation for describing and designing a complete complex transformation.

Several aspects of our proposed approach are indirectly supported by the results of the exploratory study performed by Gerpheide et al. [15] for constructing a QVTo quality model. In this work they formalize a quality model for QVTo based on the interviews with four QVTo experts. According to their results, understandability and maintainability are the most ubiquitous quality goals for QVTo experts. Moreover, among the best practices that address these goals are (1) the preference for a declarative style of programming over an imperative style (for example, avoiding loop-statements); and (2) structuring a transformation along the hierarchy of either the input or output metamodel. According to our experience, both these best practices can result from using the notation and the design principles described above in this paper. This indicates that the proposed approach can contribute to improving the quality of QVTo code with respect to the understandability and maintainability.

6   Conclusion and Future Work

According to Kurtev [18], the current QVT standard lacks a formal basis, which causes risks when using model transformations. These risks are amplified by the current lack of documentation on the QVT execution semantics and pragmatics.

   In this paper we showed how the mathematical notation of set theory and functions can be used to explain QVTo concepts, to facilitate the design process of model transformations, and to document model transformations. The resulting formulas give an overview of the organizational structure and the information flow of a transformation in an unambiguous and concise way. To assess the applicability of this approach, we applied it when designing, developing, and refactoring two model transformations[6]; one of these transformations was a non-elementary transformation bridging a wide semantic gap and involved complex structures. Moreover, we performed interviews with QVTo practitioners. While the results of these experiments and interviews are positive, the approach requires further investigation and experiments. In addition to the research questions listed in Sect. 5, we aim to examine if the proposed approach is language independent and can be used for developing in other model transformation languages, *e.g.* ATL.

Acknowledgements. We are very grateful to the QVTo experts who agreed to access our approach and provided us with very useful insights in its potential benefits and flaws. We also would like to thank Tom Verhoeff and Mark van den Brand (Eindhoven University of Technology, The Netherlands) for their useful comments on this work.

---

[6] The source code and the description of the transformation used as an example in this paper are available online at http://code.google.com/p/qvto-flatten-stm/.

References

1. OMG: Meta Object Facility (MOF) 2.0 Query/View/Transformation Specification (2015). Version 1.2
2. Guerra, E., de Lara, J., Kolovos, D., Paige, R., dos Santos, O.: Engineering model transformations with transML. Softw. Syst. Model. **12**, 555–577 (2013)
3. Visser, E.: Program transformation with Stratego/XT: Rules, strategies, tools, and systems. In: Lengauer, C., Batory, D., Blum, A., Odersky, M. (eds.) Domain-Specific Program Generation. LNCS, vol. 3016, pp. 216–238. Springer, Heidelberg (2004)
4. Etien, A., Dumoulin, C., Renaux, E.: Towards a Unified Notation to Represent Model Transformation. Research Report 6187, INRIA (2007)
5. Rahim, L.A., Mansoor, S.B.R.S: Proposed design notation for model transformation. In: ASWEC, pp. 589–598. IEEE Computer Society (2008)
6. Kalnins, A., Barzdins, J., Celms, E.: Model transformation language MOLA. In: Aßmann, U., Akşit, M., Rensink, A. (eds.) MDAFA 2003. LNCS, vol. 3599, pp. 62–76. Springer, Heidelberg (2005)
7. Idani, A., Ledru, Y., Anwar, A.: A rigorous reasoning about model transformations using the B method. In: Nurcan, S., Proper, H.A., Soffer, P., Krogstie, J., Schmidt, R., Halpin, T., Bider, I. (eds.) BPMDS 2013 and EMMSAD 2013. LNBIP, vol. 147, pp. 426–440. Springer, Heidelberg (2013)
8. Lano, K., Rahimi, S.K.: Model-transformation design patterns. IEEE Trans. Softw. Eng. **40**, 1224–1259 (2014)
9. Kolahdouz-Rahimi, S., Lano, K.: A model-based development approach for model transformations. In: Arbab, F., Sirjani, M. (eds.) FSEN 2011. LNCS, vol. 7141, pp. 48–63. Springer, Heidelberg (2012)
10. Lano, K.: Model transformation design pattern catalogue. http://www.dcs.kcl.ac.uk/staff/kcl/mtdp. Accessed August 2015
11. Jackson, M.: Designing and coding program structures. In: Stevenson, H.P. (ed.) Proceedings of a Codasyl Programming Language Committee Symposium on Structured Programming in COBOL Future and Present, pp. 22–53 (1975)
12. Jackson, M.: JSP in perspective. In: Broy, M., Denert, E. (eds.) Software Pioneers, pp. 480–493. Springer, Heidelberg (2002)
13. Snook, C., Butler, M.: UML-B: formal modeling and design aided by UML. ACM Trans. Softw. Eng. Methodol. **15**, 92–122 (2006)
14. Czarnecki, K., Helsen, S.: Feature-based survey of model transformation approaches. IBM Syst. J. **45**, 621–645 (2006)
15. Gerpheide, C.M., Schiffelers, R.R.H., Serebrenik, A.: A Bottom-Up quality model for QVTo. In: QUATIC, pp. 85–94. IEEE (2014)
16. van Amstel, M.F., van den Brand, M.G.J., Protić, Z., Verhoeff, T.: Transforming process algebra models into UML state machines: bridging a semantic gap? In: Vallecillo, A., Gray, J., Pierantonio, A. (eds.) ICMT 2008. LNCS, vol. 5063, pp. 61–75. Springer, Heidelberg (2008)
17. Mens, T., Gorp, P.V.: A taxonomy of model transformation. Electr. Notes Theor. Comput. Sci. **152**, 125–142 (2006)
18. Kurtev, I.: State of the art of QVT: a model transformation language standard. In: Schürr, A., Nagl, M., Zündorf, A. (eds.) AGTIVE 2007. LNCS, vol. 5088, pp. 377–393. Springer, Heidelberg (2008)

An Approach for the Automatic Adaptation of Domain-Specific Modeling Languages for Model-Driven Mobile Application Development

Xiaoping Jia and Christopher Jones[✉]

School of Computing, DePaul University, Chicago, IL, USA
{xjia,cjones}@cdm.depaul.edu

Abstract. The use of domain-specific modeling languages (DSMLs) is a common approach to support cross-platform development of mobile applications. However, most DSML-based approaches suffer from a number of limitations such as poor performance. Furthermore, DSMLs that are written *ab initio* are not able to access the entire range of capabilities supported by the native mobile platforms. This paper presents a novel approach of using an adaptive domain-specific modeling language (ADSML) to support the model-driven development of cross-platform mobile applications emphasizing the Android and iOS platforms. We will discuss the techniques in the design of an ADSML including meta-model extraction, meta-model elevation, and meta-model alignment. We discuss how these techniques can be incorporated into an automated process where a common, platform-independent DSML is dynamically synthesized from the native APIs of multiple target mobile platforms. Our approach is capable of generating high performance native applications; is able to access the full capabilities of the target native platforms; and is adaptable to the rapid evolutions of those platforms.

Keywords: Model-driven development · Domain-specific modeling languages · Cross-platform development · Mobile application development

1 Introduction

Mobile applications are popular and are becoming increasingly sophisticated. In addition to some unique constraints and requirements, such as high responsiveness, limited memory, and low energy consumption, mobile application development faces particular challenges with a short time-to-market, rapid evolution of technologies, and competing platforms. Currently, there are several competing mobile platforms on the market, including Google's Android and Apple's iOS, which are similar in capabilities, but drastically different in their programming languages and APIs. It is highly desirable and often necessary for a mobile application to run on all major mobile platforms. However, it is very expensive to port mobile applications from one platform to another.

P. Lorenz et al. (Eds.): ICSOFT 2015, CCIS 586, pp. 365–379, 2016.
DOI: 10.1007/978-3-319-30142-6_20

One approach for supporting *cross-platform* mobile application development is to use programming languages and virtual machines that are available on different platforms, such as HTML5 and JavaScript [1,2]. While this approach is adequate for certain types of applications, it is less than satisfactory with some serious shortcomings, including slower response times when compared to equivalent native applications [7,8]. This approach also suffers from significant limitations, such as being able to use only a small subset of the features supported by the underlying platforms. Canappi [6] uses a *domain-specific language* (DSL) to define and generate cross-platform mobile applications as front-ends to web services, but does not define the web services themselves. Other DSL-based approaches include Mobl [11] and md^2 [12].

A promising approach that may offer some solutions to the challenges of mobile application development is *model-driven development* (MDD) [27], and the use of *domain-specific modeling languages* (DSMLs) to represent the platform-independent models (PIM) [17,18]. While DSMLs can concisely represent the model entities of various target platforms, they often adopt the *least-common denominator* approach to be able to model applications in a platform-independent manner, and then transform the models into implementations on different mobile platforms. One limitation of this approach is that harnessing the full capabilities of the target platform would either lead to language "bloat", or render the language platform-specific. Consequently, DSMLs that are designed *ab initio* are not capable of harnessing the full power of the native APIs for the underlying platforms. Currently, there is no satisfactory solution to developing cross-platform mobile applications that is capable of both delivering high performance and providing full access to the API features supported by the underlying platforms.

In this paper, we present a novel approach of designing *adaptive domain-specific modeling languages* (ADSML) to support model-driven development of cross-platform mobile applications. We will discuss the techniques in the design of an ADSML for developing mobile applications targeting the Android and iOS platforms, including meta-model extraction, meta-model elevation, meta-model alignment, and meta-model unification. Our approach will be able to address the following challenges in cross-platform development of mobile applications: (a) generating high performance native applications; (b) accessing the full capabilities of the native APIs of the underlying platforms; and (c) adapting to rapid evolutions of the target platforms.

2   DSML-Based MDD

The AXIOM project [14–16] has successfully demonstrated the feasibility and effectiveness of using a DSML to support model-driven development of mobile applications. An internal DSML, hosted in Groovy, is used to represent mobile applications in the form of *abstract model trees* (AMTs). As shown in Fig. 1, a model represented as an AMT is passed through a series of transformations, resulting in new AMTs and ultimately in native Android and iOS code. Preliminary experiments have shown significantly reduced source code size, along with

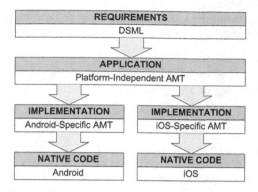

Fig. 1. AXIOM model transformations.

improved developer productivity, with the quality of the generated native code being comparable to handwritten native code produced by experienced mobile application developers.

The AXIOM DSML supports capabilities that are common across our target platforms as well as platform-specific capabilities when required. However, the mappings of the DSML elements to the native platforms is static and not easily adaptable. It requires changes to the DSML itself when there are changes to the underlying native API. Similarly, extending the AXIOM DSL to a new platform, such as the Windows Mobile OS, requires significant effort to align the DSML to the new native platform. The maintenance of such a DSML requires familiarity not only with the underlying native mobile platforms, but also the ability to synthesize a common representation across all of them, maintaining the appropriate semantics in the face of different development models. Wernik, et al. summarized these challenges when they wrote "DSL development is hard, requiring both domain and language development expertise. Few people have both." [21]

The creation of a DSML for mobile platforms would be more effective if it could evolve and adapt, automatically incorporating new elements of its target platforms and APIs. This is the motivation for an *adaptive domain-specific modeling language (ADSML)*.

3   Adaptive DSML

A *domain-specific modeling language* is a domain-specific language (DSL) designed to represent platform-independent models (PIM) for model-driven development (MDD).

3.1   Meta-Models and Mappings

The definition and design of a DSML is based on a *meta-model*. We introduce the following definitions.

Definition 1. *A* meta-model, *MM, is formally defined as* (C, R), *where C is the set of* classes *in the* meta-model, *and R is the set of relations among the classes.*

Each class contains a set of attributes and methods. We use $Att(C)$, and $Mtd(C)$ to denote the set of all attributes and methods of classes in C, respectively:

$$Att(C) = \{c.a \mid c \in C, a \text{ is an attribute of } c\}$$
$$Mtd(C) = \{c.m \mid c \in C, m \text{ is a method of } c\}$$

A *model entity* in a meta-model refers to any entity contained in the meta-model, which can be a class, an attribute, or a method. We use $E(MM)$ to denote the set of model entities in meta-model MM, that is:

$$E(MM) = C \cup Att(C) \cup Mtd(C)$$

We use MM^* to denote a platform-independent meta-model, and use MM_a to denote the platform-specific meta-model for platform a. For example, to support cross-platform development of mobile applications on Android and iOS, we will deal with platform-specific meta-models, MM_{Android} and MM_{iOS}, and platform-independent meta-model MM^*.

Definition 2. *A* simple mapping, $\Phi[MM_a, MM_b]$, *from meta-model $MM_a = (C_a, R_a)$ to another meta-model $MM_b = (C_b, R_b)$ is a function from $E(MM_a)$ to $E(MM_b)$, i.e., every model element in MM_a is mapped to a unique model element in MM_b.*

At the class level, $\Phi[MM_a, MM_b]$ is a function from C_a to C_b, that is, every class in C_a is mapped to a unique class in C_b.

$\Phi[MM_a, MM_b]$ *is the union of the following three disjoint functions:*

- $\Phi_{\text{cla}}[MM_a, MM_b]$ *is a function from C_a to C_b;*
- $\Phi_{\text{att}}[MM_a, MM_b]$ *is a function from* $\text{Att}(C_a)$ *to* $\text{Att}(C_b)$, $(c_1.a_1, c_2.a_2) \in \Phi_{\text{att}}[MM_a, MM_b]$ *implies* $(c_1, c_2) \in \Phi_{\text{cla}}[MM_a, MM_b]$;
- $\Phi_{\text{mtd}}[MM_a, MM_b]$ *is a function from* $\text{Mtd}(C_a)$ *to* $\text{Mtd}(C_b)$, $(c_1.m_1, c_2.m_2) \in \Phi_{\text{mtd}}[MM_a, MM_b]$ *implies* $(c_1, c_2) \in \Phi_{\text{cla}}[MM_a, MM_b]$.

We can also define *complex mappings*, where some classes in C_a are mapped to auxiliary classes that need to be added to the native platform.

A platform-independent meta-model, MM^*, supports both Android and iOS if there exist two mappings, Φ_{Android} and Φ_{iOS}, that map MM^* to MM_{Android} and MM_{iOS}, respectively. A DSML for representing PIMs of mobile applications can be designed based on the meta-model MM^*. We call a DSML designed based on a fixed meta-model and fixed mappings a *static* DSML.

Figure 2 shows examples of platform-specific meta-models for mobile platforms iOS and Android, MM_{iOS} and MM_{Android}. Figure 3 shows a platform-independent meta-model MM^* that supports both Android and iOS. The corresponding mappings to each platform are as follows:

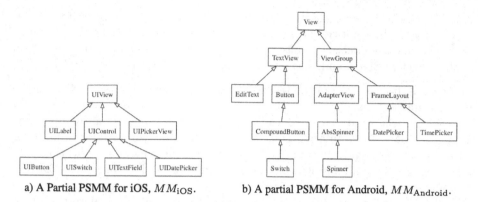

a) A Partial PSMM for iOS, MM_{iOS}.   b) A partial PSMM for Android, $MM_{Android}$.

Fig. 2. Platform-specific meta-models for iOS and Android.

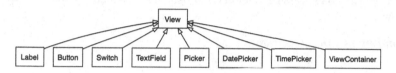

Fig. 3. A platform-independent meta-model for MM_{iOS} and $MM_{Android}$.

$$\Phi_{iOS} = \Phi[MM^*, MM_{iOS}] = \{ \text{ View} \mapsto \text{UIView, ViewContainer} \mapsto \text{UIView,}$$
$$\text{Label} \mapsto \text{UILabel, Button} \mapsto \text{UIButton, Switch} \mapsto \text{UISwitch,}$$
$$\text{TextField} \mapsto \text{UITextField, Picker} \mapsto \text{UIPickerView, DatePicker} \mapsto \text{UIDatePicker,}$$
$$\text{TimePicker} \mapsto \text{UIDatePicker, } \}$$

$$\Phi_{Android} = \Phi[MM^*, MM_{Android}] = \{ \text{ View} \mapsto \text{View, ViewContainer} \mapsto \text{ViewGroup,}$$
$$\text{Label} \mapsto \text{TextView, Button} \mapsto \text{Button, Switch} \mapsto \text{Switch,}$$
$$\text{TextField} \mapsto \text{EditText, Picker} \mapsto \text{Spinner, DatePicker} \mapsto \text{DatePicker,}$$
$$\text{TimePicker} \mapsto \text{TimePicker, } \}.$$

3.2   Characteristics of Adaptive DSML

We propose the concept of *adaptive DSMLs*, which possess the following characteristics:

- The platform-independent meta-model on which the DSML is based is adaptive and is not defined *ab initio*. The platform-independent meta-model is constructed automatically from the native platform-specific meta-models, so that it can evolve over time to accommodate changes in the native platforms.
- As the native platforms change and evolve, the mappings from the platform-independent to platform-specific meta-models are constructed automatically. The transformation and code generation tools are also adaptive to automatically accommodate the changes.

– While the basic syntactic structure of an adaptive DSML is fixed, its vocabulary may include entities in the platform-independent as well as the platform-specific meta-models. The interpretation of the vocabulary is dependent on the target platform and the current mappings among the meta-models.

We will discuss some of the techniques to implement adaptive DSML in the next several sections.

Due to the adaptive nature of the language, it is more practical to implement adaptive DSML as an internal DSL in a host language with strong support for DSL. In our prototype, the adaptive DSML for modeling mobile applications and targeting the Android and iOS platforms is implemented as an internal DSL of Groovy. Its basic syntactic rules are defined by the host language. Our adaptive DSML uses the Groovy Builder pattern to construct the object hierarchies that represent models of mobile applications. The Builder pattern offers a simple and intuitive syntax to express the model compositions. Each component is expressed as follows:

ComponentName (attributes ...) {
  ... nested child components ...
}

The components can be nested to form a hierarchy, with the root component representing the application. The allowable component names are the names of the classes in the platform-independent meta-model, MM^*, as well as the names of the classes in the platform-specific meta-models, MM_{Android} and MM_{iOS}. In other words the component names supported by the adaptive DSML can evolve over the time.

3.3 Meta-Model Evolution

A *meta-model evolution* is triggered when the API of one or more of the native platforms have been updated, such as changes or new releases of the API. The meta-model evolution process involves:

– Meta-model extraction (Sect. 4),
– Meta-model elevation (Sect. 5), and
– Meta-model alignment (Sect. 6).

Meta-model evolution constructs an updated and unified platform-independent meta-model, MM^*, and a set of updated transformation rules to transform models in MM^* to each of the platform-specific meta-models, e.g., MM_{Android} or MM_{iOS}. The updated MM^* will become the new basis of the adaptive DSML.

As shown in Fig. 4, the evolution process begins with one or more native APIs for their associated target mobile platforms. Through the processes of meta-model extraction and meta-model elevation, platform-specific meta-models, MM_A and MM_B, are generated, which can then be used as the basis for the corresponding platform-specific ADSMLs, $ADSML_A$ and $ADSML_B$. At the end

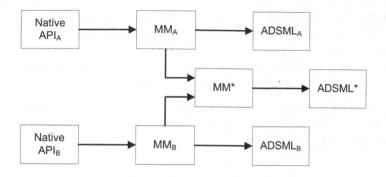

Fig. 4. AXIOM meta-model evolution.

of the meta-model alignment process, we have a derived platform-independent meta-model, MM^*, that unifies all of the original native APIs in such a way that they can be represented using a single, platform-independent DSML, $ADSML^*$.

4   Meta-Model Extraction

Meta-model Extraction is a process that extracts platform-specific meta-models from the native API of the target platforms. The primary source of input for meta-model extraction is the API documentation of the native platform in HTML. We extract the following information for each class:

- The name, inheritance, subtype, and use relation.
- The textual description of the class (in English).
- For each attribute of the class, the name, type, and textual description.
- For each method of the class, the name, signature, and textual description of the method and each parameter.

The initial platform-specific meta-model extracted from the native API of platform a is denoted as MM_a^0, which is a complete and accurate representation of the native API, and serves as the starting point of the subsequent model elevation and model alignment.

For programming languages that support reflection, part of the information can also be extracted from the binary code of the libraries. However, all information obtainable from the binaries that is useful in our analysis should also be obtainable from the API documentation. The textual descriptions and some other useful information are not available in the binaries. Hence, we choose not to use the binaries as the sources of meta-model extraction.

5   Meta-Model Elevation

Meta-model Elevation simplifies and elevates the level of abstraction of platform-specific meta-models. Meta-model elevation is carried out through the following operations on the meta-model:

1. Visibility analysis: to determine the *public* portion of the native APIs;
2. Tagging key architectural elements: to identify the key elements of the meta-models;
3. Pattern-based transformation: to simplify the meta-models through a series of semantics preserving transformations of the meta-models.

The result of meta-model elevation is a set of elevated platform-specific meta-models for each native platform. For native platform a, the elevated meta-model is denoted as MM_a^1.

5.1 Visibility Analysis

The API of a native platform typically consists of two parts: the *public* part, which is intended to be used directly by developers; and the *protected* part, which is intended for customizing and extending the native API. We will limit our DSML to support the *public* API only. It is more sensible to customize and extend the native API using the native languages supported by the platform. The additional classes for the customized or extended API can be incorporated in the DSML as auxiliary classes.

We define a set of rules to identify the classes, attributes, and methods that are intended solely for the purpose of customizing and extending the native API. These entities will be removed from the meta-model.

5.2 Tagging Key Architectural Elements

Tagging is the process of attaching tags, which are simple keywords or strings, as meta-data to model entities in a meta-model. Tagging associates model entities with key concepts in the domain. A model entity may be tagged with multiple tags.

In a given domain, there are usually a number of *key architectural elements* (KAE) that are typically present and play important roles in every application in the given domain. For example, in the domain of user interfaces (UI) of mobile applications, we can identify the following key architectural elements:

- *View:* a self-contained unit of UI, e.g., a single screen, a popup, etc. Typically contains a hierarchy of view objects.
- *Transition:* a connection between two views, the source, and the destination of the transition. It is also commonly associated with a trigger event.
- *Action:* code to be executed in response to certain event. It can also be associated with a source object that triggers the event, or a transition.

One or more tags can be associated with a key architectural element to indicate its potentially different roles and subtypes. We define a set of rules to determine whether a model entity is tagged as being associated with a key architecture element.

5.3   Pattern-Based Transformation

We start by identifying common design patterns and idioms. When a pattern is recognized, it is replaced with a more concise but equivalent representation. Some of the patterns and idioms being considered are:

- *The property pattern.* APIs often define the getter and setter methods associated with a *property* following a number of well-established naming conventions. When such a pattern is recognized, the getter and setter method can be replaced with the associated property.
- *The enumeration pattern.* APIs of mobile platforms often use integers rather than enumerations for the sake of better performance. However, enumerations are often safer and easier to use. When such a pattern is recognized, we replace the integers with enumerated types.
- *The callback pattern.* APIs often contains methods or listener (observer) objects that are designed to provide callbacks, i.e., actions or code blocks, in response to various types of events.
- *The delegation pattern.* APIs often include methods that are delegated to one of its members.

For each of the transformations of the meta-model, we also introduce code generation rules that reverse the transformation at code generation time.

6   Meta-Model Alignment

Meta-model Alignment establishes *alignment relations* among the entities in different platform-specific meta-models. Entities in different meta-models are considered *aligned* if the entities are considered to have the similar functions or behaviors, or play a similar role in their respective platform.

Definition 3. *Given two platform-specific meta-models $MM_a = (C_a, R_a)$ and $MM_b = (C_b, R_b)$, an alignment relation among the meta-models, denoted as $\Xi[MM_a, MM_b]$, is a relation that contains all the pairs of aligned entities (e_1, e_2), where $e_1 \in E(MM_a)$, and $e_2 \in E(MM_b)$. At the class level, $\Xi[MM_a, MM_b]$ is the relation of aligned classes, between C_a and C_b.*

$\Xi[MM_a, MM_b]$ is the union of the following three disjoint relations:

- *$\Xi_{cla}[MM_a, MM_b]$ is a relation between C_a and C_b, i.e., the relation of aligned classes;*
- *$\Xi_{att}[MM_a, MM_b]$ is a relation between $\text{Att}(C_a)$ and $\text{Att}(C_b)$, i.e., the relation of aligned attributes, $(c_1.a_1, c_2.a_2) \in \Xi_{att}[MM_a, MM_b]$ implies $(c_1, c_2) \in \Xi_{cla}[MM_a, MM_b]$;*
- *$\Xi_{mtd}[MM_a, MM_b]$ is a relation between $\text{Mtd}(C_a)$ and $\text{Mtd}(C_b)$, i.e., the relation of aligned methods, $(c_1.m_1, c_2.m_2) \in \Xi_{mtd}[MM_a, MM_b]$ implies $(c_1, c_2) \in \Xi_{cla}[MM_a, MM_b]$.*

Meta-model alignment is carried out through the following steps:

1. Similarity analysis: to discover the similarities between the model entities in different platform-specific meta-models.
2. Entity alignment: to determine the alignment relation among the entities in different platform-specific meta-models.
3. Meta-model unification: to construct a platform-independent meta-model by unifying the aligned entities in the platform-specific meta-models.

6.1 Similarity Analysis

We first analyze the similarity among the classes in $MM_a = (C_a, R_a)$ and $MM_b = (C_b, R_b)$. For each pair of classes $c_1 \in C_a$ and $c_2 \in C_b$, we define a class similarity function $\theta_0(c_1, c_2) \in [0, 1]$. The similarity function is calculated based on the following factors:

– the tags of each class and the relation with other classes;
– the similarity of the attributes and methods belong to the respective classes;
– the similarity of the words in the class names;
– the similarity of the textual descriptions of the classes.

We will use the text analysis techniques developed in Natural Language Processing (NLP) research [23] to calculate the semantic similarity between words and textual descriptions.

We first establish a threshold T_0^- for two classes to be considered *possibly* similar. For each pair of classes c_1 and c_2 that $\theta_0(c_1, c_2) \geq T_0^-$, we perform further similarity analysis on the attributes and methods of the classes. For each pair of attributes $c_1.a_1$ and $c_2.a_2$, we define an attribute similarity function $\theta_1(c_1.a_1, c_2.a_2) \in [0, 1]$. For each pair of methods $c_1.m_1$ and $c_2.m_2$, we define a method similarity function $\theta_2(c_1.m_1, c_2.m_2) \in [0, 1]$. The attribute and method similarity functions are calculated using the following factors:

– the tags of each attribute or method and the respective types or signature;
– the similarity of the words in the attribute or method names;
– the similarity of the textual descriptions of the attribute or method.

6.2 Entity Alignment

Entity alignment is the key step in model alignment to compute the alignment relation $\Xi[MM_a, MM_b]$ among the model entities in MM_a and MM_b.

We start with a relation of *anchored alignments* $\Xi_0[MM_a, MM_b]$, which consists of pairs of aligned model entities that are manually identified and verified. The computed alignment relation must be a super set of the anchored alignment relation, i.e., $\Xi_0[MM_a, MM_b] \subseteq \Xi[MM_a, MM_b]$.

We then establish the alignment threshold T_0^+ for similarity functions θ_0, to compute the alignment relation:

– For a pair of classes $c_1 \in C_a$ and $c_2 \in C_b$, if $\theta_0(c_1, c_2) \geq T_0^+$, we consider classes c_1 and c_2 to be aligned.

- For a pair of attributes $c_1.a_1$ and $c_2.a_2$, if $\theta_1(c_1.a_1, c_2.a_2) \geq T_1^+$ and c_1 and c_2 are aligned, we consider attributes $c_1.a_1$ and $c_2.a_2$ to be aligned.
- For a pair of methods $c_1.m_1$ and $c_2.m_2$, if $\theta_2(c_1.m_1, c_2.m_2) \geq T_2^+$ and c_1 and c_2 are aligned, we consider methods $c_1.m_1$ and $c_2.m_2$ to be aligned.

For an alignment relation, we define the following metrics to measure its degree of success in aligning the meta-models:

- *Aligned class ratio:* the ratio of the classes that are aligned with some class over the total number of classes.

$$AC_a = \frac{|\mathrm{domain}(\varXi_{cla}[MM_a, MM_b])|}{|C_a|}$$

$$AC_b = \frac{|\mathrm{range}(\varXi_{cla}[MM_a, MM_b])|}{|C_b|}$$

- *One-to-one ratio:* the ratio of the number of one-to-one class alignment pairs over the total number of class alignment pairs.
- *Degree of alignments:* the maximum number of classes that are aligned with any class.

A successful alignment relation should satisfy the following requirements:

- The aligned class ratio for both meta-models should be sufficiently high;
- A majority of the alignments should be one-to-one, i.e., the one-to-one ratio should be near 100 %
- The degree of alignments should be fairly low, typically 3 or less.

We will also apply the techniques in ontology alignment [10, 26] in entity alignment.

6.3   Meta-Model Unification

A unified platform-independent meta-model, MM^*, can be derived from the platform-specific meta-models, MM_a and MM_b, as well as the alignment relation $\varXi[MM_a, MM_b]$. Meta-model unification produces two mappings: $\varPhi[MM^*, MM_a]$ and $\varPhi[MM^*, MM_b]$.

If we have a one-to-one alignment between classes c_1 and c_2, a unified class $U(c_1, c_2)$ is added to the unified meta-model, MM^*. The class, $U(c_1, c_2)$, can be referred to using the name of c_1 or c_2 or a new unique name. All these names are considered aliases. The mappings are updated as follows:

- $U(c_1, c_2) \mapsto c_1$ is added to $\varPhi[MM^*, MM_a]$
- $U(c_1, c_2) \mapsto c_2$ is added to $\varPhi[MM^*, MM_b]$

If we have a one-to-many alignment between class c_1 and classes $c_{2,1} \ldots c_{2,n}$, and none of $c_{2,1} \ldots c_{2,n}$ is aligned with any other class, n unified classes $U(c_1, c_{2,1}) \ldots U(c_1, c_{2,n})$ will be added to the unified meta-model, MM^*. The class $U(c_1, c_{2,i})$ can be referred to using the name of c_1 or $c_{2,i}$ or a new unique name. All these names are considered aliases. The mappings are updated as follows:

– $U(c_1, c_{2,1}) \mapsto c_1, \ldots, U(c_1, c_{2,n}) \mapsto c_1$ are added to $\Phi[MM^*, MM_a]$
– $U(c_1, c_{2,1}) \mapsto c_{2,1}, \ldots, U(c_1, c_{2,n}) \mapsto c_{2,n}$ are added to $\Phi[MM^*, MM_b]$

The mappings, $\Phi[MM^*, MM_a]$ and $\Phi[MM^*, MM_b]$, produced during the unification process can be used to derive transformation rules from MM^* to MM_a and MM_b.

A similar approach is used to unify the aligned attributes and methods for each pair of aligned classes, which will produce the attribute and method level model mappings.

7   Discussion

The use of an ADSML has some practical implications to the development of software. Perhaps one of the most significant is that while the core language itself may remain more or less static, it can be extended at will by performing the various extraction, elevation, and unification processes. This means that code written using one version of $\Phi[MM^*, MM_a]$ might not work under a different version of $\Phi[MM^*, MM_a]$ because the mapping functions might be different. This suggests that we must be able to indicate the version of $\Phi[MM^*, MM_a]$ on which a model, M_a, depends.

The construction of an ADSML also comes with some significant challenges. One such challenge is that the documentation on which many of the proposed processes depend is of varying levels of completeness and utility. It is possible that additional information might be derived from an inspection of the compiled API code or even the source code, but that is by no means a certainty. Languages such as Java allow for annotations to be placed on key elements of the API. The ADSML could consume such meta-data, but that approach places the burden of defining and maintaining those annotations on API developers.

A second challenge concerns tag management and how it relates to the elements of the API. That is, people are often inconsistent in how they apply meta-data because those tags often represent their own ideas of how to organize and locate the item that they are tagging. For example, one developer might tag an entity based on its functional role within the domain, while another might tag that same entity based on its technical role within the API. This can become even more pronounced when we consider that there are different terms for similar constructs across platforms. A well-defined and maintained ontology is critical for the identification of the key architectural elements described in Sect. 5.

8   Related Work

There are many DSL-based approaches to MDD in the mobile application domain including Rhodes [24], Appcelerator, mobl, Canappi, MobDSL, DIMAG, Mobia Modeler, and md^2. Many of these have been summarized by Ribeiro [25] and each generates either VM-based or native code for their target platforms.

Appcelerator [2] and JQueryMobile [19] support the development of cross-platform mobile applications by emphasizing common languages and virtual machines such as HTML and JavaScript.

Canappi [6] uses the "m|dsl" DSL to define and generate cross-platform mobile applications as front-ends to web services. Unlike ADSML, these approaches do not allow access to native APIs or customizable code generation.

Mobl [11] is a DSL that targets mobile applications. However, it does not address the model-driven aspects of MDD. Thus while the DSL code may indeed be transformed into executable code, the models themselves are not major artifacts of the software development process.

MobDSL [20] is a DSL that uses a VM as the intermediary between the MobDSL application and the underlying platform. This is a similar approach as that taken by tools like Cannapi or Appcelerator save that the VMs are not based on existing cross-platform technologies such as HTML5 and CSS, but rather based on the native platform APIs. This provides less separation between the modeling language and the executable environments, but still requires that changes in the underlying platform APIs be re-integrated into the DSL.

DIMAG (Device Independent Mobile Application Generation framework) [22] is a framework that allows for a single, declarative application definition to be used to generate applications across a range of devices. The model is separated into the DIMAG-root language, the DIMAG-ui user interface language, and an SCXML [13] workflow description to address the behavioral aspects of the application. DIMAG can not directly take advantage of different APIs on the target platforms instead enabling the developer to provide "wrappers" that expose those APIs in a way that can be easily incorporated into the model.

Mobia Modeler [3, 4] attempts to make it possible for non-technical people to easily build their own applications. Mobia Modeler follows the standard separation of PIM from PSM while still generating native code that can be deployed to the target application. As with the other DSL-based approaches, effectively integrating with platform-specific APIs is difficult.

md^2 [12] was developed top-down and with a business-centric focus. It generates native code md^2 though with differences in the role of the developer in advising the transformation process. As with many of the previous approaches, md^2 suffers from a least-common denominator approach in terms of incorporating and accessing platform-specific capabilities.

Other work has been done on deriving DSLs from patterns. [5] provides a means of enabling end-users to construct DSLs from primitive DSL constructs. In such cases the DSL is not necessarily required to bridge to native APIs across multiple platforms, a requirements that adds significant technical complexity to the task of writing the DSL.

As described by [9, 21], the development of DSLs has traditionally followed a process of analysis and organization of the domain in question. This process can be slow to incorporate new changes. ADSML attempts to automate much of the analysis, organization and synthesis to speed up the inclusion of new elements into the DSML while keeping core syntactic elements fixed.

9   Conclusion

Domain-specific modeling languages make the development of applications for a particular domain much simpler than hand-written approaches. However, DSMLs are often "frozen" as static mappings from DSML elements to native language elements.

An adaptive domain-specific modeling language uses information about the target platforms and APIs to evolve its syntax and capabilities. Our approach extracts a meta-model for each target platform. These platform-specific meta-models undergo a process of elevation, where an appropriate subset of the extracted meta-model is selected for further analysis. Similarity analysis aligns the meta-models by mapping one platform to the other. Finally, these mappings are unified into a platform-independent meta-model on which the DSML can be based.

Our approach enables access to the full capabilities of the native platforms and is thus capable of generating high performance native applications. It is also adaptable to rapid evolutions of the target platforms. This adaptability depends on effective ontology and tag management since it is based on the derivation of semantically useful information from the documentation of the native platform and its APIs.

References

1. Apache Cordova (2015). https://cordova.apache.org/
2. Appcelerator (2015). http://www.appcelerator.com/
3. Balagtas-Fernandez, F., Tafelmayer, M., Hussmann, H.: Mobia modeler: easing the creation process of mobile applications for non-technical users. In: Proceedings of the 15th International Conference on Intelligent User Interfaces, IUI 2010, pp. 269–272. ACM, New York (2010)
4. Balagtas-Fernandez, F., Hussmann, H.: Applying domain-specific modeling to mobile health monitoring applications. In: Sixth International Conference on Information Technology: New Generations, ITNG 2009, pp. 1682–1683, April 2009
5. Barrientos, P., Martinez Lopez, P.: Developing dsls using combinators. A design pattern. In: International Multiconference on Computer Science and Information Technology, IMCSIT 2009, pp. 635–642, October 2009
6. Canappi (2011). http://www.canappi.com/
7. Charland, A., Leroux, B.: Mobile application development: web vs. native. Commun. ACM **54**(5), 49–53 (2011)
8. Corral, L., Sillitti, A., Succi, G.: Mobile multiplatform development: an experiment for performance analysis. Procedia Comput. Sci. **10**, 736–743 (2012)
9. van Deursen, A., Klint, P.: Domain-specific language design requires feature descriptions. J. Comput. Inf. Technol. **10**, 1–17 (2002)
10. Granitzer, M., Sabol, V., Onn, K.W., Lukose, D., Tochtermann, K.: Ontology alignment - a survey with focus on visually supported semi-automatic techniques. Future Internet **2**(3), 238–258 (2010)
11. Hammel, Z., Visser, E., et al.: mobl: the new language of the mobile web (2010). http://www.mobl-lang.org/

12. Heitkötter, H., Majchrzak, T.A., Kuchen, H.: Cross-platform model-driven development of mobile applications with md2. In: Proceedings of the 28th Annual ACM Symposium on Applied Computing, SAC 2013, pp. 526–533. ACM, New York (2013)
13. IETF: State Chart XML (SCXML): State Machine Notation for Control Abstraction, April 2015. http://www.w3.org/TR/scxml/
14. Jia, X., Jones, C.: Dynamic languages as modeling notations in model driven engineering. In: ICSOFT 2011, Seville, Spain, pp. 220–225, July 2011
15. Jia, X., Jones, C.: AXIOM: a model-driven approach to cross-platform application development. In: ICSOFT 2012, Rome, Italy, pp. 24–33, July 2012
16. Jia, X., Jones, C.: Cross-platform application development using AXIOM as an agile model-driven approach. In: Cordeiro, J., Hammoudi, S., van Sinderen, M. (eds.) ICSOFT 2012. CCIS, vol. 411, pp. 36–51. Springer, Heidelberg (2013)
17. Jones, C., Jia, X.: The AXIOM model framework: transforming requirements to native code for cross-platform mobile applications. In: ENASE, Lisbon, Portugal, pp. 26–37, April 2014
18. Jones, C., Jia, X.: Using a domain specific language for lightweight model-driven development. In: Maciaszek, L.A., Filipe, J. (eds.) Evaluation of Novel Approaches to Software Engineering. Communications in Computer and Information Science, vol. 551, pp. 46–62. Springer, Heidelberg (2015)
19. JQuery: JQuery mobile framework (2015). http://www.jquerymobile.com/
20. Kramer, D., Clark, T., Oussena, S.: Mobdsl: a domain specific language for multiple mobile platform deployment. In: 2010 IEEE International Conference on Networked Embedded Systems for Enterprise Applications (NESEA), pp. 1–7, November 2010
21. Mernik, M., Heering, J., Sloane, A.M.: When and how to develop domain-specific languages. ACM Comput. Surv. **37**(4), 316–344 (2005)
22. Miravet, P., Marín, I., Ortín, F., Rionda, A.: Dimag: a framework for automatic generation of mobile applications for multiple platforms. In: Proceedings of the 6th International Conference on Mobile Technology, Applications, and Systems, Mobility Conference 2009, pp. 23:1–23:8. ACM, New York (2009)
23. Noyrit, F., Gérard, S., Terrier, F.: Computer assisted integration of domain-specific modeling languages using text analysis techniques. In: Moreira, A., Schätz, B., Gray, J., Vallecillo, A., Clarke, P. (eds.) MODELS 2013. LNCS, vol. 8107, pp. 505–521. Springer, Heidelberg (2013)
24. RhoMobile, Inc.: Rhodes (2015). http://docs.rhomobile.com/en/5.1.1/home
25. Ribeiro, A., da Silva, A.: Survey on cross-platforms and languages for mobile apps. In: 2012 Eighth International Conference on the Quality of Information and Communications Technology (QUATIC), pp. 255–260, September 2012
26. Shvaiko, P., Euzenat, J.: Ontology matching: state of the art and future challenges. IEEE Trans. Knowl. Data Eng. **25**(1), 158–176 (2013)
27. Vaupel, S., Taentzer, G., Harries, J.P., Stroh, R., Gerlach, R., Guckert, M.: Model-driven development of mobile applications allowing role-driven variants. In: Dingel, J., Schulte, W., Ramos, I., Abrahão, S., Insfran, E. (eds.) MODELS 2014. LNCS, vol. 8767, pp. 1–17. Springer, Heidelberg (2014)

Automated Testing of Distributed and Heterogeneous Systems Based on UML Sequence Diagrams

Bruno Lima[1,2(✉)] and João Pascoal Faria[1,2]

[1] INESC TEC, FEUP campus, Rua Dr. Roberto Frias, s/n, 4200-465 Porto, Portugal
[2] Faculty of Engineering, University of Porto, Rua Dr. Roberto Frias,
s/n, 4200-465 Porto, Portugal
{bruno.lima,jpf}@fe.up.pt

Abstract. The growing dependence of our society on increasingly complex software systems makes software testing ever more important and challenging. In many domains, several independent systems, forming a distributed and heterogeneous system of systems, are involved in the provisioning of end-to-end services to users. However, existing test automation techniques provide little tool support for properly testing such systems. Hence, we propose an approach and toolset architecture for automating the testing of end-to-end services in distributed and heterogeneous systems, comprising a visual modeling environment, a test execution engine, and a distributed test monitoring and control infrastructure. The only manual activity required is the description of the participants and behavior of the services under test with UML sequence diagrams, which are translated to extended Petri nets for efficient test input generation and test output checking at runtime. A real world example from the Ambient Assisted Living domain illustrates the approach.

Keywords: Software testing · Distributed systems · UML sequence diagrams · Heterogeneous systems · Systems of systems

1 Introduction

Due to the increasing ubiquity, complexity, criticality and need for assurance of software based systems [2], testing is a fundamental lifecycle activity, with a huge economic impact if not performed adequately [21].

In a growing number of domains, the provision of services to end users depends on the correct functioning of large and complex systems of systems [5]. A system of systems consists of a set of small independent systems that together form a new system, combining hardware components and software systems. Systems of systems are in most cases distributed and heterogeneous, involving mobile and cloud-based platforms.

Testing these distributed and heterogeneous systems is particularly important and challenging. Some of the challenges are: the difficulty to test the system

© Springer International Publishing Switzerland 2016
P. Lorenz et al. (Eds.): ICSOFT 2015, CCIS 586, pp. 380–396, 2016.
DOI: 10.1007/978-3-319-30142-6_21

as a whole due to the number and diversity of individual components; the difficulty to coordinate and synchronize the test participants and interactions, due to the distributed nature of the system; the difficulty to test the components individually, because of the dependencies on other components.

An example of a distributed and heterogeneous system is the Ambient Assisted Living (AAL) ecosystem that was prototyped in the context of the nationwide AAL4ALL project [1]. The AAL4ALL ecosystem comprises a set of interoperable AAL products and services (sensors, actuators, mobile and web-based applications and services, middleware components, etc.), produced by different manufacturers using different technologies and communication protocols (web services, message queues, etc.). To assure interoperability and the integrity of the ecosystem, it was developed and piloted a testing and certification methodology [6], to be applied on candidate components of the ecosystem. A major problem faced during test implementation and execution was related with test automation, due to the diversity of component types and communication interfaces, the distributed nature of the system, and the lack of support tools. Similar difficulties have been reported in other domains, such as the railway domain [22]. In fact, we found in the literature limited tool support for automating the whole process of specification-based testing of distributed and heterogeneous systems.

Hence, the main objective of this paper is to propose an approach and a toolset architecture to automate the whole process of model-based testing of distributed and heterogeneous systems in a seamless way, with a focus on integration testing, but supporting also unit (component) and system testing. As compared to existing approaches, the proposed approach and architecture provide significant benefits regarding efficiency and effectiveness: the only manual activity required from the tester is the creation (with tool support) of partial behavioral models of the system under test (SUT), using feature-rich industry standard notations (UML 2 sequence diagrams), together with model-to-implementation mapping information, being all the needed runtime test components provided by the toolset for different platforms and technologies; the ability to test not only the interactions of the SUT with the environment, but also the interactions among components of the SUT, following an adaptive test generation and execution strategy, to improve fault detection and localization and cope with non-determinism in the specification or the SUT.

The rest of the paper is organized as follows: Sect. 2 describes the state of the art. Section 3 presents an overview of the proposed approach and test process. Section 4 introduces the toolset architecture. Section 5 summarizes the novelties and benefits of the proposed approach. Section 6 concludes the paper and points out future work. A running example from the AAL domain is used to illustrate the approach presented.

2   State of the Art

The highest level of test automation is achieved by automating both test generation and test execution, but the approaches for automating test generation and automating test execution are in most cases orthogonal. Hence, we analyze in separate subsections approaches for automatic test generation (from models or specifications) and automatic test execution that have the potential to be applied for distributed and heterogeneous systems.

2.1   Model-Based Test Generation

Model-based testing (MBT) techniques and tools have attracted increasing interest from academia and industry [24], because of their potential to increase the effectiveness and efficiency of the test process, by means of the automatic generation of test cases (test sequences, input test data, and expected outputs) from behavioral models of the system under test (SUT).

However, MBT approaches found in the literature suffer from several limitations [4]. The most common limitation is the lack of integrated support for the whole test process. This is a big obstacle for the adoption of these approaches by industry, because of the effort required to create or adapt tools to implement some parts of the test process.

Another common problem with existing MBT approaches is the difficulty to avoid the explosion of the number of test cases generated. In recent MBT approaches [8,18], researchers try to overcome the test case explosion problem by the usage of behavioral models focusing on specific scenarios, i.e., by following a scenario-based testing approach instead of a state-based testing approach. Being a feature-rich industry standard, UML 2 sequence diagrams (SDs) are particularly well suited for supporting scenario-based MBT approaches. With the features introduced in UML 2, parameterized SDs can be used to model both simple and complex behavioral scenarios, with control flow variants, temporal constraints, and conformance control operators. UML SDs are also well suited for modeling the interactions that occur between the components and actors of a distributed system.

In the literature it can be found some test automation approaches based on UML SDs, but those approaches has some limitations for the testing of distributed and heterogeneous systems, namely regarding the support for features specific to those systems, such as parallelism, concurrency and time constraints.

Of particular relevance in the context of this paper is the UML Checker toolset developed in recent work of the authors [7,8], with several advantages over other approaches, namely regarding the level of support of UML 2 features. The toolset supports the conformance testing of standalone object-oriented applications against test scenarios specified by means of so called test-ready SDs. Test-ready SDs are first translated to extended Petri Nets for efficient incremental conformance checking, with a limited support for parallelism and concurrency. Besides external interactions with users and client applications, internal interactions between objects in the system are also monitored using Aspect-Oriented Programming (AOP) techniques [16], and checked against the ones specified in the model. The testing of distributed systems is not supported, but some of the techniques developed have the potential to be reused for the modeling and testing of interactions between components in a distributed system, instead of interactions between objects in a standalone application.

Other examples of test automation approaches based on UML SDs are the SCENTOR tool, targeting e-business EJB applications [27], the MDA-based approach of [14], and the IBM Rational Rhapsody TestConductor AddOn [13], targeting real-time embedded applications. A comparison of the strengths and weaknesses of these approaches can be found in [8]. The main limitations of these approaches are the limited support for the new features of UML 2 SDs and the limited support for testing internal interactions (besides the interactions with the environment).

2.2   Test Execution Frameworks

Regarding test concretization and execution for distributed systems, we found in the literature several frameworks that can be adapted and integrated for building a comprehensive test automation solution.

The Software Testing Automation Framework (STAF) [20] is an open source, multi-platform, multi-language framework designed around the idea of reusable components, called services (such as process invocation, resource management, logging, and monitoring). STAF removes the tedium of building an automation infrastructure, thus enabling the tester to focus on building an automation solution. The STAF framework provides the foundation upon which to build higher level solutions, and provides a pluggable approach supported across a large variety of platforms and languages.

Torens and Ebrecht [22] proposed the RemoteTest framework as a solution for the testing of distributed systems and their interfaces. In this framework, the individual system components are integrated into a virtual environment that emulates the adjacent modules of the system. The interface details are thereby abstracted by the framework and there is no special interface knowledge necessary by the tester. In addition to the decoupling of components and interface abstraction, the RemoteTest framework facilitates the testing of distributed systems with flexible mechanisms to write test scripts and an architecture that can be easily adapted to different systems.

Zhang et al. [28] developed a runtime monitoring tool called FiLM that can monitor the execution of distributed applications against LTL specifications on finite traces. Implemented within the online predicate checking infrastructure D^3S [17], FiLM models the execution of distributed applications as a trace of consistent global snapshots with global timestamps, and it employs finite automata constructed from Labelled transition systems (LTL) specifications to evaluate the trace of distributed systems.

Camini et al. [3] proposed DiCE, an approach that continuously and automatically explores the system behavior, to check whether the system deviates from its desired behavior. At a highlevel DiCE (i) creates a snapshot consisting of lightweight node checkpoints, (ii) orchestrates the exploration of relevant system behaviors across the snapshot by subjecting system nodes to many possible inputs that exercise node actions, and (iii) checks for violations of properties that capture the desired system behavior. DiCE starts exploring from current system state, and operates alongside the deployed system but in isolation from it. In this way, testing can account for the current code, state and configuration of the system. DiCE reuses existing protocol messages to the extent possible for interoperability and ease of deployment.

One difficulty in testing distributed systems is that their distributed nature imposes theoretical limitations on the conformance faults that can be detected by the test components, depending on the test architecture used [11,12]. Hierons [11] devised a hybrid framework for solving the problem that exist in many systems that interact with their environment at distributed interfaces without the possibility in some cases to place synchronised local testers at the ports of the SUT. Before this framework existed only two main approaches to test this type of systems: having independent local testers [23] or a single centralised tester that interacts asynchronously with the SUT. The author proved that the hybrid framework is more powerful than the distributed and centralised approaches.

2.3   Synthesis

Although we didn't find in the literature an integrated approach for fully automating the testing of distributed and heterogeneous systems, the concepts used by each can be harnessed in the development of an architecture that can be fully supported by tools, so that all the testing process can be automated.

3   Approach and Process

Our main objective is the development of an approach and a toolset to automate the whole process of model-based testing of distributed and heterogeneous systems in a seamless way, with a focus on integration testing, but supporting also unit (component) and system testing. The only manual activity (to be performed with tool support) should be the creation of the input model of the SUT.

To that end, our approach is based on the following main ideas:

- the adoption of different 'frontend' and 'backend' modeling notations, with an automatic translation of the input behavioral models created by the user in an accessible 'frontend' notation (using industry standards such as UML [19]), to a formal 'backend' notation amenable for incremental execution at runtime (such as extended Petri Nets as in our previous work for object-oriented systems [8]);
- the adoption of an online and adaptive test strategy, where the next test input depends on the sequence of events that has been observed so far and the resulting execution state of the formal backend model, to allow for non-determinism in either the specification or the SUT [11];
- the automatic mapping of test results (coverage and errors) to the 'frontend' modeling layer.

Figure 1 depicts the main activities and artifacts of the proposed test process based on the above ideas. The main activities are described in the next subsections and illustrated with a running example.

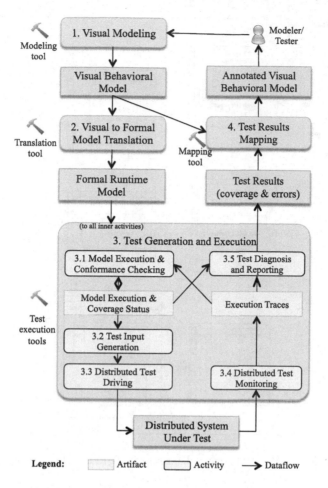

Fig. 1. Dataflow view of the proposed test process.

3.1   Visual Modeling

The behavioral model is created using an appropriate UML profile [10, 19] and an existing modeling tool. We advocate the usage of UML 2 SDs, with a few restrictions and extensions, because they are well suited for describing and visualizing the interactions that occur between the components and actors of a distributed system. UML deployment diagrams can also be used to describe the distributed structure of the SUT. Mapping information between the model and the implementation, needed for test execution (such as the actual location of each component under test), may also be attached to the model with tagged values.

To illustrate the approach, we use a real world example from the AAL4ALL project, related with a fall detection and alert service. As illustrated in Fig. 2, this service involves the interaction between different heterogeneous components

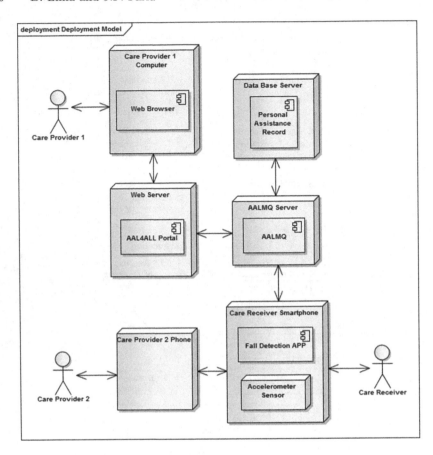

Fig. 2. UML deployment diagram of a fall detection scenario.

running in different hardware nodes in different physical locations, as well as three users.

A behavioral model for a typical fall detection scenario is shown in Fig. 3. In this scenario, a care receiver has a smartphone that has installed a fall detection application. When this person falls, the application detects the fall using the smartphone's accelerometer and provides the user a message which indicates that it has detected a drop giving the possibility for the user to confirm whether he/she needs help. If the user responds that he/she does not need help (the fall was slight, or it was just the smartphone that fell to the ground), the application does not perform any action; however, if the user confirms that needs help or does not respond within 5 s (useful if the person became unconscious due to the fall), the application raises two actions in parallel. On the one hand, it makes a call to a previously clearcut number to contact a health care provider (in this case can be a formal or informal caregiver); on the other hand, it sends the fall occurrence for a Personal Assistance Record database and sends a message to a

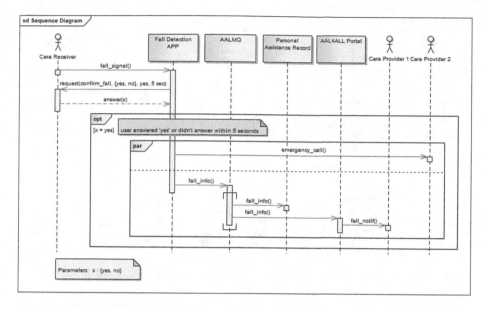

Fig. 3. UML sequence diagram representing the interactions of the fall detection scenario. The diagram is already painted after a failed test execution in which the fall detection application didn't send an emergency call.

portal that is used by a caregiver (e.g. a doctor or nurse) that is responsible for monitoring this care receiver. The last two actions are performed through a central component of the ecosystem called AALMQ (AAL Message Queue), which allows incoming messages to be forwarded to multiple subscribers, according to the publish-subscribe pattern [9]. To facilitate the representation of a request for input from the user with a timeout and a default response, we use the special syntax *request(confirm_fall, {yes, no}, yes, 5 sec)*, where the first argument identifies the message, the second argument is the set of valid answers, the third is the default answer in case of timeout, and the last argument is the timeout time.

3.2 Visual to Formal Model Translation

For the formal runtime model, we advocate the usage of *Event-Driven Colored Petri Nets* – a sort of extended Petri Nets proposed in our previous work for testing object-oriented systems [8], with the addition of time constraints as found in Timed Petri Nets. We call the resulting Petri Nets *Timed Event-Driven Colored Petri Nets*, or TEDCPN for short. Petri Nets are well suited for describing in a rigorous and machine processable way the behavior of distributed and concurrent systems, usually requiring fewer places than the number of states of equivalent finite state machines. Translation rules from UML 2 SDs to Event-Driven Colored Petri Nets have been defined in [8]. Rules for translating time and duration constraints in SDs to time constraints in the resulting Petri Net can also be defined.

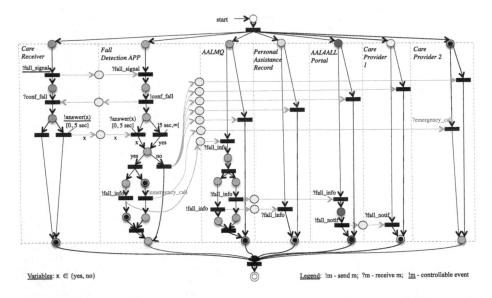

Fig. 4. TEDCPN derived from the SD of Fig. 3. The net is marked in a final state of a failed test execution in which the fall detection application didn't send an emergency call.

Figure 4 shows the TEDCPN derived from the SD of Fig. 3, according to the rules described in [8] and additional rules for translating time constraints.

The generated TEDCPN is partitioned into a set of fragments corresponding to the participants in the source SD. Each fragment describes the behavior local to each participant and the communication with other participants via boundary places.

Transitions may be optionally labeled with an *event*, a *guard* (with braces) and a *time interval* (with square brackets). Events correspond to the sending or receiving of messages in the source SD. Guards correspond to the conditions of conditional interaction fragments in the source SD. Time intervals correspond to duration and time constraints in the source SD. A transition can only fire when there is at least one token in each input place, the event (if defined) has occurred, the guard (if defined) holds, and the time elapsed since the transition became enabled (i.e., since there is a token in each input place) lies within the time interval (if defined).

Incoming and outgoing arcs of a transition may be labeled with a pattern matching expression describing the value (token) to be taken from the source place or put in the target place, respectively, being 1 the default. For example, in Fig. 4 the transition labeled "?answer(x)" has an input arc labeled "x", where "x" represents a local variable of the transition. The transition can only fire if the value of the token in the source place is the same as the value of the argument of the event. Then, the value of "x" is placed in the target place.

For testing purposes, the events in the runtime model are marked as *observable* (default) or *controllable*. Controllable events (underlined) are to be injected by the test harness (playing the role of a test driver, simulating an actor) when the corresponding transition becomes enabled. Controllable events correspond to the sending of messages from actors in the source SD. All other events are observable, i.e., they are to be monitored by the test harness. For example, when the TEDCPN of the example starts execution (i.e., a token is put in the start place), the initial unlabeled transition is executed and a token is placed in the initial place of each fragment. At that point, the only transition enabled is the one labeled with the "!fall_signal" controllable event, so the test harness will inject that event (simulating the user) and test execution proceeds.

This mechanism provides a unified framework with monitoring, testing and simulation capabilities. In one extreme case, all events in the model may be marked as observable, in which case the test system acts as a runtime monitoring and verification system. In the other extreme case, all events in the model may be marked as controllable, in which case the test system acts as a simulation system. This also allows the usage of the same model with different markings of observable and controllable events for integration and unit testing.

3.3   Test Generation and Execution

Test Generation. Using the UML 2 interaction operators, a single SD, and hence the TEDCPN derived from it, may describe multiple control flow variants, that require multiple test cases for being properly exercised.

In the running example, from the reading of the set of interactions represented in Fig. 3, one easily realizes that there are three test paths to be exercised (with at least one test case for each test path). The first test path (TP1) is the case where the care receiver responds negatively to the application and the application doesn't trigger any action. The second test path (TP2) is the situation where the user confirms to the application that he/she needs help and after that the application triggers the actions. The last test path (TP3) corresponds to the situation where the user doesn't answer within the defined time limit and the application triggers the remaining actions automatically. If one wants also to exercise the boundary values of allowed response time (close to 0 and close to 5 seconds), then two test cases can be considered for each of the test paths TP1 and TP2, resulting in a total of 5 test cases.

Equivalently, in order to exercise all nodes, edges and boundary values in the TEDCPN, several test cases are needed. In the example, one could exercise the two outgoing paths after the "?conf_fall" event, the two possible values of variable "x" in the "!answer(x)" event, and the two boundary values of the "[0, 5 sec]" interval, in a total of 5 test cases.

In general, the required test cases can be generated using an offline strategy (with separate generation and execution phases) or an online test strategy (with intermixed generation and execution phases) [25]. In an offline strategy, the test cases are determined by a static analysis of the model, assuming the SUT behaves deterministically. But that is not often the case, so we prefer an online, adaptive, strategy, in which the next test action is decided based on the current execution state. Whenever multiple alternatives can be taken by the test harness in an execution state, the test harness must choose one of the alternatives and keep track of unexplored alternatives (i.e., model coverage information) to be exercised in subsequent test repetitions.

Test Execution. Test execution involves the simultaneous execution of: (i) the set of components under test (CUTs); (ii) the formal runtime model (TEDCPN), dictating the possible test inputs and the expected outputs from the CUTs in each step of test execution; (iii) a local test component for each CUT, running in the same node of the CUT, able to perform the roles of test driver (i.e., send test inputs to the CUT, simulating an actor) and test monitor (i.e., monitor all the messages sent or received by the CUT).

The collection of monitored events (message sending and receiving events) forms an *execution trace*. Testing succeeds if the observed execution trace *conforms to* the formal behavioral model, in the sense that it belongs to the (possibly infinite) set of valid traces defined by the model.

Conformance checking is performed *incrementally* as follows: (i) initially, the execution of the TEDCPN is started by placing a token in the start place and firing transitions until a quiescent state is reached (a state where no transition can fire); (ii) each time a quiescent state is reached having an enabled transition labeled with a controllable event, the test harness itself generates the event (i.e., the message specified in the event is sent to the target CUT by the appropriate test driver) and the execution status of the TEDCPN is advanced to a new quiescent state; (iii) each time an observable event is monitored (by a test monitor), the execution state of the TEDCPN is advanced until a new quiescent state is reached; (iv) the two previous steps are repeated until the final state of the TEDCPN is reached (i.e., a token is placed in the final place), in which case test execution succeeds, or until a state is reached in which there is no controllable event enabled and no observable event has been monitored for a defined wait time, in which case test execution fails. The latter situation is illustrated in Fig. 4. Depending on the conformance semantics chosen, the observation of an unexpected event may also be considered a conformance error.

To minimize communication overheads, the TEDCPN can itself be executed in a *distributed* fashion, by executing each fragment of the 'global' TEDCPN (describing the behavior local to one participant and the communication with other participants via boundary places) by a local test component. Communication between the distributed test components is only needed when tokens have to be exchanged via boundary places.

When a final (success or failure) state is reached, the *Test Diagnosis and Reporting* activity is responsible to analyze the execution state of the TEDCPN and the collected execution trace, and produce meaningful error information.

Model coverage information is also collected during test execution, to guide the selection of test inputs and the decision about when to stop test execution, as follows: when it is reached a quiescent state of the TEDCPN with multiple controllable events enabled leading to different execution paths, the test harness shall generate an event that leads to a previously unexplored path; when a final state of the TEDCPN is reached, test execution is restarted if there are still unexplored (but reachable) paths.

3.4   Test Results Mapping

At the end of test execution it is important to reflect the test results back in the visual behavioral model created by the user. As an example, the marking shown in the net of Fig. 4 corresponds to the final state of a failed test execution in which the Fall Detection App didn't send an emergency call. By a simple analysis of this final state (and traceability information between the source SD and the TEDCPN), it is possible to point out to the tester which messages in the source SD were covered and what was the cause of test failure (missing "emergency call" message), as shown in Fig. 3.

4   Toolset Architecture

Figure 5 depicts a layered architecture of a toolset for supporting the test process described in the previous section, promoting reuse and extensibility.

At the bottom layer in Fig. 5, the SUT is composed by a set of components under test (CUT), executing potentially in different nodes [19]. The CUT interact with each other (usually asynchronously) and with the environment (users or external systems) through well defined interfaces at defined interaction points or ports [10, 11].

The three layers of the toolset are described in the following sections.

4.1   Visual Modeling Environment

At the top layer, we have a visual modeling environment, where the tester can create a *visual behavioral model* of the SUT, invoke test generation and execution, and visualize test results and coverage information back in the model.

This layer also includes a *translation tool* to automatically translate the visual behavioral models created by the user into the formal notation accepted by the test execution manager in the next layer, and a *mapping tool* to translate back the test results (coverage and error information) to annotations in the visual model.

The model transformations can be implemented using existing MDA technologies and tools [26].

4.2   Test Execution Engine

At the next layer, the test execution engine is the core engine of the toolset. It comprises a *model execution & conformance checking engine*, responsible for incrementally checking the conformance of observed execution traces in the SUT

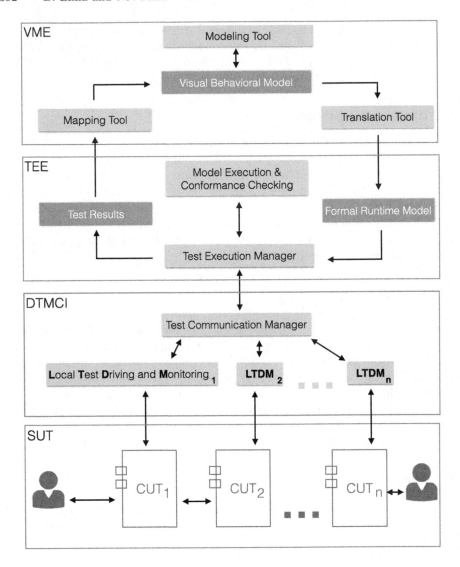

Fig. 5. Toolset architecture.

against the *formal runtime model* derived from the previous layer, and a *test execution manager*, responsible for initiating test execution (using the services of the next layer), forward execution events (received from the next layer) to the model execution & conformance checking engine, decide next actions to be performed by the local test driving and monitoring components in the next layer of the system, and produce *test results* and diagnosis information for the layer above.

The model execution & conformance checking engine can be implemented by adapting existing Petri net engines, such as CPN Tools [15].

4.3   Distributed Test Monitoring and Control Infrastructure

We adopt a hybrid test monitoring approach as proposed in [11], combining a centralized 'tester' and a local 'tester' at each port (component interaction point) of the SUT, that was shown to lead to more effective testing than a purely centralized approach (where a centralized tester interacts asynchronously with the ports of the SUT) or a purely distributed approach (where multiple independent distributed testers interact synchronously with the ports of the SUT).

Hence, the Distributed Test Monitoring and Control Infrastructure comprises a set of *local test driving and monitoring* (LTDM) components, each communicating (possibly synchronously) with a component under test (CUT), performing the roles of test monitor, driver and stub; and a *test communication manager* (TCM) component, that (asynchronously) dispatches control orders (coming from the previous layer) to the LTDMs and aggregates monitoring information from the LTDMs (to be passed to the previous layer).

During test execution, the TEDCPN may be executed in a centralized or a distributed mode, depending on the processing capabilities that can be put in the LTDM components. In centralized mode, the LTDM components just monitor all observable events of interest and send them to the central TEM; they also inject controllable events when requested from the central TEM. In distributed mode, a copy of each fragment (up to boundary places) is sent to the respective LTDM component for local execution. When there is the need to send a token to a boundary place, the LTDM sends the token to the central TEM, which subsequently dispatches it to the consumer LTDM. Because of possible delays in the communication of tokens through boundary places, the LTDM components must be prepared to tentatively accept observable events before receiving enabling tokens in boundary places.

This infrastructure may be implemented by adapting and extending existing test frameworks for distributed systems, such as the ones described in Sect. 2.2.

Different LTDM components have to be implemented for different platforms and technologies under test, such as WCF (Windows Communication Foundation), Java EE (Java Platform, Enterprise Edition), Android, etc. However, a LTDM component implemented for a given technology may be reused without change to monitor and control any CUT that uses that technology. For example, in our previous work for automating the scenario-based testing of standalone applications written in Java, we developed a runtime test library able to trace and manipulate the execution of any Java application, using AOP (aspect-oriented programming) instrumentation techniques with load-time weaving. In the case of a distributed Java application, we would need to deploy a copy of that library (or, more precisely, a modified library, to handle communication) together with each Java component under test. In the case of a distributed system implemented using other technologies (with different technologies for different components in case of heterogeneous systems), similar test monitoring components suitable for the technologies involved will have to be deployed.

5   Synthesis of Novelties and Benefits

As compared to existing approaches (see Sect. 2), the approach proposed in this paper provides the following novelties and benefits.

Our approach provides a higher level of automation of the testing process because all phases of the test process are supported in an integrated fashion. The only manual activity needed is the development in a user friendly notation of the model required as input for automatic test case generation and execution; there is no need to develop test components specific for each SUT.

This approach also provides a higher fault detection capability. The use of a hybrid test architecture allows the detection of a higher number of errors as compared to purely distributed or centralized architectures. Interactions between components in the SUT are also monitored and checked against the specification, besides the interactions of the SUT with the environment. To facilitate fault diagnosis, it is used an incremental conformance checking algorithm allowing to capture the execution state of the SUT as soon as a failure occurs. Because of the support for temporal constraints, timing faults can also be detected. Our approach has the ability to test non-deterministic SUT behaviors, using an online, adaptive, test generation strategy.

The proposed approach provides easier support for multiple test levels because the same input model can be used to perform tests at different levels (unit, integration, and system testing), simply by changing the selection of observable and controllable events in the input model. A scenario-oriented approach simplifies the level of detail required in the input models.

With this approach the test execution process is more efficient. With a distributed conformance checking algorithm, communication overheads during test execution are minimized and the usage of a state-oriented runtime model allows a more efficient model execution and conformance checking.

6   Conclusions

In this paper, it was presented a novel approach and process for automated scenario-based testing of distributed and heterogeneous systems. It was also presented the architecture of a toolset able to support and automate the proposed test process. Based in a multilayer architecture and using a hybrid test monitoring approach combining a centralized 'tester' and a local 'tester' this toolset promotes reuse and extensibility. In the approach proposed, the tester interacts with a visual modeling front-end to describe key behavioral scenarios of the SUT using UML sequence diagrams, invoke test generation and execution, and visualize test results and coverage information back in the model using a color scheme (see Fig. 3). Internally, the visual modeling notation is converted to a formal notation amenable for runtime interpretation (see Fig. 4) in the back-end. A distributed test monitoring and control infrastructure is responsible for interacting with the components of the SUT, under the roles of test driver, monitor and stub. At the core of the toolset, a test execution engine coordinates test execution and checks the conformance of the observed execution trace with the expectations derived from the visual model. For better understanding the approach and toolset architecture proposed, a real world example from the AAL domain was presented along the paper.

As future work we will implement a toolset following the architecture (represented in Fig. 5) and working principles presented in this paper, taking advantage of previous work for automating the integration testing of standalone object-oriented systems. To experimentally assess the benefits of the approach and toolset, industrial level case studies will be conducted, with at least one in the AAL domain.

With such a toolset, we expect to significantly reduce the cost of testing distributed and heterogeneous systems, from the standpoint of time, resources and expertise required, as compared to existing approaches.

References

1. AAL4ALL: Ambient Assisted Living For All (2015). http://www.aal4all.org
2. Boehm, B.: Some future software engineering opportunities and challenges. In: Nanz, S. (ed.) The Future of Software Engineering, pp. 1–32. Springer, Heidelberg (2011). http://dx.doi.org/10.1007/978-3-642-15187-3_1
3. Canini, M., Jovanović, V., Venzano, D., Novaković, D., Kostić, D.: Online testing of federated and heterogeneous distributed systems. SIGCOMM Comput. Commun. Rev. **41**(4), 434–435 (2011). http://doi.acm.org/10.1145/2043164.2018507
4. Dias Neto, A.C., Subramanyan, R., Vieira, M., Travassos, G.H.: A survey on model-based testing approaches: a systematic review. In: Proceedings of the 1st ACM International Workshop on Empirical Assessment of Software Engineering Languages and Technologies: Held in Conjunction with the 22nd IEEE/ACM International Conference on Automated Software Engineering (ASE) 2007, WEASELTech 2007, pp. 31–36. ACM, New York (2007). http://doi.acm.org/10.1145/1353673.1353681
5. DoD: Systems Engineering Guide for Systems of Systems. Technical report, Office of the Deputy Under Secretary of Defense for Acquisition and Technology, Systems and Software Engineering Version 1.0 (2008)
6. Faria, J.P., Lima, B., Sousa, T.B., Martins, A.: A testing and certification methodology for an open ambient-assisted living ecosystem. Int. J. E-Health Med. Commun. (IJEHMC) **5**(4), 90–107 (2014)
7. Faria, J.: A toolset for conformance testing against UML sequence diagrams (2014). https://blogs.fe.up.pt/sdbt/
8. Faria, J., Paiva, A.: A toolset for conformance testing against UML sequence diagrams based on event-driven colored Petri nets. Int. J. Softw. Tools Technol. Transf., pp. 1–20 (2014). http://dx.doi.org/10.1007/s10009-014-0354-x
9. Gamma, E., Helm, R., Johnson, R., Vlissides, J.: Design Patterns: Elements of Reusable Object-Oriented Software. Pearson Education, Upper Saddle River (1994)
10. Gross, H.G.: Component-Based Software Testing with UML. Springer, Heidelberg (2005)
11. Hierons, R.M.: Combining centralised and distributed testing. ACM Trans. Softw. Eng. Methodol. **24**(1), 5:1–5:29 (2014). http://doi.acm.org/10.1145/2661296

12. Hierons, R.M., Merayo, M.G., Núñez, M.: Scenarios-based testing of systems with distributed ports. Softw. Pract. Experience **41**(10), 999–1026 (2011). http://dx.doi.org/10.1002/spe.1062

13. IBM: IBM® Rational® Rhapsody® Automatic Test Conductor Add On User Guide, v2.5.2 (2013)

14. Javed, A., Strooper, P., Watson, G.: Automated generation of test cases using model-driven architecture. In: Second International Workshop on Automation of Software Test, 2007, AST 2007, p. 3, May 2007

15. Jensen, K., Kristensen, L., Wells, L.: Coloured Petri Nets and CPN tools for modelling and validation of concurrent systems. Int. J. Softw. Tools Technol. Transf. **9**(3–4), 213–254 (2007). http://dx.doi.org/10.1007/s10009-007-0038-x

16. Kiczales, G., Lamping, J., Mendhekar, A., Maeda, C., Lopes, C., Loingtier, J.M., Irwin, J.: Aspect-oriented programming. In: Akşit, M., Matsuoka, S. (eds.) ECOOP 1997. LNCS, vol. 1241, pp. 220–242. Springer, Heidelberg (1997). http://dx.doi.org/10.1007/BFb0053381

17. Liu, X., Guo, Z., Wang, X., Chen, F., Lian, X., Tang, J., Wu, M., Kaashoek, M.F., Zhang, Z.: D3S: debugging deployed distributed systems. In: NSDI, vol. 8, pp. 423–437 (2008)

18. Moreira, R.M., Paiva, A.C.: PBGT tool: an integrated modeling and testing environment for pattern-based GUI testing. In: Proceedings of the 29th ACM/IEEE International Conference on Automated Software Engineering, ASE 2014, pp. 863–866. ACM, New York (2014). http://doi.acm.org/10.1145/2642937.2648618

19. OMG: OMG Unified Modeling LanguageTM (OMG UML), Superstructure. Technical report, Object Management Group (2011)

20. STAF: Software Testing Automation Framework (STAF) (2014). http://staf. sourceforge.net/

21. Tassey, G.: The Economic Impacts of Inadequate Infrastructure for Software Testing. Technical report, National Institute of Standards and Technology (2002)

22. Torens, C., Ebrecht, L.: RemoteTest: a framework for testing distributed systems. In: 2010 Fifth International Conference on Software Engineering Advances (ICSEA), pp. 441–446 August 2010

23. Ulrich, A., König, H.: Architectures for testing distributed systems. In: Csopaki, G., Dibuz, S., Tarnay, K. (eds.) Testing of Communicating Systems. IFIP – The International Federation for Information Processing, vol. 21, pp. 93–108. Springer, US (1999). http://dx.doi.org/10.1007/978-0-387-35567-2_7

24. Utting, M., Legeard, B.: Practical Model-Based Testing: A Tools Approach. Morgan Kaufmann Publishers Inc., San Francisco (2007)

25. Utting, M., Pretschner, A., Legeard, B.: A taxonomy of model-based testing approaches. Softw. Test. Verification Reliab. **22**(5), 297–312 (2012). http://dx.doi.org/10.1002/stvr.456

26. Völter, M., Stahl, T., Bettin, J., Haase, A., Helsen, S.: Model-Driven Software Development: Technology, Engineering, Management. Wiley, Chichester (2013)

27. Wittevrongel, J., Maurer, F.: SCENTOR: scenario-based testing of e-business applications. In: Proceedings of the Tenth IEEE International Workshops on Enabling Technologies: Infrastructure for Collaborative Enterprises, 2001, WET ICE 2001, pp. 41–46 (2001)

28. Zhang, F., Qi, Z., Guan, H., Liu, X., Yang, M., Zhang, Z.: FiLM: a runtime monitoring tool for distributed systems. In: Third IEEE International Conference on Secure Software Integration and Reliability Improvement, 2009, SSIRI 2009, pp. 40–46, July 2009

Guiding Cloud Developers to Build Energy Aware Applications

Christophe Ponsard$^{(\boxtimes)}$, Jean-Christophe Deprez, and Raphael Michel

CETIC Research Centre, Gosselies, Belgium
{cp,jcd,rm}@cetic.be

Abstract. ICT energy efficiency is a growing concern. A great effort was already done making hardware more energy efficient and aware. Although a part of that effort is devoted to specific software areas like embedded/mobile systems, much remains to be done at the software level, especially for applications deployed in the Cloud. There is a increasing need to help Cloud application developers to learn to reason about how much energy is consumed by their applications on the server-side. This paper presents a set of tools which guides the developers of Cloud applications in key steps. First, at requirements stage, in order to capture energy goals in a measurable way and relate them with important Non-Functional Requirements (NFR). Second, at design level, an UML profile supporting energy Key Performance Indicators (KPI) is used in order to keep tracking off those goals and metrics across the functional design of the application. Third, at runtime, measurements probes are automatically deployed and the collected data is processed in order to be analysed at the previously goal level. Specific tools for analysing the energy behaviour and helping in making a choice among different design alternatives are also proposed.

Keywords: Cloud computing · Energy efficiency · Green IT · Goal-oriented requirements engineering · Non-functional requirements · Data visualization

1 Introduction

The expansion of ICT both at professional and personal levels induces increasingly larger amounts of data exchanged (high resolution pictures, videos) and processed (Big Data), increasing connectivity of all devices (mobile devices, Internet of Things) and higher penetration (on business domains, emerging countries). This evolution raises the energy required to run ICT to a level that would be dramatic if ICT energy efficiency was not improving simultaneously. Between 2007 and 2012, global ICT consumption raised from 3.4 % to 4.6 % of the overall energy consumption and the ratio for data centres also grew from 1 % to 1.3 % of the global energy consumption hence a 30 % increase [1]. Another US study confirms that evolution of energy consumption by data centres (+56 % Worldwide and +36 % in the US between 2005 and 2010) in the context of a large market

© Springer International Publishing Switzerland 2016
P. Lorenz et al. (Eds.): ICSOFT 2015, CCIS 586, pp. 397–414, 2016.
DOI: 10.1007/978-3-319-30142-6_22

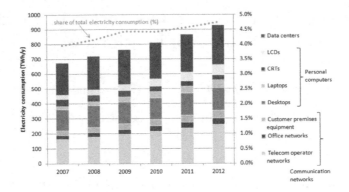

Fig. 1. Evolution of power consumption.

expansion boosted by Cloud Computing and Social Networks [2]. In contrast, the increase for the 2000-2005 period was about 200 % (Fig. 1).

A reason for the slower increase between 2007 and 2012 is the use of more efficient hardware. Virtualisation techniques also enable data centres to operate hardware at higher load. The average Power Usage Effectiveness (PUE) metric of data centres currently ranges from 1.7 to 1.1 for the most efficient ones. This metric compares the amount of energy spent by servers against the overall energy consumed by the whole infrastructure, thus the best theoretical PUE measurement is 1.0.

In order to reach another level of energy saving, it is now required to consider the software layer. Several initiatives have already studied how to reduce energy consumption of mobile or embedded devices. For the Cloud Computing domain, an important amount of work has focused on lower layers such as the physical infrastructure [3] or on the infrastructure virtualisation layer [4]. A systematic survey of sustainability showed a dedicated attention to Cloud as well as a number of proposals turned to the energy efficiency of software applications [5]. However, much remains to be done, especially to help developers to learn how much energy is consumed by their applications on the server side.

To bootstrap the process of energy based pricing model for Cloud service at infrastructure, platform or application level, it is necessary to develop a Cloud stack capable to record energy consumption at each layer and to facilitate negotiations between a customer and a provider where energy consumption is one of the factors. In a second step, self-adaptation capabilities will enable dynamic energy savings. However, such effort should not be limited to the Cloud stack middleware. Development tools that support the requirements, design and construction of Cloud applications will enable additional savings on energy consumption. This is the overall goal of projects like [6–8].

Energy requirements are part of the system Non-Functional Requirements (NFRs), i.e. constraints on the way the software-to-be should satisfy its functional requirements or on the way it should be developed [9]. A number of taxonomies have been defined to classify NFRs, such as the NFR framework [10] or the SQuaRE standard [11].

Unlike certain performance or security characteristics already understood by users and developers, the behaviour of energy consumption in server-side components is often largely unknown. Rare are those who could state quantifiable requirements on the energy consumption behaviour on the server side for particular features of their application. For example, who could say how much energy is consumed when searching for a bug in a given bug tracker and whether or not this consumption behaviour is within a normal range. In addition, energy is rarely considered as a main NFR and raising awareness in energy efficiency can only be reached by an approach considering it together with other NFRs by identifying synergies (e.g. efficient design both for energy and performance) or the best trade-off among with conflicting NFRs (like response time or availability).

Our work aims at helping developers to take more explicitly the energy dimension in consideration through the whole process of building a Cloud application and more specifically at the requirements and design stages. In order to structure our work, we defined a global framework structured across a requirements, design and run-time life-cycle phases. It is depicted in Fig. 2 and is fully detailed in [12].

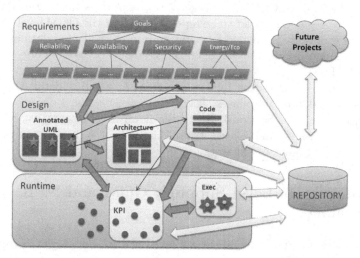

Fig. 2. Eco-aware evolution framework.

The aim of this paper is to describe how we could implement this vision based on a set of technical contributions at each phase and the validation we conducted so far based on a supporting case study. We can summarise them at each of the three key layers depicted in Fig. 2.

At Requirements Level - To structure the approach, the Goal-Question-Metric paradigm is used [13]. In particular, we proposed a way to define generic goals and questions that developers will often want answers to in order to gain a more precise knowledge of the energy consumed by various features or components of their application [14]. We also show how to rely on a number of already identified energy-related metrics [15] and how to related energy with other key NFRs, possibly related to defined Service Level Agreements (SLA).

At Design Level - To capture the information in a way that is both standard for the analyst and easy to process for further processing, an UML profile was defined and implemented on top of Papyrus [16]. This profile enhances the analysis process of a Cloud application with energy awareness both for the development of a new application or the migration of an existing application to the Cloud. It helps in identifying a set of possible application design/configuration alternatives. It also supports the automated deployment of measurement probes to monitor the specified KPI and their reporting in terms of the questions and goals of the GQM identified at requirements level.

At Runtime Level - Probes collect the specified data and report them to a monitoring infrastructure part of the energy-aware Cloud stack. This monitoring itself is efficient in terms of data collection strategy (frequency of sampling, data transmission, data aggregation). Application monitoring occurs at the SaaS level but relies on data from the lower PaaS and IaaS layers, for example, for collecting Watt-hour of a blade or CPU percentage time of a process running in a VM. The data is then aggregated in order to be reported back at the QGM level. A specific visualisation tool is also provided to navigate into the collected data and to help identifying configurations that are balanced trade-off between energy behaviour and other NFRs [17].

This paper is organized as follows. Sections 2, 3 and 4 detail the requirements, design and runtime phases sketched above. Section 3 describes our reference implementation. Section 4 illustrates it on a representative case study. Then Sect. 5 discusses some related work. Finally Sect. 6 draws conclusions and highlights the next steps of our work.

2 Requirements Level Support: GQM and NFR Reasoning

This section details, at the requirements level, the methodological support centred on energy goals. First, it details how to define energy goals in a measurable way on a target Cloud infrastructure using the Goal-Question-Metric approach. Second, it provides guidelines for reasoning with other important NFRs for Cloud applications.

2.1 Goal-Question-Metric Approach to Energy Awareness

The Goal-Question-Metric paradigm defined by Basili [13] is structured into three different levels of abstraction:

- **Conceptual Level: A Goal** is defined for an object, for a variety of reasons, with respect to various models of quality, from several points of view and relative to a particular environment. It specifies the domain vocabulary and the relationships between terms. In our context, it describes the Cloud domain (SaaS/PaaS/IaaS layers, VM and virtualised resources like CPU, RAM and storage) and captures energy goals along with other possibly related NFRs as described in Sect. 2.3.

– **Operational Level: A Set of Questions** that specifies the quality questions connecting the domain vocabulary to quality measures. In our case, they will be phrased in a way that directly relate them with measurable KPIs on the Cloud, possibly in connection with SLA.

– **Quantitative Level: A Set of Metrics**, based on the models, is associated with every question in order to answer it in a measurable way. In our case, it specifies the list of Quality-related Metrics and KPIs whose measures can be taken when running a application on the target Cloud Stack. It will also rely on standardised metrics such as surveyed by [15].

2.2 Helping a Development Team to Improve the Energy Efficiency of a Cloud Application

A development team is willing to consider improving the energy efficiency of its application when savings on energy cost can offset the cost incurred by the effort of refactoring the code. Consequently, refactoring for energy improvement would normally be considered as part of a larger refactoring effort, for example, when migrating a legacy client-server application to operate in the Cloud. In such a case, the effort for improving energy efficiency would become a small portion of the overall cost with direct benefit if the company developing the Cloud application subsequently operates it in its private Cloud. In the present context, it is assumed that the development team is willing to change the code of the Cloud application to improve its energy efficiency under several workloads (Table 1).

Table 1. GQM goal related to energy efficiency.

Energy efficiency	
Object	Server-side software features or components of a cloud application
Purpose	Characterization of the energy efficiency behaviour effectiveness on representative workloads
Quality focus	Energy efficiency
Point of view	Development team and project manager of a cloud application
Context	Identify the energy consumption of various features or components of an application to be provided as a service in the cloud to facilitate later refactoring activities to improve the application code with regards to energy consumption

For the Goal of Energy Efficiency, questions related to the operational level of the GQM depend on the variety of

– deployment alternatives considered by the service providers,
– technical characteristics of the virtual machines available at the data centre(s) of the service provider,

- workloads for representative customer profiles,
- features or components of the Cloud application for which developers want to learn the energy consumption.

As the context is application refactoring, it is important to approach the quest to learn about energy consumption behaviour of various application features or components as an integral part of the development process. As Cloud development practice commonly uses a iterative development approach based on continuous integration and continuous deployment heavily relying on nightly builds, a natural approach is to rely on this infrastructure to also gain knowledge on the energy consumption of application features or components. The continuous integration process can be used to run various workloads on a set of design/deployment alternatives that can be explored. We can characterise such a deployment alternative in the following way:

- E is a set of elements of a Cloud application where an element in E is a feature or software component
- W is a subset of workloads wl for representative customer profiles.

GQM Questions related to the Goal on Energy Efficiency, generally follow the pattern: **How much energy is consumed by an element e in E when the workload wl is applied?** This question can be asked for every element in E and every workload wl of every representative customer profile in W.

The generic question above purposely leaves room for semantic interpretations on what it means to measure the energy consumption for a feature or a component of a cloud application. To enable an incremental knowledge building of various portions of the application as well as a zoom-in approach to spot abnormal energy consumption behaviour that may later need refactoring, it is important that the development team can quickly specify what application features or components must be measured, as well as how to measure them so as to obtain new energy consumption data during the next nightly build. For example, after learning from a previous nightly built that the feature "search for a bug in a given bug tracker" under various workloads exhibits a fairly constant energy profile due to the inclusion of the energy consumed by the VM hosting the database, the development team may want to ignore the energy consumption of the database hosting VM and only obtain focus on the energy consumption for the business logic layer (on the server side) of the feature.

2.3   Capturing and Structuring Energy-Related NFRs

We will not present here an exhaustive catalogue of such NFRs but rather highlight our general design approach with a focus on Cloud computing. Given that our approach was goal-based, it is quite natural to consider a goal-oriented requirements engineering (GORE) framework to deal with such NFRs in a larger perspective, since it provides all the tools to capture NFR as well as their interrelationship like contributions or conflicts.

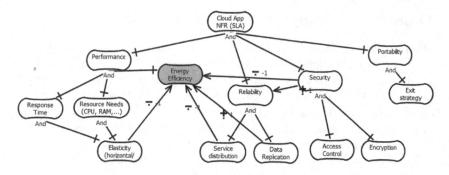

Fig. 3. High Level Structure of NFR and some relationships.

In order to identify the key NFRs, we also need to consider the concerned stakeholders, because the subsequent reasoning can be done with different sets of stakeholders, depending on the kind of deployment considered. From a service consumer's point of view, *response time* and *price* are the most common metrics used to evaluate services and applications, for these are the ones that will directly impact end users. From a service host's point of view, the *overall cost* is the most obvious parameter to minimise. This cost minimisation is subject to multiple constraints which are affected by NFRs. For the service to remain useful and profitable, the quality of service must reach a certain level. Service Level Agreements (SLAs) contractually ensure that the required quality of service is achieved consistently by defining measurements.

We rely here on the large amount of work already carried out by several European projects [18]. Figure 3 structures the most frequently NRFs encountered such as availability, performance (response time, resource and also energy), security/privacy of data, location/access/portability of data, exit strategy using a structure similar to SQuaRE. A distinctive feature of our work is of course the inclusion of energy NFRs, which also relate to "Green SLAs" that are being considered in the efficient use of resources, particularly the energy, by services and applications [19]. At this high-level, we can state some generic conflicts, e.g. redundancy will increase energy consumption, security will also require more resources (CPU, transfer volume) to cope with encryption for example and thus increase energy demand. However, other contributions might depend on the application, e.g. a good data replication strategy which can have a positive energy balance for data intensive applications. In the end, the assessment will need to be evaluated in the scope of a specific application which can be designed or deployed in different ways. This will require to explore a design space with the energy efficiency becoming a parameter of the total cost function.

Figure 3 was elaborated for a specific case study. The SQUaRE taxonomy was used as check-list and all (sub-)characteristics where not relevant here. However our belief is that some of the identified relations can be generalized in order to be reused, for example under the form of patterns which could make the link with functional requirements (e.g. requirements on availability for data storage).

3   Design Level Support: UML KPI Profile

To gather energy requirements, the design annotation and mapping with deployment time probes, we augmented UML with two stereotypes at different level of granularity. A first stereotype, *preparedForMeasurement*, provides information to prepare a UML model for a measurement session while a second stereotype, *forMeasurement*, provides information on each application elements relevant to measure (e.g. a method, a class, a deployment element such as a service, a VM,...). The definition of those two stereotypes also relies on a number of auxiliary *DataTypes* and *Enumerations*. In the rest of this section, we will use italic font to refer to concepts in the metamodel diagrams.

3.1   Stereotype for Measurement Sessions

The *preparedForMeasurement* stereotype is used to specify global information related to monitoring goals. It is depicted in Fig. 4

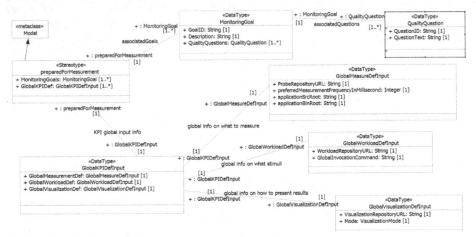

Fig. 4. Metamodel - Goal-Questions-Metrics.

Users can provide general information on a model for specifying monitoring needs. Notably, Information provided at the model level relate to

1. the explicit specification of *MonitoringGoal* and associated *QualityQuestions* to answer. Stereotyped KPIs modelled by user will then have to explicitly identify and define the questions (*QuestionID* and *QuestionText*) they help to answer.
2. a set of information (*GlobalNPIDefInput*) to define globally:
   - measures: global repository where probing information are found,
   - workload: global repository where invocation commands to exercise workloads on the application are found,
   - visualisation: global repository where visualisation information are found. The information location is implementation independent but a URL to some configuration repository is expected, e.g. [20].

3.2   Stereotype for Measured Elements

The *forMeasurement* stereotype can be attached to an UML element on which measurement can be conducted (statically or dynamically). The top of Fig. 5 shows the standard UML element to which it can be attached (operation, class, component, etc.). To address the need of dynamic measurements for those type of elements, it is necessary to define the *forMeasurement* facet which is mainly composed of a list of KPI definition and some technology specific information that will be useful at deployment time. Each KPI associated to a UML element is captured by the *KPIDefInput*. In addition to a identifying *KPIName* and *KPIRepositoryURL*, it contains a link to relevant questions it addresses (at least one) and the following defining fields:

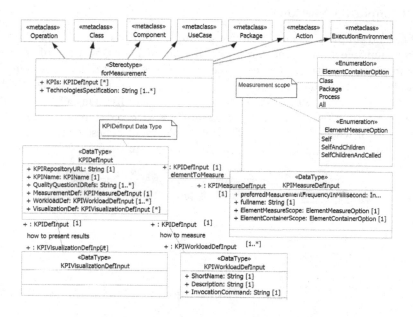

Fig. 5. Metamodel - KPI and visualisation.

- *MeasurementDef* (mandatory): defines on what to perform the measurement as *KPIMeasureDefInput*. This scope can be finely specified using strategies related to the container level (package, class, method, process,...) or inheritance/call level (self, self+children, self+children+called)
- *WorkloadDef* information (mandatory): needed to conduct dynamic test sessions on an execution environment to capture the desired measurement for relevant workload categories, defined using the *KPIWorkloadDefInput*.
- *VisualizationDef* data (optional): to further precise dashboards and other visualization widgets useful to present and to interpret measurement results. Note it is optional because all required information may already be present in the global *GlobalVisualizationDefInput*.

4   Run-Time Support: Goal-Level Data Analysis

Our approach is to keep the application designer in control of design space
exploration. However, finding the right trade-off between multiple concerns may
quickly become a daunting problem as the complexity increases dramatically
with each new parameter. To help service and application designers to find the
right balance between their different concerns, we developed a visualization tool
that allows (1) to compare how the different parameters behave on different
versions of an application or service, and (2) to easily define the trade-off and
see which versions of the application or service match the constraints set by the
trade-off.

4.1   Comparing Versions

The first and simplest visualization uses a simple chart to compare a given metric
between multiple measurement sets. A measurement set is a set of measures
taken in given conditions. For example, a measurement set may contain data
about the response time, CPU, RAM, and energy usage of one virtual machine
(VM) during one particular test, while another measurement set may contain
the same information during the same test, but with a different version of the
search code, or with a different application deployment. These tests are repeated
multiple times and measures are aggregated to obtain reasonable estimates.

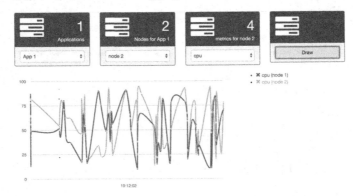

Fig. 6. CPU comparison between two nodes in the same test run.

Then, these measures can be compared on a graph. For example, the CPU
usage can be displayed using a line chart, where the CPU usage can be visualized on the duration of the test. Figure 6 illustrates a visualization comparing
CPU history on two nodes of the same experiment. This kind of graphs allows
developers to:

– identify potential peaks or long CPU intensive operations that could be investigated further and optimized locally.
– compare two versions or deployments of their code to see the actual effects of
  a change.

4.2   Trade-Off Definition

The second view approaches the data set from the opposite side. Instead of taking different tests and versions and showing how they compare on one specific aspect, this view takes multiple aspects and for each of them, displays how the various measurement sets are distributed, then it allows to filter out the unwanted parts of the distributions and see which measurements sets match the filter.

Figure 7 illustrates this: three bar graphs display the distributions of the measurements sets over the Energy consumption, Cost, and Time dimensions. On each chart, the X axis represents the measurement range (in the relevant unit, e.g. Wh for Energy), and the Y axis represents the corresponding number of measurements sets. We selected those three dimensions as the most relevant in our current experiments but other dimensions can be explored too. Our visualization is also not restricted to three dimensions.

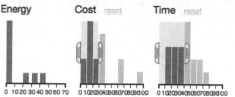

| Fig. 7. Filtering on aspects. | Fig. 8. Energy (kWh) vs Time (s). |

Figure 7 also shows the filtering mechanism. Using sliders on each graph, the user can easily select the parts of each chart that he wants to include in the filter. The user can immediately see the impact of the filters on a scatter plot restricted to two selected parameters. Figure 8 shows the result of the filtering on cost and time on the energy versus time plot. We can clearly see that the time dimension (Y axis) has been capped at a given level: all the blue points are under the level selected by the filter. We can also see however that not all the points under that line are blue. On the left side for example, a few dots are grey, even though there is no filter on the energy (X axis) aspect. This is an effect of the filter on the cost. The grey dots on the left side of the graph (low energy) had a higher cost, and they were excluded by the filter on the cost aspect.

The list of corresponding measurements sets and versions of the service that match the filters is also updated, so that the user can then make an informed choice about which version of his service he can ship and deploy.

5   Reference Implementation

Our work is part of the ASCETiC toolbox [6] which aims at improving the lifecycle of Cloud services to reduce carbon footprint and optimise energy efficiency. The toolbox relies on Open Source component and will be released under Open Source terms. The platform is an energy-enhanced OpenStack. The design tools are based on the Eclipse IDE while the runtime components are integrated within a web portal based on Bootstrap [21].

The Requirement level tooling is based on the jUCMNav Eclipse plugin [22]. It takes the form of a catalogue of goal-question-metric refinements from high level goals (such as Energy Efficiency presented in Sect. 2.2 and also covering key relationship across NFR. This work is specific to the Cloud domain.

The KPI UML profile was developed on top of Papyrus, an Open Source Eclipse-based UML tool [16]. Papyrus supports the definition of profiles through *.profile* projects that can be specified with the tool itself and can then be applied to normal UML projects. Papyrus automatically generates all the input forms required to captures the structured and typed information specified in the profile. In order to retrieve the energy-related information encoded in an instantiated model, we used [23] which provides a nice declarative language to transform the source UML model into some target such as the monitoring deployment descriptor in an OVF format for instance.

Finally, the data visualisation relies on the BIRT Eclipse plugin [24] and is also available as a web-portal using D3 [25] and SVG [26].

6 Photo Album Case Study

6.1 Case Study Description

Photo Album is a 3-tier web application that is designed to be desktop-like on-line photo manager [27]. It provides social services for uploading photos, storing and previewing them, creating albums and sharing them with other users. The visualisation layer is implemented in JavaScript while the business logic in Java runs on the server side and a database for storing issue data can run on the same server or on a different machine. It is very representative of applications that can be deployed in SaaS mode on a Cloud and that can benefit of the PaaS and IaaS layers elasticity/reconfigurability features.

6.2 GQM Energy Analysis

We restrict ourselves to a simple goal together with related questions as described in Table 2. Those elements are encoded into a *preparedForMeasurement* entry which is directly attached the to the Photo Album UML design project.

Table 2. Goal and question definition for the Photo Album.

Type	ID	Description

Goal	EE	Study the impact of executing the following features and components of Photo Album on the energy consumption to determine if a refactoring effort is worth undertaking:
		  – Upload a multimedia item in an album
		  – Compile an album

Questions	EE_TQ1	What is the **overall energy consumed** when exercising the given feature or component for each workload category?
	EE_SQ1	How does the **energy consumed every second** varies when exercising the given feature or component for each workload category?
	...	...

6.3   Use Case Annotation

The UML Use Case diagram is the simplest to use because it easily relates to business level services typically in the application server. Figure 9 shows the two identified features of our GQM analysis.

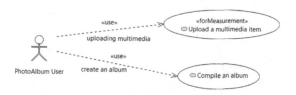

Fig. 9. Annotated use case for the Photo Album.

The first use case *Upload a multimedia item* is annotated with a *forMeasurement* stereotype. This was done using the *KPIDefInput* partly shown in Fig. 10. It is worth noting that such appropriate dialogue windows are automatically generated by Papyrus from information described in the metamodel.

For the PhotoAlbum Use Case, the recommended measurement strategy is coarse grained, i.e. measuring all the contained elements and following both the inheritance and call graphs. Note that the *fullName* field can accept a specific language for specifying the deployment target to monitor with some facilities like regular expression. It is used to specify a *upload* entry-point method and a *samba* process performing the file upload.

6.4   Deployment Annotations and Monitoring Process

Figure 11 shows a deployment view. It should normally only show the photo album related VM, i.e. the application VM *PA-APP-VM* and the database VM) *PA-BD-VM* along side the *Test VM* is used to inject specific workloads in a controlled way on the application under energy monitoring. However, to give some insight on the monitoring process, Fig. 11 also represents the infrastructure VMs managing the energy monitoring: the *SaaS Modelling VM* offers developer front-end tools such as Papyrus, aggregation, reporting and visualisation tools and the *PaaS Infrastructure VM* runs a global efficient monitoring service.

Regarding the deployment process, information for generating the probe descriptor and the test load specification is extracted from the UML model using Acceleo. Those elements are then passed respectively to the probe deployment and load generator services.

Beside application features of components, as illustrated earlier, a UML model can also use annotated application VMs with *forMeasurement* information, for example to capture VM level monitoring and measure the impact of specific Cloud architectural components, in our case, it could be used to determine the energy consumption of a load balancer which distributes the load to keep good response times and therefore identify explicitly a time-energy trade-off that could take place.

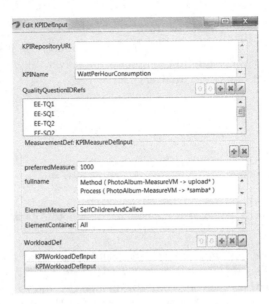

Fig. 10. KPI Definition for photo upload.

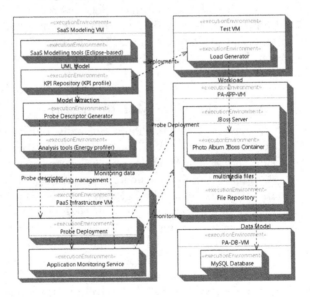

Fig. 11. Deployment view.

6.5 Reporting the Results

Figure 12 shows a typical report generated from BIRT. It shows historical data gathered from the monitoring service on virtualised components such as CPU, IO, memory access. Those are transparently translated into Watt history and total Joule consumption based on an energy model. The link with the related question and goal is also reported. The data can then be analysed, for example to correlate the Watt consumption with some element (CPU, network access...) and/or some specific load event. Based on this measurement information, bottlenecks could be identified and improvements to a specific service or more globally to an architecture refactoring can be triggered.

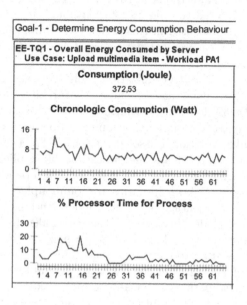

Fig. 12. Reporting at KPI level (partial).

7 Related Work and Discussion

As already mentioned, much work has been devoted to energy efficiency in the embedded domain given the limited resource available. The MARTE profile is capturing a lot of resource categories, including energy [28]. In a SysML context, they can be related to requirements however the profile does not support our richer traceability to KPI and based on a systematic GQM approach. Further extensions dealing more specifically with energy have been developed [29]. Their aim is more directed towards design time energy estimation rather than runtime monitoring and evolution as ours.

Concerning energy requirements and goals, there is little room for them in the current analysis literature: standards structuring non-functional requirements like the ISO9126 and even the more recent SQuaRE essentially captures them from a performance efficiency point of view and do not enable any reasoning on them [11]. They are also not present in goal-oriented frameworks like Chung's NFRs [10] or KAOS [9]. However, they provide very effective reasoning means that were applied to Energy requirements in this work. As pointed by a Microsoft report, most of the time energy consideration are simply not present in software specifications, except for specific systems like embedded systems, and fail to address fundamental issues such as the available power budget, the impact of energy in the selection of a specific design, or the resolution of conflicts with other requirements. At the organisation level, the situation is different, with a current trend to help organisations in their energy management strategies, for example using goal-oriented techniques [30]. Although this work seems farther away from the context presented in this article, the framework presented could be well used to collect measurement data needed as evidence for compliance to [31] on Energy Management.

Overall, the SaaS KPI and visualization tools propose an operational approach to perform a particular assessment of the architecture trade-off analysis method (ATAM) [32] focused on runtime quality characteristics of various deployment alternatives of a SaaS application to be operated in Cloud infrastructures. However, unlike traditional assessment with ATAM or other approaches to quantify NFRs, our approach assumes an executable application, e.g. a legacy application being migrated to operate in the Cloud or a SaaS application being developed incrementally. As both scenarios are commonplace, we believe that we will cover a significant percentage of Cloud application development projects.

On the visualization side, there exists other tools like the ClaferMoo Visualizer, a tool aimed at visualizing Pareto fronts to help making a choice between optimal configurations of a product line in [33]. This work uses a 4 dimensional bubble chart by using the size and the colour of the bubble as additional visual variables. Our work, while similar in appearance, takes a different approach. Our constraints can take the form of boundaries on different dimensions and we limit to use 2-dimensional charts to keep the comparison simple. Also, we do not address the issue of optimisation.

This work can to some extend be generalized to other kinds of software applications as the GQM analysis and UML profile are generic, as well as the visualization tool. However, the elaborated models are specific to the Cloud domain. This domain knowledge is part of the tool delivered to the Cloud application developer. The global approach can of course be applied to other domains but will only be worth the investment if it exhibits enough specificities/constraints and has a large enough developer base (e.g. mobile ecosystems, smart card product families, etc.).

8 Conclusion and Future Work

In this paper, we presented an integrated approach to guide Cloud developers in building their applications in a more energy-aware way and helping them to make the right trade-offs among different energy related non-functional requirements. Our approach consists of a requirements phase where relationships and impacts among NFR are identified, a design phase where design alternatives are specified in a measurable way, and a run-time phase where the collected data are visualised for the specified set of alternatives and an appropriate trade-off is identified inside the explored design space. Our work is supported by an Open Source tooling.

Our experimentation so far is still limited to partial data sets, which have been manually collected from a news publication application currently being migrated to the Cloud, and complemented by a test data generator. The next steps in our work will be to achieve a complete integration with the ASCETiC test-bed and validate the approach on two other case studies (microservice-based shopping cart and numeric simulation for building optimization). In this process, we also enrich our goal refinement pattern database to document links between NFR and energy effectiveness. In order to provide the best assistance to the Cloud application developer, we also plan to further develop the visualization capabilities of the tool and to integrate some data analysis capacities helping with the identification of interesting trade-offs. Finally, we also plan to develop specific support for the coding phase under the form of a static code analysis tool able to detect possible energy "hotspots" and inform developers about green code patterns that can address them.

Acknowledgement. This work was partly funded by the European Commission under the FP7 ASCETiC project (nr 610874).

References

1. Internet Science NoE: D8.1. Overview of ICT energy consumption (2013). http://www.internet-science.eu
2. Masanet, E.R., Brown, R.E., Shehabi, A., Koomey, J.G., Nordman, B.: Estimating the energy use and efficiency potential of u.s. data centers. Proc. IEEE **99**, 1440–1453 (2011)
3. Dougherty, B., White, J., Schmidt, D.C.: Model-driven auto-scaling of green cloud computing infrastructure. Future Gener. Comp. Syst. **28**, 371–378 (2012)
4. Mastelic, T., et al.: Cloud computing: survey on energy efficiency. ACM Comput. Surv. **47**, 33:1–33:36 (2014)
5. Penzenstadler, B., et al.: Systematic mapping study on software engineering for sustainability (SE4S). In: 18th International Conference on Evaluation and Assessment in Software Engineering, EASE 2014, pp. 14: 1–14: 14, London, UK, May 2014
6. ASCETIC: Adapting Service lifeCycle towards EfficienT Clouds - FP7 Project. http://www.ascetic.eu
7. ENTRA: Whole-Systems ENergy TRAnsparency (2013). http://entraproject.eu/
8. ECO2Cloud: Experimental Awareness of CO2 in Federated Cloud Sourcing (2012). http://eco2clouds.eu
9. Van Lamsweerde, A.: Requirements engineering: from system goals to UML models to software specifications, Wiley (2009)
10. Chung, L., Nixon, B.A., Yu, E., Mylopoulos, J.: Non-Functional Requirements in Software Engineering. Kluwer Academic Publishers, Hardbound (2000)
11. ISO/IEC: 25010: 2011: Systems and software engineering - Systems and software Quality Requirements and Evaluation (SQuaRE) -Quality models (2011)

12. Deprez, J.C., Ramdoyal, R., Ponsard, C.: Integrating energy and eco-aware requirements engineering in the development of services-based applications on virtual clouds. In: First International Workshop on Requirements Engineering for Sustainable Systems (2012)

13. Basili, V.R., Caldiera, G., Rombach, D.H.: The Goal Question Metric Approach. Wiley, UK (1994)

14. Deprez, J.C., Ponsard, C.: Energy related goals and questions for cloud services, measurement and metrics for green and sustainable software. In: Measurement and Metrics for Green and Sustainable Software (MeGSuS 2014) (2014)

15. Bozzelli, P., Gu, Q., Lago, P.: A systematic literature review on green software metrics. Technical report, VU University Amsterdam (2013)

16. Foundation, E.: Papyrus graphical editing tool for UML2. http://www.eclipse.org/papyrus

17. Ponsard, C., Michel, R., Saadaoui, S.J.C.D.: Guiding cloud application developers in designing balanced trade-off among energy impacting requirements. In: Measurement and Metrics for Green and Sustainable Software (MeGSuS 2015) (2015)

18. Commission, E.: Cloud Computing Service Level Agreements - Exploitation of Research Results (2013)

19. Haque, M.E., et al.: Providing green SLAs in high performance computing clouds. In: International Green Computing Conference, IGCC 2013, Arlington, USA (2013)

20. Chef: Automation for Web-Scale IT. http://www.getchef.com/chef

21. Twitter: Bootstrap. http://getbootstrap.com

22. University Ottawa: jUCMNav: juice up your modelling (2001). http://goo.gl/gyElGB

23. Foundation, E.: Acceleo, a pragmatic MOF Model to Text Language Implementation. http://www.eclipse.org/acceleo

24. BIRT: Business Intelligence and Reporting Tool (2005). http://eclipse.org/birt

25. Bostock, M.: D3 - data driven documents. http://d3js.org

26. W3C: Scalable vector graphics (svg) 1.1 2nd edn (2011). http://www.w3.org/TR/SVG

27. Tsebro, A., Mukhina, S., Galkin, G., Sorokin, M.: Rich faces photo album application (2009). http://tinyurl.com/ncd77zp

28. OMG: The UML Profile for MARTE: Modeling and Analysis of Real-Time and Embedded Systems. http://www.omgmarte.org

29. Shorin, D., Zimmermann, A.: Evaluation of embedded system energy usage with extended uml models. Softwaretechnik-Trends 33 (2013)

30. Stefan, D., Letier, E., Barrett, M., Stella-Sawicki, M.: Goal-oriented system modelling for managing environmental sustainability. In: 3rd International Workshop on Software Research and Climate Change (2011)

31. ISO 50001: Energy Management (2011). http://www.iso.org

32. Kazman, R., Klein, M., Clements, P.: Atam: method for architecture evaluation. Technical report CMU/SEI-2000-TR-004, SEI, Carnegie Mellon University (2000)

33. Murashkin, A.: Web-based gui for pareto front visualization and analysis

SPACES: Subjective sPaces Architecture for Contextualizing hEterogeneous Sources

Daniela Micucci, Marco Mobilio$^{(\boxtimes)}$, and Francesco Tisato

Department of Informatics, Systems and Communication,
University of Milano-Bicocca, Milano, Italy
{micucci,marco.mobilio,tisato}@disco.unimib.it
http://www.sal.disco.unimib.it

Abstract. The growing use of sensors in smart environments applications like smart homes, hospitals, public transportation, emergency services, education, and workplaces not only generates constantly increasing of sensor data, but also rises the complexity of integration of heterogeneous data and hardware devices. Existing infrastructures should be reused under different application domain requirements, applications should be able to manage data coming from different devices without knowing the intrinsic characteristics of the sensing devices, and, finally, the introduction of new devices should be completely transparent to the existing applications. The paper proposes a set of architectural abstractions aimed at representing sensors' measurements that are independent from the sensors' technology. Such a set can reduce the effort for data fusion and interpretation, moreover it enforces both the reuse of existing infrastructure and the openness of the sensing layer by providing a common framework for representing sensors' readings. The abstractions rely on the concepts of *space*. Data is localized both in a positing and in a measurement space that are subjective with respect to the entity that is observing the data. Mapping functions allow data to be mapped into different spaces so that different entities relying on different spaces can reason on data.

Keywords: Sensor heterogeneity · Modularisation · Software architecture · Knowledge representation

1 Introduction

Smart environments are usually instrumented with various typologies of sensors. Sensors may have a fixed position, like a thermometer or a light sensor, or they may move inside the environment, like the sensors embedded in smartphones. Moreover, sensors are heterogeneous, thus producing measurements that are semantically linked to their sources. Applications that rely on sensors' measurements usually fall under the umbrella of Ambient Intelligence (AmI) that includes specific domains like smart homes, health monitoring and assistance, hospitals, transportation, emergency services, education, and workplaces [1].

© Springer International Publishing Switzerland 2016
P. Lorenz et al. (Eds.): ICSOFT 2015, CCIS 586, pp. 415–429, 2016.
DOI: 10.1007/978-3-319-30142-6_23

Such applications often are required to know the specific device that originated the measurement in order to understand and use the information provided. This leads to vertical systems, which feature low modularity and scarce openness.

When modeling sensors and related measurements, architectural solutions should face the challenge related to both heterogeneity and semantics. For example, authors in [7] propose a layered architecture that provides the low-level software, the middleware, and the upper-level services with detailed specifications of the involved sensors. This way sensors are well modeled, but their knowledge is distributed throughout all the system.

Authors in [2] focus on issues related to the management of large amount of data from sensors: the proposed approach consists in transforming sensor data in what authors call a *set of observations* that are meaningful for the applications. Lower levels embed semantics that is strictly related to the specific application. This lead to scarce reusability as the same abstraction rules for a specific sensor may not be applicable in different contexts.

Finally, database approach is growing interest. Indeed, the database approach allows heterogeneous applications to access the same sensor data via declarative queries. This kind of solutions may resolve data heterogeneity at the application level, but there still persists the issue of sensor data management, since most of the existing solutions suppose homogeneous sensors generating data according to the same format [4].

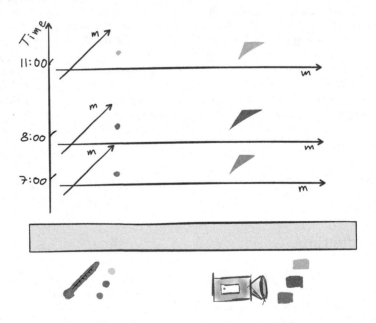

Fig. 1. Abstraction of sensed information.

The identification of a suitable set of architectural abstractions, able to represent sensor measurements independently from the hardware characteristics of the source, could improve reusability, openness, and modularity of software systems. In this paper we present SPACES (Subjective sPaces Architecture for Contextualizing hEterogeneous Sources), a set of architectural abstractions that remove the dependency from the sensor by contextualizing the measurements in a spatio-temporal frame. In detail, measurements have a time-stamp and are localized in both a measurement and a positioning space. Such spaces are subjective to the software components that manage them. For example, a sensor component that is in charge of acquiring temperature expressed in a Celsius measurement unit, will localize the sensed data in a Celsius measurement space and in a Cartesian 2D space that is local to the sensor. Mapping functions allow to project localizations defined in source spaces in target spaces (possibly different) that are in turns subjective to the software component interested in managing the sensed data. In the example above, a software component that controls the temperature of a room reasoning on Fahrenheit degrees and by operating on actuators placed in the room, will reason on a Fahrenheit measurement space and on a Cartesian positioning space.

The general concept is that a space is the source with respect to a target space. A mapping function is in charge of mapping the couple of spaces. This hold for both the measurement and the positioning spaces. The general pattern defined by the abstractions can be replicated many times, at different abstraction layer.

Figure 1 sketched a visual representation of the core concepts of SPACES. In the example, a temperature sensor and a camera are the sensing devices. Data acquired are localized in the subjective spaces of the acquisition components at different time-stamps. Moreover, data is also localized in the subjective space of a software components that reason in terms of room. In this example, only the localization spaces have been changed (the measurement spaces remain unchanged). As it can be possible to notice, images acquired by the camera are localized in a bi-dimensional Cartesian Space (image plane). A mapping function projects the image plane in a cone on the Cartesian 2D space representing the room.

Measurements may also result in spatio-temporal events that can be stored inside a Data Base Management System (DBMS) or streamed inside a Data Stream Management System (DSMS) [6], as proposed in [4]. The main benefit is that applications no longer need to know the kind and the numbers of deployed sensors. Upon the occurrence of an event of interest, applications can decide to access all the other events that are related both spatially and temporally. In this paper neither the storage nor distribution of data is handled, but the focus is on the definition of such a set of architectural abstractions that could solve sensors heterogeneity issue, in order to be able to apply one of the mentioned approaches for data distribution, storage, and usage.

This paper will present the basic concepts along with the following simplified case of study. Consider a smart building composed by different rooms; in each room different sensors are located. In our example, we consider a room only (room1) that is instrumented as follow: in the top corner there is a camera (cam1) facing the centre of the room. Hanged on the wall there is also a thermometer (therm1). Moreover, a person in the room owns a smartphone with the accelerometer `acc1`. In this kind of contexts, smartphones are usually considered as extensions of the user, which means that their position is the same. Several applications can rely on the above listed sensors: a tracking application could try to follow the user (either a specific one or any user) and could make the position available to the system; an application could exploit the locations of the users to control the temperature in the rooms accordingly, based on their needs or preferences. These are just a few examples that can benefit from the proposed approach.

The paper is organized as follows: Sect. 2 introduces core concepts related to spaces and zones; Sect. 3 discusses stimuli as measurements from the sensors and their contextualization in the measurement space and the positioning space; Sect. 4 presents how sources have been modeled be they sensors or software components reasoning on their subjective spaces; Sect. 5 presents the way subjective spaces can be related; finally Sect. 6 sketches some conclusions and future directions.

2   Spaces and Zones

Spatial contextualization have been derived from previously defined concepts [5,8]. Those concepts have been revisited and enriched in order to capture and model the meta representation of a space.

A *Space* is defined as a set of potential locations, that are all the locations that could be theoretically considered in that space. In a graph, the potential locations are all the nodes and the edges. On the other hand, if a Cartesian space is used to localize entities within a room, then the potential locations are every point in $\mathbb{R}^2$ of the area delimited by the room perimeter. Applications, when dealing with a space, explicitly manage effective locations, which are a subset of space's potential locations. For example, an application that calculates the trajectory of a mobile entity will only explicitly consider a finite number of locations in the Cartesian space, that is, the locations belonging to the trajectory (known as effective locations). Each space defines at least a *premetric*. The premetric defines the distance between two locations as a positive, non-zero number if the two locations are distinct, and zero if the locations are the same.

The main extension to the original model consists in defining spaces as an aggregation of *Dimension*s. A Dimension literally represents a dimension in a space: it is characterized by a *UnitOfMeasure*, a *Precision* related to its values, and a set of *Boundaries* related to the values that each dimension can assume. Locations are aggregations of dimension values. For example a location in a 3 dimensional Cartesian space, would be represented as an aggregation of 3 values, one for each dimension of such space. Considering the scenario introduced in Sect. 1, `room1` is represented by a 3D Cartesian Space (a positioning space). Suitable locations for this kind of space are 3D points.

Spaces and (effective) locations are respectively created from *Space Model* and *Location Type* as depicted in Fig. 2: a space model thus specifies the type of allowable locations and at least one premetric that can be applied to a

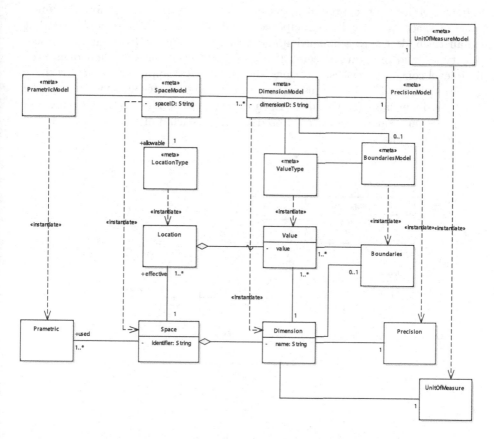

Fig. 2. Core concepts: meta representation and instances.

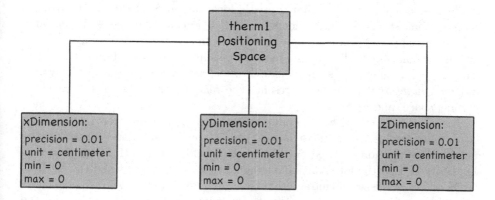

Fig. 3. 3D Cartesian space example.

pair of locations. Of course, if a space is defined as an aggregation of dimensions, a space model will be composed by at least one *Dimension Model* that exhaustively describes a dimension and all its components. Space models, location types, and premetric specifications are meta-level concepts that define the base-level concepts (spaces, locations and premetrics) applications deal with.

For example, Fig. 3 pictures a three dimensional Cartesian space, composed by three dimensions (x, y and z). Each dimension has its own unit of measure and precision. Boundaries are expressed as values, each dimension has a *min* and a *max* admissible value.

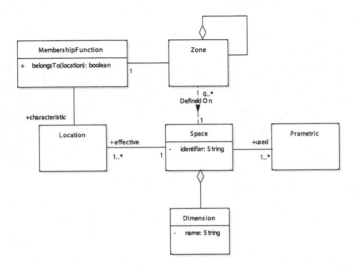

Fig. 4. Space, location, and zone.

A *zone* Z_S is a subset of potential locations of a space S. It is defined by a set of effective locations termed characteristic locations in S and by a membership function that states if a given location of S belongs to the zone. Essentially, the membership function is a boolean function that is true when a location falls within the zone. According to the membership function used, different kinds of zones can been identified, such as: *enumerative, premetric declarative, polygonal,* and *pure functional.* Figure 4 represents the relationship between the concepts of zone, space, and location.

A zone characterized by an enumerative membership function (also defined as an enumerative zone) has a non-empty set of characteristic locations: the membership function is based on the standard belonging relationship defined in set theory and all the locations belonging to the zone are identified through the enumeration of the set of characteristic locations. As an example, a specific area of a grid space can be represented with an enumerative zone by listing all the cells included in such area. On the other hand, a polygonal membership function is related to a polygonal zone in which the characteristic locations are the vertexes of a polygon, and indicates the inclusion of a location in such polygon. As an example, the zone representing a specific room within a two dimension space that depicts a floor of a building can be obtained by a polygonal membership function with the vertexes of the polygon as the zone's characteristic locations. A premetric declarative zone, which is a zone that has a premetric membership function, only features a single characteristic location. Its membership function thus includes all and only the locations situated at a given distance from the characteristic locations. A clear example of this kind of zone can be the representation of the detection area of a RFID reader in a Cartesian space. Finally, a pure functional zone has a functional membership function that uses mathematical expressions defined in terms of the space coordinate system. An example can be the following one: for each pair of locations (x, y) in a space S and for any given location (x_0, y_0) and (x_1, y_1),

$$f(x) = \begin{cases} true, & \text{if } x_0 < x < x_1 and y_0 < y < y_1 \\ false, & \text{otherwise} \end{cases}$$

This example defines a rectangular zone, in which all locations between (x_0, y_0) and (x_1, y_1) are included. Figure 4 also pictures that a zone can be seen as an aggregation of other zones. This allows to create a zone that contains sub-zones, this can be useful in many cases, as an example, when dealing with continuous spaces and locations defined by real values, a simple enumeration can be an issue: it is impossible to get a positive response when using an enumeration of numbers with infinite precision. Using the concept of sub-zones, the enumeration of real numbers can be expressed as an enumeration of zones, where each zone features a premetric declarative membership function with each real value as characteristic location and a distance ϵ as small as needed that defines the precision of acceptance.

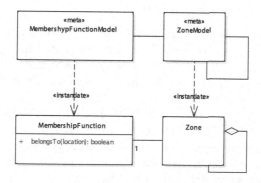

Fig. 5. The zone model.

As pictured in Fig. 5, zones and membership functions are build respectively from the meta level descriptors *ZoneModel* and *MembershipFunctionModel*.

3   Stimuli

Usually, data coming from physical or software sensors, is strictly related to the sensor itself. This means that without the knowledge of the characteristic of the source it is difficult, if not impossible, to understand and manipulate such data. One of the main contribution of this work deals with the representation of data from sensors that have been completely dissociated from the sensing devices exploiting the concepts of spaces, zones, and locations introduced in Sect. 2. Figure 6 represents the general structure of a *Stimulus*.

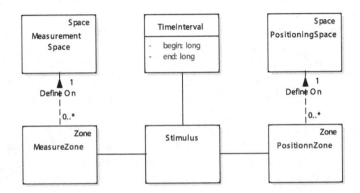

Fig. 6. The stimulus.

A stimulus is defined as any information related to a physical event and it is composed by three main information:

- *Time Interval*, the acquisition time.
- *Measure Zone*, the reading payload.
- *Position Zone*, the reading location.

The time interval represents the instant of acquisition and, thus, of validity, of the sample. The concept of Time Interval is presented in [3].

As pictured in Fig. 6, the measure zone is a specialization of zone and it is referred to a *Measurement Space*, which is a special kind of space, devoted to represent all the possible values that an information source can produce. Within the measurement space are represented all the characteristics of the allowable locations. As an example, Fig. 7 pictures the details of a possible representation of the *Temperature Space* subjective to the thermometer *therm1*. In this example, the space features a single dimension, which is the dimension of temperature values, the precision is referred to the precision with which values are expressible and their unit of measure is Celsius. The dimension also has its boundaries specified as two temperature values, -10 and 40 that represents respectively the lowest and highest temperatures sensible by the sensor. From this example it is clear that all the information of the sensor `therm1` that are related to the values it can provide, are embedded within the specification of its measurement space.

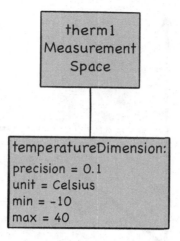

Fig. 7. Therm1 temperature space example.

The definition of a zone on a measurement space can be seen as expressing the payload of a single reading. At first, the use of a zone instead of a single location in order to represent the payload of a stimulus may seem an over-complication, but after a more careful examination this choice allows the representation of more meaningful information. For example, a simple temperature probe such as the one in the thermometer defined in the example scenario, is composed by a metal component that is physically designed to output a voltage signal that is linearly proportional to the local temperature. The most intuitive approach would be to use a temperature value representing the conversion from the voltage signal to the corresponding Celsius value. However, the precision of sensors may differ with respect of the values read. As an example, the data sheet of `therm1` could reasonably states something like:

$$Accuracy = \begin{cases} \pm 0.2^\circ \ C, & \text{from } -10^\circ \ C \text{ to } 0^\circ C \\ \pm 0.1^\circ \ C, & \text{from } 0^\circ \ C \text{ to } 30^\circ C \\ \pm 0.2^\circ \ C, & \text{from } 30^\circ \ C \text{ to } 40^\circ C \end{cases}$$

Using a location to represent the current reading, such information would be needed at any level, in order to correctly interpret and use the temperature value. On the other hand, by using a premetric declarative zone, the accuracy of each reading could be embedded within the measure itself: so for a value between -10° C and 0° C, the value of the ϵ parameter would be 0.2.

The positioned zone, represents where, by the sensor's perspective, the measure zone is placed. A simple thermometer like `therm1`, does not provide (or know) any information about where its readings are positioned: in this scenario, the position zone, would be irrelevant and usually corresponds to the origins of the position space. A more interesting scenario, is the one where the sensor is a different kind of thermometer, like an infrared thermometer, which infers

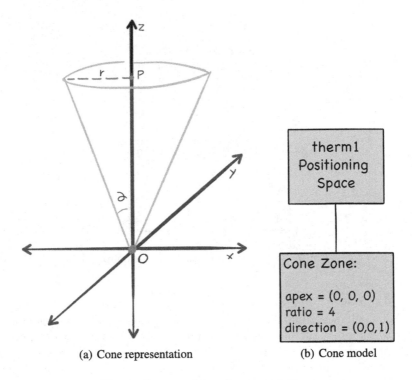

(a) Cone representation   (b) Cone model

Fig. 8. Cone model and representation.

the temperature from the thermal radiation emitted by the object toward it is pointed at. In this case, the position zone is represented by a cone as in Fig. 8.

Figure 8(b) pictures a cone in a three dimension Cartesian space, the apex of the cone is placed on the origin of the axes and it opens toward the positive Z axis. The opening angle α determines the radius r at the height z_p. In sensors it is usually expressed as a *ratio* between height of the cone section and depth of the base, also known as distance to spot ratio. Infrared thermometers usually do not provide distance measures, which is why the representation in Fig. 8(b) does not includes the point P: the cone is supposed to extend itself indefinitely, but it consider the apex of the cone in $(0,0,0)$ and the direction represented by the vector $(0,0,1)$ (it opens toward the positive Z axis).

It is worth noting that the distinction between positioning and measurement concepts is purely conceptual: they are all spaces and zones, as defined in Sect. 2.

4   Sources

Section 3 introduced the concept of stimulus. This section deals with the way sources of information (such as the physical devices) are modeled. One of the main issue of currently available proposals is the fact that the knowledge of low level physical devices is spread at each level of the system, up to the applications. In this work the more general concept of *Source* is introduced. A source is intended as a role, instead of a physical object. For example, when considering the thermometer `therm1`, it acts as a source with respect to the component that manages the temperature in room `room1`; at the same time, the temperature component manager could act as a source to another component that regulates the temperature in the floor.

As pictured in Fig. 9 a source can be fully defined by:

- A *MeasurementSpaceModel*, which defines the characteristics of the measurements that the source provides.
- One or more *MeasureZoneModel*, which states how the measurements belonging to the measurement space are expressed.
- A *PositioningSpaceModel*, representing the positioning space in which those measurements are contextualized.
- One or more *PositionZoneModel*, which expresses how measurements are positioned inside the po4sitioning space.

A source can feature more than one measure and position zone model, this allows for more complex sources that could represent their data in different manners.

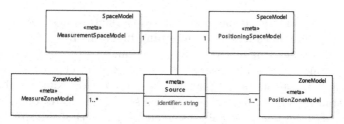

Fig. 9. The source model.

5   Mapping Functions

Given two different spaces, the concept of *Mapping* relates one zone defined on one space with another zone defined on the other one. Starting from [8] three kind of mappings can be defined:

- Explicit Mappings.
- Projective Mapping.
- Implicit Mappings.

An explicit mapping is an ordered pair of zones defined of different spaces, possibly build from different models: given the spaces S_1 and S_2, with $S_1 \neq S_2$, the ordered pair (Z_{S_1}, Z_{S_2}) is an explicit mapping between the zones $(Z_{S_1}) \subseteq S_1$ (the source) and $(Z_{S_2}) \subseteq S_2$ (the target). It is important to note that the target zone may be defined independently from the source zone. If, on the other hand, the target zone is the result of the application of a projection to the source zone, the mapping is a projective mapping, and it is described by the types of the involved spaces and the types of the respective zones. Finally, defined SM the set of all the defined mappings and Z_a and Z_b defined as two zones referred to different spaces, an implicit mapping (Z_a, Z_b) is derived if there exist n zones $Z_1, ..., Z_n$ such that $(Z_a, Z_1), (Z_1, Z_2), ..., (Z_n, Z_b) \in SM$ for $n \geq 1$ (Fig. 10).

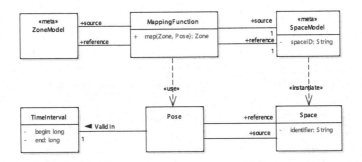

Fig. 10. The mapping function.

As mentioned, an explicit mapping is used to relate zones that are independent, projective mappings functions (mapping functions from now on) are thus the best choice, because the zones they produce can be seen as the representation of the source zone in the target space. In this work, mapping functions are used as connecting components between abstraction layers: for example, they can be used to abstract stimuli coming from physical sensors that are contextualized in subjective spaces, into other stimuli, referred to spaces that are subjective with respect to the software component interested in the readings. This pattern can be repeated many times as required by the abstractions needed.

For example, the stimuli produced by the simple thermometer therm1 represents the temperature in a specific position of the sensor subjective space. By applying a projection mapping to the position zone of the therm1 it is possible to obtain a new position, that represents the same information within the position space of room1.

With the aim of using a mapping function in order to position a stimuli (for example, from a sensor subjective space, to a space representing a room), the real *position* of the sensor itself inside the room comes in place. Since the aim of this work is to move from physical devices toward the concept of spaces, the position of a generic source with respect to a destination space is expressed as the *Pose* of the source position space with respect to its reference (target) space. For example Fig. 11 gives a graphical representation of the concept of pose of the therm1 positioning space within the room1 positioning space, it also gives a glimpse of how the conical zone defined in Fig. 8(a) needs to be represented with respect of the room1 perspective. The pose of a space with respect to another

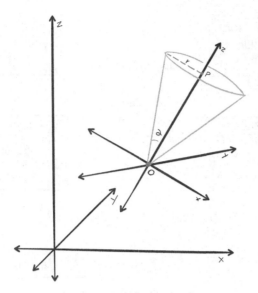

Fig. 11. The pose of the `therm1` space.

space is strictly dependent on the types of the two spaces: for example, when dealing with Cartesian spaces, the most common information needed to define a pose are:

a rotation and translation matrix
- a set of multipliers, in order to address the differences in scales between the two spaces. It may be one for each dimension, or a single one for all of them.

Figure 12 shows the mapping of the cone zone from the subjective space of `therm1` to the equivalent zone in the `room1` space. The conversion of the apex location its base on the roto-translation matrixes (they are not reported here, but can be calculated by different tools already available). The ratio of the destination zone depends on a interpolation of the scale values and the direction, finally, the destination direction vector is calculated applying to it the same rotation matrixes. What could also be included in the room perspective is the point P as showed in Fig. 11 as it is reasonable to delimit the cone to the boundaries of the room, nonetheless this could need a different and more complex polyhedric representation if the cone intersects the corners of the space.

While it is more common to think about the concepts of pose and mapping with positioning spaces, the same paradigm can be applied to measurement spaces. Referring to the temperature measurements considered until now, it is possible to define, as an example, the mapping between the measure contextualised in the subjective space of `therm1`, in a measure contextualised in a different temperature space, like the one referred to `room1`. Considering that `therm1`'s temperature space is expressed in Celsius degrees, while the `room1`'s is in Fahrenheit degrees, the mapping function can be seen as the conversion function, while the pose are the parameters that `align` the Celsius scale with respect to the Fahrenheit scale.

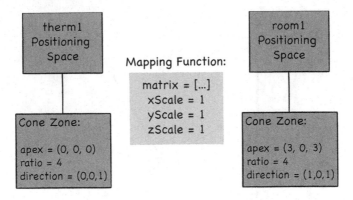

Fig. 12. The mapping of a cone.

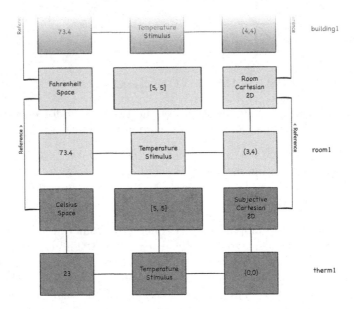

Fig. 13. The stimulus mapping chain.

By putting together both a positioning and a measurement mapping function, it is then possible to completely contextualize a stimulus in a different space. Figure 13 shows how abstraction of information works under the presented paradigm.

6   Conclusions

The proposed model has been object of a proof-of-concept Java implementation. It has proved the effectiveness and the feasibility of the proposal, while highlighting the aspects that require further investigations, such as how complex mapping function can been easily included into the model.

The first experimentation has dealt with static configuration of all the actor involved. Dynamic presentation of sources is also under development, by allowing a source to present itself to an upper layer by providing an exhaustive description of the spaces upon which it contextualize the data it provide.

A first experimentation with real world sensors is also being carried on: a number of heterogenous sources are being used. For example, the image information and the skeleton structure from a Kinect and onboard sensors from a Samsung Galaxy S5 smartphone, which dynamically present themselves to an integration component. The acquisition is currently controlled by a web application. A solid and wider implementation is still required, as the realisation of data-flow mechanisms that domain applications can exploit in order to consistently access and query stimuli at different levels of abstraction.

References

1. Cook, D.J., Augusto, J.C., Jakkula, V.R.: Ambient intelligence: technologies, applications, and opportunities. Pervasive Mob. Comput. **5**(4), 277–298 (2009)
2. Dasgupta, R., Dey, S.: A comprehensive sensor taxonomy and semantic knowledge representation: energy meter use case. In: 2013 Seventh International Conference on Sensing Technology (ICST), pp. 791–799. IEEE (2013)
3. Fiamberti, F., Micucci, D., Morniroli, A., Tisato, F.: A model for time-awareness. In: Bajec, M., Eder, J. (eds.) CAiSE Workshops 2012. LNBIP, vol. 112, pp. 70–84. Springer, Heidelberg (2012)
4. Gurgen, L., Roncancio, C., Labbé, C., Bottaro, A., Olive, V.: Sstreamware: a service oriented middleware for heterogeneous sensor data management. In: Proceedings of the 5th International Conference on Pervasive Services, pp. 121–130. ACM (2008)
5. Micucci, D., Vertemati, A., Fiamberti, F., Bernini, D., Tisato, F.: A spaces-based platform enabling responsive environments. Int. J. Adv. Intell. Syst. **7**(1), 179–193 (2014)
6. Motwani, R., Widom, J., Arasu, A., Babcock, B., Babu, S., Datar, M., Manku, G., Olston, C., Rosenstein, J., Varma, R.: Query processing, resource management, and approximation in a data stream management system. CIDR (2003)
7. Pirkl, G., Munaretto, D., Fischer, C., An, C., Lukowicz, P., Klepal, M., Timm-Giel, A., Widmer, J., Pesch, D., Gellersen, H., et al.: Virtual lifeline: multimodal sensor data fusion for robust navigation in unknown environments. Pervasive Mob. Comput. **8**(3), 388–401 (2012)
8. Tisato, F., Simone, C., Bernini, D., Locatelli, M., Micucci, D.: Grounding ecologies on multiple spaces. Pervasive Mob. Comput. **8**(4), 575–596 (2012)

Author Index

Printed in the United States
By Bookmasters